This chart correlates the Council for Exceptional Children's content standards for teachers to specific chapters of this text.

CEC content standard	Description	Chapter
1. Foundations	Understands the field as an evolving and changing discipline based on philosophies, evidence-based principles, theories, authorities, laws, and history	1 3 4
2. Development and characteristics of learners	Respects students as unique human beings; understands the similarities and differences in human development and the characteristics of exceptional learning needs	3 5 14
3. Individual learning differences	Understands the effects that an exceptional condition can have on an individual's learning in school and throughout life	1 3 5
4. Instructional strategies	Possesses a repertoire of evidence-based instructional strategies to individualize instruction for individuals with special learning needs	10 11 12 14
5. Learning environments and social interactions	Creates learning environments for individuals' special needs that foster cultural understanding, safety and emotional well being, positive social interactions, and active engagement	4
6. Language	Understands typical and atypical language development and the ways in which exceptional conditions can interact with an individual's experience with and use of language	10
7. Instructional planning	Knows individualized decision making and instruction; develops long-range, individualized instructional plans anchored in both general and special curricula	2 3 4
8. Assessment	Knows and uses multiple types of assessment information for a variety of educational decisions; uses the results of assessment to help identify exceptional learning needs and to develop and implement individualized instructional programs, as well as to adjust instruction in response to ongoing learning progress	2
9. Professional and ethical practice	Is guided by the profession's ethical and professional practice standards; practice in multiple roles and complex situations across wide age and development ranges; attention to legal matters	1 3 4
10. Collaboration	Collaborates with families, other educators, related service providers, and personnel from community agencies in culturally responsive ways	4 7 8 9

Source: Council for Exceptional Children, Professional Standards (2001). Arlington, VA, Council for Exceptional Children

For further discussion on these content standards, see the section titled "Current Directions" in Chapter 1, "Learning Disabilities: Definitions, Characteristics, and Current Directions."

Learning Disabilities and Related Disorders

Characteristics and Teaching Strategies

TENTH EDITION

Janet W. Lerner
Northeastern Illinois University

with Frank Kline
Seattle Pacific University

Houghton Mifflin Company
Boston   New York

To Eugene

Publisher: Patricia A. Coryell
Senior Sponsoring Editor: Sue Pulvermacher-Alt
Senior Development Editor: Lisa A. Mafrici
Editorial Assistant: Dayna Pell
Senior Project Editor: Margaret Park Bridges
Manufacturing Coordinator: Chuck Dutton
Senior Marketing Manager: Jane Potter
Marketing Assistant: Erin Lane

Cover Image: Celia Gullett, Rhythm 1/Tim Olsen Gallery

Chapter opening photographs: Chapter 1: © Bob Daemmrich; Chapter 2: © Jean-Claude
Lejeune; Chapter 3: © Bob Daemmrich; Chapter 4: © Jean-Claude Lejeune; Chapter 5:
© Jean-Claude Lejeune; Chapter 6: © Michael Newman/PhotoEdit; Chapter 7: © Elizabeth
Crews; Chapter 8: © Mary Kate Denny/PhotoEdit; Chapter 9: © Cleo/PhotoEdit; Chapter 10:
© Elizabeth Crews; Chapter 11: © Index Stock Photography; Chapter 12: © Elizabeth Crews;
Chapter 13: © Steve Skjold/PhotoEdit; Chapter 14: © Dana White/PhotoEdit.

Credits continue after the Reference Guide, on page C-1.

Printed in the U.S.A.

Library of Congress Control Number: 2004110351

ISBN: 0-618-47402-1

1 2 3 4 5 6 7 8 9–MP–09 08 07 06 05

BRIEF CONTENTS

CONTENTS

The title of the tenth edition of this textbook is changed to *Learning Disabilities and Related Disorders: Characteristics and Teaching Strategies*. This new title reflects the shifts in the field of learning disabilities. These shifts occurred with the realization that many students with learning disabilities exhibit coexisting related disorders, such as attention deficit disorder, Asperger's syndrome, nonverbal learning disabilities, and other related conditions. The condition of learning disabilities is widely recognized as a problem that leads to serious difficulties in school learning, and those difficulties often continue into adulthood. The field of learning disabilities continues to be dynamic, influential, and responsive to the advances in research, policy, and societal changes. This edition of *Learning Disabilities and Related Disorders* reflects these rapid advances and modifications. Individuals with learning disabilities encounter unexpected difficulties in certain types of learning. Learning disabilities can impede learning to talk, listen, read, write, spell, reason, recall, organize information, or achieve in mathematics. Described as a weakness among a sea of strengths, the condition of learning disabilities is especially perplexing because each individual has a unique combination of talents and characteristics and of strengths and weaknesses. Students with learning disabilities are found in every classroom; however, because learning disabilities cannot be seen, the condition often is neglected. Unless these students are recognized and treated, they are destined to become educational discards. Identifying students with learning disabilities and helping them to succeed are the primary concerns of this textbook.

AUDIENCE AND PURPOSE

Learning Disabilities and Related Disorders, Tenth Edition, is an introductory textbook written for undergraduate and graduate students who are majoring in general education or special education. This textbook provides a comprehensive view of the field; describes the characteristics of learning disabilities; and offers teaching strategies to general education teachers, special education teachers, school psychologists, administrators, language pathologists, counselors, and related professionals. *Learning Disabilities and Related Disorders* is particularly useful for preservice teachers and in-service classroom teachers who increasingly are responsible for teaching students with learning disabilities in inclusive classrooms. In addition, this textbook provides parents with the necessary background information to better understand their child and their child's problems.

A varied approach to learning disabilities and related disorders enables readers to gain a comprehensive overview of this complex subject. Teachers must understand the diverse theoretical approaches within the field. They must know the procedures to assess and evaluate students; possess skills in the art of clinical teaching; and be familiar with teaching methods, strategies, and materials. In addition, teachers must know the requirements of the special education laws. *Learning Disabilities and Related Disorders* addresses each of these essential topics.

REVISIONS IN THIS EDITION

- *The 2004 reauthorization of the Individuals With Disabilities Education Improvement Act (IDEA–2004).* This edition includes information about IDEA–2004 and its influence on the field of learning disabilities. An explanation of the features of IDEA–2004 that affect students with learning disabilities is included in Chapter 1 and Chapter 2, as well as in other chapters of the textbook.

- *Expanded coverage of standards-based education.* The standards are addressed in several chapters of this book. A correlation chart that summarizes the Council for Exceptional Children's content standards for special education and indicates the chapters in which the standards are addressed is included in Chapter 1, as well as adjacent to the inside back cover of this book. In addition, standards for language from the Council for Exceptional Children are included in Chapter 10. Mathematics Principles and Standards from the National Council of Teachers of Mathematics are included in Chapter 13.

- *Increased website information.* Students today want to investigate certain topics further through the Internet. Throughout this textbook, marginal icons graphically signal relevant websites. These icons enable students to identify website content more easily. In addition, greater coverage of certain topics is provided on the website that accompanies this textbook. The website for *Learning Disabilities and Related Disorders* is located at **http://www.college.hmco.com/education**.

- *Teaching students with learning disabilities in the general education classroom.* The educational setting for the majority of students with learning disabilities is in the general education classroom, and teaching these students becomes the responsibility of the general education teacher. Each chapter of the textbook addresses strategies for the general education teacher to teach students with learning disabilities. In addition, each chapter contains an "LD in Practice" box that summarizes various methods to teach students with special needs in the general education classroom.

- *New approaches to assess students with learning disabilities.* Chapter 2 explores new assessment approaches and discusses response-to-intervention. In addition, the chapter provides recent information about the use of intelligence tests in the identification process, and discusses accommodations for assessment and alternate assessment.

- *Thoroughly revised and renamed Chapter 6.* Entitled "Attention Deficit Disorder and Related Neurodevelopmental Conditions," this chapter includes information about new research and medications for attention deficit disorder and attention deficit hyperactivity disorder. Chapter 6 also addresses related neurodevelopmental conditions, such as nonverbal learning disorders and Asperger's syndrome.

- *Recent brain research.* Chapter 9, "Medical Aspects of Learning Disabilities," reports on the exciting recent findings about the brain and learning. The chapter includes information about recent research on the brain and dyslexia and research using functional magnetic resonance imaging (fMRI).

- *Coverage of the findings from the National Reading Panel.* Chapter 11, "Reading" covers the National Reading Panel's findings about successful teaching methods for reading and the need for explicit and structured instruction for teaching phonological awareness, phonics, fluency, vocabulary, and comprehension. This chapter also incorporates the value of literacy-based instruction in the teaching of reading.

- *Inclusion.* Most students with learning disabilities are now served in general education classroom settings. Chapters 1 through 4, Chapter 6 and Chapter 8 contain expanded and up-to-date information about responsible inclusion practices and describe how special education teachers and general education teachers can work together to make inclusion work.

- *Cultural and linguistic diversity.* Chapters 1, 3, 5, 7, and 10 discuss the changing demographics of the children in our schools and address the growing number of linguistically and culturally diverse students who also have learning disabilities. This revision also explores methods for assessing and teaching these students.

- *Young children with learning disabilities.* Chapters 7 and 10 examine the early signs of learning disabilities exhibited by young children, including problems with phonological awareness, rapid naming, and early literacy instruction. In addition, Chapter 7 provides many early intervention strategies for use with young children.

- *Adolescents and adults with learning disabilities.* Chapter 8 provides current information about the problems of adolescents and adults with learning disabilities and offers strategies to help these individuals. Learning strategies instruction is emphasized in this chapter.

- *The use of computer technology.* Chapters 1, 3, 7, and 8, and Chapters 10 through 13 discuss the rapid advances in computer technology and how students with learning disabilities can use computer technology as an aid to learning.

- *The role of parents.* Chapter 4 covers current perspectives on the essential role of parents, the problems that parents face, and the importance of establishing healthy home–school partnerships.
- *Updated citations.* Current citations, with many updated citations, appear throughout the textbook.

Learning Disabilities and Related Disorders, strives to provide a fair and clear explanation of the new and controversial issues in the field of learning disabilities. This textbook presents the basic foundations, concepts, and strategies that have helped teachers, parents, and students over the years.

Boxes, entitled LD Stories, provide accounts of students with learning disabilities. "LD in Practice" boxes offer practical applications for instruction. A new feature on teaching students with special needs in the general education classroom is included in each chapter.

A three-part case study follows a student, Rita G., from prereferral through placement. This case study appears in Chapters 2 through 4. The Reference Guide section at the end of the text provides a second comprehensive case study of another student, Adam Z.

COVERAGE AND ORGANIZATION

Learning Disabilities and Related Disorders is organized into four major parts. Part I provides an overview of learning disabilities. Chapter 1 includes important features of the 2004 Individuals With Disabilities Education Improvement Act. This chapter also provides an overview of learning disabilities, the characteristics of learning disabilities, the history of the field of learning disabilities, and current directions.

Part II, which is comprised of Chapters 2 through 4, examines the assessment-teaching process. Viewed as interrelated parts of a continuous process, assessment and clinical teaching involve trying to understand students and to help them learn. Assessment is discussed in Chapter 2, with special emphasis on how the 2004 Individuals With Disabilities Education Improvement Act affects the individualized education program (IEP). Chapter 3 examines clinical teaching, the elements that make teaching successful, and the relationship between teaching and assessment. Chapter 4 provides coverage of the educational settings for teaching students with learning disabilities, the growing inclusion movement, the various educational settings, and ways for general education teachers and special education teachers to collaborate.

Part III, which is comprised of Chapters 5 through 8, addresses theoretical issues and expanding directions. Chapter 5 examines the basic psychological theories of learning disabilities, including the contributions of developmental psychology, behavioral psychology, and cognitive psychology. Chapter 6 looks at attention deficit disorder and related neurodevelopmental conditions, which is a new feature of this edition. In Chapter 7, the focus is on early childhood, with an examination of the early signs of learning disabilities in young children. This chapter also includes a discussion of perceptual problems, motor problems, and the topic of early literacy. Chapter 8 focuses on adolescents and adults with learning disabilities and includes a discussion of the transition from school to adult life. In addition, Chapter 8 covers inclusion in high school and the transition to college. Chapter 9 discusses the medical aspects of research, assessment, and treatment.

Part IV bridges the gap from theories to teaching strategies, dealing with the heart of the challenges that accompany teaching children and adolescents with learning disabilities. The chapters are organized by academic areas. Every chapter in Part IV has two sections: (1) Theories and (2) Teaching Strategies. Each Theories section examines the theoretical framework for teaching the particular content area covered in the chapter; each Teaching Strategies section offers practical suggestions and methods to teach the academic subject covered in the chapter. Chapters 10 through 12 discuss language in its various forms. Chapter 10 looks at oral language, specifically listening and speaking. Chapter 11 investigates reading skills and reading comprehension, in addition to the important findings of the National Reading Panel. Chapter 12 addresses written language, including written expression, spelling, and handwriting. Chapter 13 analyzes disorders in mathematics concepts, skills, and problem solving, and presents NCTM standards. The final chapter, Chapter 14, discusses social and emotional behavior, including nonverbal learning disorders, social disorders, and the emotional implications of learning disabilities.

SPECIAL FEATURES   To make this textbook easy to study and more appealing to use, the following features are included:

- **Chapter outlines** for each chapter present the major headings as an advanced organizer for students to use in learning the chapter material.
- **Quotations** at the beginning of each chapter help to focus the reader and to provide interesting insights.
- **LD Stories** boxes are interspersed throughout most chapters. These short illustrative vignettes demonstrate real-life situations.
- **LD in Practice** boxes provide examples of practical instruction models, methods and stratagies. These boxes also include teaching tips for the general education teacher in the form of strategies for the general education classroom.
- **Website logos** provide marginal alerts to pertinent websites.
- **Case Study of Rita G.** in Chapters 2 through 4 offers a detailed account of one student's experience from prereferral through placement. The comprehensive case study of Adam Z. appears in the Reference Guide section at the end of the text.
- **Chapter Summaries** at the end of each chapter highlight, in a clear point-by-point format, the major ideas presented in the chapter.

- **Discussion and Reflection** sections follow the summary section at the end of each chapter and offer an opportunity to pull together and elaborate on the major ideas of the chapter.

- **Key Terms** conclude each chapter and list important terminology, providing an opportunity for students to review their knowledge of key concepts.

- A new **Reference Guide** section contains useful information for teachers and includes (1) an extended case study of Adam Z.; (2) a listing of tests for assessment of students with learning disabilities, with a brief description of these commonly used tests; and (3) an additional resource section that includes a listings of key websites, video resources, print resources, and professional organizations for learning disabilities and related disorders.

- A **Glossary** of important terms appears at the end of the text and includes the definitions of all key terms listed at the end of each chapter.

COMPANION WEBSITE

The tenth edition of *Learning Disabilities and Related Disorders* is accompanied by extensive websites for students and instructors. Each is described. They are located at **http://www.college.hmco.com/education.**

The Student Website

The website for students is a *Study Guide*. Each chapter includes: (1) objectives, (2) key terms and definitions, (3) major points, (4) matching questions, and (5) multiple-choice rapid review questions. The student website also contains more detailed information for several chapters: the history of learning disabilities (Chapter 1), identifying learning disabilities through the discrepancy between intellectual ability and achievement level (Chapter 2), and a phonics quiz and phonic generalization (Chapter 11).

The Instructor Website

The website for instructors is a Resource Manual. Each chapter contains a number of files to help instructors in teaching the course: (1) learning objectives, (2) key terms and definitions, (3) major points, (4) suggested activities, (5) short answer questions, (6) essay/discussion questions, (7) PowerPoint presentations, and (8) pages for making transparencies. The instructor website also contains more detailed information for several chapters: the history of learning disabilities (Chapter 1), identifying learning disabilities through the discrepancy between intellectual ability and achievement level (Chapter 2), and a phonics quiz and phonics generalization (Chapter 11). In addition, the TestBank contains two sets of multiple-choice questions for each chapter: TestBank Set A and TestBank Set B.

HM Computerized Test Bank

The assessment items in the *Instructor's Resource Manual With Test Bank* are also available in an electronic format for use with PC and Macintosh computers. There are two sets of multiple choice questions, Test Bank A and Test Bank B, for each chapter.

ACKNOWLEDGMENTS   *Learning Disabilities and Related Disorders: Characteristics and Teaching Strategies* grew out of experiences from working in public schools with students who had reading and learning disabilities as well as from teaching courses in learning disabilities and special education in colleges and universities. This textbook was influenced greatly by the feedback from students in our courses. Students; colleagues; and organizations also alerted us to new concepts, programs, assessment instruments, and intervention strategies. We are indebted to many scholars, researchers, authors of books and articles, to speakers at conferences, and to educators in school districts and universities with whom we have worked.

We extended our thanks to the following reviewers who read the manuscript at various stages and provided helpful suggestions and criticisms.

Jerome J. Ammer, University of California at San Diego
Lynda Conover, Western Illinois University
Howard Falk, National Louis University
Karen S. Y. Lee, Western Connecticut State University
Diane L. Miller, Emporia State University
Jayne E. Sullivan, Virginia Wesleyan University

We also wish to acknowledge the editors at Houghton Mifflin who skillfully guided us through the processes of writing this book: Sue Pulvermacher-Alt, Senior Sponsoring Editor, and Lisa Mafrici, Senior Development Editor. Also, thanks to Kristen LeFevre, Development Editor.

Thanks to Laura Lerner for creating the student and instructor websites for this book.

As my first college instructor in special education and as a stimulating and provocative scholar and writer, the late Dr. Samuel A. Kirk played a significant role in the inception of this book. I also thank my family—Susan, Laura, Dean, James, Aaron, Lee, Sue, Anne, and Sarah. Finally, I thank my husband, Eugene, who continues to provide the encouragement and support every author needs. —Janet W. Lerner

I am grateful for the help that I have received over the years from the parents of my students, the students themselves, and the many teachers I have had the privilege of learning from in various classes. I am especially thankful for the mentoring from Don Deshler and Jean Schumaker. Thanks also are due to Janet Lerner, whose text has been a major influence on my professional life both as a student and as a teacher. —Frank M. Kline

1

Learning Disabilities: Definitions, Characteristics, and Current Directions

CHAPTER OUTLINE

> Life is not so much a matter of holding good cards but of playing a poor hand well.
>
> —*Robert Louis Stevenson*

This is a book about learning disabilities and related disorders, problems that impede learning for many children, adolescents, and adults, which affects their schooling and their adult lives.

Part I of this book consists of Chapter 1, *Learning Disabilities: Definitions, Characteristics, and Current Directions*. Here, we describe the travails of some famous people with learning disabilities, discuss several definitions of learning disabilities, and present the characteristics of learning disabilities. We also look briefly at the history of the field of learning disabilities and give a more detailed account of the history on the website for this book, **http://college.hmco.com/education.** Part I also contains an analysis of the effect the law has on the field of learning disabilities and we discuss some major current directions in the field.

THE ENIGMA OF LEARNING DISABILITIES

The term **learning disabilities** refers to a neurobiological disorder in one or more of the basic processes involved in understanding spoken or written language. This brain variance may influence an individual's ability to speak, listen, read, write, spell, reason, organize information, or do mathematical calculations. If provided with the right support and intervention, a child with learning disabilities can succeed in school and have a successful, and often distinguished, career later in life. Parents and teachers can help the child achieve success by both fostering the child's strengths and knowing the child's weaknesses.

The enigma of the youngster who encounters extraordinary difficulty in learning, of course, is not new. Throughout the years, children from all walks of life have experienced serious difficulties in learning. Moreover, the condition we call learning disabilities occurs in all cultures, nations, and language groups.

"Zachary—The Puzzle of Learning Disabilities," in the LD Stories box, shows the effects of learning disabilities and the problems that parents encounter in identifying the problem. Throughout the text, you will encounter boxes containing LD Stories. These LD Stories are first-hand accounts of individuals with learning disabilities.

ZACHARY—THE PUZZLE OF LEARNING DISABILITIES

The case of Zachary illustrates the enigma of learning disabilities and the difficulty parents encounter. Zachary's parents have long been aware that their son has severe problems in learning. As an infant, Zachary was colicky and had difficulty in learning to suck. His early speech was so garbled that no one could understand him and, frequently, his inability to communicate led to sudden temper tantrums. The kindergarten teacher reported that Zachary was "immature"; his first-grade teacher said he "did not pay attention"; and succeeding teachers labeled him "lazy" and then "emotionally disturbed." Zachary's distraught parents attempted to find the source of his learning problems to alleviate his misery and theirs. They desperately followed suggestions from many sources, which led to a succession of specialists and clinics dedicated to treating such difficulties.

One clinic detected a visual problem and, as a result, Zachary received visual training exercises for several years. An opinion of emotional disturbance at another agency led to years of psychotherapy for both Zachary and his parents. Another expert placed Zachary on a special diet for a period of time. The family pediatrician said that the boy was merely going through a stage and would grow out of it. Yet, despite this wealth of diagnosis and treatment, Zachary still cannot learn. He is unhappily failing in school, and, understandably, he has lost faith in himself.

The problems encountered by Zachary and his parents are typical. Each profession viewed Zachary's problem from its own perspective and saw only part of the picture. What is needed instead is a unified, interdisciplinary approach to the problem of Zachary's learning disabilities—a coordinated effort by members of the various participating professions.

Some Eminent People With Learning Disabilities

The life stories of eminent individuals who eventually became successful contributors to society reflect their travails with serious learning disabilities.

Nelson Rockefeller, who served as vice president of the United States and governor of the state of New York, suffered from severe dyslexia, a type of learning disability in which the individual encounters extreme difficulty in learning to read. His poor reading ability kept him from achieving good grades in school, and the affliction forced him to memorize his speeches during his political career.

In describing his feelings about growing up with a learning disability, Rockefeller (1976) recalled,

> I was dyslexic . . . and I still have a hard time reading today. I remember vividly the pain and mortification I felt as a boy of eight when I was assigned

to read a short passage of scripture at a community vesper service and did a thoroughly miserable job of it. I know what a dyslexic child goes through . . . the frustration of not being able to do what other children do easily, the humiliation of being thought not too bright when such is not the case at all. But, after coping with this problem for more than 60 years, I have a message of hope and encouragement for children with learning disabilities and their parents. (pp. 12–14)

Charles Schwab, the founder of the successful and innovative stock brokerage firm, struggled with severe reading problems throughout his life. Schwab explained that he coped by developing his other abilities, such as the capacities to envision, to anticipate where things are going, and to conceive a solution to a business problem. He believes that his reading problem forced him to develop these skills at a higher level than that attained by people for whom reading comes easily (Kantrowitz & Underwood, 1999; West, 1997). More information about Charles Schwab can be found at **http://www.schwablearning.org.**

As a child, Thomas Edison, the ingenious American inventor, was called abnormal, addled, and mentally defective. Writing in his diary that he was never able to get along at school, he recalled that he was always at the foot of his class. His father thought of him as stupid, and Edison described himself as a dunce. Auguste Rodin, the great French sculptor, was called the worst pupil in his school. Because his teachers diagnosed Rodin as uneducable, they advised his parents to put him out to work, although they doubted that he could ever make a living. Woodrow Wilson, the scholarly twenty-eighth president of the United States, did not learn his letters until he was 9 years old and did not learn to read until age 11. Relatives expressed sorrow for his parents because Woodrow was so dull and backward (Thompson, 1971).

Albert Einstein, the mathematical genius, did not speak until age 3. His search for words was described as laborious and, until he was 7, he formulated each sentence, no matter how commonplace, silently with his lips before speaking the words aloud. Schoolwork did not go well for young Albert. He showed little facility with arithmetic, no special ability in any other academic subject, and great difficulty with foreign languages. One teacher predicted that "nothing good" would come of him. Einstein's language disabilities persisted throughout his adult life. When he read, he heard words. Writing was difficult for him, and he communicated badly through writing. In describing his thinking process, he explained that he rarely thought in words; it was only after a thought came that he tried to express it in words at a later time (Patten, 1973).

These persons of eminence fortunately were somehow able to find appropriate ways of learning, and they successfully overcame their initial failures. Many youngsters with learning disabilities are not as fortunate.

The Cross-Cultural Nature of Learning Disabilities

The condition of learning disabilities is a universal problem that occurs in all languages, cultures, and nations in the world. The problem is neither confined to the United States nor to English-speaking countries. Accumulating research shows that in all cultures there are children who seem to have normal intelligence, but they have severe difficulty in learning oral language, acquiring reading or writing skills, or doing mathematics. The International Academy for Research in Learning Disabilities (IARLD), an organization dedicated to fostering international research on learning disabilities, publishes a journal called *Thalamas* and has a website at **http://www.iarld.net.**

 Clinical reports of the personal travails of children from all corners of the world are remarkably similar. In the following excerpt, for example, a Chinese adult remembers his first baffling failure in a Chinese school; the story parallels the bewildering episodes that children with learning disabilities face in our own schools (Lerner & Chen, 1992).

> My first recollection of learning problems occurred at age 7, when I entered the first grade in school in Taiwan. My teacher wrote [characters] on the blackboard and the pupils were to copy this board work into their notebooks. I vividly remember that I was simply unable to perform this task. Observing how easily my classmates accomplished the assignment, I was perplexed and [troubled] by my inability to copy the letters and words from the board.

Research reports about learning disabilities come from many parts of the world: Great Britain (Wedell, 2001), Scandinavia (Lundberg & Höien, 2001), the Netherlands (Stevens & Werkhoven, 2001), New Zealand (Chapman, 1992), Germany (Opp, 2001), Italy (Fabbro & Masutto, 1994), Mexico (Fletcher & DeLopez, 1995), Portugal (da Fonseca, 1996), Canada (Wong & Hutchinson, 2001), Australia (Elkins, 2001), Russia (Korkunov, Nigayev, Reynolds, & Lerner, 1998), South America (Bravo-Valdivieso & Müller, 2001), and Israel (Shalev, Manor, Auerbach, & Grodd-Tour, 1998). The problem appears in children learning an alphabet-based system of written language, such as English, and with children learning a logographic (pictorial) system of written language, such as Chinese (Hsu, 1988) or Japanese (Tsuge, 2001).

DEFINITIONS OF LEARNING DISABILITIES

The term *learning disabilities* was first introduced in 1963. A small group of concerned parents and educators met in Chicago to consider linking the isolated parent groups active in a few communities into a single organization. Each of these parent groups identified the children of concern under a different name, including perceptually handicapped, brain-injured, and neurologically impaired. If these groups were to unite, they needed to agree on a single term to identify the children. When the term *learning disabilities* was suggested at this meeting (Kirk, 1963), it met with immediate approval. The organization today known as the Learning Disabilities Association of America (LDAA) was born at this historic meeting. The LDAA website can be found at **www.ldaamerica.org.**

Although the term learning disabilities had immediate appeal and acceptance, the task of developing a definition of learning disabilities proved to be a formidable challenge. Indeed, defining this population is considered such an overwhelming task that some have likened learning disabilities to Justice Potter Stewart's comment on pornography: impossible to define, "but I know it when I see it."

Formulating a definition of learning disabilities that is acceptable to all has been difficult. Three of the influential definitions are: (1) the definition in the federal law (IDEA–2004) (PL 108–446), (2) the Interagency Committee on Learning Disabilities definition, and (3) the National Joint Committee on Learning Disabilities definition.

The Federal Definition

The most widely used definition of learning disabilities first appeared in 1975 in **Public Law 94–142, the Education for all Handicapped Children Act.** It was also incorporated in revisions of this law: in 1990, in the **Individuals With Disabilities Education Act (IDEA–1990) (Public Law 101–476);** in 1997, in the **Individuals With Disabilities Education Act of 1997 (IDEA–1997) (Public Law 105–17);** and most recently in the **Individuals with Disabilities Education Improvement Act (IDEA–2004) (Public**

Law 108–446). The definition of learning disabilities in the federal law is the basis of most state definitions, and it is used by many schools.

The definition of learning disabilities in the federal law IDEA–2004 is:

> The term "specific learning disability" means a disorder in one or more of the basic psychological processes involved in understanding or in using language, spoken or written, which disorder may manifest itself in imperfect ability to listen, think, speak, read, write, spell, or to do mathematical calculations. Such term includes such conditions as perceptual disabilities, brain injury, minimal brain dysfunction, dyslexia, and developmental aphasia. Such term does not include a learning problem, that is primarily the result of visual, hearing, or motor disabilities; of mental retardation; of emotional disturbance; or of environmental, cultural, or economic disadvantage.

In addition, there is an operational definition in the federal law, which first appeared in a separate set of regulations for children with learning disabilities (U.S. Office of Education, 1977). These regulations state that a student has a specific learning disability if: (1) the student does not achieve at the proper age and ability levels in one or more specific areas when provided with appropriate learning experiences and (2) the student has a severe discrepancy between achievement and intellectual ability in one or more of these seven areas: (a) oral expression, (b) listening comprehension, (c) written expression, (d) basic reading skills, (e) reading comprehension, (f) mathematics calculation, and (g) mathematics reasoning.

To summarize, the federal definition of learning disabilities includes the following major concepts:

1. The individual has a *disorder in one or more of the basic psychological processes.* (These processes refer to mental abilities, such as memory, auditory perception, visual perception, oral language, and thinking.)

2. The individual has *difficulty in learning,* specifically, in speaking, listening, writing, reading (word-recognition skills and comprehension), and mathematics (calculation and reasoning).

3. The problem is *not primarily due to other causes,* such as visual or hearing impairments; motor disabilities; mental retardation; emotional disturbance; or economic, environmental, or cultural disadvantage.

4. To determine eligibility, the school may consider whether a severe discrepancy exists between the student's apparent ability for learning and his or her low level of achievement. As noted in this chapter and in the chapter on assessment, the school may also consider the student's *response-to-intervention.*

IDEA–2004 (Public Law 108–446) offers a fresh approach for determining a child's eligibility for learning disability services. This law indicates that when determining whether a child has a specific learning disability, schools shall *not* be required to take into consideration whether the child has a severe

THE NJCLD DEFINITION OF LEARNING DISABILITIES

The **National Joint Committee on Learning Disabilities (NJCLD)** is an organization of representatives from several professional organizations and disciplines involved with learning disabilities.

The main points of the NJCLD (1997) definition are as follows:

1. *Learning disabilities are a heterogeneous group of disorders.* Individuals with learning disabilities exhibit many kinds of behaviors and characteristics.

2. *Learning disabilities result in significant difficulties in the acquisition and use of listening, speaking, reading, writing, reasoning, and/or mathematical skills.*

3. *The problem is intrinsic to the individual.* Learning disabilities are due to factors within the person rather than to external factors, such as the environment or the educational system.

4. *The problem is presumed to be related to a central nervous system dysfunction.* There is a biological basis to the problem.

5. *Learning disabilities may occur along with other disabilities or conditions.* Individuals can have several problems at the same time, such as learning disabilities and emotional disorders.

Source: Reprinted with the permission of the National Joint Committee on Learning Disabilities.

discrepancy between achievement and intellectual ability in oral expression, listening comprehension, written expression, basic reading skill, reading comprehension, mathematics calculation, or mathematics reasoning.

Further, IDEA–2004 indicates that when determining whether a child has a specific learning disability, a school *may* use a process that determines if the child responds to scientific, research-based interventions as part of the evaluation process, a procedure called *Response-to-Intervention (RTI)*. After receiving instruction with scientific, research-based materials, those students who do not respond or learn adequately are given more intensive research-based interventions. After several trials, the non-responding student can then be considered for an evaluation for learning disabilities (Fletcher, Coulter, Reschly, & Vaughn, 2004; Fuchs, Moch, Morgan, & Young, 2003; Vaughn & Fuchs, 2003). This procedure is discussed in greater detail in the chapter on assessment.

In effect, IDEA–2004 permits two approaches to determining eligibility for learning disabilities services.

Other Significant Definitions

Other influential definitions of learning disabilities have been recommended. The two most significant are those by the National Joint Committee on Learning Disabilities (NJCLD) and the Interagency Committee on Learning Disabilities (ICLD). These two definitions have been summarized in the boxes above.

COMMON ELEMENTS IN THE DEFINITIONS

The various definitions of learning disabilities have several elements in common: (1) central nervous system dysfunction, (2) psychological processing deficits, (3) difficulty in academic and learning tasks, (4) discrepancy between potential and achievement, and (5) exclusion of other causes. The nature of each of these elements and the problems that surround them are examined in the following sections.

Central Nervous System Dysfunction

Although not always stated directly, implied in many of the definitions is the view that learning disabilities are related to neurological factors. All learning originates within the brain and, consequently, a disorder in learning can be caused by a dysfunction in the central nervous system, which is an organic system comprising the brain and the spinal cord. In many cases, the neurological condition is difficult to detect by medical examination or external medical tests. Central nervous system dysfunction is therefore usually determined through observation of behavior. Neuroscience and medical research show growing evidence that learning disabilities have a neurological basis. (See the chapter on the medical aspects of learning disabilities.) Although teachers are chiefly concerned with behavioral and educational aspects, the medical contributions remain important.

Psychological Processing Deficits

Psychological processing deficits refer to an uneven development of the various components of mental functioning. Mental ability is not a single capacity; rather, it is composed of many underlying mental abilities. For the individual with learning disabilities, these component abilities or subabilities do not develop in an even fashion. That is, while some of the components are maturing in an anticipated sequence or rate, others are lagging in their development, thereby appearing as symptoms of the learning problem. Students with learning disabilities manifest strengths and weaknesses in different mental processes. A key phrase in the federal definition—*a disorder in one or more of these basic psychological processes*—refers to this component of the definition.

The concepts of an uneven growth pattern, intraindividual differences, and psychological processing disorders are often considered in assessment and instruction in learning disabilities. About 88% of the states include a process/language component in their state definition (Frankenberger & Fronzaglio, 1991; Mercer et al., 1996).

Difficulty in Academic and Learning Tasks

Individuals with learning disabilities encounter different types of problems in learning. One child's obstacle may be in the acquisition of speech and oral language; another's may be in reading, arithmetic, handwriting, motor skills, written expression, thinking, or nonverbal learning. As noted earlier, the operational portion of the federal definition identifies seven specific academic areas in which learning disabilities can be detected.

Discrepancy Between Potential and Achievement

Another element common to many definitions of learning disabilities is the identification of a gap between what the student is potentially capable of learning and what the student has in fact learned or achieved. The operational portion of the federal definition states that the child with learning disabilities has a **severe discrepancy** between achievement and intellectual ability in one or more of seven areas.

To determine if a discrepancy exists between potential and achievement, one must ask three essential questions (each of which raises serious problems):

1. *What is the individual's potential for learning?* Judgments about a child's potential, ability level, or capacity are usually based on such measurements as intelligence tests, tests of cognitive abilities, clinical judgments, or other means. Often an intelligence, or IQ, test is used. IQ tests are criticized as being inaccurate measures of intelligence, as being racially and culturally biased, and as measuring achievement rather than intelligence.

2. *What is the individual's current achievement level?* The **current achievement level** refers to a student's current performance. Tests that are used to measure the individual's performance have imperfections. Many academic tests have poor validity, reliability, and standardization (Farr & Carey, 1986; Salvia & Ysseldyke, 2001), and the score may not reflect the child's actual achievement level.

3. *What degree of discrepancy between potential and achievement is "severe"?* The important word here is *severe*. A one-year discrepancy at the second-grade level is more severe than a one-year discrepancy at the eleventh-grade level. Further, should a *severe discrepancy* be measured by a fixed amount of time (such as one year or three years), or should a ratio or some statistical measure or formula be used?

Each state, school district, or evaluation team can establish its own method of defining a "severe" discrepancy. Many states (about 66%) quantify the learning disability using one of several forms of "discrepancy formulas" to determine if a child is eligible for learning disabilities services (Frankenberger & Fronzaglio, 1991; Mercer et al., 1996). See the website **http://college.hmco.com/education** for more information on these eligibility formulas.

There are questions about the validity of identifying students with learning disabilities through a discrepancy between ability and achievement (Fletcher et al., 2004; Lyon, 1997; Vellutino, Scanlon, & Lyon, 2000) for the following reasons:

■ The criterion of IQ-achievement discrepancy is predicated on failure. This procedure (coined the "wait-and-fail" model) requires that a child fall behind a predicted level of performance to be eligible for services. This practice often results in services being delayed until third grade and beyond. Unfortunately, while the child waits to cross a threshold of failure to be eligible for services, the child can develop many negative conditions resulting from school failure, such as low self-esteem and loss of interest and motivation.

- The **response-to-intervention** method is permitted under IDEA–2004 in the prereferral stage to identify children with learning disabilities. As defined, students considered to be at-risk for learning disabilities are given instruction with scientific, research-based curriculum materials. Those pupils who do not respond favorably to these methods are considered at-risk for learning disabilities (Fletcher, et al., 2004; Fuchs et al., 2003; Vaughn & Fuchs, 2003).

- This discrepancy component of the definition stresses the criterion of underachievement and, thus, minimizes other aspects of the definition, especially the concept of disorders in basic psychological processes and phonological problems. Because there are many reasons besides learning disabilities for an individual to be underachieving—such as poor teaching, lack of motivation or interest, or psychological or emotional factors—the criterion of underachievement alone is insufficient.

Exclusion of Other Causes

This component of the definition reflects the notion that learning disabilities are not primarily the result of other conditions, such as mental retardation; emotional disturbance; visual or hearing impairments; or cultural, social, or economic environments.

In practice, however, the exclusion component of the definition of learning disabilities becomes difficult to implement because children often exhibit coexisting problems. Teachers who work with children with other disabilities often observe that many students appear to have two problems—their primary impairment plus their learning disabilities. It is hard to determine which problem is primary and which is secondary. There is growing acceptance of the idea that other conditions often co-occur with learning disabilities, as indicated in the NJCLD and ICLD definitions.

DIFFERENT VIEWS OF LEARNING DISABILITIES

Learning disabilities are recognized as a category of disabilities under the special education law IDEA–2004. Moreover, children identified with learning disabilities comprise over 50% of the special education population. However, some new views of children with learning problems are emerging, which are related to new philosophies and policies.

Learning Differences/Learning Difficulties

The term **learning differences,** which is the concept that all individuals have variations in learning abilities in various areas, was proposed by Levine

(2002, 2003) to describe a broad group of children who are struggling to learn and are failing in school. Arguing against the use of labels such as learning disabilities, Levine contends that we should focus on determining where the student is experiencing a breakdown in learning. He believes that these children have different kinds of minds and that educators and parents must understand the individual differences and needs of these students. The website for Levine's work on learning differences is **http://www.allkindsof minds.org.**

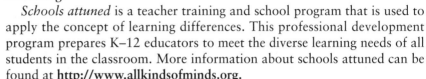

Schools attuned is a teacher training and school program that is used to apply the concept of learning differences. This professional development program prepares K–12 educators to meet the diverse learning needs of all students in the classroom. More information about schools attuned can be found at **http://www.allkindsofminds.org.**

The term learning difficulties is proposed in the website **http:// www.schwablearning.org,** which is a product of the Charles and Helen Schwab Foundation. The mission of this foundation is to help students with learning difficulties to be successful in their learning, as well as in their life. The website provides a parent's guide to helping children with learning difficulties. A special website designed for students with learning difficulties, which is geared to students ages 12–18 is **http://www.sparktop.org.**

It is important not to confuse the term learning disabilities with other proposed terms, such as *learning differences* or *learning difficulties*. The notion of learning differences applies to *all* children in the general population. Learning disabilities, however, refers to a small group of children with underlying neurological disorders. The rights of children with learning disabilities are recognized as a category of special education in the special education law and should be protected. The terms learning differences and learning difficulties are not recognized in the law (Silver, 2001).

Mild/Moderate Disabilities

The term **mild/moderate disabilities** refers to groupings of children with several different disabilities: learning disabilities, mild mental retardation, emotional disabilities, attention deficit disorders, and other syndromes. This approach clusters students who are identified with several different disabilities into cross-categorical classes for instruction. To be eligible for special education instruction, these children, of course, must be first identified with their primary disability through their **individualized education program (IEP),** which is the written plan for the education of an individual student with disabilities. The plan must meet the requirements specified in the rules and regulations of IDEA.

The concepts presented in this text are extremely broad in scope and have applications to many children with special needs. The topics and coverage on the law, assessment, characteristics, and instructional strategies readily apply to children with mild/moderate disabilities.

Gifted and Talented Children With Learning Disabilities

Some children with learning disabilities also may be gifted and talented (Fletcher, et al., 2004). Characteristics of giftedness include spontaneity, inquisitiveness, imagination, boundless enthusiasm, and emotionality; and these same traits are often observed in children with learning disabilities. Often, children with learning disabilities, like gifted children, seem to require a great deal of activity. They may find the general education classroom environment uninviting, or they may have trouble attending to the classroom instruction. If their learning needs are not being met, they may respond by becoming fidgety, inattentive, and even disruptive. It is especially important that difficulty with school for these children does not lead to the withholding of learning opportunities, which can develop into frustration, failure, or depression. Teachers can meet the unique needs of students whose strengths and talents lie outside the narrow view of knowledge by

- Helping students bypass their deficits as they access their area of strengths
- Modifying assignments and curricula for these students so that their true abilities may be demonstrated
- Creating an environment that nurtures personal creativity and intellectual characteristics

Multiple Intelligences   In line with the concept of strengths and weaknesses, many parents and teachers have observed that their children with learning disabilities have incredible talents that are generally undervalued or not well represented in school curricula. Howard Gardner (1983, 1993, 1999) has popularized the notion that people possess **multiple intelligences** in at least eight different types of intelligence (Table 1.1).

Highly Successful Adults With Learning Disabilities   Successful adults with learning disabilities find the world of work is quite different from the world of school. Studies show that many highly successful people have learning disabilities. In fact, about 30% to 40% of 300 individuals who had achieved a high level of financial success had learning difficulties in school (West, 2003). A major business magazine, *Fortune* (Morris, 2002), did a cover story on chief executive officers (CEOs) of major corporations who have learning disabilities. Thus, there appears to be a strong, positive side to learning disabilities and dyslexia that requires further research (West, 2003).

CHARACTERISTICS OF LEARNING DISABILITIES

Many different characteristics are associated with learning disabilities, but each individual is unique and will present only some of these characteristics.

TABLE 1.1

Gardner's Multiple
Intelligences

Type of intelligence	Description	Symbol
Verbal/linguistic	Related to words and language (qualities of *writers* and *poets*)	
Logical/mathematical	Abilities with quantitative thinking, numbers, and logical patterns (qualities of *mathematicians* and *scientists*)	$\sum \sqrt{} \;^{+}\; ^{1}/_{8}$ % =
Visual/spatial	Abilities to visualize objects and to create internal mental images and pictures (qualities of *artists, architects,* and *engineers*)	
Musical/rhythmic	Sensitivities to tonal patterns, rhythms, and musical expressiveness (qualities of *musicians*)	
Bodily/kinesthetic	Related to abilities to control one's physical movement (qualities of *athletes* and *dancers*)	
Interpersonal	Skills in dealing with other people (qualities of *salespeople* and *politicians*)	
Intrapersonal	Inner states of being, self-reflection, and knowledge of one's self (qualities of *persons with accurate self-knowledge*)	
Naturalistic	Attuned to nature, animals, and plant life (qualities of *farmers, forest rangers,* and *gardeners*)	

Source: Adapted from *Frames of mind: The theory of multiple intelligences,* by Howard Gardner, 1983, New York: Basic Books.

Varied Characteristics

Students with learning disabilities exhibit many kinds of learning and behavioral traits, and no individual displays all of the traits. Some students have disabilities in mathematics, whereas others excel in mathematics. Attention disorders are symptomatic problems for many students with learning disabilities, but not for all. Further, certain kinds of characteristics are more likely to be exhibited at certain age levels. Young children are more

TABLE 1.2

Common Learning
and Behavioral
Characteristics of Learning
Disabilities and Related
Disorders

Characteristic	Description
Disorders of attention	Does not focus when a lesson is presented; short attention span, easily distracted, poor concentration; may display hyperactivity
Poor motor abilities	Difficulty with gross motor abilities and fine motor coordination (exhibits general awkwardness and clumsiness)
Psychological processing deficits	Problems in processing auditory or visual information (difficulty interpreting visual or auditory stimuli)
Lack of phonological awareness	Poor at recognizing sounds of language (cannot identify phoneme sounds in spoken language)
Poor cognitive strategies for learning	Does not know how to go about the task of learning and studying; lacks organizational skills; passive learning style (do not direct their own learning)
Oral language difficulties	Underlying language disorders (problems in language development, listening, speaking, and vocabulary)
Reading difficulties	About 80% of students with learning disabilities have disabilities in reading (problems in learning to decode words, basic word-recognition skills, or reading comprehension)
Writing difficulties	Poor in tasks requiring written expression, spelling, and handwriting
Mathematics	Difficulty with quantitative thinking, arithmetic, time, space, and calculation facts
Social skills	Does not know how to act and talk in social situations; difficulty with establishing satisfying social relationships and friendships

likely to be hyperactive than adolescents. In addition, deficits are manifested in different ways at different age levels. For example, an underlying language disorder may appear as a delayed speech problem in the preschooler, as a reading disorder in the elementary pupil, and as a writing disorder in the secondary student.

These characteristics are also found among children with other disorders and disabilities. The implications of each of these learning and behavioral characteristics are complex, and they are discussed in detail throughout this book. Table 1.2 shows the common learning and behavioral characteristics displayed by children with learning disabilities and related disorders.

Gender Differences

Clinics and schools identify four times as many boys as they do girls who have learning disabilities. However, gender research shows that actually there are as many girls with learning disabilities as boys, but they are not being identified. Boys tend to exhibit more physical aggression and loss of control; however, they also exhibit visual-motor abilities, spelling ability, and written language mechanical aptitude. Girls with learning disabilities tend to have more cognitive, language, and social problems and to have severe academic achievement deficits in reading and math (Lyon, 1997; Shaywitz, Fletcher, & Shaywitz, 1995; Shaywitz, Shaywitz, & Fletcher, 1990; Shaywitz & Shaywitz, 1988; Vogel, 1990). Girls tend to be more verbal and display less physical aggression. Girls with learning disabilities who are not identified are an underserved group that is at significant risk for long-term academic, social, and emotional difficulties.

Explanations of why more boys than girls are identified with learning disabilities include *biological causes* (males may be more vulnerable to learning disabilities), *cultural factors* (more males may be identified because boys tend to exhibit more disruptive behaviors that are troublesome to adults), and *expectation pressures* (the expectations for success in school may be greater for boys than for girls).

Characteristics at Different Stages of Life

When the initial small group of concerned parents and professionals first sought to obtain help for their children and to promote the field of learning disabilities, their efforts focused on the pressing needs of the elementary-level child. Today, we recognize that learning disabilities become evident at many stages of life and that the problem appears in a different form at each stage.

Figure 1.1 illustrates the number of children identified with specific learning disabilities at different age levels, ranging from age 6 through age 21 (U.S. Department of Education, 2002). The number of students gradually increases from age 6 to 9, a majority of students are in the 9 to 14 age range, and the number decreases sharply from ages 16 to 21. This pattern suggests that substantial numbers of children with learning disabilities are identified in the age range of 9 through 14. Most children are not identified until age 9, and the decrease during the teen years may relate to the large dropout rate of adolescents with learning disabilities.

Each age group (preschoolers, elementary children, adolescents, and adults) needs different kinds of skills. Therefore, certain characteristics of learning disabilities assume greater prominence at certain age levels.

The Preschool Level   Because growth rates are so unpredictable at young ages, educators are generally reluctant to identify preschoolers under a categorical label such as *learning disabilities*. Very young children (under age 6) who appear to have learning disabilities are often identified under a noncategorical label such as *developmental delay*. However, experience and research show that intervention for young children is very effective and that educational efforts have a high payoff (Lerner, Lowenthal, & Egan, 2003).

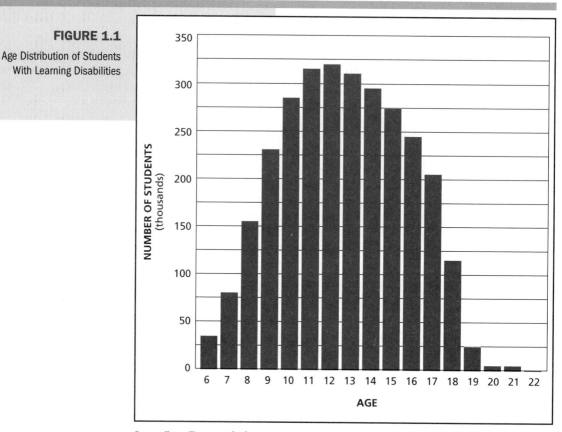

FIGURE 1.1

Age Distribution of Students With Learning Disabilities

Source: From *To assure the free appropriate public education of all children with disabilities.* Twenty-fourth Annual Report to Congress on the Implementation of the Individuals With Disabilities Act, by the U.S. Department of Education, 2002. Washington, DC: U.S. Government Printing Office, Table AA4, AA5.

Among the characteristics displayed by preschool children with learning disabilities are inadequate motor development, language delays, speech disorders, and poor cognitive and concept development. Common examples of problems at the preschool level are the 3-year-old child who cannot catch a ball, hop, jump, or play with manipulative toys (poor motor development); the 4-year-old child who does not use language to communicate, has a limited vocabulary, and cannot be understood (language and speech disorders); and the 5-year-old who cannot count to 10, name colors, or work puzzles (poor cognitive development). In addition, preschoolers often exhibit behaviors of hyperactivity and poor attention. The problems and treatment of the preschool child are so unique that a special chapter of this text is devoted to the topic (see the chapter on young children with learning disabilities). Data for 3–5-year-old children are not counted by category of disabilities (e.g., learning disabilities), but 5% of all children receiving

LD STORIES

FRED'S ELEMENTARY SCHOOL EXPERIENCE

That day stands out starkly in my memory. I was at the blackboard, carefully printing the words that my first-grade teacher had asked me to write. As I stepped back from my work, the laughter of my classmates told me I'd done something terribly wrong. What was so funny? I was confused by the laughter. "Fred," the teacher admonished, "you wrote all of your *e*'s backward."

During second grade, things became worse. No matter how hard I tried, I couldn't grasp simple math—even adding 2 and 2 was difficult. I kept wondering, What's wrong with me?

By the third grade, my parents became increasingly concerned. I remember my mother plaintively asking, "What'll become of Fred?"

Note: This child became one of the world's leading brain surgeons and pioneered many surgical techniques.

Source: Based on "What'll become of Fred?" by F. Epstein, 1994, *Reader's Digest*, February, 46–50.

special education services are in the 3–5 age group (U.S. Department of Education, 2002).

The Elementary Level   For many children, learning disabilities first become apparent when they enter school and fail to acquire academic skills. The failure often occurs in reading, but it also happens in mathematics, writing, or other school subjects. Among the behaviors frequently seen in the early elementary years are inability to attend and concentrate; poor motor skills, as evidenced in the awkward handling of a pencil and in poor writing; and difficulty in learning to read. "LD Stories: Fred's Elementary School Experience" describes one student's difficulties.

In the later elementary years, as the curriculum becomes more difficult, problems may emerge in other areas, such as social studies or science. Emotional problems also become more of an impediment after several years of repeated failure, and students become more conscious of their poor achievement in comparison with that of their peers. For some students, social problems and the inability to make and keep friends increase in importance at this age level. About 40% of all children with learning disabilities are in the 6–11 age group (U.S. Department of Education, 2002).

The Secondary Level   A radical change in schooling occurs at the secondary level, and adolescents find that learning disabilities begin to take a greater toll. The tougher demands of the middle school and high school curricula and teachers, the turmoil of adolescence, and the continued academic failure combine to intensify the learning disability. Adolescents are also concerned about life after completing school. They may need counseling and guidance for college, career, and vocational decisions. To worsen

AN ADULT'S STRUGGLE WITH LEARNING TO READ

When I left school at the age of 15, the only qualifications I possessed besides years of failing was the reading ability of a 6-year-old. I could not even spell my own name. It was like living in a dark shadow, and at times it was like hell. If I didn't know or understand what was being said, I would never ask for clarification. I was too scared and nervous.

I was frustrated and tired of people humiliating me. I tried to hide my illiteracy by doing things like carrying a card in my wallet with the different amounts of money spelled on it so I could slip it out and withdraw some money from the four banks in town.

I couldn't trust my own reading ability when reading instructions on medicine bottles. I had checks returned to me many times because the words and figures didn't match. I couldn't read the instructions on how to use the public telephone in an emergency. I applied for a horticultural apprenticeship, but was turned down five times in five years.

I decided to enroll in the Adult Learning Assistance Program. My dream was to learn to read and write. I had three wonderful tutors who gradually helped me learn to read and write. Gradually, I became more confident and convinced that I could learn to read successfully.

Source: Based on "Overcoming illiteracy: The toughest marathon," by Michael Marquet, 1994, *Reading Today* 12 no. 2:17.

---

the situation, a few adolescents find themselves drawn into acts of juvenile delinquency (Learning Disabilities Association of America, 1995).

Because adolescents tend to be overly sensitive, some emotional, social, and self-concept problems often accompany a learning disability at this age. Most secondary schools have programs for adolescents with learning disabilities. Although this age group is considered throughout this text, some of its unique features and some special programs for adolescents are discussed in the chapter on adolescents and adults with learning disabilities. About 60% of all children with learning disabilities are in the 12–17 age group (U.S. Department of Education, 2002).

The Adult Years By the time they finish schooling, some adults overcome their learning disabilities, are able to reduce them, or have learned how to compensate or circumvent their problems. For many adults, however, the learning problems continue, and vestiges of their disorder continue to hamper them as they grow older. Both reading difficulties and nonverbal social disabilities may limit their career development and may also hinder their ability to make and keep friends. Many adults are voluntarily seeking help in later life to cope with their learning disabilities, as illustrated in "LD Stories: An Adult's Struggle With Learning to Read."

What percentage of the children in our schools have learning disabilities? Estimates of the prevalence of learning disabilities vary widely—ranging from 1% to 30% of the school population, with about 5% receiving services in the schools. The number of children and youth identified as having learning disabilities depends largely on the criteria used to determine eligibility for services. The more stringent the identification criteria, the lower the prevalence rate. If only severe cases of learning disabilities are admitted to the program, a low percentage of pupils in the school will be identified. Conversely, the more lenient the criteria, the higher the prevalence rate. If mild as well as severe learning disabilities are admitted for service, the prevalence rate will rise.

Increase in Children Identified With Learning Disabilities

Before the passage of Public Law 94–142 in 1975, there were only estimates of the number of children with disabilities who were being served in our schools. With this law, a nationwide count was accomplished through the individualized education program (IEP), which was written for each student in special education. This child-count information indicates that the number of students identified as having learning disabilities has increased steadily. The first year the law was implemented (1977–1978), fewer than 800,000 children (or 1.8% of the enrolled school population) had received services under the category of learning disabilities in 1977. The percentage had increased to 5.8%, or over 2.6 million, by the 2000–2001 school year (U.S. Department of Education, 2002). Figure 1.2 shows the steady increase in the percentage of students identified with learning disabilities from the year 1978 to 2001.

Why has the category of learning disabilities experienced such a rapid increase? Several explanations are suggested.

1. *More awareness of learning disabilities.* Public awareness of the condition of learning disabilities has increased. As a consequence, parents, educators, and students are exerting additional pressure on the schools to provide adequate services for students with learning disabilities.

2. *More procedures for identifying and assessing learning disabilities.* Evaluation and assessment techniques identify many children who previously would have gone unidentified.

3. *Social acceptance and preference for the learning disabilities classification.* Many parents and administrators prefer the classification of learning disabilities because it does not carry the stigma of other areas of disability. Some students who once would have been classified as having mental retardation or behavior disorders are increasingly being classified under the rubric of learning disabilities. For example, as

FIGURE 1.2

Percentage of Students With
Learning Disabilities

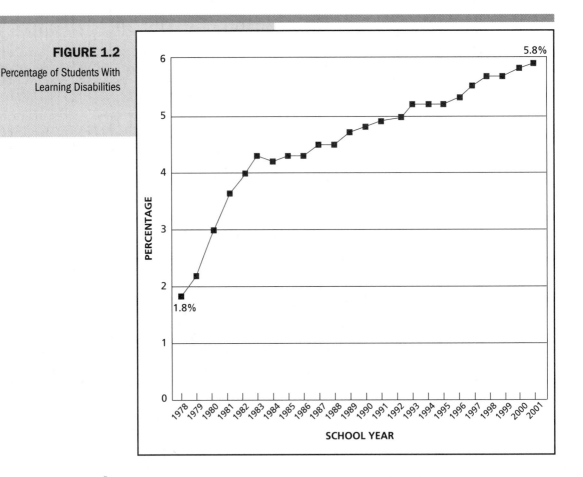

noted in point 4, the number of children classified under *mental retardation* has decreased significantly.

4. ***Court orders.*** A number of court decisions found that the classification of minority children as mentally retarded was discriminatory. Some of these children may be identified under the classification of learning disabilities. In contrast with the increases in learning disabilities, there has been a long-term decrease in the number and relative proportion of children and youth identified with mental retardation.

Comparison of Learning Disabilities and Other Categories of Disability

Comparisons of learning disabilities with other categories of disability are revealing. In Table 1.3, the first column lists each type of disability or impairment, and the second column shows the percentage of each disability

TABLE 1.3

Percentage of Children
With Disabilities,
Ages 6–17

Type of disability	Percentage of total school enrollment	Percentage of all disabilities
Learning disabilities	5.74	50.0
Language impairment	2.28	20.0
Mental retardation	1.14	9.9
Emotional disturbance	.94	8.2
Hearing impairment	.14	1.2
Orthopedic impairment	.14	1.1
Other health impairment	.59	5.1
Visual impairment	.05	0.4
Autism	.16	1.4
Traumatic brain injury	.03	0.3
Developmental delay	.06	0.5
Other	.23	1.9
All disabilities	11.50	100.0

Source: From *To assure the free appropriate public education of all children with disabilities.* Twenty-fourth Annual Report to Congress on the Implementation of the Individuals With Disabilities Education Act, by the U.S. Department of Education, 2002. Washington, DC: U.S. Government Printing Office.

or impairment in terms of school enrollment. The third column shows the portion of each disability or impairment as a percentage of all children identified under special education; Figure 1.3 displays this information as a pie chart. Learning disabilities is the largest category, accounting for one-half of the children receiving special education services.

HISTORY OF THE FIELD OF LEARNING DISABILITIES

The field of learning disabilities has had a relatively short history. This section offers a brief review of the important events. A more detailed history of the field of learning disabilities appears on the student website for this text at **http://www.college.hmco.com/education.**

Three phases of this history are (1) the foundation phase, (2) the transition phase, and (3) the integration phase (Figure 1.4).

Foundation Phase: Early Brain Research

The foundation phase (1800–1930) occurred prior to the establishment of the field of learning disabilities. This was a period of broad scientific

FIGURE 1.3

Composition of Students
With Disabilities

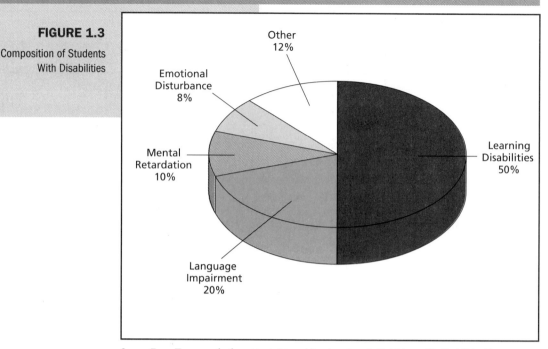

Source: From *To assure the free appropriate public education of all children with disabilities.* Twenty-fourth Annual Report to Congress on the Implementation of the Children With Disabilities Education Act, by the U.S. Department of Education, 2002. Washington, DC: U.S. Government Printing Office.

research on the functions and disorders of the brain. Many of the early brain researchers were physicians who were involved in investigating the brain damage of adult patients who had suffered a stroke, an accident, or a disease. These scientists gathered information by studying the behavior of patients who had lost some function, such as the ability to speak or read. In the autopsies of many of these patients, the scientists were able to link the loss of functions to specific damaged areas of the brain. Overall, the brain research conducted during this phase set the foundation of the field of learning disabilities.

Transition Phase: Clinical Study of the Child

During the transition phase (1930–1960), scientific studies of the brain were applied to the clinical study of children and were then translated into ways of teaching. Psychologists and educators developed instruments for assessment and methods for teaching, and they analyzed specific types of learning disabilities. During the transition phase, terminology changed

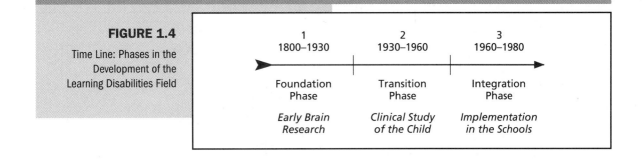

FIGURE 1.4

Time Line: Phases in the
Development of the
Learning Disabilities Field

	1 1800–1930	2 1930–1960	3 1960–1980
	Foundation Phase	Transition Phase	Integration Phase
	Early Brain Research	*Clinical Study of the Child*	*Implementation in the Schools*

many times, with various terms being used to describe the problem—*brain-injured children, Strauss syndrome, minimal brain dysfunction* and, finally, *learning disabilities*. The progression of these terms reflects the historical progress of the field.

The Brain-Injured Child   The term **brain-injured child** was first used by Alfred Strauss and Laura Lehtinen (1947), pioneers who identified brain-injured children as a new category of exceptional children. Strauss and Lehtinen hypothesized that a brain injury could occur during one of three periods in the child's life: *before* birth (prenatal stage), *during* the birth process, or at some point *after* birth (postnatal stage). They believed that as a result of such organic impairment, the normal learning process was prevented or impeded. Many of these children previously had been classified as mentally retarded, emotionally disturbed, autistic, aphasic, or behaviorally maladjusted. A large number of children exhibited such severe behavioral characteristics that they were excluded from the public schools.

One characteristic of the brain-injured child is a **perceptual disorder,** which is a disturbance in the ability to perceive objects, relations, or qualities—a difficulty in the interpretation of sensory stimulation. For example, one teacher noted that when she wore a particular dress with polka dots, the children with perceptual disorders seemed compelled to touch it to verify what they thought they perceived. Figure 1.5 illustrates the ambiguity in perception that the normal observer senses, which helps one understand the unstable world of the child with a perceptual disorder. In Figure 1.5, one is to determine whether the picture is the face of an old woman or a young woman. Do you see a young woman or an old woman in this picture? In Figure 1.6, one is asked to look at the drawing and then to sketch it from memory. (Even copying this figure while viewing it may prove to be difficult.) These illustrations produce a perceptual confusion, much like that experienced by a child with perceptual disorders.

Strauss's work with brain-injured children laid the foundation for the field of learning disabilities by perceiving similar characteristics in a diverse

FIGURE 1.5

Do you see a young woman or an old woman in this picture?

Source: Illustration by W. E. Hill in *Puck*, 1915.

group of children who had been misdiagnosed by specialists, misunderstood by parents, and often discarded by society.

Strauss Syndrome   In seeking another way to identify these children, the term **Strauss syndrome** was recommended to recognize the pioneering work of Strauss (Stevens & Birch, 1957). The *Strauss syndrome* child exhibits the following behaviors:

1. Erratic and inappropriate behavior on mild provocation
2. Increased motor activity disproportionate to the stimulus
3. Poor organization of behavior
4. Distractibility of more than the ordinary degree under ordinary conditions
5. Persistent faulty perceptions
6. Persistent hyperactivity
7. Awkwardness and consistently poor motor performance

Minimal Brain Dysfunction   The term **minimal brain dysfunction (MBD)**, which is defined as a mild or minimal neurological abnormality that causes learning difficulties, was recommended by the Department of Health, Edu-

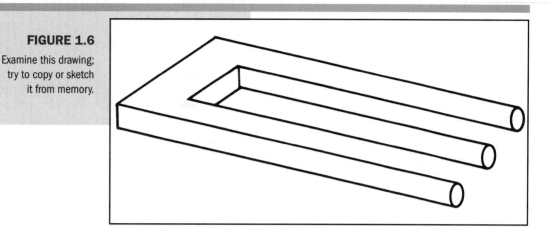

FIGURE 1.6

Examine this drawing;
try to copy or sketch
it from memory.

cation, and Welfare (Clements, 1966). MBD was used to describe children with near-average intelligence and with certain learning and behavioral disorders associated with deviations or dysfunctions of the central nervous system. Many medical professionals employed the term MBD when diagnosing children.

Learning Disabilities   None of the recommended terms for describing these children received general acceptance, and it was clear that another term was needed to more meaningfully describe these children. As noted earlier, Samuel Kirk (1963) first proposed the term learning disabilities at a meeting of concerned professionals and parents. Accepted immediately, the term gained rapid acceptance among parents, teachers, and governmental bodies. This term encompasses many diverse types of learning problems. It focuses on the educational problems and avoids the medical implications. In 1975, the term learning disabilities became part of the special education law in the United States, and it is now used in many other countries throughout the world. Learning disabilities successfully serves as a recognized way to refer to individuals with problems that are the concern of this text.

Integration Phase: Implementation in the Schools

During the integration phase (1960–1980), learning disabilities became an established discipline in schools throughout the United States. The field grew rapidly as programs for learning disabilities were developed, teachers were trained, and children began to receive services.

One of the first public school programs for learning disabilities was established in Syracuse, New York (Cruickshank, Bentzen, Ratzebbugh, &

Tannhauser, 1961). The Syracuse curriculum called for: (1) reducing unessential visual and auditory environmental stimuli, (2) providing a highly structured schedule, and (3) increasing the stimulus value of the teaching materials.

By the 1960s and 1970s, public school programs for learning disabilities were rapidly established throughout the nation. Several strong forces promoted this development, including parental pressures, an increase of professional information, the availability of teacher training programs, and state laws requiring services for students with learning disabilities. All of this took place before the passage of the first comprehensive special education law in 1975, which was, as noted previously, the Education for All Handicapped Children Act (PL 94–142).

Most of the early programs were for students at the elementary level. In these early programs, children with learning disabilities were placed in separate classes, which followed the traditional delivery system in special education at that time. Later in this period, resource room programs were introduced, and the secondary schools also began to serve adolescents with learning disabilities. Many new tests and teaching materials were developed during this period to serve the growing number of students identified under the category of learning disabilities.

Special Education Laws: Individuals With Disabilities Education Improvement Act

The legislation that had the greatest influence on the establishment of learning disabilities services in our public schools was the 1975 federal special education law, which, as noted earlier in this chapter, was known as Public Law 94–142 (or the Education for All Handicapped Children Act). This law was updated as the Individuals With Disabilities Education Act (IDEA; PL 101–476) in 1990 and IDEA was revised with PL 105–17 in 1997. In 2004, IDEA was again revised (PL 108–446). Under this series of laws, summarized in Table 1.4, all children and youth ages 3 through 21 with disabilities have the right to a free and appropriate public education. Further, each state must have a plan that is in compliance with the federal law. Table 1.4 shows these laws.

Individuals With Disabilities Education Act of 1990 and 1997 continued the mandates of the earlier 1975 law, PL 94–142, but added several important features. The term *disabilities* was used instead of *handicaps*, which is now considered a pejorative term. The word *individuals* replaced the word *children*. The law recognized two additional categories of disabilities: *autism* and *traumatic brain injury*. It also required transition plans for adolescents with learning disabilities. The Individuals With Disabilities Education Improvement Act of 2004 sharpened the law by (see the website http:www.cec.sped.org for a summary of IDEA–2004):

	Public law number	Name of law	Date passed
TABLE 1.4 Series of Special Education Laws	PL 94–142	The Education for All Handicapped Children Act	1975
	PL 101–476	Individuals With Disabilities Education Act (IDEA) of 1990	1990
	PL 105–17	Individuals With Disabilities Education Act (IDEA–1997) of 1997	1997
	PL 108–446	Individuals With Disabilities Education Improvement Act (IDEA–2004) of 2004	2004

- Strengthening the role of parents
- Extending the full rights and protections to preschool children with disabilities
- Ensuring access to the general education curriculum
- Giving more attention to racial, ethnic, and linguistic diversity to prevent inappropriate identification and mislabeling
- Encouraging parents and educators to work out their differences through nonadversarial means, such as mediation or a dispute resolution process

Basic Concepts of the Individuals With Disabilities Education Act   IDEA is considered civil rights legislation that guarantees education to individuals with disabilities. The law alters former educational practices that had led to exclusion, neglect, and substandard treatment of students with disabilities. The critical features of IDEA that have implications for identifying, assessing, and serving students with learning disabilities are discussed in relevant sections of this book. Among them are the *individualized education program* or IEP (see the chapter on assessment), *procedural safeguards* (see the chapter on assessment), *least restrictive environment* (see the chapter on educational settings), *continuum of alternative placements, parental involvement* (see the chapter on assessment and educational settings), and attention deficit disorders (see the chapter on attention deficit disorder and related conditions).

IDEA–2004 recognizes that individuals with disabilities need special education or related services. Federal categories of disabilities under IDEA–2004 include learning disabilities, mental retardation, hearing impairments including deafness, language impairments, visual impairments including blindness, emotional disturbances, orthopedic impairments, other health impairments, autism, and traumatic brain injuries.

Other Special Education Laws: Section 504 and the Americans With Disabilities Act   Two additional laws affect students with disabilities in the schools. Section 504 of the Rehabilitation Act requires that accommodations be made for individuals with disabilities in institutions that receive federal funds. The Americans With Disabilities Act (ADA) protects people with disabilities from discrimination in the workplace. Both laws are discussed further in the chapters on educational settings and adolescents and adults with learning disabilities.

No Child Left Behind Act

In 2001, Congress passed the **No Child Left Behind Act (NCLB)** to ensure that all children have a fair, equal, and significant opportunity to obtain a high-quality education and to reach a minimum proficiency on challenging state academic achievement standards. The centerpiece of NCLB is the requirement that public schools bring students to proficiency in reading and math. The law includes sanctions for schools that fail to make acceptable progress.

Some of the highlights of the NCLB Act (Wright, Wright, & Heath, 2004) are:

- Every state needs to adopt challenging academic standards and curriculum guidelines. Every state also needs to develop coherent "proficiency" levels to be attained by all children. Every state needs to develop an accountability system in which the consequences fall on responsible adults. Success should be reward. Failing schools should be closed, restructured, or taken over. All students should have the right to leave poor schools for better schools.

- Each school's progress is measured with reading and math proficiency tests of all students. The school is to report on students by subgroups (i.e., ethnicity, disabilities, English-language learners, and low-income). To meet the NCLB standard, all subgroups must make sufficient academic progress to ensure that all students are proficient by 2014. If the school does not educate any subgroup, the school will fail to meet this standard.

- NCLB requires schools to teach all children to proficiency in reading, math, and science by 2014. The key requirements of the law—annual proficiency tests in grades 3–8; highly qualified teachers in every classroom; research-based instruction; increased parental rights; public school choice; and state, district, and school report cards—are strategies to accomplish this goal.

- Schools and school districts are required to meet the educational needs of all children, including poor children, children with disabilities, English-language learners, minority and migratory children, and other neglected groups of children, and to publicly report their progress in educating children every year.

- Children will have access to effective, scientifically based instruction and challenging academic content. Children are to receive an enriched, accelerated educational program that includes additional services that increase instructional time.

- NCLB covers all states, school districts, and schools that accept federal Title I grants. Title I grants provide funding for remedial education programs for poor and disadvantaged children in public schools and in some private programs. States shall give priority to school districts that serve the lowest-achieving schools and that demonstrate the greatest need and strongest commitment to improve.

For students with learning disabilities, the tests required by the act provide a formidable challenge. Often, the areas being tested are the areas of their disability, and students with learning disabilities often do poorly on these tests because the NCLB procedures do not take into account their unique individual differences (Johns, 2003).

CURRENT DIRECTIONS A number of issues currently affect students with learning disabilities. In this section, we look at the issues of standards-based education, high-stakes testing, the inclusion practices, cultural and linguistic diversity, and computer technology.

Standards-Based Education

Standards-based education refers to the setting of certain standards for the curriculum content and teacher education. For the field of special education, the Council for Exceptional Children, with the approval of the National Council for the Accreditation of Teacher Education (NCATE), developed 10 content standards, as well as knowledge and skill-based standards for special education teachers. For more information, visit their website at **http://www.cec.sped.org/ps/perf_based_stds/standards.html.** These content standards refer to all areas of special education. Table 1.5 shows the 10 content standards for special education and where each standard is addressed in this text.

High-Stakes Testing

The call for accountability in today's schools profoundly affects students with learning disabilities and all students with special needs. All states now have state-level assessments. These standards-based assessments are called **high-stakes testing** because they have significant consequences for districts, schools, administrations, teachers, and students. Schools, administrators,

TABLE 1.5	CEC content standard	Description	Chapter
Content Standards for Special Education	Foundation	Understands the field as an evolving and changing discipline based on philosophies, evidence-based principles, theories, authorities, laws, and history.	Chapters 1, 3, and 4
	Development and characteristics of learners	Respect for students as unique human beings. Understands the similarities and differences in human development and the characteristics of exceptional learning needs.	Chapters 3, 5, and 14
	Individual learning differences	Understands the effects that an exceptional condition can have on an individual's learning in school and throughout life.	Chapters 1, 3, and 5
	Instructional strategies	Possesses a repertoire of evidence-based instructional strategies to individualize instruction for individuals with special learning needs.	Chapters 10, 11, 12, 13, and 14
	Learning environments and social interactions	Creates a learning environment for individuals' special needs that fosters cultural understanding, safety and emotional well-being, positive social interactions, and active engagement.	Chapter 4
	Language	Understands typical and atypical language development and the ways in which exceptional conditions can interact with an individual's experience with and use of language.	Chapter 10
	Instructional planning	Knows individualized decision making and instruction. Can develop long-range individualized instructional plans anchored in both general and special curricula.	Chapters 2, 3, and 4
	Assessment	Knows and uses multiple types of assessment information for a variety of educational decisions. Uses the results of assessment to help identify exceptional learning needs, to develop and implement individualized instructional programs, as well as to adjust instruction in response to ongoing learning progress.	Chapter 2
	Professional and ethical practice	Guided by the profession's ethical and professional practice standards. Practice in multiple roles and complex situations across wide age and development ranges. Attention to legal matters.	Chapters 1, 3, and 4
	Collaboration	Collaborates with families, other educators, related service providers, and personnel from community agencies in culturally responsive ways.	Chapters 4, 7, 8, and 9

Source: Reprinted with permission of the Council for Exceptional Children, *Professional Standards*, 2001. Arlington, VA: Council for Exceptional Children.

HIGH-STAKES TESTING

The Oregon Statewide Assessment System (OSAS) measured performance in the area of written language assessment (e.g., spelling). These tests did not allow the use of word processors and spell-checkers, even for students with learning disabilities who were using these accommodations in their classrooms. Due to the method of scoring the spelling subtests, many students with learning disabilities failed to achieve the certificate of mastery. Furthermore, Oregon had not developed alternate assessments for students with learning disabilities, nor was there a fully developed appeals process.

The Oregon legal case involved students with learning disabilities who were denied the certificate of mastery because they had failed the written language test. The parents of these children filed a class-action lawsuit against the Oregon Department of Education. The settlement of this lawsuit required that appropriate accommodations for students with learning disabilities be developed. Students with disabilities in the area of written language were given the opportunity to use a word processor and a spell-checker for the written language test.

Source: From *Do no harm: High-stakes testing and students with learning disabilities,* by Disabilities Rights Advocates, 2001, Oakland, CA: Disabilities Rights Advocates.

and teachers can be rewarded or punished based on student performances on these tests. For students, the test results often determine whether they will pass to the next grade or graduate from high school (Thurlow, 2000). The No Child Left Behind Act (2001) has fueled the testing accountability with annual reading and math assessments in grades 3 through 8.

Prior to the Individuals with Disabilities Education Act of 1997, students with disabilities (including learning disabilities) could be excluded from the state and district-wide assessments. IDEA–2004 requires that students with disabilities be included in these tests. Two additional IDEA–2004 requirements for testing affect students with disabilities:

1. *Accommodations.* Students with disabilities may be provided with *accommodations* in the testing, such as changes in presentation, response, timing, scheduling, or setting. These accommodations are to be included in the student's IEP.

2. *Alternate assessments.* States must develop guidelines for *alternate assessments* to be used with students unable to participate in the general state assessment. Alternate assessments refer to another way to measure performance; these should be included in the students' IEP.

Inclusion Practices

Inclusion refers to the policy of placing children with disabilities into the general education classrooms for instruction. **General education placement** for students with disabilities has grown rapidly in our schools in recent years. Support for placing children with disabilities in general education classrooms is based on a component of the law called the **least restrictive environment (LRE)**. The least restrictive environment is a term in special education law that indicates that, to the greatest extent appropriate, children with disabilities should receive instruction in an educational setting with children who do not have disabilities. Some suggestions for general education teachers are given in LD in Practice: Strategies for Teaching Students With Special Needs in the General Education Classroom, later in this chapter.

Instructing students with disabilities in general education classrooms can provide students with greater access to their general education peers, raise expectations for student performance, help general education students be more accepting of diverse students, and improve coordination between regular and special educators (Cawley, Hayden, Cade, & Baker-Krocynski, 2002; Elbaum, 2002; Stainback & Stainback, 1992).

Concerns about inclusion practices focus on whether children with learning disabilities will receive the intensive, direct, and individualized teaching they need. Special education requires discovering what is unique about each child with learning disabilities and providing individually designed instruction to meet the particular needs of that child. Several research studies show that students with learning disabilities are poorly served in inclusion classrooms (Holloway, 2001; Johns, 2003; McLeskey et al., 2004; Zigmond, 2003). Inclusion is discussed further in the chapter on educational settings.

Cultural and Linguistic Diversity

In our schools today, children from many different backgrounds, cultures, environments, and languages receive instruction through learning disabilities programs. Understandably, difficulty in school learning may occur when the language, values, or customs of the child's culture differ substantially from those of the school. However, the problem is compounded when the child also has learning disabilities. For students with culturally diverse backgrounds, the problems arising from the cultural differences and those from learning disabilities are difficult to untangle (Ortiz, 1997; Taylor & Leonard, 1999). Some parents reflect cultural attitudes that a child with a disability is a personal failure. These parents may not wish to admit that their child has a disability, they may refuse to attend individualized education program (IEP) meetings, or they may even keep a child with a disability at home as a face-saving gesture.

The school population is rapidly changing in the United States and Canada. Schools must be responsive to an increasingly diverse society. In the United States, nearly one of every three students is from a minority background—African American, Hispanic, Asian American, or Native American. Children who are **English-language learners** have limited English proficiency and are a rapidly growing group of the school population. In the school districts of New York and Chicago, students who are English-language learners make up almost one-half of the students initially entering school at the kindergarten level.

One of the greatest challenges our schools face is the ability to educate students from all cultures, whatever their geographic origin, socioeconomic status, or language. Cultural pluralism recognizes the rich contributions of the participating cultures in our schools and promotes the conviction that each culture can make worthy contributions to the overall society. The differences that exist among the various cultural populations in our schools can be a positive force in society. Children benefit by maintaining their cultural identities, and society is enriched by the mosaic created by this diversity (Taylor & Leonard, 1999).

Because learning disabilities occur in all cultures and ethnic groups, the population of students with learning disabilities reflects the **cultural and linguistic diversity** of our society. Teachers must appreciate the cultural contributions of each group, understand the differences in assessment procedures, and be fair in considering each child's culture, language, and background.

Learning English is particularly challenging for children with learning disabilities whose native language is not English. These children actually have two difficulties: limited English proficiency and learning disabilities. Many do not have a good grasp of their native language, yet they are expected to learn and function in English. For these children, teachers must draw upon instructional methods from both bilingual education and special education. Strategies for helping children with limited English proficiency and learning disabilities are presented in the chapter on oral language.

In 2002, the U.S. Department of Education reported the number of children with disabilities served by race or ethnicity. Five race/ethnicity categories were used in presenting these data: Native American, Asian/Pacific Islander, black (non-Hispanic), Hispanic, and white (non-Hispanic). The percentage of students by race/ethnicity with learning disabilities and in the general school population is shown in Table 1.6.

Computer Technology

Our children live in a computer society with an ever-changing influx of new computer-based technologies. Children today have more comprehensive and faster worldwide links to commerce, communication, and culture.

Race/ethnic group	Percentage with learning disabilities
Native American	1.3
Asian/Pacific Islander	1.9
Black (non-Hispanic)	19.9
Hispanic	14.5
White (non-Hispanic)	62.4

Source: From *To assure the free appropriate public education of all children with disabilities.* Twenty-fourth Annual Report to Congress on the Implementation of the Individuals with Disabilities Education Act, by the U.S. Department of Education, 2002. Washington, DC: U.S. Government Printing Office.

Schools must prepare students to deal with these dramatic changes so that they can fully participate and compete in the increasingly complex technological workplace.

Society readily recognizes the benefits of computer-based technologies for typically functioning children. However, there are even greater benefits that computer-based technologies may afford children with learning disabilities. Computer applications can help level the playing field for students with learning disabilities, allowing them to succeed in the general education environment. For many students with learning disabilities and related disorders, their ease in operating computers is an area of strength that helps them overcome areas of severe difficulty, such as their abilities to read and write. Research shows that often students with learning disabilities who have academic problems have a special facility with computers (Belson, 2003; Hasselbring & Glaser, 2000; Raskind & Higgins, 1998a, 1998b). Specific uses of computer applications are discussed throughout this book in pertinent sections.

Assistive Technology   Technology for students with disabilities is defined in federal law as "any item, piece of equipment, or product system, whether acquired commercially off the shelf, modified, or customized, that is used to increase, maintain, or improve functional capabilities of individuals with disabilities" (Individuals With Disabilities Education Act, 1997). The **Assistive Technology Act** recognizes the need for persons with disabilities to access and use assistive technology devices and provides funding to support **assistive technology** (PL 108–364, 2004).

Assistive technology devices enable users with disabilities to move, play, communicate, write, speak, and participate in many activities that would be inaccessible without the computer. Assistive technology can help these individuals overcome barriers in print, in communication, and in learning. Students who have problems with reading and writing can use assistive technology such as CDs or taped books, devices that read printed books aloud, and "talking" computer programs. Students who have difficulty

COMPUTERS AS AN AREA OF STRENGTH

Jason is a young adult with serious learning disabilities who is severely dyslexic; his reading and writing skills are at the first-grade level. Despite participating in numerous kinds of reading programs and working with many tutors over the years, he still virtually cannot read or write. In a computer class, he was taught how to use spreadsheets for budgeting and PowerPoint to make presentations. Jason successfully learned and began using these computer programs within a very short time. Apparently, these computer applications did not tap his linguistic disability areas; instead, they used his strengths in visual areas. It has long been known that many students with learning disabilities do extremely well in the arts. Perhaps this phenomenon is also true of their facility with computer technology.

with written communication can use word processing programs, spelling and grammar aids that provide editing help, programs that assist writers in organizing their thoughts during the planning stage of the writing process, and voice input devices to dictate written messages.

Universal Design for Learning   A new model of technology use was developed by the organization **Universal Design for Learning (UDL)**. This organization investigates new views of technology for teaching, learning, assessment, and curriculum development, UDL emphasizes the idea that every curriculum should include alternatives to make learning accessible and appropriate for individuals with different backgrounds, learning styles, abilities, and disabilities in widely varied learning contexts. The website for UDL is **http://www.cast.org.**

UDL points out that designing for the diverse needs of special populations increases usability for everyone. All learners should have the tools to complete the tasks they encounter. Thus, the findings of assistive technology should be broadened to all learners. A good example of how Universal Design for Learning has a broad scope of applications for all people is the use of "curb cuts." Originally intended for wheelchair users, people quickly discovered that they were useful for many purposes in the general population: strollers, bicycles, roller skates, luggage carts, etc.

Computer Uses   Descriptions of several current and emerging computer uses that have important implications for students with learning disabilities follow.

E-mail   E-mail is widely used by students with learning disabilities and its use should be part of the curriculum. With e-mail, students can send and

receive electronic messages, make friends, communicate with other students, and teachers can communicate with the entire class through a list-serv. Unlike snail mail, e-mail allows people to send and receive messages at any time of the day or night. It encourages students to engage in meaningful peer-to-peer writing and join interest bulletin boards.

The Internet The World Wide Web provides a way to display information on the Internet. The Web is made up of interconnected pages or sites, each containing textual and graphic information on specific topics. Users can link up to pages that interest them. For example, students can go to the White House and visit its occupants at **http://www.whitehouse.gov.**

CD-ROM Technology CD-ROM drives and compact discs make multimedia-based applications possible through their large storage and retrieval capability. With CD-ROM software, programs can use text, speech, graphics, pictures, audio, and video, and students can interact with the computer program as they solve problems and make choices. With electronic reference materials, such as encyclopedias on CD-ROM, students can explore and obtain information by browsing through topics or searching for specific information. Electronic storybooks on CD-ROM offer high-interest stories, and words can be highlighted or read aloud by the computer.

Word Processing Word processing is a boon for students with learning disabilities who have difficulty in handwriting, spelling, and written composition. One student with learning disabilities wrote:

LD IN PRACTICE

STRATEGIES FOR TEACHING STUDENTS WITH SPECIAL NEEDS IN THE GENERAL EDUCATION CLASSROOM

- Begin each lesson with a review of what has been learned.
- Tell students the goal of the lesson.
- Reorganize the seating to help students by placing students with special needs near the teacher.
- Provide positive support for all students.
- Teach all students study skills.
- Allow sufficient practice of the concepts or skills for all students.
- Work with special education teachers to help all students.
- Use differentiated instruction to take into account the learning styles and learning needs of all students in the class.
- Summarize what has been learned at the end of each lesson.

I didn't learn how to write until I learned how to use a computer. This sounds ironic, but in my past, writing was spelling, and since I could not spell, I could not write. When I discovered a word processing system with a spell check, I finally understood that writing involved putting thoughts and ideas into some kind of written form. Knowing that the computer would catch my spelling errors, I began to ignore my spelling. Then I began to look at writing as content. (Lee & Jackson, 1992, p. 23)

Computers can help students with learning disabilities by providing a one-on-one interactive environment in which students can practice recently acquired reading skills as often as they wish and spend more time in learning tasks.

Voice Recognition Devices and Text Readers   A voice recognition device allows the user to dictate through a microphone. The device then translates the user's speech into a form that the computer can say. Each user must participate in a teaching session before the computer can recognize the user's speech. One specifically used speech recognition is Dragon Naturally Speaking. More information can be found on the website, **http://www. scansoft.com/naturallyspeaking.**

Text reader devices are known as text-to-speech applications. Such devices convert printed text into synthetic or digital speech. An excellent text reader program is the Kurzweil Reading Program. More information can be found on the website, **http://www.Kurzweiledu.com.**

Other Computer Applications Students also need to know how to use spreadsheets and charts, presentation software (such as PowerPoint), databases, desktop publishing software, and how to develop webpages. Knowing how to use these applications will enhance their learning in content areas and in the curriculum. Moreover, employers expect employees to be familiar with these applications, at which students with learning disabilities often excel (Belson, 2003).

Specific applications of computer technology appear in the chapters on young children with learning disabilities, reading, written language, and mathematics.

CHAPTER SUMMARY

1. Learning disabilities have affected the lives of many eminent people.

2. Learning disabilities occur in all cultures, affecting individuals of all nations and languages.

3. The definition of learning disabilities in federal law is the basis for most state definitions, but other definitions have been proposed.

4. Common elements of the definitions include neurological dysfunction, processing deficits, difficulty in academic and learning tasks, discrepancy between achievement and intellectual ability, and/or response-to-intervention exclusion of other causes.

5. Students with learning disabilities have many different characteristics.

6. The history of the field of learning disabilities includes the foundation phase, the transition phase, and the integration phase.

7. Laws that affect students with learning disabilities include the Individuals With Disabilities Education Improvement Act (IDEA–2004) and the No Child Left Behind (NCLB) Act.

8. Current directions include standards-based education, high-stakes testing, inclusion practices, cultural and linguistic diversity, and computer technology.

DISCUSSION AND REFLECTION

1. What are the various definitions of learning disabilities that have been proposed? How do they differ?

2. What are the components that are common to most of the definitions of learning disabilities? Discuss the nature of each component and the controversies surrounding each.

3. How has the role of the learning disabilities teacher changed? Discuss the new responsibilities.

4. Describe three distinct historical phases in the development of the field of learning disabilities. Discuss how each phase has contributed to the discipline of learning disabilities.

5. What is meant by high-stakes testing? What is the implication for students with learning disabilities?

6. Describe some ways that computers can be used for students with learning disabilities.

KEY TERMS

assistive technology *(p. 36)*

Assistive Technology Act *(p. 36)*

brain-injured child *(p. 25)*

cultural and linguistic diversity *(p. 35)*

current achievement level *(p. 11)*

English-language learners *(p. 35)*

general education placement *(p. 34)*

high-stakes testing *(p. 31)*

inclusion *(p. 34)*

individualized education program (IEP) *(p. 13)*

Interagency Committee on Learning Disabilities (ICLD) *(p. 9)*

learning differences *(p. 12)*

learning disabilities *(p. 2)*

least restrictive environment (LRE) *(p. 34)*

mild/moderate disabilities *(p. 13)*

minimal brain dysfunction (MBD) *(p. 26)*

multiple intelligences *(p. 14)*

National Joint Committee on Learning Disabilities (NJCLD) *(p. 8)*

No Child Left Behind Act (NCLB) *(p. 30)*

perceptual disorder *(p. 25)*

Public Law 94–142, Education for All Handicapped Children Act (1975) *(p. 6)*

Public Law 101–476, Individuals With Disabilities Education Act (IDEA–1990) *(p. 6)*

Public Law 105–17, Individuals With Disabilities Education Act of 1997 (IDEA–1997) *(p. 6)*

Public Law 108–446, Individuals With Disabilities Education Improvement Act (IDEA–2004) *(p. 6)*

response-to-intervention *(p. 12)*

severe discrepancy *(p. 11)*

standards-based education *(p. 31)*

Strauss syndrome *(p. 26)*

Universal Design for Learning (UDL) *(p. 37)*

2 Assessment

Assessment today is on the forefront of education. Parents, federal and state legislators, executive leaders, and the general public want to know the extent to which students are profiting from their school experiences. Schools are increasingly held accountable for the performance of pupils.

—J. Salvia & J. Ysseldyke

Part II, The Assessment–Teaching Process, includes the three chapters that highlight the interrelated elements of the assessment–teaching process. They are "Assessment," "Clinical Teaching," and "Educational Settings."

Assessment must be linked with teaching if one is to understand and help a troubled student. Attention to only one of these components splinters the effort and shortchanges the student. For example, routinely teaching skills or using methods or materials without considering a student's unique problems may be ineffective because such teaching does not address the student's needs. Similarly, if assessment only results in selecting a diagnostic label, the procedure will not provide guidelines for aiding the student's learning.

Chapter 2 focuses on assessment. We examine the uses of assessment, investigate the influence of the law on the assessment process, and look at ways to obtain assessment information. We also provide examples of tests and review the issue of standards and accountability. Finally, in this chapter we begin a case study, which continues in the chapters on clinical teaching and educational settings, to illustrate the assessment–teaching process.

USES OF ASSESSMENT INFORMATION

Assessment is the process of collecting information about a student that will be used to form judgments and make decisions concerning that student. Two major reasons for conducting an assessment in special education are classification and planning instruction. First, in order to be eligible for special education services, a student must be identified—or classified—as having a disability (such as a learning disability). The second, more important reason for assessment is to obtain information that can be used to plan ways to help the student learn.

The closer the connection between educational assessment and instruction, the more effective the assessment–teaching process will be. Assessment that focuses on curriculum and teaching is needed for guiding instruction. The astute clinical teacher continues to probe and evaluate during the teaching process. Even after the initial assessment, the teacher should remain alert to the student's responses and changing needs. During the teaching process, the evaluation should continue through discerning observation and questioning.

The assessment process serves several purposes:

1. *Screening.* The screening process is used to detect pupils who may need a more comprehensive examination. In the screening process, a cursory evaluation is given to ascertain which students need a more intensive evaluation.

2. *Referral.* The referral process seeks additional assistance from other school personnel. On the basis of observation and classroom performance, the teacher (or others) requests an evaluation of a student.

3. *Classification.* The classification process is used to determine a student's eligibility for services. Students are assessed to judge the need for services and to classify the category of disability.

4. *Instructional planning.* The instructional-planning process is used to assist in planning an educational program for an individual student. The assessment information is used to formulate instructional goals and objectives, to decide on placement, and to make specific plans for teaching.

5. *Monitoring pupil progress.* This process is used to review a student's achievement and progress. Many approaches can be used, including standardized formal tests and alternate or informal measurements.

THE INFLUENCE OF THE LAW ON THE ASSESSMENT PROCESS

Special education laws have significantly shaped the assessment process. As noted earlier, there have been a series of special education laws since 1975, with each law revising an earlier law.

1. 1975, All Handicapped Children Education Act (PL 94–142)

2. 1990, Individuals With Disabilities Education Act (IDEA; PL 101–476)

3. 1997, Individuals With Disabilities Education Act of 1997 (IDEA–1997; PL 105–17)

4. 2004, Individuals With Disabilities Education Improvement Act of 2004 (IDEA–2004; PL 108–446)

Information about the special education law (IDEA) can be obtained at **http://www.ideapractices.org.** In addition, the No Child Left Behind (NCLB) Act impacts the assessment of students with disabilities, particularly with regard to statewide testing and performance standards. See **http://www.wrightslaw.com** for more information.

IDEA–2004 (PL 108–446) provides all students with disabilities a *free, appropriate public education (FAPE).* This means special education and related services that have been provided at public expense:

■ Meet the standards of the state education agency

- Include an appropriate preschool, elementary school, or secondary school education in the state involved
- Are provided in conformity with the individualized education program (IEP)

A major provision of the law is the requirement that each public school child who receives special education and related services must have an **individualized education program (IEP).** The IEP is a written statement for each child with a disability; this statement is developed, reviewed, and revised in accordance with the law (IDEA–2004). Each IEP is designed for one student and should be a truly *individualized* document. The IEP creates an opportunity for teachers, parents, school administrators, related services personnel, and students (when appropriate) to work together to improve educational results for children with disabilities. The IEP is the cornerstone of a quality education for each child with a disability (IDEA–2004 [PL 108–446]).

Purposes of the IEP

The IEP serves two purposes:

1. *The IEP is a written plan for an individual student.* It is a written statement developed by the IEP team that prescribes specific educational goals and placement for an individual student.

2. *The IEP is a management tool for the entire assessment–teaching process.* In this sense, the IEP also serves a much broader purpose. As the core of the entire assessment–teaching process, the IEP involves all assessment evaluations as well as teaching procedures. It becomes the critical link between the student with learning disabilities and the special teaching that the student requires.

Thus, the IEP is intended to be a management tool for ensuring that the education designed for an individual student is appropriate for that student's special learning needs and that the special education services are actually delivered and monitored. The IEP represents an entire accountability system in miniature—an outline of learner expectations, assessment strategies, and performance standards (Bateman & Linden, 1998; Erickson, Ysseldyke, & Thurlow, 1998).

Procedural Safeguards and Parents' Rights

Procedural safeguards are regulations in federal law that are designed to protect the rights of children and parents. The term **parents' rights** was used in IDEA as a procedural safeguard to protect the rights of parents; these rights have been considerably expanded and are summarized in Table 2.1.

TABLE 2.1

Parents' Rights and
Procedural Safeguards

1. Parents must *consent in writing* to several phases of the IEP process: (1) to having their child evaluated; (2) to the IEP, including plans and placement as set forth in the written IEP; and (3) to the three-year reevaluation plan.

2. The assessment must be conducted in the student's language and form most likely to yield accurate information on what the child knows or can achieve academically, developmentally, and functionally. The findings must be reported in the parents' native language.

3. The school or local education agency (LEA) must ensure that tests are *not racially or culturally discriminatory*.

4. Parents have the *right to see all information* that is collected and used in making decisions. Parents can request an explanation of all evaluation procedures, tests, records, and reports.

5. Parents have the *right to mediation* at no cost. **Mediation** is voluntary; it is defined as a process of resolving disputes between the school district and the parents of a child with a disability in a nonadversarial fashion.

6. An additional dispute resolution process called a "resolution session" can be convened.

7. Parents and students have the *right to an impartial, due process hearing* if they disagree with the IEP decision or if the voluntary mediation is unsatisfactory. There are certain provisions to have the school pay attorneys' fees if the parents prevail in a lawsuit.

8. The *confidentiality* of the student's reports and records is protected under the law.

STAGES OF THE IEP

The IEP follows a sequence of stages. As shown in Figure 2.1, there are three broad stages: referral, assessment, and instruction. Each of these stages is subdivided, making six stages in all. These six stages meet the legislative mandates of the IEP. The case study described at the end of this chapter and continued in the chapters on clinical teaching and educational settings for services, illustrates the stages of the IEP process.

Referral Stages

The **referral stages** begin the IEP process and involve two components: the prereferral activities and the referral activities.

Stage 1: Prereferral Activities **Prereferral activities** are preventive intervention measures taken by general education classroom teachers to meet the needs of students who are encountering difficulties in their classrooms. Teachers take these measures before referring students for a special education case study. If the prereferral measures are successful, the prereferral interventions make the referral unnecessary. Most school districts and some states now require evidence that prereferral activities have occurred before a referral is initiated.

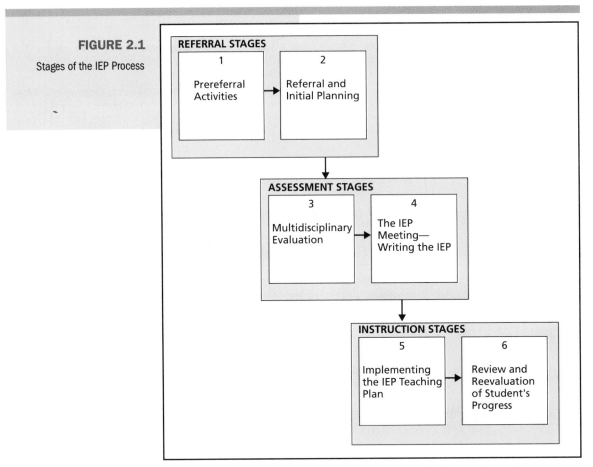

FIGURE 2.1

Stages of the IEP Process

REFERRAL STAGES

1

Prereferral Activities

2

Referral and Initial Planning

ASSESSMENT STAGES

3

Multidisciplinary Evaluation

4

The IEP Meeting— Writing the IEP

INSTRUCTION STAGES

5

Implementing the IEP Teaching Plan

6

Review and Reevaluation of Student's Progress

Source: Reprinted with permission from J. Lerner, D. Dawson, and L. Horvatch, *Cases in Learning and Behavior Problems: A Guide to Individualized Education Programs* (Salem: W. I. Sheffield Publishing, 1980), p. 3. Copyright 1979 by Houghton Mifflin Company.

Prereferral intervention is a less cumbersome means of gathering data about a student's performance than the formal multidisciplinary evaluation. A peer group of colleagues helps the classroom teacher analyze the student's academic and/or behavioral problems and recommends interventions and accommodations for the classroom. The classroom teacher then tries the suggested methods to help the student. The prereferral stage is important because the decision to refer a student for a multidisciplinary evaluation has serious consequences. Once a student is referred, the probability is high that the student will be declared eligible for services (Salvia & Ysseldyke, 2004).

For the prereferral intervention, a general education teacher refers a child of concern to a prereferral collaboration team in the school building. This team responds to the teacher's prereferral requests, using the general steps listed in "LD in Practice: Tasks of the Prereferral Collaboration Team" (Chalfant & Pysh, 1993; F. Clark, 2000; Spinelli, 2002).

LD IN PRACTICE

TASKS OF THE PREREFERRAL COLLABORATION TEAM

1. A general education classroom teacher requests help from a school collaboration team for a student of concern.
2. The collaboration team explores possible interventions for the child with the classroom teacher.
3. The classroom teacher tries suggested interventions in the general education classroom.
4. If further decisions are needed, a member of the collaboration team observes the student in the classroom and then consults with the classroom teacher.
5. If the student's problem persists, the teacher makes a formal referral for a special education evaluation.
6. A response-to-intervention procedure can be used to provide scientific research based interventions.

The procedure known as *response-to-intervention* is a prereferral intervention, which is discussed later in this chapter in the section "Determining Eligibility for Learning Disabilities."

Stage 2: Referral and Initial Planning   The initial **referral** of a student for special education evaluation can come through several sources: the parent, the teacher, other professionals who have contact with the student, or a self-referral by the student. After a referral is made, school personnel must follow it up. Parents must be notified of the school's concern and must give written permission for an evaluation. In addition, decisions must be made about the general kinds of evaluation data needed and the people who will be responsible for gathering this information.

Assessment Stages

The **assessment stages** are the core of the process and involve the tasks of evaluation and developing and writing the IEP.

Stage 3: Multidisciplinary Evaluation   At this stage, specialists representing various disciplines obtain pertinent information by assessing academic performance and behavior in areas related to the suspected disability. For example, specialists for the **multidisciplinary evaluation** might include a school psychologist, school social worker, school nurse, speech and language pathologist, learning disabilities specialist, or reading specialist.

The law (IDEA–2004; PL 108–446) outlines the procedures for gathering information for the evaluation. Several features of the law regulate the evaluation. The tests must be appropriate, validated for the purpose used, and as free as possible from cultural or racial bias. Evaluation materials must be administered in the student's native language. The evaluation team must represent several disciplines and must include at least one teacher or specialist in the area of the suspected disability. This means that if the condition of being learning disabled is suspected, at least one person knowledgeable about learning disabilities will be involved in the multidisciplinary evaluation. The multidisciplinary evaluation team specialists administer tests and obtain other evaluation data. The qualified professionals on this team and the parents determine the student's eligibility for learning disabilities services.

Stage 4: The IEP Meeting—Writing the IEP   After the multidisciplinary evaluation has been conducted, the information is gathered, and the parents are contacted for the **IEP meeting.** It is at this meeting that the IEP is written.

The Participants at the IEP Meeting   According to IDEA–2004, the participants on the IEP team must include the following:

1. The parents of the child with a disability
2. Not less than 1 regular education teacher of such child (if the child is, or may be, participating in the regular education/special education environment)
3. Not less than 1 special education teacher, or where appropriate, not less than 1 special education provider of such child
4. A representative of the school or school district who
   a. Is qualified to provide, or supervise the provision of, specially designed instruction to meet the unique needs of children with disabilities
   b. Is knowledgeable about the general education curriculum
   c. Is knowledgeable about the availability of resources of the school or school district
5. An individual who can interpret the instructional implications of evaluation results, who may be a member of the team
6. At the discretion of the parent or the agency, other individuals who have knowledge or special expertise regarding the child, including related services personnel as appropriate
7. Whenever appropriate, the child with a disability

Contents of the Child's IEP   The contents of the IEP must include these components (IDEA–2004):

1. A statement of the child's present levels of academic achievement and functional performance

    a. How the disability affects the child's involvement and progress in the general education curriculum

    b. For preschool children, how the disability affects the child's participation in appropriate activities

    c. For children with disabilities who take alternate assessments aligned to alternate achievement standards, a description of benchmarks or short-term objectives

2. A statement of measurable annual goals, including academic and functional goals designed to

    a. Meet the child's needs, that result from the child's disability, in order to enable the child to be involved in and make progress on the general education curriculum

    b. Meet each of the child's other education needs that result from the child's disability

3. A description of how the child's progress toward meeting the annual goals will be measured, and when the periodic reports, on the progress the child is making toward meeting the annual goals (such as through the use of quarterly or other periodic reports, concurrent with the issuance of report cards), will be provided

4. A statement of the special education and related services and supplementary aids, based on peer-reviewed research to the extent practicable, to be provided to the child, and a statement of the program modifications or supports for school personnel that will be provided for the child

5. An explanation of the extent to which the student will not participate with nondisabled children in the regular class and in regular class activities

6. A statement of individual appropriate modifications that are necessary to measure the academic achievement and functional performance of the child on state and districtwide assessments

7. The projected date for the beginning of the services and modifications, and the anticipated frequency, location, and duration of those services and modifications

8. Appropriate transition assessments and services, beginning not later than the first IEP to be in effect when the child is 16, and updated annually (transition is described in more detail in the chapter on Adolescents and Adults with Learning Disabilities).

Related Services   In addition to determining the necessary special education services, the IEP team also determines the need for related services that may be required to enable a child with a disability to benefit from special education. These may include transportation and developmental, corrective, and other supportive services. Such assistance may include speech-language specialists and auditory services, psychological services, physical and occupational therapy (including therapeutic recreation), social work services, counseling services (including rehabilitation counseling), orientation and mobility services, and medical services for diagnostic and evaluation purposes.

Instruction Stages

The **instruction stages** occur after the written document (the IEP) has been completed, and they involve the teaching and monitoring of the student's progress.

Stage 5: Implementing the IEP Teaching Plan   This is the teaching portion of the assessment–teaching process. It occurs after the IEP document has been written. During this stage, the student is taught in the agreed upon setting and receives instruction designed to help the student reach the goals set forth in the IEP. This stage involves implementing the IEP plan through teaching (see the chapters on clinical teaching and educational settings).

Stage 6: Review and Reevaluation of the Student's Progress   This stage calls for the review and reevaluation of the IEP plan in terms of the student's progress. The IEP must include explanations that show how this evaluation will be accomplished, who will conduct the evaluation, and what assessment instruments and criteria will be used. IDEA requires that the child's parents be informed of their child's progress toward reaching annual goals as frequently as parents of nondisabled children are informed. One way to do this is to send the parents IEP report cards.

DETERMINING ELIGIBILITY FOR LEARNING DISABILITIES

It is necessary to determine if a student has a learning disability and is eligible for special education services. Two models for determining eligibility are: (a) the *discrepancy between achievement and intellectual ability method*, and (b) *the response-to-intervention* method. Each is discussed in this section.

The Discrepancy Between Achievement and Intellectual Ability Method to Determine Eligibility for Learning Disabilities

The discrepancy between achievement and intellectual ability method has been generally used in schools to determine eligibility for learning disabilities. With this method learning disabilities are identified, if the student has a severe discrepancy between the score of intellectual ability and the score on achievement in oral expression, listening comprehension, written expression, basic reading skill, reading comprehension, mathematical calculation, or mathematical reasoning, their learning disabilities are identified. The student's achievement, which is what the student has actually learned, is compared to the student's intellectual ability, which is what the student is potentially capable of learning. A significant difference between the two measures indicates that the student has a learning disability. One procedure for measuring this gap is to compare a student's standard score on an achievement test, such as a reading achievement test, with the student's standard score on a capacity of learning test, such as an intelligence test or a test of cognitive ability. A difference between these two standard scores greater than 1.5 or 2 standard deviations indicates that the student has a learning disability and is eligible for special services (Salvia & Ysseldyke, 2004; Spinelli, 2002).

There are several different formulas for determining a discrepancy score. A **discrepancy score** is a mathematical calculation for quantifying the discrepancy between achievement and intellectual ability, or potential for learning. Formulas for determining a discrepancy score are explained and illustrated in the website accompanying this book, **http://college.hmco.com.**

Concerns About Discrepancy Formulas   There are a number of concerns about using aptitude-achievement discrepancy formulas.

- *Quantitative and qualitative information should be combined.* Many parents and teachers are concerned about the use of quantitative discrepancy scores for making decisions about their children, contending that there is no substitute for clinical judgment and actual experience (Chalfant, 1989; Mastropieri, 1987). Indeed, decisions about eligibility for learning disabilities services should not be made solely on the basis of a discrepancy formula. Discrepancy scores ignore other learning characteristics that are unique for individuals with learning disabilities, and do not consider many significant human and clinical factors. Fortunately, the clinical judgment of the evaluation team can override the discrepancy formulas in identifying a student with learning disabilities.

- *How useful is the IQ score in measuring an individual's potential?* IQ tests do not necessarily measure intelligence. Moreover, an IQ score can be adversely affected by the student's culture or native language. In addition, the student could have a lowed IQ score because of the nature of the disability itself (Fletcher, Coulter, Reschly & Vaughn, 2004).

- *Children who are poor achievers have similar characteristics, whether they have high IQ scores or low IQ scores.* Research shows there are many similarities between these two groups (Fletcher et al., 2004).

- *Using the IQ-achievement discrepancy score implies that children must fail before they can be identified as having a learning disability.*

- *Discrepancy formulas vary from state to state.* States and school districts differ in their discrepancy formulas for identifying learning disabilities. Thus, a child could be identified as having a learning disability in one state but may be declined for services after moving to another state.

Determining the Present Levels of Achievement   When applying a discrepancy formula, the IEP team must also determine the student's **present levels of achievement,** which are the levels that the student is currently performing in various developmental and academic areas. This task involves the following activities:

1. Reviewing the information gathered by the multidisciplinary team
2. Determining the subject and skills areas for which an IEP should be developed
3. Deciding whether sufficient evaluation data are available and, if necessary, gathering additional evaluation information through standardized tests, alternative assessment measures, or observations
4. Designating the student's current achievement level in the skill areas to be developed. The achievement level can be stated in terms of norm-referenced test scores (such as grade level) or alternative measures (such as criterion-referenced measures or portfolio information).

The Response-to-Intervention Method to Determine Eligibility for Learning Disabilities

Another approach for determining eligibility for learning disabilities is described in the Individuals With Disabilities Education Improvement Act of 2004 (Public Law 108–446) and is called the *response-to-intervention* procedure for determining eligibility for learning disabilities. According to the law, when determining whether a child has a specific learning disability, schools shall *not* be required to take into consideration whether a child has a severe discrepancy between achievement and intellectual ability.

The *response-to-intervention* approach is used during the prereferral stage to determine if a child responds to scientific, research-based interventions. Students who are thought to be at risk of academic failure are taught using scientific, research-based instructional materials. If students respond well to these interventions, they are not thought to have a learning disability. Students who do not respond positively to this instruction or who do not learn adequately are given more intensive teaching in scientific research-based instruction. If the child still does not respond or learn after several trials, the child can then be considered for an evaluation for learning disabilities (Fletcher et al., 2004; Fuchs, Mock, Morgan, & Young, 2003; Vaughn & Fuchs, 2003).

Scientific Research-Based Instruction   The response-to-intervention method is based on using *scientific research-based instruction*. For the subject of reading, the *No Child Left Behind Act*, 2001, defines scientifically based research for reading instruction in this way:

1. It applies rigorous, systematic, and objective procedures to obtain valid knowledge relevant to reading
2. It includes research that
   a. Employs systematic, empirical methods that draw on observation or experiment
   b. Involves rigorous data analyses that are adequate to test the stated hypotheses and justify the general conclusions drawn
   c. Relies on measurements or observational methods that provide valid data across evaluators and observers and across multiple measurements and observations
   d. Has been accepted by a peer-reviewed journal or approved by a panel of independent experts through a comparably rigorous, objective, and scientific review

 Some state websites provide guides for CORE instructional materials that meet these criteria, for example, **www.isbe.net/curriculum/reading/html/read_first.htm** and **www.ncpublicschools.org/readingfirst/corelist.html.**

EVALUATING A STUDENT WITH LEARNING DISABILITIES

There are a number of dimensions to be considered in the process of evaluating a student with learning disabilities.

Observing the Student in the Classroom

A classroom **observation** of the student is required to provide information about the student's behavior in school and the ways in which that behavior affects academic problems. For example, the observation would consider what the student with learning disabilities does during the independent reading activity period.

Recognizing the Student's Strengths and Clusters of Characteristics

Students with learning disabilities have many strengths. It is important to recognize and to encourage these strengths. For example, some children with learning disabilities do well in math or computer applications, yet they may have difficulty with reading skills. Some children have strong social skills and acquire many friends, others do well in artistic and creative endeavors, and some children excel at physical activities and sports. It is important to recognize the child's strengths and to use those recognized strengths when determining the child's teaching plan (Gardner, 1999; Levine, 2002, 2003).

It is also helpful to look for clusters of characteristics in evaluating a student with learning disabilities. For example, a student with a severe handwriting problem may also have difficulty with other fine-motor skills. Likewise, a student with a reading problem may also have an underlying oral language disorder. A student who does poorly in oral expression may have a history of delayed speech, speech–motor difficulties that affect articulation, and difficulty with remembering words.

Considering the Concerns of Parents

IDEA–2004 emphasizes strengthening the role of parents and ensuring that families have meaningful opportunities to participate in the education of their child at home and at school. The law recognizes the key role that parents have in their child's education.

Setting Annual Goals

What **annual goals** should be set for the student? Annual goals are general estimates of what the student will achieve in one year. These goals should represent the student's most essential needs and priorities for each subject area. For example, an annual goal in mathematics could be that the student learns to multiply and divide. Interim goals could include the following:

1. The student will add numbers that involve carrying in two digits (e.g., 578 + 389).
2. The student will subtract numbers that involve regrouping in two digits (e.g., 311 − 289).
3. The student will multiply and divide through products of 81.
4. The student will multiply two-digit numbers by one-digit numbers (e.g., 25 × 9).
5. The student will divide numbers by two-digit divisors (e.g., 237 ÷ 25).

Periodic reports to parents could report on the progress to meet this annual goal.

Determining Educational Settings and Services

What specific special education and related services are to be provided? To what extent will the student attend general education classes? These decisions are related to where the student will be placed or to the educational setting. (The various options for placement are discussed in the chapter on educational settings.) In addition, decisions must be made about the extent to which the student will be placed in the least restrictive environment (i.e., with students who do not have disabilities). In IDEA, the general curriculum is presented to be the appropriate beginning point for planning an IEP for a student, and the general education curriculum is the preferred course of study for all students.

What teaching plan is appropriate for the student? Although not required in the IEP, a plan must be developed for teaching. This plan should take into account all the information about the student: (1) strengths and weaknesses, (2) developmental levels, (3) skills learned as well as those not yet assimilated, (4) age, (5) interests, and (6) attitudes. Teachers should have a broad knowledge of methods, materials, approaches, curriculum areas, child development, and, most important, the students themselves.

Monitoring Progress

How will the student's progress be monitored and measured? It is necessary to determine whether annual goals are being met. What measurement instruments will be used? Who will be responsible for administering them? Also, any accommodations that will be needed for the statewide tests must be included in the IEP. A sample format for evaluating annual goals appears in Table 2.2.

SPECIAL FACTORS TO CONSIDER IN THE IEP FOR STUDENTS WITH LEARNING DISABILITIES

A number of special factors must be considered in the evaluation of students with learning disabilities, according to the provisions of IDEA.

Functional Behavioral Assessment and Positive Behavioral Intervention and Support

IDEA–2004 indicates that if the child's *behavior* interferes with his or her learning or the learning of others, the IEP team will consider strategies and supports to address the child's behavior. If a child with disabilities displays behavior that impedes his or her learning or that of others, the IEP team

TABLE 2.2

Sample Format for IEP
Annual Goal in Mathematics

Instructional area: Mathematics

Annual goal: Student will learn multiplication and division computation skills

Meeting the annual goal

Progress reports to parents	Tests, materials, and evaluation procedures to be used	Criterias of successful performance	Evaluation schedule	Educational accommodations
1. Student will add numbers involving two renamings	Student will compute 20 addition problems requiring two renamings	85% accuracy	End of first grading period	■ Student will participate in statewide assessment in mathematics
2. Student will subtract numbers involving two renamings	Student will compute 20 subtraction problems requiring two renamings	85% accuracy	End of second grading period	■ Allow double time for math assessment ■ Permit student to use a calculator during the math test
3. Student will multiply and divide through products of 81	Student will compute a fact sheet containing 20 multiplication and division facts and products through 81 within a specified time	65% accuracy	End of third grading period	
4. Student will multiply two-digit numbers by one-digit numbers	Appropriate mastery test will be included in mathematics text	75% accuracy	End of fourth grading period	
5. Student will divide numbers by two-digit divisors	Appropriate mastery test will be included in mathematics text	75% accuracy	End of fifth grading period	

Source: "Percentage of Students with Learning Disabilties by Race/Ethnicity" from United States Department of Education, *To Assure the Free Appropriate Education for All Children with Disabilities,* Twenty-Fourth Annual Report to Congress on the Implementation of the Individuals with Disabilities Act (Washington, DC: United States Government Printing Office, 2002).

must be able to evaluate the child's behavior through a *functional behavioral assessment* and to design a *positive behavioral support* to change the student's troublesome behavior (Center for Effective Collaboration and Practice, 1998; Smith, 2000; Sugai & Homer, 1999; U.S. Department of Education, 2000a). Also see the websites at **http://www.cecp.air.org, http://www.pbis.org, http://www.fape.org** and **http://www.behavioradvisor.com.**

Functional Behavioral Assessment   A **functional behavioral assessment** includes a number of steps: (1) identify the target problem behavior, (2) develop a hypothesis about what conditions provoke the problem behavior, and (3) determine what seems to maintain the occurrence of the behavior. This procedure is not new; it is based on the applied behavior analysis procedure called *ABC:* antecedent, behavior, consequence. Figures 2.2 and 2.3 illustrate these three behavioral events. Also, if the student is suspended or expelled, the IEP team must make a *manifestation determination.* This means that they must decide whether the troublesome behavior is part of the student's disability. If it is, services must continue for the student with disabilities who has been suspended or expelled because of his or her behavior (Sugai & Homer, 1999).

Positive Behavioral Support   IDEA–2004 stipulates that if a child's behavior impedes the child's learning or the learning of others, the IEP shall consider strategies, including positive behavioral interventions and supports, to address the behavior. **Positive behavioral support** as a general term refers to the culturally appropriate applications of positive behavioral interventions and systems to achieve socially important behavior change (Center for Effective Collaboration and Practice, 1998; U.S. Department of Education, 2002). The following can be done to implement positive behavioral interventions:

- A desirable replacement behavior should be taught to the student. For example, if the student throws a math book, he or she would be removed from the math class.

- A replacement behavior would be to give the student an alternative math assignment.

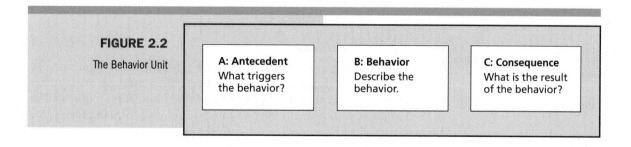

FIGURE 2.2

The Behavior Unit

A: Antecedent
What triggers
the behavior?

B: Behavior
Describe the
behavior.

C: Consequence
What is the result
of the behavior?

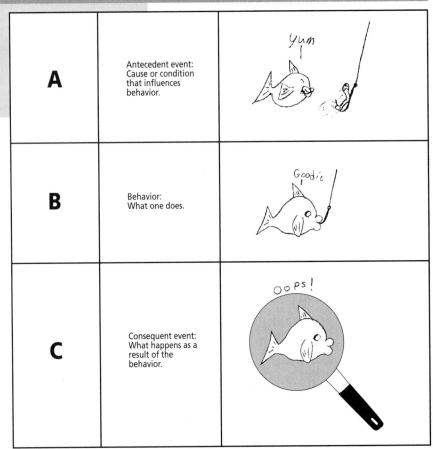

FIGURE 2.3

Example of ABC:
Antecedent Event,
Behavior, Consequent Event

A	Antecedent event: Cause or condition that influences behavior.	
B	Behavior: What one does.	
C	Consequent event: What happens as a result of the behavior.	

Source: Artist: Anne Lerner, Age 9.

- The environment could be modified to increase the effectiveness of the replacement behavior. For example, the student would receive a consequence for throwing the book, but the student could not avoid attending the math class.

English-Language Learners

Society is becoming more responsive to the growing needs of an increasingly diverse society. **English-language learners (ELL)** (students with limited English proficiency) comprise the fastest growing population in our nation. In the largest school districts in the United States, English-language learners make up almost one-half of the children entering school at the kinder-

Race/ethnicity	Percentage of population
White (non-Hispanic)	61.3
Black (non-Hispanic)	18.0
Hispanic	17.6
Asian/Pacific Islander	1.6
Native American	1.5

Source: From *To Assure the Free Appropriate Public Education of All Children With Disabilities.* Twenty-Fourth Annual Report to Congress on the Implementation of the Individuals With Disabilities Education Act, by the U.S. Department of Education, 2002, Washington, D.C.: U.S. Government Printing Office, Table 22-5.

garten level. IDEA requires that if the child has limited proficiency in English, the IEP team must consider the child's language needs as they relate to the child's IEP. IDEA requires that states report by race ethnicity the number of children with disabilities served. For children with learning disabilities, the percentages reported by race/ethnicity are listed in Table 2.3.

Assistive Technology

IDEA requires that the IEP team must consider whether the child needs assistive technology devices or services. **Assistive technology** is defined as any technology that enables an individual with a disability to compensate for specific deficits. It includes low- and high-tech equipment.

- The term *assistive technology devices* refers to equipment or products designed to help the functional capabilities of a child with a disability. For example, a speech-recognition system that allows a person to operate a computer by speaking into it, is such a device.
- The term *assistive technology services* refers to any service that directly assists a child with a disability in the selection, acquisition, or use of an assistive technology device. For example, teaching a child who has a disability in writing the needed keyboarding skills for word processing would be an assistive technology service.

The IEP team should describe the nature of the child's disability and the required assistive technology devices and services in the IEP.

"*I'm* not *an underachiever. You're an overexpecter.*"

To find answers to the many questions involved in the process when obtaining assessment information, evaluators gather information from several major sources: (1) the case history or interview; (2) observation; (3) rating scales; (4) standardized norm-referenced tests; (5) curriculum-based measurement and progress monitoring; and (6) alternate or informal measures. Often, several kinds of information are compiled at one time or one assessment procedure may lead to another. For example, observation of a student may suggest that a specific test should also be used. Likewise, detection of speech misarticulation accompanied by the student's frequent misunderstandings of the examiner's conversation could suggest an auditory difficulty and lead to a decision to administer a test of auditory acuity or auditory discrimination.

Case History

The information obtained through a **case history** contributes insights and clues about the student's background and development. During an interview, parents share information about the child's prenatal history, birth conditions, neonatal development, the age of developmental milestones (sitting, walking, toilet training, and talking), the child's health history (including illnesses and accidents), and learning problems of other members of the family. The student's school history can be obtained from parents, school records, and school personnel (e.g., teachers, nurses, and guidance counselors).

The interviewer must try to establish a feeling of mutual trust, taking care not to ask questions that might alarm parents or make them defensive by indicating disapproval of their actions. The interviewer should convey a spirit of cooperation, acceptance, and empathy while maintaining a degree of professional objectivity to guard against excessive emotional involvement and consequent ineffectiveness.

Skillful interviewers are able to obtain much useful information during the case history interview. They gather information in a smooth, conversational manner and go beyond routine questions, garnering more information and impressions than the questions themselves ask. Case history information and impressions are integrated with knowledge obtained through clinical observation, traditional tests, and alternative assessment measures. Table 2.4 illustrates the kind of information obtained through the case history interview.

TABLE 2.4 Case History Information	**Identifying information**
	Student: Name, address, telephone, date of birth, school, grade
	Parents: Father's name and occupation, mother's name and occupation
	Family: Siblings' names and ages, others in the home
	Clinic: Date of interview, referral agency, name of examiner
	Birth history
	Pregnancy: Length, condition of mother, unusual factors
	Birth conditions: Mature or premature, duration of labor, weight, unusual circumstances
	Conditions following birth: Normal, needing special care
	Physical and developmental data
	Health history: Accidents, high fevers, other illnesses
	Present health: Habits of eating and sleeping, energy and activity level
	Developmental history: Age of sitting, walking, first words, first sentences, language difficulties, motor difficulties
	Social and personal factors
	Friends
	Sibling relationships
	Hobbies, interests, recreational activities
	Home and parental attitudes
	Acceptance of responsibilities
	Attitude toward learning problem
	Educational factors
	School experiences: Skipped or repeated grades, moving, change of teachers
	Preschool education: Kindergarten, nursery school
	Special help previously received
	Teachers' reports
	Student's attitude toward school

Case History Interview Forms   Many case history interview forms are available. Some forms are quite lengthy and complete, procuring information in many domains. **Adaptive behavior scales** that question the extent to which individuals adapt themselves to the expectations of nature and society are often used. An informant (usually the mother) provides the information during an interview. The following list contains some commonly used adaptive behavior scales. "Tests for Assessing Students With Learning Disabilities," in the Reference Guide at the back of this book, contains additional information about these instruments.

- *Vineland Adaptive Behavior Scales.*   There are three different versions of these scales: (1) the Interview Edition, Survey Form; (2) the Interview Edition, Expanded Form; and (3) the Classroom Edition. They all assess the domains of communication, daily living skills, socialization, and motor functions for ages birth to 19.

- *Adaptive Behavior Inventory.*   This inventory is used to interview an informant, and it yields information about self-help skills, communication skills, social skills, academic skills, and occupational skills for ages 6 to 9.

Observation

According to Yogi Berra, "Sometimes you can observe a lot just by watching." *Observation* of the student is a required part of the assessment of learning disabilities, and the information that it produces can make a valuable contribution. Although many attributes of the student may be inadequately identified through testing or case study interviews, the skillful observer can often detect important characteristics and behaviors of the child in the classroom setting.

Observation of student behavior often corroborates findings of other assessment measures. For example, a skillful observer can note whether the student is attending to the lesson or is engaged in other activities. One astute observer overheard Richard, who was being evaluated because of poor reading, warning another child that for his bad behavior he would no doubt get "H-A-L-L." The observer perceptively inferred that Richard's incorrect spelling might be related to problems in phoneme awareness and auditory processing. Later testing confirmed that hypothesis.

Observation is also useful for shedding light on a student's general *personal adjustment*. How does the student react to situations and people? What is the student's attitude toward the learning problem? Has the school problem affected the student's social life and home life? Has it drained the student's energy? Is the student's attitude one of interest or seeming indifference? During one testing situation, the teacher observed three children in the class—Ricky, Pat, and Duster. When the work became difficult, Ricky gave up completely and simply filled in the blank spaces with any answer. Pat tensed up and refused to continue his work. Duster refused to guess and was afraid to make a mistake, so she struggled with a single item on the test for as long as she was permitted. These observations gave the teacher valuable information about each student.

Motor coordination and development can be appraised by observing the student's movements and gait. Can the student hop, skip, or throw and catch a ball? How does the student attack a writing task? Is there a contortion of the body while writing? What is the general appearance of the student's handwriting? How does the student hold a pencil? Must the student expend an inordinate effort in trying to make the handwriting presentable?

The child's *use of language* is readily assessed through observation. Is there evidence of articulation problems or infantile speech patterns? Does the student have difficulty finding words? Does the student possess an adequate vocabulary? Does the student speak easily, haltingly, or perhaps excessively? Does the student use complete sentences or single words and short, partial phrases? Is the sequence of sounds correct in words (e.g., *aminal* or *psghetti*)? The student's native language is an important consideration in today's culturally diverse school population. What is the student's primary language and facility with English?

Games and toys offer activities for making observations of the student and also serve as a way to build rapport. For example, one can observe the student's ability to zip a zipper, tie a shoelace, button clothing, or lock a padlock for clues about *fine-motor coordination* and *eye–hand relationships*. Games such as phonic rummy or phonic bingo give clues to the student's *phonics abilities* and *auditory skills*.

Observations of everyday classroom behavior provide much authentic information. For example, while reading, how does the student react to an unknown word? Does the student stop and look to the teacher for help, look at the initial consonant and then take a wild guess, attempt to break the word into syllables, or try to infer the word from the context?

Rating Scales

Rating scales require teachers or parents to record their observations and impressions of students in a measurable fashion. Using these rating scales, teachers or parents check off their impressions of a student's behavior characteristics. Rating scales are frequently used to make judgments about students with learning disabilities and are considered a valuable addition to the assessment process.

Two scales, the Pupil Rating Scale (Revised): Screening for Learning Disabilities and the Devereaux Elementary School Behavior Rating Scale are described in "Tests for Assessing Students With Learning Disabilities." Another commonly used rating scale is the Conners Rating Scale, of which there are several versions.

Rating scales are frequently completed by parents or by teachers when assessing attention deficit hyperactivity disorder (ADHD). These rating scales are described in the chapter on attention deficit disorder, in Table 6.2.

Another rating scale is shown in Figure 2.4. It is a 24-point rating scale designed to help teachers identify pupils with learning disabilities in their classes. Teachers rate the 24 behaviors, from auditory comprehension to motor skills, on a 5-point scale (with 1 indicating poor behavior; 5, good behavior; and 3, average behavior). The highest possible score is 120 (5 × 24). In one study, the mean score of the children classified as normal was 81, and the score of the children identified as having learning disabilities was 61 (Myklebust & Boshes, 1969).

FIGURE 2.4

Rating Scale of Student Behavior

	POOR 1	2	3	4	GOOD 5	
AUDITORY COMPREHENSION						
1. Ability to follow oral directions						1
2. Comprehension of class discussion						2
3. Ability to retain auditory information						3
4. Comprehension of word meaning						4
SPOKEN LANGUAGE						
5. Complete and accurate expression						5
6. Vocabulary ability						6
7. Ability to recall words						7
8. Ability to relate experience						8
9. Ability to formulate ideas						9
ORIENTATION						
10. Promptness						10
11. Spatial orientation						11
12. Judgment of relationships						12
13. Learning directions						13
BEHAVIOR						
14. Cooperation						14
15. Attention						15
16. Ability to organize						16
17. Ability to cope with new situations						17
18. Social acceptance						18
19. Acceptance of responsibility						19
20. Completion of assignments						20
21. Tactfulness						21
MOTOR						
22. General coordination						22
23. Balance						23
24. Ability to manipulate						24

Standardized Norm-Referenced Tests

In the evaluation process, the student's performance and achievement are measured. One approach for measuring student skills is standardized norm-referenced tests.

Standardized **norm-referenced tests** are frequently used in our schools. To develop a standardized test, the test questions are given to a large number of children of the same age. This group is called the *norm-referenced group* because the test norms are based on their performance. When the results of a standardized test are analyzed, the scores of an individual student are compared with the scores of students of comparable age or grade in the norm-referenced group.

Formal standardized tests are statistically designed so that one-half of the student scores will be below the mean (average), and one-half will be above the average. Of course, communities want all of their children to score above average. The humorist Garrison Keillor lampoons this notion in his tales of the mythical town of Lake Wobegon, where "all of the children are above average."

Standardized tests require strict procedures in administration, scoring, and interpretation. They also have the following characteristics:

- The test is usually available in more than one form so that a student can be tested more than once without being able to obtain a higher score due to practice.
- The test is accompanied by a manual giving directions for administration, scoring, and interpretation.
- The manual contains grade norms, age norms, percentile ranks, or some other form of scaled scores.
- The manual has information on validity (the degree to which the test measures what it is supposed to measure). The manual also shows reliability (consistency or similarity of performance). A reliability coefficient of 0.90 indicates that if the test were given to the student again, it is 90% likely that the student would obtain a score in the same range.

The examiner should know the techniques of using and interpreting tests and be thoroughly familiar with the specific test being used. Frequently, the value of a test may not be so much in the final test score as in the measurement of a particular subtest performance, the profile of all the subtest scores, or the clinical observations of the student during the test. The evaluator who has had extensive experience with a test may find that some parts used alone yield the necessary information.

Adequacy of Formal Tests Used in Learning Disabilities In interpreting test scores, it is important to follow certain precautions. The score indicates only a small sample of behavior at one moment in time. By their very nature, all tests give only a limited measure of a person's abilities.

The integrity of formal tests is judged on: (1) *standardization*—on what group was the test standardized? (2) *reliability*—are the test results consistent? and (3) *validity*—does the test measure what it claims to measure? Many of the tests used to assess learning disabilities are inadequate by these criteria (Salvia & Ysseldyke, 2004). Nevertheless, these tests can still be useful in the assessment process. It is important to know the limitations of a test and to use its information in proper perspective. A single score provides only a small part of the information, so teachers should not overgeneralize the implications of a specific test. If multiple sources of data are used in the assessment, test scores can provide a rich harvest of leads for assessment and teaching.

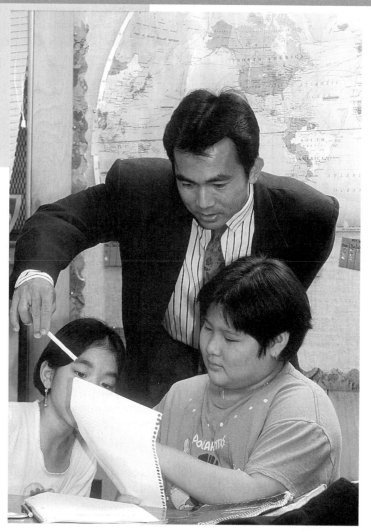

Alternate and informal assessment measures are useful and practical alternative assessment procedures that test students on the ordinary materials that they are currently working with in the classroom.
(© Bob Daemmrich)

Standardized tests can be viewed as a means of providing two levels of information about a student. **General tests** are tests that provide overall scores, but not diagnostic information. They sample general, or global, areas of functioning and indicate whether a student is performing at, above, or below age level in a given area. **Diagnostic tests** provide specific evaluative information about a child's functioning. They give a microscopic view of the components of some area of performance, enabling the teacher to analyze the student's functioning in specific subskills and to supply direction for teaching.

Some commonly used standardized tests of both types are described in this chapter and in the chapters on oral language, reading, written language, mathematics, and social and emotional behavior. A listing of tests and their publishers is presented in "Tests for Assessing Students With Learning Disabilities" in the Reference Guide at the back of this book.

Standardized testing is criticized for a number of reasons:

1. Many educators find that standardized tests do not provide enough information about the students

2. The tests may not assess what students are learning in class

3. Standardized tests may be biased against culturally diverse populations

4. The pressure for students to attain high test scores may sway teachers to use class time to prepare students for taking the tests

5. The tests emphasize segmented skills instead of higher order thinking and creativity

Curriculum-Based Measurement and Progress Monitoring

Curriculum-based measurement (CBM) and progress monitoring are measurement procedures designed to test what a student actually does in the student's school or classroom curriculum. The assessment requires that the student actively perform some task through frequent and repeated measures.

Curriculum-Based Measurement   **Curriculum-based measurement (CBM)** is a procedure for assessing the growth of basic skills (Deno, 2003). First, the teacher determines the area of the curriculum or the goal for the student in the student's IEP. Then, the student's progress is measured through frequent, systematic, and repeated measures of that learning task. Performance results are graphed or charted so that the student's progress is clearly observable to both the teacher and the student. CBM performance samples are 1 min to 3 min, and they are charted to display the student's performance changes over successive time periods, such as days or weeks.

In Figure 2.5, CBM is used to monitor growth in reading through frequent measurements of the number of words the student reads aloud during 1 min reading samples, which is the base-line period over 3 successive

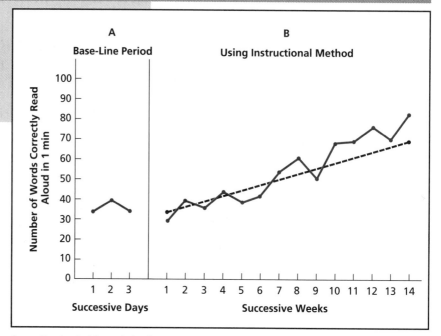

FIGURE 2.5

A Curriculum-Based Measurement Chart Monitoring an Individual Student's Progress

Source: Reprinted with permission from W. Otto, R. McMenemy, and R. Smith, *Corrective and Remedial Teaching, Third Edition.* Copyright 1980 by Houghton Mifflin Company.

days, as shown in the left side of the figure. The right side of Figure 2.5 shows the progress achieved after a targeting instructional program is used for 14 successive weeks, with measurements taken weekly. It demonstrates the improvement in oral reading performance over the 14-week period by showing the number of words read correctly in successive 1 min reading samples. The dashed line shows the IEP goal, which is reading 65 words per minute within 14 weeks (Deno, 2003). A website describing curriculum-based measurement procedures is **http://www.aimsweb.com.**

Progress Monitoring   An extension of CBM for the inclusive classroom is **progress monitoring,** which is an assessment procedure that is used to measure a student's academic performance and to evaluate the effectiveness of instruction. Progress monitoring can be implemented with individual students or an entire class. Like CBM, the teacher first determines the student's current levels of performance and then identifies the goals for learning that will take place over time. The teacher measures the student's academic performance on a regular basis (weekly or monthly) and charts the academic performance. The teacher then measures academic growth by comparing the expected rates of learning against the actual rates of learning (Council for Exceptional Children, 2004). For more information, visit the website for the National Center on Student Progress Monitoring at **http://www.studentprogress.org.**

In the progress monitoring procedure, the teacher gives a short assessment, taking only 1 min to 10 min, and determines the long-term goal. The data are graphed, displaying the current performance level and the long-term goal. By plotting the student's score at each testing, the teacher can determine the actual rate at which the student is progressing. When the teacher sees a student is not making adequate progress, the teacher tries another instructional method and continues to monitor the student's progress. Progress monitoring is a useful means to inform parents of student progress on IEP goals.

Most progress monitoring programs are prepackaged, and many of these programs enable teachers to use computers to produce the graphs and charts they need to see how individual students are progressing. Some websites that provide information about materials for progress monitoring are AIMSweb/Edformation, **http://www.aimsweb.com**; DIBELS, **http://dibels.uoregon.edu**; and McGraw-Hill, **http://www.mhdigitallearning.com**.

Informal Assessment Measures

Disenchantment with standardized testing led educators to turn to alternate and informal assessment procedures. Interest in alternate assessment is growing because it evaluates the student in the natural setting, uses the school curriculum, and capitalizes on what the student actually does in the classroom. Informal assessment approaches encourage students to produce, construct, demonstrate, or perform a response.

Informal assessment measures are useful and practical assessment procedures that test students on the ordinary materials and activities they are currently working with in the classroom. A major advantage of using classroom materials for informal tests is that the assessment is as close as possible to the expected behaviors. Informal tests also give teachers freedom in administration and interpretation. For example, a teacher can encourage the student during the assessment or give the student more time to complete the test. Such adjustments put students at ease and help ensure that they will give their best effort. Informal assessment measures can also be given more frequently than formal tests, and they can be administered over a period of time rather than in a single session. In addition, informal assessment measures can use a variety of materials and procedures, they can be given during regular instruction periods, and they are less expensive than formal tests.

In this section, we present several alternate and informal measures for teachers to use, such as: (1) portfolio assessment, (2) dynamic assessment, (3) diagnostic teaching, (4) informal graded word-recognition tests, (5) informal arithmetic tests, and (6) criterion-referenced tests. Some informal tests are also provided in other pertinent chapters, such as informal reading tests (see the chapter on reading), informal motor tests (see the chapter on young children with learning disabilities), and tests of phonological awareness (see the chapter on oral language).

Portfolio Assessment   In **portfolio assessment,** multiple samples of a student's actual classroom work are collected over an extended period of time. This portfolio is used to evaluate the student's current achievement level and progress over time. Portfolio assessment is often used to measure reading and writing progress. Samples of student work can be used to determine achievement and progress in all academic areas.

A portfolio might contain the following kinds of materials: selected samples of daily work done in the classroom, academic classroom tests (e.g., in spelling or mathematics), checklists of behavior, sample stories, writing drafts at various stages of development, science projects, art samples, a teacher's observational notes, or the results of group projects.

In deciding what samples to collect, the teacher must first consider the goals of the instructional program, and the samples should then reflect these goals. For example, the portfolio might include samples of the objectives in the IEP. Students can be responsible for organizing their own portfolios. Because portfolios serve as mirrors of the process of learning in the classroom, they should be available for student–teacher conferences or for parent conferences (Salend, 1998).

Dynamic Assessment   In **dynamic assessment,** the teacher evaluates the student's ability to learn in a teaching situation rather than determining what the student has already learned. The procedure is: (1) to engage in instruction that is active and flexible and then (2) to observe how well the student can learn under favorable conditions.

A key element in dynamic assessment is the social environment in which the learning occurs. When a healthy reciprocal relationship exists among teacher and students, the student's ability to learn will grow and flourish. The teacher can evaluate how well a student performs in an interactive teaching environment and can make a subjective judgment rather than rely on test scores (Feuerstein, 1979; Palinscar, Brown, & Campione, 1991). Reciprocal teaching offers the teaching side of dynamic assessment (see the chapter on clinical teaching; Palinscar & Brown, 1984).

Diagnostic Teaching   **Diagnostic teaching** is an extension of the assessment process, whereby a perceptive teacher continues to collect assessment information while teaching the student. Typically, after giving tests, the teacher still has much to learn about the student and can do so by developing lessons that teach and test simultaneously and by noting the student's reactions to these lessons. Diagnostic teaching is also referred to as "trial lessons" or "teaching probes."

Assessment information about the student's learning styles can be obtained through short lessons. For example, the following procedure can indicate whether the student learns well through a sight-word method. First, the teacher teaches some words visually by putting a few words on cards. The teacher then says the word while the student is looking at the word. A short time later, the student is tested to see if she or he remembers a certain word. Students who have fairly good visual memories will have little difficulty remembering the word after a few repetitions. A similar procedure can be used in a diagnostic teaching session to assess a student's auditory and phonetic learning abilities.

Informal Graded Word-Recognition Test   This type of test can be used as a quick method to determine the student's approximate reading level. It is also useful in detecting the student's errors in word analysis. An informal graded word-recognition test can be constructed by selecting words at random from graded basal reader glossaries. Table 2.5 illustrates such a list; the words were selected from several basal reader series and from graded reading vocabulary lists. The informal graded word-recognition test can be given as follows: (1) type the list of words selected for each grade on separate cards; (2) duplicate the entire test on a single sheet; (3) have the pupil read the words from the cards while the examiner marks the errors on the sheet, noting the pupil's method of analyzing and pronouncing difficult

TABLE 2.5

Informal Graded
Word-Recognition Test

Preprimer	Primer	Grade 1	Grade 2
see	day	about	hungry
run	from	sang	loud
me	all	guess	stones
dog	under	catch	trick
at	little	across	chair
come	house	live	hopped
down	ready	boats	himself
you	came	hard	color
said	your	longer	straight
boy	blue	hold	leading

Grade 3	Grade 4	Grade 5	Grade 6
arrow	brilliant	career	buoyant
wrist	credit	cultivate	determination
bottom	examine	essential	gauntlet
castle	grammar	grieve	incubator
learned	jingle	jostle	ludicrous
washed	ruby	obscure	offensive
safety	terrify	procession	prophesy
yesterday	wrench	sociable	sanctuary
delight	mayor	triangular	tapestry
happiness	agent	volcano	vague

A collaboration team considers a student's strengths and weaknesses and explores possible interventions for that student. (© Elizabeth Crews)

words; and (4) have the pupil read from increasingly difficult lists until three words are missed. The level at which the student misses only two words suggests the instructional level at which the pupil is able to read with help. The level at which one word is missed suggests the pupil's independent reading level (i.e., the level at which the pupil can read alone). The level at which three words are missed suggests a frustration level, and the material is probably too difficult.

Informal Arithmetic Test An informal arithmetic test can be easily devised to point out weaknesses in a student's basic computational skills. The informal survey test, which is illustrated in Figure 2.6, can be used for sixth-grade students. The difficulty level of the test could be increased or decreased, depending on the grade level being tested.

FIGURE 2.6

Informal Survey Test: Sixth-Grade Level

ADDITION	300 60 406 + 3	35 24 6 +18	271 +389	234 573 +261	123 324 +452
SUBTRACTION	765 −342	751 −608	7054 −3595	8004 −5637	90327 −42827
MULTIPLICATION	37 ×10	45 ×83	721 ×346	483 ×208	802 ×357
DIVISION	2/̅3̅6̅	12/̅3̅6̅	6/̅9̅6̅6̅	16/̅1̅0̅6̅1̅	13/̅8̅7̅2̅6̅

The informal arithmetic test should include several items of each kind so that a simple error will not be mistaken for a more fundamental difficulty.

Criterion-referenced tests *describe* rather than *compare* performance, measuring mastery levels rather than grade levels. In contrast, *norm-referenced tests* (traditional standardized tests) compare the pupil's performance to that of other children of the same age. This difference can be illustrated in a nonacademic area of learning, such as swimming. In criterion-referenced terms, a child would be judged as being able to perform certain tasks, such as putting his or her face in the water, floating, or doing the crawl stroke. In contrast, in norm-referenced terms, the child would be tested and judged to swim as well as an average 9-year-old child.

Criterion-referenced tests are useful because they provide a way to show growth. It is often difficult to show that a student has improved in terms of percentiles, stanines, or even grade-level scores, but the teacher can show that the student has learned certain specific skills, in terms of mastery, of criterion-referenced measures.

Some commercial criterion-referenced tests used in special education are the Brigance Comprehensive Inventory of Basic Skills—Revised, the Key Math—Revised, the Standard Reading Inventory, and the Prescriptive Reading Inventory (see "Tests for Assessing Students With Learning Disabilities" in the Reference Guide at the back of this book).

EXAMPLES OF TESTS In this section, we provide examples of some of the assessment tests and discuss tests of: (1) intelligence and cognitive abilities, (2) reading tests, (3) motor tests, (4) language tests, and (5) screening tests for visual and auditory acuity.

Tests of Intelligence and Cognitive Abilities

Intelligence tests and tests of cognitive abilities provide information about the student's aptitude for learning and specific cognitive attributions. Certain intelligence tests are administered by psychologists; others may be given by teachers with appropriate training.

Commonly used individual intelligence tests that are typically administered by psychologists are the Wechsler Intelligence Scale for Children—Fourth Edition (WISC-IV), the Stanford-Binet Intelligence Scale—Fourth Edition, and the Kaufman Assessment Battery for Children (K-ABC). The *WISC-IV* has 16 subtests of mental ability. The Stanford-Binet has 15 subtests grouped into four areas: (1) verbal reasoning, (2) quantitative reasoning, (3) abstract/visual reasoning, and (4) short-term memory. The Kaufman Assessment Battery for Children (K-ABC) classifies mental abilities as sequential processing or simultaneous processing.

Some tests of cognitive ability that can be given by teachers with training are listed in Table 2.6 (see "Tests for Assessing Students With Learning Disabilities" for a further description of these tests).

- Tests of Cognitive Ability of the Woodcock-Johnson Psychoeducational Battery—Revised (this test is described in greater detail later).

- The Kaufman Brief Intelligence Test (K-BIT) is a short test that measures two distinct cognitive functions through two subtests: the Vocabulary subtest (verbal, uses expressive vocabulary and definitions) and the Matrices subtest (nonverbal, uses pictures and abstract designs).

- The Slosson Intelligence Test—Revised is a relatively short screening test.

- The Detroit Tests of Learning Aptitude—4 (DTLA-4) are intended for use with children ages 6 through 17.

- The Detroit Tests of Learning Aptitude—Primary—2 are intended for younger children, ages 3 through 12.

- The McCarthy Scales of Children's Abilities are designed to assess young children, ages 2.5 to 8.5.

- The Illinois Test of Psycholinguistic Abilities—Third Edition (ITPA-3) was one of the first tests of mental processes designed expressly to analyze subskills of mental function.

- The Goodenough-Harris Drawing Test estimates intellectual maturity through an analysis of a child's drawing of a person.

Woodcock-Johnson Psychoeducational Battery—III, Complete Battery
The Woodcock-Johnson Psychoeducational Battery—III, Complete Battery (WJ-III) provides a co-normed set of tests for measuring general intellectual ability, specific cognitive abilities, scholastic aptitude, oral language, and academic achievement. It can be used on subjects from 2 years old to 90+ years and for Grade K through graduate school. The WJ-III consists of two assessment instruments: (1) tests of cognitive abilities and (2) tests of achievement. The WJ-III can be administered by teachers with appropriate training, and it is designed so that a discrepancy analysis can be developed by comparing cognitive test scores and achievement test scores. The test uses clusters of scores for interpretation, and a computer program is available to assist the user in calculating and interpreting the student's performance. The WJ-III Tests of Cognitive Abilities are shown in Table 2.7. The WJ-III Cognitive Performance Clusters are shown in Table 2.8.

Analysis of the Subtest Scores of Intelligence Tests   Intelligence is not a single general factor, but rather it is comprised of many separate abilities (Sternberg, 1985). The WISC-IV has four factors: (1) verbal comprehension, (2) perceptual reasoning, (3) working memory, and (4) processing speed. Another intelligence test, the K-ABC, divides intelligence into (1) sequential thinking (thinking in logical order) and (2) simultaneous thinking (an immediate grasp of an idea). The multiple-intelligence theory of Gardner (Gardner & Hatch, 1989) conceives of eight separate intelligences:

TABLE 2.7

WJ-III Tests of
Cognitive Abilities

Category/factor	Standard battery	Extended battery
Verbal ability		
Comprehension/ knowledge	Test 1. Verbal comprehension	Test 11. General information
Thinking ability		
Long-term retrieval	Test 2. Visual–auditory learning	Test 12. Retrieval fluency
		Test 13. Picture recognition
Visual–spatial thinking	Test 3. Spatial relations	Test 14. Auditory attention
Auditory processing	Test 4. Sound blending	Test 15. Analysis–synthesis
Fluid reasoning	Test 5. Concept formation	
Cognitive efficiency		
Processing speed	Test 6. Visual matching	Test 16. Decision speed
Short-term memory	Test 7. Numbers reversed	Test 17. Memory for words
Supplemental		
	Test 8. Incomplete words	Test 18. Rapid picture naming
	Test 9. Auditory working memory	Test 19. Planning
	Test 10. Visual–auditory learning-delayed	Test 20. Pair cancellation

TABLE 2.8

WJ-III Cognitive
Performance Clusters

The WJ-III cognitive performance clusters

The WJ-III cognitive tests include certain clusters representing broad categories of cognitive abilities that are casually related to cognitive performance. The clusters are the result of a combination of tests. They include

- Verbal ability—Standard scale
- Verbal ability—Extended scale
- Comprehension/knowledge
- Long-term retrieval
- Visual–spatial thinking

Other clinically useful clusters

Phonemic awareness
Working memory

CHARLIE

"... I can't go bowling tonight, Freddie, I'm cramming for an IQ test tomorrow..."

(1) linguistic, (2) logical–mathematical, (3) spatial, (4) musical, (5) bodily–kinesthetic, (6) intrapersonal, (7) interpersonal, and (8) naturalistic.

Many of the intelligence tests and cognitive tests provide scores for components or factors in addition to the overall IQ score. Clinicians find it useful to analyze the factors to obtain clinical information about a student's component cognitive abilities. In some cases, the analysis of scores might show wide variability (or "scatter") in different components of mental functioning. In other cases, clusters of scores might indicate a student's strengths and weaknesses in specific areas of learning.

Bias in Intelligence Testing   The use of IQ tests continues to be controversial. School policies about the use of intelligence tests have been influenced by class-action lawsuits that found bias in intelligence testing. In an early lawsuit, *Larry P. v. Riles* (1979), the court ruled that IQ testing was racially and culturally discriminatory when used as the sole criterion for placing students in classes for mentally retarded children. As a result of this case, and others, the state of California stopped using standardized intelligence tests to identify educable, mentally retarded African American children. It is critical to consider cultural and linguistic bias in administering intelligence tests. The student's language and background experience can affect the score in an intelligence test (Salvia & Ysseldyke, 2004).

Reading Tests: Survey-Type Tests and Diagnostic Tests

General Reading Tests   General survey-type tests of reading yield a general score of silent reading and give an indication of the level at which a child reads. Table 2.9 lists some of the widely used general survey reading tests, and they are described in the Reference Guide at the back of this book in "Tests for Assessing Students With Learning Disabilities."

Diagnostic Reading Tests   Diagnostic reading tests differ from general reading tests in that they analyze the processes by which the child attempts to read, providing information on *how* the child reads rather than indicating only the reading level. By analyzing specific errors, the examiner can determine whether the problem is poor word-attack skills, a lack of familiarity with certain phonic elements (such as vowels, consonant blends, and diphthongs), inadequate sight vocabulary, or a slow reading rate. A few of the useful diagnostic reading tests are listed in Table 2.9; they are also discussed in the chapter on oral language and described in "Tests for Assessing Students With Learning Disabilities."

Comprehensive Batteries of Academic Tests   General test batteries measure performance in academic skills in reading, arithmetic, spelling, and grammar. These comprehensive batteries are also listed in Table 2.9, and they are described in the Reference Guide at the back of this book in "Tests for Assessing Students With Learning Disabilities."

Diagnostic Academic Tests and Test Batteries   Diagnostic tests for academic areas are designed to provide more in-depth information than the general tests. They can be given to one child, rather than to a group, and they provide information on several academic areas. Commonly used tests are listed in Table 2.9, and they are described in the Reference Guide at the back of this book in "Tests for Assessing Students With Learning Disabilities."

TABLE 2.9

Commonly Used
Survey-Type and
Diagnostic Tests

General reading tests

- California Achievement Tests: Reading
- Gates-MacGinitie Reading Tests—Fourth Edition
- Metropolitan Achievement Tests: Reading
- SRA Achievement Series: Reading
- Stanford Achievement Test: Reading

Diagnostic reading tests

- Analytic Reading Inventory
- Diagnostic Assessment of Reading with Trial Strategies (DARTTS)
- Diagnostic Reading Inventory
- Gates-McKillop-Horowitz Reading Diagnostic Tests
- Stanford Diagnostic Reading Test—Fourth Edition
- Test of Reading Comprehension (TORC)—Third Edition
- Woodcock Reading Mastery Tests—Revised

Comprehensive batteries of academic tests

- California Achievement Tests
- Iowa Tests of Basic Skills
- Metropolitan Achievement Tests
- SRA Achievement Series
- Stanford Achievement Test
- Wide-Range Achievement Test—III (WRAT—III)

Diagnostic academic tests and test batteries

- Brigance Comprehensive Inventory of Basic Skills—Revised
- Kaufman Test of Educational Achievement (K-TEA)
- Key Math—Revised
- Peabody Individual Achievement Test—Revised (PIAT-R)
- Stanford Diagnostic Mathematics Test—Third Edition
- Test of Written Spelling—3 (TOWS-3)
- Woodcock-Johnson Psychoeducational Battery III—Achievement Tests

Motor tests

- Bruinicks-Oseretsky Test of Motor Proficiency
- Peabody Development Motor Scales
- Southern California Perceptual–Motor Tests

Language tests

- Ammons Full-Range Picture Vocabulary Test
- Carrow Elicited Language Inventory
- Clinical Evaluation of Language Fundamentals—Revised (CELF-R)
- Goldman-Fristoe Test of Articulation
- Houston Test for Language Development
- Peabody Picture Vocabulary Test—III
- Templin-Darley Test of Articulation
- Test of Adolescent Language—3 (TOAL-3)
- Test of Language Development—3: Intermediate (TOLD-3: Intermediate)
- Test of Language Development—3: Primary (TOLD-3: Primary)
- Test of Written Language—3 (TOWL-3)
- Test for Auditory Comprehension of Language—Revised

The Woodcock-Johnson Psychoeducational Battery III—Tests of Achievement is a battery consisting of 22 achievement tests that can be combined to form score clusters. The clusters include: (1) oral expression, (2) listening comprehension, (3) basic reading skills, (4) reading comprehension, (5) phoneme/grapheme knowledge, (6) math calculation, (7) math reasoning, and (8) written expression.

Motor Tests

Examples of diagnostic tests that evaluate motor performance are listed in Table 2.9; they are also discussed in the chapter on young children with learning disabilities and described in the Reference Guide at the back of this book in "Tests for Assessing Students With Learning Disabilities."

Language Tests

Speech-screening tests of articulation include tests of articulation, tests of the ability to understand words, tests of syntax, tests of language comprehension, and tests of written language. These tests are listed in Table 2.9, and they are discussed further in the chapter on oral language and described in the Reference Guide at the back of this book in "Tests for Assessing Students With Learning Disabilities."

Screening Tests for Visual and Auditory Acuity

Students with learning disabilities should be checked for sensory deficits. Visual- and auditory-screening tests may be given by learning disabilities teachers who are trained in the administration of these tests or by the school nurse or some other specially trained school staff member. Students who fail the screening tests are referred to an eye or ear specialist for a professional examination.

Visual-screening instruments are the Keystone Visual Survey Service for Schools and the Ortho-Rater. These instruments use stereoscopic slides to screen for near-vision and far-vision acuity, eye-muscle balance, and fusion (see the chapter on medical aspects of learning disabilities and "Tests for Assessing Students With Learning Disabilities").

The *audiometer* is an auditory screening instrument that is used to detect hearing problems. Students who fail the screening should be referred for a professional hearing examination.

STANDARDS AND ACCOUNTABILITY

As a nation, we take education very seriously. In fact, educational accountability has become a political issue as our nation's leaders at the federal and state level call for more accountability. In education, the call for accountability has led to a system for informing those inside and outside the education arena about how our schools are doing. The states are setting high standards, and most of them now administer statewide assessments to measure the progress of students in meeting these standards. The U.S. law, the No Child Left Behind Act of 2001, requires annual testing in reading and math for all pupils in Grades 3 through 8 by the school year 2005–2006.

Including Students With Learning Disabilities in Statewide Testing

IDEA–2004 specifically requires that, as a condition of a state's eligibility for educational funding, children with disabilities must be included in general statewide and districtwide assessment programs. The law also addresses timelines and reporting requirements. The law mandates that states

- Provide for the participation of children with disabilities in general statewide and districtwide assessments, with appropriate accommodations and modifications in administration, if necessary
- Provide for the conducting of alternate assessment of children who cannot participate in the general assessment programs
- Make available and report to the public on results of the assessment of disabled children with the same frequency and in the same detail as they report the assessment results of nondisabled children

This regulation means that children with learning disabilities must participate in the statewide tests and that any accommodations that are needed for this testing must be included in each student's IEP. Further, reports to parents about the child with learning disabilities must be made in the same detail and with the same frequency as reports about other children. Thus, if report cards are issued on a semester basis for all children, then report cards must be issued for students with learning disabilities.

Accommodations for Assessment

IDEA–2004 permits *accommodations* in statewide testing for students with learning disabilities. However, these **accommodations for assessment** must be written in the student's IEP. Teachers need much support and guidance in planning for and implementing these accommodations. Figure 2.7 provides examples of common assessment accommodations for students with disabilities.

IDEA–2004 requires that states develop guidelines for accommodations that allow students with learning disabilities and other special education students the opportunity to participate in state-level assessments. Accommodations for students with disabilities serve to level the playing field for these

TIMING	SETTING
■ Allow frequent breaks during testing	■ Give to small groups
■ Alter time of day that test is administered	■ Give in hospital setting
■ Extend time allotted to complete the test	■ Use study carrel
■ Administer test in several sessions over the course of the day	■ Use separate room
■ Administer test in several sessions over several days	
PRESENTATION	**RESPONSE**
■ Use audiocassettes	■ Use computer for written tests
■ Read test aloud to student	■ Dictate to scribe
■ Use large-print versions	■ Record answers
■ Give repeated directions	■ Put answers in booklet instead of answer sheet
■ Use magnification devices	
■ Use computers to read test	

Source: Adapted from Erickson, Ysseldyke, Thurlow, and Elliot, "Inclusive Assessment and Accountability Systems" from *Teaching Exceptional Children* 31 (1998): 8. Copyright 1998 by The Council for Exceptional Children. Reprinted with permission.

students. A concern about accommodations is whether they invalidate the psychometric qualities of the test. For example, does giving extended time on a test nullify the validity of the test (Johnson, Kimball, & Brown, 2001)? There are several studies on the effects of extended time on the test scores of postsecondary students with learning disabilities. Students with learning disabilities had significantly better scores after being allowed extended time, while students without learning disabilities did not improve their scores by using extended time (Weaver, 2000).

In addition, IDEA–2004 requires states to develop guidelines for alternate assessments for children who cannot participate in regular assessment.

TEST-TAKING STRATEGIES IN THE GENERAL EDUCATION CLASSROOM

The general education teacher, with the collaboration of the special education teacher, is responsible for administering their state's standard performance tests to all students in the inclusion class. The following box, "LD in Practice: Test-Taking Strategies in the General Education Classroom," offers some strategies to help students to prepare for and to take these tests (Spinelli, 2002). Websites with useful information on test-taking strategies are **http://www.ucc.vt.edu/stdysk/strategi.html** and **http://www. as.wvu.edu/~scidis/learning.html.**

LD IN PRACTICE

TEST-TAKING STRATEGIES IN THE GENERAL EDUCATION CLASSROOM

- Prepare students for test taking by suggesting that they get enough rest and nourishment before taking the test.

- Provide students with opportunities to practice working under standardized conditions in simulated situations.

- Give students practice in filling in the appropriate circle with quick, dark strokes inside the circle or bubble. Most standardized tests require students to record their responses by filling in circles on separate answer sheets.

- Separate answer sheets from the test. Instruct students to mark answers on the test booklet and then have the students practice transferring their marked responses to the answer sheet.

- Instruct students to eliminate any answers that they know are incorrect. Provide students practice in eliminating wrong answers and discuss why they are wrong.

- Explain to students that guessing at an answer is usually better than leaving the question blank.

- Teach students to use their time efficiently by not wasting time on items they do not know. Students should have practice in monitoring their time as they take the test.

- Encourage students to request accommodations, as appropriate, for students with disabilities, such as extended time, assistive technology, and testing in smaller groups.

- Ensure that the teacher checks the modifications for testing that are written in the students' IEP.

This chapter presents the first part of an extended case study. Every case is influenced by the theoretical orientation of the case investigators, which affects many factors: (1) how the student's learning problems are analyzed, (2) the kinds of assessment questions asked, (3) the selection of evaluation measures and tests, (4) the interpretation of case data, (5) the recommended educational settings, and (6) the proposed instructional strategies. Because solving the puzzle of a learning disabilities case is an art as well as a science, professionals may differ about many aspects of a case. (Another extended case study is presented in "Case Study: The Process of Referral, Assessment, and Teaching of Adam Z" in the Reference Guide at the back of this book.

The following case study of Rita G. illustrates the stages of the assessment–teaching process. The information presented in this case study is based on an actual case. Identifying information has been altered to maintain confidentiality. This case study is broken into three segments, which are presented in this chapter and the following two chapters. With reference to the stages of the IEP, the case study is presented as follows:

Case study	*Stages of the IEP*	*Chapter*
Part I	*Prereferral and Referral*	"Assessment"
	• Prereferral information and activities	
	• Referral and initial planning	
Part II	*Multidisciplinary evaluation*	"Clinical Teaching"
	• Classroom observation	
	• Auditory and visual acuity	
	• Developmental and educational history	
	• Measures of intellectual aptitude	
	• Present levels of academic functioning	
	• Adaptive behavior	
Part III	*Case conference: IEP meeting*	"Educational Settings"
	• Writing the IEP	
	• Implementing the teaching plan	
	• Monitoring progress and review	

RITA G.'S PREREFERRAL AND REFERRAL

Identifying Information
Name of Student: Rita G.
Age: 9.0 (9 years, 0 months)
Current placement: Grade 3.6, general
education third-grade class

Prereferral Information and Activities

Rita G.'s third-grade teacher, Steve Martinez, requested a prereferral staffing for her. In his request, Mr. Martinez reported that Rita cannot work independently; she seems unable to organize and plan when faced with a problem task, such as thinking through an arithmetic word problem or solving problems in other curriculum areas. When doing a class assignment, she answers one or two items and then becomes distracted by other activities going on in the classroom and does not complete her work. Although Rita recognizes words in reading, her reading comprehension is inconsistent, and her work is usually not completed. On the day Mr. Martinez made the prereferral request, Rita's total morning's work consisted of writing four spelling words five times each. Mr. Martinez also reported that Rita never engaged in conversations with him and rarely asked questions either in class or of him personally. He did note that in her school records her first-grade teacher had described Rita as inquisitive, but she showed no evidence of that quality in his class.

The prereferral team meeting was held soon afterward. The team consisted of Mr. Martinez, the school principal, and the fourth-grade teacher. After discussing Rita's performance in class, the team concluded that the assigned work in the class may be too difficult for Rita. The team made several suggestions: (1) Provide Rita with texts and workbooks at the second-grade level and give her individual assignments in

these materials; (2) change Rita's seating to the front of the class so that Mr. Martinez would have closer contact with her; (3) talk to the second-grade teacher about Rita's work last year; (4) obtain some high-interest, low reading-level books from the library for Rita to use; and (5) check to see that she has her assignment book before she goes home.

Mr. Martinez followed up on these suggestions for several weeks. Unfortunately, Rita objected to being given different assignments from those of her classmates. She complained that she was being given "baby" work. She did not read the library books. She also began to hide her papers at home and lost her assignment notebook. Her mother reported that Rita purposely broke pencils when doing homework. Also, Mr. Martinez could not contact Rita's second-grade teacher because she had moved out of town. Rita's academic functioning at school grew worse; she was failing in several subjects. Mr. Martinez decided to call in Rita's mother to discuss recommending an educational evaluation.

Referral and Initial Planning

Mr. Martinez met with Rita's mother to discuss her daughter's problems in school. Mrs. G. said that she was worried because the problem was becoming critical. Rita kept saying she was dumb and hated school, and it was becoming increasingly difficult to get her to go to school. She frequently complained of stomachaches in the morning. Mr. Martinez and Mrs. G. agreed to refer Rita for an educational evaluation in the hope that it would provide information to help plan an appropriate educational program for her. Mrs. G. signed the informed consent form so that the evaluation could proceed.

Mr. Martinez submitted a referral and discussed Rita's problem with the special education coordinator in the school. The initial planning for Rita's evaluation included the following kinds of assessment information: classroom observation; auditory and visual acuity; a relevant developmental and educational history; measures of intellectual aptitude; measures of present levels of academic functioning; a measure of adaptive behavior, learning strengths, and weaknesses; and an interest inventory.

Note: The information gained from this evaluation is presented in the continuation of the case of Rita G. in the chapter on clinical teaching.

CHAPTER SUMMARY

1. Assessment is the process of gathering pertinent information about the student in order to make critical decisions about teaching.

2. The federal law, the Individuals With Disabilities Education Improvement Act (IDEA–2004), influences the assessment process.

3. The individualized education program (IEP) is written for an individual student and regulates the entire assessment–teaching process.

4. Parents' rights or procedural safeguards must be considered during the assessment process.

5. The assessment–teaching process has six stages: (1) prereferral activities, (2) referral and initial planning, (3) multidisciplinary evaluation, (4) the IEP meeting—writing the IEP, (5) implementing the IEP teaching plan, and (6) review and reevaluation of the student's progress.

6. Those creating the IEP for students with learning disabilities should consider special factors: (1) the ways of determining eligibility of students, (2) functional behavioral assessment and positive behavioral intervention and support, (3) English-language learners (ELL), and (4) assistive technology.

7. Those creating the IEP should take into account, when identifying the student for learning disabilities, the student's: (1) present levels of performance, (2) observed behavior, (3) strengths and clusters of characteristics, (4) parent concerns, (5) annual goals, (6) the educational setting for instruction, and (7) monitoring progress.

8. Assessment information can be obtained in several ways through: (1) case history or interviews, (2) observations, (3) rating scales, (4) standardized norm-referenced tests, (5) curriculum-based measurement and performance monitoring, (6) alternate and informal assessment measures, and (7) curriculum-based measurement (CBM) and progress monitoring.

9. The demand for accountability is increasing in our schools. Students with learning disabilities must now be included in statewide testing. Accommodations for such testing must be written into a student's IEP.

DISCUSSION AND REFLECTION

1. Describe the six stages of the individualized education program (IEP) process. What is the purpose of each stage?

2. The Individuals With Disabilities Education Improvement Act (IDEA–2004) requires that important procedural safeguards be used with students with learning disabilities. Discuss four parents' rights or procedural safeguards.

3. IDEA specifies the participants for the IEP meeting. Describe each of the participants.

4. What are the five ways to obtain data for an evaluation of a student with learning disabilities? Give examples of information that might be obtained by using each method.

5. Compare and contrast standardized norm-referenced tests with informal or alternate assessment measures.

6. Describe several accommodations that can be made for testing students with learning disabilities.

KEY TERMS

accommodations for assessment (p. 82)

adaptive behavior scales (p. 64)

annual goals (p. 56)

assessment stages (p. 49)

assistive technology (p. 61)

case history (p. 62)

criterion-referenced tests (p. 75)

curriculum-based measurement (CBM) (p. 69)

diagnostic teaching (p. 72)

diagnostic tests (p. 69)

discrepancy between achievement and intellectual ability (p. 53)

discrepancy score (p. 53)

dynamic assessment (p. 72)

English-language learners (ELL) (p. 60)

formal standardized tests (p. 67)

functional behavioral assessment (p. 59)

general tests (p. 69)

IEP meeting (p. 50)

individualized education program (IEP) (p. 46)

informal assessment measures (p. 71)

instruction stages (p. 51)

mediation (p. 47)

multidisciplinary evaluation (p. 49)

norm-referenced tests (p. 67)

observation *(p. 55)*

parents' rights *(p. 46)*

portfolio assessment *(p. 72)*

positive behavioral support *(p. 59)*

prereferral activities *(p. 47)*

present levels of achievement
  (p. 54)

procedural safeguards *(p. 46)*

progress monitoring *(p. 70)*

rating scales *(p. 65)*

referral *(p. 49)*

referral stages *(p. 47)*

response-to-intervention *(p. 54)*

3

Clinical Teaching

CHAPTER OUTLINE

> A teacher affects eternity: One can never tell where a teacher's influence stops.
>
> —*Henry Adams*

This chapter reviews the teaching portions of the assessment–teaching process. Assessment is only a starting point; the process continues with teaching—a special kind of teaching required to help students with learning disabilities. We call it **clinical teaching.**

CLINICAL TEACHING

The goal of clinical teaching is to tailor learning experiences for the unique needs of a particular student. Using all the information gathered in the assessment, including an analysis of the student's specific learning characteristics, the clinical teacher designs a special teaching program. Assessment does not stop when teaching begins. In fact, the essence of clinical teaching is that assessment and instruction are continuous and interwoven. The clinical teacher modifies the teaching as new needs become apparent.

Many different intervention strategies can be used in clinical teaching. A clinical teacher is a "child watcher." Instead of concentrating solely on what the student *cannot* do, the teacher observes in detail what the student *does* do. For example, by observing the kinds of errors a student makes, the clinical teacher can obtain much information about the student, such as the student's current level of development, way of thinking, or underlying language system. A student's oral reading errors also can provide insight into the student's way of thinking.

Clinical teaching can be seen as an alternating test-teach-test process, with the teacher alternating roles as tester and teacher. First, the student is tested; a unit of work based on the resulting information is then taught. After teaching, the student is again evaluated to determine what has been learned. If the student performs well on the evaluation, the clinical teacher knows that the teaching has been successful and plans for the next step of learning. If the student performs poorly on the evaluation, the teacher must reassess the teaching plan, analyze the errors to try to determine the cause of the failure to learn, and develop a new course of action for teaching.

Clinical teaching, then, implies a concept of and an attitude about teaching. It does not require any one particular instructional system, educational setting, or style of teaching. It can be used by special education teachers, by general education classroom teachers, or in team collaboration. Clinical teaching can also be applied in many settings: a general education classroom, a resource room, or a one-to-one setting. It can be used with many different intervention strategies or teaching methods. A variety of terms are used to describe this instruction, such as *remediation, intervention, educational therapy, instructional strategies,* or simply *good teaching;* and these terms are often used interchangeably.

Stages of the Clinical Teaching Cycle

The clinical teaching process can be viewed as a cycle, with each stage of the process represented as a point along a circle, as shown in Figure 3.1.

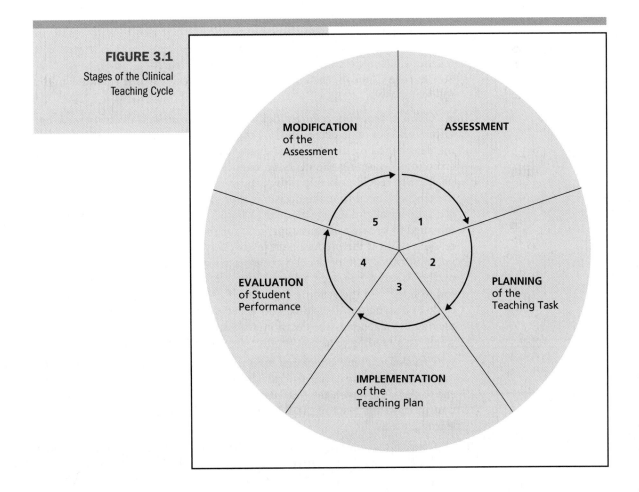

FIGURE 3.1

Stages of the Clinical Teaching Cycle

The five stages of the clinical teaching cycle are:

1. *Assessment.* This is the process of gathering evidence about a student's skills or knowledge. It can be administered through a test or as an integral part of instruction.

2. *Planning of the teaching task.* The assessment information is used to plan the teaching task.

3. *Implementation of the teaching plan.* This stage involves the actual teaching.

4. *Evaluation of student performance.* The teacher now evaluates how well the student has responded to the teaching.

5. *Modification of the assessment.* Now, it may be necessary to modify the assessment.

Qualities of Clinical Teaching

Many critical decisions must be made about what and how to teach. In many respects, teaching remains an art. One can never tell where a teacher's influence stops. Examples of clinical teaching are given in "LD Stories: The Clinical Teaching Approach." Clinical teaching is unique in the following ways:

■ *Clinical teaching requires flexibility and continual decision making.* Often, instruction is determined by the material that is used, instead of being determined by the teacher. In many classes, textbooks dominate the instruction, becoming the de facto curriculum. The search for the *perfect* package to teach academic skills can be viewed as an attempt to minimize the teacher's need to make decisions. For example, the **basal reader,** which is a sequential and interrelated set of books and supportive material that is intended to provide the basic material for the development of fundamental reading skills, is the predominant instruction tool that is used to teach reading in 90% to 95% of the classrooms across the country. Once the reading textbook series has been selected, many of the teaching decisions can be found largely in the reading series itself. The reading textbook has many built-in instruction decisions, and it becomes the curriculum, thereby replacing the teacher as the decision maker. Clinical teachers should not rely solely on a reading textbook to meet the needs of an individual student.

■ *Clinical teaching is planned for a unique student rather than for an entire class.* Lessons in the general education classroom are designed for the entire class. However, the *best* method for teaching a class may not be the best method for teaching individual students with unique behaviors and learning needs.

■ *Clinical teaching can be accomplished in a variety of settings.* Clinical teaching can occur in a group or in an individual setting, in a general education classroom or in a special education classroom. Clinical teaching re-

THE CLINICAL TEACHING APPROACH

- Sammy was having difficulty going from the overhead transparency the teacher was showing to the class to the work he was doing at his desk. His teacher realized that this difficulty reflected Sammy's visual–motor perceptual problem. The teacher gave Sammy a copy of the material on the transparency so that he did not have to make the transfer from the transparency to the work at his desk.

- Debby failed the arithmetic word problem on the test. Her teacher observed that Debby could read the words and perform the arithmetic calculations, but she could not picture the items to be calculated in the word problem. The clinical teacher recognized that Debby's arithmetic failures were related to her difficulty in spatial orientation. Debby could not remember how to get to school, to the store, or to her friend's house; and she constantly lost her way. Her teacher directed the teaching toward strengthening Debby's visualization skills and her ability to visualize the situation in the word problem.

- Saul, a high school student, was failing in most of his subjects. He appeared to be uninterested and uninvolved in his school courses. Although his word-recognition skills were good, his reading comprehension was very poor. When questioned in class, Saul usually blurted out his first answer, which was typically wrong. His reactions were the same in his written work. Saul did not have a dependable system for learning. He did not know how to become actively involved in the learning task and responded impulsively. Saul's teacher recognized that he lacked learning strategies. The teaching that ensued taught Saul strategies for learning.

flects an attitude on the part of the teacher. What is important is the teacher's ability to integrate feedback information and be ready to make decisions. Teachers should be sensitive to the individual student's learning style, interests, shortcomings, strengths, levels of development, and feelings.

A Remembrance of Grace Fernald: A Remarkable Clinical Teacher

Grace Fernald was a remarkable teacher and educational therapist who had a long-lasting influence on her students. In her book, which was first published in 1943, she described the multisensory methods she used (Fernald, 1943/1988). Fernald created one of the first reading clinics for students with reading problems at UCLA, and she also had a private practice. Fernald died in 1960, at the age of 70. In a remembrance of her influence on their lives, many of her former students wrote about their memories in tribute to their teacher. A poignant remembrance of this remarkable clinical teacher is given in "LD Stories: A Tribute to a Remarkable Clinical Teacher, Grace Fernald."

ECOLOGICAL CONSIDERATIONS

The **ecological system** refers to the various environments within which a person lives and grows. The environments of the home, the school, the social group, and the culture influence a student's desire and ability to learn. Learning competencies depend on positive interactions with the various environments. Recognizing the effects of the ecological system, realizing that learning, attitudes, and progress depend on positive interactions with the various environments, is an important feature of clinical teaching.

Home Environment

The home is the child's first environment. The child's experiences at home during the first 5 or 6 years influence cognitive development and lay the foundation for later school performance. As the child's first teachers, parents can provide intellectual stimulation and emotional well-being. The development of self-concept, self-esteem, interest in literacy, and a curiosity about learning all depend on the support and encouragement parents provide within the home. Parents become role models for their child, and when their child experiences school difficulties, a supportive family relationship becomes especially important. A dysfunctional home environment contributes to school problems. The child's learning disabilities also have an impact on members of the family (Turnbull, Turnbull, Shank, & Smith, 2004).

School Environment

A substantial portion of a student's day is spent in school, and school experiences exert dramatic effects. An integral part of the school experience is the student's relationships with peers and with school personnel (including teachers, aides, administrators, office personnel, and maintenance staff). The school environment encompasses more than teaching and learning academic subject matter. In addition to the academic curriculum, students must cope with a "hidden curriculum" of expected values and behaviors. They must learn complex rules for participating in a classroom, such as learning how to be recognized and how to demonstrate what they know.

Many students with learning disabilities not only encounter academic difficulty, but often have problems acquiring appropriate school behaviors. They often have unsatisfactory relationships with teachers and classmates in the school environment, receive much less praise and acknowledgment for their efforts, and are more likely to be criticized, shown disapproval, and even ignored (Brooks, 2000; Haager & Vaughn, 1995). Teachers who are sensitive to the ways in which such negative factors can discourage learning can take measures to provide a nurturing school atmosphere.

A TRIBUTE TO A REMARKABLE CLINICAL TEACHER, GRACE FERNALD

Grace Fernald: A Remembrance
by a Student

I was the oldest in a family that came to have eight children. Even when very young, my parents talked with me about the world and the politics of the day—we were in the middle of World War II. I liked learning about things. With my second-grade teacher, my otherwise happy world seemed to come to an end. While I was well behaved in school, everything I did or said, from the teacher's perspective, was wrong. While only a second grader, I knew I wanted to be a doctor and a medical researcher and, in my heart, I believed I would be able to do those things well. She asked to see my parents. Because of all the young children at home, my father came alone. It was after school, and I was at one end of the room sitting quietly. I can remember hearing her tell my father I was retarded and, of course, would never be a doctor. I can also remember him patiently, but very firmly, telling her he disagreed about my intelligence and that I would be whatever I wanted.

My parents revered education. They called UCLA and were given the name of Grace Fernald, who agreed to see me in her private practice. I remember Dr. Fernald's house from the first visit somewhat differently than does my mother. I thought it was grand. It was, to me, a very big Spanish home in a very nice area of Westwood (what is now called Little Holmby Hills). It had a tall, vaulted ceiling of wood and big timbers with a huge stone fireplace. I was amazed by the furniture, which I thought must be antique, and enjoyed looking at the oriental carpets. There were many shelves with books. Everything was very neat and very quiet.

Dr. Fernald was friendly, gray-haired, with a wonderful smile. After talking to my parents, she took me into her office. It was a small office with a big desk and many, many books. It seemed quite cozy and comfortable. We talked. She then told me I would be given an IQ test. It was fun. At a couple of points we both laughed at some of the questions: "If you fire two bullets at somebody and the first bullet kills the person, what does the second bullet do?" She also did some other testing. I did not feel at all nervous. At the end, she told me that I had done just fine and would be learning to read and spell very quickly. She and I were going to impress Miss Potter (a pseudonym). And, we did!

Dr. Fernald's kinesthetic approach involved writing in the air as well as tracing words in large written or scripted format. My mother was very interested in the method and we worked hard on it after school between my visits to Dr. Fernald. In those visits, Dr. Fernald was always cheerful and always smiling. As a child, I felt I had a new friend, one who I knew was helping me in very important ways. I wanted to do well.

By the summer, Dr. Fernald decided I should enroll in the class being taught at UCLA for children with my type of problem. My parents taught me to take the big blue bus from Pico and Robertson in West Los Angeles directly to the UCLA bus stop and to navigate to the other side of campus across its various little ravines to the wood school building near Sunset Boulevard that housed Dr. Fernald's program. The building was a simple, barracks-style green structure that smelled very much of wood, cheap drawing paper, and the type of paint that children used to use many years ago. In the course of getting back and forth to her building I, of course, explored many buildings and many ravines!

The class had fewer than 16 pupils. We sat two pupils to a table. There was a student teacher who was a UCLA trainee for every two pupils. Dr. Fernald was in the background circulating among the pupils and the student teachers. She did not run the class, but was clearly in charge. The student teachers rotated being in charge of the class. The method of instruction was quite interesting. Every day, each pupil had to dictate a story to his or her student teacher. It could be as long as you wanted—mine were quite long! The teacher wrote it all down. The next day she (all the student teachers were, as I remember, young women) would bring the story back, typed up on a special typewriter that made letters that I recall as being about a half inch in height. We then read our stories to the student teachers from the neatly typed manuscript. I appreciated what a nice job the student teacher had done. We then would practice some of the words of the story, which were written on big cards (in my mind's eye, the cards were about 2- or 3-in high and about 10-in long). We would trace the words and learn to spell them. While one of the student teacher's pupils was reciting his story (most of the pupils were boys), the other pupil was doing the word practice, including softly repeating his story and tracing words. There was some work involving the group as a whole with larger cards.

Dr. Fernald always seemed to be in a good mood and, as I look back on it, seemed to have an individual relationship and concern for each of the pupils and student teachers. Nevertheless, some of the students also had trouble behaving themselves. She was stern about the class being a place to learn. Students who could not behave in the class had to leave and go outside. I remember one or two of those students had to leave the class permanently.

The sessions lasted a half day. They included recess breaks as well as some time for painting. Much of that was finger painting, dipping our hands into chalky paints, which had a rather nice smell.

Once I got the notion of reading, I became quite avid. I tried to explain to Miss Potter what I was learning from Dr. Fernald. But Miss Potter made it quite clear that she was not interested.

Forty-five years after the experiences in this story, I was again at UCLA. Having spent 25 years on the Stanford faculty and holding an endowed chair there, I was invited to become Dean for Neuroscience and Research at the UCLA Medical School. I spent 4 years there before coming to New York. The ravines at UCLA have been filled in. There are far more buildings, and Grace Fernald's simple wood classrooms have recently been torn down for a new business school. But UCLA still has a Grace Fernald School, and it is considered one of the crown jewels of the institution.

Before meeting Professor Monaghan, I had episodically thought of Grace Fernald—particularly as I made various professional transitions. In my current positions as Chair of Psychiatry at the New York Hospital Cornell Medical Center with responsibility for its Payne Whitney Clinic and editor of one of the major scientific journals of psychiatry, I have sometimes wondered what Grace Fernald would have thought. How did life change for some of the other boys as a result of her help and ministrations? I still use aspects of the Fernald method to this day. It, thus, is a great pleasure to be able to pay homage to her here. I did not know her as a leader in her field—though I came to recognize that. Rather, I knew Dr. Fernald as a teacher who clearly loved helping children who had problems and who—with my two remarkable parents—made possible for me the future I dreamed of.

Jack D. Barchas is Chair of Psychiatry at the New York Hospital Cornell Medical Center and editor of *Archives of General Psychiatry*. This remembrance appeared at http://history literacy.org/98_spring/Fernald_stu.html. Reprinted with the permission of Dr. Jack D Barchas.

Social Environment

A student's social environment also has significant consequences. Everyone needs mutually satisfying relationships with friends. Friendships serve as the basis for further social growth, and they provide opportunities to build confidence in the social realm. Children who develop normally in the social sphere learn social skills in a casual and informal manner, assimilating through incidental experiences appropriate ways of acting with people.

For many students with learning disabilities, however, the social environment becomes another sphere of dismal failure. Often, they are not socially perceptive or adept at discerning the nuances of everyday living. They are unaware of how their actions affect others and how their behavior is interpreted. Their unsatisfying social experiences, in turn, can adversely affect school learning. Many of the characteristics that underlie academic learning disabilities also create the disability in the social sphere (Brooks, 2000; Bryan, Sullivan-Burnstein, & Mathur, 1998). Strategies for helping students with learning disabilities to cope with social problems and nonverbal learning disabilities are further discussed in the chapter on social and emotional behavior. Also see "LD Stories: Learning Disabilities in the Social Environment."

LD STORIES

LEARNING DISABILITIES IN THE SOCIAL ENVIRONMENT

Betsy is a first grader who encountered difficulty in the social environment (Osman, 1987). Betsy had trouble understanding verbal communication and talking to her classmates. She hugged and touched every prospective friend until the classmate backed away. She made connections with people by feeling and touching—a behavior characteristic of much younger children. When Betsy liked someone, she wanted to show it and did so by hugging, kissing, and grabbing. The other first graders were able to play together and convey thoughts to one another by talking. They did not need to touch to feel liked, and they thought Betsy was strange. When Betsy sensed the other children's rejection, she became even more possessive. The more she was rebuffed, the more she tried to make a friend—the wrong way. By age 7, Betsy expected to be rebuffed by her classmates and unconsciously provoked them. She would ask, "Do you like me?" at inappropriate times, inviting a negative response. Because of her complaints of mistreatment at the school bus stop, Betsy's mother drove her to school. This provoked taunts from the other children, which she hated. Eventually, her claim that "nobody likes me" was based more on reality than on Betsy's imagination.

Cultural and Linguistic Diversity in the Environment

In today's pluralistic society, the student's cultural and language environment is an extremely critical consideration. Our nation's school population consists of students from many different ethnic, language, and cultural populations. One of our nation's greatest challenges is to educate all students regardless of culture, geographic origin, socioeconomic status, or native language. The school is a place where all children of all cultures can share in the heritage and life of the nation. For students with learning disabilities, problems stemming from disabilities are compounded by dimensions of the student's cultural system (Hernandez, 2001; Montgomery, 2001; Ortiz, 1997).

Understanding the student's culture and language background is essential for effective teaching, and teachers should appreciate the unique contributions of each culture. By the time children enter school, they have already absorbed many of the values and behaviors of the culture in which they were raised, which have major ramifications for school success. The child's language is one obvious consideration. If the school expects all students to be fluent in English, students from families that speak another language will be at a disadvantage. Another consideration is that many schools expect students to work independently and to compete for grades and recognition. This expectation may be in conflict with the attitudes of cultures in which cooperation and peer orientation are valued more than the qualities of independence and competitiveness. A similar assumption—that students should do their own work and that helping others is cheating—may also produce conflicts if the culture of the students makes them less willing to

In many respects teaching remains an art. One can never tell where a teacher's influence stops. (© Ed Kashi/CORBIS)

compete and more interested in cooperating with their peers (Cummins, 1996; Hernandez, 2001; Montgomery, 2001).

Teachers should create an atmosphere that builds on cultural and linguistic diversity (Montgomery, 2001). Culturally responsive teachers:

- Accept and welcome culturally diverse students into their classrooms and recognize the need for these students to find relevant connections among themselves and with the subject matter of the tasks teachers ask them to perform

- Establish a classroom atmosphere that respects individuals and their cultures by providing

  a. Current and relevant bulletin boards that display positive and purposeful activities and events involving culturally diverse people

  b. A book corner with a variety of culturally diverse literature

  c. Cross-cultural literature and discussion groups

  d. Language arts and social studies programs that offer opportunities to showcase written and oral reports pertaining to student heritage and cultural traditions

- Use a range of culturally sensitive instruction materials and methods, including

  a. Explicit strategies instruction

  b. Interdisciplinary arts

  c. Instructional scaffolding

  d. Journal writing

- Foster an interactive classroom environment so that students can engage in shared inquiry and discovery by providing

  a. Cooperative learning groups that bring students with diverse backgrounds together

  b. Guided and informal group discussions that offer opportunities for students to learn from one another

  c. Internet opportunities so that children can express cultural exchanges with online penpals. A website to locate e-mail connections is at **http://www.stolaf.edu/network/iecc.**

- Collaborate and communicate with culturally diverse families and professionals

DIFFERENTIATED INSTRUCTION TO MEET LEARNING DIFFERENCES

Some children confront obstacles in learning because the curriculum is not geared to their *learning differences*. They do not respond to a one-size-fits-all curriculum; they need teaching that responds to their personal talents, interests, and proclivities. It may be that their brains are wired differently; the wiring of the brain may have been laid down in a different way, causing a glitch in the pattern of learning (Levine, 2003; Shaywitz, 2003). Levine (2002) suspects that the biggest mistake we make in teaching is to treat everyone equally when it comes to learning. Children process information differently from one another; some form images, others form words, and others form sentences. Children with learning differences need another approach to learning; one that takes their individual needs into account.

An approach to teaching called **differentiated instruction** reflects a philosophy of teaching that enables teachers to reach the unique needs of each student, capitalizing on the student's strengths and weaknesses. In differentiated instruction, the teacher seeks to find that special method that will be successful for an individual student to help that student learn (Bender, 2002). A website for differentiated instruction is **http://www.cast.org/ncac/index.cfm?i=2876.**

In this section, we describe some of the differentiated special methods and the theories that underlie these teaching approaches. Teachers should know and have at their disposal many techniques to meet the needs of an individual student, and they should not be overly dependent on a single teaching approach. Such a flaw is exemplified in "LD Stories: A Fable for Teachers." The point of the fable is that each student is different, and that one method cannot be relied on as the *best* way for teaching in every case. There is no magic formula for teaching a child. Teachers need to have a wide range of instructional approaches at their disposal, and they need to be imaginative and flexible enough to adapt them to the particular needs of each child.

In the next section, we discuss several types of differentiated instruction, such as: (1) psychological processing, (2) cognitive strategies for learning, (3) direct instruction and mastery learning, (4) special teaching techniques, and (5) psychotherapeutic teaching.

Psychological Processing

Psychological processing refers to the mental processes of perception, memory, and attention. Perceptual disorders include visual, auditory, tactile, and kinesthetic learning. For example, Jeff's teacher is aware of his difficulty with auditory processing, and she understands why Jeff has so much difficulty in learning phonics. Jeff's teacher therefore makes accommodations in teaching phonics for his auditory processing difficulty. Susan has difficulty with visual perception and cannot remember written words. Her teacher uses strategies to help her recognize written words.

The concept of psychological processing appeared early in the field of learning disabilities, and it has become an integral part of the field of learning disabilities. In fact, the definition of learning disabilities in federal law (IDEA–2004; PL 108–446) contains the phrase *psychological processing disorders*. The idea of psychological processing continues to be useful for understanding a child's learning differences.

A Fable for Teachers

Once upon a time the animals decided they must do something educational to help their young meet the problems of the world. A school was organized where they adopted a curriculum consisting of running, climbing, and swimming. To make it easier to administer, all of the animals took all the subjects. Of course, the duck was excellent in swimming—in fact, he was better than the instructor; running, however, was a weak area for him. Therefore, he had to stay after school and drop swimming in order to practice running. Now, this was kept up until his webbed feet were badly worn, and soon he became only average in swimming. However, average was an acceptable criterion in this school, so no one was concerned about it—except, of course, the duck. While the rabbit was good in running, he was not up to par in swimming and suffered a nervous breakdown because of the makeup work required to improve his swimming. By the end of the year, an abnormal eel that could swim exceedingly well and also run and climb had the highest average overall and was consequently named valedictorian of the class.

Source: From "A fable for teachers," 1974, *Reading Today International,* International Reading Association, 3(2), p. 1. Reprinted with permission of the publishers.

Cognitive Strategies for Learning

A **cognitive strategy** is a procedure, or group of procedures, that a student uses to perform academic tasks. Cognitive strategies involve higher order thinking skills involved in problem solving, organizing, self-monitoring, self-questioning, monitoring and self-checking, and rule learning (Council for Exceptional Children, 2002).

Students with learning differences tend to process information differently, using an inefficient route to access information. In teaching cognitive strategies, students are taught to use the cognitive strategies that effective learners use, such as organizational skills, planning, asking themselves questions, and monitoring their own performance (Meltzer & Montague, 2001).

Direct Instruction and Mastery Learning

In **direct instruction,** which is also referred to as *explicit teaching,* the focus is on teaching the academic skills of the curriculum in a structured and controlled manner. The curriculum and the tasks that the student is to learn are analyzed. Then the desired academic curriculum skill is carefully scheduled so that each step can be taught in sequence by the teacher. The student can practice and repeat each step of the sequence until the student masters the skill. Research shows that direct instruction is very effective, and the students do learn the academic curriculum skills (Carnine, Silbert, & Kame'enui, 1990; Mainzer, Deshler, Coleman, Kozleski, & Rodriguez-Walling, 2003; Swanson, 1999b).

Procedures for direct instruction include:

1. Break tasks into small steps
2. Administer probes
3. Supply feedback
4. Provide diagrams and pictures to enhance comprehension
5. Provide ample independent practice

Mastery learning is an outcome of direct instruction. This perspective presumes that the student must learn each of a sequence of skills in order to learn a task. Learning each skill of a task is likened to climbing the rungs on a ladder. Each rung must be touched in climbing to the top; the student who misses some rungs may fall off. The skill of reading, for example, is analyzed as consisting of many subskills; by mastering the component subskills, the student should master the skill of reading.

Special Teaching Techniques

Unlike the usual developmental methods used in the general education classroom, a number of methods offer a highly differentiated way of teaching. A *special teaching technique* is sometimes the name of the originator, or the popularizer, of the approach (e.g., the Orton-Gillingham method). These special teaching techniques are often used as remedial methods, and they are often used for one-to-one instruction. Some of these special teaching techniques are described in the chapter on reading.

Psychotherapeutic Teaching

The **psychotherapeutic teaching** approach concentrates on the student's feelings and relationship with the teacher. Failing students are unhappy in the learning situation, and their frustrations, poor ego development, and feelings of inadequacy all lead to a continued failure in learning. What is needed, this view suggests, is a reversal of this downward cycle of failure by building feelings of success and establishing a healthy psychodynamic relationship between a student and a teacher.

The goal of psychotherapeutic teaching is to rebuild self-concept, to foster hope and assurance, and to let the student know that the teacher understands the problem and has confidence in the student's ability to learn and succeed. Despite the obvious need for considering psychodynamic factors, an exclusive concentration of the psychodynamic approach, without teaching the student the needed skills, may result in the creation of *happy fail-ures* (students who have learned to be content with their academic failure).

CONTROLLING INSTRUCTIONAL VARIABLES

The teacher and the school can do relatively little about many factors related to learning disabilities. The home environment or the genetic or biological makeup of the student may be key elements contributing to the learning problem, but usually such variables cannot be modified by the teacher. Other factors that can be changed by teachers should receive careful consideration. Variables in learning that can be readjusted by teachers include the difficulty level, space, time, language, and interpersonal relationship between student and teacher.

Difficulty Level

The *difficulty level* of material is an extremely important consideration. Difficulty level can be modified to meet a student's present performance and tolerance levels. The concept of **readiness,** which is defined as the state of maturational development that is necessary before a skill can be learned, applies here. Vygotsky's notion of the **zone of proximal development (ZPD),** which is a term that envisions a range of difficulty levels for a student, with the ZPD at the midpoint of a student's capacity and an appropriate level for learning, applies here as well (Vygotsky, 1962; see the chapter on theories of learning). Many students fail tasks simply because the tasks are too difficult and the required level of performance is beyond their present skill level. Expecting a student to perform a task far beyond her or his skill level can result in a complete breakdown in learning. A synthesis of intervention research shows that "control of task difficulty" is a critical feature of effective intervention (Vaughn, Gersten, & Chard, 2000, p. 160).

Many skills or responses must be overlearned so that they can become automatic. Many skills must be internalized or become automatic before they can be used quickly in new situations or transferred to new situations. The internalization permits a shift from the conscious, cognitive level to the automatic response, or habitual level. For example, in reading, the student initially may use phonic skills in a conscious, deliberate way to decode words; later, the process must become automatic for effective reading.

Space

Space refers to the physical setting, which should be conducive to learning. Among the ways to modify space are using partitions, cubicles, screens, special rooms, quiet corners, and removing distracting stimuli. Space also involves the student's work area, such as the size of the paper and the desk surface. The school environment should not be a distraction from learning.

The goal of space control is to slowly increase the amount of space with which the student must contend. Gradually, students must internalize their own controls so that they can get along in an unmodified space environment.

Time

There are a number of ways to control *time* in the teaching setting. Lessons for students with a very short attention span can be limited so that they can be completed in less time. For example, one row of mathematics problems can be assigned instead of an entire page. The work page can be cut into squares or strips to shorten the time required to complete one section. Fewer spelling words can be given to learn. In timed exercises, the allotted time can be increased. Time can be broken into shorter units by varying the types of activity so that quiet activities are followed by livelier ones. Planned activity changes, such as having the student come to the teacher's desk or walk to a shelf to get supplies, can be useful breaks during long lessons. Homework assignments can be shortened. The goal is to gradually increase the time that the student works on a task.

Language

Language can also be modified to enhance student learning. To ensure that language clarifies rather than confuses, teachers should examine the wording of their directions. The language should match the student's level of understanding. For students whose first language is not English, it is especially critical that the teacher's language be clear, precise, and unambiguous. Using a visual support, such as a chart, can be helpful.

For students with severe disabilities, the language quantity must be reduced to the simplest statements. Techniques to simplify language include: (1) reducing directions to "telegraphic speech," or using only essential words; (2) maintaining visual contact with the learner; (3) avoiding ambiguous words and emphasizing meaning with gesture; (4) speaking in a slow tempo; (5) touching the student before talking; and (6) avoiding complex sentence structure, particularly negative constructions.

The Interpersonal Relationship

The *interpersonal relationship factor,* or the **rapport** between the student and teacher, which is based on total acceptance of the student as a human being worthy of respect, is of paramount importance. Without it, learning is not likely to take place; with it, learning frequently occurs in spite of the use of inappropriate techniques and materials or other shortcomings. The importance of a good student–teacher relationship is discussed in the next section on building self-esteem.

Robert Louis Stevenson once observed that life is not so much a matter of holding good cards but of playing a poor hand well. This observation expresses the plight of students with learning disabilities and the need for teachers to help them learn how to play their hand well. Clinical teaching requires an affirming and positive teacher–student relationship. Although effective teaching requires objectivity and a thorough knowledge of the curriculum, skills, and methods, it also requires a subjective understanding of the student as an individual with feelings, emotions, and attitudes (Brooks & Goldstein, 2002; Brooks, 2000). Students with learning disabilities often feel lost and frightened because they have suffered years of despair, discouragement, and frustration. They frequently experience feelings of rejection, failure, and hopelessness about the future that affect every subject they study in school and every aspect of their lives. The emotional plight of students with learning disabilities is further explored in "LD Stories: The Emotional Plight of the Failing Student."

Teachers should realize that learning disabilities may influence every aspect of the student's world. It is important to recognize the emotional impact of failure on the student. Not only are parents and teachers displeased with the child, but the parent's anxiety also often becomes uncontrollable. The parents wonder whether their child is unable to learn or is just plain lazy. If they are assured that their child's intelligence is normal, even the most loving parents can become so alarmed at their child's inability to learn

LD STORIES

The Emotional Plight of the Failing Student

- For 12 long years of school and after, the student contends with a situation for which he or she can find no satisfactory solution. When schoolwork becomes insurmountable, the student has few alternative resources. An adult who is dissatisfied with his job may seek a position elsewhere or find solace outside of work or may even choose to endure these difficulties because of a high salary or other compensations. For the student, however, there is no escape; he or she is subjected to anything from degradation to long-suffering tolerance. Proof

of inadequacies appears daily in the classroom. In the end, the student is held in low esteem, not only by classmates, but also often by his or her family (Roswell & Natchez, 1977).

- Learning disabilities do not begin and end at the classroom door; they pervade every aspect of the child's life. They interfere with everything important to the child—from riding a bicycle to making friends, from knowing how to behave at recess to being an effective student (Silver, 2003).

that they will tend to punish, scold and threaten, or even reward with the hope of producing desired results. Teachers also feel frustrated by their inability to reach the child.

The child tries to function under these adverse conditions. Then, when failure continues, the child can become overwhelmed and devastated. These feelings linger after school and on weekends. The notion that he or she does not measure up hangs over the child relentlessly.

An important responsibility for the clinical teacher, therefore, is to motivate students who have been failing, to build their self-concept and **self-esteem,** and to interest them in learning. Success in learning has a beneficial effect on personality, enhances feelings of self-worth, and rekindles an interest in learning. Such teaching can be considered therapeutic (Brooks, 2000). The following principles of: (1) rapport, (2) shared responsibility, (3) structure, (4) sincerity, (5) success, and (6) interest offer guidelines for therapeutic teaching.

Rapport

A good relationship between the teacher and student is an essential first step in clinical teaching. Much of the success in clinical teaching depends on the establishment of such rapport. The teacher must accept the student as a human being worthy of respect in spite of a failure to learn. A healthy relationship implies compassion without overinvolvement, understanding without indulgence, and a genuine concern for the student's development. Because the student lives in a continuing atmosphere of rejection and failure, the relationship with the clinical teacher should provide a new atmosphere of confidence and acceptance. It is extremely difficult for a parent to retain an accepting yet objective attitude, and the student becomes very sensitive to the parent's disappointment. Parents are often unaware of their child's reaction to their efforts. For example, one well-intentioned father, observed in a public library helping his son pick out a book and listening to him read, was overheard saying, "I'll tell you that word one more time, and then I don't want you to forget it for the rest of your life." This is not an attitude that is conducive to learning. Children need to see a word dozens of times before they readily recognize the word.

Shared Responsibility

Involvement of both the student and the teacher is another factor in clinical teaching. Students should participate in both the analysis of their problems and the evaluation of their performance. In the same collaborative spirit, the student should also take an active role in designing lessons and choosing materials.

Structure

Providing structure and establishing routines are important factors for introducing order into the chaotic lives of students with learning disabilities. Many students need and welcome such order. Structure and routine can be provided in many aspects of teaching—in the physical environment, in the sequence of activities, and in the manner in which lessons are taught.

Sincerity

Students are skillful in detecting insincerity, and they will soon detect dishonesty if a teacher tells them they are doing well when they know otherwise. Instead, the teacher might try to minimize anxiety about errors by saying that many students have similar difficulties and by conveying confidence that together they will find ways to overcome them.

Success

Success is similar to a vitamin. If you don't get enough of it growing up, you suffer a very severe deficiency that could result in long-term problems (Levine, 2002).

Self-esteem cannot be injected or taught; it is a result of success (Richardson, 2003). It is important that students become aware of and appreciate their successes. Students should be aware of what they can do well, and teachers and parents should help them pursue their areas of strengths. Many students and adults with learning disabilities achieve success by understanding the nature of their learning problems and learning to use their strengths.

Achieving goals in learning and acquiring a feeling of success are of paramount importance. Lessons must be designed and materials selected to permit students to experience success. For example, the teacher can obtain books at the reading level that meets the students' areas of interest. In addition to selecting the appropriate level of difficulty of teaching materials, the teacher can make students conscious of their success and progress by:

- Praising good work
- Using extrinsic rewards as reinforcement
- Developing visual records of progress through charts and graphs

Interest

The chance of successful achievement increases when a teacher provides materials based on the student's special interests. Student interests can be determined through conversations with the student or by administering interest inventories. Using materials in the student's area of interest gives the student a strong motivation to learn.

Students have diverse reading interests that include sports, adventure and action, history, science, biography and memoir, mysteries, and humor. Teachers can develop valuable reading lessons from materials that students have an interest in—*TV Guide,* newspapers, baseball and football programs, CD inserts, popular magazines, and even computer manuals. The first real interest in reading shown by some high school students is stimulated by the need to pass a written test in order to get a driver's license. Engaging this interest, some teachers have successfully used the driver's manual to teach reading. A favorite author or series books have been the impetus for other youngsters to become readers.

The following are some examples of students who made great strides once an interest had been tapped.

- Antonio, an eighth-grade boy with learning disabilities, found the first book he ever read from cover to cover, *The Incredible Journey,* so fascinating that he was completely oblivious to class changes, ringing bells, and classroom incidents from the time he started the book until he completed it.

- Maria developed an interest in successful women who had, in her words, "made it." Her teacher helped her find many books and articles that related stories of successful women in many fields. Her reading improved dramatically after she read these materials.

- Dave had a keen interest in the Chicago Cubs baseball team. His teacher helped him find newspaper stories about the games and biographies of the players. His interest led him to read more, and his reading improved.

- Sometimes a television show or a movie based on a book can spark an interest. After seeing a television show about *Robinson Crusoe,* Juan, who had severe reading problems, was introduced to a simplified version of this book. His teacher reported that he became so immersed in the story that he would grab the book as soon as he entered the room for their daily session.

Once in a while, dramatic changes occur in a student's attitude and outlook because of clinical teaching. When such a change occurs because of a book the child has read, it is sometimes called **bibliotherapy.** Learning about the experiences of others can foster release and insight as well as hope and encouragement. Students with personal problems (e.g., children who are short, overweight, unpopular, or who have physical or academic disabilities) identify with book characters who suffer similar problems. Such students can be helped by the characters' resolution of their problems (Sridhar & Vaughn, 2002).

Peter, a seventh-grade student with learning disabilities, was fascinated by Houdini, the great escape artist. Peter read all the books he could find on Houdini in the school library and in the public library. During this

Acceptance and self-respect are important to any student's self-esteem and motivation. (© Jeffrey W. Myers/FPG International)

period, Peter's teachers observed personality and attitude changes, as well as tremendous improvement in his reading.

The right book can be a powerful tool to build interest, provide motivation, and improve academic learning.

TEACHING STUDENTS WITH LEARNING DISABILITIES IN THE GENERAL EDUCATION CLASSROOM

In this section, we will examine some instructional strategies for students with learning disabilities, which include: (1) accommodations for students with learning disabilities, (2) peer tutoring, (3) explicit teaching, (4) promoting active learning, (5) scaffolded instruction, (6) reciprocal teaching, and (7) learning strategies instruction.

Most students with learning disabilities (83%) spend at least a portion of their school day in general education classrooms. About 46% of these students have full placement in the general education class, while 38% are in resource rooms for a portion of the day and in the general education class for the rest of the day (U.S. Department of Education, 2002).

In addition, accommodations in general education classrooms must be made for students identified under **Section 504 of the Rehabilitation Act,** which is the federal law that covers all agencies and institutions that receive financial assistance and that requires that no otherwise qualified handicapped individual shall be excluded from participation. These students have disabilities that "limit one or more of life's major activities," but they are not eligible for special education under the school's criteria for eligibility. For students identified under Section 504, **"reasonable accommodations,"** the phrase which is used to describe what can easily be done in a setting for an individual with a disability, must be made in general education classrooms. States must have accommodation guidelines.

The boxed feature, "LD in Practice: Accommodations for the General Education Teacher," offers general ways for accommodating students with learning disabilities in the general education classroom (Council for Exceptional Children, 2001; U.S. Department of Education, 2000b).

Accommodations for Students With Learning Disabilities

Accommodations for teaching students with learning disabilities in the general education classroom include the following: (1) improve organizational skills, (2) increase attention, (3) improve the ability to listen, (4) adapt the curriculum, and (5) help students manage time.

Improve Organizational Skills   Difficulty in organizing their lives is characteristic of students with learning disabilities. The lack of organization re-

LD IN PRACTICE
ACCOMMODATIONS FOR THE GENERAL EDUCATION TEACHER

- *Modify the setting.*   Give instructions or tests in a separate room, in a carrel, or in a small group.
- *Modify the scheduling.*   Extend the time and the breaks for testing and instruction.
- *Modify the presentation.*   Use large print; give verbal directions instead of written directions or tape-record the directions.
- *Modify responses.*   Have students answer questions orally or point to the answer; students can mark in a booklet instead of on an answer sheet.

sults in incomplete assignments. These students need to learn how to plan ahead, how to gather appropriate materials for school tasks, how to prioritize the steps to complete an assignment, and how to keep track of their work. The following steps are useful to help students organize.

- Provide clear routines for placing objects—especially regularly used objects such as books, assignments, and outdoor clothes—in designated places so that they can be found easily
- Provide students with a list of materials needed for a task; limit the list to only those materials necessary to complete the task
- Provide a schedule so that students know exactly what to do for each class period
- Make sure students have all homework assignments before leaving school; write each assignment on the board and have students copy it, or write the assignment for a student in a pocket notebook
- Provide students with pocket folders to organize materials—for example, place new work on one side and completed work in chronological order on the other
- Use a different color folder for each subject

Increase Attention　A short attention span is a characteristic of many students with learning disabilities. These students may initially be attentive, but their attention soon wanders. The following activities will help students attend and prolong their concentration.

- Shorten the task by breaking a long task into smaller parts; assign fewer problems—for example, fewer spelling words or mathematics problems
- Shorten homework assignments by giving fewer problems
- Use distributed practice; instead of a few long and concentrated practice sessions, set up more short, spaced, and frequent practice sessions
- Make tasks more interesting to keep students' interest; encourage students to work with partners, in small groups, or in interest centers
- Alternate highly interesting tasks and less interesting tasks
- Increase the novelty of the task; tasks that are new or unique are more appealing and will increase attention

Improve the Ability to Listen　We erroneously assume that students know how to listen. Students with learning disabilities frequently miss important instructions and information because they are not actively listening. They may even be unaware that a message is being given. Teachers expect students not just to hear or recognize the words that are spoken, but also to comprehend the message. The following strategies can help students acquire better listening skills.

- Make instructions simple by using short, direct sentences; give one instruction at a time, and repeat it as often as necessary; make sure students know all the vocabulary being used

- Prompt students to repeat instructions after listening to them; later, have the students repeat to themselves information they have just heard to build listening and memory skills

- Alert students by using key phrases—for example, "This is important," "Listen carefully," or "This will be on the exam"; some teachers use prearranged signals, such as hand signals or switching the lights on or off before giving directions

- Use visual aids (such as charts, pictures, graphics, key points on a chalkboard, or overhead transparencies) to illustrate and support verbal information

Adapt the Curriculum   Often the teacher can change, modify, or adapt the curriculum without sacrificing its basic integrity. Even a small change can be beneficial for the student.

- Select high-interest materials to reinforce the basic curriculum; use manipulatives, or hands-on materials, whenever possible; create activities that require active participation, such as talking through problems and acting out steps—many students learn better when they actually do something in addition to just listening and observing

- Use visual aids to supplement oral and written information; use learning aids, such as computers, calculators, and tape recordings to increase motivation

- Modify tests, allowing students to take tests orally instead of writing the answers; teach students how to cross out incorrect answers on multiple-choice tests

Help Students Manage Time   Managing time is a common problem area for many students with learning disabilities. They get pulled away from the task at hand and become involved with new challenges. They become procrastinators, a trait they retain into their adult lives. The following activities are designed to help students with time management.

- The "How I Spend My Time" chart (Figure 3.2) can be kept by students to develop a sense of time and what must be accomplished in a given time span; students can make a spreadsheet, bar chart, or pie chart with a computer to illustrate time use

- Set up a specific routine and adhere to it; when disruptions occur, explain the situation to students, as well as appropriate ways to respond

- During the school day, alternate activities that are done sitting and those that involve standing and moving about

- Make lists that will help students organize their tasks; have students check off tasks as they complete them

- Use behavior contracts that specify the amount of time allotted for specific activities

FIGURE 3.2

How I Spend My Time

NAME				DATE			
ACTIVITY	Mon	Tues	Wed	Thurs	Fri	Sat	Sun
Attending Classes							
Studying							
Socializing							
Watching T.V.							
Exercising							
Working							
Reading							
Sleeping							

Peer Tutoring

Peer tutoring is a strategy for the general education classroom in which two children work on learning tasks together. One child is the *tutor* and serves as a teacher; the other child is the *tutee* and serves as the learner. The children work in pairs, so peer tutoring supports one-to-one teaching in the general education classroom. The peer tutor helps the tutee learn, practice, or review an academic skill that the classroom teacher has planned. Examples of peer tutoring tasks are saying aloud or writing spelling words, reading sentences, or solving a mathematics problem. Types of peer tutoring include *same-age peer tutoring* (in which one student in the classroom tutors a classmate) and *cross-age peer tutoring* (in which the tutor is several years older than the tutee; Greenwood, Maheedy, & Delquardi, 2002).

Both the tutor and the tutee benefit from the peer-tutoring experience. For the tutee, there are gains in academic achievement. The child is able to learn more effectively from a classmate whose thinking process is closer to that of the child than that of an adult. For the tutor, there are also academic benefits because the best way to really learn something is to teach it to someone else. The experience also offers the tutor a sense of accomplishment. In addition, there are other advantages of peer tutoring. The tutor serves as a model of appropriate academic and nonacademic behavior, and the relationship between the two children provides opportunities for establishing additional social relationships within the classroom.

Research consistently shows that peer tutoring is a successful and valid strategy (Fischer, Schumaker, & Deshler, 1995; Fuchs & Fuchs, 1998; Greenwood et al., 2002). It is also relatively easy for teachers to implement.

Peer tutoring is a practical way to provide support for children with learning disabilities in the inclusive classroom, and *more* importantly, children like it.

Classwide peer tutoring is a more organized version of peer tutoring that involves the entire class. For this activity, tutor–tutee pairs work together on a classwide basis. At the beginning of each week, all students are paired for tutoring, and these pairs are then assigned to one of two competing teams. Tutees earn points for their team by responding to the tasks presented to them by their tutors. The winning team is determined daily and weekly on the basis of the team with the highest point total (Greenwood, 1996; Utley, Mortweet, & Greenwood, 1997).

Explicit Teaching

Many students with learning disabilities need explicit teaching. Like *direct instruction,* **explicit teaching** means that teachers clearly state what is to be taught and explain what needs to be done. Students are not left to make inferences from experiences that are unmediated by such help. In explicit instruction, students are provided with models of appropriate methods for solving problems or explaining relationships. They are amply supported during the stages of the learning process, and they are provided with ade-

In peer tutoring, two children work on a learning task together, with one child serving as the teacher (tutor) and the other child as the learner (tutee). (© Anne Dowle/The Picture Cube)

TABLE 3.1 Principles of Explicit Teaching	■ Provide students with an adequate range of examples to exemplify a concept or problem-solving strategy ■ Provide models of proficient performance, including step-by-step strategies (at times) or broad generic questions and guidelines that focus attention and prompt deep processing ■ Provide experiences where students explain how and why they make decisions ■ Provide frequent feedback on quality of performance and support so that students persist in performing activities ■ Provide adequate practice and activities that are interesting and engaging

Source: From "Recent Advances in Instructional Research for Students With Learning Disabilities: An Overview," by R. Gerstein, 1998, *Learning Disabilities Research & Practice, 13*(13), pp. 162–170. Reprinted with the permission of Laurence Erlbaum Associates, Inc.

quate practice (Gerstein, 1998; U.S. Department of Education, 1997). Table 3.1 provides some principles of explicit teaching.

Promoting Active Learning

Learning is not a spectator sport. The importance of instruction that promotes **active learning** is advanced by research in contemporary cognitive psychology. Active learners (1) attend to instruction, (2) attribute results to their own efforts, (3) relate tasks and materials to their knowledge and experience, and (4) actively construct meaning during learning. Instruction for active learning capitalizes on the child's interests, stresses the importance of building background knowledge prior to teaching, and encourages the active involvement of students. The theory emphasizes the concept that learning and behavior emerge from the interaction of three components: the learning environment, the learner, and the teaching material (Resnick, 1987; Wittrock, 1988). The boxed feature "LD in Practice: Guidelines for Promoting Active Learning" provides guidelines for promoting active learning.

Scaffolded Instruction

Scaffolding refers to abundant teacher supports at the initial stage of a student's learning of a task. An analogy is made to the scaffold used by builders. A scaffold is a temporary structure used to support a building in the early stages of construction and then removed when it is no longer needed. In teaching the student, the metaphor of a scaffold is used to describe supports that the teacher provides for the student in the early stages of learning a task that is beyond the student's level of competency. These supports are removed when they are no longer necessary (Rosenshine, 1997; Stone, 1998a).

LD IN PRACTICE

GUIDELINES FOR PROMOTING ACTIVE LEARNING

Encourage interactive learning	Learning emerges from the interaction of three components: the environment, the learner, and the teaching material. Teachers should interrelate these three components.
Recognize the importance of prior experience	Integrate the children's background knowledge and experience into the learning activities. Learning is dependent on what children already know.
Prepare children for the lesson	Preparation for learning leads to improved understanding, motivation, and storage of information. Expose children to key concepts before they are presented in the lesson.
Encourage active involvement	When children are actively involved in their learning, they are more successful learners than when they take a passive role in the learning process.
Structure lessons for success	There is a positive correlation between learning, self-concept, and positive attitudes. Teachers should structure lessons to provide opportunities for children to experience success.
Teach "learning to learn" strategies	Teachers can help children become aware of their learning processes. For example, asking children how they found a solution to a problem will assist them in understanding the strategies they use to learn.

The concept of **scaffolded instruction** is often linked to Vygotsky's (1962) notion of the zone of proximal development (ZPD). The term *ZPD* refers to the difficulty level for effective learning; it is neither too easy nor too difficult for the child (the "Goldilocks" approach to instruction; see the section titled "Developmental Psychology" in the chapter on theories of learning). Also, Vygotsky notes that learning depends upon the social interaction of an experienced adult (teacher) and the learner (student). The teacher provides the support or scaffolding that the student needs during the initial stage of learning the task (Rosenshine, 1997; Stone, 1998a).

For scaffolding to be successful, a child must enter an exchange with some prior understanding of what is to be accomplished. The scaffolding procedure uses an ongoing interaction in which the teacher provides carefully calibrated assistance at the child's leading edge of competence (Stone, 1998a). Examples of scaffolds include: (1) simplified problems, (2) modeling of the procedures by the teacher, (3) thinking aloud by the teacher, and (4) teacher mediation to guide the student to think through the problem. Reciprocal teaching, described next, is an example of scaffolded instruction.

Reciprocal Teaching

In the chapter on assessment, we discussed the model of dynamic assessment. **Reciprocal teaching** is the instructional link of dynamic assessment. In teaching reading comprehension, reciprocal teaching assumes the form of a dialogue in which teachers and students take turns leading discussions about a shared reading text (Palinscar et al., 1991). The initial study on reciprocal teaching was conducted by Palinscar and Brown (1984). The researchers used reciprocal teaching to train a group of seventh-grade poor readers, whose scores were about 2.6 years below grade level, in reading comprehension. The students were trained in four learning strategies: *summarizing* the content of a passage, *asking questions* about a central point, *clarifying* the difficult parts of the material, and *predicting* what would happen next.

The reciprocal teaching procedures follow four steps: (1) the teacher and students read the material silently; (2) the teacher explains and then models the strategies of summarizing, questioning, clarifying, and predicting by saying out loud the thoughts that she or he used in those learning strategies; (3) everyone reads another passage, and the students are given the responsibility of demonstrating out loud for the other students in the group. At first, many of the students may be hesitant and their demonstrations imperfect. The teacher provides guidance, encouragement, and support (scaffolding) to help the students perfect their demonstrations. Finally, (4) each student demonstrates abilities in the strategies of summarizing, questioning, clarifying, and predicting.

The reciprocal teaching procedure has been investigated in a number of studies, and it has been shown to be an effective approach to instruction. Students improved in their ability to summarize, question, clarify, and predict using reading passages. Students also showed improvement in their scores in reading comprehension (Palinscar et al., 1991).

The key principles of reciprocal teaching instruction are (Palinscar et al., 1991) these:

- Learning is considered a social activity, initially shared among people; but learning is gradually internalized to reappear again as individual achievement

- The dialogue or conversations between teachers and students guide the student's learning

- The teacher plays a mediating role, shaping learning opportunities and bringing them to the attention of the learner

- Assessment is a continuing, ongoing process that occurs during the reciprocal teaching

Learning Strategies Instruction

Instruction in learning strategies is increasingly being used as a teaching method for students with learning disabilities. These students tend to be inefficient learners because they lack systematic ways of learning, remembering, or directing their learning. **Learning strategies instruction** helps students with learning disabilities learn the secrets of being a successful student, how to study, how to integrate new materials with what they already know, how to monitor their learning and problem solving, and how to remember or to predict what is going to happen. Research supports learning strategies as an effective way to teach students with learning disabilities (Mainzer et al., 2003; Swanson, 1999b).

Instruction in learning strategies helps students take charge of their own learning; thus, they become active learners and acquire a repertoire of learning strategies (Deshler, Ellis, & Lenz, 1996). The model for teaching learning strategies to students with learning disabilities, which was developed at the University of Kansas Institute for Research on Learning, has eight steps: (1) pretesting, (2) describing the strategy, (3) teaching modeling, (4) verbal practice, (5) controlled practice, (6) advanced practice, (7) posttesting, and (8) generalization.

Learning strategies are discussed in several sections of this textbook—in the chapters on theories of learning, in adolescents and adults with learning disabilities, and in reading (in the context of reading). These chapters provide examples of learning strategies instruction.

The procedures for learning strategies instruction include the following:

1. Provide elaborate explanations
2. Model learning processes
3. Provide prompts to use strategies
4. Engage in teacher–student dialogue
5. Ask process-type questions

The next section of this chapter introduces task analysis as a component of clinical teaching.

TASK ANALYSIS The purpose of **task analysis** is to plan the sequential steps for learning a specified skill. Task analysis breaks down the complexity of an activity into easier steps; these steps are organized as a sequence, and the student is taught each step of the sequence. The goal is to move the student to the desired level of skill achievement. The skill of buttoning, for example, entails a sequence of component subskills: grasping the button, aligning the button with the buttonhole, and so forth. The teacher must consider the following: (1) What are the important, specific educational tasks that the

LD IN PRACTICE

STEPS OF TASK ANALYSIS

Step 1 Clearly state the learning task (the behavioral objective).

Step 2 Break the learning task into the steps necessary to learn the target skill, and place these steps into a logical teaching sequence.

Step 3 Test informally to determine the steps that the student can already perform.

Step 4 Begin teaching, in sequential order, each step of the task analysis sequence.

student must learn? (2) What are the sequential steps in learning this task? and (3) What specific behaviors does the student need to perform this task? See "LD in Practice: Steps of Task Analysis."

The following list provides examples of the task analysis of instruction sequences to reach a curriculum goal:

- *Task analysis of long division* includes the steps (or subskills) of estimating, dividing, multiplying, subtracting, checking, bringing down the next digit, and then repeating the process. Each step must be planned for, taught, and assessed.

- *Task analysis of writing a report* by using the school library includes the skills of knowing alphabetical order, using the card catalog (or a computer terminal), finding books on a subject, using a book index to find information on a topic, getting a main idea from reading, and knowing language usage skills (Slavin, 2000).

- *Task analysis of recognizing a word* might include the skills of recognizing initial consonants, recognizing short vowels, and blending.

The case study that follows is a continuation of the case of Rita G., which was begun in the chapter on assessment. Part II of the case study covers Stage 3 of the IEP process, the multidisciplinary evaluation.

RITA G.'S MULTIDISCIPLINARY EVALUATION

The multidisciplinary team for Rita's case consisted of the school psychologist, school nurse, social worker, and learning disabilities teacher. Each member of the team was responsible for administering certain tests and gathering specific evaluation information. Here is a summary of the multidisciplinary evaluation.

Classroom Observation

The learning disabilities teacher and the social worker observed Rita in her third-grade class. The learning disabilities teacher's observation took place during an arithmetic lesson. Mr. Martinez was giving the class practice in solving word problems in two-digit addition and subtraction, using place value. He read a problem to the class; students were expected to visualize the situation and then perform the calculations on paper to find the answer. The lesson was followed with practice on similar written word-story problems in a workbook, and students were asked to complete five problems. Rita did not volunteer the answer to any of the oral problems, and she did not write the calculations to find the answer to the problems during the lesson. In the seatwork portion of the lesson, Rita attempted the first problem but had difficulty staying on task. She did not even attempt the other four problems. Inspection of her work showed she could not line up the numbers in the addition problem and, consequently, made mistakes in addition. She had many erasures and crossouts.

The social worker observed Rita during a 15-minute "free" period. During this time, none of her classmates interacted with Rita, and she just stared out of the window for the entire period.

Auditory and Visual Acuity

The school nurse tested Rita for hearing and visual impairments.

Hearing   The school nurse administered an audiometer hearing screening test. Rita's hearing tested within the normal range.

Vision   The school nurse used the Keystone Visual Survey Service for Schools to screen Rita's vision. No visual difficulties were noted.

Developmental and Educational History

The social worker interviewed Mrs. G. to obtain the case history information. Rita is the older of two daughters in an English-speaking household. Her father is a salesman; her mother a homemaker. Rita's birth and prenatal history were reported as normal. Her birth weight was 7 lbs 10 oz. Rita had a high fever at 6 months of age and was hospitalized for 2 days. She had chicken pox at age 5. Otherwise, her medical history appears to be normal.

Mrs. G. said that Rita's motor development seemed to be normal. Rita crawled at 6 months and walked at 1 year, but she seemed to fall and bump into things frequently. She had much difficulty learning to feed and dress herself. She still has trouble with certain tasks, such as tying shoelaces. She did not like to play with educational types of toys that had to be put together. Mrs. G. described Rita as *klutzy*. Language development seemed to be normal; Rita had babbled at 6 months, said her first word at about 1 year, and used two-word sentences at 18 months.

Rita attended a nursery school at age 4 but, according to Mrs. G., was not enthusiastic about going to preschool. Rita began to experience problems in kindergarten. The kindergarten teacher told Mrs. G. that Rita showed difficulty in fine-motor coordination and seemed *immature* for a 5-year-old. The first-grade teacher said she did not always pay attention and did not complete her work. The second-grade teacher said she did not try hard enough, and her work was very *sloppy*. Rita does not have any close friends and usually plays with younger children.

Mrs. G. felt the major problem now was that Rita was failing third grade and that she did not want to go to school.

Measures of Intellectual Aptitude

The school psychologist administered the Wechsler Intelligence Scale for Children—Third Edition (WISC-III). Rita's overall performance was within the average range with a full-scale IQ score of 109. Her verbal IQ score was 128 and her performance IQ score was 87. These WISC-III scores suggest a discrepancy between Rita's verbal and performance abilities. Her aptitude strengths were in areas that use language; her weaknesses were in tests in which she had to visualize objects in space or plan and manipulate objects, and in arithmetic. (The mean for the IQ scores on the WISC-III is 100; the mean for the subtest scores on the WISC-III is 10. The school psychologist noted that Rita seemed to give up as soon as items became difficult and did not seem to have any system for attacking challenging problems. When items became hard for her, Rita seemed helpless and simply said, "I can't do that. It's too hard for me." Her WISC-III scores were as follows:

WISC-III Full Scale IQ: 109
Verbal IQ: 128
Performance IQ: 87

Verbal subtest scaled scores

Information	13
Similarities	14
Arithmetic	8
Vocabulary	14
Comprehension	11
Digit Span	13

Performance subtest scaled scores

Picture Arrangement	7
Coding	6
Picture Completion	8
Block Design	8
Object Assembly	7
Symbol Search	7
Mazes	5

Present Levels of Academic Functioning

Rita's current academic achievement levels were determined by assessment in the areas of mathematics, reading, handwriting, spelling, adaptive behavior, learning strengths and weaknesses, and interest. In addition, her classroom work was observed and analyzed. Curriculum-based assessment was given in reading and mathematics. Assessment results are summarized next.

Mathematics Mathematics testing included the mathematics tests of the Peabody Individual Achievement Test—Revised (PIAT-R), the Key Math—Revised, and the Brigance Comprehensive Inventory of Basic Skills—Revised. Rita scored substantially below grade level in all these mathematics tests. Her grade placement at the time of the test was 3.8, and her mathematics scores ranged between Grade 1.8 and 2.5, making her between 1 and 1.5 years to 2 years below her present grade in mathematics. Her most serious mathematics difficulties were in the areas of numerical reasoning and word problems. She also did poorly in addition, subtraction, and multiplication. Her scores were low in fractions and division, but she has not had instruction in these areas in the classroom.

Reading Rita was given the reading tests of the Brigance Comprehensive Inventory of Basic Skills—Revised, the PIAT-R, the Woodcock

Reading Mastery Tests—Revised, and the Gray Oral Reading Tests, Fourth Edition, to test reading achievement. In general, Rita scored satisfactorily in tests of word recognition, but her performance dropped considerably when reading comprehension was required. When she was observed during the reading, she seemed to lose her place and had difficulty concentrating on the material. Her word identification, phonics skills, and reading vocabulary are adequate. Difficulties in reading appear when she is required to use higher conceptual skills in reading comprehension. Her reading comprehension is at the independent reading level of second grade. Her word-recognition skills are at the fourth-grade level.

Handwriting Rita's handwriting skills were assessed with the Brigance Comprehensive Inventory of Basic Skills and through observation. Handwriting poses a major problem for her. The third-grade handwriting curriculum calls for shifting from manuscript to cursive writing. However, Rita has resisted making the change and asked Mr. Martinez if she could continue using manuscript writing. She is left-handed and has always had much difficulty performing this visual–motor task. Her written papers are a painstaking assignment for her to complete and require much effort and time. Even then, the final product is usually illegible and has a very sloppy appearance. She begins many letters from the bottom, moving to the top of a line. Tall letters are the same size as small letters. Her pencil grasp is unusual, and she keeps her nonwriting right hand in a folded, tense position. Written expression could not be tested because of her extremely poor handwriting skills.

Spelling Rita's spelling was tested with the spelling tests of the PIAT-R, the Brigance Comprehensive Inventory of Basic Skills—Revised, the Woodcock-Johnson Psychoeducational Battery—III (WJ-III), and the Wide-Range Achievement

Test—3 (WRAT-3). She scored at the second-grade level. Analysis of her spelling errors showed that she usually spelled words according to phonics rules, for example, *frend* for *friend, laf* for *laugh,* and *tok* for *talk.* She showed poor visual memory for irregularly spelled words.

Adaptive Behavior

Information on Rita's adaptive behavior was obtained by the social worker, who used the Vineland Adaptive Behavior Scales in interviewing Rita's mother. Rita's lowest scores were in the areas of daily living skills and socialization. These scores supported her mother's comments that Rita relies on other people to tell her what to do and that she has made no friends and plays mostly with her younger sister. They also support Mr. Martinez's observation that Rita lacks the motivation to organize herself to complete school work and will often "just sit there."

Learning Strengths and Weaknesses Rita was given the Developmental Test of Visual–Motor Integration by the learning disabilities teacher. Rita's score was equivalent to that of a 6-year-old child, or 3 full years below her chronological age. Although she could copy simple designs, such as the circle and plus sign, she had difficulty with the triangle, diamond, and other more complicated shapes. She appears to have a weakness in visual perception abilities.

Rita's auditory discrimination was tested with the Goldman-Fristoe-Woodcock Test of Auditory Discrimination. Her scores were adequate on this test, suggesting a strength in auditory discrimination.

Other learning strengths included good phonics skills, an adequate sight vocabulary, and good verbal skills. All the specialists on the multidisciplinary team noted Rita's weaknesses in attention and concentration. They also noted that she lacked cognitive strategies to approach learning situations. Rita had become a passive learner and did not actively seek out ways to enhance her learning.

Interest Inventory The learning disabilities teacher gave Rita an informal interest inventory. Rita indicated that she likes to watch television and eat. She said that her playmates include her younger sister and her sister's friend. Rita does not receive an allowance, but she earns money by taking out the garbage. She spends the money she earns on candy. In response to the question "Do you like school?" she said, "Sometimes and sometimes not." After some prompting, she admitted that a good school day meant that the teacher had not yelled at her. Rita's favorite subject is music; she dislikes gym and arithmetic.

Note: The case study of Rita G. is continued in the chapter on educational settings, where the case conference will be discussed.

CHAPTER SUMMARY

1. Clinical teaching is an integral part of the assessment–teaching process. The concept of tailoring learning experiences to the unique needs of a particular student is the essence of clinical teaching.

2. The clinical teaching process can be viewed as a five-stage cycle of decision making that consists of assessment, planning of the teaching task, implementation of the teaching plan, evaluation of student performance, and modification of the assessment.

3. The student's ecological system includes the home environment, the school environment, the social environment, and cultural and linguistic diversity in the student's environment. Each has an impact on the student's learning.

4. Differentiated instruction is required to meet the individual needs of students with learning disabilities.

5. One of the critical options available to teachers is to change certain variables in the school setting: difficulty level, space, time, language, and the interpersonal relationship between teacher and student. By modifying these elements, the teacher controls certain variables that affect learning.

6. Clinical teaching requires not only a sound foundation in methods and practices, but also the ability to establish an understanding and empathic relationship with the pupil. Six therapeutic principles—rapport, shared responsibility, structure, sincerity, success, and interest—can help in creating such a relationship.

7. Emerging instructional trends include accommodations for students with learning disabilities, peer tutoring, explicit teaching, promoting active learning, scaffolded instruction, reciprocal teaching, and learning strategies instruction.

8. Task analysis involves analyzing the small sequential steps of a specific skill.

1. What is meant by the term clinical teaching?

2. Teachers should consider the student's ecological system. Discuss the various environments in which students live that can affect their learning. What changes are occurring in today's society in terms of the ecological system of children?

3. Teachers can do little about many of the factors related to learning disabilities. Some variables, however, can be controlled or adjusted by the teacher. Describe and give an example of three instructional variables that teachers can change.

4. Why is it important to consider ways to accommodate students with learning disabilities in the general education classroom? Name three ways that general education classroom teachers can make modifications for students with learning disabilities.

5. Other students in the classroom may complain that it is not fair to make modifications and accommodations for students with disabilities because the students are not all being treated in the same way. How would you respond to these comments?

6. Describe task analysis. Give an example of an instructional sequence (or the steps to learning a specific skill).

KEY TERMS

active learning *(p. 117)*

basal reader *(p. 94)*

bibliotherapy *(p. 110)*

clinical teaching *(p. 92)*

cognitive strategy *(p. 103)*

differentiated instruction *(p. 102)*

direct instruction *(p. 103)*

ecological system *(p. 96)*

explicit teaching *(p. 116)*

learning strategies instruction
 (p. 120)

mastery learning *(p. 104)*

peer tutoring *(p. 115)*

psychological processing *(p. 102)*

psychotherapeutic teaching
 (p. 104)

rapport *(p. 106)*

readiness *(p. 105)*

reasonable accommodations
 (p. 112)

reciprocal teaching *(p. 119)*

scaffolded instruction *(p. 118)*

Section 504 of the Rehabilitation
 Act *(p. 112)*

self-esteem *(p. 108)*

task analysis *(p. 120)*

zone of proximal development
 (ZPD) *(p. 105)*

4 Educational Settings

Students with learning disabilities and related disorders have a right to learn skills they will need in the competitive world they will be entering. Instruction for these students requires systematic, intensive, and explicit teaching by teachers who are skilled in such teaching.

—*Anonymous*

This chapter examines the educational settings for teaching students with learning disabilities and related disorders. The educational setting is the third element of the assessment–teaching process. In this chapter, we focus on: (1) the important concepts about educational settings, (2) educational settings, (3) promoting partnerships between general education teachers and special education teachers, and (4) parents and the family of students with learning problems. Finally, this chapter contains the conclusion of the case study of Rita G.

IMPORTANT CONCEPTS ABOUT EDUCATIONAL SETTINGS

Determining the setting where a student with learning disabilities will receive instruction is a key decision that is made by the IEP team. For students with learning disabilities, as well as other disabilities, the placement increasingly is in the general education classroom. The term *inclusion* is often used to describe the placement of students with disabilities in the general education classroom setting, along with suitable supports for students with disabilities. The Individuals With Disabilities Education Improvement Act of 2004 calls for instructing students with disabilities in the *least restrictive environment*; that is, with peers who do not have disabilities, to the greatest extent appropriate. IDEA–2004 emphasizes that students with disabilities should have access to the general education curriculum.

Inclusion placements continue to expand, even though research evidence for one special education delivery model over another is still inconclusive (Zigmond, 2003). There are several differing viewpoints about the issue of general education placement and inclusion:

1. One perspective is that children with disabilities, including those with learning disabilities, have a right to participate in environments as close to normal as possible and to benefit socially and academically from being in the mainstream of school and society. Moreover, this view suggests that

placing students with disabilities in other settings for instruction is harmful and stigmatizing (McLeskey, Hoppey, Williams, & Rentz, 2004; Rea, McLaughlin, & Walter-Thomas, 2002; Stainback & Stainback, 1996; Waldron & McLeskey, 1998).

2.   An alternative perspective is that students with learning disabilities need intensive, systematic, and explicit instruction from teachers who are trained and highly skilled in delivering such services. Such instruction is most effective in small instructional groups, which is difficult to provide in a general education class (Vaughn, Elbaum, & Boardsman, 2001; Zigmond, 2003).

3.   Still another view suggests that the issue of where students with learning disabilities should receive instruction is complex and there are no simple answers. Moreover, it is important to recognize that the placement or setting is not a treatment, and the setting itself is less important than what goes on in the setting. Schools differ in their models of inclusion classes and in their models of pull-out instruction. General education teachers and special education teachers can work together to provide individualized instruction within a regular education classroom setting (Holloway, 2001; McLeskey et al., 2004; Murawski & Dieker, 2004; Murawski & Swanson, 2002).

The inclusion movement is rapidly escalating within our schools. The steady increase of the placement of students with learning disabilities in general education classes is striking. Between 1990 and 2002, the percentage of students with learning disabilities who had only general education class placement increased from 17% to 45%. During the same 12-year period, the percentage of students with learning disabilities placed in resource rooms decreased from 59% to 38% (U.S. Department of Education, 2002). The pie chart in Figure 4.1 shows the placement of students with learning disabilities.

To appreciate the full implications of the inclusion movement, it is necessary to know certain basic concepts about educational settings for instruction in special education. The child's placement is determined when the case study team holds the IEP meeting. The type of educational setting, or the place where the student will receive services, is written into the IEP.

The federal special education law, IDEA–2004, contains two significant provisions related to placement for services: (1) the continuum of alternative placements and (2) the least restrictive environment. The implications of these two provisions differ significantly.

Continuum of Alternative Placements

The **continuum of alternative placements** provision specifies that schools make available an array of educational settings to meet the varied needs of students with disabilities for special education and related services. The

FIGURE 4.1

Educational Settings of
Students With Learning
Disabilities

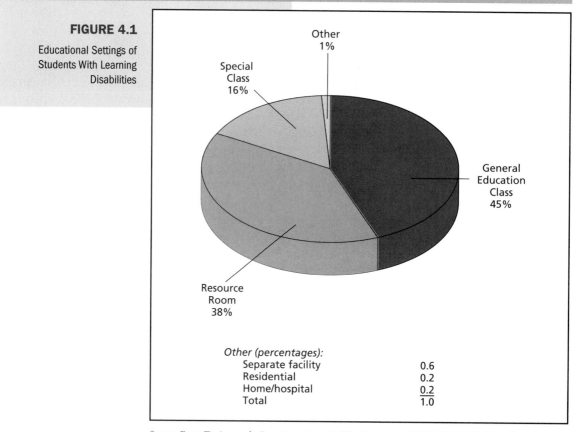

Other (percentages):
Separate facility	0.6
Residential	0.2
Home/hospital	0.2
Total	1.0

Source: From *To Assure the Free Appropriate Public Education of All Children With Disabilities.* Twenty-Fourth Annual Report to Congress on the Implementation of the Individuals With Disabilities Education Act, by the U.S. Department of Education, 2002, Washington, DC: U.S. Government Printing Office.

placement options include: (1) general education classes, (2) resource rooms, (3) separate classes, (4) separate schools, and other types of placements as needed, such as a (5) residential facility, or (6) a homebound or hospital setting.

Table 4.1 contains a brief list, with explanations, of alternative placements for students with all categories of disabilities. The placement options are ordered from the least restrictive to the most restrictive environment. The term *restrictive* refers to the placement of students with disabilities with nondisabled students. The placement of students with disabilities with nondisabled students in general education classes is therefore considered the least restrictive option. Placement in a separate class or a separate school in which only students with disabilities are served is a more restrictive environment. It is important that teachers not lose sight of the continuum of services and the fact that some students with learning disabilities

TABLE 4.1	General education class	Includes students who receive most of their education program in a general education classroom and receive special education and related services outside this classroom for less than 21% of the school day. It includes children placed in a general education class and receiving special education within this class, as well as children placed in a general education class and receiving special education outside this class.
Continuum of Alternative Placements		
	Resource room	Includes students who receive special education and related services outside the general education classroom for at least 21%, but not more than 60% of the school day. This may include students placed in resource rooms with part-time instruction in a general education class.
	Separate class	Includes students who receive special education and related services outside the general education classroom for more than 60% of the school day. Students may be placed in a separate class with part-time instruction in another placement or placed in separate classes full-time on a regular school campus.
	Separate school	Includes students who receive special education and related services in separate day schools for more than 50% of the school day.
	Residential facility	Includes students who receive education in a public or private residential facility for more than 50% of the school day.
	Homebound or hospital setting	Includes students placed in and receiving special education in homebound or hospital programs.

need more than an inclusive setting can offer (Crockett & Kauffman, 2001; Langone, 1998; Zigmond, 2003).

Least Restrictive Environment

The second important provision in special education law regarding educational settings is the least restrictive environment (LRE), which has been the cornerstone of the inclusion movement. The argument is that successful adults with disabilities have learned to function comfortably in society and in the community—in an unrestricted environment composed of all people. To promote normalization and experiences in the greater society, the LRE provision aims to ensure that, to the extent appropriate, students with disabilities have experiences in school with students who do not have disabilities. Translated into practice, this means that when the IEP team makes decisions about educational settings, the team must attempt to choose the least restrictive environment for each student. Educational settings that include students who do not have disabilities are less restrictive. IDEA–2004 also requires that students with disabilities have access to the general education curriculum.

Integrating General Education and Special Education

Over the years, a progression of practices has been designed to integrate general education and special education. In the early days of special education, special classes or schools were established for each category of disability. There were special classes for students with mental retardation, for students who were blind or deaf, and for students with learning disabilities. An influential article by Lloyd Dunn (1968) is credited with initiating the idea of integrating special education students into less restrictive settings. In the years since Dunn's article, we have seen many changes in the type of educational settings and more integration with general education students.

Mainstreaming   Mainstreaming was an early procedure in which students with learning disabilities were placed selectively in the general education classroom for instruction, particularly if teachers believed the children would benefit from an integrated placement. Students with learning disabilities were carefully integrated into general education classrooms, perhaps for a single subject or for a portion of the day. The goal was to increase slowly the amount of time that the students would spend in the general education classroom. The mainstreaming plan was carefully worked out and monitored for each student by special and general educators.

Inclusion   As noted, inclusion refers to the instruction of students with disabilities in the general education classroom, which should be accomplished with appropriate supports to meet the students' individual needs. Some proponents of inclusion have an underlying aim of restructuring the schools to eliminate special education, which is viewed as an unnecessary "second system" (Association for Persons With Severe Handicaps, 1995; Villa, Thousand, Meyers, & Nevin, 1996).

The philosophical ideologies of inclusion are the normalization of children through integrated regular classes and the elimination of labels for children with disabilities. An added argument for inclusion is the notion that society artificially constructs the disability labels of children; the belief is that a large part of a child's problem would disappear by doing away with labels.

Many parents and professionals worry that inclusion will not meet the needs of all students with learning disabilities. Does the stigma come from the label or from the child's failure to learn? For example, reading disabilities would not exist in a society that does not value literacy. The reality is, however, that we live in a society that does value literacy, and a person who does not know how to read suffers in this society (Kauffman & Hallahan, 1997). The heart of IDEA–2004 is the *individualized education program* (IEP). Many students with learning disabilities and related disorders need individualized instruction and intensive teaching, which is difficult to provide in a general education classroom setting. As a result, research shows that students with learning disabilities are often neglected (Zigmond, 1997, 2003). The concern is that one size does not fit all, and lumping all students with learning disabilities into the general education classroom ignores the notion of individualized instruction (Crockett & Kauffman, 2001; Foorman & Torgesen, 2001; Johns, 2003).

Guidelines for Effective Inclusion

To make inclusion settings more effective, it is essential to provide sufficient support through multidisciplinary teams of professionals who mutually adjust their collective skills and knowledge to create unique, personal programs for each student. Ideally, all staff members should be involved in making decisions, teaching, and evaluating the student's needs and progress.

Effective inclusion requires that teachers: (1) consider the student and the family, (2) be committed to the goals of inclusion, (3) have adequate resources and supports, and (4) engage in ongoing professional development (Friend & Bursuck, 2002; Langone, 1998; Smith, Polloway, Patton, & Dowdy, 2002).

Specific strategies for effective inclusion in the general education classroom are described in "LD in Practice: Strategies for Effective Inclusion in the General Education Classroom."

EDUCATIONAL SETTINGS

In selecting an **educational setting** for a particular student, the IEP team should consider: (1) the severity of the disability, (2) the student's need for related services, (3) the student's ability to fit into the routine of the selected setting, (4) the student's social and academic skills, and (5) the student's level of schooling (primary, intermediate, or secondary). Teams often recommend a placement that combines elements of several types of educational settings.

Parents must agree to the placement in writing. If parents and school personnel disagree, parents can ask for mediation at no cost to them, the school can request a "resolution session," or either party can request a due process hearing (Individuals With Disabilities Education Improvement Act, 2004).

In what type of settings are students with learning disabilities currently receiving instruction? In the Twenty-Fourth Annual Report to Congress, the U.S. Department of Education (2002) reported educational environments of students with disabilities in terms of the percentage of time students were outside the general education class. Table 4.2 shows how the

LD IN PRACTICE

STRATEGIES FOR EFFECTIVE INCLUSION IN THE GENERAL EDUCATION CLASSROOM

- *Use a team approach.* General education classroom teachers are sometimes hesitant and even fearful about providing for the needs of special students in their classrooms. The general education classroom teacher should use a team approach and share responsibility with special education teachers and related professionals.

- *Provide supportive services.* When students with learning disabilities are served in the general education classroom, they often need supportive services. The special education teacher can be helpful in obtaining and providing supportive services.

- *Plan for social acceptance.* Many students with learning disabilities experience difficulty in being accepted socially by their peers in the general education classroom. By itself, placement in a general education classroom may not lead to greater social interaction or increased social acceptance. Social planning is needed.

- *Teach students appropriate classroom behavior.* Acceptable classroom behaviors are even more important than academic competencies as predictors of success in the classroom. Important behaviors for classroom success include: (1) interacting positively with other students, (2) obeying class rules, and (3) displaying proper work habits.

- *Use coteaching strategies.* The general education teacher and the special education teacher should use collaborative planning and teaching in the classroom.

TABLE 4.2

Percentage of Children Served in Different Educational Environments

Placement type	General education class	Resource room	Special class
Percentage of time all special education students spent outside of general education classrooms	Less than 21%	21%–60%	More than 60%
Percentage of students with learning disabilities in educational environments	46%	38%	15%

Department of Education classifies the percentage of time that students with disabilities spend in the general education class, the type of educational environment, and the percentage of students with learning disabilities in each educational environment.

As indicated in Figure 4.1, most students with learning disabilities (84%) spend much, most, or all of their time in general education classes. This number includes students whose educational placement is in the general education classroom only (46%) and those students who are in both a resource room for part of the day (38%) and in a general education classroom for the rest of the day. About 15% of students with learning disabilities are placed in separate classes. A small percentage (1%) are in other settings (separate schools, residential facilities, or homebound/hospital settings; U.S. Department of Education, 2002). The various placement options are described in this section. Most students with learning disabilities receive services through general education classrooms, resource rooms, or special classrooms.

Sometimes a combination placement may be a viable alternative for particular students. For example, a student could be in a special class for a portion of the day or the week and in a general education classroom for the remainder of the time.

Significant changes have occurred in the placement of students with learning disabilities. As shown in Figure 4.2, over a 12-year period, the percentage of students with learning disabilities who were placed in general education classrooms increased from 17% to 46%. During this time period, the percentage of students with learning disabilities placed in resource rooms decreased from 59% to 38%. The percentage of children in separate classes also decreased from 21% to 15%. In addition, there was a decrease in other placements from 2% to 1%.

General Education Class

Placement in the **general education classroom** is the least restrictive environment for students with learning disabilities. Successful integration of students with learning disabilities into the general education classroom requires careful planning, teacher preparation, team effort, and a complete support system. Mere physical placement in a general education classroom is not enough to ensure academic achievement or social acceptance. Students with learning disabilities have specific needs that require targeted instruction and attention. Such students in general education classes receive special education and related services outside this classroom for less than 21% of the day (U.S. Department of Education, 2002).

Ideally, general and special educators share responsibility for teaching. The special educator may collaborate with the general education classroom teacher, provide materials for the student, or actually teach the student within the general education classroom. The general education classroom

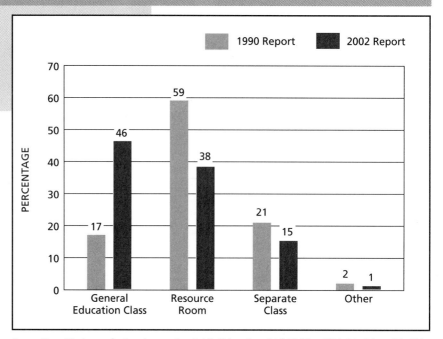

FIGURE 4.2

Changes in Placements for Students With Learning Disabilities

Source: From *To Assure the Free Appropriate Public Education of All Children With Disabilities.* Twelfth and Twenty-Fourth Annual Reports on the Implementation of the Individuals With Disabilities Education Act, by the U.S. Department of Education, 1990, 2002, Washington, DC: U.S. Government Printing Office.

teacher must also have the skills, knowledge, and willingness to work with students with learning disabilities who are placed in the teacher's classroom. In-service training and the continuing education of classroom teachers are critically important, as is the coordinated effort of all school personnel—general education teachers, special education teachers, related staff, and administrators.

It is crucial to recognize that the composition of students in the general education classroom is dramatically changing. Most students in the general education classroom do not have disabilities. Some students will have disabilities that have been diagnosed through an individualized educational program (IEP). Other students will not have an IEP for special education services, but they will still be eligible to receive accommodations under *Section 504 of the Rehabilitation Act.* These students will have a Section 504 Plan, which is shown in Figure 4.3.

Resource Room

A **resource room** is an educational setting that provides educational services to students with disabilities on a regularly scheduled basis for approximately

| Student: _____ | School: _____ | Grade: _____ |

Date of
Implementation: _____ Termination: _____ Review: _____

Statement of Student's Achievement as it Relates to this "Plan": _____

_____

INTERVENTION/ STRATEGY	IMPLEMENTOR(S)	MONITORING DATE	COMMENTS

21%–60% of the school day (U.S. Department of Education, 2002). Students placed in resource rooms spend the remainder of the school day in a general education classroom. The resource room offers flexibility in terms of the curriculum offered, the time students spend in the program, the number of students served, and the teacher's time. The resource room is a supporting element for general education instruction. As noted in Figure 4.2, the percentage of students receiving resource room instruction is decreasing.

Care must be taken in scheduling students for a resource room session. For example, if the pupil enjoys physical education, the teacher should avoid preempting this period for the resource room session. In addition, the classroom teacher must be consulted about the optimum time for the student to leave the classroom. Resource rooms should be pleasant and have an abundant supply of materials. Because students with learning disabilities often have short attention spans, it is wise to provide a change of pace by planning several activities during a teaching session.

Separate Class

The **separate class** within the school was one of the first placements used in the public schools to provide education to students with learning disabilities. These classes are typically small, containing about 6 to 15 students at a time. The separate class offers the opportunity for highly individualized and closely supervised intensive instruction. It serves students for more than 60% of the day (U.S. Department of Education, 2002). Even with the growing inclusion movement, the percentage of students with learning disabilities placed in special classes is about 15%.

Some separate classes are *categorical* (consisting only of students with learning disabilities); others are *cross-categorical* (consisting of students with various disabilities, usually learning disabilities, emotional disturbance, or mental retardation).

The separate class is beneficial for certain students with learning disabilities. They appear to have a better self-concept than similar students in general education classrooms, possibly because regular class competition sets achievement criteria that these students cannot meet. In separate classes, certain students with learning disabilities make greater strides in both academic and social areas. With its lower teacher–pupil ratio, this setting offers more intensive individualized instruction in which students spend more time learning. The separate classroom may provide the most appropriate setting for the kind of intensive and comprehensive intervention needed by students with the most serious and severe learning disabilities.

A goal of separate class placement is to help students organize themselves for increased independent learning so that eventually they will be able to take part in a less restrictive environment. Sometimes, the first step in the transition involves having the student receive some instruction in the resource room. Students may continue the transition by participating in a limited way in a general education class for a selected subject; their participation is then gradually increased. If the transition is to be effective, a good working relationship must be maintained between the teacher of the separate class and the teacher of the general education class.

Separate School

Separate schools are special educational facilities established specifically for students with learning disabilities. These schools are often private, but they may be publicly supported. Some students attend the separate school full time. Other students attend the separate school only half a day and may spend the balance of the school day in the public school.

The disadvantages of separate schools include the high expense to parents, the traveling distance, and the lack of opportunity to be with other students for some portion of the school day. The advantages of separate schools are that they often serve students with learning disabilities well, and they sometimes provide the only feasible option for certain students. Successful pilot programs are often developed at separate schools, which are then used in other settings.

Residential Facility

Residential facilities provide full-time placement for students away from their homes. The students receive education in a public or private residential facility. Relatively few students have disabilities that are severe enough to warrant such placement. However, in some cases—if the community lacks adequate alternative facilities, if the behavioral manifestations are extremely severe, and if the emotional reaction among other members of the family is debilitating—residential placement on a 24-hour basis may be the best solution for both the student and the family.

The disadvantages of residential facilities are that they remove the student from home and neighborhood, emphasize the student's disability, and provide fewer opportunities for social experiences in the larger community. However, for certain youngsters, residential placements remain the most appropriate choice, and they have successfully helped students learn, adjust to the world, and achieve very rewarding careers and lives.

Homebound or Hospital Setting

Students in homebound or hospital settings usually have a medical condition requiring these placements. The school sends teachers to these settings to provide instruction.

One-to-One Instruction

One-to-one instruction occurs when one adult works with one student. It is one of the most effective types of teaching, and the research shows that it leads to substantial improvement in student achievement. One-to-one instruction works because the teaching is highly individualized, and the student receives intensive instruction over a period of time by a skilled teacher who can tailor the instruction to the specific student's needs. Sometimes students with learning disabilities need one-to-one instruction, and they tend to do well with this individualized instruction (Slavin, 2000; Vaughn, Gersten, & Chard, 2000).

In the real world, of course, the cost for schools to provide a teacher for each student is impractical, so parents must often turn to private specialists or clinics to receive this highly individualized form of instruction. Therefore, it is important for schools to seek ways to get as close as possible to one-to-one instruction. Methods for doing this include using computer instruction and using other aides and volunteers as tutors in the classroom (Slavin, 2000).

Computers offer a way to individualize teaching. A good computer software program is like a tutor because it presents the information, gives students abundant practice, assesses their level of understanding, and provides additional information if it is needed. Computer programs can be quite effective in presenting ideas and in using pictures or graphics to reinforce concepts. Because most students are motivated by the computer, they will work longer and harder than they will with paper-and-pencil tasks.

Using aides and volunteers offers another procedure to approximate one-to-one instruction. The volunteer movement is alive and growing.

Some 60 reading and literacy groups support one-to-one programs, using volunteer adult tutors. Moreover, research demonstrates that tutoring works by increasing a student's reading achievement, confidence, and motivation, in addition to providing a sense of control of the student's reading ability. Even when a student receives the very best in-class instruction, some students still require extra time and assistance to meet the high levels of reading skills needed in school, in the workplace, and throughout life. Tutors can provide the explicit instruction that produces positive results (Center for the Improvement of Early Reading Achievement, 1998; Snow, Burns, & Griffin, 1998a). Tutoring is especially critical during long school breaks, such as summer vacation. Research shows that during these vacation periods, students lose many skills they have learned (Wasik, 1998).

PROMOTING PARTNERSHIPS BETWEEN GENERAL EDUCATION TEACHERS AND SPECIAL EDUCATION TEACHERS

Procedures that promote partnerships between general education teachers and special education teachers become especially important as a greater number of students with learning disabilities are placed in general education classrooms for instruction. Finding ways to facilitate a team effort is necessary for successful inclusion of students with learning disabilities and related disorders.

Student teamwork is a style of interaction that provides a way for individuals to work together. *(© Bill Aron/ PhotoEdit)*

Collaboration

Collaboration is a style of interaction that provides a way for individuals or groups to work together. Through collaboration, two or more individuals interact in a supportive manner that benefits each member, as well as the people they are supporting. The process of collaboration involves people with diverse areas of expertise (such as classroom teachers, special education teachers, and speech–language specialists) who work together to find creative solutions to mutually defined problems. As more students are placed in the inclusive setting of the general education classroom, collaboration becomes essential for effective inclusion (Friend & Cook, 2003; Walther-Thomas, Korinek, & McLaughlin, 2000). Successful collaboration requires the following (Friend & Cook, 2003):

- Mutual goals
- Voluntary participation
- Equality among participants
- Shared responsibility for participation and decision making
- Shared responsibility for outcomes
- Shared resources

Table 4.3 presents a summary of the principles of effective collaboration and activities that work.

TABLE 4.3

Principles of Effective Collaboration

Principles	Activities that work
Establish common goals Successful partners share mutual goals and a common philosophy.	■ Develop a relationship ■ Engage in small-scale efforts initially ■ Develop common perceptions
Participation should be voluntary Collaboration cannot be forced by directives from superiors. Individuals must take mutual responsibility for a problem and freely seek solutions.	■ Involve key stakeholders ■ Invite participation
Recognize equality among participants Each person's contribution is equally valued. Each person has equal power in decision making.	■ Use names, not titles, when interacting ■ Rotate and share team roles ■ Structure ways to facilitate participation

	Principles	Activities that work
TABLE 4.3 (cont.) Principles of Effective Collaboration	**Share responsibility for participation and decision making** Each person should share the responsibility for participation and decision making.	■ Share perspectives about the problem ■ Balance between coordination of tasks and division of labor ■ Brainstorm before decision making ■ Establish clear delineation of agreed-upon actions as follow-up procedures
	Share accountability for outcomes Everyone shares, whether the outcome is successful or not. If the outcome is successful, they share the credit. When it is unsuccessful, they share responsibility for the failure.	■ Acknowledge risks and potential failure ■ Celebrate success together ■ Learn from the failure together
	Share resources Each person has resources to contribute.	■ Identify respective resources ■ Use joint decision making about resource allocation

What the General Education Teacher Needs

The responsibilities of the general education classroom teacher are increasing as the inclusion movement continues to expand. Classroom teachers are accountable for a wider range of students, including more children with disabilities and other special needs. Teachers need many supports if inclusion is to work. What kinds of supports should be provided for general education teachers who are responsible for inclusion?

■ *Participation in the IEP.* The Individuals With Disabilities Education Improvement Act of 2004 requires that general education classroom teachers be part of the individualized education program (IEP) team. Being on the IEP team helps these classroom teachers understand the problems, strengths, and needs of students with disabilities.

■ *Reduced class size.* Having many students with special needs in a general education classroom makes the teaching task more difficult. A smaller class size could help teachers cope with this added responsibility.

■ *Time for planning.* Time should be allocated during the school day for general education classroom teachers to plan with the special education teacher and other professionals for meeting the needs of students with disabilities.

- *Paraprofessionals.* Paraprofessional personnel and aides in the classroom can help general education classroom teachers meet the needs of each student.
- *Volunteers.* Many schools are successful in attracting volunteers to help in the classroom. Senior citizens and volunteers from business organizations sometimes can be recruited to assist.
- *Collaboration with special educators.* It is essential that special educators are available to help general education classroom teachers solve problems, discuss issues, and manage the many situations that they confront in the classroom.
- *Continuum of alternative services.* Some students with special needs require more than the inclusive, general education classroom can offer. For these students, other placement options, such as the resource room or special classes, are needed.
- *Availability of related professional.* The IEP may indicate that the services of related professionals, such as speech–language experts or occupational therapists, are needed. It is important that such services be provided.
- *Opportunities for learning.* General education classroom teachers need to be supported when seeking additional training by attending conferences, seminars, or related activities.

What the Special Education Teacher Needs

The responsibilities of special educators and learning disabilities teachers are difficult to define because they are changing so rapidly. Learning disabilities teachers are expected to wear many hats because they are responsible for: (1) setting up programs to identify, assess, and instruct students; (2) participating in the screening, assessment, and evaluation of students; (3) collaborating with general education classroom teachers to design and implement instruction; (4) knowing both formal assessment measures and alternate assessment methods; (5) participating on IEP teams; (6) implementing the IEP through direct intervention, coteaching, and collaboration; (7) interviewing and holding conferences with parents; and, perhaps most important, (8) helping students to develop self-understanding and to gain the hope and the confidence that is necessary to cope with and to overcome their learning disabilities.

To accomplish these goals, effective special education teachers need to have two different kinds of competencies: (1) competencies in professional knowledge and skills (having the information and proficiencies for testing and teaching) and (2) competencies in human relationships (the art of working with people).

Coteaching

Coteaching occurs when two or more teachers deliver instruction to a diverse group of students in a general education classroom. Coteaching between general educators and special educators has become a common method for delivering instruction to all students in a general education classroom. Both teachers share the teaching. Coteaching can be mutually satisfying, but both teachers must be willing to share and accept responsibility. In fact, coteaching has been likened to a marriage. To be successful, both partners have to make a 100% effort (Friend & Bursuck, 2002; Friend & Cook, 2003; Gately & Gately, 2001). Actually, there are several types of coteaching, and they are described in Table 4.4.

TABLE 4.4

Types of Coteaching

Type	Description
One teaches, one supports One group: One lead teacher, one supportive teacher	One teacher has primary instructional responsibility. The other teacher serves in a supportive role (e.g., observes, tutors, manages behavior).
Station supportive teaching Two groups: Each teacher teaches one group	Divide the content into two parts; then divide the groups into two groups (A and B). Teacher 1 teaches half of the content to Group A, while Teacher 2 teaches the rest of the content to Group B. Then the groups switch. Teacher 2 teaches the rest of the content to Group A, and Teacher 2 teaches the rest of the content to Group B.
Parallel teaching Two groups, two teachers: Each teacher teaches one-half of the class	Each teacher instructs half of the class. Both teachers use the same instructional materials. Teachers may differ in their instructional styles. Essentially, the class is smaller, so students have more opportunities to participate.
Alternative teaching Two groups: One small, one large	The class is divided into two groups—a large group and a small group. One teacher teaches the large group; one teacher teaches the small group. More intensive and direct instruction is usually used in the small group.
Team teaching Both teachers share leadership in teaching the group	Both teachers are equally engaged in the instructional activities. For example, Teacher 1 may begin the lesson by introducing vocabulary while Teacher 2 provides examples to place the words in context.

Strategies to Make Coteaching Work

The following activities can help promote the spirit of coteaching.

- *Make time for coteaching activities.* Productive work requires space, time, and the assurance of uninterrupted sessions. If planning, communicating, and evaluating are not specifically scheduled, there will be insufficient time in the busy school day for these purposes.

- *Recognize that the skills in coteaching and collaboration are learned through developmental processes.* Coteachers must go through developmental stages as they learn to understand each other and to work together.

- *Use coaching strategies.* Coaching is a way to help students with learning disabilities. The special education teacher might take on the role of a coach, giving instructions or demonstrating a specific skill, while the general education classroom teacher learns the skill. The coteachers then decide on the skills they wish to teach.

- *Encourage open communication.* Communication is key to coteaching. If problems are allowed to persist without an opportunity for face-to-face communication, dissatisfaction increases and misunderstandings develop. To avert such situations, oral and written communication must be clear. Effective coteachers are active listeners; they are sensitive to the contributions and ideas of others and recognize nonverbal messages. In addition, effective coteachers give and ask for continuous feedback; they are willing to say "I don't know," and they also give credit to others, when applicable.

"LD in Practice: Strategies for Two Teachers Working Together" describes some ways that two teachers can work cooperatively.

PARENTS AND THE FAMILY   Children with learning disabilities and related disorders claim a tremendous emotional toll on parents. Parents of these children face many of the same problems as teachers do, but in greatly magnified intensity. The child is in school for a few hours a day in a limited and controlled situation; but, for the parents, their responsibility encompasses 24 hours a day, 7 days a week, with no vacations, in all types of situations, and with all types of demands.

It is important for school personnel to consider the strengths of the family. Involvement of parents and families through family–school collaboration is encouraged by informal communication, such as written notes between school and home, parental involvement in the classroom and in extracurricular activities, through face-to-face conferences, telephone contact, and e-mail messages (Turnbull et al., 2004).

LD IN PRACTICE
STRATEGIES FOR TWO TEACHERS WORKING TOGETHER

Activities of first teacher	Activities of second teacher
Lecturing to the class	Writing notes of key ideas on the board during the lecture
Giving instructions orally	
Checking for understanding with the large group	Writing instructions on the board
	Checking for understanding with a small group or individual students
Working with one half of the class in preparing for a debate	Working with the other half of the class in preparing for a debate
Creating basic lesson plans for standards, objectives, and content curriculum	Providing suggestions for modifications, accommodations, and diverse learners
Providing large group instruction	Reviewing homework with small groups
Providing enrichment activities	Providing modifications

Source: Adapted from "Tips and Strategies for Coteaching at the Secondary Level," by W. Murawski & L. Dieker, 2004, *Teaching Exceptional Children, 36,* p. 56. Reprinted with permission of the Council for Exceptional Children.

Parents can play a crucial role in helping their child. They must: (1) be informed consumers, continually working to learn more about the problem of learning disabilities; (2) be assertive advocates, seeking the right programs for their child at home, in school, and in the community; (3) work to ensure that their child's legal rights are being recognized; and (4) be firm in managing their child's behavior while remaining empathetic to their child's feelings, failures, fears, and tribulations. Parents must also give time and attention to other members of the family and try to make a life for themselves. There are no easy answers or simple solutions for parents of children with learning disabilities. For several accounts of a parent's role in helping their child with learning disabilities, see "LD Stories: Mothers' Thoughts."

Parenting a child with learning disabilities is challenging, but it can also be rewarding. Parents need support from the school, the extended family, and other professionals. With this support, encouragement, and the sharing of expertise, the child can emerge from the school years academically, emotionally, and socially intact, as well as prepared for the challenges ahead.

A child's self-esteem benefits from a parent's support of a child's interests, talents, and related activities.
(© Elizabeth Crews)

Suggestions for Parents

Some useful things parents *can* do are presented in "LD in Practice: Suggestions for Parents." Teachers may also wish to recommend reading materials to parents to help them become better acquainted with the problem of learning disabilities and with ways of helping their children. A selection of appropriate books for parents is provided in Table 4.5 on page 152. Three useful websites for parents are **http://www.shwablearning.org, http://www.ldaamerica.org,** and **http://www.chadd.org.**

MOTHERS' THOUGHTS

- All during the evaluation process, I continued to search for a school for Allegra. I applied to many schools in the city, and one by one they rejected her. It was the same each time, a voice on the phone telling me "She doesn't belong here." With each rejection came a deeper sense of despair. As the list grew shorter, my despair began to be overcome by something close to panic.

  I was frightened. I didn't know what to do. What in the world can anyone do if a child is denied a basic education? Her future was falling apart before my eyes. I knew the only chance she stood of making it in this world was to find a school, *any* school, that would accept her; yet, with each one I continued to hear, "She doesn't belong here."

  Source: From *Laughing Allegra* (p. 40), by A. Ford, 2003, New York: New Market Press.

- My son has a learning disability. . . . I remember his coming home from first grade and crying over his reader. He could not decode! The only way he managed to get through first grade was to memorize the readers he brought home. He accomplished this by going over and over them with me. I don't think his teacher was ever aware that he memorized.

  Teacher comments were predictable: "He is just immature." "He could do it if he would just try." "He's just sloppy because he rushes through his work." "He's just lazy." If only they had been with him as he cried over his homework.

  Source: From "A mother's thoughts on inclusion," by M. Carr, 1993, *Journal of Learning Disabilities, 26*(9). p. 590.

- No one would accuse Kerri . . . of lacking smarts or motivation. The . . . fifth grader has an IQ of 118 and enthusiasm to spare. Unfortunately, she's never had an aptitude for linking letters to sounds. She recognizes many words by their appearance on the page, but at 11 she still can't spell or write. Common sense says she's dyslexic. But (by the standards set in her state) Kerri is not entitled to special help. It's sad. She may waste her time in school until she fails badly enough to qualify as learning disabled.

  Source: From *Overcoming dyslexia* (p. 29), by S. Shaywitz, 2003, New York: Alfred A. Knopf.

Parents' Rights

IDEA–2004 strengthens the rights of parents and families in the educational process of their children. A fundamental provision of the law is the right of parents to participate in the educational, decision-making process. Parents have the right to:

- A free, appropriate public education for their child
- Request an evaluation of their child

LD IN PRACTICE
SUGGESTIONS FOR PARENTS

1. *Be alert to any hint that your child is good at something.* By discovering an area of interest or a talent, you can give your child a new chance for success. Even small tasks, such as folding napkins or helping with specific kitchen chores, can give your child a sense of achievement.

2. *Do not push your child into activities for which the child is not ready.* The child may react by trying half-heartedly to please you; rebelling, either actively or passively; or just quitting or withdrawing into a world of daydreams. When a child is forced to meet arbitrary and inappropriate standards imposed by the adult world, learning becomes painful rather than pleasurable.

3. *Simplify family routine.* For some children, mealtime can be an extremely complex and stimulating situation. Your child may be unable to cope with the many sounds, sights, smells, and so on. It may be necessary at first to have the child eat earlier and then gradually join the family meal—perhaps starting with dessert. Search for other such examples in your routines.

4. *Try to match tasks to the child's level of functioning.* Think about the child's problem and find some way to help. For example, easy-to-wipe surfaces and break-proof containers can reduce mess and breakage when the child uses these materials. Drawing an outline of the child's shoes on the closet floor can indicate left and right.

5. *Be direct and positive in talking to your child.* Try to avoid criticizing; instead, be supportive and provide guidance. For example, if your child has trouble following directions, ask him or her to look at you while you speak and then to repeat what you have said.

6. *Keep the child's room simple and in a quiet part of the house.* As far as possible, make the room a place to relax and retreat.

7. *Help your child learn how to live in a world with others.* When a child does not play well with other children, parents may have to go out of their way to plan and guide social experiences. This may mean inviting a single child to play for a short period of time, arranging with parents of other children for joint social activities, or volunteering to be a den mother or Brownie leader.

8. *Children need to learn that they are significant.* They must be treated with respect and allowed to do their own work. They should learn that being a responsible and contributing member of the family is important—probably more important than learning the academic skills demanded by the school.

9. *Keep your outside interests.* Try to relinquish your child's care to a competent baby sitter periodically. Parents need time off for independence and morale boosting.

TABLE 4.5

Books for Parents

Barkley, R. (1995). *Taking charge of ADHD: The complete authoritative guide for parents.* New York: Guilford Press.

Ford, A. (2003). *Laughing Allegra.* New York: New Market Press.

Goldstein, S., & Mather, N. (1998). *Overcoming underachievement: An action guide to helping your child succeed in school.* New York: John Wiley.

Hall, S., & Moats, L. (1999). *Straight talk about reading: How parents can make a difference during the early years.* Chicago: Contemporary Press.

Lerner, J., Lowenthal, B., & Lerner, S. (1995). *Attention deficit disorders: Assessment and teaching.* Pacific Grove, CA: Brooks/Cole.

Osman, B. (1997). *Learning disability and ADHD: A family guide to learning and learning together.* New York: John Wiley.

Silver, L. (1998). *The misunderstood child: A guide for parents of children with learning disabilities.* New York: Times Books.

Smith, S. (1991). *Succeeding against the odds: Strategies and insights from the learning-disabled.* Los Angeles: Jeremy P. Tarcher.

- Notification whenever the school wants to evaluate their child or change the child's educational placement
- Informed consent (parents understand and agree in writing to teaching plans and may withdraw their consent at any time)
- Obtain an independent evaluation of their child
- Request a reevaluation of their child
- Have their child tested in the language that the child knows best
- Review all of their child's school records
- Be informed of *parents' rights*
- Participate in their child's individualized education program (IEP) or Individual Family Service Plan (IFSP) for young children
- Be informed of their child's progress at least as often as parents of children who do not have disabilities are informed
- Have their child educated in the least restrictive environment possible
- Use voluntary mediation, dispute resolution, or a due process hearing to resolve differences with the school

The Family System

A family of five is like five people lying on a waterbed. Whenever one person moves, everyone feels the ripple (Lavoie, 1995).

It is useful to view the family as a system. The fundamental idea of the family systems theory is that whatever happens to one part of a family or system affects all the other parts. In the family system, all members of the extended family are interdependent, and each member has an interactive effect on all other members. The family system involves the child, parents, siblings, grandparents, other people living in the home, or those who are part of the child's family.

The entire family system is affected by a child with learning disabilities. Day-to-day living can be stressful from the start. As infants, these children may be irritable, demanding, and difficult to soothe, which can make parents feel incompetent, confused, and helpless. As the child enters school and begins to face learning failure, the parents may have feelings of guilt, shame, or embarrassment. As they become frustrated, they may blame each other for their child's problems. One parent may accuse the other of being too strict or too lenient in raising their child, putting extra strain on the marital relationship. Siblings and other family members are also affected when a brother or sister has learning disabilities. The siblings may be embarrassed or feel angry or jealous if their parents pay more attention to the sibling with learning disabilities.

For these reasons, in some cases it is necessary to include the entire family in the treatment process, with counseling for the family system as an important part.

Stages of Acceptance

When parents are faced with the quandary of a child with learning disabilities, they are likely to pass through a series of predictable **stages of acceptance** (Kübler-Ross, 1969; Lavoie, 1995). These stages are universal and apply to anyone who experiences a loss. In this case, the parents have lost their hope for a normal child.

The parents go through a mourning process when first told that their child has learning disabilities. The stages in the process are shock, disbelief, denial, anger, bargaining, depression, and acceptance. There is no factor that predicts the order in which the parent experiences these stages, the number of stages that the parent goes through, or the length of time that is spent in each stage. Nor is the process linear; the parent often returns to an earlier stage.

- *Shock* is the numb, distancing feeling that engulfs the parents when the bad news is being delivered.
- *Disbelief* is the stage in which parents do not believe the diagnosis.
- *Denial* is a stage in which parents refuse to even consider that the child has a learning disability, and they may seek an alternative diagnosis. Some examples of statements of denial include "There's nothing wrong," "That's the way I was as a child—not to worry," and "He'll grow out of it."
- *Anger* occurs as the denial breaks down and the child's condition becomes more real and apparent. Angry feelings are exhibited when

parents say things like "Why did this happen to me?" or "It isn't fair," "The teachers don't know anything" or "I hate the neighborhood, this school, and this teacher."

- *Bargaining* is evident when the parent decides that dedication will somehow alleviate their child's condition. For example, they may say, "Maybe the problem will improve if we move."

- *Depression* is evident when the parent makes statements like "What's the use?" "Why even bother?" "Nothing is going to change." or "What will happen to my child?" The parent may despair of ever finding a solution and feel sad and helpless.

- *Acceptance* is the stage at which the parents can look past the disability and accept the child as he or she is. A stage beyond acceptance is to *cherish* the child for those differences and for how that child has made the parents' lives better.

This roller coaster of emotions has a profound impact upon the parent and upon interactions with the child. Because the two parents will probably not go through these stages at the same time, each parent must learn to respect the other's right to travel through the stages at a different rate.

The goal is to reach acceptance so that the parent is able to make placement decisions that are unclouded by undue emotionality. When parents accept their child along with their child's disabilities, they are then able to provide for the child's special needs while continuing to live a normal life and tending to family, home, civic, and social obligations.

Parent Support Groups and Family Counseling

Establishing healthy parental attitudes and ensuring parent–teacher cooperation are, of course, desirable goals. Two procedures—parent support groups and family counseling—can help in meeting these goals.

Parent support groups offer parents a way to meet regularly in small groups to discuss common problems. They can be organized by the school, family service organizations, professional counselors, or parent organizations, such as the Learning Disabilities Association (LDA). The opportunity to meet with other parents whose children are encountering similar problems tends to reduce the parents' sense of isolation. Furthermore, such parent support groups have been useful in alerting the community, school personnel, other professionals, and legislative bodies to the plight of their children. To find local parent groups, see the LDA website at **http://www.ldaamerica.org.**

Family counseling offers parents help in accepting the problem, in developing empathy for the child, and in providing a beneficial home environment. Guidance counselors and social workers often play important roles in providing such help. Often, the first step in parent or family counseling is to help the parents get over their initial feelings. In addition to the feelings already mentioned, the initial period of reaction may include feelings of mourning, misunderstanding, guilt, self-deprecation, or even shame. Parents may respond to these feelings by turning away in confusion, or they may overreact, become aggressive, and try to break down doors to get things done. These aggressive parents are needed in our profession because they keep educators moving. Educators should empathize with parents to help them get through the initial reaction period.

Parent support groups and family counseling offer the following benefits:

- Helps parents to understand and to accept their child's problem
- Reduces anxieties stemming from apprehension about the psychological and educational development of their child; parents can discover that they are not alone; other parents have similar problems and have found solutions
- Helps parents to realize that they are an integral part of their child's learning, development, and behavior; they can learn to perceive their children differently and to deal with their problems more effectively
- Helps parents learn about discipline, communication skills, behavioral management, parent advocacy, special education legislation, social skills development, helping one's child make friends, home management, and college and vocational opportunities

Two useful websites for parents are **www.schwablearning.org** and **www.allkindsofminds.org**.

Parent–Teacher Conferences

Parent–teacher conferences are a bridge between the home and school. Both parents and teachers tend to shy away from these private conferences, parents fearing what they will hear and teachers fearing that parents will react negatively. Yet, these conferences, at which the student's progress and problems are discussed, should be viewed as an opportunity to help the student. Parents and teachers can work together to enhance progress.

In setting up a conference, teachers should reassure parents that they are going to communicate with someone who cares about their child. Teachers must impart a sense of confidence without being arrogant and should convey a sincere interest in the student and respect for the parents. They should discuss problems in a calm manner, avoiding technical jargon. Parents want to understand the nature of their child's problems, and diagnostic data and current teaching approaches should therefore be interpreted and explained. The parents must also be helped to become sensitive to the nature of their children's learning problems and to those tasks that are difficult for them. Parents also want to know what they can do at home.

RITA G.'S CASE CONFERENCE—IEP MEETING

The IEP or case conference team that met to discuss Rita included the school psychologist, the learning disabilities teacher, Mr. Martinez (her third-grade teacher), and Rita's parents, Mr. and Mrs. G.

The case conference team agreed that Rita has a number of strengths. They include facility with oral language; intelligence within the overall normal range, with high abilities in verbal areas; an understanding and supportive family and a playful relationship with her sister; good word-recognition skills in reading; a grasp of phonics skills; and an above-average listening–speaking vocabulary.

Her weaknesses include poor problem-solving skills in mathematics computation and word problems; slow, laborious, and illegible handwriting, related to general visual-motor and spatial problems; and difficulty in reading comprehension. Rita has developed a passive attitude toward learning, and she cannot attend to a task without becoming distracted. She lacks organizational skills and does not use efficient learning strategies. In addition, Rita has inept social skills.

The case conference team concluded that Rita has learning disabilities. She has a severe discrepancy between her intellectual ability and her achievement in academic areas. Her learning problems are not primarily the result of other known disabilities, such as mental retardation or due to economic or cultural disadvantages. Rita has difficulties with visual–motor perception, social interactions, attention, and learning strategies.

The annual goals developed for Rita focused on improving skills for written communication, improving mathematics skills—calculation and word problems, improving reading comprehension, developing cognitive learning strategies, and developing better social skills.

The case conference team recommended that Rita be placed in the general education third-grade class. The general education third-grade teacher and the special education teacher would coordinate their efforts through coteaching and other classroom supports. Rita's father said that he thought this would be a good arrangement because Rita would receive the special teaching she needed and still be part of the third-grade class.

Writing the IEP

The information and decisions were written into Rita's individualized education program (IEP), and the IEP was signed by all of the case conference team members, including Rita's mother and father. The annual goal concerning improvement in the skills of writing for cursive follows. A few selected short-term objectives for this goal are also presented.

Annual goal   Writes legibly, using cursive writing, one paragraph consisting of 10 sentences.

Progress Measures: Cursive Writing

1. Traces two cursive letters using a stencil
2. Copies 10 letters using cursive writing in uppercase and lowercase on a chalkboard
3. Writes all letters legibly using cursive writing in uppercase and lowercase on paper
4. Writes name in cursive writing
5. Writes five short words legibly in cursive writing from a model
6. Writes a sentence legibly from a model
7. Writes a five sentence paragraph legibly
8. Writes a 10 sentence paragraph legibly

Implementing the Teaching Plan

The learning disabilities teacher and Mr. Martinez, Rita's third-grade teacher, developed more specific plans to meet the goals and progress measures identified in the IEP.

Rita would be placed in Mr. Martinez's third-grade classroom. Through a team partnership between the learning disabilities teacher and Mr. Martinez, the two could share the activities for Rita's instruction. Coteaching would allow Rita's learning disabilities teacher and general education teacher to work with her in different kinds of groups. The use of peer tutoring would provide Rita with more individual practice and instruction. In addition, Rita would receive some resource room help if it were needed.

The instruction in mathematics and reading would be linked to the curriculum-based assessment data. Rita's deficits in visual–motor skills were taken into account in planning a skills approach to mathematics. The learning disabilities teacher and Mr. Martinez decided to use concrete materials and manipulatives to establish basic number concepts for addition, subtraction, and multiplication. Opportunity for drill and practice was planned by using a number of different manipulative materials and some computer mathematics drill-and-practice software.

A computer typing software program would also be used to teach Rita keyboarding (or typing) skills. The plan was that after she learned to type, she would be taught word processing and then would move into lessons in written expression. It was felt that it would be worthwhile to try to teach Rita cursive writing because many occasions in daily life require handwriting. However, because her writing problem is so severe, Rita's progress should be monitored very carefully and her plan reevaluated continually.

Another specific plan was to help Rita develop more efficient learning strategies. She would be taught to self-monitor her attention to keep herself on task and self-rehearsal strategies to improve her approach to learning. The plan also included the provision of more opportunities for social interaction in the classroom through assigning Rita to committees and through peer work. (These are only a few of the implementation activities.)

Monitoring Progress and Review

The learning disabilities teacher and Mr. Martinez will review Rita's progress informally on a monthly basis. An annual review is planned for the middle of the following year, when Rita will be in fourth grade. She will be tested in mathematics computation, mathematics reasoning, written expression, and reading comprehension. Also, the information gathered through instruction linked to curriculum-based assessment will serve to monitor progress continuously.

CHAPTER SUMMARY

1. Important concepts for planning the educational settings for students with learning disabilities are (1) the continuum of alternative placements and (2) the least restrictive environment.

2. The term *continuum of alternative placements* refers to the array of educational placements in the schools to meet the varied needs of exceptional students.

3. The Individuals with Disabilities Education Improvement Act of 2004 (IDEA–2004) requires that students be placed in the *least restrictive environment*. This means that, to the greatest extent appropriate,

students with disabilities should be with students who do not have disabilities. Students with disabilities should have access to the general education curriculum.

4. The continuum of alternative placements available to meet the needs of students with learning disabilities includes: (1) the general education classroom, (2) the resource room, (3) the separate class, (4) the separate school, (5) the residential facility, and (6) the home or hospital setting. Each of the placements is successively more restrictive in terms of the student's opportunity to interact with students without disabilities. One-to-one instruction between teacher and student is very effective, but also very costly.

5. Methods for promoting the partnership between general education and special education include: (1) collaboration and (2) coteaching.

6. Collaboration is the coordinated effort of the learning disabilities teacher and the general classroom teacher to provide services for students with learning disabilities in the general education classroom. Collaboration is a growing responsibility for learning disabilities teachers and general education teachers.

7. In coteaching, two instructors, a general education classroom teacher and a special education teacher, teach a diverse group of students in the general education classroom.

8. Families and parents are vital components of the student's education. In the family system, all members of the extended family are interdependent, and each member has interactive effects on all other members of the family system. Parents go through stages of mourning before they reach the acceptance stage. Parent support groups and family counseling are effective in helping parents understand their children and their problems and in finding ways to help their children within the home.

DISCUSSION AND REFLECTION

1. Discuss two key concepts about educational settings that are features of the special education law. Do you think these two features are compatible or in conflict? Explain your position.

2. Discuss some of the recent trends in educational settings for students with learning disabilities. How do you think these trends will affect students with learning disabilities?

3. Inclusion is one of the recommended placement plans for students with learning disabilities. Describe the advantages and shortcomings of the inclusion placement model. What do you think the future holds for inclusion?

4. What are the three most common educational settings for students with learning disabilities? Compare and contrast these settings.

5. Discuss activities for coteaching between the special education teacher and the general education teacher.

6. Discuss the various needs of the general education teacher and the special education teacher.

KEY TERMS

collaboration *(p. 143)*

continuum of alternative placements *(p. 131)*

coteaching *(p. 146)*

educational setting *(p. 135)*

general education classroom *(p. 137)*

one-to-one instruction *(p. 141)*

parent support groups *(p. 154)*

residential facilities *(p. 140)*

resource room *(p. 138)*

separate class *(p. 139)*

separate schools *(p. 140)*

stages of acceptance *(p. 153)*

5

Theories of Learning: Implications for Learning Disabilities

> If you don't know where you're going, any road will take you there. Theories are working concepts to be modified in the light of new knowledge. Those who teach without theories may follow the road that leads nowhere.
>
> —*John Dewey*

P art III examines underlying theories and new directions in the field of learning disabilities. It covers the key psychological theories that underlie the study of learning disabilities, in this chapter. Three special populations of students with learning disabilities are reviewed: (1) children with attention deficit disorders, and other neurodevelopmental disorders, in Chapter 6, Attention Deficit Disorder and Related Neurodevelopmental Conditions; (2) young children with learning disabilities, in Chapter 7, Young Children With Learning Disabilities; and (3) learning disabilities in adolescents and adults, in Chapter 8, Adolescents and Adults With Learning Disabilities. We also look at the significant medical aspects of learning disabilities in Chapter 9, Medical Aspects of Learning Disabilities.

In this chapter, we explore the contributions of theories from three branches of psychology to the field of learning disabilities. Fundamental concepts from developmental psychology, behavioral psychology, and cognitive psychology have advanced our understanding of learning disabilities, with implications for assessment, instruction, and research.

THE ROLE OF THEORY

"If you don't know where you are going, any road will take you there." This advice is as applicable to learning disabilities as it is to other facets of life. **Theories** help us to understand the foundations of learning disabilities. By shedding light on the nature of the learning problems encountered by the student, theories suggest a basis for instructional methods. Those who teach without theories may follow the road that leads nowhere.

The purpose of theory is to bring form, coherence, and meaning to what we observe in the real world. Underlying any assessment or instructional procedure should be a theory of teaching or learning. Theory is helpful in sorting and evaluating the bewildering deluge of new materials, technology, machines, gadgets, methods, and media confronting the educator.

Theories, in this context, are meant to be working statements. Theories are not meant to be ideas "frozen into absolute standards masquerading as eternal truths" or "programs rigidly adhered to" (Dewey, 1946, p. 202, 1998). Theories are meant to serve as guides in systematizing knowledge and as working concepts to be modified in the light of new knowledge. John Dewey considered theory the most practical of all things because it provides a guide for action, clarifies and structures thought, and creates a catalyst for further research.

Theory building is a process. Every discipline is built on the concepts and ideas contributed by earlier theorists. Theories are challenged, modified, and strengthened as researchers and practitioners test the theory's relevance and usefulness. The modified theory in turn leads to changes in assessment and instructional practices. The theories generated in the field of learning disabilities also have significant applications in other areas of special education and in general education.

THEORIES OF LEARNING

We now turn our attention to three major theories in psychology and their implications for learning disabilities: (1) developmental psychology, (2) behavioral psychology, and (3) cognitive psychology. Let's take a look at each theory.

DEVELOPMENTAL PSYCHOLOGY

Developmental psychology offers an important theory for understanding learning disabilities. A key notion in developmental psychology is that the maturation of cognitive skills (or thinking) follows a sequential progression. A child's ability to learn depends on the child's current maturational status. Further, this theory implies that attempts to speed up or bypass the developmental process may actually create problems. Jean Piaget, the celebrated Swiss developmental psychologist, remarked, "Every time I describe a maturational sequence in the United States, an American asks 'How can you speed it up?'" In this section, we discuss: (1) developmental variations, (2) Piaget's maturational stages of development, (3) stages of learning, and (4) the implications of developmental psychology for learning disabilities.

Developmental Variations

The term **developmental variations** refers to a slowness in specific aspects of development. According to this point of view, each individual has a preset rate of growth for various human functions, including cognitive abilities (Levine, 1994). Discrepancies among the various abilities indicate that the abilities are maturing at different rates, with some abilities lagging in their development; Bender (1957) called these "maturational lags." Thus, many children with learning disabilities are not so different from other children; rather, their developmental differences are more a matter of *timing.*

The developmental perspective suggests that society actually creates many learning disabilities. The school curriculum may have set expectations for student performance in terms of age. Learning problems occur when children are pushed into performing academic tasks before they are able to do so. Therefore, the demands of schooling can cause failure by requiring students to perform beyond their readiness, or ability, at a given stage of maturation.

Vygotsky (1978), the Russian developmental psychologist, recognized the important part that social context has in learning. He reasoned that children learn when instruction is directed toward, what Vygotsky called, their *zone of proximal development (ZPD)*. The ZPD is comprised of the tasks that are in the range of difficulty between what a person can do independently and what he or she can do with assistance. Some call this level the "Goldilocks" level because it is neither too easy nor too hard; rather, it is just right. If a child's abilities do not mesh with the instructional level, learning cannot occur.

The following studies demonstrate that many young children manifest variations in development that lead to academic problems as they get older:

■ Koppitz (1973) studied students with learning disabilities over several years, and she concluded that these children were immature and needed more time to learn and to grow up. When given the needed extra time, along with the help necessary to compensate for their slowness in maturation, many did well academically. Koppitz observed that these children may require 1 or 2 more years than other pupils do to complete their schooling.

■ Silver and Hagin (1966, 1990) found evidence of maturational lags in young children, including delays in spatial orientation of symbols, auditory discrimination, and left–right discrimination. When these children were reevaluated as young adults, ages 16 to 24, many no longer had maturational lags. Many of the problems had disappeared.

■ De Hirsch, Jansky, and Langford (1966) conducted an extensive study aimed at finding factors that predicted reading failure in kindergarten children. They found that the tests that were most sensitive to differences in maturation were the ones that best predicted reading and spelling achievement in second grade. They concluded that maturational status is the crucial factor in predicting reading achievement.

■ Levine (2002, 2003) described how neurodevelopmental variations led to academic failure. Levine emphasized the importance of recognizing developmental variations in children and providing instruction to ameliorate these learning differences.

■ The collection of studies from the National Institute of Child Health and Human Development (Lyon, 1996; Lyon, Alexander, & Yaffee, 1997; Lyon, Shaywitz, & Shaywitz, 2003; NICHD, 1999; Torgesen, 1998; Vellutino et al., 2001) showed that children who were likely to have difficulty in learning to read exhibited developmental delays in several areas of maturational development, including phonological awareness. The NICHD studies showed that explicit instruction during the preschool and early primary years helped these children to overcome these developmental delays and to achieve academically. More information about this topic can be found at **http://www.nichd.nih.gov.**

Piaget's Maturational Stages of Development

Jean Piaget, who is recognized as a pioneer in developmental psychology, spent his life studying the intellectual development of children. Piaget's observations of the maturational stages of thinking in children showed that cognitive growth occurs in a series of invariant and interdependent stages. At each stage, the child is capable of learning only certain cognitive tasks. As the child goes through a series of maturational or developmental stages, the child's ability to think and learn changes with age. The quantity, quality, depth, and breadth of learning that occurs depends upon the stage during which the learning takes place (Piaget, 1970). For a more complete representation of Piaget, see Brainerd (2003) or Meece (2002). Additional information about this topic can be found at **http://www.piaget.org.** Piaget provided a schematic description of the typical child's stages of development:

1. *Sensorimotor stage: Birth to age 2.* The first 2 years of life are called the **sensorimotor stage.** During this stage, children learn through their senses and movements and by interacting with the physical environment. By moving, touching, hitting, biting, and so on, as well as by physically manipulating objects, children learn about the properties of space, time, location, permanence, and causality. Some children with learning disabilities need more opportunities for motor exploration. (Motor learning is discussed in Chapter 7, Young Children With Learning Disabilities.)

2. *Preoperational stage: Ages 2–7.* Piaget called the next 5 years of life, ages 2 to 7, the **preoperational stage.** During this stage, children make intuitive judgments about relationships, and they also begin to think with symbols. Language now becomes increasingly important, and children learn to use symbols to represent the concrete world. They begin to learn about the properties and attributes of the world about them. Their thinking is dominated largely by the world of perception. (The subject of perception is one of the concerns of Chapter 7, Young Children With Learning Disabilities.)

One characteristic of the preoperational stage is that young children can attach only one attribute or function to an object. For example, 3-year-old Josephine was confused when her mother was the emergency substitute teacher in her nursery school class. Josephine was visibly baffled and upset as she exploded, "You can't be a teacher; you're a mother!"

3. *Concrete operations stage: Ages 7–11.* The period between ages 7 and 11 is called the **concrete operations stage.** Children are now able to think through relationships, to perceive consequences of acts, and to group

In the preoperational stage (ages 2–7), children make intuitive judgments about relationships, and language becomes increasingly important.
(© Elizabeth Crews)

entities in a logical fashion. They are better able to systematize and organize their thoughts. However, their thoughts are shaped in large measure by previous experiences, and they are linked to the concrete objects that they have manipulated or understood through the senses. For example, at this stage, a child can recognize a set of four objects without physically touching and counting them.

4. *Formal operations stage: Age 11.* The fourth stage, the **formal operations stage,** commences at about age 11 and reflects a major transition in the thinking process. At this stage, instead of observations directing thought, thought now directs observations. Children now have the capacity to work with abstractions, theories, and logical relationships without having to refer to the concrete. The formal operations period provides a generalized orientation toward problem-solving activity.

The transition from one level to the next depends on maturation, and the stages are sequential and hierarchical. An implication for teaching is that students need ample opportunities and experiences to stabilize behavior and thought at each stage of development. Yet, the school curriculum frequently requires students to develop abstract and logical conceptualizations in a given area without providing sufficient opportunity for students to go through the preliminary levels of understanding. Attempts to teach abstract, logical concepts divorced from any real experiential understand-

DEVELOPMENTAL THEORY AND MATURATION

- Illustrations of young children who have surface verbal skills without an in-depth understanding of concepts are frequently amusing. One kindergarten child explained with seemingly verbal proficiency the scientific technicalities of a spaceship being shot into orbit. His apparently precocious explanation ended with "and now for the blastoff . . . 10-3-8-5-6-1!"

- The maturation of the cognitive ability to categorize objects was apparent when each of three children, ages 7, 9, and 11, was asked to pack clothes for a trip in two suitcases. Sue, the 11 year old, was adultlike in her thinking, packing day clothes in one suitcase and night clothes in another. Dean, the 7 year old, had no organizational arrangement and randomly proceeded to stuff one suitcase with as much as it would hold and then to stuff the second with the remainder. Laura, the 9 year old, made an organizational plan that called for clothes above the waist to go in one suitcase and clothes below the waist to go in the second. The top parts of pajamas and a two-piece bathing suit were placed in one suitcase and the bottoms in the other. Each child had categorized in a manner appropriate to the individual's maturational stage.

- Children must understand early learning concepts before moving to more difficult abstract concepts and logical thinking in the primary grades. For example, one-to-one correspondence is an essential concept for learning mathematics—understanding that one object in a set is the same number as one object in a different set. In working with 6-year-old Jennine, the teacher placed five small buttons in a glass, one at a time, and then placed five large buttons in another glass, one at a time. Jennine said the glass with the large buttons contained more buttons. She had not grasped the concept of one-to-one-correspondence.

Piaget used the following experiments to illustrate that children's concepts about *conservation* develop according to their maturational stage of thinking. In one of Piaget's conservation experiments, two balls of clay of equal size were placed on a scale to demonstrate to the child that they were equal. When one ball of clay was then flattened, 8-year-olds were likely to predict that they were still the same weight. Four-year-olds, however, said that the flattened ball weighed more. In another experiment, an equal amount of liquid was poured in each of two identical glasses. When the liquid from one glass was then emptied into a tall, thin container, 5-year-olds were convinced that the tall, thin glass contained more liquid, but 7-year-olds knew there was no difference in volume. From experiments such as these, Piaget concluded that the child's ability to understand the principles of conservation develops naturally through the maturational process.

ing on the part of the students may lead to inadequate and insecure learning. The teacher may think students are learning the concepts, but they may be giving only surface verbal responses. Some examples of surface learning without understanding are given in "LD Stories: Developmental Theory and Maturation."

Stages of Learning

Students need a period of time to *know* a concept that is being taught. All learners, including those with learning disabilities, do not fully comprehend, or know, a concept the first time that they are exposed to the concept. Rather, they go through the developmental stages of learning before they grasp the concept completely. As indicated in Figure 5.1, the developmental **stages of learning** include: (1) exposure, (2) grasping the knowledge, (3) independence, and (4) application. Teachers need to provide appropriate instruction to help students with learning disabilities move from one learning stage to the next. These students need abundant support at each stage, and they may move from one stage to the next at a slower rate than other students. The types of practice that are most effective also vary with the stage of learning. In the early stages of acquisition, students need frequent feedback that elaborates and explains the intricacies of the new skill or information. In the later stages of learning, where students are building facility with the new skill or consolidating the new knowledge, massed practice is the most effective. Students with learning problems often need support in the generalization or application of new skills as well. Simple acquisition does not insure that a person can use the skills flexibly in a variety of contexts. The *strategies intervention model* (SIM), which is an instructional method for teaching learning strategies to adolescents with learning disabilities, includes specific instructional techniques to assist the

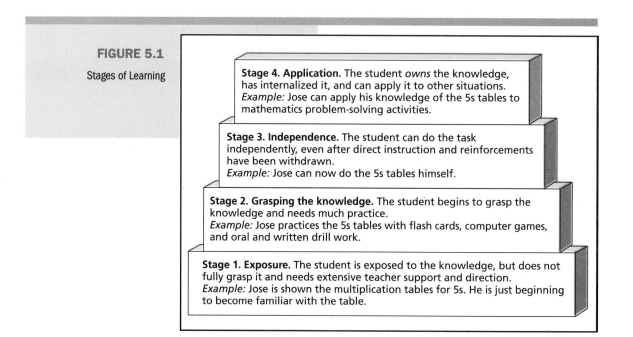

FIGURE 5.1

Stages of Learning

Stage 4. Application. The student *owns* the knowledge, has internalized it, and can apply it to other situations. *Example:* Jose can apply his knowledge of the 5s tables to mathematics problem-solving activities.

Stage 3. Independence. The student can do the task independently, even after direct instruction and reinforcements have been withdrawn. *Example:* Jose can now do the 5s tables himself.

Stage 2. Grasping the knowledge. The student begins to grasp the knowledge and needs much practice. *Example:* Jose practices the 5s tables with flash cards, computer games, and oral and written drill work.

Stage 1. Exposure. The student is exposed to the knowledge, but does not fully grasp it and needs extensive teacher support and direction. *Example:* Jose is shown the multiplication tables for 5s. He is just beginning to become familiar with the table.

student in generalizing his or her new skills (Deshler et al., 1996; see Chapter 8, Adolescents and Adults With Learning Disabilities, for a more complete discussion of the strategies intervention model).

Implications of Developmental Psychology for Learning Disabilities

Some implications of developmental psychology for students with learning disabilities follow. A major cause of these students' school difficulties is immaturity. All individuals have a natural development time for the maturation of various skills. What is sometimes thought to be a learning problem may be merely a lag in a student's maturation of a certain process.

1. Research shows that younger children in the early grades tend to have more learning problems than older children placed in those grades, which is a phenomenon called the *birth-date effect*. When each student's month of birth was compared with the percentage of children referred for learning disabilities services, the younger children (those born near the cutoff date for school entrance) were much more likely to be referred for learning disabilities services (Diamond, 1983; DiPasquale, Moule, & Flewelling, 1980).

2. The educational environment may actually hinder rather than assist the child's learning by making intellectual demands that require cognitive abilities that the child may not have yet developed. Cognitive abilities are qualitatively different in children from those of adults. Cognitive abilities develop sequentially; as children mature, their ways of thinking continually change. Schools must design learning experiences to enhance children's natural developmental growth.

3. The concept of *readiness* refers to the state of maturational development and prior experiences that are needed before a target skill can be learned. For example, readiness for walking requires a certain level of development of the neurological system, adequate muscle strength, and the development of certain prerequisite motor functions. Until a toddler has these abilities, attempts to teach the skill of walking are futile. To illustrate readiness in a very different area of learning, a student must have acquired certain mathematics skills and knowledge to profit from a course in calculus.

Readiness skills are picked up in an incidental fashion by some learners. For young students with learning disabilities, special instruction is needed to help them strengthen the precursor or readiness abilities they need for their next step of learning. Sensitive teachers can help students acquire these abilities by being aware of the young students' stage of maturation and of any developmental delays that they have.

Ironically, with all our attempts to be *scientific* about decisions made in education, one of the most important decisions—when to teach a child to read—is based on *astrology*. The star under which the child is born, the birth date, is the key determining factor of this crucial decision because it determines when the child enters school and begins formal school learning.

We now turn to another major theory in psychology, behavioral psychology, and its implication for learning disabilities.

BEHAVIORAL PSYCHOLOGY

Behavioral psychology helps us to understand how behavior is learned, and this branch of psychology significantly influences the way we teach. For over 50 years, since the seminal work of B. F. Skinner, who is considered to be the father of behavioral psychology, the concepts of behavioral psychology have flourished, creating major and productive applications for promoting learning. In special education, the individual education program (IEP) is an application of the behavioral approach. The IEP requires the use of observable and measurable behavior. In the IEP, the student's current levels of performance are measured and documented, goals and objectives are determined, and plans for measuring the achievement of these goals and objectives are formulated. Behavioral theories thus provide a systematic foundation for research, assessment, and instruction (Bauer, Keefe, & Shea, 2001; Scotti & Meyer, 1999).

In this section, we discuss: (1) the behavioral unit, (2) functional behavioral assessment and positive behavioral support, (3) explicit teaching and direct instruction, (4) behavioral analysis, and (5) implications of behavioral psychology for learning disabilities.

The Behavioral Unit

Behavioral psychology is based on the **behavioral unit,** which has three key events called A, B, and C. The ABC model is illustrated in Figure 5.2. A is the **antecedent event** (or stimulus), B is the **target behavior** (or response), and C is the **consequent event** (or reinforcement).

To illustrate the relationship among the three behavioral events, the teacher's goal, in this example, is to have Bonnie lengthen the time she engages in silent reading. The *antecedent event* (or stimulus) is the teacher's action, which is assigning a silent reading period. The *target behavior* (or response) occurs when Bonnie reads for 2 min. The *consequent event* (or

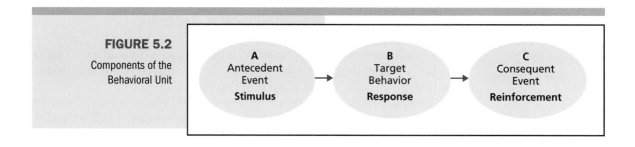

FIGURE 5.2

Components of the Behavioral Unit

| A Antecedent Event **Stimulus** | B Target Behavior **Response** | C Consequent Event **Reinforcement** |

reinforcement) occurs when the teacher reinforces Bonnie's reading behavior by praising her or giving her a reward.

There are critics of reinforcement theory. In his popular book, *Punished by Rewards: The Trouble With Gold Stars, Incentive Plans, A's, Praise, and Other Bribes,* Alfie Kohn (1995) derides rewards as bribes that do not lead to long-term changes in behavior.

Functional Behavioral Assessment and Positive Behavioral Support

A feature of the Individuals With Disabilities Education Improvement Act of 2004 (IDEA–2004) is the requirement that the individualized education program (IEP) for a student with a disability who also has problem behaviors must include a functional behavioral assessment and positive behavioral supports. *Functional behavioral assessment* is the evaluation of the child's behavior, and *positive behavioral support* is the intervention to change the behavior. Because students with learning disabilities sometimes display behavior problems in the school setting, this ruling may apply to some students with learning disabilities (Lewis & Sugai, 1999; Polloway, Patton, & Serna, 2001; U.S. Department of Education, 2000a; Yell, Rozalski, & Drasgrow, 2001).

Functional Behavioral Assessment   When a student displays a challenging behavior, it is serving a purpose or function for the student. In the three events of the behavioral unit (refer to Figure 5.2), this is the antecedent event that triggers the student's observable behavior. Through the functional behavioral assessment, the child's antecedent behavior is described and analyzed to discover what needs this challenging behavior is fulfilling for the student. For example, Joshua makes jokes and loud noises whenever he is asked to read aloud. His functional behavioral assessment reveals that Joshua acts this way to avoid reading aloud because his poor reading ability embarrasses him.

Positive Behavioral Support   Once the teacher understands the reason for the student's antecedent behavior, the teacher looks for a substitute activity for reading aloud—a positive behavioral support. For example, the teacher could privately inform Joshua ahead of time about the passage that he will be asked to read, and then have him practice reading the passage with a peer. A functional behavioral support would prepare Joshua for being called upon to read aloud. This support would eliminate the need for Joshua's interruptive behavior.

Explicit Teaching and Direct Instruction

Instructional practices stemming from behavioral theory are called *explicit teaching* or *direct instruction*. Both terms refer to a similar approach to teaching, with a focus on the tasks to be learned.

Explicit teaching means that teachers are clear about the specific skills to be taught, and they explicitly teach each step or skill rather than leave it up to the student to make inferences from the student's own experiences in order to learn (Gersten, 1998). Table 3.1 in the chapter on clinical teaching illustrates the principles of explicit instruction.

Direct instruction is similar to explicit teaching. It is also based on a behavioral orientation, focusing on the academic skills that the student needs to learn and structuring the environment to ensure that the student learns these skills (Algozzine, 1991). According to Rosenshine (1986) and Rosenshine and Stevens (1986), direct instruction:

- Teaches academic skills directly
- Is teacher directed and controlled
- Uses carefully sequenced and structured materials
- Provides students mastery of basic skills
- Sets goals that are clear to students
- Allocates sufficient time for instruction
- Uses continuous monitoring of student performance
- Provides immediate feedback to students
- Teaches a skill until mastery of that skill is achieved

Behavioral Analysis

Behavioral analysis is another application of behavioral psychology to teaching. It requires that teachers analyze a specific task that students are to learn to determine the skills needed to accomplish that task. These subskills are then placed in an ordered and logical sequence. Teaching involves helping the students accomplish the specific task by learning each skill they have not yet mastered. Students are taught each of the subskills that they do not know. By learning all of the subskills, the students accomplish the desired complex behavior. For more information, visit the website at **http://www.state.ky.us/agencies/behave/homepage.html.**

The steps involved in teaching a child to swim illustrate the behavioral analysis approach. First, analyze the steps involved in swimming (e.g., floating, treading water, holding one's breath under water, and kicking). Next, teach the child each skill in its sequence, help the child combine the skills, and finally, observe the child swimming across the pool. Although this example does not demonstrate an academic task, the same behavioral procedures would apply to teaching reading, mathematics, or writing.

The following steps are involved in behavioral analysis:

1. State the objective to be achieved or the task to be learned in terms of student performance
2. Analyze the subskills needed to perform that task

3. List the subskills to be learned in their sequential order

4. Determine which of these subskills the student does not know

5. Teach one subskill at a time; when one subskill has been learned, teach the next subskill

6. Evaluate the effectiveness of the instruction in terms of whether the student has achieved the objective or learned the task

Implications of Behavioral Psychology for Learning Disabilities

Behavioral theories have important implications for teaching a student with learning disabilities:

1. *Explicit teaching and direct instruction are effective.* It is important for the student with learning disabilities to receive direct instruction in academic tasks. Teachers should understand how to analyze the components of a curriculum and how to structure sequential behaviors.

2. *Explicit teaching and direct instruction can be combined with many other approaches to teaching.* When the teacher is sensitive to a student's unique style of learning and particular learning difficulties, direct instruction can be even more effective. For the student who lacks phonological awareness, for example, the sensitive teacher can anticipate difficulties in learning phonics during a direct instruction lesson. To learn the skill, this student will need more time, practice, review, and alternative presentations of the concepts. The sensitive clinical teacher will use knowledge of the curriculum and of the individual student in planning instruction.

3. *Functional behavioral assessment and positive behavioral support can help a student with behavioral problems.* These methods provide a valuable means to understand undesirable behavior and a way to meet a student's needs.

For a summary of strategies based on behavioral psychology for the general education classroom, see "LD in Practice: Strategies Based on Behavioral Psychology for the General Education Classroom."

Let's now turn to a third major theory of psychology, cognitive psychology, and its implications for learning disabilities.

COGNITIVE PSYCHOLOGY

Cognitive psychology focuses on the human processes of learning, thinking, and knowing. **Cognitive abilities** are clusters of mental skills that are essential to human functions. They enable one to know, be aware, think, conceptualize, use abstractions, reason, criticize, and be creative. Theories about the nature of cognitive and mental processes lead to a better understanding of how human beings learn and how the cognitive

LD IN PRACTICE

STRATEGIES BASED ON BEHAVIORAL PSYCHOLOGY FOR THE GENERAL EDUCATION CLASSROOM

Set goals and objectives

- Structure learning tasks as clear academic goals
- Use task analysis to break goals into manageable steps

Provide rapidly paced lessons and carefully sequenced materials

- Sequence and structure materials and lessons to help students master one step at a time
- Use a fast pace so that learning becomes automatic through overlearning

Offer a detailed explanation and many examples

- Make sure the student understands the task
- Provide detailed and redundant instructions and explanations
- Use many examples
- Ask many questions

Provide many opportunities to practice the new skill

- Offer many practice activities
- Help students develop automaticity so that they can do the activity with ease

Give students feedback and correction

- Help students learn new material through teacher feedback
- Give immediate, academically focused feedback and correction

Monitor student progress

- Actively monitor student progress to check on learning
- Make adjustments in teaching as necessary

characteristics of learning disabilities affect learning. Cognitive theory also suggests a guide for teaching students with learning disabilities.

Concepts in cognitive psychology have been broadly elaborated over the years, and changes in the field of learning disabilities reflect these elaborations. A progression of ideas from cognitive psychology has influenced the field of learning disabilities: (1) the term *disorders of psychological process-*

ing refers to the idea that launched the field of learning disabilities and continues to be an influential concept; (2) the *information-processing model* is a model of learning that emphasizes the flow of information within a person's mind and memory systems; and (3) *cognitive learning theories* emphasize activity in learning and thinking as well as acquisition of a contemporary view of how people learn, think, and acquire knowledge.

Disorders in Psychological Processing

As noted earlier, a critical element of the federal definition of learning disabilities in the Individuals With Disabilities Education Improvement Act of 2004 (IDEA–2004) is that students with learning disabilities have disorders in one or more of the *basic psychological processes* that are needed for school learning. Psychological processes refer to underlying abilities in such areas as visual, auditory, and tactile–kinesthetic perception; motor competence; linguistic abilities; or memory functions. Disorders in psychological processes are intrinsic limitations that interfere with a student's learning.

The recognition that disorders in psychological processing are related to a student's difficulty in learning provided the foundation for the field of learning disabilities. For educators, psychologists, and other professionals, the notion of **psychological processing disorders** offered a refreshing and hopeful new way to view students who were failing to learn, as well as a new way to teach these students. For parents, it offered an encouraging and logical means for understanding a child's difficulty in learning, without blaming the child for not trying, the teachers for not teaching, or themselves for poor parenting (Smith, 2001; Vail, 1992; Vaughn et al., 2000). In most states, the criteria for identifying students with learning disabilities include psychological processing disorders (Mercer et al., 1996).

Teachers may be able to ascertain a student's psychological processing abilities and disabilities through observations, samples of their work, or tests. Knowledge about the student's processing strengths and weaknesses may help the teacher plan appropriate instruction for that student. For example, a student with difficulty in auditory processing might have trouble with instructional approaches that are primarily auditory, such as phonics. A student with difficulty in visual processing might experience obstacles in learning by methods that are primarily visual.

An example of a school curriculum that makes good use of information about the student's psychological processing difficulties is the Lab School of Washington, DC, which is a school for students with learning disabilities (Smith, 2005). Sally Smith, the founder and director of the Lab School, recognized that many of the children attending the school displayed much difficulty with auditory and linguistic learning, yet they excelled in the visual arts. Therefore, she used the arts and experiential, hands-on learning to teach these students. Instead of learning through typically structured, text-based lessons in social studies and history, these children are taught through academic clubs for Grades 1 through 6. These clubs include the Cave Club, the God's Club, the Knights and Ladies Club, the Renaissance Club, the Museum Club, and the Industrialists Club. The children participate in a single club for an entire year during one half of the school day. The clubs teach content, vocabulary, history, and geography through the visual arts. For example, in the Renaissance Club, the children build scaffolding and actually paint a replica of the ceiling of the Sistine Chapel.

The Information-Processing Model of Learning

The **information-processing model** of learning traces the flow of information during the learning process, from the initial reception of information, through a processing function, and then to an action. There are *inputs,* such as auditory stimuli; *processing functions,* which are cognitive processes such as associations, thinking, memory, and decision making; and *outputs,* which are actions and behaviors. Thus, like a computer, the human brain takes in the information (input), stores and locates the information (memory systems), organizes the information and facilitates operations and decisions (central processing system—executive functions), and generates responses to the information (output; Mayer, 1996).

Figure 5.3 is a pictorial diagram of the information-processing system. The model pulls together many of the concepts contributing to cognitive theory and provides a useful way to conceptualize the processes and characteristics of learning. The information-processing model depicts the components of input, output, memory, and an executive control function (Greeno, Collins, & Resnick, 1996; Lyon & Krasnegor, 1996; Swanson, 1996). To illustrate this flow of information, a student is shown a word (input stimulus). The student searches his or her memory to recognize the word and to determine its sound and its meaning (processing and executive function) and, finally, the student says the word (output performance). If the memory of the word has decayed or is lost, the student will be unable to recognize or say the word.

Central to the information-processing model is the **multistore memory system.** The multistore memory system conceptualizes a flow of information among three types of memory: (1) sensory register, (2) short-term memory (or working memory), and (3) long-term memory (Atkinson & Shiffrin, 1968; Broadbent, 1958). For more information about information processing, visit **http://chiron.valdosta.edu/whuitt/col/cogsys/infoproc.html.** The three memory types are shown in Figure 5.3 within the dotted frame. The components and the flows of information of the information-processing model of learning are discussed next.

Sensory Register Information is first received through the senses—vision, hearing, touch, smell, taste, and so on. Stimuli can be from internal sources or from external sources. Most of the stimuli that bombard one's input re-

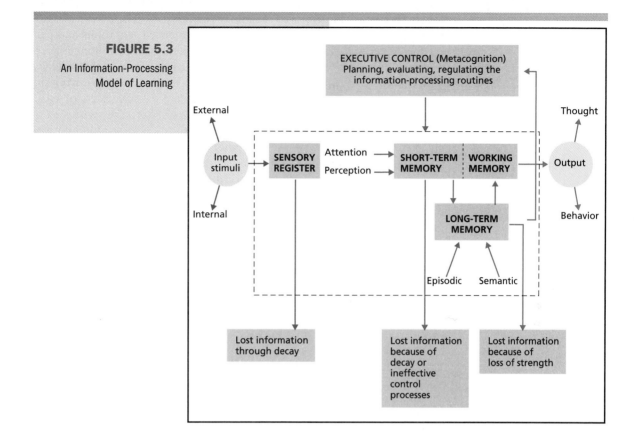

FIGURE 5.3

An Information-Processing Model of Learning

EXECUTIVE CONTROL (Metacognition)
Planning, evaluating, regulating the information-processing routines

External

Internal

Input stimuli

SENSORY REGISTER

Attention

Perception

SHORT-TERM MEMORY

WORKING MEMORY

LONG-TERM MEMORY

Episodic   Semantic

Output

Thought

Behavior

Lost information through decay

Lost information because of decay or ineffective control processes

Lost information because of loss of strength

ceptors are unimportant, are not attended to, and do not reach the sensory register. However, once the mind attends to selected input stimuli, that information flows into the first memory system, the **sensory register.** The sensory register system serves as an input buffer, which helps to interpret and maintain the information from the input receptor long enough for it to be perceived and analyzed. **Perception** is important at this stage because it gives meaning to the stimuli. Perception depends upon the individual's past experiences and ability to organize and attach meaning to the stimulus event. To illustrate how past experiences shape perception, a 3-year-old child was asked to identify a square shape printed on a page. His personal and unique perception of the shape was clear when he responded, "That's a TV."

Along with perception, attention is critical at this stage. Subconscious decisions about what stimuli should receive attention are constantly being made. Attention and associated disorders are covered in more depth in the chapter on attention deficit disorders and related neurodevelopmental conditions.

Sensation, attention, and perception take place when the stimulus is present; they are ongoing activities. Memory pertains to sensations and data *already* received and perceived. Memory (imagery or "the mind's eye") is our ability to store and retrieve previously experienced sensations and perceptions when the stimulus that originally evoked them is no longer present. Examples of sensations and perceptions that occur only in the mind are a musician *listening* to music played at an earlier time, a cook *tasting* the sourness of a lemon to be used, a carpenter *feeling* the roughness of sandpaper used yesterday in a job, and a gardener *smelling* the sweetness of lilacs while looking only at the buds on the tree. A 3-year-old child was helped to understand the nature of memory. Her mother asked the child to close her eyes and think about a peanut butter and jelly sandwich. Yes, the child said she could "see" the jelly dripping down the sides of the bread, she could "smell" the peanut butter, and she could even "taste" the first bite. The sandwich that had become so vivid existed in her memory.

Significance for Teaching   Information-processing theory suggests that a copy of an experience is stored very briefly, perhaps for a few seconds, in the sensory register. Unless there is an effort to pay attention to it, the information is immediately lost from the sensory register. The significance for teaching is that the student must be attending; the lesson must be planned to initially spark the attention of the student. Teachers use a number of verbal and nonverbal cues to get students' attention. These include flicking the lights, ringing a bell, or saying "This information is important" or even "This will be on the test." Other more subtle cues, such as pointing, placing the index finger to the lips, or even where the teacher stands can also be used to direct or redirect students' attention. Children are always attending to something. The teacher's challenge is to focus the attention on the material being taught.

Short-Term or Working Memory   Short-term memory is also a temporary storage facility. With the first system, the sensory register, the individual is not consciously aware of information. In short-term memory, however, the individual becomes very consciously aware of information. **Short-term memory** is considered **working memory.** The pertinent information or current problem is receiving the person's conscious attention, and the individual can act on it. When a person thinks of a new problem, the new information replaces the old information in working, or short-term, memory. The old information either decays and is lost or is placed into long-term storage (Swanson, 1996). Short-term memory is similar to the material you work with on the computer screen. To return to the computer analogy, the information is temporary, and it will be lost when the power is turned off unless the information has been saved.

Significance for Teaching   In terms of teaching, we should recognize that information remains in short-term memory for a short period of time. Unless it is acted on in some way, information in short-term memory will be lost. A common characteristic of students with learning disabilities is their problems remembering verbal information (Mastropieri & Scruggs, 1998).

Some of the strategies or actions that can extend the time that information stays in short-term memory, as well as help to move it to long-term memory include:

1. *Rehearsal, or repeating the information.* Rehearsal slows the forgetting process and helps in transferring the information to long-term memory. For example, when you look up a telephone number, repeating the number may help you to remember it long enough to dial it.

2. *Chunking, or grouping the information.* It is easier to remember grouped information than isolated bits of information. For example, a social security number can be chunked into three groups: a chunk of three numbers, a chunk of two numbers, and a group of four numbers, as in 123-44-1830.

3. *Organizing the information.* The organization of information makes the information less complicated and relates the parts to one another. For example, food can be organized in four basic food groups—dairy, grains, fruits and vegetables, and meats.

4. *Key words.* This is a mnemonic technique in which a word is linked to another word that is familiar (Mastropieri & Scruggs, 1998). The linkage is that part of the word (e.g., the initial sound or rhyming element) that is similar to the key word. The key-word method is useful when pairs of items, such as foreign language words, technical words, or names, have to be learned. For example, when you are introduced to someone, you will more easily recall the person's name if you link the name with a characteristic, such as "tall Tony" or "blue-eyed Bonnie."

Long-Term Memory and Retrieval **Long-term memory** is the permanent memory storage. To learn and retain information for long periods of time, information must be transferred from short-term memory to long-term memory. It is thought that information placed into long-term memory remains there permanently. It is evident from neurological research and clinical experiences that memories remain in long-term storage for a very long time (Semb & Ellis, 1994). The problem people face in long-term memory is not storage, but **retrieval;** that is, how to recall (or remember) information stored in long-term memory. As was shown in Figure 5.3, information from short-term memory is lost unless it is saved in long-term memory. Before one can think about a problem, the stored information must be retrieved from long-term memory and placed into short-term or working memory (or consciousness). Using the computer as an analogy, when one wishes to work on a saved file, the file from long-term storage must be loaded into the desktop (short-term or working memory).

There are two types of long-term memory: *episodic* and *semantic.* Episodic memories are images—visual and other sensory images of events in one's life. The episodic memory of one's first carnival, for example, might be triggered by the sound of a merry-go-round. Semantic memories consist of the storage of general knowledge, language, concepts, and generalizations. The retrieval of odd bits of long-term memory is sometimes triggered by strange events. One such event occurred at a recent national education conference when a participant noted a vaguely familiar woman in the lobby. After observing her for several minutes, he walked up to her and blurted out "Hilltop 5-4260." Indeed, that had been her telephone number some 25 years earlier. Although the conference participant recalled the telephone number, he could not remember her name.

Significance for Teaching   The way information is stored in long-term memory helps with the process of retrieval. Through instruction in learning strategies, teachers can help students with the retrieval process (Scruggs & Mastropieri, 1998; the chapter on adolescents and adults with learning disabilities discusses learning strategies, and the chapter on reading discusses some of the strategies used in reading to improve semantic memory). The following strategies help with the storage and retrieval of information in long-term memory:

1. *Organizing schemes.*   Many of the recommended study techniques are methods of organizing information to make it easier to recall from long-term memory. For example, in studying a country in social studies, use a word web to link key information about the country, such as the weather, crops, rivers, and so on.

2. *Using prior knowledge.*   New information that is linked to something the student already knows is much easier to retrieve. To know something is not only to have received information, but also to have interpreted the information and related it to other knowledge. Teachers must recognize that learning depends on what the student already knows, and that the student must build links between old and new knowledge. For example, Abe already knows quite a lot about dinosaurs. A new type of dinosaur has just been discovered, so Abe links this new dinosaur information with the old information that he already knows.

3. *Making the information meaningful.*   Students can strengthen their long-term memory if they make the information meaningful by linking it to something they already know. Learning depends on what one already knows or on prior knowledge. Teachers can help students by providing background knowledge and linkages to what is already in the long-term memory. For example, Betty has come across the concept of the electoral college in the news. That term becomes more meaningful when she links it with information she already knows about elections. Betty has developed a spreadsheet of electoral college votes for each state and the total number of electoral votes for each presidential candidate. She can illustrate this spreadsheet with a bar graph chart.

Executive Control   **Executive control** is the component of the information-processing model that refers to the ability to control and direct one's own learning, thinking, and mental activity. The term *metacognition* is often used in conjunction with executive control. (Metacognition is discussed in more detail later in this chapter, in the section on learning strategies.) Executive control: (1) directs the flow of thinking, (2) manages the cognitive processes during learning, and (3) keeps track of what information is being processed. It involves the planning, evaluating, and regulating of the information-processing routines. It determines which mental activities occur and which processing components receive system attention resources, or one's concentration. One's motivation and goals are important factors in directing the priorities and the problems that will receive attention (Lyon & Krasnegor, 1996; Swanson, 1996).

The executive function is similar to the operating system of a computer. The operating system intervenes and controls the allocation and interface between the program and the resources of the system. It keeps track of what each program is doing and when the program needs to use some system resources, such as a disk drive or print instructions.

Executive decisions require *metacognitive* skills, which are skills that involve *thinking about thinking*. Metacognitive functions require that students: (1) have knowledge of strategies to control their learning and (2) are able to select the appropriate method for the problem at hand.

Significance for Teaching   It is not enough to memorize information; students must also have the metacognitive skills to decide to use the information. Research with students with learning disabilities shows that these students must learn to activate and select the strategies to use the information they have (Deshler et al., 1996; Lenz, Ellis, & Scanlon, 1996). Learning strategies instruction for metacognitive skills are discussed later in Chapter 8, Adolescents and Adults With Learning Disabilities.

Cognitive Learning Theories

Contemporary theories of cognitive learning extend and elaborate the earlier psychological processing concepts of learning. To succeed in the general education classroom, students with learning disabilities must learn the complex concepts and fundamental problem-solving skills of the content areas in the general education curriculum. Students confront a number of challenges in the content areas, such as organizing information on their own, having limited background knowledge for many academic activities, and needing sufficient feedback and practice to retain abstract information (Gersten, 1998; Greeno et al., 1996; Vaughn et al., 2000).

A number of instructional strategies stem from cognitive theories of learning, which help students with learning disabilities grasp the concepts and subject matter of the general education curriculum. Some of these effective and validated instructional approaches were discussed in the chapter on clinical teaching, such as scaffolded instruction, learning strategies instruction, and peer tutoring. In this section, we will discuss several additional effective cognitive learning strategies, such as: (1) apprentice-ships, (2) graphic organizers, (3) concept maps, and (4) mind mapping.

Apprenticeships   Apprenticeships refer to the kind of teaching that occurs in a setting in which a knowledgeable adult and a learner work jointly on a real-life problem. Learning in such a setting is geared to solving a genuine problem rather than just reading about the problem. Apprenticeships are motivating for learners, and apprentices increase generalization because student apprentices learn through experience how the knowledge they have acquired applies to the real world (Gersten, 1998).

Graphic Organizers   **Graphic organizers** are visual representations of con-cepts, knowledge, or information that incorporate both text and pictures. They make it easier for a person to understand the information by allowing the mind to see complex relationships. Research shows that graphic orga-nizers have proven to be very useful for students with learning disabilities (Fisher et al., 1995; Sabbatino, 2004). Graphic organizers commonly used include:

- Venn diagrams
- Hierarchical (top-down) organizers
- Word webs
- Concept maps
- Mind mapping

In the following section, we discuss concept maps and mind mapping, which also are effective cognitive learning strategies.

Concept Map   With a concept map, a student or a teacher can cluster ideas and words that go together. The activity serves to activate the student's con-struction of a concept. Figure 5.4 shows a concept map that a 13-year-old student created on the topic of team sports to prepare for a writing project.

Mind Mapping   **Mind mapping** is a technique that employs a pictorial method to transfer ideas from a student or from a group of students onto a large piece of paper, a transparency, or a large class chart. Ideas are pro-duced randomly, and certain words or ideas will trigger other ideas, which will lead to other suggestions or pictures. It is much easier to mind map than to create an outline because the ideas do not have to be organized or sequenced. Figure 5.5 shows a mind map that a group of students con-structed on the topic of homework.

Metacognition

Metacognition refers to the awareness of one's systematic thinking about learning. It is the ability to facilitate learning by taking control and direct-ing one's own thinking processes. People exhibit metacognitive awareness

FIGURE 5.4

Graphic Organizer: Concept
Map on Team Sports

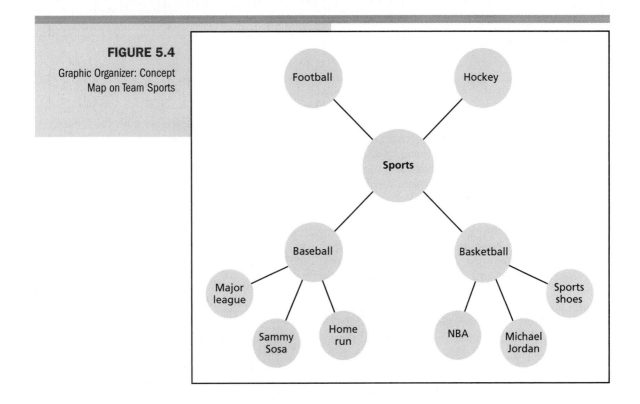

FIGURE 5.5

Mind Mapping
on Homework

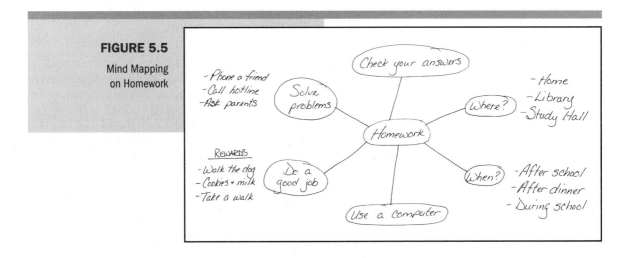

METACOGNITIVE SHOPPING BEHAVIOR

A common example of metacognitive behavior that is familiar to most people is the activity of planning for grocery shopping. Most people must engage in this activity, and they have developed plans that work for them. The following grocery-shopping plans are metacognitive behaviors that are based on prior knowledge and experience. They include ways to enhance memory (e.g., through writing, visualization, or review) and to organize and prepare for future activities (e.g., making meals, eating, and entertaining). When groups of people were asked how they plan for their grocery shopping, their answers differed widely, revealing a correspondingly wide range of metacognitive styles. Some of their answers follow.

■ I keep a pad of paper in a convenient spot; as I discover needs during the week, I jot them down on the notepad. I take this list with me to the store, and it becomes my guide for shopping.

■ I think about what I need, and I write a list just before going shopping. I take this list with me and then check each item on the list as I take it off the grocery shelf.

■ I open my kitchen cabinets just before going shopping, and the visualization of missing items gives me enough information to complete my grocery shopping.

■ I walk up and down the aisles, and items that I need just pop up.

■ I buy only items that are on sale, and I stock up on these items.

■ I carefully plan my shopping to use the coupons I have acquired.

■ I go to the store and just buy food that looks as though it would be good to eat. When I get home, I usually find that I forgot to buy the necessary items, so I have to go back to the store again. I guess I do not plan well for shopping.

■ To avoid impulsive buying, I always eat something before I go shopping.

■ I plan on how much money I will spend, use a calculator, and stop when that amount is reached.

when they do something to help themselves learn and remember, such as compiling shopping lists to remember what to buy, outlining difficult technical chapters to help themselves understand and recall the material, or rehearsing and repeating what they have just learned to help stabilize and strengthen their learning. These behaviors indicate an awareness of one's own limitations and the ability to plan for one's own learning and problem solving (Swanson, 1996). "LD Stories: Metacognitive Shopping Behavior" offers other examples of metacognition.

Efficient learners use metacognitive strategies, but students with learning disabilities tend to lack the skills to direct their own learning. However, once they learn the metacognitive strategies that efficient learners use, students with learning disabilities can apply them in many situations. The metacognitive strategies needed for school learning include: (1) classification, (2) checking, (3) evaluation, and (4) prediction (Gersten, 1998; Kluwe, 1987).

Classification Classification is a technique for determining the type, status, or mode of a learning activity. Individuals ask themselves "What am I doing here?" or "Is this activity important to me?" For example, Jose, while comparing words in Spanish with words in English, says to himself, "Knowing this will help me learn English."

Checking Checking involves taking steps during the process of problem solving to determine one's progress, success, and results. For example, a person may say, "I remember most of the lesson," "My planning is pretty detailed and careful," "I still have a long way to go before I get there," or "There is something I do not understand here."

Evaluation Evaluation goes beyond checking and provides information about quality. For example, an individual may think, "My plan is not good enough to rule out any risks" or "I have done a good job."

Prediction Prediction provides information about the possible alternative options for problem solving and possible outcomes. The person may think, "If I decide to work on this problem, the technical details will be hard to accomplish. I will have to get someone to help me with them" or "I should be able to finish the paper in 4 days."

Implications of Cognitive Psychology for Learning Disabilities

Cognitive psychology analyzes how people learn and, therefore, it offers strategies for teaching students with learning difficulties. Teaching strategies based on cognitive psychology can help students learn to attend, to remember, to understand, to think, and to enjoy learning. "LD in Practice: Strategies Based on Cognitive Psychology for the General Education Classroom" presents ways that the general education teacher can apply cognitive strategies.

LEARNING STRATEGIES INSTRUCTION In this section, we discuss some instructional applications of cognitive theories. We review: (1) learning strategies, (2) cognitive styles of learning, (3) the social interactions of learning, (4) interactive dialogues, and (5) implications of learning strategies instruction for learning disabilities.

Learning Strategies

The **learning strategies approach** to instruction is a series of methods that focuses on *how* students learn rather than on *what* they learn. Efficient

LD IN PRACTICE
STRATEGIES BASED ON COGNITIVE PSYCHOLOGY FOR THE GENERAL EDUCATION CLASSROOM

Link new information to prior knowledge

- Learning is a cumulative process that depends on prior knowledge and past experiences. New knowledge is built upon what is already known. The more one knows about a subject, the more one can acquire through a learning experience.
- Start with what the student already knows and help them build and link new information. For example, a child who knows that $2 + 2 = 4$ can learn the new number fact $2 + 3$ more easily if it is linked to the existing knowledge of $2 + 2$.

Begin instruction at the appropriate level

- Find the right difficulty level at which to aim the lesson.
- Vygotsky's zone of proximal development (ZPD) points out that there are several levels of learning. At the lower end, students can learn independently. At the upper end, the level is beyond the students' capabilities and students will not be able to grasp the skill and transfer the skill to themselves. The midpoint is the ZPD, which is where instruction should take place. This level is not too hard nor too easy, and students can successfully learn under adult guidance.

Provide a guiding social environment

- The social and reciprocal relationship between the teacher and the student is a critical element in learning. The teacher serves as a coach, providing the support necessary for the student to learn and grow.
- This support is called *scaffolded instruction* because it offers support until the student can do the task independently.

Develop automaticity in certain skills

- Students need much practice and repetition for developing certain automatic responses. Some kinds of knowledge must become automatic, almost subconscious, requiring little processing effort.
- Examples of **automaticity,** which is defined as the condition in which learning has become almost subconscious, include recognizing sight words, rapid recall of arithmetic facts, or knowing the sequence of the days of the week.
- When students exert so much effort on tasks that should be automatic, they have less effort remaining to attack other areas of learning.

Use activities that motivate students to want to learn

- Make learning enjoyable for the students.
- Show pleasure and pride with student accomplishments and project sincerity and enthusiasm.
- Find topics of interest for the students.
- Supply extrinsic incentives for which students will want to work.
- Use novelty and variety to keep the students' interest.

learners can count on a number of learning strategies to help them learn and remember. Students with learning disabilities do not have such a repertoire of learning strategies. When teachers help students acquire learning strategies, students *learn how to learn.* What strategies are employed by people who learn in an efficient and well-functioning manner? Successful learners control and direct their thinking processes to facilitate learning. They are **active learners.** They ask themselves questions, and they organize their thoughts. They connect and integrate the new materials that they are trying to learn with prior experience and with knowledge that they already possess. They also try to predict what will come next, and they try to monitor the relevance of the new information. In other words, good learners have discovered how to go about the business of learning, and they have at their disposal a repertoire of cognitive strategies that work for them (Deshler et al., 1996; Lenz et al., 1996).

In contrast, students with learning disabilities usually lack these functional learning strategies. They are **passive learners.** They do not know how to control and direct their thinking in order to learn, how to gain more knowledge, or how to remember what they have learned. They may lack interest in learning because past learning experiences were dismal exercises in failure and frustration. Not believing that they can learn, these students do not know how to go about the task of learning. As a consequence, they become passive and dependent learners, exhibiting a style that is called **learned helplessness.**

Students with learning disabilities must first become aware of and acquire learning strategies to facilitate their learning and remembering. Fortunately, research shows that once they have received learning strategies instruction, they become privy to the best-kept secrets about how to achieve academic success, and they consequently use these strategies in many contexts (Desher, 2003; Gersten, 1998; Mainzer et al., 2003; Swanson, 1999b).

As mentioned earlier in this chapter, a widely used model of strategy instruction for students with learning disabilities is the strategies intervention model (SIM). The SIM learning strategies were developed over many years at the University of Kansas Center for Research on Learning (Deshler et al., 1996; Lenz et al., 1996). Because SIM is geared for adolescents with learning disabilities, the SIM model is discussed in the chapter on adolescents and adults with learning disabilities (see **http:www.ku-crh.org** for more information).

Learning strategies can be used in every area of the curriculum—in the teaching of reading, writing, mathematics, social studies, and science. In addition, learning strategies for specific academic areas are woven throughout various parts of this textbook, especially in the teaching strategies sections; see "Reading Comprehension" in the chapter on reading and "Adolescents With Learning Disabilities" in the chapter on adolescents and adults with learning disabilities.

Cognitive Styles of Learning

Cognitive styles are stable variations in perceiving, organizing, processing, and remembering information (Shipman & Shipman, 1985; Sigel & Brodzinsky, 1977). Cognitive style is different from ability. Ability is an issue of capacity, while cognitive style is a matter of habit. Cognitive styles reflect individual differences in organizing or processing the information required to do a variety of tasks. Learning styles link cognitive, affective, and social functioning and are associated with receptivity to different types of instruction (Messick, 1984).

A number of different systems of learning styles that have been proposed. Field dependence and field independence refer to the extent that one depends on or is distracted by the context or perceptual field in which an event occurs (Witkin, Moor, Goodenough, & Cox, 1977). Categorization is another way of examining cognitive style. The attribute that people use to categorize a set of objects is used to establish learning style (Sigel & Brodzinsky, 1977). Kagan (1966) and Shipman and Shipman (1985) identify cognitive tempo as a cognitive style that categorizes individuals by how quickly they respond to various stimuli. Students who are more impulsive do not do as well in school as those who are more reflective. The extent to which an individual sharpens or levels (blurs) distinctions between stimuli, how willing an individual is to take a risk, and sensory modality preferences (i.e., kinesthetic, visual, auditory) have all been investigated as systems of cognitive style (Schunk, 2004).

Each of these cognitive styles shows developmental differences. As children mature, their cognitive style appears to become more sophisticated and more of a habit. Some research shows gender differences in cognitive styles. Cognitive styles have educational implications, and some are malleable. For example, Meichenbaum and Goodman (1971) found that self-instruction training decreased errors in impulsive children.

Cognitive styles are not without significant criticism. Intuitively, they seem important for teaching and learning. However, distinctions between the various styles are often tenuous at best and are controversial. Furthermore, links of cognitive style to academic achievement are not clearly established (Schunk, 2004; Snider, 1992; Tiedeman, 1989).

Behavioral Temperaments   Research shows that even infants have a variety of personalities and behavioral temperaments. Thomas and Chess (1977) verified this common observation of parents. Some babies are alert and responsive; others are irritable or passive. Moreover, the research shows that these temperamental patterns set the stage for the child's later reaction to the world. Temperamental differences are important for understanding children with learning disabilities and their reactions to school learning (Keogh & Bess, 1991).

The Social Interactions of Learning

The social environment significantly influences learning. The learning process is more than an individualistic, student-centered activity. The social interactions between the teacher and the student, as well as those among students, are critical ingredients in the learning process. Theories that emphasize the social context of learning include Vygotsky's (1978) social influences of learning and interactive dialogues. These theories are reviewed in this section.

Vygotsky: Social Influences of Learning The social nature of cognitive development and the role that interpersonal relationships play in this development were observed more than 70 years ago by Lev Vygotsky, a Russian psychologist. Vygotsky's concept of the zone of proximal development was discussed earlier in this chapter, in the section on cognitive psychology. Vygotsky (1978) observed that social influences are crucial in the learning processes. Learning is an interpersonal, dynamic social event that depends on at least two people, with one person better informed or more skilled than the other. Human learning occurs as a transfer of responsibility, be it learning to play the violin, doing arithmetic, learning Spanish, reading, writing, or repairing an automobile. All of these learning abilities pass along the interpersonal plane. While much learning and development occurs naturally, students who are not learning well require a more careful analysis of the task relative to the student's current ability. Learning and cognitive development are enhanced when the student works collaboratively with a slightly more skilled learner. Tudge and Scrimsher (2003) provide a more complete discussion of Vygotsky's contribution to educational psychology. For additional information, visit the website at **http://www. kolar.org/vygotsky.**

Interactive Dialogues

Interactive dialogues are conversations between students and a teacher. Research shows that the use of interactive dialogues is an effective intervention strategy, particularly in teaching reading comprehension and writing, and research also shows that interactive dialogues are most effective when used with small, interactive groups of six or fewer students. The role of the teacher and the students is to explore ideas and to think critically about the topics under discussion (Vaughn et al., 2000; Wong, 1999). Interactive dialogues are often used as a strategy to improve reading comprehension. The students discuss a story they have read. The teacher listens to what the students say and guides the discussion. The following list provides examples of interactive dialogue (Jennings, Caldwell, & Lerner, 2006):

- The student creates a story map with visual diagrams showing: (1) the characters, (2) the setting, (3) the problem, and (4) the solution. The teacher and student discuss the story map.
- The student discusses her or his personal reaction to the story or the student compares the story with previously read stories.
- The student discusses the traits of a character in the story and then develops a graphic web to illustrate the character's traits.

An application of the interactive dialogue, called *reciprocal teaching,* has been used to teach reading comprehension strategies (Palinscar et al., 1991). Palinscar and colleagues successfully taught the following reading comprehension strategies through reciprocal teaching:

1. The teacher and the students read the material silently.
2. The teacher explains and models summarizing, questioning, clarifying, and predicting by saying aloud the thoughts that are used.
3. The students read another passage and take the responsibility of modeling and saying their thoughts aloud.
4. Each student demonstrates abilities in summarizing, questioning, clarifying, and predicting.

The social environment significantly influences learning. Social interactions between the teacher and students are central ingredients to the learning process. (© Stone/Getty Images)

Implications of Learning Strategies Instruction for Learning Disabilities

The approaches of learning strategies instruction have practical teaching implications. Once students have been taught effective learning strategies, they can use them in learning situations; they can become active, involved learners who accept responsibility for their own learning. Effective learning occurs in a social context where the interrelationship between a student and a teacher is critical.

CHAPTER SUMMARY

1. Theories about learning and teaching are needed to understand learning disabilities. Theory building implies a progression of ideas that builds upon the contributions of earlier theories.

2. Developmental psychology stresses the natural progression of the child's growth and the sequential development of cognitive abilities. A state of readiness is needed for the child to acquire certain abilities. Forcing a child into trying to learn before that state of readiness has been reached can lead to academic failure.

3. Behavioral psychology provides an approach to learning disabilities that emphasizes: (1) explicit teaching and (2) direct instruction. The behavioral unit consists of: (1) the antecedent event, (2) the target behavior, and (3) the consequent event. Explicit teaching means that teachers are clear about what needs to be accomplished. Direct instruction focuses on the teaching of needed academic skills.

4. Through behavioral analysis, teachers examine an academic task in terms of the subskills that lead to the achievement of that task.

5. Cognitive psychology deals with the human processes of: (1) learning, (2) thinking, and (3) knowing. A group of theories about learning disabilities stem from cognitive psychology: (1) disorders in psychological processing, (2) the information-processing model of learning, and (3) cognitive learning theories.

6. Theories about disorders in psychological processing focus on the unique learning characteristics of students with learning disabilities and how they affect achievement. Analysis emphasizes the processing deficiencies and inadequacies in prerequisite skills, particularly various types of auditory and visual processing.

7. The information-processing model of learning describes the flow of information within the individual. It includes: (1) internal or external input, along with attention and perception; (2) the processing function, in which the individual uses an executive function; and, finally, (3) outputs in the form of performance.

8. The multistore model of three types of memory is the core of the information-processing model. The three memory systems are: (1) the sensory register, (2) short-term (or working) memory, and (3) long-term memory. Executive control is another important component of the model.

9. Cognitive learning theories emphasize the learner's own elaborations of knowledge and ways to help students grow in their capacity to monitor and guide their own thinking. Cognitive psychology emphasizes that new learning builds upon prior knowledge and that students construct their own knowledge.

10. The learning strategies approach focuses on *how* students learn rather than on *what* they learn. Students learn to use strategies that enable them to control their own learning.

11. Learning occurs in a social environment, and the relationship between teacher and student is a critical element.

DISCUSSION AND REFLECTION

1. Why is theory important in the study of learning disabilities?

2. Discuss developmental psychology as it applies to learning disabilities. How can developmental delays lead to learning disabilities?

3. How do the principles of behavioral psychology apply to teaching students with learning disabilities?

4. What are the basic concepts of cognitive psychology?

5. What are the three memory systems of the information-processing model? How are these systems related? How can the information-processing model of learning be applied to teaching students with learning disabilities?

6. What is meant by the term *metacognition?* Discuss the problems of students with learning disabilities with regard to metacognitive strategies.

7. What are interactive dialogues? How can they be used to teach students with learning disabilities?

active learners *(p. 187)*

antecedent event *(p. 170)*

automaticity *(p. 186)*

behavioral analysis *(p. 172)*

behavioral unit *(p. 170)*

cognitive abilities *(p. 173)*

concrete operations stage *(p. 165)*

consequent event *(p. 170)*

developmental variations *(p. 163)*

executive control *(p. 180)*

formal operations stage *(p. 166)*

graphic organizers *(p. 182)*

information-processing model
  (p. 176)

interactive dialogues *(p. 189)*

learned helplessness *(p. 187)*

learning strategies approach
  (p. 185)

long-term memory *(p. 179)*

metacognition *(p. 182)*

mind mapping *(p. 182)*

multistore memory system
  (p. 176)

passive learners *(p. 187)*

perception *(p. 177)*

preoperational stage *(p. 165)*

psychological processing disorders
  (p. 175)

retrieval *(p. 179)*

sensorimotor stage *(p. 165)*

sensory register *(p. 177)*

short-term memory *(p. 178)*

stages of learning *(p. 168)*

target behavior *(p. 170)*

theories *(p. 162)*

working memory *(p. 178)*

6

Attention Deficit Disorder and Related Neurodevelopmental Conditions

CHAPTER OUTLINE

> You mean I'm not lazy, hazy, or crazy? Attention deficit disorder is a distinct syndrome greatly in need of detection and treatment. Untreated, it leaves thousands of children and adults misunderstood and unnecessarily floundering and incapacitated.
>
> —*Anonymous*

We devote a separate chapter to the condition of attention deficit disorder (ADD) and related neurodevelopmental conditions. ADD or attention deficit hyperactivity disorder (ADHD) is a common co-occurring condition for children with learning disabilities. Research indicates that between 25% and 40% of the children with learning disabilities have co-occurring ADD/ADHD and that between 30% and 65% of the children with ADD/ADHD have co-occurring learning disabilities (Fletcher, Aram, Shaywitz, & Shaywitz, 2000; Mayers, Calhoun, & Crowell, 2000; Silver, 1998).

Attention deficit disorder (ADD) or **attention deficit hyperactivity disorder (ADHD)** is a condition of the brain that makes it difficult for children to control their behavior in school and social settings. It is one of the most common chronic conditions of childhood and affects between 4% and 12% of all school-age children. About three times more boys than girls are diagnosed with ADHD (American Academy of Pediatrics, 2001).

Two different terms are used to refer to this condition: (1) *attention deficit disorder (ADD),* which is used by the U.S. Department of Education and many of the schools, and (2) *attention deficit hyperactivity disorder (ADHD),* which is taken from the diagnostic criteria in the *Diagnostic and Statistical Manual of Mental Disorders, Fourth Edition Revised (DSM–IV–TR)* (American Psychiatric Association, 2000) and is used by physicians and psychologists. Both terms refer to the same difficulty. With increasing frequency, physicians and psychologists are identifying children with ADD or ADHD.

There are several active support groups for parents and professionals of children with ADD that can provide additional information:

- *CHADD.* Children and Adults With Attention Deficit Disorders. Phone: (800) 233-4050. Website: **http://www.chadd.org.**
- *ADDA.* National Attention Deficit Association. Phone: (847) 432-ADDA. Website: **http://www.add.org.**
- *AD-IN.* Attention Deficit Information Network, Inc. Phone: (781) 455-9895. Website: **http://www.addinfonetwork.com.**

RYAN, A CHILD WITH ADD/ADHD

Ryan's parents have come to dread the phone calls from his teacher. He is only 6 years old, but he is already viewed as a discipline problem. When Ryan was age 3, his nursery school teacher informed his parents that Ryan's pushy behavior interfered with the play of his classmates. The nursery school teacher described him as an undisciplined child. At age 4, his preschool teacher said that the other children complained about Ryan's aggressive behavior. At age 5, his kindergarten teacher described him as a wild boy who ran about the room knocking toys off the shelf and interrupting other children. His classmates did not want to play with him because he was so aggressive.

Now Ryan's first-grade teacher compares him to a tornado. When Ryan enters a room, he changes the tone from a peaceful and quiet class to total pandemonium. Ryan's distraught parents are reluctant to take him anywhere because of his sudden tantrums. He has never been invited to a birthday party and has no playmates.

Ryan's parents finally sought help from a pediatric neurologist, who diagnosed Ryan as having ADD/ADHD.

CHARACTERISTICS OF ADD/ADHD

ADD/ADHD is a chronic neurological condition characterized by: (1) developmentally inappropriate attention skills, (2) impulsivity, and, in some cases, (3) hyperactivity. **Inattention** is the inability to concentrate on a task. **Impulsivity** is the tendency to respond quickly without thinking through the consequences of an action. **Hyperactivity** refers to behavior that is described as a constant, driving motor activity in which a child races from one endeavor or interest to another.

Children with ADD/ADHD have difficulty staying on task, focusing attention, and completing their work. Roughly one half of all children with ADD/ADHD have a co-occurring learning disability (Centers for Disease Control and Prevention, 2002). They are easily distracted, rushing from one idea or interest to another, and they may produce work that is sloppy and carelessly executed. They give the impression that they are not listening or have not heard what they have been told. Children with ADD/ADHD have attention problems and/or problems with hyperactivity, displaying symptoms of age-inappropriate behavior (Accardo, Blondis, Whitman, & Stein, 2000; Barkley, 1998; Haber, 2000; Lerner, Lowenthal, & Lerner, 1995; Rappley, 2004; Silver, 2004). "LD Stories: Ryan, a Child With ADD/ADHD" provides an example of a young child with ADD/ADHD.

Symptoms of ADD/ADHD

For a diagnosis of ADD/ADHD, symptoms must meet the following criteria (American Psychiatric Association, 2000):

1. *Severity.* The symptoms must be more frequent and severe than are typical of other children at similar developmental levels.

2. *Early onset.* At least some of the symptoms must have appeared before the child reaches age 7.

3. *Duration.* The child's symptoms must have persisted for at least 6 months prior to the diagnosis.

Symptoms of ADD/ADHD change at different stages of life. Young children, elementary-age children, adolescents, and adults tend to exhibit different sets of behaviors.

- *Young children* with ADD/ADHD exhibit excessive gross-motor activity, such as running or climbing. They are described as being "on the go," "running like a motor," and having difficulty sitting still. They may be unable to sit still for more than a few minutes at a time before beginning to wriggle excessively. It is the *quality* of the motor behavior that distinguishes this disorder from ordinary overactivity because hyperactivity tends to be haphazard and poorly organized. For example, 4-year-old Jerry grabs a toy from another child, and he hits the child if the toy is not given to him.

- *Elementary-age children* with ADD/ADHD may be extremely restless and fidgety. They are likely to talk too much in class and may constantly fight with friends, siblings, and classmates. For example, 8-year-old Sarah always blurts out the answer without raising her hand or waiting to be recognized.

- For *adolescents* with ADD/ADHD, hyperactivity may diminish, but other symptoms may appear, such as behavioral problems, low self-esteem, inattentiveness, or even depression. For example, 13-year-old Lorraine has such low self-esteem that she believes even her imaginary friend is too busy to talk to her.

- *Adults* with ADD/ADHD often have organizational problems, social relationship difficulties, and job problems. For example, 27-year-old Joshua cannot keep a job because he does not follow through in completing job assignments.

ADD/ADHD affects children in all areas, disrupting the child's home life, education, behavior, and social life. At home, children with this condition have difficulty accommodating home routines and parental expectations. They may resist going to bed, refuse to eat, or break toys during play. At school, they have trouble completing their class work, often missing valuable information because of their attention problems. They speak aloud out of turn and find themselves in trouble for their behavior. Their social interactions may be undermined by their impulsivity, hyperactivity, and inattention, which hampers their ability to make and keep friends. In terms of gender, more boys than girls are diagnosed with ADD/ADHD. However, research suggests that the prevalence rate is equal for boys and girls, but boys are more likely to be identified (Shaywitz et al., 1995).

ASSESSMENT OF ADD/ADHD

The assessment of ADD/ADHD is a necessary step before decisions can be made about treatment and eligibility for services. The diagnosis of ADD or ADHD is usually based on the observation of behaviors. The criteria for these behaviors are described in the *Diagnostic and Statistical Manual of Mental Disorders, Fourth Edition Revised (DSM–IV–TR)* (American Psychiatric Association, 2000).

Types of ADHD in the *Diagnostic and Statistical Manual of Mental Disorders, Fourth Edition, Revised*

The American Psychiatric Association publishes a reference manual entitled the *Diagnostic and Statistical Manual of Mental Disorders (DSM-IV)* that provides criteria for the diagnosis of all mental disorders, and it is used by medical specialists and psychologists. The fourth edition of this publication revised the criteria for assessing ADD/ADHD. As previously noted, the term used in *DSM-IV* is *attention deficit hyperactivity disorder (ADHD)*, and three types of ADHD are specified. Each type requires that the individual display at least six of nine specified symptoms, which are shown in Table 6.1.

1. *ADHD-IA: Primarily inattentive.* The ADHD-IA subtype refers to children who have problems primarily with attention.

2. *ADHD-HI: Primarily hyperactive and impulsive.* The ADHD-HI subtype refers to individuals who display behaviors of hyperactivity and impulsivity, but who do not manifest problems with attention.

3. *ADHD-C: Combination of ADHD-IA and ADHD-HI.* The ADHD-C subtype refers to individuals who have attention problems and display symptoms of hyperactivity and impulsivity. About 5% are primarily inattentive; about 15% are primarily hyperactive and impulsive; about 80% are combined (Rappley, 2004).

The American Academy of Pediatrics (2001) has published a similar set of assessment guides. See the discussion later in this chapter for these guidelines.

TABLE 6.1

Criteria for Subtypes of
ADHD in *DSM-IV-TR*

ADHD-IA subtype: Symptoms of inattention

- Fails to give close attention to details, makes careless mistakes
- Has difficulty sustaining attention
- Does not seem to listen
- Does not follow through or finish tasks
- Has difficulty organizing tasks and activities
- Avoids or dislikes tasks that require sustained effort
- Loses things needed for tasks
- Is easily distracted by extraneous stimuli
- Is often forgetful in daily activities

ADHD-HI subtype: Symptoms of hyperactivity and impulsivity

Hyperactivity

- Fidgets with hands or feet, squirms in seat
- Leaves seat in classroom or in other situations
- Runs about or climbs excessively
- Has difficulty playing or engaging in leisure activities quietly
- Talks excessively
- Acts as if "driven by motor" and cannot sit still

Impulsivity

- Blurts out answers before questions are completed
- Has difficulty waiting in line or awaiting turn in games or activities
- Interrupts or intrudes on others

ADHD-C: Combined subtype

- Symptoms of both IA and HI

Source: From *Diagnostic and statistical manual of mental disorders, Fourth Edition, Text Revision.*
Copyright 2000 by the American Psychiatric Association. Reprinted with permission.

Rating Scales

A variety of behavioral assessment methods are used to identify children
with ADD/ADHD. Methods of assessing behavior include: (1) teacher rating scales, (2) parent rating scales, and (3) direct observation (Barkley,
1998). *Rating scales* are assessment measures based on reports of behavior
observed by teachers and parents. Rating scales that are frequently used are
shown in Table 6.2.

TABLE 6.2

Rating Scales for Assessing
ADD/ADHD

Rating scale	Publisher
Attention Deficit Disorder Evaluation Scale	Hawthorne Educational Services
Behavior Assessment System for Children (BASC)	American Guidance Services
Child Behavior Checklist for Ages 2–3	University of Vermont, Department of Psychiatry
Child Behavior Checklist for Ages 4–16	University of Vermont, Department of Psychiatry
Conners Rating Scales	Multi-Health Services

Eligibility of Children With ADD/ADHD for Special Services

The condition of ADD/ADHD is not identified as a separate category of disability in Individuals With Disabilities Education Improvement Act of 2004 (IDEA–2004). However, due to the hard work of parents and professionals concerned about children with ADD/ADHD, significant laws were passed by the U.S. Department of Education that allow children with ADD/ADHD to be eligible for special education services under the existing categories of disabilities. These laws are:

1991   Clarification of Policy to Address the Needs of Children With Attention Deficit Disorders Within General and/or Special Education

1999   The Regulations for the Individuals With Disabilities Education Act of 1997 (IDEA–1997)

Implications of the Law for Children With ADD/ADHD

The following laws provide legal protections for students with ADD/ADHD:

1. *Special education services.* Children with ADD or ADHD may be eligible for special education services under the category of *other health impaired* in IDEA–2004. The law describes "other health impaired," when

applied to children with ADD/ADHD, as heightened alertness to environmental stimuli that results in limited alertness with respect to the educational environment (U.S. Department of Education, 1999).

A child with ADD or ADHD may also be eligible for special education services under other existing categories of special education, in addition to "other health impaired," such as the categories of learning disabilities or emotional disturbance.

2. *Section 504 services.* A child with ADD or ADHD may be eligible for services under the legislation of Section 504 of the Rehabilitation Act of 1973, even if that child is not eligible for special education services. Section 504 mandates that any agency receiving federal funds must provide reasonable accommodations for people with disabilities.

According to Section 504, if the child is found to have "a physical or mental impairment that substantially limits a major life activity," such as learning, the school must make an individualized determination of the child's educational needs, and reasonable accommodations must be provided within the general education classroom (IDEA–2004).

Increase in the Number of Children Identified With ADD/ADHD

The number of children identified under the category other health impaired has increased substantially since the passage of the 1991 Clarification of Policy to address the needs of children with ADD/ADHD within general and/or special education. More children with ADD/ADHD are now identified under other health impaired, with the number increasing from 53,165 in 1991 to 291,850 in the year 2001, as shown in Figure 6.1.

TREATMENTS FOR ADD/ADHD Many different kinds of treatments are prescribed for children with ADD/ADHD.

Multimodal Treatment Plan

A **multimodal treatment plan** combines several approaches for treating children with ADD/ADHD: (1) effective instruction (utilizing useful teaching methods), (2) behavior management strategies (utilizing a system of reinforcements to modify childrens' behavior), (3) family and child counseling (receiving therapy and counseling), (4) home management (parents use strategies at home to modify the child's behavior), and (5) medication

FIGURE 6.1

Increase in "Other Health Impaired"

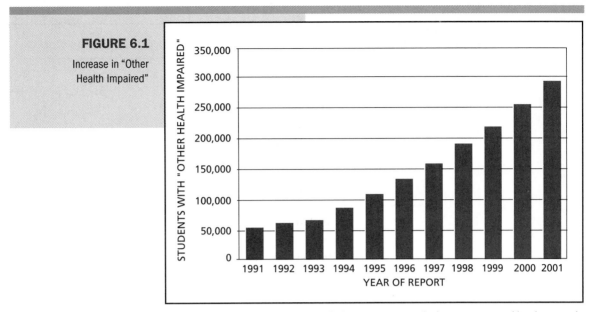

Source: From United States Department of Education, *To assure the free, appropriate public education of all children with disabilities.* Twenty-fourth Annual Report to Congress on the Implementation of the Individuals With Disabilities Education Act. (Washington, DC: U.S. Government Printing Office, 2002.)

(working with a physician to find the right treatment). A child's improvement is greatest when all components of the treatment are present and are working in conjunction (Accardo et al., 2002).

Medication

Many children with ADD/ADHD receive medication to improve their attention and to control their hyperactive behavior. In fact, medication is prescribed in 96.4% of all cases of ADD/ADHD (National Institutes of Health, 1998). The ideal medication should control hyperactivity, increase attention span, and reduce impulsive and aggressive behavior without inducing insomnia, loss of appetite, drowsiness, or other serious toxic effects. Finding the ideal medication for a child is not an easy task, and it requires close cooperation among physicians, school personnel, and family members (Accardo & Blondis, 2000; Powers, 2000).

Psychostimulant Medications **Psychostimulant medications** are the most widely used type of medication prescribed for ADD/ADHD. They are very effective for most children. About 75% to 85% of individuals with

TABLE 6.3

Psychostimulant Medications
Used for Treatment of
ADD/ADHD

Brand name	Generic name	Onset of action	Duration of action
Ritalin	Methylphenidate	30 min	3–5 hr
Dexedrine	Dextroamphetamine	30 min	3–5 hr
Cylert	Pemoline	2–4 weeks	long-lasting
Adderall	Combination of dextroamphetamine and amphetamine	30 min	8 hr
Concerta	Contains a type of Ritalin	30 min	8–12 hr

ADD/ADHD improve with psychostimulants. Psychostimulant medications include Ritalin, Dexedrine, Cylert, Adderall, and Concerta (Accardo & Blondis, 2000; Rappley, 2004). Table 6.3 provides more details about these psychostimulant medications.

The usefulness of psychostimulants in reducing hyperactivity was first reported more than 50 years ago when children taking the psychostimulant Benzedrine showed longer attention spans and an improved ability to concentrate, with a corresponding decrease in hyperactivity and oppositional behavior (Bradley, 1937).

Research on ADD/ADHD suggests that psychostimulant medications affect the brain of children with ADD/ADHD by increasing the arousal or alertness of the central nervous system (Accardo & Blondis, 2000; Barkley, 1998; Powers, 2000). It is thought that these individuals do not produce sufficient **neurotransmitters**—chemicals within the brain that transmit messages from one cell to another across a gap, or synapse—and that the psychostimulants work by stimulating the production of the chemical neurotransmitters needed to send information from the brain stem to the parts of the brain that deal with attention. The psychostimulant medications appear to lengthen the children's attention spans, control impulsivity, decrease distractibility and motor activity, and improve visual–motor integration (Barkley, 1998; Powers, 2000; Rappley, 2004).

The psychostimulant medications most frequently prescribed for ADD/ADHD are Ritalin, Dexedrine, Concerta, and Adderall. Ritalin and Dexedrine become effective in less than 30 min.

The duration of effect for Ritalin and Dexedrine is 3 to 5 hr. Consequently, unless a second dose is taken during the school day, the effects of a morning dose of either of these two medications will wear off during the course of the day. The psychostimulants Cylert and Adderall are taken in one daily dosage, and their effects are long-lasting. Concerta, a newer medication that contains Ritalin, is purported to last 8 to 12 hr because it is released throughout the day.

The side effects of stimulant medications include insomnia and loss of appetite, but these effects are usually transient and diminish as tolerance develops (Barkley, 1998). For a few children, a more serious side effect of Ritalin is that it can trigger tics or Tourette's syndrome. If one of these side effects occurs, the medication must be changed.

A *rebound effect* sometimes occurs with children on psychostimulants. The child's behavior can significantly deteriorate in the late afternoon or evening after a daytime dose of the stimulant. This wearing off of the medication can cause the child to temporarily exhibit more impulsivity, distractibility, and hyperactivity than was previously observed (Barkley, 1998). If this occurs, additional low doses may be needed in the late afternoon.

Strattera   A new medication that is not a psychostimulant for the treatment of ADD/ADHD was approved by the Food and Drug Administration (FDA) in the year 2000. The medication is atomoxetine, and the brand name is Strattera. Because Strattera is not a psychostimulant medication, it is not subject to the same restrictions as psychostimulant medications, and unlike the psychostimulant medications, the FDA does not list Strattera as a Schedule II drug nor does it define Strattera as having a potential for addiction. In addition, Strattera only needs to be given once daily (Kratochvil et al., 2002; Rosenthal, 2003).

Other Medications   As noted previously, about 75% to 85% of children with ADD/ADHD show general improvement with psychostimulant medications. For those who do not improve, other medications are used. These include antidepressant medications, such as Norpramin, Tofranil, Elavil, Prozac, Pamolar, and Wellbutin. Also, an antihypertensive medication, such as Clonidine, may be prescribed (Accardo & Blondis, 2000; Barkley, 1998; Powers, 2000; Rappley, 2004).

American Academy of Pediatrics Guidelines for Treatment

In 2001, guidelines for clinical practice treatment for children with ADHD were established by the American Academy of Pediatrics (2001). These guidelines are:

- Primary care clinicians should establish a treatment program that recognizes ADHD as a chronic condition.

- The treating clinician, parents, and child, in collaboration with school personnel, should specify appropriate target outcomes to guide management.

- The clinician should recommend stimulant medication and/or behavior therapy as appropriate to improve target outcomes for children with ADHD.

- When the selected management for a child with ADHD has not met target outcomes, clinicians should evaluate the original diagnosis, use all appropriate treatments, and adhere to the treatment plan and presence of coexisting conditions.

- The clinician should provide a systematic follow-up for the child with ADHD. Monitoring should be directed to target outcomes and adverse effects, with information gathered from parents, teachers, and the child.

Alternative Therapies

Several alternative, nonmedication therapies are also used to treat children with ADD/ADHD. These therapies are based on **diet-related theories,** which are concepts of controlling hyperactivity and behavior through diet control. Among them are theories of: (1) the removal of food additives, (2) the control of blood-sugar levels, and (3) the treatment of allergies.

Removal of Food Additives   One of the most controversial and widely discussed diet-related theories is that of Feingold (1975), who proposed that food additives in a child's diet induce hyperactivity. Feingold noted that artificial flavors, preservatives, and colors have increased in the American diet and that children today consume a large variety of food additives. Therapy consists of the **Feingold diet,** which controls the child's diet and removes food additives.

Although numerous studies have been conducted on the Feingold diet, most have found that the method is not effective in controlling hyperactivity (Silver, 1998). Nevertheless, the Feingold diet continues to enjoy popularity and has many supporters among parents of hyperactive children.

Control of Blood-Sugar Level   Another diet-related theory of the cause of learning disorders suggests that many children with learning disabilities have hypoglycemia, which is a deficiency in the level of blood sugar (Runion, 1980; Silver, 1987). Therapy consists of controlling the child's eating pattern. Without diet control, according to the theory, the blood-sugar level decreases about an hour after eating, and the child's energy for learning is drained. Several research studies show that sugar in the diet does not increase hyperactivity (Barkley, 1995).

Treatment for Allergies   According to some researchers, many children develop both diet- and environment-related allergies that adversely affect learning. The treatment in this approach is the removal of the element that causes the allergy. Crook (1983) and Rapp (1986) reported success with this treatment. Among the food ingredients thought to impair learning and to induce hyperactivity are sugar, milk, corn, eggs, wheat, chocolate, and citrus (Crook & Stevens, 1986; Lowenthal & Lowenthal, 1995). According to Silver (1998), the current research does not clarify the relationship between allergies and learning disabilities.

NEUROCHEMISTRY OF PSYCHOSTIMULANT MEDICATIONS

In this section, we look at the neurochemistry of psychostimulant medications, which are often prescribed for children with ADD/ADHD.

Individuals with ADD/ADHD do not release enough of the needed chemicals to send information from the brain stem to other parts of the brain. A deficiency in the production of the neurotransmitters *dopamine* and *norepinephrine* results in decreased stimulation and a consequent dysfunction of the neural circuits underlying attention.

The brain is a complex information network made up of millions of nerve cells called **neurons.** Information moves through the brain as nerve impulses that are transmitted from cell to cell by neurotransmitters. An impulse travels along the cell body from a sending neuron to a receiving neuron. A small space, which is called a *synapse,* is between the sending neuron and the receiving neuron. The impulse causes the sending cell to release chemicals—or neurotransmitters—from tiny sacs located at the synapse between the sending cell and the receiving cell. A diagram of the neurotransmitter system is shown in Figure 6.2.

Individuals with ADD/ADHD have an insufficiency in the neurotransmitter activity within the brain stem. The psychostimulant medications increase the production of the chemicals, leading to a decrease in the behaviors associated with ADD/ADHD, such as inattention, impulsivity, and hyperactivity. Thus, medication, through its action on the neurotransmitters, improves the child's attention, motivation, motor responses, activity level, restlessness, and responsibility (Lerner et al., 1995; Powers, 2000; Rappley, 2004).

The use of psychostimulants for ADD/ADHD is associated with rapid improvement in attentiveness, hyperactivity, impulsivity, scholastic performance, handwriting skills, family life, and socialization based on objective tests and subjective evaluations by parents, teachers, and clinicians. In addition, psychostimulant therapy appears to help children with ADD/ADHD improve their self-esteem and self-image, and it enables children with ADD/ADHD to express feelings of greater control over themselves and their lives (Powers, 2000).

FIGURE 6.2

The Neurotransmitter System

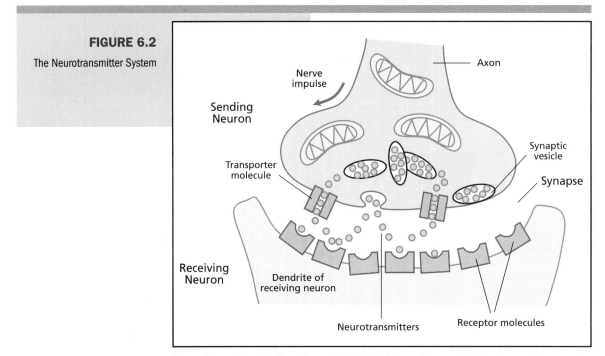

Source: Adapted from *The Dana Sourcebook of Brain Science: Resources for Secondary and Postsecondary Teachers and Students* (New York: Dana Press, 2003), p. 138.

METHODS FOR TEACHING STUDENTS WITH ADD/ADHD

To accommodate students with ADD/ADHD, teachers must be able to manage the three primary traits of ADD/ADHD: (1) inattention, (2) impulsivity, and (3) hyperactivity. Because most students with ADD/ADHD are in a general education classroom setting, it is important for the special education teacher and the general education classroom teacher to be familiar with these methods (Lerner et al., 1995). Let's take a look at each.

Increasing Attention

Inattention is a major symptom of individuals with ADD/ADHD. The student may be attending, but attending to the wrong stimuli. For example, the student may be attending to what is going on outside, to noises in the classroom, or even to his or her own thoughts. There are several distinct but interrelated phases of attention.

1. *Coming to attention.* The first phase, coming to attention, requires students to be alert, steady, and motivated for the lesson.

2. *Focusing attention.* The next phase, focusing attention, requires vigilance and the energy to examine problems carefully and to develop an interest in the problems to be solved. Students with ADD/ADHD must learn to focus their attention, to slow down, to become more deliberate and reflective, and to monitor their responses before answering.

3. *Sustaining attention.* The third phase, sustaining attention, requires that students concentrate for an extended period of time. The ability to focus and attend to a task for a prolonged period is essential for the students to receive the necessary information and to complete certain academic activities.

To learn many academic skills, such as reading, students must work hard and keep attending over many days, weeks, or even months. Some methods for increasing attention appear in the following list:

Methods for Increasing Attention

- Place the student near the front of the room.
- Place the student away from noisy or distracting locations, such as windows and hallways.
- Place the student away from students with behavior problems.
- Place the student with well-behaved students.
- Keep the routines simple and direct.
- Alert the student by using key words, such as "this is important."
- Use visual aids; write out key points.
- Increase the novelty of the task.

Managing Impulsivity

Impulsive students act out physically and/or verbally. Often, they will shout out answers without raising their hands or waiting for recognition. Particularly challenging for impulsive students are transition times, when class activities shift from unstructured activities to structured activities. After a stimulating activity, such as recess or a physical education period, impulsive students have difficulty settling down. The following list includes suggestions for managing impulsivity:

Methods for Managing Impulsivity

- Adapt the curriculum. Small changes in the curriculum can be helpful. Students with ADD/ADHD need a stimulating, active curriculum that will hold their attention and motivate them to complete the activity at hand.
- Help the student learn to wait. Give the student some substitute verbal or motor responses to use while waiting. Instruct the student about how

To accommodate students with ADD/ADHD, teachers must provide ways of managing the three primary traits of ADD/ADHD: inattention, impulsivity, and hyperactivity. (© Elizabeth Crews)

to continue on easier parts of tasks, or how to do a substitute task, while awaiting the teacher's help.

- Help the student manage time. Give short assignments and tasks and reduce the amount of work involved. Alternate activities that are done while sitting with those that involve standing and moving about.

Reducing Hyperactivity

Students who are hyperactive present challenges for classroom teachers. These students cannot sit in their seats for prolonged periods; they may get up to sharpen their pencils 12 times during each class. They need to move and be active. Such students may simply pace back and forth because they cannot sit quietly. The following suggestions offer methods for managing hyperactivity in the classroom.

Methods for Managing Hyperactivity

- Permit the students to move about during class by providing opportunities for students to move about the room. For example, ask students to place their completed papers in a designated area of the classroom.

- Allow the students to leave their seats to make a wall chart after completing a task.
- Give passes that allow students to get a drink, to sharpen a pencil, or to go to workstations or computers.
- Use computers. For example, students can go to a computer to do many tasks, such as writing, planning, or playing games.

ACCOMMODATIONS FOR THE GENERAL EDUCATION CLASSROOM

Teachers must make accommodations in the general education classroom to adjust for the behaviors of students with ADD/ADHD. "LD in Practice: Strategies for Students With ADD/ADHD in the General Education Classroom" lists some of the target behaviors, along with accommodations that can be made to achieve those behaviors. Almost one half of all students with ADD/ADHD are in general education classrooms.

RELATED NEURO-DEVELOPMENTAL CONDITIONS

In this section, we discuss several neurodevelopmental conditions that are often associated with learning disabilities. For many of these neurodevelopmental conditions, the characteristics and treatment procedures overlap with those of learning disabilities.

LD IN PRACTICE

STRATEGIES FOR STUDENTS WITH ADD/ADHD IN THE GENERAL EDUCATION CLASSROOM

Limit distractions
- Seat student near the teacher
- Seat student away from noisy places
- Seat student with well-behaved students and away from students with problem behaviors
- Keep routines simple and direct

Increase attention
- Shorten the task—break it into smaller parts
- Shorten homework assignments
- Use distributed practice (i.e., many shorter sessions)
- Make tasks more interesting (e.g., work with partners, interest centers, groups)
- Increase the novelty of the task

Improve organization

- Provide clear classroom rules and teacher expectations
- Establish routines for placing objects in the room
- Provide a list of materials for each task
- Check that student has homework before leaving school; use assignment books
- Use a different colored folder for each subject

Improve listening skills

- Keep instructions simple and short
- Have students repeat instructions aloud, then to themselves
- Alert students by using key phrases, such as "this is important" or "listen carefully"
- Use visual aids, charts, pictures, graphics, transparencies; write key points on chalkboard

Help students manage time

- Set up a specific routine and adhere to it
- Make lists to help students organize tasks
- Use behavior contracts that specify the time allotted for activities

Provide opportunities for moving

- Permit students to move in class (e.g., sharpen pencils, get papers, get materials)
- Alternate activities (e.g., standing, sitting, moving)
- Allow students to work while standing or while leaning on their desks
- Have work centers in the classroom
- Use computers (e.g., allow children to go to computers during work time)

Asperger's Syndrome

The recognition and use of the clinical term **Asperger's syndrome (AS),** which is defined as a developmental disorder that is characterized by difficulty with social interactions and difficulty in dealing with other people, has increased significantly in the last several years. Virtually unknown until recently, the disorder of AS is now recognized as a relatively common developmental disability. The impact of AS on children and their families is profound. Although AS is not recognized as a disability under federal special education legislation, it is recognized as a mild form of autism, which is an identified category of federal special education law, IDEA–2004. AS is also identified as a mental disorder in the *Diagnostic and Statistical Manual of Mental Disorders, Fourth Edition Revised (DSM-IV–TR)* by the American Psychiatric Association (2000).

AS was first brought to the attention of the psychiatric community in 1944 by Hans Asperger (1944), a Viennese physician. Asperger described the unusual social isolation of a group of children with whom he was working. However, AS did not gain wide recognition until 50 years later when the disorder was included in the American Psychiatric Association's *DSM-IV* (American Psychiatric Association, 1994). Today, AS is widely known, and the number of children identified with this condition is increasing dramatically (Baker & Welkowitz, 2005; Myles & Simpson, 2001a, 2001b).

As noted earlier, AS is characterized as a developmental disorder, with problems ranging from social withdrawal to unskilled social activeness. Children with AS lack an understanding of the rules of social behavior, such as eye contact, proximity to others, gesture, and posture. They display emotional vulnerability and stress, and, as a result, problems of poor self-esteem, poor self-concept, and depression are common. Children with AS have normal or even superior intellectual abilities and language skills.

Usually, children with AS receive instruction in the general education classroom, but they often have academic difficulties. Their poor organizational skills, poor problem-solving skills, and poor motor skills interfere with their academic achievement. To succeed in the general education classroom, children with AS need the support of special educators and related service staff. They need help in developing social skills, in academic planning and programming, and in sensory issues. With suitable support and instruction, most children with AS can be successful in school. Many students with AS are able to attend college and enjoy a variety of successful careers (Baker & Welkowitz, 2005; Myles & Simpson, 2001a, 2001b; Myles, Cook, Miller, Rinner, & Robins, 2000). See the chapter on social and emotional behavior for additional information.

 Helpful tips to prepare a child with AS to return to school after a summer break are given on the website **http://www.udel.edu/bkirby/asberger.** These tips are also presented in "LD in Practice: Ten Tips for Helping Your Child With AS Prepare to Return to School."

Because AS is defined as a mild form of autism, it is important to discuss the characteristics of autism.

LD IN PRACTICE

TEN TIPS FOR HELPING YOUR CHILD WITH AS PREPARE TO RETURN TO SCHOOL

1. Reestablish school-year home routines
2. Establish homework routines
3. Discover how to motivate your child
4. Address the issue of school clothes
5. Set the stage for a good relationship
6. Implement student orientation activities
7. Call your school contact person and review plans for staff training
8. Leave time in your fall schedule for telephone calls and meetings
9. Orchestrate a few social gatherings for your child
10. Plan a relaxing day just for you

Source: From the Online Asperger Syndrome Information and Support (O.A.S.I.S). **http://www.udel.edu/bkirby/asperger.** Reprinted with the permission of O.A.S.I.S. and Diane Adreon, University of Miami Center for Autism and Related Disorders.

Autism

The term *austistic spectrum disorder* is often used because of the wide range of symptoms with autism. **Autism** is a lifelong developmental disability that is best described as a collection of behavioral systems that affect verbal communication, nonverbal communication, and social interaction. It is generally evident before age 3, and autism adversely affects educational performance. Characteristics that often are associated with autism include: (1) engagement in repetitive activities and stereotyped movements, (2) resistance to environmental change or daily routines, and (3) unusual responses to sensory experiences (Klin, Lang, Cicchetti, & Volkmar, 2000).

Austism was first identified as a category of disability in the federal legislation, IDEA, in 1990. Austism is also identified in the *DSM-IV–TR* (American Psychiatric Association, 2000). The forms of autism range from severe to mild. In severe autism, the difficulty appears during the first 3 years of a child's life. A major difficulty for children with autism is communication problems, with many of these children never learning to speak. In its milder forms, only a few of the characteristics of autism are present or they are in a very mild form. As noted earlier, Asperger's syndrome is a mild type of autism.

Nonverbal Learning Disorders

The condition of **nonverbal learning disorders (NVLD)** is widely recognized in the field of neuropsychology. Children with NVLD differ from children with learning disabilities who have academic, linguistic, and cognitive disabilities. NVLD are believed to have a neurological basis that involves a dysfunction in the brain's right hemisphere. Children with NVLD have difficulty understanding the subtle cues that are inherent in nonverbal communication and that play such an important role in social interaction. For example, these children cannot read facial expressions to discern if a person is sad, happy, or angry. Children with NVLD also may not know how to initiate friendships nor recognize the idea of personal space. These social cues are normally grasped intuitively through observation, but children with NVLD need to be taught these social skills through direct and explicit instruction (Rourke, 1995; Thompson, 1997). These children often have a high verbal intelligence, they tend to be early talkers, and they are highly verbal. Because they do well reading and decoding in the primary years, their nonverbal learning problems are frequently missed. These children often have poor visual–spatial abilities, poor nonverbal problem-solving abilities, and low arithmetic skills. Problems with NVLD become more evident in the later elementary school years, during adolescence, and in the adult years (Dimitrovsky, Spector, Levy-Shiff, & Vakil, 1998; Rourke, 1995; Thompson, 1997). A useful website for NVLD is **www.nldline.com**.

Many of the characteristics of AS appear to be similar to NVLD. However, Roman (1998) claims they are different disorders and that AS is part of the autistic spectrum. NVLD are not recognized in IDEA–2004 or in the *DSM-IV–TR*, although they are recognized by the field of neuropsychology. For more information, see the chapter on social and emotional behavior strategies for teaching social skills.

CHAPTER SUMMARY

1. Attention deficit disorder and learning disabilities are a common co-occurring condition.

2. The term *attention deficit disorder (ADD)* is used by the U.S. Department of Education and in the schools. The term *attention deficit hyperactivity disorder (ADHD)* is defined by the American Psychiatric Association and used by physicians and psychologists. The two terms refer to the same condition.

3. The characteristics of ADD/ADHD change with age. Young children, elementary-age children, adolescents, and adults all display different characteristics of ADD/ADHD.

4. For a diagnosis of ADD/ADHD, symptoms must meet the criteria of: (1) severity (2) early onset, and (3) duration.

5. The *Diagnostic and Statistical Manual of Mental Disorders, Fourth Edition, Revised (DSM-IV–TR)* describes three types of ADHD: (1) primarily inattentive, (2) primarily hyperactive and impulsive, and (3) a combination of (1) and (2).

6. Two laws that make children with ADD/ADHD eligible for special education services are: (1) the 1991 Clarification of Policy to Address the Needs of Children With Attention Deficit Disorders Within General and/or Special Education, and (2) the 1999 Regulations for IDEA-1997.

7. The number of children identified with ADD/ADHD is increasing.

8. Medication is important part of the treatment therapy for children with ADD/ADHD. A group of psychostimulant medications are widely used and are effective medications for ADD/ADHD. There are also other medications and alternative therapies used for children with ADD/ADHD.

9. Teaching methods for students with ADD/ADHD are used by special education teachers and general education teachers. These teaching methods include strategies of: (1) increasing attention, (2) managing impulsivity, and (3) reducing hyperactivity.

10. Related neurodevelopmental conditions that are often associated with learning disabilities include Asperger's syndrome and nonverbal learning disorders.

DISCUSSION AND REFLECTION

1. Many children today are diagnosed with ADD/ADHD. Describe the characteristics of children with ADD/ADHD at different developmental stages.

2. What are some of the settings for serving children with ADD/ADHD in the schools?

3. Many children with ADD/ADHD receive medication as part of their treatment. Discuss the kinds of medication that children with ADD/ADHD receive.

4. Describe two related neurodevelopmental conditions.

KEY TERMS

Asperger's syndrome (AS) *(p. 212)*

attention deficit disorder (ADD) *(p. 196)*

attention deficit hyperactivity disorder (ADHD) *(p. 196)*

autism *(p. 214)*

diet-related theories *(p. 206)*

Feingold diet *(p. 206)*

hyperactivity *(p. 197)*

impulsivity *(p. 197)*

inattention *(p. 197)*

multimodal treatment plan *(p. 202)*

neurons *(p. 207)*

neurotransmitters *(p. 204)*

nonverbal learning disorders (NVLD) *(p. 215)*

psychostimulant medications *(p. 203)*

7

Young Children With Learning Disabilities

Early intervention is beneficial for young children with disabilities and their families, but it is also profitable for society because research shows that young children who receive early intervention services become tax payers rather than tax receivers, and they grow up to become citizens who contribute to society.

—Anonymous

Young children with disabilities and young children who are at risk for disabilities (children who have conditions that indicate they are prone to having disabilities) need to be identified early and provided with appropriate interventions. Because national and state policies now support early intervention services for children with disabilities, schools and agencies are expanding their services for young children. In this chapter, we review: (1) the importance of the early years, (2) developmental indicators of problems in young children, (3) motor development and learning, (4) perception, (5) assessing young children, (6) early childhood curriculum and practices for young children with special needs, (7) early intervention strategies, and (8) strategies for preschool inclusion.

THE IMPORTANCE OF THE EARLY YEARS

The early childhood years are crucial for all children, but for the child with special needs in terms of mental, physical, behavioral, developmental, or learning characteristics, these years are especially critical. Research from several disciplines confirms what early childhood educators have long observed—that the early years of life are crucial for establishing a lifelong foundation for learning. If the opportunity for children to develop intellectually and emotionally during these critical years is missed, precious learning time is lost forever.

Children do not *begin* to learn when they enter formal schooling at age 6. During the first 6 years of their lives, young children learn at a rapid pace. They need continuous and intense learning from the moment of birth. By the time they reach school age, they should have mastered many kinds of learning. Parents and others involved with young children need to be actively engaged in promoting learning during the preschool years. Otherwise, their child's intellectual abilities will not grow optimally during these vital years. Children who start school already behind their peers may never be able to catch up, to keep up, or to take advantage of all the efforts schools make to help them.

Benefits of Early Intervention

Perhaps the most promising success stories in education today are the reports of special programs for young children who have disabilities or who are at risk for disabilities because of environmental and other conditions that make them likely to develop disabilities. The formative stages in child development and family life occur during the early years. These early years make a significant difference in a child's growth and development (Wolery & Bailey, 2003). When a child's problems are recognized early, school failure can, to a large extent, be prevented or reduced.

Early childhood special education programs: (1) first *identify* young children, ages birth through 5, who have special needs and are likely to encounter difficulty in academic learning and then (2) provide an immediate early intervention program. "LD Stories: A Preschooler With a Disability" illustrates such a situation.

Research demonstrates that early comprehensive and intensive intervention is beneficial for children with disabilities, for their families, and for society (Guralnick, 1997; Wolery & Bailey, 2003).

Children at risk dramatically improve when early intervention and work with families are provided. (© *Elizabeth Crews)*

LD STORIES

A PRESCHOOLER WITH A DISABILITY

Lorinda was identified during the local school district's preschool screening program as a high-risk child who needed further assessment and intervention. She performed poorly on tests requiring expressive language skills and on social measures. Lorinda's age was 3 years 9 months at the time of her testing.

During the interview with Lorinda's mother, the school obtained additional information. Born 6 weeks prematurely, Lorinda weighed a little more than 4 lb at birth and had trouble breathing. She frequently suffered from colds during her first 2 years, and between the ages of 2 and 3, she had at least eight serious ear infections. Motor development seemed to be normal; she sat up, walked, and crawled at the same ages that her siblings had performed these activities. Her language development, however, was slower than theirs. Although she seemed to understand language when spoken to, she could not use it to make her wants known. She did not use any words until she was 2 years old and even now uses only very short sentences, such as "Me want pizza" or "Him break cup." She often uses the wrong word or simply points to what she wants. She still has temper tantrums, which seem to be triggered by her inability to communicate her needs.

Her mother described her as an "overactive" child compared with the other children. She would "tear the house apart," break the crib, and take all her toys apart. She never sat down, except to watch television, and that activity usually lasted for only a few minutes. When Lorinda turned 3, her mother tried to enroll her in a small play school, but after a few days the director said she could not stay because of her extreme hyperactivity. Without provocation, she grabbed toys from other children and hit or scratched her classmates.

Lorinda's mother had suspected that Lorinda was different, but everyone had told her not to worry—that Lorinda would outgrow her disruptive behavior. The mother expressed relief at having her daughter in the special preschool program. At last, someone else recognized Lorinda's problem and would be working to help her. The hours Lorinda would be in school would offer her mother the first break since Lorinda was born, and her mother was looking forward to receiving help from the school on home behavior management.

- **Early intervention helps children with disabilities.** Early intervention accelerates cognitive and social development and reduces behavioral problems. Many conditions can be alleviated, other disorders can be overcome to a large extent, and some problems can be managed so that the child can live a better life. Early intervention can avert the occurrence of secondary problems that compound the original difficulty.

- **Early intervention benefits the families of young children with special needs.** In the family-centered intervention approach, the child is viewed as part of a family system. When the parents are empowered to be an integral part of the intervention process, the family becomes an essential element in the process of teaching the child and improving child–adult interactions.

■ *Early intervention benefits society.* Early intervention programs offer a substantial financial savings for the community by reducing the number of children who need special education services. In summary, early intervention accomplishes the following (Guralnick, 1997; Lerner et al., 2003; Schweinhart, Barnes, & Weikart, 1993; Wolery & Bailey, 2003):

a. Enhances intelligence

b. Promotes substantial gains in all developmental areas (physical, cognitive, language, psychosocial, and self-help)

c. Inhibits or prevents secondary disabilities

d. Reduces family stress

e. Reduces dependency and institutionalization

f. Reduces the need for special education services at school age

g. Saves the nation and society substantial health care costs and education costs

THE LAW AND YOUNG CHILDREN WITH DISABILITIES

The special education law, Individuals With Disabilities Education Improvement Act (IDEA–2004), incorporates two earlier early childhood laws (i.e., PL 99–457 and PL 102–119). These laws identify two different age groups of young children with disabilities: (1) *preschoolers,* ages 3 through 5 and (2) *infants* and *toddlers,* birth through age 2. The provisions in the law are different for each of these age groups. Table 7.1 compares the provisions of the early education law for children ages 3 through 5 in **Part B of IDEA–2004** and birth through age 2 in **Part C of IDEA–2004.**

TABLE 7.1

Comparison of Legislation for Preschoolers and for Infants and Toddlers

	Preschoolers	Infants and toddlers
Age	Ages 3 through 5	Birth through age 2
Eligibility	Category of disability or developmental delay	Developmental delay
Plan	IFSP or IEP	IFSP
Law	Part B, mandatory	Part C, permissive
Lead agency	State education agency	Agency appointed by governor
Transition	To regular class or special education class	To program for preschool special education
Primary orientation	Developmental learning	Family–infant interaction
Personnel	Early childhood special education teacher	Service coordinator

Preschool Children: Ages 3 Through 5

Preschool children, ages 3 through 5, with disabilities are eligible to receive the same full rights under the law that older children have. These provisions are specified in Part B of IDEA–2004. Preschoolers may have a developmental delay in one or more of the following areas:

1. Physical development
2. Cognitive development
3. Communication development
4. Social or emotional development
5. Adaptive development

The following list provides a summary of the provisions in the law for preschoolers with disabilities:

- Each state must provide a free, appropriate public education, along with related services, to all eligible children with disabilities, ages 3 through 5.

- States may select to identify preschool children either noncategorically, such as by *developmental delay,* or by the category of disabilities, such as *learning disability.* Any state that adopts the term *developmental delay* has the option to apply it to children ranging from age 3 to age 9.

- For children ages 3 through 5, the child study team may use either the IEP or the **individualized family service plan (IFSP),** which is a plan for young children that includes the family as well as the child. The plan used must ensure due process, confidentiality, and the child's placement in the least restrictive environment.

- The lead agency for preschool children ages 3 through 5 is the state education agency. The law gives each state's education agency the responsibility of implementing Part B of IDEA–2004 for preschool children by working with local education agencies or other contracted service agencies.

Infants and Toddlers: Birth Through Age 2

The policies for infants and toddlers, birth through age 2, with disabilities are contained in Part C of IDEA–2004. Services for infants and toddlers with disabilities are not mandated, but Part C authorizes financial assistance to the states through state grants. Financial assistance is offered to develop and implement a statewide comprehensive and coordinated multidisciplinary interagency program of early intervention services for infants and toddlers with disabilities and for their families. The family system is recognized as critical in the child's development. The teams must use an IFSP, which includes plans for the family as well as for the child.

The number of infants and toddlers with disabilities is increasing. Recent advances in medical technology have allowed neonates with very low birth weights and substantial health problems to survive. Newborns may have other kinds of problems. For example, there are 375,000 drug-exposed babies and 2,000 HIV-infected babies born each year. These fragile infants usually need highly specialized medical attention, and they and their families also require services that medical professionals cannot provide. Infant specialists and infant/toddler service coordinators (or case managers) are key members of the interdisciplinary team in neonatal intensive care units and in child-care centers (U.S. Department of Education, 2000b).

Number of Preschool Children Receiving Special Education Services

The number of preschool children receiving special education services has been increasing. Over 5% of all preschool children (ages 3 through 5) currently receive special education services through the schools. About 1.5% of infants and toddlers (birth through age 2) and their families receive services, as shown in Table 7.2 (U.S. Department of Education, 2002).

For the preschool-aged children, the breakdown by ages of preschool children receiving special education services is shown in Table 7.3 (U.S. Department of Education, 2002).

TABLE 7.2

Percentage of Young Children Receiving Special Education Services

Age group	Percentage of general population
Infants and toddlers (birth through age 2)	1.5
Preschoolers (ages 3 through 5)	5.0

Source: From United States Department of Education, *To assure the free, appropriate public education for all children with disabilities,* Twenty-Fourth Annual Report to Congress on the Implementation of the Individuals With Disabilities Education Act, (Washington, DC: U.S. Government Printing Office, 2002).

TABLE 7.3

Breakdown by Ages of Preschool-Aged Children Receiving Special Education Services

Age	Percentage receiving special education services
3	21
4	35
5	44

The U.S. Department of Education (2002) reported the disabilities for preschool children. Figure 7.1 shows that the most frequently identified disabilities for children ages 3 through 5 are: (1) speech or language impairment, (2) developmental delay, (3) mental retardation, (4) learning disabilities, (5) other health impairments, (6) multiple disabilities, (7) autism, and (8) other. The "other" category includes hearing impairment, orthopedic impairment, visual impairment, deaf–blindness, and traumatic brain injury.

Considerations of Cultural Diversity

Many children and families who participate in programs for young children with special needs are from diverse linguistic and cultural backgrounds. Early childhood special educators need to be sensitive to the cultural differences that may occur in parent–child interactions, values, perceptions of the family unit, perceptions of disabilities, and attitudes toward seeking help. Professionals must have the ability to communicate with family members in a way that is respectful and clear (Lerner et al., 2003).

Early childhood special education teachers should respect the child's culture and recognize that the cultural values can affect how the family views the disability. In some cultures, the family may be ashamed that they have a child with a disability and they may neglect their child with special needs. Teachers should understand that the family may be reluctant to accept suggestions from the school. Teachers should encourage children from diverse cultures and languages to demonstrate their knowledge through drawing, collaboration, or performance in small group discussions (Lowenthal, 2003).

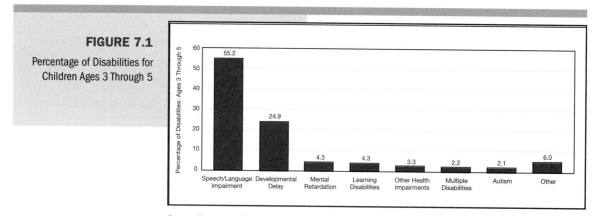

FIGURE 7.1

Percentage of Disabilities for Children Ages 3 Through 5

Source: From United States Department of Education, *To assure the free, appropriate public education for all children with disabilities,* Twenty-Fourth Annual Report to Congress on the Implementation of the Individuals With Disabilities Education Act, (Washington, DC: U.S. Government Printing Office, 2002).

The U.S. Department of Education (2002) reports data on the race/ethnicity of young children with disabilities. For children ages 3 through 5, the race/ethnicity percentages are shown in Table 7.4.

A website for student diversity can be found at **http://www.urban.com.**

Children at Risk

Children **at risk,** which is defined as children who are at risk for poor development and learning failure, pose another concern. Children who are at risk presently may not be eligible under the law for services, but they are at high risk for becoming children with disabilities if early intervention services are not provided. States may choose to serve children who are at risk; however, they are *not required* to provide services for them.

Research shows that children who are at risk dramatically improve when early intervention and work with families are made available. For example, low-birth-weight infants show significant gains in cognitive and behavioral function when they receive comprehensive early intervention consisting of home visits, parent training, parent group meetings, attendance at a child development center, pediatric surveillance, and community referral services (Gopnick, Meltzoff, & Kuhl, 1999; Keogh, 2000).

Research also shows the critical effect of the infant's environment on the early development of the brain (Gopnick et al., 1999; Huttenlocher, 1991). During the early months and first years of life, the *synapses,* or interconnecting links between the neurons in the brain, grow at a phenomenal rate. The brain rapidly increases in size and becomes more efficient. The environmental influences and the child's experiences during the earliest years of life play a major role in brain development and affect intelligence and the ability to learn. Research on early brain development shows that:

- Environment affects the number of brain cells, the connections among the brain cells, and the way the brain cells are wired. Brain development is much more vulnerable to environmental influences than was previously suspected.

TABLE 7.4

Percentage of Young Children With Disabilities by Race/Ethnicity

Race/ethnicity	Percentage
White (non-hispanic)	60.5
Hispanic	20.0
Black (non-hispanic)	15.4
American Indian/Alaskan Native	0.9

- Brain development before age 1 is more rapid and extensive than previously realized.
- The influence of the early environment on brain development is long lasting.
- Early stress has a negative impact on brain function.

Among the factors that affect young children at risk are poverty, disrupted families, or abusive parents. Other risk factors are prenatal substance exposure; exposure to alcohol, tobacco, and nicotine; and illegal drug use (Keogh, 2000; U.S. Department of Education, 2000b).

Educational Environments

The term *educational environments* refers to the primary educational setting for young children with disabilities. The U.S. Department of Education (2002) reports that preschool children with disabilities are served through many different educational environments. As shown in Figure 7.2, the educational environments include: (1) general early childhood classes, 36%; (2) early childhood special education classes, 34%; (3) split general early childhood classes/early childhood special education classes, 13%; (4) separate school, 4%; (5) itinerant services outside the home, 7%; (6) home instruction, 4%; and (7) reverse mainstreaming, 2%.

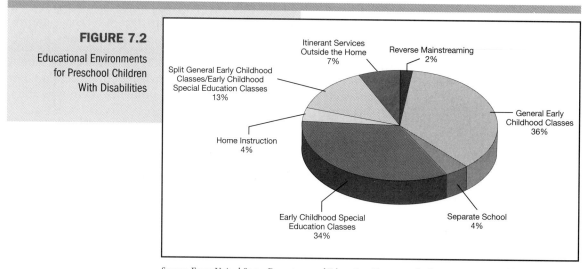

FIGURE 7.2

Educational Environments for Preschool Children With Disabilities

Source: From United States Department of Education, *To assure the free, appropriate public education for all children with disabilities,* Twenty-Fourth Annual Report to Congress on the Implementation of the Individuals With Disabilities Education Act. (Washington, DC: U.S. Government Printing Office, 2002).

DEVELOPMENTAL INDICATORS OF PROBLEMS IN YOUNG CHILDREN

Developmental indicators are early signs of problems (or learning disabilities) in young, preschool children. Signs of problems can be observed in the child's motor development, auditory processing, visual processing, speech and language development, or attention abilities. Often, the child will excel in some areas of development, while displaying significant difficulty in others. These precursors of problems are predictive of later difficulty in academic achievement, but early intervention can help preschool children reduce or overcome these potential problems (Lerner et al., 2003). Some early warning signs in preschool children (**http://www.ldonline.org**) are:

- Late talking, compared with other children
- Pronunciation problems
- Slow vocabulary growth, often unable to find the right word
- Difficulty rhyming words
- Trouble learning numbers, the alphabet, days of the week
- Extremely restless and easily distracted
- Trouble interacting with peers
- Poor ability to follow directions

Learning disabilities may not be identified in young children if the definition of learning disabilities emphasizes failure in academic subjects by seeking a discrepancy between the child's ability and the child's academic achievement. This approach is called the "wait and fail method" because the child must first fail before she or he is eligible for identification and services. Preschoolers may not be identified as having learning disabilities because they have not yet been exposed to formal academic learning. Waiting for a child to fail in order to consider the child eligible for services is a costly approach. A more appropriate approach for identifying learning disabilities in young children is to evaluate precursors of learning disabilities (Lerner et al., 2003).

Accumulating research shows the importance of early identification of young children who show signs of learning difficulty and the value of providing early intervention.

Unfortunately, young children with learning disabilities are not being identified or being given appropriate instruction. In fact, data from the U.S. Department of Education (2002) show that most children with learning disabilities are not identified until ages 9 through 14. Very few 6-year-old children and relatively few 7- and 8-year-old children receive special learning disabilities services. It is only when children actually fail at ages 9–14 that they are finally identified and thus eligible to receive special instruction.

Developmental indicators of disabilities may appear as difficulties in the following areas:

- *Gross-motor skills.* A common precursor for some children with learning disabilities is an awkwardness in gross-motor skills, which require children to use large muscles when moving their arms, legs, torso, hands, and feet. Young children with gross-motor problems appear clumsy in walking, jumping, hopping, running, skipping, throwing, and catching skills.

- *Fine-motor skills.* Fine-motor activities involve the small muscles used to move fingers and wrists, as well as eye–hand coordination and coordination of the two hands. Children with problems in fine-motor skills tend to be slow in learning to dress themselves, in learning eating skills, in using buttons and zippers, and in using pencils and crayons. Problems in fine-motor development are evident when children have difficulty doing puzzles, playing building games, accomplishing art projects, and using scissors in cutting activities. In the later elementary years, fine-motor difficulties are evident in slow and laborious handwriting.

- *Auditory processing.* An important precursor of learning disabilities involves auditory processing. The ability to interpret what is heard provides an important pathway for learning. Children who have difficulty learning to read show early signs of difficulties with auditory processing abilities. These children can hear, but their difficulty lies in several dimensions of auditory processing, including phonological awareness, auditory discrimination, auditory memory, and auditory sequencing and blending.

- *Visual processing.* Visual processing abilities play a significant role in school learning, particularly in reading. Children with visual processing difficulties can see, but they encounter problems in visual discrimination of letters and words, visual memory, or visual closure. Visual processing and orthographic problems in young children are early signs of learning disabilities, and these precursors are predictive of later reading difficulties.

- *Communication and language skills.* Difficulty in acquiring speech and understanding and using language are among the most common precursors of learning disabilities. The ability to use language to communicate one's thoughts is central to learning. Children with communication or language disorders have difficulty understanding the language of others (listening), responding to instructions, initiating communications, explaining, engaging in conversations, and communicating with others. Delays in speech and language acquisition are discussed in the chapter on oral language.

- *Problems with attention.* Some young children with learning disabilities display behaviors related to attention deficit disorder. They display behaviors of hyperactivity, inattention, and impulsivity. These children cannot regulate or manage their activity levels to meet the demands of the moment. They act as if they were driven by a motor, running and climbing about excessively, being in constant motion, fidgeting and squirming when sitting, and making loud noises. Young children with inattention problems have difficulty concentrating on a task, are easily distracted, shift from one activity to another, and do not finish what they start. Parents and teachers complain that these children do not listen and often lose things. Impulsive young children have problems inhibiting their responses to immediate events and do not think reflectively before acting. They act before considering the consequences of their behavior. They tend to blurt out answers before their teachers have finished the question. These youngsters also find it difficult to share and take turns with their classmates (Warner-Rogers, Taylor, Taylor, & Sandberg, 2000). The chapter on attention deficit disorder addresses these learning disabilities.

MOTOR DEVELOPMENT AND LEARNING

Parents, teachers, physicians, and other professionals often describe a young child with learning disabilities as awkward or as lacking manual dexterity. Parents frequently report that their child was slow in acquiring motor skills, such as using eating utensils, putting on clothes, buttoning a coat, catching a ball, or riding a bicycle. "LD Stories: Motor Coordination Problems" describes a student with motor coordination difficulties.

The special education law (IDEA–2004) recognizes the need for physical education for all exceptional children. The child's IEP can designate the use of adapted physical education, occupational therapy (OT), or physical therapy (PT) as a needed related service. Occupational therapists (OTs) and physical therapists (PTs) are medically trained health professionals who provide therapy for a variety of motor and physical disorders. Motor activities are typically part of the curriculum in early childhood special education programs.

The Importance of Motor Development

Throughout history, philosophers and educators have written about the close relationship between motor development and learning. Plato placed gymnastics at the first level of education in the training of the philosopher–king. Aristotle wrote that a person's soul is characterized by both body and mind. Spinoza advised, "Teach the body to do many things; this will help you to perfect the mind and to come to the intellectual level of thought." Piaget (1936/1952) emphasized that early sensorimotor learning establishes the foundation for later, more complex perceptual and cognitive development. Indeed, a recurring theme throughout the history of special education is the concern for motor development (Francks et al., 2003; Itard, 1801/1962; Montessori, 1912; Sequin, 1866/1970).

MOTOR COORDINATION PROBLEMS

Jim is an example of a student with academic learning disabilities who also shows signs of immature motor development, laterality confusion, and poor awareness of his own body. Jim was brought to a learning disabilities clinic at age 12 for an evaluation because he was doing poorly in school, particularly in reading and arithmetic. An individual intelligence test indicated that Jim's intelligence was above average, and a screening test for auditory and visual acuity showed no abnormalities. His oral language skills seemed good for his age. At first, Jim's posture gave the impression of being unusually straight, almost military in bearing. During the motor testing, however, it was evident that this seemingly straight posture was actually rigidity. When a change in balance occurred because of a required movement, Jim was unable to make the correction within his body position and his relationship to gravity. He lost his balance and fell when he tried to walk in a straight line on the floor. When a ball was thrown to him, he was unable to catch it and lost his balance. Jim's attempts at catching the ball were similar to those of a child of 4 or 5. He worked at times with his left hand, at other times with his right hand; he had not yet established hand preference. Although he had been given swimming lessons several times, he was still unable to swim. All the neighborhood children played baseball after school and on weekends, but Jim could not participate in this sport with youngsters his own age. Consequently, he had no friends, and his teacher identified him as a loner. Evidence of poor motor skills appeared in many academic activities. For example, his handwriting was almost illegible, reflecting his perceptual-motor dysfunction. Jim's father, who had excelled in athletics and had won several sports championships in high school and college, had little patience for playing with a son who did not learn motor skills easily. In fact, because of Jim's abysmal failure in sports, his father was convinced his son was either mentally retarded or not "a real boy." For Jim, then, reading was only one part of the difficulty he had in relating to the world. A comprehensive assessment should take into account his poorly developed motor skills, and an individualized instructional plan should help Jim acquire motor experiences to establish a motor awareness of the world.

The *Diagnostic and Statistical Manual of Mental Disorders (DSM-IV)* classifies severe problems in motor skills as a *developmental coordination disorder (DCD)* (American Psychiatric Association, 1994). The criteria for developmental coordination disorder include: (1) delays in developmental milestones, (2) dropping things, (3) clumsiness, (4) poor performance in sports, or (5) poor handwriting (Fox, 1998).

Early childhood educators view motor growth as a cornerstone of child development (Lerner et al., 2003). Motor activities are typically included in the general education curriculum for preschool children. For preschoolers with disabilities who have deficits in motor coordination, balance, rhythm, or body image, the intervention strategies include methods for building

motor skills, spatial awareness, and motor planning (Cook, Tessier, & Klein, 2000).

Providing motor activities can bring about many unanticipated and probably immeasurable improvements for the young child. It can help a child become happier, more confident, and more available for learning; it can also foster social interactions. When the motor curriculum requires the child to go *through, under, over, between,* and *around* obstacles, the child is also learning important cognitive skills and language skills.

Concepts of Motor Development

Movement and motor experiences are crucial for human development. For many children with disabilities, difficulty in motor coordination is a serious problem. Some children exhibit motor behaviors that are typical of much younger children. Examples of such motor behaviors are overflow movements (when the child performs a movement with the right arm, the left arm involuntarily performs a shadow movement), poor coordination in gross-motor activities, difficulty in fine-motor coordination, poor body image, and lack of directionality. These children are so poor in the physical education activities for their age that they are easily spotted in gym class. They frequently disturb others in the classroom by bumping into objects, falling off chairs, dropping pencils and books, and appearing generally clumsy.

Gross- and Fine-Motor Development   *Gross-motor skills* involve the large muscles of the neck, trunk, arms, and legs. Gross-motor development involves postural control, walking, running, catching, and jumping. To provide stimulation for gross-motor development, children need safe environments that are free from obstacles, and they need much encouragement from parents and teachers.

Fine-motor skills involve the small muscles. Fine-motor coordination includes coordination of the hands and fingers and dexterity with the tongue and speech muscles. Children develop fine-motor skills as they learn to pick up small objects, such as beads or chunks of food, cut with a scissors, grasp and use crayons and pencils, and use a fork and spoon. They need ample opportunities for building with blocks, manipulating small toys, stringing beads, buttoning, and rolling and pounding (Cook et al., 2000).

Motor Development Through Play   Through the normal activities of play, children have many opportunities for motor activity. On the playground, children's muscles move as they reach, grasp, run, stoop, or stretch. In the typical play environment, the child develops motor skills by playing with toys, using clay, or painting. Playing games can also help build self-concept, social relationships, and acceptance by peers. Motor activities—such as riding bicycles, playing games, and dancing—signal the emergence of various developmental levels. The inability to accomplish these activities with reasonable proficiency may precipitate a chain of failure (Bricker, 1998; Linder, 1993).

Sometimes children with learning disabilities receive instruction in motor skills through an adapted physical education program, which is a special physical education program that has been modified to meet the needs of children with disabilities. Helping children with disabilities take advantage of the same physical, emotional, and social benefits of exercise, recreation, and leisure activities that other children enjoy is important in inclusive environments.

Movement games can help children with learning disabilities adjust to general classroom learning. For example, the child's attention span can be lengthened through games and physical activities that require increasing the ability to pay attention. The learning of letters can become a physical activity if large letters made of rope are placed on a playground and games are devised in which the student runs or walks over the shapes of letters. Activities that involve the total body may also serve to focus the attention of the hyperactive child (Cratty, 1988).

Perceptual Motor Development

The idea of the relationship between **perceptual motor learning** and learning disabilities was formulated by one of the pioneers in the field of learning disabilities, Newell Kephart (1963, 1967, 1971). This view suggests that through perceptual motor learning, the child integrates motor behaviors and perception (visual, auditory, tactile, and kinesthetic perception). Children who have normal perceptual motor development establish a solid and reliable concept of the world, a stable perceptual motor world, by the time they encounter academic tasks at age 6.

In contrast, children with atypical perceptual motor development must contend with a perceptual motor world that is unstable and unreliable. In order to deal with symbolic materials, these children must make some rather precise observations about objects and events. Children with perceptual motor problems encounter confusion when confronted with symbolic materials because they have not established a stable perceptual motor world. For example, one child could not understand or perceive a *square* because he lacked sufficient motor experiences with squares. Another child could not rely on her visual observations, so she had to touch things to assure herself that what she was seeing was real.

Sensory Integration

Sensory integration (SI) provides another approach to motor development and learning disabilities. This theory comes from the field of occupational therapy (OT). Sensory integration is a theory about the relationship between the neurological processes and motor behavior (Ayres, 1994; Fisher, Murray, & Bundy, 1991; Goldey, 1998; Williamson & Anzalone, 1997).

Occupational therapists (OTs) are trained in brain physiology and function. They prescribe specific physical therapies and exercises designed to modify the motor and sensory integration functions of patients. Occupational therapists use sensory integration therapy with children who have disorders in several sensory integration functions, which interfere with the awareness of their body and body movements. These methods are often used in early childhood special education programs.

Three systems are involved in sensory integration: (1) the tactile system, (2) the vestibular system, and (3) the proprioceptive system (Clark, Mailloux, & Parham, 1989; Fisher et al., 1991; Silver, 1998).

Tactile System   The *tactile system* involves the sense of touch and the stimulation of skin surfaces. Some children have problems in *tactile defensiveness;* they experience discomfort when touched by another person. Infants with tactile defensiveness do not like to be held or touched. Older children may complain about being bothered by a tag on the back of a shirt, by a seam on a sock, or by clothes that are uncomfortable. These children may lash out and fight when they are brushed against while they are lining up. Children who suffer from touch deprivation need more body contact.

Methods of sensory integration used by occupational therapists for tactile defensiveness include touching and rubbing skin surfaces, using lotions, and brushing skin surfaces.

Vestibular System   The *vestibular system* involves the inner ear and enables individuals to detect motion. The vestibular system allows children to know where their head is in space and how to handle gravity. Children with

Source: PEANUTS. Reprinted with permission of UFS, Inc.

vestibular disorders fall easily and do not know how to adjust their bodies for the position of their heads or for other body movements.

Therapy for vestibular disorders used by occupational therapists consists of exercises in body planning and balance. It includes activities such as spinning in chairs, swinging, and rolling on a large ball to stimulate the vestibular system.

Proprioceptive System The *proprioceptive system* involves stimulation from the muscles or within the body itself. Disorders in this system may involve *apraxia,* which is a difficulty in intentional performance of certain body movements. Children with an apraxia problem cannot plan how to move their bodies without bumping into walls, and they cannot direct movements, such as buttoning, tying, skipping, or writing.

Therapy for proprioceptive stimulation used by occupational therapists includes having the child use scooter boards and engage in other planned motor behaviors.

Assessing Motor Development

Tests for assessing motor development are listed in Table 7.5. Additional information on these tests appears in "Tests for Assessing Students With Learning Disabilities" in the Reference Guide at the back of this book.

PERCEPTION Learning does not suddenly begin when a child reaches age 5 or 6 and enters school. During the preschool years, children are earnestly and actively engaged in learning. During these early years, they master many preacademic skills and acquire a vast amount of knowledge, information, and abilities that are needed later for learning academic subjects (Kirk, 1987). In the preschool years children acquire skills in visual and auditory

TABLE 7.5

Tests for Assessing
Motor Development

- Bruinicks-Oseretsky Test of Motor Proficiency
- Peabody Developmental Motor Scales
- Southern California Test Battery for Assessment of Dysfunction (This battery consists of five tests: Southern California Kinesthesia and Tactile Perception Tests, Southern California Figure–Ground Visual Perception Test, Southern California Motor Accuracy Test, Southern California Perceptual–Motor Tests, and Ayres Space Test.)
- Test of Gross-Motor Development

perception, extend their facility to attend, expand memory and thinking skills, and learn to understand and use language.

Perception is the process of recognizing and interpreting sensory information. It is the intellect's ability to give meaning to sensory stimulation. For example, a *square* must be perceived as a whole configuration, not as four separate lines. Because perception is a learned skill, the teaching process can have a direct impact on the child's perceptual facility.

The concept of perception was one of the productive ideas of Gestalt psychology, which is a body of study that was influential in the early 1900s in Western Europe, particularly in Germany. (The word *gestalt* refers to the ability to grasp the wholeness of an experience.) A tenet of Gestalt psychology is that people have an innate inclination to organize information taken from the environment and to make sense of the world by bringing structure and organization to what they perceive.

Ideas from Gestalt psychology influenced the early development of the field of learning disabilities because many of the field's first scholars, such as Alfred Strauss, were trained in Gestalt theory. They recognized that perceptual disorders were a common characteristic of the children they examined and taught (Strauss & Lehtinen, 1947). The strong influence of the concept of perceptual disorders is evident in the federal definition of learning disabilities (i.e., IDEA–2004) within the phrase *disorder in one of the basic psychological processes.*

Several dimensions of perception have implications for understanding learning disabilities: (1) the perceptual modality concept, (2) overloading the perceptual systems, (3) auditory perception, (4) visual perception, and (5) tactile and kinesthetic perception.

Perceptual Modality Concept

The **perceptual modality concept** is based on the premise that children learn in different ways. Some learn best by listening (auditory), some by looking (visual), some by touching (tactile), and some by performing an action (kinesthetic). Adults, too, have individual learning styles. Some learn best by listening to an explanation; others know that to learn something they must read about it or watch it being done. Still others learn best by writing something down or by going through the action themselves. Some students with learning disabilities appear to have a much greater facility in using one perceptual or learning style over another. "LD Stories: Perceptual Problems" describes two children's perceptual problems.

Research on brain function, using brain imaging technologies (such as fMRIs), shows that different perceptual systems do exist in different areas within the brain. Sensitive teachers use information about a child's style of learning and perceptual strengths and weaknesses in teaching academic skills. For example, the child who has great difficulty with the auditory perception of the sounds in words (or a deficit in awareness of phonemes)

PERCEPTUAL PROBLEMS

Sandra: Auditory Perception Problems

Eight-year-old Sandra failed many tasks that involved auditory learning. She could not learn nursery rhymes, was unable to take messages correctly over the telephone, forgot spoken instructions, and could not discriminate between pairs of spoken words with minimal contrast or a single phoneme difference (*cat-cap*). She could not tap out the number of sounds in words and found phonics instruction baffling. Sandra was failing in reading, yet she had passed the reading readiness test with ease because it tested performance skills that required visual learning. At first, Sandra could not remember the arithmetic facts, but there was a sudden spurt in her arithmetic achievement during the second half of first grade. She explained that she solved her arithmetic problems by putting the classroom clock in her head. By *looking* at the minute marks on the clock to perform arithmetic tasks, Sandra did well with visual tasks, but poorly in auditory processing, particularly in recognizing sounds in words.

John: Visual Perception Problems

In contrast, John, at age 8, performed several years above his age level on tasks that required auditory processing. He had easily learned to say the alphabet in sequence. He also learned poems and nursery rhymes; remembered series of digits, phone numbers, and verbal instructions; and quickly learned to detect phonemes or sounds in words. Visual tasks, however, were difficult. John had much trouble putting puzzles together, seeing and remembering forms in designs, doing block arrangements, remembering the sequence and order of things he saw, and recalling what words looked like in print.

is likely to have difficulty learning phonics. Of course, the child will have to learn to decode words to acquire reading fluency. However, recognizing the child's auditory difficulties alerts the teacher to the child's area of difficulty and helps in teaching the child. The child may need additional practice in recognizing sounds in words.

Another important variable to consider is the child's culture and language background. Learning styles differ in various cultures, and the behavior of children will reflect these differences. Children whose first language is not English may have difficulty with auditory perception and recognizing the sounds or phonemes of the English language.

Overloading the Perceptual Systems

For a few children, the reception of information from one input system interferes with information coming from another. These children have a lower tolerance for receiving and integrating information from several input systems at the same time. An analogy might be made to an overloaded circuit that blows out when it cannot handle any more electrical energy. Unable to accept and process an excess of data, the perceptual system becomes overloaded. Symptoms include: (1) confusion, (2) poor recall, (3) retrogression, (4) refusal of the task, (5) poor attention, (6) temper tantrums, (7) seizures, or (8) "catastrophic responses."

If a child presents such symptoms, teachers should be cautious about using multisensory techniques and should change the method of instruction. One teacher reported that a second-grade girl with learning disabilities was not making progress when taught through simultaneous auditory and visual instruction. The teacher reduced the auditory input by not talking and instead taught reading and arithmetic through visual pictures and examples. The girl now could understand and made great strides in both reading and arithmetic.

Sometimes children learn by themselves to adapt their own behavior to avoid overloading. One boy avoided looking at an individual's face when he engaged in conversation. When asked about this behavior, the boy explained that he found he could not understand what was being said if he watched the speaker's face while listening. The visual stimuli, in effect, interfered with the boy's ability to comprehend auditory information.

Auditory Perception

Auditory perception, which is the ability to recognize or interpret what is heard, provides an important pathway for learning. Accumulating research shows that many poor readers have auditory, linguistic, and phonological difficulties (Lyon, 1998; Stahl & Murray, 1994). These children do not have a problem in hearing or in auditory acuity. Rather, they have difficulty with auditory perception. Because abilities in auditory perception normally develop during the early years, many academic teachers mistakenly presume that all students have acquired these skills. Auditory subskills include: (1) phonological awareness, (2) auditory discrimination, (3) auditory memory, (4) auditory sequencing, and (5) auditory blending.

Phonological Awareness   A necessary ability for learning to read is the ability to recognize that the words we hear are composed of individual sounds within the word. This ability is called **phonological awareness.** For example, when an individual hears the word *cat,* the ear hears it as one pulse of sound. But the individual who has acquired phonological awareness knows that the word *cat* is made up of three sounds (or *phonemes*): /c/a/t/. The child who lacks phonological awareness does not recognize that *cat* has three separate sounds.

Children who have trouble learning to read are often completely unaware of how language is put together. They are unable to recognize or isolate the sounds of words or the number of sounds in a word. For example, when hearing the word *kite,* they cannot tap out three sounds. These children also cannot recognize similarities in words. They have difficulty recognizing words that rhyme (e.g., *right, fight,* and *night*) and alliteration in words (e.g., *cat* and *cap*). As a result, these children cannot understand or use the alphabetic principle needed for learning phonics and decoding words.

Skills in phonological awareness abilities are formed during the preschool years. It is very important to assess these abilities before children are taught to read and to provide training for children who have not acquired phonological abilities. Fortunately, research shows that young children can develop phonological awareness through specific instruction and that such teaching has a positive effect on reading achievement (Ball & Blachman, 1991; Bradley, 1988; Lerner, 1990; Liberman & Liberman, 1990; Stahl & Murray, 1994; Williams, 1991). Phonological awareness as it relates to reading is also discussed in the chapters on oral language and reading. An informal test of phonological awareness is shown in the chapter on oral language.

Auditory Discrimination   **Auditory discrimination** is the ability to recognize a difference between phoneme sounds and to identify words that are the same and words that are different when the difference is a single phoneme element. In testing for this problem, the student is faced away from the examiner (so there will be no visual cue of watching the speaker's mouth) and then asked whether a pair of words are the same or different. The two words (e.g., *mitt-mat* or *big-pig*) have a minimal sound difference or contrast of a single phoneme.

Auditory Memory   *Auditory memory* is the ability to store and recall what one has heard. For example, the student could be asked to do three activities, such as close the window, open the door, and place the book on the desk. Is the student able to store and retrieve through listening to such directions?

Auditory Sequencing   *Auditory sequencing* is the ability to remember the order of items in a sequential list. For example, the alphabet, numbers, and the months of the year are learned as auditory sequences.

Auditory Blending   **Auditory blending** is the ability to blend single phonic elements or phonemes into a complete word. Many students have difficulty blending (e.g., the phonemes *m-a-n* to form the word *man*).

Tests of Auditory Perception   Some formal tests of auditory perception are listed in this chapter (refer to Table 7.6) and they are described in "Tests for Assessing Students With Learning Disabilities" in the Reference Guide at the back of this book.

Visual Perception

Visual perception, which is the identification, organization, and interpretation of sensory data received by the individual through the eye, plays a significant role in school learning, particularly in reading. Students have difficulty in tasks requiring the visual discrimination of letters and words, as well as of numbers, geometric designs, and pictures. Within the broad scope of visual perception, several subareas of skills can be identified.

Visual Discrimination   **Visual discrimination** refers to the ability to differentiate one object from another. In a preschool readiness test, for example, the child may be asked to find the rabbit with one ear in a row of rabbits with two ears. Or, when asked to distinguish visually between the letters *m* and *n,* the child must perceive the number of humps in each letter. The skill of matching identical letters, words, numbers, pictures, designs, and shapes is another visual discrimination task. Objects may be discriminated by color, shape, pattern, size, position, or brightness. The ability to discriminate letters and words visually becomes essential in learning to read. Children who can recognize letters when they are preschoolers do better in reading.

Figure–Ground Discrimination   *Figure–ground discrimination* refers to the ability to distinguish an object from its surrounding background. The student with a deficit in this area cannot focus on the item in question apart from the visual background. Consequently, the student is distracted by irrelevant stimuli.

Visual Closure   *Visual closure* is a task that requires the individual to recognize or identify an object even though the total stimulus is not presented. For example, a competent reader is able to read a line of print when the top half of the print is covered. There are enough letter clues in the remaining portion for the reader to provide visual closure to read the line.

Letter Recognition   The ability to recognize objects includes recognition of alphabetic letters, numbers, words, geometric shapes (e.g., a square), and entities (e.g., a cat, a face, or a toy). The kindergartner's ability to recognize letters, numbers, and geometric patterns is a dependable predictor of reading achievement (Richek et al., 2002).

Several examples of visual perception tasks used in tests or lessons are shown in Figure 7.3.

Visual Perception and Reversals   There is an important difference between the perceptual world of *objects* and the perceptual world of *letters* and *words.* During the prereading stage of development, children make a perceptual generalization that an object retains the same name or meaning regardless of the position it happens to be in, the direction it faces, or the modification of slight additions or subtractions. A chair, for example, is a chair regardless of whether it faces left or right, back or front, upside down or right side up. Whether it is upholstered, has additional cushions, or even has a leg missing, it is still called a *chair.* The child makes similar

FIGURE 7.3

Examples of Visual
Perception Tasks

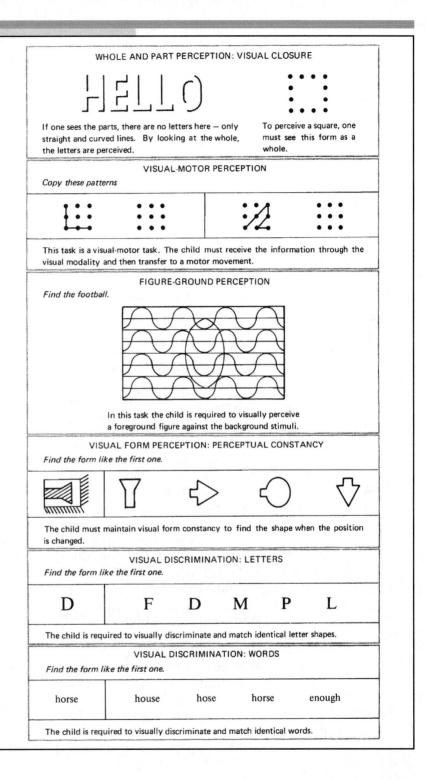

WHOLE AND PART PERCEPTION: VISUAL CLOSURE

If one sees the parts, there are no letters here — only straight and curved lines. By looking at the whole, the letters are perceived.

To perceive a square, one must see this form as a whole.

VISUAL-MOTOR PERCEPTION

Copy these patterns

This task is a visual-motor task. The child must receive the information through the visual modality and then transfer to a motor movement.

FIGURE-GROUND PERCEPTION

Find the football.

In this task the child is required to visually perceive a foreground figure against the background stimuli.

VISUAL FORM PERCEPTION: PERCEPTUAL CONSTANCY

Find the form like the first one.

The child must maintain visual form constancy to find the shape when the position is changed.

VISUAL DISCRIMINATION: LETTERS

Find the form like the first one.

| D | F | D | M | P | L |

The child is required to visually discriminate and match identical letter shapes.

VISUAL DISCRIMINATION: WORDS

Find the form like the first one.

| horse | house | hose | horse | enough |

The child is required to visually discriminate and match identical words.

generalizations about dogs; no matter what its position, size, color, or quantity of hair, a dog is still called a *dog.*

When beginning to deal with letters and words, however, the child finds that this perceptual generalization no longer holds true. The placement of a circle on a stick from left to right or top to bottom changes the name of the letter from *b* to *d* or to *p* or *q.* The addition of a small line changes *c* to *e.* The direction the word is facing changes it from *was* to *saw,* from *no* to *on,* and from *top* to *pot.*

Some students with learning disabilities fail to make the necessary amendments to earlier perceptual generalizations they have formulated. One incident of such confusion happened during a teachers' strike. A boy with this type of difficulty looked at the picket signs and asked why the teachers were picketing if the strike had been called off. The sign was lettered *ON STRIKE,* but the boy read it as *NO STRIKE.* In another such example, a student reversed the letters when making a Christmas card. He printed *LEON* instead of *NOEL.*

Tactile and Kinesthetic Perception

The tactile and kinesthetic systems are two perceptual systems for receiving information. The term *haptic* is sometimes used to refer to both systems.

Tactile Perception   **Tactile perception** is obtained through the sense of touch via the fingers and skin surfaces. The ability to recognize an object by touching it, to identify a numeral that is drawn on one's back or arm, to discriminate between smooth and rough surfaces, and to identify which finger is being touched are all examples of tactile perception.

Kinesthetic Perception   **Kinesthetic perception** is obtained through body movements and muscle feeling. The awareness of positions taken by different parts of the body and bodily feelings of muscular contraction, tension, and relaxation are examples of kinesthetic perception.

The tactile and kinesthetic systems are important sources of information about object qualities, body movement, and their interrelationships. Most school tasks, as well as most acts in everyday life, require both touch and body movement. Tactile and kinesthetic perception play important roles in learning.

Assessing Perceptual Development

Tests of perception are listed in Table 7.6. Additional information on these tests appears in "Tests for Assessing Students With Learning Disabilities" in the Reference Guide at the back of this book.

ASSESSING YOUNG CHILDREN   A major trend in assessment practices today is to use informal, functional assessment measures instead of relying solely on formal standardized tests and testing procedures. There is more authentic assessment and obser-

TABLE 7.6 Tests for Assessing Perceptual Development	**Auditory perception**

Auditory perception

- Detroit Tests of Learning Aptitude—Primary—2
- Detroit Tests of Learning Aptitude—4 (reversed letters, word sequences)
- Goldman-Fristoe-Woodcock Auditory Skills Test Battery
- Goldman-Fristoe-Woodcock Test of Auditory Discrimination
- Illinois Test of Psycholinguistic Abilities (ITPA–3; auditory sequential memory, sound blending, and auditory closure)
- Test of Auditory Skills Analysis
- Wepman Test of Auditory Discrimination

Visual perception

- Bender-Gestalt Test
- Detroit Tests of Learning Aptitude—Primary—2
- Detroit Tests of Learning Aptitude—4 (design sequences, design reproduction, picture fragments)
- Developmental Test of Visual–Motor Integration
- Developmental Test of Visual Perception
- Frostig Developmental Test of Visual Perception
- Illinois Test of Psycholinguistic Abilities (ITPA–3; visual reception, visual association, visual closure, and visual sequential memory)
- Motor-Free Test of Visual Perception
- Test of Visual–Motor Integration
- Visual Retention Test—Revised

Tactile and kinesthetic perception

- Southern California Kinesthesia and Tactile Perception Tests

 vation of the child in a natural environment (Lerner et al., 2003). The website **http://www.ldonline.org/ld_indepth/assessment/assess-nichcy.html** provides an overview for the assessment of a disability.

Phases of Early Identification and Assessment

As Figure 7.4 shows, there are four separate but related phases of identification and assessment of preschoolers with disabilities: (1) child-find, (2) screening, (3) diagnosing, and (4) evaluating (Lerner et al., 2003). Many different tests and assessment procedures can be used during each of these phases.

FIGURE 7.4

Stages of the Assessment Process for Young Children With Disabilities

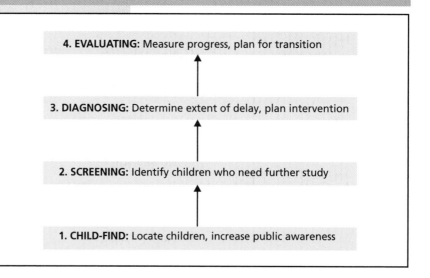

4. **EVALUATING:** Measure progress, plan for transition

3. **DIAGNOSING:** Determine extent of delay, plan intervention

2. **SCREENING:** Identify children who need further study

1. **CHILD-FIND:** Locate children, increase public awareness

Child-Find   This first phase, **child-find,** refers to ways of finding young children with disabilities in the community. Emphasis is on making initial contact and increasing the public's awareness of services. Preschool children are not usually in the public school system, and communities must therefore make a concerted effort to seek them out. Communities develop methods, such as radio announcements, posters, signs in day-care centers and libraries, and local newspaper articles to alert families of young children.

Screening   This second phase, **screening,** attempts to identify children who need further study. Emphasis is on ways of quickly surveying many children to identify those who *may* need special services. School districts often encourage families to bring *all* 3- through 5-year-old children in for free evaluation services, even if the family does not suspect a disability. The screening is a short, low-cost assessment of children's vision and hearing, speech and language, motor skills, self-help skills, social–emotional maturity, and cognitive development.

Many school systems use screening interviews or questionnaires with the parents of all incoming kindergarten children. Questions are designed to detect those children who are likely to have learning difficulty. The hope is that early detection of high-risk cases will permit plans to be made to help prevent the development of learning disabilities. Table 2.5 in the chapter on assessment provides some questions that might be used in such a screening interview.

Diagnosing   The third phase, diagnosing, consists of determining the extent of **developmental delay** and devising an intervention program. The emphasis is on methods of comprehensively examining a child through formal and authentic measures to determine whether the child's problems warrant special education services. A multidisciplinary team determines the nature of the problem, its severity, and the intervention and placement that the child needs.

Evaluating   The fourth phase, evaluating, concentrates on measuring progress, judging whether a child should remain in a special education program, and planning for transition. This stage of the assessment helps determine whether the child still needs special education services, what skills the child has learned and still lacks, and what new placement will be needed.

Areas of Assessment

To evaluate a child's developmental delay, the assessment typically includes an evaluation of cognitive, motor, communication, social–emotional, and adaptive development (Bagnoto, Neisworth, & Munson, 1997; Lerner et al., 2003).

Cognitive Development   This evaluation includes the assessment of the child's abilities in thinking, planning, and concept development. Examples of cognitive tasks are identifying colors; naming parts of the body; rote counting (up to 10 or so); showing an understanding of one-to-one correspondence ("Show me three blocks"); demonstrating place concepts (on, under, corner, between, middle); identifying given concepts (round, bigger); naming letters; or sorting chips by color, size, and shape.

Motor Development   This category includes the child's overall physical development, gross-motor skills, and fine-motor development. Examples of tasks the child is asked to perform include catching a ball or bean bag, jumping, hopping, skipping, building a four-block design, touching fingers (copying the tester's demonstration by consecutively touching each finger on one hand to the thumb of the same hand and then repeating the task on the other hand), cutting various patterns with scissors, matching and copying shapes and letter formations, and writing one's own name. The child's visual and auditory acuity are also often assessed.

Communication Development   This evaluation includes speech and language skills and the abilities to understand and use language. Testers might assess articulation by having children say certain words. They can be asked to repeat numbers and sentences spoken by the tester; to describe pictures; to answer problem-solving questions; or to state their first and last names, gender, age, address, and phone number. An auditory test—for example, that has children copy a series of clapping patterns—may also be included.

Social and Emotional Development The child's social and affective interactions are recorded through observational notes made by the testers. Typical observations include how well the child relates to adults and to other children.

Adaptive Development This category refers to the child's self-help skills. It includes such areas as independent toileting skills, dressing skills, eating skills, and the ability to separate from parents.

Problems Related to Early Identification

The assessment process for young children has some flaws. Many instruments used in early intervention programs fail to demonstrate adequate reliability and test validity, and many have not been subjected to the evaluation procedures required to determine whether a test is psychometrically sound (Meisels & Fenichel, 1996; Wolery & Bailey, 2003). During a screening program in which many children are being tested, errors in judgment are often made, as are errors in the testing procedures and in scoring. Children can be either falsely identified or missed, as illustrated in "LD Stories: Errors in Testing and Identification."

LD STORIES

ERRORS IN TESTING AND IDENTIFICATION

The following example illustrates how test errors can occur and how faulty diagnoses and judgments are made. The parents of a 4-year-old boy were called to a staffing, where a school representative told them that their child performed significantly below the norm on all measures during the district's preschool screening. The parents were informed that mental retardation was suspected, and placement in a special school was recommended. A friend, who was a teacher, accompanied the parents to the staffing and asked to see the test. Upon "eyeballing" the front page of the test, the teacher noted that the child performed either at or above age level on all areas of the test, suggesting that the diagnosis of mental retardation was questionable. Further, the test indicated that the child did not recognize letters and could not count, whereas the child was actually able to do both quite well. When questioned about the scoring and interpretation of the test results, the school representative conducting the staffing explained that she was unfamiliar with the test and that her responsibility was to report to the parents and make placements. As this example illustrates, errors in evaluation and diagnosis do occur, and data should be carefully checked and monitored before any conclusions are drawn.

Philosophy of the Early Childhood Curriculum for Young Children With Special Needs

The philosophy underlying the curriculum for young children with special needs considers the following (Lerner et al., 2003):

- *Content.* It should foster the development of the child and encourage self-directed learning and positive relationships.
- *Child's stage of development.* The curriculum and stage of design should be appropriate for the child's stage of development.
- *Intervention strategies.* The methods should be effective for teaching young children with special needs.
- *Social relationships.* Activities should nourish social relationships and encourage social interactions with other children and adults.

Division for Early Childhood Recommended Practices

The professional organization for early childhood special education is the Division for Early Childhood (DEC), which is a component of the Council of Exceptional Children. The website for the Division of Early Childhood of the Council of Exceptional Children is **http://www.dec-sped.org.** DEC has proposed the following recommended practices for early childhood special education:

- *The right of all children to be included in natural settings.* This means that teaching should occur within the context of daily routines in natural environments.
- *The importance of individualization.* The teaching should meet the individual needs of each child.
- *The assessment procedures should be informal and in natural environments.* The use of standardized assessment tests should be de-emphasized.
- *The assessment and curriculum should be integrated.* Testing and teaching should not be isolated, they should be combined.
- *Encourage child-initiated activities.* A child-centered approach to teaching young children with special needs is encouraged.
- *Use active engagement to learn independent functioning.* In activity-based instruction, the teacher follows the child's lead to discover the child's interests, motivation, and choice of activities.

Head Start Programs

Head Start was first launched in 1964 under the administration of President Lyndon Johnson, within the Office of Economic Opportunity, and

Learning activities and materials should be concrete, real, and relevant to the lives of young children. (© *Elizabeth Crews/Stock Boston*)

it is now administered by the Administration for Children and Families. **Head Start** was intended to provide preschool education to the nation's low-income children ages 4 and 5 and to offer early educational experiences to low-income children who might otherwise come to school unprepared and unmotivated to learn. Head Start has become one of the most influential and massive federal social experiments in the history of early childhood education. In 1972, Head Start legislation was amended to include children with disabilities, reserving 10% of its total enrollment for children with disabilities.

Head Start created a fortuitous opportunity to investigate the impact of early intervention. Several heartening longitudinal studies followed up with children in Head Start programs in later life. The research showed impressive long-term effects of early intervention for environmentally at-risk children. Individuals who had participated in Head Start were evaluated some 15 years later (Lazar & Darlington, 1982). The study followed up on 820 Head Start participants, comparing them with a group of children who did not have the Head Start experience. The results demonstrate that the Head Start program was very successful. Head Start participants were less likely to be placed in special education classes, were less likely to be retained and required to repeat a grade, consistently scored higher on intelligence tests, and were more likely to finish high school by the age of 18. The research showed that early intervention prevents school failure and reduces the need for remedial programs (Head Start Bureau, 1993). In addition to education,

Head Start offers services for health, parental involvement, and social services (Administration for Children and Families, 2001).

The Head Start studies and other early intervention research demonstrates the benefits of early intervention. In terms of cost–benefit analysis, society has gotten its money back with interest. On the completion of schooling, students who received early intervention are more likely to be gainfully employed—to be taxpayers rather than tax receivers—and to be citizens who contribute to society.

Using Computer Technology

For young children with learning disabilities, the computer offers many opportunities to explore, play, and learn. The experiences become an integral part of their overall development. The computer bestows a unique magic on children who have special needs by empowering them with a sense of independence and control. The value of the computer may be greater for exceptional youngsters than for others in the population. It is widely acknowledged that computers enable ordinary people to do extraordinary things. But for the child who has special needs, the computer does even more. It enables extraordinary people to do ordinary things.

Computers can help young children develop independence, self-help skills, motor control, visual and auditory concepts, language skills, cognitive skills, and other precursor skills. With the computer, young children with disabilities are able to control their environment and to make decisions. Even social skills can be encouraged through cooperative computer activities. Computer activities can help families and teachers meet IEP and IFSP goals (Raskind, Higgins, Slaff, & Shaw, 1998c). "LD Stories: Using

LD STORIES

USING A COMPUTER WITH A PRESCHOOL CHILD

Twenty-month-old Julia was delighted when she found that the computer allowed her to control her environment by letting her make and implement decisions and practice some newly acquired computer words: *more, all gone, orange,* and *broke.*

By age 3, Julia was playing with the alphabet games on the Muppet Learning Keys and with the Sticky Bear Shapes program. During lunch one day, she displayed her generalizations derived from computer learning. Holding up her diagonally cut half of a peanut butter-and-jelly sandwich, she said, "triangle." Then she took two bites from the sandwich from the diagonal side, looked at it, and announced, "walrus" (the picture identification for *W* on the software program).

a Computer With a Preschool Child" presents a preschooler learning by using a computer.

The computer can creatively present colors; distinguish differences, such as *larger* and *smaller;* illustrate concepts, such as *above* and *below;* and help with shape and letter recognition, counting, matching, and sequencing.

Adaptive peripherals are particularly useful with young children. Speech synthesizers allow the computer to talk to the child. Switches can be plugged into the computer, allowing the child to use the computer without the keyboard. Alternative keyboards such as the Muppet Learning Keys, Power Pad, and Intellikeys are especially useful with young children. With the Touch Window, the child can directly touch the screen to control the computer. Most important, young children with disabilities like using the computer. It is an enjoyable, motivating way of learning.

Table 7.7 offers some recommended software for preschool children with learning disabilities (Forgan, 1996). The software programs are divided into the categories of: (1) early learning, (2) exploration, (3) communication, (4) beginning users, (5) emergent literacy, and (6) keyboarding skills.

TABLE 7.7

Computer Software for Young Children With Learning Disabilities

Program name	Publisher
Early learning	
Putt-Putt Joins the Parade	Humongous
Putt-Putt Goes to the Moon	Humongous
The Tree House	Broderbund
Millie's Math House	Edmark
Trudy's Time and Play House	Edmark
Berenstain Bears Get in a Fight	Broderbund
Exploration	
Just Grandma and Me	Living Books
The Playroom	Broderbund
Little Monster at School	Broderbund
Sammy's Science House	Edmark
Thinking Things Collections I	Edmark
In Grandma's Attic	Soft Key
Communication	
Exploring First Words	Laureate
Exploring First Words II	Laureate
Let's Go to the Moon	Laureate
Beginning users	
Adventures of Quinn	Edmark
Cause/Effects	Judy Lynn Software
Children's Switch Progressions	J. J. Cooper
Clowns	Colorado Easter Seal Society
Creative Chorus	Laureate
Dino-Maze	Academic Skillbuilders

Program name	Publisher
Beginning users *(continued)*	
Early and Advanced Switch Games	R. J. Cooper
Early Concepts Skillbuilders	Edmark
Fundamental Concepts	Judy Lynn Software
Katie's Farm	Lawrence Productions
McGee	Lawrence Productions
Mickey's Colors and Shapes	Disney Software
New Cause and Effects	Colorado Easter Seal Society
Noises	Colorado Easter Seal Society
Old MacDonald II	UCLA Intervention Program
Peek-a-Book on Fundamental Concepts	Judy Lynn Software
This Is the Way We Wash Our Face	UCLA Intervention Software
Where's Puff?	UCLA Intervention Software
Emergent literacy	
New Kid on the Block	Living Books
Harry and the Haunted House	Living Books
Dr. Seuss's ABC CD	Broderbund
Sesame Street Letters	EA*Kids
Kid Works 2	Davidson
Bailey's Book House	Edmark
K. C. & Clyde	Don Johnston
Keyboarding skills	
Kids Keys	Davidson
Stickybear Typing	Optimum Resources
Mavis Beacon Teaches Typing	Mindspace
Dinosoft Typing Tutor	Maverick

EARLY INTERVENTION STRATEGIES

In this section, we describe representative activities for teaching young children with learning difficulties. The activities include: (1) motor development activities, (2) auditory processing, (3) visual processing, and (4) tactile and kinesthetic processing.

Motor Development Activities

Motor development activities are a particularly useful part of the early childhood curriculum. The teaching strategies in this section are subdivided into three target areas: (1) gross-motor activities, (2) fine-motor activities, and (3) body awareness activities.

Gross-Motor Activities   Gross-motor activities involve the ability to move various parts of the body. The purpose of these activities is to develop smoother, more effective body movements and to increase the child's sense of spatial orientation and body consciousness. Gross-motor activities are grouped as: (1) walking activities, (2) throwing and catching activities, and (3) other gross-motor activities.

Walking Activities

1. *Forward, backward, and sideways walk.*   Children walk to a target goal on a straight or curved path marked on the floor. The path may be wide or narrow, but the narrower the path, the more difficult the task. A single line requiring tandem walking (heel-to-toe) is more difficult than a widely spaced walk. A slow pace is more difficult than a running pace. Walking without shoes and socks is more difficult than walking with shoes. Students walk through the same course backward and sideways. In variations, children walk with arms in different positions, carrying objects, dropping objects such as balls into containers along the way, or focusing eyes on various parts of the room.

2. *Stepping-stones.*   Put objects on the floor for stepping-stones, identifying placements for right foot and left foot by colors or by the letters *R* and *L*. The student is to follow the course by placing the correct foot on each stepping-stone.

3. *Box game.*   The student has two boxes (the size of shoe boxes), one behind and one in front. The student steps into the front box with both feet, moves the rear box to the front, and then steps into that. The student can use either hand to move the boxes and can use alternating feet. The student should be moving toward a finish line.

4. *Line walks.*   Draw lines in colors on the floor. Lines can be curved, angular, or spiral. Place a rope on the floor and have the students walk along the side of the rope. A variation is to place a ladder flat on the ground. Students walk between the rungs, forward and backward, and then hop through the rungs.

Throwing and Catching Activities

1. *Throwing.*   Balloons, wet sponges, beanbags, yarn balls, and rubber balls of various sizes can be used to throw objects at targets, to the teacher, or to one another.

2. *Catching.* Catching is a more difficult skill than throwing. Students can practice catching the previously mentioned objects thrown by the teacher or by other students.

3. *Ball games.* Various types of ball games help develop motor coordination. Examples include balloon volleyball or rolling-ball games, bouncing balls on the ground, and throwing balls against the wall.

4. *Rag ball.* If children find that throwing and catching a rubber ball is too difficult, a rag ball can be used. Rag balls are made by covering rags or discarded nylon hosiery with cloth.

Other Gross-Motor Activities

1. *Balance beam.* The balance beam is commonly used in the early childhood curriculum. Each end of the board is fitted into a bracket that serves as a brace and prevents the board from tipping over. The board can be set flat with the wide surface up or set on its edge with the narrow surface up.

2. *Skateboard.* The child rides a skateboard lying on the stomach, kneeling, or standing; the surface can be flat or can slope downhill.

3. *Jumping jacks.* Children jump, putting feet wide apart, while clapping the hands above the head. To vary this activity, the children can make quarter turns, half turns, and full turns or jump to the left, right, forward, or back.

4. *Hopping.* Children hop on one foot at a time and alternate feet while hopping. Use rhythmical patterns: left, left, right, right; or left, left, right; or right, right, left.

5. *Bouncing.* Children bounce on a trampoline or on a large truck tire tube.

6. *Skipping.* A difficult activity for children with poor motor coordination, skipping combines rhythm, balance, body movement, and coordination. Many children need help to learn to skip.

7. *Rope skills.* A length of rope can be used in a variety of exercises. Have the child put the rope around designated parts of the body, such as knees, ankles, and hips to teach body image. Have the child follow directions to put the rope around chairs, under a table, or through a lampshade; to jump back and forth or sideways over the rope; or to make shapes, letters, or numbers with the rope.

Fine-Motor Activities The following activities give young children experiences with fine-motor activities.

1. *Tracing.* Students trace lines, pictures, designs, letters, or numbers on tracing paper, plastic, or stencils. Use directional arrows, color cues, and numbers to help children trace the figures.

2. *Water control.* Children carry and pour water into measured buckets from pitchers to specified levels. Smaller amounts and finer measurements make the task more difficult. Coloring the water makes the activity more interesting.

3. *Cutting with scissors.* Choose cutting activities that are appropriate for the child's developmental level. The easiest activity is cutting straight lines marked near the edge of the paper. A more difficult activity is cutting a straight line across the center of the paper. A piece of cardboard attached to the paper helps guide the scissors. Children can cut out marked geometric shapes, such as squares, rectangles, and triangles. By drawing lines in different colors, the teacher can indicate changes of direction in cutting. Children can cut out curving lines and circles, then pictures, and finally patterns made with dots and faint lines.

4. *Stencils or templates.* Children draw outlines of geometric shapes. Templates can be made from cardboard, wood, plastic, or foam containers. Two styles of templates are (1) a solid shape and (2) frames with the shape cut out.

5. *Lacing.* A piece of cardboard punched with holes or a pegboard can be used for this activity. A design or picture is made on the board, and then the student follows the pattern by weaving or sewing through the holes with a heavy shoelace, yarn, or cord.

6. *Paper-and-pencil activities.* Coloring books, readiness books, dot-to-dot books, and kindergarten books frequently provide good paper-and-pencil activities to practice fine-motor and eye–hand development.

7. *Clipping clothespins.* Clothespins can be clipped to a line or to a box. The child can be timed in this activity by counting the number of clothespins clipped in a specified time.

8. *Copying designs.* The child looks at a geometric design and copies it on paper.

Body Awareness Activities   The purpose of these activities is to help children develop accurate images of the location and function of the parts of the body.

1. *Pointing to body parts.* Children point to the various parts of the body: nose, right elbow, left ankle, and so forth. This activity is more difficult with the eyes closed. The child can also lie on the floor and be asked to touch various parts of the body. This activity is more difficult if performed to a rhythmic pattern—using a metronome, for example. As a variation, make a robot from cardboard that is held together at the joints with fasteners and can be moved into various positions. The child can move the limbs of the robot on command and match the positions with his or her own body movements.

2. *"Simon says."* This game can be played with the eyes open or closed.

3. *Life-size drawing.* Children lie on a large sheet of paper, and the teacher traces an outline around them. Next, the children fill in and color the clothes and the details of the face and body.

4. *Games.* Games such as "Lobby Loo," "Hokey-Pokey," and "Did You Ever See a Lassie?" help develop concepts of left, right, and body image.

5. *Following instructions.* Instruct the child to put the left hand on the right ear and the right hand on the left shoulder. Other instructions might be to put the right hand in front of the left hand or to turn right, walk two steps, and turn left.

6. *Twister.* Make rows of colored circles on the floor, an oilcloth, or a plastic sheet, or use the commercial game. Make cards instructing the student to put the left foot on the green circle, the right foot on the red circle, and so on.

7. *Water activities.* Gross-motor movements in a pool or lake allow some freedom from the force of gravity. Some activities are easier to learn in the water because it affords greater control, and activities can be done at a slower pace. Swimming is also an excellent activity to strengthen general motor functioning.

Auditory Processing

Many children with learning disabilities need specific instruction to acquire auditory processing skills. Considered in this section are phonological awareness, listening to sounds, auditory discrimination, and auditory memory.

Phonological Awareness For success at the beginning stages of reading, the child must hear the individual sounds (phonemes) in words and in language. The child must be aware of the fact that the words we hear comprise individual sounds within the words.

Listening to Sounds

1. *Listening for sounds.* Children close their eyes and listen to environmental sounds—for example, sounds of cars, airplanes, animals, and other outside sounds; and sounds in the next room. Recorded sounds of planes, trains, animals, and bells can be played back to the students, who are then asked to identify them.

2. *Sounds made by the teacher.* Children close their eyes and identify sounds that the teacher makes. Examples of such sounds include dropping a pencil, tearing a piece of paper, using a stapler, bouncing a ball, sharpening a pencil, tapping on a glass, opening a window, snapping

the lights, leafing through a book, cutting with scissors, opening a drawer, jingling money, or writing on a blackboard.

3. *Food sounds.*   Ask the children to listen for the kind of food that is being eaten, cut, or sliced—such as celery, apples, or carrots.

4. *Shaking sounds.*   Place small, hard items, such as stones, beans, chalk, salt, sand, or rice into containers with covers. Have the children identify the contents by shaking the containers and listening.

5. *Listening for sound patterns.*   Have the children close their eyes or sit facing away from the teacher. Clap hands, play a drum, or bounce a ball. Rhythmic patterns can be made—for example, slow, fast, fast. Ask students how many counts there were, or ask them to repeat the patterns. As a variation on the previous suggestion, use a cup and a book, for example, to tap out sound patterns.

Auditory Discrimination

1. *Near or far.*   With eyes closed, the students judge from what part of the room a sound is coming and whether it is near or far.

2. *Loud or soft.*   The students learn to judge and to discriminate between loud and soft sounds that the teacher produces.

3. *High and low.*   Students learn to judge and to discriminate between high and low sounds that the teacher produces.

4. *Find the sound.*   One student hides a music box or a ticking clock, and the other students try to find it by locating the sound.

Auditory Memory

1. *Do this.*   Place five or six objects in front of the student and give the student a series of directions to follow. For example, "Put the green block in Jean's lap, place the yellow flower under John's chair, and put the orange ball into Joe's desk." The list can be increased as the student improves in auditory memory.

2. *Following directions.*   Give the student several simple tasks to perform. For example, "Draw a big red square on your paper, put a small green circle underneath the square, and draw a black line from the middle of the circle to the upper right-hand corner of the square." Such activities can be tape recorded for use with earphones at a listening center.

3. *Nursery rhymes.*   Have children learn nursery rhymes and poems and play finger games.

4. *Television programs.*   Ask students to watch a television program and remember certain things. For example, "Watch *The Wizard of Oz* tonight and tomorrow tell me all the different lands that Dorothy visited."

5. *Going to the moon.*   Update the game of "Grandmother's Trunk" or "Going to New York." Say, "I took a trip to the moon and took my spacesuit." The student repeats the statement, but adds one item, for example, "helmet." Pictures may be used to help with auditory memory.

Visual Processing

Abilities in visual perception are necessary for academic learning. Children who can read letters and numbers, copy geometric patterns, and match printed words tend to do well in first-grade reading.

Visual Perception

1. *Pegboard designs.*   Using colored pegs, students reproduce colored visual geometric patterns on a pegboard from a visual model made by the teacher or shown on a printed page.

2. *Blocks.*   Children reproduce models using parquetry blocks. Have children use wood or plastic blocks that are all one color or have faces of different colors to match geometric shapes and have them build copies of models.

3. *Finding shapes in pictures.*   Children are asked to find all the round objects or designs in a picture, then all the square objects, and so forth.

4. *Puzzles.*   Students assemble puzzles that are made by the teacher or commercially. Subjects such as people, animals, forms, numbers, or letters can be cut into pieces to show functional parts.

5. *Classification.*   Students group or classify objects by shapes, sizes, and colors. The objects can be placed in a box or bowl. They can be chips, coins, buttons, beans, and so on.

6. *Matching geometric shapes.*   Place shapes on cards and have the students play games requiring the matching of these shapes. Collect jars of different sizes with lids, mix the lids, and have students match the lids with the jars. Make a domino-type game by making sets of cards decorated with sandpaper, felt, self-adhesive covering, or painted dots; have students match the cards with one another.

7. *Playing cards.*   A deck of playing cards provides excellent teaching material to match suits, pictures, numbers, and sets.

8. *Letters and numbers.*   Visual perception and discrimination of letters are important reading readiness skills. Games that provide opportunities to match, sort, or name shapes can be adapted to letters and numbers. Bingo cards can be made with letters. As letters are called, the student recognizes and covers up the letters.

Visual Memory

1. *Identifying missing objects.* Expose a collection of objects. Cover and remove one of the objects. Show the collection again, asking the student to identify the missing object.

2. *Ordering from memory.* Expose a short series of shapes, designs, or objects. Have the student place another set of these designs in the identical order from memory. Playing cards, colored blocks, blocks with designs, or mahjongg tiles are among the materials that might be used for such an activity. Show a toy, number, letter, or word for a brief time and then have the child recall it.

3. *Stories from pictures.* On a flannel board, place pictures of activities that tell a story. Remove the pictures and have the pupil tell the story by depending on visual memory of the pictures.

Tactile and Kinesthetic Processing

For children who do not learn easily through the visual or auditory systems, tactile and kinesthetic perception provides a way to strengthen learning. The following activities stimulate tactile and kinesthetic perception.

1. *Feeling various textures.* Children feel various textures, such as smooth wood, metal, sandpaper, felt, flocking, sponge, wet surfaces, and foods. Attach different materials to small pieces of wood. The student touches the boards without looking and learns to discriminate and match the various surfaces.

2. *Feeling shapes.* Place various textures that are cut into geometric patterns or letters on boards. Children can touch them and discriminate, match, and identify the shapes. The shapes can also be made of plastic, wood, cardboard, clay, or the like.

3. *Feeling weights.* Fill small cardboard spice containers to different levels with beans, rice, and so on. Have the child match weights through shaking and sensing the weights.

STRATEGIES FOR PRESCHOOL INCLUSION

As noted earlier, the most frequent placement for young children with special needs is in an inclusion education setting in the general education preschool classroom. This means that the early childhood teacher must plan for early childhood students without special needs and early childhood students with special needs. "LD in Practice: Strategies for Children With Special Needs in the General Education Preschool Classroom" offers some suggested strategies.

LD IN PRACTICE

STRATEGIES FOR CHILDREN WITH SPECIAL NEEDS IN THE GENERAL EDUCATION PRESCHOOL CLASSROOM

- The early childhood general education teacher and the special education teacher should work together in planning the curriculum for all children in the preschool class.
- Young children with special needs and young children without special needs should share a common curriculum.
- Make adaptations for diverse learning styles and abilities.
- Use both child-initiated activities and teacher-initiated activities.
- Play experiences should foster active engagement and interaction of all children.
- Activities should be appropriate for each child's stage of development.
- Activities should nourish social relationships for all children.
- Use activities that promote communication among children.
- Consider the cultural and linguistic diversity of all children.

CHAPTER SUMMARY

1. The early preschool years are critical to a child's development. Early identification and intervention for young children with disabilities are two successful means to avert or reduce later failure.

2. The Individual with Disabilities Education Improvement Act (IDEA–2004) incorporates provisions for preschool children with disabilities (ages 3 through 5) and also for infants and toddlers with disabilities (ages birth through 2).

3. Developmental indicators of problems are early signs of disabilities in preschool children.

4. Many young children are clumsy in their motor skills. Motor learning is a developmental skill, and it is considered a key curriculum activity in the general education setting for young children.

5. Perception is an important domain for young children with disabilities. Consideration should be given to auditory and visual processing.

8

Adolescents and Adults With Learning Disabilities

C H A P T E R   O U T L I N E

> If you give a starving man a fish, you feed him for a day. But if you teach the man *how* to fish, you feed him for a lifetime. If you teach a students with learning disabilities a fact, you help the student for the moment. But if you teach that student *how* to learn, you help the student for a lifetime.
>
> —*Donald Deshler*

For many individuals, a learning disability is a lifelong problem that continues into the adolescent and adult years. As secondary schools try to meet this challenge, they are serving more adolescents with learning disabilities. In this chapter, we discuss: (1) adolescents with learning disabilities, (2) special issues at the secondary level, (3) the transition from school to adult life, (4) the approaches to teaching adolescents with learning disabilities in secondary schools, (5) learning strategies instruction, (6) the adult years, and (7) computer technology for adolescents and adults.

ADOLESCENTS WITH LEARNING DISABILITIES

The period of adolescence is well documented as a stage of turmoil and difficult adjustment. The physical, mental, and emotional adjustments that characterize adolescence affect learning. Teenagers with learning disabilities and related disorders have difficulty in school and in their social life, not only because of their learning problems, but also because they must cope with the normal challenges and adjustments of adolescence. Because many characteristics of learning disabilities and adolescence overlap, it is hard to know whether a particular behavior stems from the learning disability or from normal adolescent development. In many cases, the difficulties stem from both, thus complicating the learning, social, and behavioral problems.

Characteristics of Adolescence

The period of adolescence is marked by conflicting feelings about: (1) freedom and independence versus security and dependence, (2) rapid physical changes, (3) developing sexuality, (4) peer pressure, and (5) self-consciousness. Many of the characteristics of adolescence can affect the processes of learning (Snowman & Biehler, 2000).

Freedom and Independence Versus Security and Dependence Adolescents want to become independent and separate themselves from their families; however, at the same time, they also need to keep these ties. According to Erikson's (1968) psychosocial model of development, adolescents must resolve a conflict between their desire for freedom and independence and their desire for security and dependence.

Rapid Physical Changes Adolescence is a period of rapid changes in physical growth and in appearance, including dramatic changes in facial and body structure. Adolescents must develop a new self-image and learn to cope with a different physical appearance, as well as new psychological and biological drives.

Developing Sexuality The adolescent period is also one of developing sexuality—another change to which the adolescent must learn to adjust. The sexual dimensions of adolescence may be very demanding in terms of time, energy, and worry.

Peer Pressure Adolescents are greatly influenced by peer pressure and peer values. When the values of friends differ from those of parents, family confrontation and conflict may result.

Self-Consciousness Teenagers tend to be very conscious of themselves, of how they look and of how they compare with group norms. This self-consciousness can lead to feelings of inferiority and withdrawal.

Characteristics of Adolescents With Learning Disabilities

For adolescents with learning disabilities and related disorders, the problems of adolescence are compounded by their learning difficulties. As illustrated in "LD Stories: Tim, an Adolescent With Learning Disabilities," the adolescent can find it devastating to cope with learning disabilities, in addition to the difficulties created by normal adolescent development.

It is critical to know the characteristics of adolescents with learning disabilities, but it is equally important to recognize the demands of the setting within which the adolescent lives and learns (Deshler et al., 1996; Lenz & Deshler, 2003). The characteristics of learning disabilities vary. Many adolescents do not display the characteristics described here, and they may even excel and possess strengths in some of these areas. Nevertheless, when one considers the combination of academic difficulties, the traits of adolescents, and the characteristics of learning disabilities, it is small wonder that these years are often trying. The following characteristics are seen in some, but certainly not in all, adolescents with learning disabilities:

Tim, an Adolescent With Learning Disabilities

Tim, a 14-year-old freshman at Washington High School, has learning disabilities. His first-semester grades confirmed what he had feared: He failed three subjects—English, algebra, and history. He made only a *D* in general science, and he received a *C* in physical education and mechanical drawing.

Tim finds that he cannot cope with the assignments, the work load, and the demands of his courses. Even worse, he cannot read the textbooks, and he does not understand all that goes on in his classes. Tim also does poorly on the written exams. He feels as though he is drowning, and he knows he needs help.

When Tim was in elementary school, he received intermittent help from the learning disabilities resource teacher. Last year, in eighth grade, Tim was placed in general education, content-area classes, and he received no resource help or direct special education services. The special education teacher, his eighth-grade homeroom teacher, and his other subject-area teachers informally discussed Tim's academic progress and planned his program. Tim was very involved in these planning sessions. In general, he had a successful year in eighth grade, passing all his subjects with above-average grades, although he had to work hard to accomplish this.

Over the summer, Tim grew so rapidly that he had to buy a complete set of new clothes. His voice changed, and he found that he must now shave the dark hair sprouting over his upper lip about once a week. Tim has made new friends at the high school and has kept many of his old friends from eighth grade. However, he has not told any of them about his grades. In fact, he is so embarrassed about his grades that he has stopped seeing his friends.

At this point, Tim does not know where to turn. In a conference that the school counselor held with Tim and his parents, they were told that the tests show he has the ability and that he should try harder. His parents are disappointed and angry. Tim is discouraged and depressed. Since the grades were mailed to his parents, he has cut a number of classes. Clearly, without help, there is danger that Tim will become another dropout statistic.

■ *Cultural and linguistic diversity.* Learning difficulties can be related to the adolescent's cultural and language background. The family's cultural views about school, academic performance, reading, studying, and test taking can shape the student's attitude. Some families will not acknowledge any failure or disability and refuse to seek help for their student. In some cultures, adolescents are expected to take on many family responsibilities and, therefore, they have less time for school work. Some cultures are not as time oriented as the mainstream American culture, and they may not see the importance of being on time or turning in work at a specified time. Many classes stress competition, while the adolescent's culture may reward group or teamwork, rather than individual accomplishment.

For adolescents whose first language is not English, they may still be considered *English-language learners*. Their lack of English proficiency leads to obstacles in many academic subjects that involve language, such as reading, writing, and language arts. In addition, the testing demands of the school can be particularly challenging. It is important for secondary teachers to recognize the impact of these cultural and linguistic differences and to understand the hurdles that these adolescents face.

 A website that is designed to help teachers with special students who have cultural and linguistic differences is **http://iris.peabody.vanderbilt.edu/CLDE/chalcycle.htm.**

■ *Passive learning.* Many adolescents with learning disabilities are *passive learners*. In response to failure-producing experiences, they develop an attitude of *learned helplessness*. They learn to be passive instead of active learners. Instead of trying to solve a problem, these adolescents tend to wait passively until the teacher directs them and tells them what to do. In an academic task, they fail to associate new information with what they already know, and they do not elaborate in their thinking (Deshler et al., 1996; Lenz & Deshler, 2003). In addition, adolescents who experience repeated failures may also begin to exhibit acting-out behaviors or other types of behavioral problems. This acting out may be one of the reasons that adolescent students with learning disabilities are adjudicated at a higher rate than other groups.

■ *Poor self-concept.* Poor self-concept and low self-esteem result from years of failure and frustration. Many adolescents with learning disabilities have little confidence in their ability to learn and achieve. Often, emotional problems also develop from their lack of successful experiences. Adolescents with learning disabilities often have low self-esteem and little self-confidence (Deshler et al., 1996; Lenz & Deshler, 2003; Silver, 1998).

■ *Social and behavioral problems.* During these critical adolescent years, when friendships and peer approval are so important, problems with social skills create another impediment for adolescents with learning disabilities. Because some adolescents with learning disabilities display social ineptitude, they have difficulty making and keeping friends. The social and behavioral problems become even more troublesome than the academic problems. The years of failure, low self-esteem, poor motivation, inadequate peer acceptance, and disruptive and maladaptive behavior take their toll (Bryan, 2003; Cole & McLeskey, 1997; Dohrn & Bryan, 1998; also see the chapter on social and emotional behavior).

When social malfunctions are extremely disabling and include problems in social interactions and nonverbal communication, students may be diagnosed as having nonverbal learning disorders or *Asperger's syndrome* (Roman, 1998; Thompson, 1997; also see the chapter on social and emotional behavior). Websites for these two social conditions are located at **http://www.nldline.com** (for nonverbal learning disorders) and at **http://www.asperger.org** (for Asperger's syndrome).

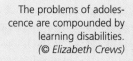
The problems of adolescence are compounded by learning disabilities.
(© Elizabeth Crews)

■ *Attention deficits.* Many adolescents with learning disabilities lack the attentional capacity to meet the demands of secondary school. High school heightens the demand for students to sustain cognitive effort and to concentrate for extended periods. The requirements of the secondary curriculum can place a strain on the adolescent's capacity to attend to the varied sources of input from teachers, instructional materials, and peers. Given the long periods of concentration needed for studying and listening in class, deficits in attention can seriously impede progress (Barkley, 1998; Lerner et al., 1995).

Levine (1988, p. 15) relates how a 14-year-old described his attention problem: "I'll tell you just what my head is like. It's like a television set. Only one thing, it's got no channel selector. You see, all the programs keep coming over my screen at the same time." The websites **http://www. adders.org** and **http://www.chadd.org** offer more information about ADD/ADHD.

■ *Lack of motivation.* By the time students with learning disabilities reach secondary school, they have experienced many years of failure. Many begin to doubt their intellectual abilities. They lack resiliency and come to believe that their efforts to achieve are futile. These feelings, in turn, lead to a low-persistence level; these adolescents give up quickly as soon as something appears to be difficult (Brooks & Goldstein, 2001). **Attribution theory** suggests that even when these adolescents do have successes, they do not believe that they were responsible for the achievement. Instead, they attribute their success to some outside force, such as luck, something the teacher did, or an easy task (Licht & Kistner, 1986; Yasutake & Bryan, 1995). Therefore, even success does not bring much satisfaction or raise their confidence level. It is difficult to motivate such students to exert the effort needed to learn. Yet, the best-made decisions about what to teach and the most skillful applications of how to teach will be successful only if the students are motivated to learn and can attribute success to their own efforts (Scanlon, Deshler, & Schumaker, 1996; Zigmond, 1997; see the chapter on social and emotional behavior for a further discussion of attribution theory and motivation).

Secondary School Students With Learning Disabilities in Different Educational Environments

The inclusion movement is growing at the secondary level, as more adolescents with learning disabilities are placed in general education, content-area classes for instruction. Table 8.1 shows the placement or educational environment for students with learning disabilities, ages 12 through 18. The percentage of adolescents placed in full-time, general education, content-area classes increased to 44% (from 19%, as reported 8 years ago). The placement of adolescents in resource rooms decreased to 38% (from 58%, as reported 8 years ago). As noted previously, resource room students spend part of their school day in general education classes. Thus, including general education class and resource room settings, about 82% of secondary students are in a general education, content-area class for at least a portion of the day. About 17% of the secondary students with learning

TABLE 8.1

Percentages of Secondary School Students With Learning Disabilities, Ages 12 Through 18, Served in Different Educational Environments

Educational environment	Percentage of adolescents with learning disabilities
General education class	44
Resource room	38
Separate class	17
Other placements	1

Source: From U.S. Department of Education, *To assure the free, appropriate public education of all children with disabilities,* Twenty-Fourth Annual Report to Congress on the Implementation of the Individuals With Disabilities Education Act. (Washington, DC: U.S. Government Printing Office, 2002.)

disabilities are in special classes, and about 1% of secondary students are in other settings (U.S. Department of Education, 2002).

What Happens to High School Students With Learning Disabilities?

A report by the U.S. Department of Education (2002) about why high school students with learning disabilities leave school showed that:

- 62% graduate with a standard diploma
- 28% drop out of school

In addition, the U.S. Department of Education (2002) noted that there are several different types of diplomas or certificates that schools offer:

1. *Standard diploma.* Students must meet the same criteria as all general education students, including adequate performance on tests.
2. *Standard diploma with multiple criteria for earning the diploma.* Students can earn the diploma by meeting different criteria, such as completing IEP goals.
3. *Certificate of attendance, completion, or achievement.* Students with IEPs may be allowed to meet the criteria in different ways.
4. *Special education certificate.* Available only to students with IEPs.

The high dropout rate of students with learning disabilities suggests that schools are failing to serve these students appropriately. Moreover, dropout rates have increased as a consequence of the high-stakes testing movement. Studies show that there are significant differences in terms of employment and postschool adjustments between students with learning disabilities who drop out and those who graduate (Thurlow, 2000; Ysseldyke, 2001). Students who stay in school and graduate fare much better than those who leave. Unfortunately, many students with learning disabilities drop out of school, and they face an uncertain and grim future.

Not only do a disproportionate number of students with learning disabilities drop out of school, but many of these adolescents also display a broad array of performance and adjustment problems (Deshler et al., 2001).

SPECIAL ISSUES AT THE SECONDARY LEVEL There are now more students with learning disabilities served at the secondary level than at the elementary level. According to the U.S. Department of Education (2002), 56% of all students with learning disabilities are in the 12 through 18 age group. For these adolescents, the issues at the secondary level involve special challenges, including:

(1) inclusive classes, (2) dealing with performance standards and high-stakes testing for secondary school students, and (3) adapting to content-area secondary teachers.

Challenges for Adolescents With Learning Disabilities

The demands of secondary school differ significantly from those of elementary school. Students move from a pupil-oriented elementary school environment to a content-driven secondary school setting. Often, the secondary students with learning disabilities lack the requisite skills needed to meet high school academic expectations. If methods used to teach content areas are not suited to the adolescent's particular learning strengths and interests, the prospect of graduating with a high school diploma becomes increasingly problematic (Deshler et al., 2001; Wagner, Cameto, & Newman, 2003).

Adolescents with learning disabilities experience numerous problems, ranging from mild to severe, that interfere with their mastering many of the subjects of the secondary curriculum. In addition to academic problems, these students have difficulties with cognitive skills, social behaviors, and emotional stability. Many adolescents who have received learning disabilities services at the elementary level continue to need help when they reach junior and senior high school. In some cases, problems are not identified until the adolescent enters the secondary school because of the subtle nature of the problem and the increased demands of the secondary curriculum.

Almost one of every three youths with learning disabilities fails content-area, general education high school courses (Blackorby & Wagner, 1997). The problems faced by adolescents with learning disabilities are summarized in Table 8.2 (Reith & Posgrove, 1994).

TABLE 8.2

Problems Faced by Adolescents With Learning Disabilities

- Severe deficits in basic academic skills, such as reading, spelling, and math
- Generalized failure and below-average performance in content-area courses, such as science, social studies, and health
- Deficient work-related skills, such as listening well in class, taking notes, studying for and taking tests
- Passive academic involvement and a pervasive lack of motivation
- Inadequate interpersonal skills

Inclusion at the Secondary Level

Although 82% of secondary school students with learning disabilities are in general education, content-area classes for at least a portion of the day, secondary schools have been slower to develop policies for inclusion than elementary schools. Secondary schools face several obstacles in providing inclusion programs, including: (1) the complex, content-area curriculum; (2) the large gap between student skill levels and classroom demands; (3) content-area secondary school teachers not trained to meet the needs of students with learning disabilities; and (4) the standards-based, high-stakes testing movement (Beckman, 2001; Cole & McLeskey, 1997; Deshler et al., 2000; Friend & Cook, 2003; Lenz & Deshler, 2003; Orkwis, 2003). One example of successful inclusion at the secondary level is presented in "LD Stories: Successful Inclusion at the Secondary Level, Trusting One's Strengths."

Effective Inclusion Practices for Secondary Teachers

To make *inclusion* work at the secondary level, it is necessary to establish partnerships between the **content-area teachers,** who are high school teach-

---

LD STORIES

SUCCESSFUL INCLUSION AT THE SECONDARY LEVEL, TRUSTING ONE'S STRENGTHS

For some secondary students, inclusion works well. Michael's learning disability was detected by his school in first grade. He vividly recalls that when the first-grade teacher asked the pupils to copy words from the blackboard, he simply could not perform the task. He was unable to recognize words, and he still has severe reading problems. However, Michael said he soon learned to trust his strengths. He had many friends and excellent social skills. He also did well in sports. Because his learning disability—poor reading skills—had been identified before he entered high school, when he reached the secondary level, he was placed in the general education inclusion class. His reading deficits continued in high school, but so did his strengths. At high school,

Michael was elected president of his class, and he was an effective member of the football team. He also excelled at debate and was a valuable member of the debate team. The school's support system gave him the kind of help he needed for his reading problem, so his reading performance slowly improved. Upon completing high school, Michael was accepted at the state university, and he made the college football team and debate team. In reflecting about his learning disabilities, Michael stressed the importance of "knowing and trusting his strengths."

Source: From P. Rodis, A. Garrod, and M. Boscardin. *Learning disabilities: Life stories.* Copyright 2001 by Pearson Education. Adapted with permission of the publisher.

---

ers whose primary orientation and expertise is the subject matter of their specialty, and the special education teachers. Partnerships consist of two or more professionals working together to plan and deliver instruction in general education classes that include adolescents with disabilities. There are several models for secondary professionals working together (Friend & Cook, 2003; Gately & Gately, 2001; McLeskey et al., 2004; Murawski & Dieker, 2004).

"LD in Practice: Inclusion Strategies for the Secondary General Education Classroom" offers a number of effective inclusion practices.

Performance Standards and High-Stakes Testing

Accountability has become the watchword in education. The standards-based criteria, known as **performance standards,** are an influential force in our secondary schools today, with directives about academic levels coming from national, state, and local sources. Secondary schools have established performance standards in the high school content areas (English, mathematics, and science), which are standards that all students are expected to meet. Most states have developed performance standards and assessment tests to determine whether students meet these set academic standards. Assessment tests, which are statewide tests given to all students, are often called **high-stakes testing** because so many critical decisions are based on the test results. There are rewards and punishments for students, teachers, administrators, and schools.

Holding students responsible for their performance on state and district tests is increasing in popularity among governors and legislators. When tests are used to make high-stake decisions, such as whether a student will graduate or be promoted to the next grade level, dropout rates often increase. Many educators are concerned about the large number of students with learning disabilities who are not passing these assessment tests. They frequently drop out of school and, consequently, these students have poor prospects for employment and postsecondary education (Thurlow, 2000; Ysseldyke, 2001).

In the past, students with disabilities were excluded from such statewide and districtwide assessments. All of this changed with the IDEA–1997, the Individuals With Disabilities Education Improvement Act (IDEA–2004), and the No Child Left Behind Act (NCLB–2001). These laws require that students with disabilities be included in statewide and districtwide assessments and that the results be reported.

IDEA–2004 also requires that states develop alternate assessment guidelines and policies on **accommodations** for students with disabilities. The law outlines several requirements for including students with disabilities in the statewide or districtwide assessments. Each student's IEP must include

LD IN PRACTICE

INCLUSION STRATEGIES FOR THE SECONDARY GENERAL EDUCATION CLASSROOM

- *Establish partnerships between content-area teachers and special educators.* Two or more professionals work together to plan and deliver instruction.

- *Use collaborative teams.* In this ongoing process of **collaborative teaming,** teachers with different areas of expertise work together to develop creative solutions to problems that may be impeding a student's progress. Collaborative team members develop supportive and mutually beneficial relationships and share their resources.

- *Use a coteaching model.* The content-area teacher and the special education teacher instruct students in the classroom jointly. Ingredients for successful coteaching include:
  a. Determining each teacher's strengths and preferences
  b. Developing trust and respect
  c. Receiving strong administrative support
  d. Providing adequate communication and time

- *Provide differentiated instruction.* Individualized instruction is given to *all* students in the classroom, both students who do not have disabilities and students who have special needs. According to Beckman (2001), the principles for differentiated instruction include:
  a. Content-area teacher and special educator should share responsibility
  b. Content-area teacher and special educator should be familiar with the student's IEP
  c. Content-area teacher and special educator should be aware of the student's strengths and weaknesses
  d. Sufficient coplanning time should be built into the day
  e. Student expectations should be set by student abilities, not by classification

a plan that details how the student will be assessed and what accommodations the student will need for assessment (Thurlow, 2000; Individuals With Disabilities Education Improvement Act, 2004).

The goal for standards-based testing is the desire to improve teaching and learning so that all students can demonstrate their mastery of the knowledge and skills needed to participate in the global economy of today and the future. We should not lose sight of these goals. Assessment is only one part of the picture. The most critical piece is providing all students with the chance to learn. Unless students are given adequate opportunities to learn, holding them to higher standards will only further victimize those students already being harmed by gross inequities in the educational system (Kauffman & Wiley, 2004; Lenz & Deshler, 2003; Thurlow, 2000; Ysseldyke, 2001).

In addition to meeting these performance standards, problems for adolescents with learning disabilities are magnified by the complex set of curriculum demands in high school. When adolescents with learning disabilities are in general education, content-area classes for four periods a day, they are expected to meet the same requirements that all other students meet. There are heavy expectations of reading proficiency that many adolescents with learning disabilities cannot meet. In spite of their learning problems, they are expected to learn, integrate, manage, and express large amounts of information (Deshler et al., 1996, 2001; Kauffman & Wiley, 2004).

Students with disabilities may be eligible for accommodations in taking high-stakes tests. The Educational Testing Service (ETS) offers information on obtaining accommodations. The website for ETS is **http://www.ets.org/ disability.**

The following "LD in Practice: Test-Taking Tips" offers some helpful advice for taking tests.

Content-Area Secondary Teachers

Many content-area secondary teachers, whose training was in their content specialization, are not prepared to work with students with learning disabilities. Because their training was in their content specialization, be it mathematics, French, physics, or English literature, their specialized training may not have prepared them to provide the needed support for students with disabilities. Therefore, an important collaborative role for the special educator in the high school is to work with content-area teachers to help them develop a sensitivity to the needs of students with learning problems and to provide them with strategies for teaching these students. Collaboration involves helping the high school, content-area teacher understand the nature of a specific student's problem and how to

LD IN PRACTICE

Test-Taking Tips

- Get enough sleep and try to remain calm.
- Look over the entire test and read the directions carefully.
- Read each question carefully and note key words and phrases.
- Read each question all the way through. Do not read into the question what is not there.
- If you are unsure about a question re-read it and try to eliminate one or two of the answers.
- Budget the time allotted for the test and do not waste time by getting stuck on one question.
- Take all authorized breaks. Also, periodically take a few breaks by stopping for a moment, shutting your eyes, and taking some deep breaths.
- Have a sheet of scrap paper to help track lines of print.
- Allow time at the end to look over the test and make sure you did not skip any questions.

make the needed accommodations for that student. For example, if the student has a severe reading disability, that student may be helped by recording the lesson. Recordings for the Blind and Dyslexics are books on audiotapes and on CDs that are accessible to students with learning disabilities. In fact, about 75% of those who use Recordings for the Blind and Dyslexics are individuals with learning disabilities. (For further information, contact Recordings for the Blind and Dyslexics at **http://www.rfbd.org.**) During examinations, the student with a severe writing problem might be allowed to give answers orally, to tape answers, or to dictate answers to someone else. Students who process very slowly might be allowed additional time.

TRANSITION FROM SCHOOL TO ADULT LIFE

The transition from school to adult life is full of complexities for all adolescents. To successfully negotiate this transition, all adolescents require varying degrees of assistance from friends, family, and school personnel.

Adolescents with learning difficulties need extra support and assistance to successfully make this challenging transition.

Transition refers to a change in status from behaving primarily as a student to assuming emerging adult roles. These new roles include employment, becoming a student in postsecondary school, maintaining a home, and experiencing satisfactory personal and social relationships (National Information Center for Children and Youth [NICHCY], 1999). The research shows that adolescents with learning disabilities receive inadequate **transition planning,** which does not help them in seeking employment. They are most likely to find a job on their own, with little support from schools or adult agencies. Relatively few adolescents with learning disabilities go to college. Only 27% actually enroll in any postsecondary school (i.e., 4-year college, 2-year college, or vocational school; National Council on Disability Social Security Administration, 2000). Significant training in self-advocacy is helpful because students with learning disabilities are expected to take increasingly more responsibility for their own decisions and lives.

Transition Legislation

The Individuals With Disabilities Education Improvement Act (IDEA–2004) contains requirements in regard to transition (U.S. Department of Education, 2004).

Beginning not later than the first IEP to be in effect when the student is 16, and then updated annually, IDEA requires:

1. appropriate measurable postsecondary goals based upon age appropriate transition assessments related to training, education, employment, and, where appropriate, living skills

2. the transition services (including courses of study) needed to assist the student in reaching those goals

3. beginning not later than 1 year before the student reaches the age of majority under State law, a statement that the student has been informed of the student's rights under this title, if any, that will transfer to the student on reaching of majority

Transition, according to IDEA–2004, is designed to be within a results-oriented process that is focused on improving the academic and functioning achievement of a student with a disability; to facilitate movement from school to postschool activities, including postsecondary education, vocational education, integrated employment (including supported employment), continuing and adult education, adult services, independent living, or community participation (IDEA–2004).

The law views **transition** as a set of activities that are based on the needs of the individual student and that are designed to prepare the student for the years beyond secondary school. To ensure that the student completes secondary school prepared for employment or postsecondary education, as well as for independent living, the law requires that an *individualized transition plan (ITP)* be written for students with disabilities, beginning at age 16, as part of the IEP. Many school districts use an attachment to the student's IEP to indicate transition goals and activities designed to meet those goals. Other schools develop a separate ITP. The special education teacher may need to take the lead in developing the ITP.

Content of the Transition Plan   The transition plan (IEP/ITP) should include the following (Brown, 2000; NICHCY, 1999):

1. *Current levels of performance.*   The transition plan should document the student's current levels of achievement so that the transition team knows where to begin.

2. *Interests and aptitude.*   The plan should take into account the student's interests, aptitudes, potential, and vision for the future.

3. *Postschool goals.*   The plan should define and project desired postschool goals as identified by the student, parents, and transition teams for community living, employment, postsecondary education, and/or training.

4. *Transition activities.*   The plan should include specific transition activities in areas such as vocational and career education, work experience, and community-based instruction.

5. *Designate responsible persons.*   The plan should designate a person or agency that is responsible for the continuation of the transition after the student's high school years.

6. *Review.*   The transition plan should be reviewed and revised as necessary.

Developing Transition Plans

The goals for transition planning for adolescents with learning disabilities follow several paths.

Competitive Employment   About 57% of students with learning disabilities plan to go into competitive employment after high school (Wagner et al., 2003). Vocational educators need to be an integral part of the transition team to help these students explore occupations and to gain at least a basic knowledge within the various fields. Parents and educators must work together to help students identify areas of interest and potential fields of employment and also to determine how the students can meet the entry-level requirements of those fields. Students will benefit from job experience by participating in a *co-op* project (Brown, 2000; Gerber & Brown, 1997).

Vocational Training and Apprenticeship Programs   Some students with learning disabilities prepare for a trade after high school by going to a vocational training school or by entering an apprenticeship program.

Postsecondary and College Attendance   In the past, many students with learning disabilities did not consider postsecondary education options. However, recent studies show that as many as 50% of these students plan to attend either a 2-year or a 4-year college at some point (Wagner et al., 2003). However, meeting these goals requires transition plans that are carefully laid out and that include significant encouragement toward college (National Joint Committee on Learning Disabilities, 1994; Stewart & Lillie, 1995).

Supported Employment   Some transition programs offer a bridge from school to work through supported employment. In this type of program, transition educators seek potential employers to hire special education students. In some cases, a job coach works at the employment site, supervising and helping the students over the inevitable rough spots. Job coaches work for the business that employs the student and for the school or agency (Rusch & Phelps, 1987). Table 8.3 shows the results of a national survey of the transition goals of students with learning disabilities.

Guidelines for transition plans appear in "LD in Practice: Guidelines for Developing Transition Plans for Secondary Students With Learning Disabilities."

TABLE 8.3

Transition Goals for Students With Learning Disabilities

Transition goal	Description	Percentage
Competitive employment	Seeking job in competitive sector or going into military service	59.0
Vocational training	Enrolling in a vocational training program	43.4
College attendance	Furthering their education at a 4-year college or at a 2-year or community college	54.3
Supported employment	Seeking noncompetitive employment in agencies with job coaches and with other types of support	1.6

Source: Table compiled from data published in M. Wagner, R. Cameto, and L. Newman, *Youth with disabilities: A changing population. A report of findings from the National Longitudinal Transition Study-2.* (Menlo Park, CA: SRI International, 2003.)

LD IN PRACTICE

GUIDELINES FOR DEVELOPING TRANSITION PLANS FOR SECONDARY STUDENTS WITH LEARNING DISABILITIES

- Form an individual transition team for each student to develop the individual transition plan (ITP). Identify resources that are available to meet the goals of the plan.

- Work with business and industry representatives and build relationships for students to meet the goals of the transition plan.

- Develop a transition curriculum. Include communication skills, self-esteem development, decision-making skills, career exploration, community-living skills, and time-management skills to help students during the transition.

- Teach self-advocacy skills. Help students understand the legislative mandates that support requests for accommodations, both in the classroom and on the job. Adolescents can use this information in making decisions about their futures. Teach students to advocate for themselves. Many of their interactions require a constructive request for accommodations and services. Students must interact with teachers in high school, in postsecondary school, and with employers. They may need to get services from other agencies. By learning to speak for themselves and to bear the consequences of their actions or inactions, students learn the skills necessary for adulthood.

- Build competencies in academic skills. Ensure that students have competencies in reading, writing, mathematics, and computer usage.

- Teach study skills. Adolescents need help in test preparation, test-taking strategies, and learning strategies.

- Teach students to use accommodations and modifications appropriately and effectively.

- Teach social skills and interpersonal communication skills.

APPROACHES TO TEACHING ADOLESCENTS WITH LEARNING DISABILITIES IN SECONDARY SCHOOLS

Several different instructional approaches and curriculum models are being used with students with learning disabilities in junior and senior high school (Cole & McLeskey, 1997; Sitlington, 1996; Swanson & Hoskyn, 2001).

Features of Effective Secondary Programs

According to Zigmond (1990, 1997, 2003), essential features of effective secondary programs for students with learning disabilities include the following methods.

Intensive Instruction in Reading and Mathematics   Many students with learning disabilities receive failing grades in general education courses because of their poor skills in reading, writing, and mathematics. These students still require basic instruction in reading, writing, vocabulary development, and mathematics (Fuchs & Fuchs, 2001a).

Instruction in Survival Skills   Several **functional skills or survival skills** that are needed for successful functioning in a high school include: (1) strategies to help students stay out of trouble in school; (2) skills to help students acquire behavioral patterns that will make teachers consider them in a positive light; and (3) study and test-taking skills, such as organizing time, approaching a textbook, taking notes from a lecture or text, organizing information, studying for tests, and taking tests (Zigmond, 1990).

Curriculum Models for Serving Adolescents With Learning Disabilities at the Secondary Level

A range of curriculum models are used with adolescents with learning disabilities in junior and senior high schools (Cole & McLeskey, 1997; Deshler et al., 1996; Lenz & Deshler, 2003; Sitlington, 1996). These include: (1) basic academic skills instruction, (2) tutorial instruction, (3) functional skills or survival skills instruction, and (4) work–study programs. Learning strategies instruction, an important instructional model, is discussed in the next major section of this chapter.

Basic Academic Skills Instruction   The objective of teaching basic skills is to remediate the student's academic deficits. **Basic academic skills instruction** usually focuses on improving the student's abilities through direct teaching, especially in reading and mathematics. Students receive instruction at a level that approximates their achievement or instructional level. For example, if a 16-year-old student is reading at fifth-grade level, reading instruction for that student would be geared to the fifth-grade level (Fuchs & Fuchs, 2001b).

Tutorial Programs   The objective of **tutorial instruction** is to help students in their specific academic-content subjects and to achieve success in the regular curriculum. For example, if Alex experiences failure or difficulty in his American history class, his instruction will focus on the specific history material he is studying. The goal is to help Alex succeed in the general education curriculum. The special education resource teacher must know the requirements of all academic subjects in which students may have difficulty.

Functional Skills or Survival Skills Instruction   The objective of the functional skills instruction model is to equip students to function in society. Survival skills enable adolescents to get along in the world outside of school. The curriculum includes such subjects as consumer information; the completion of application forms, such as job applications; banking and money skills, such as understanding interest rates and installment purchases; life-care skills, such as grooming; and computer literacy. Academic content is geared to the students' careers and life needs. For example, reading is directed toward relevant areas, such as directions, want ads, or a driver's instruction manual. Guidance and counseling for self-identity and career planning are also often part of the curriculum.

Work–Study Programs   The objective of a **work–study program** is to provide adolescents with job- and career-related skills, as well as actual on-the-

High school curricula can incorporate work–study and vocational programs to teach job skills.
(© Bob Daemmrich/ The Image Works)

job experience. Students in work–study programs typically spend half the day on the job and the remainder of the day in school. While in school, they may study materials that are compatible with their jobs. Sometimes these students take general education courses and also work with a special education teacher. The work–study approach is particularly successful for students who are not motivated by the high school environment. The special education teacher serves as a coordinator who integrates education with desired job skills and supervises students on the work site.

LEARNING STRATEGIES INSTRUCTION

Learning strategies instruction offers a viable and promising approach to help adolescents with learning disabilities learn to take control of their own learning. The objective of this instruction is to teach students how to learn, rather than what is contained in a specific curriculum. Effective learning strategy instruction involves helping students learn and use procedures that will empower them to accomplish important academic tasks, to solve problems, and to complete work independently. With proficiency in learning strategies, students can overcome or lessen the effects of learning disabilities. Learning strategies are tools that students can use to approach tasks in content-area classes or other learning situations. In effect, the teacher helps students learn how to learn (Deshler et al., 1996, 2001; Lenz & Deshler, 2003).

A *learning strategy* is an individual's approach to a task that includes how a person thinks and acts when planning, executing, and evaluating performance on a task and its outcome. It includes both cognitive (thinking processes) and behavioral (overt actions) elements that guide the student's planning, performance, and evaluation of strategy engagement (Lenz et al., 1996).

Learning strategies research shows that adolescents with learning disabilities are *inefficient learners*. These adolesecents do not lack the ability to learn, but, rather they go about learning in an inefficient manner. For example, Maria's memory may be adequate for remembering the facts in a history lesson, but she has to put the right kind of learning effort into remembering those facts. For Sam, who is having difficulty in science, learning strategies instruction would teach some techniques for organizing his materials for learning, rather than teach him the content of the subject. Thus, the emphasis is on teaching students how to adapt and cope with the changing world; that is, the emphasis is on how to learn how to learn. (See "LD Stories: The Power of Learning Strategies, a Parable" and also the chapter on theories of learning.) Instruction in learning strategies is particularly effective with adolescents with learning disabilities who are above third-grade reading level, are able to deal with symbolic as well as concrete learning tasks, and have an average intellectual ability (Deshler et al., 1996, 2001; Lenz et al., 1996). Learning strategies can be applied to all academic areas of the secondary curriculum, as well as to social and behavioral learning.

Guidelines for Teaching Learning Strategies

The intense interest in learning strategies instruction has generated a significant amount of research (Deshler et al., 1996; Lenz & Deshler, 2003; Palinscar & Brown, 1984; Slavin, 2000). The following list provides some practical guidelines for putting learning strategies instruction into practice.

- *Use background knowledge.* Students get more from instruction when their **background knowledge**, which is defined as information or experiences that are gained about the topic of instruction or about a reading selection, is activated or when the teacher elicits, builds, and focuses on appropriate background knowledge. Background knowledge is the strongest predictor of a student's ability to learn new material. The more students know about a topic, the better they comprehend and learn about the topic from the text.

- *Monitor progress.* Successful learners monitor their own progress. They have an idea of how they are doing. In reading, for example, they use their knowledge of text features and appropriate strategies to monitor their own learning.

- *Teach generalization.* Successful learners use skills and knowledge in new situations, adapting it to particular contexts. Providing students with direct instruction about situations when a skill will be useful, and monitoring their implementation, can improve their generalization.

- *Create active learners.* Students who are actively involved in their learning are more successful than students who play a more passive role. Effective learners generate questions, make summaries, and help determine the direction of the lesson.

- *Enhance self-concept.* There is a strong correlation between successful learning and the student's self-concept and positive attitude. Students with high levels of achievement tend to have high self-concepts, while low achievers have poor self-concepts. Success in learning enhances self-concept.

- *Use memory strategies.* Successful learners use effective memory strategies. Memory is related to background; those who know more are able to remember more. Short-term memory is limited in capacity. Most of what is learned is forgotten quickly if it is not acted upon or linked with previous learning.

- *Use interactive learning.* The opportunity for students to interact with other students is important. Cooperative learning and peer tutoring increase achievement and motivation, as well as improve interpersonal relationships. When one student teaches another student, the achievement of both students can improve.

- *Develop questions.* Questioning helps comprehension. Students learn more effectively when they generate their own questions. Students exposed to higher order questions understand more than students who are exposed only to lower order questions. They tend to give more thoughtful, reflective responses to questions when teachers allow more time for responses and encourage follow-up.

Strategies Intervention Model

One widely used model of strategy instruction, the **strategies intervention model (SIM)**, was developed and validated through many years of programmatic research with adolescents with learning disabilities by Deshler and colleagues (2001) at the Kansas Center for Research on Learning. SIM is a recognized, fully developed procedure for teaching learning strategies to adolescents with learning disabilities (Deshler et al., 1996; Ellis et al., 1991; Lenz & Deshler, 2003; Lenz et al., 1996; Oas, Schumaker, & Deshler, 1995). This practical and useful model has two phases for helping students cope with the demands of the high school curriculum: (1) teachers must identify the curriculum demands of their students and (2) teachers must match these school demands with specific learning strategies.

Steps for Teaching Learning Strategies

Central to the SIM model is a series of eight instructional stages (Clark, 2000; Deshler et al., 1996; Lenz & Deshler, 2003). The integrated series of overt acts and cognitive behaviors enables students to solve a problem or to complete a task. The steps for teaching a learning strategy are summarized in Table 8.4, and they are illustrated in the steps presented in the following steps:

Step 1: Elena Martinez (the teacher) pretests Andrew Fleming (the student) to determine his current learning habits, and she obtains a commitment from him to learn.   Andrew is asked to perform a task that requires the target learning strategy. For example, for the strategy of self-questioning, Ms. Martinez asks Andrew to read a passage and answer the comprehension questions. Ms. Martinez and Andrew discuss the results of his performance and she helps him see his need for acquiring the learning strategy. Seeing the benefit, Andrew readily commits to learning the new strategy.

Step 2: Ms. Martinez describes the new learning strategy.   Next, Ms. Martinez explains to Andrew the steps and behaviors involved in performing the learning strategy: "First, Andrew, you will read a paragraph. Then you will stop reading and ask yourself some questions. As you think of a question, you will either answer it yourself or go back to the paragraph to find the answer. After you have answered all the questions you can think of, you will read the next paragraph." She also explains to Andrew the situations in which the strategy will be useful.

Step 3: Ms. Martinez models the new learning strategy.   She demonstrates all the steps described in Step 2. While doing so, Ms. Martinez *thinks aloud* so that Andrew can witness the entire process. In subsequent modeling, Ms. Martinez includes Andrew by asking appropriate questions.

Step 4: Andrew verbally rehearses the steps of the learning strategy.   Andrew rehearses the steps by talking aloud until he reaches the goal of 100% correct without prompting from Ms. Martinez. Andrew becomes familiar with the steps through a self-instruction procedure.

Step 5: Andrew practices with controlled materials and obtains feedback.   Elena Martinez provides materials for Andrew to practice the new learning strategy. By carefully selecting practice materials, she keeps other intervening problems to a minimum. For example, to practice the strategy of self-questioning in reading material, she selects material that is easy enough for Andrew to practice the target strategy without getting bogged down in very difficult vocabulary.

Step 6: Andrew practices with classroom materials and obtains feedback.   Once Andrew has gained proficiency in the strategy with controlled materials, Ms. Martinez applies the strategy to materials used in his general education classroom. This step is a stage in developing an application and generalization of the learning strategy. After using the strategy successfully in the resource room, Andrew must learn to generalize the technique to broader learning situations.

TABLE 8.4

Steps for Teaching a
Learning Strategy

Stage 1. Teacher pretests students and obtains a commitment

Phase 1. Orientation and pretest

Phase 2. Awareness and commitment

Stage 2. Teacher describes the learning strategy

Phase 1. Orientation and overview

Phase 2. Presentation of strategy and system for remembering

Stage 3. Teacher models the strategy

Phase 1. Orientation

Phase 2. Presentation

Phase 3. Student enlistment

Stage 4. Students verbally practice the strategy

Phase 1. Verbal elaboration

Phase 2. Verbal rehearsal

Stage 5. Students have controlled practice and feedback

Phase 1. Orientation and overview

Phase 2. Guided practice

Phase 3. Independent practice

Stage 6. Students have advanced practice and feedback

Phase 1. Orientation and overview

Phase 2. Guided practice

Phase 3. Independent practice

Stage 7. Teacher posttests students and obtains a commitment

Phase 1. Confirmation and celebration

Phase 2. Forecast and commitment to generalize

Stage 8. Students generalize the learning strategy

Phase 1. Orientation

Phase 2. Activation

Phase 3. Adaptation

Phase 4. Maintenance

Source: Adapted from E. Ellis, D. Deshler, B. Lenz, J. Schumaker and F. Clark. (1991). An instructional model for teaching learning strategies, *Focus on Exceptional Children, 23*(6), p. 11. Reprinted by permission of Love Publishing Company, Denver.

Step 7: Ms. Martinez posttests to determine Andrew's progress, and she obtains his permission to generalize. Instruction is successful if Andrew has progressed sufficiently to cope with curricular demands in the target area.

Step 8: Andrew generalizes the learning strategy. The real measure of effective strategy instruction is the degree to which students generalize the acquired strategy to the real world and maintain its use in new settings and situations. Ms. Martinez assists Andrew in generalization by monitoring his performance of the strategy in other settings, reviewing the steps as necessary, helping him brainstorm appropriate adaptations to the strategy, and encouraging him in its use.

In summary, the goal of the learning strategies approach is to teach adolescents with learning disabilities to become involved, active, and independent learners. After identifying the demands of the curriculum that the student cannot meet, the teacher provides instruction to meet those demands. The cognitive aspects of learning, rather than specific subject matter content, are emphasized. Research shows that this is an effective teaching approach because students "learn how to learn." For additional information about the strategies intervention model, contact the Center for Research on Learning, University of Kansas, 3061 Dole Human Development Center, Lawrence, KS 66045. Phone: (785) 864-4780. Website: http://www.ku-crl.org.

THE ADULT YEARS

For many individuals, a learning disability is a lifelong problem. In this section, we consider posthigh school and college programs and adults with lifelong learning disabilities. Postsecondary education includes community colleges, vocational–educational training, nondegree postsecondary programs, and 4-year colleges.

Legislation for Adults With Disabilities

The protections of the *Individuals with Disabilities Education Improvement Act (IDEA–2004)* end when the student graduates from high school or when the student has reached the maximum age of 22. Two other laws come into play for protection of adults with disabilities; they are: (1) the **Americans With Disabilities Act** and (2) *Section 504 of the Rehabilitation Act.* In addition, assistance with job training and placement can be obtained through the Job Training Partnership Act (JTPA) and through Job Corp. The Americans With Disabilities Act (ADA) is a federal law that was passed in 1990. The ADA ensures the rights of individuals with disabilities to nondiscriminatory treatment in aspects of their lives other than education. It provides protections of civil rights in the specific areas of employment, transportation, public accommodations, state and local government, and telecommunications. It also can protect the rights of adults with disabilities in educational settings. This law has been used to provide accommodations for individuals with disabilities taking licensing exams. Citing the Americans With Disabilities Act, a recent Supreme Court decision gave a professional golfer, Casey Martin, the right to use a golf cart in professional tournaments because his disability affected his capacity to walk.

Section 504 of the Rehabilitation Act of 1973 has been a major factor that triggered the proliferation of postsecondary and college programs. Section 504 of the Rehabilitation Act of 1973 (PL 93–112) states that:

> "No otherwise qualified handicapped individual . . . shall, solely, by reasons of his/her handicap, be excluded from participation in, be denied the benefits of, or be subject to discrimination under any program or activity receiving federal financial assistance."

Further clarification and interpretation of Section 504, with regard to the requirements of schools and educational institutions, are provided by case law. Because most colleges receive some federal financial assistance, they are subject to the Section 504 regulation (Rothstein, 1998).

The Job Training Partnership Act (JTPA) was established to prepare youth and adults facing serious barriers to employment by providing job training and other services designed to: (1) increase employment and earnings, (2) increase educational and occupational skills, and (3) decrease welfare dependency. The goal of the JTPA is to help its clients move toward self-sufficiency in the work force. This goal is pursued through a program of eligibility, assessment training, job search, and employment.

Job Corp provides a training and employment program in a residential setting for students between the ages of 16 and 21 who are from a low-income home (students with disabilities qualify under the family of one), have a condition that keeps them from getting a job, and are able to benefit from the service. Services provided can include: (1) basic education, (2) vocational skills training, (3) work experience, (4) counseling, (5) leadership training, (6) health care, and (7) related support services.

Nondegree Postsecondary Programs

Some young adults with learning disabilities may not be eligible for college programs, yet they still need postsecondary transitional programs that will provide them with opportunities to learn independence; social experiences; practical activities, such as budgeting; computer skills; life experiences; and work experiences. A few colleges have developed such programs for these students. One is the PACE program, located at National-Louis University in Evanston, Illinois.

Another is the Threshold Program, which is part of Lesley University in Cambridge, Massachusetts. Both are 2-year programs that provide students with a college-like experience of living in dormitories. Students take classes in consumer math, critical thinking, health and wellness, human development, music and art appreciation, social strategies, assertiveness training, independent living, and computer technology. They also gain experience working at jobs throughout their 2-year program, with the support of a job coach. The Threshold Program conducted a follow-up study of its graduates for the past 12 years and found that 69% were living independently in apartments and 82% were employed (Yuan & Reisman, 2000). A study of graduates of the PACE program showed that 82% were employed, a figure that is much higher than that for other adults with learning disabilities (Harth & Burns, 2004). The website for the PACE program is **http://www2.nl.edu/pace.**

College Programs

Only a few years ago, attending college was out of the question for most adults with learning disabilities. Today, however, the prospects for getting a college education have brightened considerably, and there are now many college opportunities for such young adults. Many individuals with learning disabilities can look forward to enrolling at a college and to being better prepared for their future (Vogel, 1998; Vogel & Adelman, 1993, 2000). Community colleges are often a good choice for young adults with learning disabilities. They bridge the gap between high school and college and may offer special programs for individuals with learning disabilities. "LD Stories: Darlene, a College Student With Learning Disabilities" illustrates such a situation.

According to Section 504 of the Rehabilitation Act and the Americans With Disabilities Act, educational institutions are required to make reasonable accommodations for students with learning disabilities (Rothstein, 1998). Learning disabilities are recognized as a category of disability under both of these laws. As this legislation is increasingly being implemented at educational institutions, adults with learning disabilities are able to enroll at colleges and postsecondary schools in steadily growing numbers, and they are eligible to receive a variety of services there.

Accommodations Compliance with the regulations of Section 504 and the Americans With Disabilities Act require that colleges allow for modifications and make **reasonable accommodations.** The most frequent accommodation within the general education program is providing extended time on an examination. Research conducted on the efficacy of allowing extended time for postsecondary students with learning disabilities shows that these individuals performed significantly better when provided with extended time. It was also noted that the performance of individuals who did not have learning disabilities did not significantly improve under extended time provisions (Weaver, 2000).

DARLENE, A COLLEGE STUDENT WITH LEARNING DISABILITIES

Darlene was the youngest of three children. Her older sister and brother were model students—they received good grades in school with little effort. For Darlene, however, school was difficult. At first her parents would say, "Why can't you get *As* like your brother and sister?" Finally, in sixth grade, her parents realized that Darlene had learning disabilities. She received help during her middle school years, and her grades improved. During her high school years, Darlene, her parents, and the transition team developed a transition plan for college. She wanted to major in art, an area in which she excelled. She worked with her high school counselor and selected a college with a good arts curriculum and a supportive learning disabilities program. Darlene requested special accommodations for the college entrance examinations, and she was admitted to the college of her choice. At the college, she worked with the learning disabilities staff in planning her courses. When she needed any special accommodations in her courses, she knew her rights under the law and was able to advocate for herself. She decided to take three courses each semester instead of four so that she would graduate in 5 years instead of 4 years. Darlene is now a college senior, and she looks forward to her graduation. With careful planning and preparation, her college education has been a challenging, but happy experience.

Some common accommodations in college programs are listed in Table 8.5 (Bursuck, Rose, Cowen, & Yahaya, 1989; Vogel, 1998):

College Entrance Testing for Individuals With Learning Disabilities Special accommodations are also available for students with learning disabilities who are taking college entrance examinations. Information on accommodations for the Scholastic Aptitude Test (SAT) can be obtained at **http://www.collegeboard.org,** and for the GRE and the GMAT from the Educational Testing Service (ETS), Rosedale Road, Princeton, NJ, 08541. Phone: (609) 921-9000, Fax: (609) 734-5410. Website: **http://www.ets.org.** Information on special accommodations on the American College Test (ACT) is described in ACT Assessment Special Testing Guide (available from ACT Universal Testing Special Testing: 61, P.O. Box 4028, Iowa City, IA, 52243-4028. Phone: (319) 337-1332, Fax: (319) 337-1285. Website: **http://www.act.org.**

Special Problems at the College Level College poses many problems for students with disabilities that they do not encounter during the high school years. There is less student–teacher contact, and college has long-range assignments and evaluations, rather than the day-to-day monitoring that

TABLE 8.5

Suggested Accommodations in College Programs

- Extending the time allowed to complete a program
- Adapting the method of instruction
- Substituting an alternative course for a required course
- Modifying or substituting courses for the foreign language requirements
- Allowing for part-time, rather than full-time, study
- Modifying examination procedures to measure achievement without contamination from areas of deficit
- Providing audiotapes or CDs of student textbooks
- Providing note takers to help students with lectures
- Offering counseling services to the students
- Developing IEPs for the students
- Providing basic skills instruction in areas of reading, mathematics, and language

occurs in high school. The student does not have the support network of family and friends that was available during high school. Students also have more unstructured time they must manage, and they also must learn to advocate for themselves. In addition, the physical environment is very different, with classes in different buildings, adjustments to roommates, and acclimation to the eating and sleeping patterns of the dormitories. To meet these new demands, students may need a period of transition activities before the college year begins. Some colleges offer an intensive transition program to prepare such students for college challenges. The University of Wisconsin—Whitewater transition program, which occurs over a 5-week summer period, is described by Dalke (1993). A resource of college transition programs is in the *K & W Guide for the Learning Disabled* (Kravetz & Wax, 2001).

Another problem many students encounter in college is the foreign language requirement. For many students with learning disabilities, the foreign language requirement becomes a major stumbling block, and it may even prevent them from completing their college work. Colleges need to develop policies for students with learning disabilities who are unable to complete the foreign language requirement. Such policies could include a method for students to petition for a substitution, a procedure for waiving the foreign language requirement, or a provision of accommodations in foreign language classes (Ganschow, Sparks, & Javorsky, 1998; Ganschow, Philips, & Schneider, 2000).

One of the greatest challenges faced by college students with learning disabilities is gaining and maintaining the acceptance and cooperation of the academic faculty. Research shows that faculty members often support the concept of providing accommodations for students with learning dis-

TABLE 8.6

Guidelines for Helping College Students With Learning Disabilities

1. Make the syllabus available 4 to 6 weeks before the beginning of the class and, when possible, be available to discuss the syllabus with students with learning disabilities who are considering taking the course.

2. Begin lectures and discussions with reviews and overviews of the topics to be covered.

3. Use a chalkboard or overhead projector to outline lecture material, reading what is written, or what is on previously prepared transparencies.

4. Use a chalkboard or overhead projector to highlight key concepts, unusual terminology, or foreign words (being mindful of legibility and of the necessity to read what is written).

5. Emphasize important points, main ideas, and key concepts orally in lecture.

6. Give assignments in writing, as well as orally, and be available for further clarification.

7. Provide opportunities for student participation, question periods, and/or discussion.

8. Provide time for individual discussion of assignments and questions about lectures and readings.

9. Provide study guides for the text, study questions, and review sessions to aid in mastering material and preparing for exams.

10. Allow oral presentations or tape-recorded assignments instead of a written format.

11. Modify evaluation procedures. For example, permit untimed tests and oral, taped, or typed exams instead of written exams. Allow alternative methods to demonstrate course mastery and provide adequate scratch and lined paper for students with overly large or poor handwriting. Offer alternatives to computer-scored answer sheets.

12. Assist students in obtaining CDs or recorded textbooks. Contact RFB & D (Recording for the Blind and Dyslexic), Phone: (800) 221-4792. Website: **http://www.rfbd.org.**

abilities, but they need help to understand the needs of these students and to become familiar with the accommodations that can be made (Rose, 1993). Table 8.6 lists the ways that college faculty members can help college students with learning disabilities (Vogel, 1998).

Many colleges establish an office for disabled student services to meet the needs of all students with disabilities on the campus. The office staff is involved with student admission, assessment, counseling, program planning, and communication with faculty.

Finding Colleges for Students With Learning Disabilities   It is difficult to list college programs for students with learning disabilities because these programs continually are being started and changed. However, several available guidebooks that can help prospective students, their families, and counselors are listed in Table 8.7. Many of these guides listed in the table can be located in libraries.

TABLE 8.7	■ "Dispelling the Myths: College Students With Learning Disabilities," by Katherine Garnett and Sandra La Porta, 1990, *A Monograph for Students and Educators That Explains What Learning Disabilities Are and What Faculty Members Can Do to Help Such Students Succeed in College.* Call NCLD at (888) 575-7373.
College Guides and Resources for Learning Disabilities	■ *Assisting college students with learning disabilities: A tutor's manual,* by Pamela Adelamna and Debbie Olufs. Call AHEAD at (614) 488-4972.
	■ *College students with learning disabilities: A handbook,* by Susal Vogel, 1997, A handbook about college-related issues, including Section 504. For students with learning disabilities and college personnel. Contact LDA by phone at (414) 341-1515 or on the internet at **http://www.ldanatl.org.**
	■ *K & W guide to colleges: For students with learning disabilities or attention deficit disorder: A state-by-state guide* by Marybeth Kravets and Imy Wax, New York: Princeton Review, 2001. Call NCLD at (212) 545-7510.
	■ *Peterson's guide to colleges with programs for students with learning disabilities: A state-by-state guide,* 4th ed. Princeton, NJ: Peterson's Guides, 1997. Call NCLD at (888) 575-7373.
	■ *School/search guide to colleges with programs for students with learning disabilities: A state-by-state guide,* by Midge Lipkin, Belmont, MA: SchoolSearch Press, 1994. Call (617) 489-5785.
	■ *Unlocking potential: College and other choices for learning disabled people: A step-by-step guide,* by Barbara Scheiber (1992). A book that assists the reader through the postsecondary school selection process. Call Woodbine House at (800) 843-7323.

Source: From "College Guides and Resources for Learning Disabilities" *Their World,* (New York: NCLD, 1999). Reprinted with the permission of the National Center for Learning Disabilities, 381 Park Avenue South, New York, NY 10016. http://www.ld.org.

Professional Licensing and Learning Disabilities

Individuals entering professions such as law, medicine, and optometry must pass licensing examinations. Under the Americans With Disabilities Act, individuals with learning disabilities may receive accommodations when taking these exams. A frequently requested accommodation is an extension of time on the exam. Research shows that extended time is beneficial to such people (Weaver, 2000). Unfortunately, individuals with learning disabilities trying to enter professions are too often denied the opportunity for accommodations (Hagin & Simon, 2000).

Such barriers are all the more cruel because these young adults are usually among the most promising graduates. They are individuals whose intelligence, motivation, and perseverance, together with the supports and accommodations supplied by families and teachers, have enabled them to succeed in higher education and in their professional education despite the vicissitudes of a learning disability. Given the opportunity to serve society as professionals, they could make substantial contributions (Hagin & Simon, 2000).

Adults With Learning Disabilities

The problems created by learning disabilities may not disappear when individuals leave school. For many, difficulties continue throughout their lives. Through public awareness programs about learning disabilities, as seen on television and reported in newspapers and magazine articles, many adults come to recognize that their problems are related to learning disabilities. For example, an article in *Newsweek* brought information about learning disabilities to the general public (Wingert & Kantrovitz, 1997).

What is the life of an adult with learning disabilities like? These adults sometimes have great difficulty finding their niche in the world. They have trouble finding and keeping a job, developing a satisfying social life, and even coping with individual daily living. Many adults with learning disabilities have developed amazing strategies for avoiding, hiding, and dealing with their problems. Such a situation is described in "LD Stories: Frank, an Adult With a Learning Disability."

LD STORIES

FRANK, AN ADULT WITH A LEARNING DISABILITY

Frank is a 36-year-old man with a learning disability. He is of average intelligence, but he has much difficulty with reading. Frank sought help at a university learning disabilities clinic. Employed as a journeyman painter, and supporting his wife and two children, he has learned to cope with many daily situations that required reading skills. Although he was unable to read the color labels on paint cans, and he could not decipher street and road signs nor find streets, addresses, or use a city map to find the locations of his house-painting jobs, Frank had learned to manage by compensating for his inability to read. He visually memorized the color codes on paint cans to determine their color. He tried to limit his work to a specific area of the city because he could not read street signs. When he was sent into an unfamiliar area, he would ask a fellow worker to provide directions and accompany him, or he would request help from residents of the area to reach his destination. He watched television to keep abreast of current affairs, and his wife read and answered his correspondence. However, Frank finally realized that advancement was not possible unless he learned to read. Moreover, his children were rapidly acquiring the reading skills that he did not possess. His disability was a continual threat to him and finally led him to search for help. It is remarkable that after so many years of failure and frustration, Frank recognized that his problem is a learning disability and that he had the fortitude and motivation to attempt once again the formidable task of learning to read.

Surveys of adults with learning disabilities indicate that their major needs are in the areas of: (1) social relationships and skills; (2) career counseling; (3) developing self-esteem and confidence; (4) overcoming dependence; (5) survival skills; (6) vocational training; (7) job procurement and retention; and (7) reading, spelling, management of personal finances, and organizational skills. When these adults lose a job, they are uncertain about what has gone wrong (Gerber & Brown, 1997).

What is unique about adults with learning disabilities? They are usually self-identified and self-referred. To succeed, they must be intimately involved in both the diagnosis and the remediation process. They are likely to be highly motivated to learn the skills they know they need in life. They want to know what test results mean and what the goals and purposes of the remediation program are. It is their commitment to the remediation program that enables them to succeed. Because adults are no longer in school, they usually must find other agencies for services. Most clinics are not geared to serving adults with learning disabilities. Thus, learning disabilities specialists must enlarge their scope to provide service to adults, who are a very neglected population. Adults with learning disabilities should learn about their rights under the law (Latham & Latham, 1997).

Literacy Organizations for Teaching Adults to Read   Often adults are motivated to seek instruction in learning to read. The problem is that after individuals with learning disabilities leave school, there are fewer educational options open to them. Some literacy programs designed for adults include

- *Literacy Volunteers of America.*   Literacy Volunteers of America (LVA) is a national, nonprofit organization that has a network of volunteer tutors to teach reading, writing, and English-speaking skills to adults. LVA can be contacted at 1320 Jamesville Ave., Syracuse, NY 13210. LVA can also be reached by phone at (800) 448-8878 or at **http://www. literacyvolunteers.org** or **http://www.proliteracy.org.**

- *The Laubach program.*   The objective of this private organization is to teach literacy to people around the world. Write to Laubach Literacy Action, P.O. Box 131, 1320 Jamesville Ave., Syracuse, NY 13210. The Laubach program can also be reached by phone at (800) 528-2224 or at **http://www.laubach.org.**

- *Adult Basic Education (ABE) and General Education Degree (GED).* These government-sponsored programs offer education for adults. A person passing the GED examination is awarded a high school equivalency degree.

LD STORIES

How Computers Changed My Life

Computers changed my experience of being dyslexic and dysgraphic. Computers allow me to compensate (some might say overcompensate) for my writing and organizational problems so well, that aside from the few times when people see my handwriting, my dyslexia and dysgraphia is not evident in my daily life.

Further, I've been lucky enough to actually build a career out of talking about this with audiences all over the world. The very tools that I talk about are those that allow me to organize and give these presentations.

Source: From Richard Wanderman. (2003). "Tools and dyslexia," *Perspectives, 29*(4), 5–9.

COMPUTER TECHNOLOGY FOR ADOLESCENTS AND ADULTS

The ability to use common computer applications is an absolute necessity. If you can't use a computer, you can't function in life. People *talk* through e-mail, write with a word processor, think with spreadsheets, and create PowerPoint presentations. Individuals with learning disabilities can learn to use these technologies, and they often excel in this aspect of learning. Facility with a computer can go a long way toward bringing people with learning disabilities into the mainstream. Experience with computers helps people develop the unique technological skills needed for many types of jobs. Many individuals with learning disabilities, who have great difficulty with reading, writing, and spelling, do well with computers. Computer skills seem to require abilities that many individuals with learning disabilities have (Belson, 2003; Raskind, 1998).

Young adults with severe learning disabilities, according to Zilla & Lerner, 2004, do well with a syllabus that includes the following computer technologies:

- E-mail
- Word processing
- Inspiration
- Spreadsheets (e.g., Excel)
- Charting with spreadsheets
- Finding and using graphics
- Presentation programs (e.g., PowerPoint)
- Creating web pages
- Scanning photographs and graphics

1. Adolescents with learning disabilities must cope with the dramatic changes in their lives caused by puberty, as well as with problems related to their disabilities.

2. More adolescents with learning disabilities are being placed in general education classes. Several special problems occur at the high school level. Performance standards create pressure for high school graduation.

3. The transition from school to adult life is full of complexities for all adolescents. Adolescents with learning disabilities need extra support and assistance to successfully make this challenging transition. Transition refers to a change in status from behaving primarily as a student to assuming emergent adult roles in the community. Students with disabilities must have written transition plans beginning when they reach age 16.

4. Important features for success in high school include intensive instruction in reading and mathematics, explicit instruction in survival skills, and completion of all required high school courses for graduation. Curriculum models for learning disabilities in the secondary schools include basic skills instruction, tutorial instruction, functional skills instruction, and work–study programs.

5. Learning strategies instruction helps adolescents with learning disabilities learn how to learn and become active, efficient learners. The learning strategies approach teaches students how to learn rather than what to learn. Students can apply learning strategies to all areas of the secondary curriculum.

6. Postsecondary and college programs for young adults with learning disabilities are growing, and an increasing number of colleges have developed special services for college students with learning disabilities. The Americans With Disabilities Act and Section 504 of the Rehabilitation Act provide protection for college students with learning disabilities.

7. For many individuals, learning disabilities do not end with high school graduation. Rather, they continue as a lifelong problem. Adults with learning disabilities are receiving a growing amount of attention.

1. Describe three characteristics of adolescents with learning disabilities, and discuss how these characteristics affect high school achievement.

2. Why do special problems that occur at the secondary level affect adolescents with learning disabilities? How do these problems differ for elementary-age students?

3. More secondary students with learning disabilities are being educated in general education content-area classes. How can content-area teachers and special education teachers work together?

4. What is a transition plan for secondary students with learning disabilities? What are some of the possible goals for such a transition plan?

5. Several different curriculum models are used for teaching adolescents with learning disabilities. Describe three of these approaches.

6. What is the purpose of using learning strategies instruction for adolescents with learning disabilities? Describe each of the eight steps in learning strategies instruction.

7. How does Section 504 of the Rehabilitation Act affect the education of college students with learning disabilities? Describe three accommodations in college for students with learning disabilities.

KEY TERMS

Americans With Disabilities Act (ADA) *(p. 290)*

accommodations *(p. 275)*

attribution theory *(p. 270)*

background knowledge *(p. 286)*

basic academic skills instruction *(p. 283)*

collaborative teaming *(p. 276)*

content-area teachers *(p. 274)*

functional skills or survival skills *(p. 283)*

high-stakes testing *(p. 275)*

learning strategies instruction *(p. 285)*

performance standards *(p. 275)*

reasonable accommodations *(p. 292)*

strategies intervention model (SIM) *(p. 287)*

transition *(p. 279)*

transition planning *(p. 279)*

tutorial instruction *(p. 284)*

work–study program *(p. 284)*

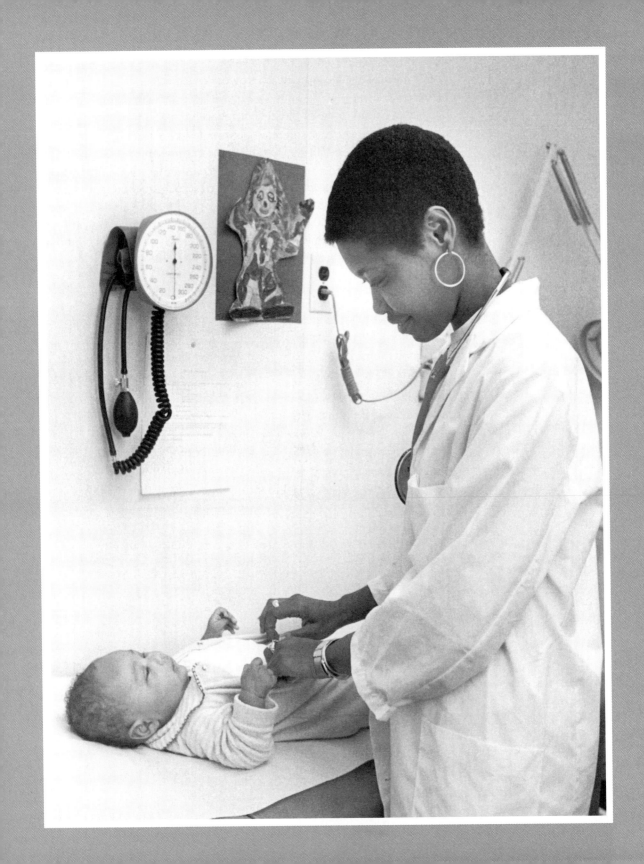

9

Medical Aspects of Learning Disabilities

> Only recently have neuroscientists had the technology to study the brain and its role in learning. The neurobiological correlates of learning disabilities are slowly being uncovered.
>
> *—Anonymous*

This chapter examines the medical aspects of learning disabilities. We will discuss: (1) the value of medical information for educators, (2) the neurosciences and the study of the brain, (3) neuropsychology, (4) the neurological examination, and (5) medical specialties involved with learning disabilities and related disorders.

The medical profession has long been an indispensable participant in the field of learning disabilities. Medical scientists conducted basic brain research that became central to the early development of the learning disability field. The current research in the neurosciences is especially exciting, providing new discoveries about how the brain functions and its relationship to learning.

Physicians who deal with children often are the first professionals to come into contact with a child with learning difficulties. They often become involved with the child's assessment, diagnosis, and treatment; and they may contribute to a student's individualized education program (IEP). Moreover, physicians tend to monitor these children with learning difficulties over a long period of time.

THE VALUE OF MEDICAL INFORMATION FOR EDUCATORS

No one discipline can remain productive in isolation. Training programs for pediatricians today recognize the multidisciplinary nature of child health and include relevant educational concepts and procedures about learning disabilities. There is a corresponding need for teachers to learn about relevant medical aspects of the field for the following reasons:

- *Learning occurs in the brain.*   Teachers need basic information about the **central nervous system**, which is the organic system that comprises the brain and the spinal cord, and its relationship to learning and to learning disabilities. All learning involves the neurological process that occurs within the brain, which is a major part of the central nervous system. A dysfunction in that system can seriously impair the processes of learning. We cannot artificially separate behavior and learning from what happens in our bodies.

- *Physicians are actively involved in treating children with learning disabilities.*   As noted previously, medical specialists often participate in the assessment and the treatment of children with learning disabilities. Teachers must therefore understand the vocabulary and concepts of the medical sciences to interpret medical reports about their students and to discuss the findings with physicians and parents. When medications are prescribed, teachers should be asked to provide feedback to parents and physicians about the child's reaction to the medication.

■ *Advances in medical technology affect children with learning disabilities.* Medical procedures now save the lives of many children who probably would not have survived only a few years ago, but sometimes these treatments lead to learning disabilities. For example, the treatment for childhood leukemia may lead to problems in attention and concentration, memory, sequencing, and comprehension on school tasks. Advances in neonatology may lead to increases in the survival rates of babies with very low birth weights, but some of these infants encounter learning disabilities later in life.

■ *Awareness of current brain research.* Informed educators need up-to-date information about the brain and learning. Scientific investigations that attempt to unravel the mysteries of the human brain and learning are fascinating in themselves. Knowledge about the brain is increasing rapidly and promises to further our understanding of the enigma of learning disabilities.

NEUROSCIENCES AND THE STUDY OF THE BRAIN

The **neurosciences** are the cluster of disciplines that investigate the structure and function of the brain and the central nervous system. In this section, we briefly examine two facets of the neurosciences: (1) the structure and functions of the brain and (2) recent brain research.

The Brain: Its Structure and Functions

All human behavior is mediated by the brain and the central nervous system. The process of learning is one of the most important activities of the brain. From a neurological perspective, learning disabilities represent a subtle malfunction in this most complex organ of the human body. Figure 9.1 shows the structure of the brain. Further information about the structure of the brain can be found at **http://serendip.brynmawr.edu.**

The Cerebral Hemispheres   The human brain is composed of two halves, the right hemisphere and the left hemisphere, which appear on casual inspection to be almost identical in construction and metabolism. Each **cerebral hemisphere** contains: (1) a frontal lobe, (2) a temporal lobe, (3) an occipital lobe, (4) a parietal lobe, and (5) a motor area, as shown in Figure 9.1. The motor area of each hemisphere controls the muscular activities of

FIGURE 9.1

The Brain

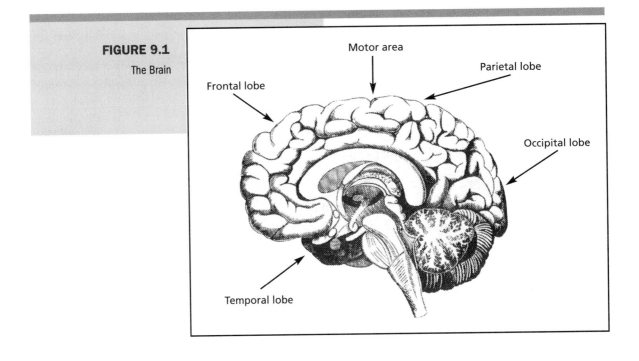

the opposite side of the body. Thus, the movements of the right hand and foot originate in the motor area of the left hemisphere. Both eyes and both ears are represented in each hemisphere (Kibby & Hynd, 2001).

Right Brain, Left Brain: Differences in Function   Although the two halves of the brain appear almost identical in structure, they differ in function, and these differences appear very early in life.

The left hemisphere reacts to and controls language-related activities. For more than 90% of adults, language function originates in the left hemisphere, regardless of whether the individual is left-handed, right-handed, or a combination of the two. Language is located in the left hemisphere in 98% of right-handed people and in about 71% of left-handed people (Hiscock & Kinsbourne, 1987).

The right hemisphere deals with nonverbal stimuli. Spatial perception, mathematics, music, directional orientation, time sequences, and body awareness are located in the right hemisphere.

Thus, even though visual and auditory nerve impulses are carried to both cerebral hemispheres simultaneously, it is the left hemisphere that reacts to linguistic stimuli, such as words, symbols, and verbal thought. Consequently, adult stroke patients with brain injury in the left hemisphere often suffer language loss, in addition to an impairment in the motor function of the right half of the body.

This duality of the brain has led to speculation that some people tend to approach the environment in a "left-brained fashion," whereas others use a "right-brained approach." Left-brained individuals are strong in language and verbal skills, while right-brained individuals have strengths in spatial, artistic, and mechanical skills. These differences in brain function warrant further discussion because the concept may provide some insight into differences in learning styles.

Cerebral Dominance Samuel Orton, a physician and early investigator of reading and language difficulties, theorized that the reversal of letters and words (which he called *strephosymbolia,* or twisted symbols) was symptomatic of a failure to establish *cerebral dominance* in the left hemisphere, which is the location of the language area (Orton, 1937). Current findings support Orton's early theories, showing that the left hemisphere does specialize in the language function and the right hemisphere controls nonverbal functions. However, the two hemispheres of the brain do not operate independently; there are many interrelating elements and functions. The learning process depends on both hemispheres and their interrelating functions. Inefficient functioning of either hemisphere reduces the total effectiveness of individuals and affects their acquisition and use of language (Cotman & Lynch, 1988; Hiscock & Kinsbourne, 1987; Kibby & Hynd, 2001).

Lateral Preference The issue of **lateral preference** is the subject of a related controversial theory, which proposes a relationship between learning disorders and a tendency to use either the right or left side of the body or a preference for the right or left hand, foot, eye, or ear. The term *consistent laterality* refers to the tendency to perform all functions with one side of the body. *Mixed laterality* is a tendency to mix the right and left preference in the use of hands, feet, eyes, and ears. A student's laterality may be tested through observation of simple behaviors—such as throwing a ball, kicking a stick, seeing with a tube, and listening to a watch—or through more sophisticated means used in neuropsychology. There are mixed research findings about the relationship between reading ability and lateral preferences (Biegler, 1987; Obrzut & Boliek, 1991).

Recent Brain Research

Research on the brain and its relationship to behavior and learning has accumulated slowly, in part because some technologies for studying the structure and function of the brain have only recently become available. Today, neuroscientists can vastly extend their studies of the structure and functions of the brain because of technological advancements that have created opportunities for a better understanding of the brain and its relationship to learning disabilities.

Many of the brain research investigations have involved studies of individuals with **dyslexia,** which is a puzzling type of learning disability that interferes with learning to read. (See the chapter on reading for more information about reading disabilities.) Individuals with dyslexia have severe difficulty with reading; however, it is not a matter of intelligence. Instead, dyslexia appears to be related to brain structure and function. Additional information about dyslexia can be found at **http://www.interdys.org.**

Reading is an extremely complex human task that requires an intact and well-functioning brain and central nervous system. "LD Stories: Recollec-

---

LD STORIES

RECOLLECTIONS OF INDIVIDUALS WITH DYSLEXIA

The following statements by individuals with this severe reading problem reveal the frustration they faced in school and the strengths they developed as they met the challenges of life.

- Charles Schwab, the founder of the successful and innovative stock brokerage firm, observed that his struggle with dyslexia led him to develop other abilities. "I've always felt that I have more of an ability to envision, to be able to anticipate where things are going, to conceive a solution to a business problem than people who are more sequential thinkers."

Source: From "Slow Words, Quick Images—Dyslexia as an Advantage in Tomorrow's Workplace," by T. West, in *Learning disabilities and employment,* p. 349, by P. Gerber & D. Brown (Eds.), 1997, Austin, TX: Pro-Ed.

- Tom Cruise, the successful movie actor, recalls, "When I was about 7 years old, I had been labeled dyslexic. I'd try to concentrate on what I was reading, then I'd get to the end of page and have very little memory of anything I'd read. I would go blank, feel anxious, nervous, bored, frustrated, dumb. I would get angry. My legs would actually hurt when I was studying. My head ached. All through

school, and well into my career, I felt like I had a secret."

Source: From "My Struggle to Read," by Tom Cruise, *People,* July 21, 2003, pp. 60–64.

- *Two students reflect on the effect of having the label of dyslexia.*

Mary said she was "thrilled" when told that she had dyslexia. She said that the diagnosis and label brought her relief. She could now better assess her abilities and recognize why and where she was having difficulty learning. Also, the label positively affected her parents, prompting them to realize the struggle she underwent in order to do well in school.

Jackie said the label of dyslexia gave her a "feeling of peace and assurance that [she] wasn't an oddity." She noted, "The label of LD is a label, and as [with any] label[,] stereotypes will always surface. But that label is also part of me. It's as much a part of me as my middle name, as my smile, as my love of lilacs."

Source: From H. McGrady, J. Lerner, and M. Boscardin, "The Educational Lives of Students With Learning Disabilities", in P. Rodis, A. Garrand, and M. Boscardin, *Learning disabilities and life stories,* pp. 177–193. Copyright 2001 by Pearson Education. Adapted with the permission of the publisher.

---

tions of Individuals With Dyslexia" illustrates the serious challenges for people with dyslexia.

For almost a century, scientists conjectured that there was a neurological basis for dyslexia and that the difficulty in acquiring reading skills stemmed from differences in brain function. With growing knowledge about the brain and its relationship to reading, there is now convincing evidence that the brains of people with dyslexia do indeed differ in structure and function from the brains of persons who do not have reading problems (Lyon et al., 2001; Shaywitz, 2003; Zeffrino & Eden, 2000).

A series of research studies to investigate the mystery of dyslexia occurred in a relatively short period of time. This research involved: (1) postmortem anatomical studies, (2) the genetics of learning disabilities, (3) computed tomography, (4) positron-emission tomography, and (5) functional magnetic resonance imaging. Each of these research studies revealed a piece of the puzzle.

Postmortem Anatomical Studies   **Postmortem anatomical studies** showed strong evidence that the brain structure of dyslexic individuals was different from that of individuals without dyslexia. These autopsy studies analyzed the brain tissue of deceased individuals who had dyslexia. Some of these individuals were young men who died suddenly, such as in motorcycle accidents. At the time of death, their brains were donated for study to an ongoing dyslexia research center at Harvard Medical School's Department of Neurology at Beth Israel Hospital in Boston. The brain tissue of eight people—six men and two women—was studied. The postmortem anatomical brain studies found a remarkable and consistent abnormality in the structure of the brain in these individuals. This abnormality was found in an area of the brain known as the *planum temporale,* which lies on the superior surface of the temporal lobe. In the left hemisphere, this area is the center of language control. In the postmortem studies of dyslexic cases, this area (i.e., the language area) of the left hemisphere was smaller and had fewer brain cells than that of nondyslexic individuals. However, this same area in the right hemisphere was larger and contained more cells than are found in nondyslexic individuals (Filipek 1995; Galaburda, 1990; Powers, 2000).

Genetics of Learning Disabilities   Knowledge of the **genetics of learning disabilities** and its role in the inheritability of learning disabilities and dyslexia increased significantly in the last decade (Pennington, 1995). Two types of genetic studies are: (1) family studies and (2) twin studies.

- *Family studies.*   The family studies began with a study conducted in Scandinavia, which showed that dyslexia aggregates in families (Hallgren, 1950). Since then, more extensive family studies continue to show strong evidence that the tendency for severe reading disabilities is inherited and appears to have a genetic basis (Pennington, 1995).

- **Twin studies.** The twin studies research provides further evidence that genetics plays a significant role in dyslexia. Research showed that twins have similar characteristics in terms of reading disabilities, even when they are raised separately (DeFries et al., 1997).

Computed Tomography **Computed tomography (CT)** is a computerized series of X-rays that build a three-dimensional image of the brain. Using this technology, researchers were able to see the structure of the brain for the first time (Shaywitz, 2003).

Positron-Emission Tomography **Positron-emission tomography (PET)** was the first technology developed to measure the brain at work. PET measures blood flow to the brain regions through the use of a radioactive compound that is injected into the bloodstream (Hauser et al., 1993). Much has been learned about the brain through PET technology. However, this technology is difficult to use because it is an invasive procedure, and it also requires elaborate equipment.

Advances with Functional Magnetic Resonance Imaging

A tremendous breakthrough in the study of the brain during the reading process came about in the 1990s with the development of **functional magnetic resonance imaging (fMRI)**. This device has several advantages: (1) it allows neuroscientists to view regions of the human brain as the person is reading, (2) it is a noninvasive procedure, and (3) it is a relatively easy procedure for use with children. The fMRI shows which parts of the brain are receiving the most blood or are the most active at any point in time. The studies conducted at Yale University with the fMRI provide much information about the human brain during reading tasks (Gorman, 2003; Shaywitz, 2003; Shaywitz et al., 2004). Further information about fMRI can be found at **http://www.fmri.ox.ac.uk.**

Figure 9.2 shows three areas of the left hemisphere of the brain that are used during the act of reading (Gorman, 2003; Kotulak, 2004; Shaywitz, 2003; Shaywitz & Shaywitz, 1999).

1. In the frontal lobe *(left interior front gyrus)* is the phoneme producer. This region of the brain, called *Broca's area,* is used to link letters to sounds and is associated with the ability to say words out loud.

2. In the parietal lobe *(left parieto-temporal area)* is the word analyzer. This region of the brain, called *Wernicke's area,* is involved with analyzing words.

3. In the occipital lobe *(left occipito-temporal area)* is the automatic detector. This region of the brain is involved with integrating learned words and storing and retrieving words.

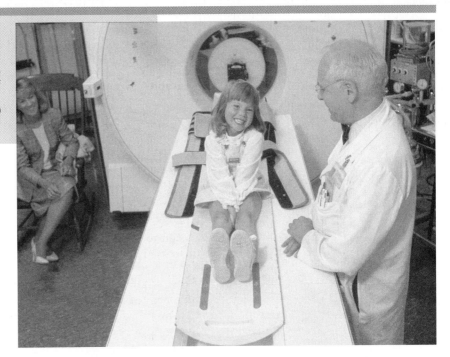

Neuroscientists are using functional magnetic resonance imaging (fMRI) to study the working brain of children as they read. *(© David A. Wells/Corbis)*

FIGURE 9.2

An fMRI image shows activation patterns in the brain while a person is engaged in an activity. This illustration shows the activation locations of some reading activities.

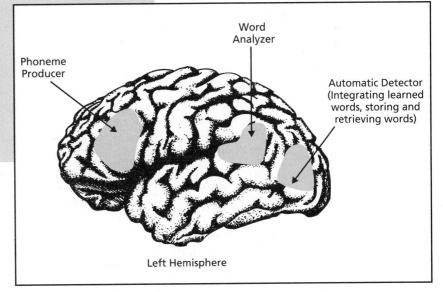

Phoneme Producer

Word Analyzer

Automatic Detector (Integrating learned words, storing and retrieving words)

Left Hemisphere

All of these areas work simultaneously during reading, much like "sections of an orchestra playing a symphony" (Shaywitz, 2003).

The fMRI studies show that beginning readers and children with reading disabilities or dyslexia rely heavily on the front of the brain, which is the *phoneme producer* region, as they concentrate on, and try to say, the sounds of phonemes. They also rely heavily on the *word analyzer* region of the brain, as they try to decode words. As the readers became more skilled, they activate the *automatic detector* region of the brain, as they automatically recognize familiar words on sight. The fMRI research suggests that physical changes occur as a result of academic intervention with children who are dyslexic (Aylward et al., 2003; Shaywitz, 2003). The fMRI research also shows that individuals with dyslexia, even after gaining reading skills, continue to have difficulty accessing the reading areas at the back of the brain (i.e., the automatic detector region of the brain), and they rely more heavily on the phoneme producer region and the front of the brain. Hence, there is a neurological explanation for why these individuals read more slowly and require extended time (Shaywitz, 2003).

One of the fMRI studies conducted at Yale University found that the areas of the brain changed after children were given intensive reading instruction, using phonologically based reading instruction. The study showed that the brains of poor readers started off with only the first two areas of the brain activated; however, after a year of reading instruction, their reading ability leaped ahead, as did the word storage area of the brain, which began to activate, just like that of the good readers (Shaywitz et al., 2004).

A research study using the fMRI was conducted in China on children as they read using the Chinese writing system. Similar to fMRI western studies, the Chinese study also showed differences between the brain scans of normal and dyslexic readers. However, the Chinese writing system puts demands on different parts of the brain than western alphabetic writing systems. The western alphabetic writing system requires abilities in phonological awareness of spoken words. The Chinese writing system requires abilities with pictorial and visual symbols. The fMRI study with Chinese dyslexic children showed that they had difficulty in the left middle frontal gyrus, located in front of the brain on the left, the area of the brain that maps written symbols to meaning. The researchers suggest that dyslexic children using the Chinese writing system need instruction in linking visual shapes, sound, and meaning of visual characters (McGough, 2004).

We now turn to a branch of psychology known as neuropsychology to investigate the relationship between brain function and behavior.

NEUROPSYCHOLOGY   **Neuropsychology** is a branch of psychology that combines psychology and neurology. The neuropsychologist assesses the development and integrity of the individual's central nervous system and the relationship between brain function and behavior. Most of the research in neuropsychology has been applied to the behavior of adults with brain injury. However, recent work in this specialized field has been directed toward research and applications in the area of learning disabilities (Fennel, 1995; Kibby & Hynd, 2001; Swanson, 1996).

A neuropsychological examination is specifically designed to identify subtle or overt neurobehavioral problems that contribute to the child's difficulty in making normal academic progress. Several broad domains in functioning are addressed in the neuropsychological examination: intellectual, attentional, memory, learning, language, sensorimotor, frontal executive, and social–emotional (Fennel, 1995). Neuropsychological evaluations also analyze hemispheric differences, that is, differences in functions between the left and right hemispheres of the brain (Kibby & Hynd, 2001).

Neuropsychological test batteries that assess brain functions in children include the Halstead-Reitan Neuropsychological Test Battery for Children (ages 9 to 14) and the Reitan-Indiana Neuropsychological Battery for Children (ages 5 to 8). Use of these tests requires training in neuropsychology and in administering tests. A test of information processing functions is the Swanson Cognitive-Processing Test (see "Tests for Assessing Students With Learning Disabilities" in the Reference Guide at the back of this book).

THE NEUROLOGICAL EXAMINATION

Neurological examinations can be conducted by several medical specialists—the family practice physician, the pediatrician, the developmental pediatrician, the pediatric neurologist, or the child psychiatrist. (The roles of these specialists are discussed in more detail later in this chapter.) The neurological examination of a child or adolescent suspected of having learning disabilities has two distinct components: the conventional neurological assessment and the examination for **soft neurological signs,** which are minimal or subtle neurological deviations, such as coordination difficulties in visual–motor, fine-motor, or gross-motor activities.

A carefully performed and judiciously interpreted neurological examination can contribute to the understanding of the functional status of a child with learning disabilities. However, parents and schools should not have unrealistic expectations about the results of neurological examinations. Often, the conventional neurological examination will fail to find any overt abnormalities in patients whose primary complaint is the inability to learn (Accardo & Blondis, 2000; Levine, 1994; Rapkin, 1995). There are a number of difficulties in interpreting neurological findings:

1. A wide range of soft signs of minimal neurological dysfunction occurs among students who *are* learning satisfactorily.

2. Because the student's neurological system is not yet mature and is continually changing, it is often very difficult to differentiate between a developmental lag and a dysfunction of the central nervous system.

3. Many of the tests for soft signs are psychological or behavioral, rather than neurological.

The ultimate test of healthy neurological function is efficient learning. The unique human ability to learn is attributable to the highly complex organization of the brain and nervous system. This section gives a brief overview of: (1) the conventional neurological assessments and (2) the neurological examinations for soft signs. More information can be found at **http://www.lpch.org/diseasehealthinfo/healthlibrary/neuro/neuroexam. html.**

Conventional Neurological Assessment

In the conventional neurological examination, the physician first obtains a careful, detailed medical history. The information includes a family history (for clues of a genetic nature); details of the mother's pregnancy, the birth process, and the neonatal development; and the child's developmental history. The physician obtains information about all illnesses, injuries, and infections that the child has had. The developmental history includes information about motor behavior (the age at which the child crawled, stood, and walked) and language skills. Additional information about the child's hearing, vision, feeding, sleeping, toilet-training, and social and school experiences is collected (Accardo & Blondis, 2000; Rapkin, 1995).

An examination of the *cranial nerves* gives information relating to vision, hearing, taste, and vestibular function (the sense of balance), as well as such characteristics as facial expression, chewing, swallowing, and the ability to speak. The function of the various cranial nerves is evaluated by noting the child's responses to certain stimuli, the condition of various organs, and the child's ability to perform certain tasks.

The conventional neurological examination also assesses the control of *motor function.* The child's reflexes are tested, and sensory nerves are assessed through tests of perception or tactile stimulation.

Other special medical procedures that might be requested include an EEG to measure the electrical activity of the brain, X-rays of the skull and the blood vessels of the brain, biochemical studies, endocrinologic studies, or genetic examinations.

Examination for Soft Neurological Signs

Soft neurological signs can be detected through a neurological examination that goes beyond the conventional examination. As noted earlier, the neurological anomalies most often seen in people with learning disabilities are not gross deviations, but rather fine, subtle, and minor symptoms. These

soft signs include mild coordination difficulties, minimal tremors, motor awkwardness, visual–motor disturbances, deficiencies or abnormal delay in language development, and difficulties in reading and arithmetic skills. Another soft sign is hyperactivity, which is also recognized as a characteristic of attention deficit disorder.

Neurologists use a number of tests to detect soft signs of central nervous system dysfunction (Accardo & Blondis, 2000; Levine, 1987). Some of these tests could also be used by teachers as informal motor tests. Many of the tests used to detect soft neurological signs have been borrowed or adapted from psychological assessment procedures. We will look at: (1) visual–motor, (2) gross-motor, and (3) fine-motor tests.

Visual–Motor Tests A number of visual–motor tests are used to evaluate a patient's ability to copy various geometric forms. Children can copy the forms shown in Figure 9.3 at the following ages:

FIGURE 9.3

Geometric Forms

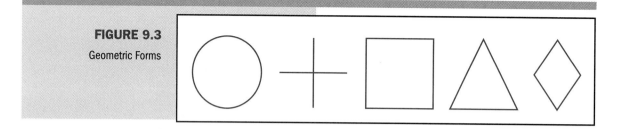

Figure	Age
Circle	3
Cross	4
Square	5
Triangle	6–7
Diamond	7

Other commonly used visual–motor tests are the Bender-Gestalt Test, in which the patient is asked to copy nine geometric forms, and the Goodenough-Harris Drawing Test, which requires the patient to draw a picture of a human figure. The scoring of the Goodenough-Harris test depends on the body detail represented.

Gross-Motor Tests   Gross-motor tests assess postural skills, movement, and balance. The child's walking gait is also observed. Children can normally perform the following tasks at the ages indicated:

Task	Age
Hopping on either foot. The child is asked to hop on the right foot, then on the left.	5
Standing on one foot. The child is asked to stand on one foot (first the right, then the left) and to maintain balance.	6
Tandem walking (heel-to-toe). The child is asked to walk by placing the heel of one foot directly in front of the toe of the other.	9

Two tests of crossing the midline in the execution of movements are also given:

Touching nose and left ear and then nose and right ear.   Observers note the rapidity with which the automatic takeover of motor movements is introduced.

Finger–nose test.   The child is asked to touch a finger to his or her nose and to the examiner's finger repeatedly. Facility in alternating movement is observed.

Fine-Motor Tests   The *finger-agnosia* test assesses the child's ability to use tactile sensation to recognize, often with eyes closed, which finger is being touched by the examiner. The tasks and the normal age at which each task can be performed follow:

Task	Age
Recognition of thumb	4
Recognition of index finger	5–6

Other tests of tactile perception are recognition of objects by touch, recognition of two simultaneous contacts as the examiner touches two parts of the child's body (such as face and hand), recognition of letters or numbers by touch, recognition of letters or numbers drawn in the palm of the hand, and facility in moving the tongue (vertically and horizontally).

The *finger dexterity* test requires the child to touch each finger in turn to the thumb. Each hand is tested separately.

MEDICAL SPECIALTIES INVOLVED WITH LEARNING DISABILITIES AND RELATED DISORDERS

Many medical specialists become responsible for the diagnosis and treatment of the child with learning disabilities and related disorders. We briefly review some of these medical specialties, which include: (1) pediatrics and family practice medicine, (2) neurology, (3) ophthalmology, (4) otology, and (5) psychiatry.

Pediatrics and Family Practice Medicine

Pediatricians and family practice physicians who deal with children and adolescents see their role as extending beyond the child's physical health to include the total management of the child in terms of physical and mental health, in addition to language development, school adjustment, and academic learning. Pediatricians are increasingly aware of learning disabilities. *Developmental and behavioral pediatrics* is an emerging subspecialty within pediatrics that combines expertise in child development with medical knowledge, especially in the areas of genetics, neurology, and psychiatry (Accardo & Blondis, 2000).

Neurology

Neurology is a field of medicine that studies the structure, functions, and abnormalities of the nervous system. The neurologist is a physician who specializes in the development and function of the central nervous system. The subspecialty within neurology that deals with learning disabilities is called *pediatric neurology.* These specialists have the experience, training, and professional perspective to diagnose and treat children and adolescents with learning disabilities and related disorders.

Ophthalmology

When a child has difficulty in school, parents often contact an eye specialist, particularly if the problem is poor reading. Two specialties that deal with eye care are ophthalmology and optometry. An **ophthalmologist** is a medical eye specialist who is concerned with the organic health of the eye, as well as with refractive errors. An *optometrist* is the nonmedical eye specialist concerned with measuring and correcting vision, as well as with the correct use of the eyes.

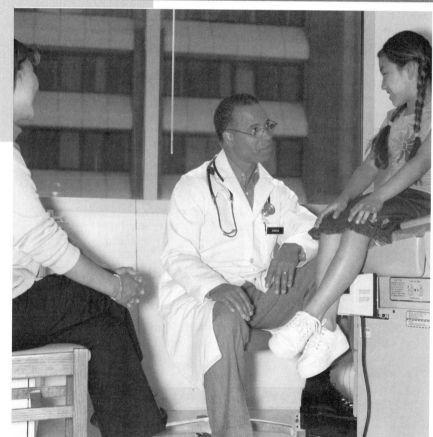

Many medical specialists become responsible for students with learning disabilities and related disorders in terms of diagnosis and treatment. *(© Ryan McVay/ Getty Images)*

Otology

Otology is a field of medicine that is concerned with the ears and auditory disorders. Our ability to hear sounds and language is a crucial factor in the learning of language. The medical specialist responsible for the diagnosis and treatment of auditory disorders is the *otologist*. The nonmedical specialists who deals with hearing is the *audiologist*. A common ear condition in children is *otitis media*, which is an inflammation of the middle ear. This condition can cause a mild and fluctuating hearing loss that interferes with language development.

Psychiatry

Children with learning disabilities are often referred to a child **psychiatrist,** who is a medical specialist who considers the complex relationships between organic factors, emotional elements, and mental health. The child psychiatrist plays an important role in the diagnosis and treatment of children with learning disabilities (Silver, 1998).

"LD in Practice: Strategies for Using Medical Information in the General Education Classroom" offers strategies for using medical information in the general education classroom.

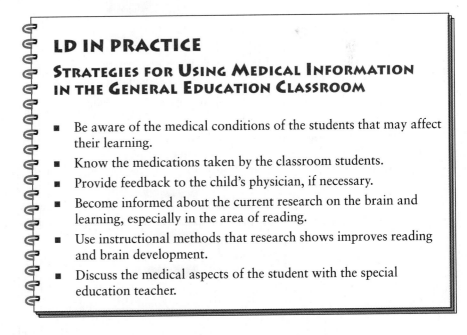

LD IN PRACTICE
STRATEGIES FOR USING MEDICAL INFORMATION IN THE GENERAL EDUCATION CLASSROOM

- Be aware of the medical conditions of the students that may affect their learning.
- Know the medications taken by the classroom students.
- Provide feedback to the child's physician, if necessary.
- Become informed about the current research on the brain and learning, especially in the area of reading.
- Use instructional methods that research shows improves reading and brain development.
- Discuss the medical aspects of the student with the special education teacher.

1. Medical information about learning disabilities has value for teachers because learning occurs within the brain, and what happens in the central nervous system affects a student's learning. Physicians often participate in the assessment and treatment of a student with learning disabilities.

2. The neurosciences consist of various specialties that study the structure and function of the brain. Functional magnetic resonance imaging (fMRI) technology has produced important research studies.

3. The brain has two hemispheres—the right and the left. Each hemisphere controls different kinds of learning, although the learning process depends on both hemispheres and their interrelationships. Theories about cerebral dominance, lateral preference, and hemispheric differences are applied to learning disabilities. Recent brain research provides evidence that dyslexia has a neurological basis. Familial and twin studies suggest that a tendency for severe reading disabilities is genetic.

4. Neuropsychology combines neurology and psychology and studies the relationship between brain function and behavior. Neuropsychologists are beginning to apply their knowledge to the field of learning disabilities.

5. The neurological examination for learning disabilities is conducted by a family practice physician, pediatrician, neurologist, or psychiatrist. It consists of two parts: (1) the standard neurological assessment and (2) the examination for soft signs, which are minimal neurological deviations.

6. The medical professionals who typically serve students with learning disabilities include pediatricians, family practice physicians, developmental pediatricians, pediatric neurologists, and child psychiatrists.

1. Why should teachers be informed about the function and dysfunction of the brain?

2. What are the neurosciences discovering about the brain in relation to dyslexia? What kinds of research are being conducted?

3. What medical specialties are involved with learning disabilities? What role do they play?

Oral Language:
Listening and Speaking

> "Then you should say what you mean," the March Hare went on. "I do," Alice hastily replied, "at least—at least I mean what I say—that's the same thing, you know." "Not the same thing a bit!" said the Hatter. "You might just as well say that 'I see what I eat' is the same thing as 'I eat what I see'!"
>
> —*Alice's Adventures in Wonderland*, Lewis Carroll

Part IV considers the major areas of learning that affect children and youth with learning disabilities: (1) oral language, (2) reading, (3) written language, (4) mathematics, and (5) social and emotional behavior. In each of these chapters, there are two major sections: "Theories," which describes the concepts underlying that area of learning, and "Teaching Strategies," which describes methods for improving skills in that area of learning.

The three chapters on language constitute an integrated segment. Each chapter focuses on a different form of language, from oral language, to reading, to written language. Their organic unity comes from the underlying integrated language system.

This chapter highlights oral language, which includes listening and speaking. In the "Theories" section, we review: (1) oral language, reading, and writing as an integrated system; (2) language as a communication process; (3) how children acquire language; (4) the components of the language system; (5) the types of language problems; (6) cultural and linguistic diversity in oral language; (7) early literacy and oral language; and (8) assessing oral language. The "Teaching Strategies" section provides instructional methods of: (1) listening, (2) speaking, (3) computer technology for oral language, and (4) teaching language in the general education classroom.

THEORIES

Language is a wondrous thing. It is recognized as one of the greatest of human achievements—more important than all the physical tools invented in the past 2,000 years. The acquisition of language is unique to human beings. Although other animals have communication systems, only humans have attained the most highly developed system of communication—speech. Language fulfills several very human functions: It provides a means of communicating and socializing with other human beings, it enables the culture to be transmitted from generation to generation, and it is a vehicle of thought.

An untreated language deficit, then, may diminish an individual's capacity to experience the full range and depth of communicating through language. Many individuals with learning difficulties manifest some aspect of language inadequacy. Unlike physical disabilities, a language disorder cannot be seen. Yet its effects are often more pervasive and insidious than are the effects of acute physical impairments.

We know that language is essential for development, thinking, and human relationships; yet many aspects of language remain mysterious. How is language acquired by the child? What is the connection between symbolic language and the thinking process? What are the links between language and cognitive and social learning? How does a language impairment affect learning? Language researchers continue to investigate these complicated issues.

ORAL LANGUAGE, READING, AND WRITING: AN INTEGRATED SYSTEM

Language appears in several forms: (1) *oral language* (listening and speaking), (2) *reading*, and (3) *writing;* all are linked through an integrated language system. Concepts about teaching oral language, reading, and writing have undergone tremendous change. The interrelationships of oral language, reading, and writing serve to build the core of the language system. As children gain competence and intimacy with language in one form, they also build knowledge and experience with the underlying language core, which are then carried into learning language in another form. What the child learns about the language system through oral language provides a knowledge base for reading and writing, and what the child learns about language through writing improves reading and oral language. Moreover, these interrelationships also affect language difficulties. When a child exhibits language difficulty in one form, the underlying language deficit often reappears in other forms. For example, a child who has a language delay at age 5 may have a reading disorder at age 8 and a writing disorder at age 14 (Adams, Foorman, Lundberg, & Beeler, 1998; Mann & Foy, 2003; Mather & Goldstein, 2001).

Early experiences in listening, talking, and learning about the world provide the foundation for reading and writing. Through experience with oral language, children learn about the linguistic structures of language, expand their vocabularies, and become familiar with different types of sentences. They are building vocabulary (or semantic knowledge) and an awareness of sentence structure (syntactic knowledge) that they will use in reading and writing. Examples of oral language experiences that help children develop such knowledge include learning words; hearing stories, songs, and rhymes; and recognizing repeated refrains in books. Functional knowledge about sentence sequences or the formation of plurals in one form of language carries over to other forms (Adams et al., 1998; Richek et al., 2002).

By becoming familiar with the sounds of language, children develop a language base for reading. Poor readers who lack an awareness of phonological sounds need specific practice with language sounds. Phonological experiences promote familiarity with language sounds, establishing the basis for word-recognition skills in reading (Adams et al., 1998; Blachman, Tangel, & Ball, 2004; Moats, 1998).

In summary, language is an integrated system, and many areas of learning depend upon mastery of language and facility with verbal symbols. As the child matures, language plays an increasingly important part in the development of the thinking processes and in the ability to grasp abstract concepts. Words become symbols for objects, groups of objects, and ideas. Language permits human beings to speak of things unseen, of the past, and of the future.

Forms of the Language System

The language system encompasses the language forms of listening, speaking, reading, and writing. The acquisition of these language skills follows a general sequence of development: (1) listening, (2) speaking, (3) reading, and (4) writing. As shown in Figure 10.1, the different language forms have an underlying language core that integrates the four forms of language. Moreover, experiences with each language form strengthen the underlying language core, which in turn improves the individual's facility in other language forms.

Historically, as civilization evolved, oral language systems for listening and speaking developed hundreds of thousands of years before the creation

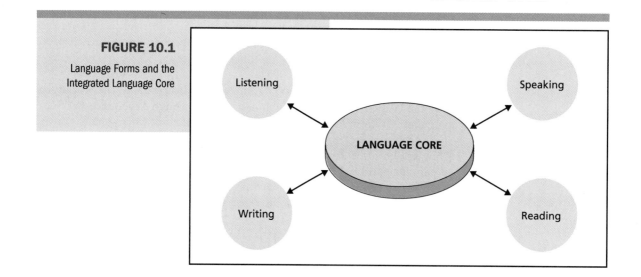

FIGURE 10.1

Language Forms and the Integrated Language Core

Listening

Speaking

LANGUAGE CORE

Writing

Reading

LANGUAGE AND LEARNING

HELEN KELLER

One of the most dramatic illustrations of the dependency of thought on language is the experience of Helen Keller as she became aware that things have symbolic names that represent them. The impact of this discovery, made at age 7, changed her behavior from that of an intractable, undisciplined, animal-like child to that of a thinking, language-oriented human being. Her teacher, Anne Sullivan, described the events (Keller, 1961):

> I made Helen hold her mug under the spout while I pumped. As the cold water gushed forth, filling the mug, I spelled "w-a-t-e-r" in Helen's free hand. The word coming so close upon the sensation of cold water rushing over her hand seemed to startle her. She dropped the mug and stood as one transfixed. A new light came into her face. She spelled "water" several times. Then she dropped to the ground and asked for its name and pointed to the pump and the trellis and suddenly turning around she asked for my name. . . . All the way back to the house she was highly ex-cited, and learned the name of every object she touched, so that in a few hours she had added 30 new words to her vocabulary. (pp. 273–274)

Helen Keller also described the transformation caused by her own awareness of language:

> As the cool water gushed over one hand she spelled into the other the word *water,* first slowly, then rapidly. I stood still, my whole attention fixed upon the motion of her fingers.
>
> Suddenly I felt a misty consciousness as of something forgotten—a thrill of returning thought; and somehow the mystery of language was revealed to me. I knew then that "w-a-t-e-r" meant the wonderful, cool something that was flowing over my hand. That living word awakened my soul, gave it light, hope, joy, set it free. . . . I left the wellhouse eager to learn. Everything had a name, and each name gave birth to a new thought. (p. 34)

Helen Keller had learned that a word can be used to signify objects and to order the events, ideas, and meaning of the world about her. Language had become a tool for her to use.

---

of written systems for reading and writing. In fact, in historical terms, the written form of language is relatively recent; even today, many societies in the world have only a spoken language and no written language.

Because the oral skills of listening and speaking are developed first, they are considered the **primary language system.** Reading and writing are considered the **secondary language system** because we are dealing with a symbol of a symbol. Whereas the spoken word is a symbol of an idea or a concrete experience, the written word is a symbol of the spoken word. Helen Keller's primary language system was finger spelling because she learned it first, and Braille was her secondary system. "LD Stories: Language and Learning" illustrates Helen Keller's first experiences in language learning.

Two of the four forms of the language system can be categorized as input or *receptive language modes,* and the other two are output or *expressive language modes.* Listening and reading are input or *receptive* skills, feeding information into the central nervous system. Speaking and writing are output or *expressive* skills in which ideas originate in the brain and are sent outward.

One implication for teaching is that abundant quantities of input experience and information are needed before output skills can be effectively executed. This principle has been concisely stated as *"intake* before *outgo."* Students should not be assigned to produce output, such as a written theme or an oral report, before they have been exposed to adequate input experiences, such as discussions, graphic organizers, field trips, or reading. These experiences will enhance the productivity of the output. The integrating mechanism between the input and the output is the brain, or the central nervous system. The relationship of the four language forms is shown in Figure 10.2.

Council for Exceptional Children Standards for Language

The Council for Exceptional Children (CEC) has developed a knowledge and skill base for language, which was written for teachers of students with learning disabilities. There are two sections: (1) the *common core language standards* for all special education students and (2) the *learning disabilities standards,* which are specific to learning disabilities. These standards are presented in Table 10.1. The website for these standards is **http://www.cec.sped.org/ps/.**

Language as a Communication Process

Language provides a way for people to communicate with one another. There are other methods of communication, such as gesturing, using body

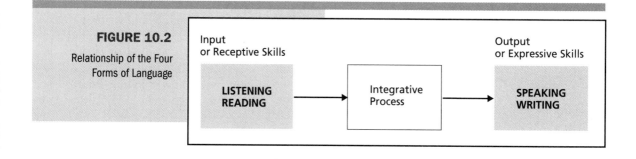

FIGURE 10.2

Relationship of the Four Forms of Language

Input or Receptive Skills

LISTENING READING → Integrative Process → **SPEAKING WRITING**

Output or Expressive Skills

TABLE 10.1	*Common core* language standards (for all special education students)
CEC Knowledge and Skill-Based Standards for Language	**Knowledge**
	■ Effects of cultural and linguistic differences on growth and development
	■ Characteristics of one's own culture and use of language and the ways in which these can differ from other cultures and use of languages
	■ Ways of behaving and communicating among cultures that can lead to misinterpretation and misunderstanding
	■ Augmentative and assistive communication strategies
	Skills
	■ Use strategies to support and enhance communication skills of individuals with exceptional learning needs
	■ Use communication strategies and resources to facilitate understanding of subject matter for students whose primary language is not the dominant language
	Learning disabilities **standards (for students with learning disabilities)**
	Knowledge
	■ Typical language development and how that may differ for individuals with learning disabilities
	■ Impact of language development and listening comprehension on academic and nonacademic learning of individuals with learning disabilities
	Skills
	■ Enhance vocabulary development
	■ Teach strategies for spelling accuracy and generalization
	■ Teach methods and strategies for producing legible documents
	■ Teach individuals with learning disabilities to monitor for errors in oral and written communication

Source: From Council for Exceptional Children, "Knowledge Skill Base for Language: Common Core Language Standards and Learning Disabilities Standards," http://www.cec.sped.org/ps. Copyright 2000 by Council for Exceptional Children. Reprinted with permission.

language, and using sign language. The communication process between two people consists of sending a message (*expressive language*) and receiving a message (*receptive language*). As Figure 10.3 illustrates, Person A, who is transmitting an idea to Person B, must convert her idea into language symbols. She encodes (or converts) the message into either sound symbols (speaking) or visual graphic symbols (writing). Person B, who receives the message, must then convert the symbols back into an idea. He decodes (converts) either the sound symbols (listening) or the visual graphic symbols (reading).

A breakdown can occur anywhere in this process. For example, in the expressive portion of the communication process, the impairment could be in formulating the idea, in coding it into spoken and written language symbols, or in remembering the sequences of previous speaking or writing. In the receptive portion of the communication process, the impairment could be in the reception and perception of the symbols through the eye or ear, in the integration of these stimuli in the brain, or in the recall or memory as it affects

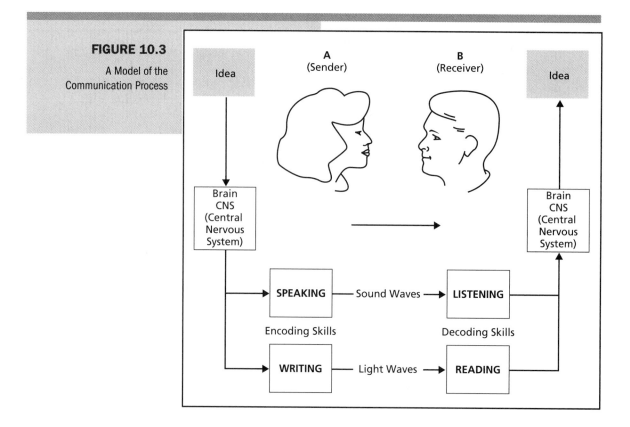

FIGURE 10.3

A Model of the
Communication Process

the ability to translate the sensory images into an idea. Understanding the communication process helps teachers deal with the communication problems of students with learning disabilities.

HOW CHILDREN ACQUIRE LANGUAGE

Several factors play a role in the acquisition of language: (1) behavioral, (2) biological, (3) cognitive, and (4) social factors all contribute to how children learn language. Each factor suggests a different way of teaching language.

Behavioral Factors

Environmental influences and behavioral principles shape a child's language learning. B. F. Skinner (1957), the pioneering behavioral psychologist, explained that children learn language through the behavioral processes of imitation and reinforcement. As young children try to imitate the sounds they hear in their environment and are reinforced for their attempts, they begin their learning of language.

For example, Peter's mother was worried about her 22-month-old son who was not, as yet, saying words. During a Thanksgiving dinner, Peter was sitting in a high chair at the family gathering of about 25 people. When Peter gestured that he wanted to get up, his mother said the word *up,* and Peter tried to imitate the word. When Peter attempted to say the sound, all 25 people stood up and said "up." Peter looked around and was delighted with the response he had generated. He uttered the sound "up" again and again, each time eliciting the same response from the group. By the end of the Thanksgiving meal, Peter had learned his first word.

Using the behavioral learning principle of positive reinforcement, the adults rewarded the child for a language attempt with attention and praise. Teachers also can encourage language development through positive reinforcement (Mather & Goldstein, 2001; Lerner et al., 2003).

Biological or Innate Factors

Language learning is also affected by biological factors. Lenneberg (1967) first observed that children are biologically predisposed to learn and use language. Further, human beings have an innate capacity for dealing with linguistic universals that are common to all languages. In the process of learning a language, the child has a limited number of primary language experiences. At a rather young age, the child hears speech and begins to understand and to repeat certain words and sentences. The mystery of language learning is that, from these limited experiences, the child soon is able to understand and to produce new sentences (Chomsky, 1965; Pinker, 1995). To add to this puzzle of language learning, children in all cultures have the ability to perform this feat in their native language at about the same chronological and developmental stage. When it is time to enter school, children who are developing along normal language growth patterns use language nearly as well as the adults in their immediate environment, using and understanding almost all the common sentence patterns.

The child learning a language does not merely learn a set of sentences, but rather internalizes the total language system, which is needed for understanding and making new sentences. The transition in language learning from the simple stages of comprehension and expression to the stage at which the child uses a complex mechanism of language is so rapid that accurate notation of the child's language acquisition and development by observation alone is very difficult. In that brief period of transition, the child suddenly learns to use the mechanisms of grammar. The biological or innate view is that the task of learning human language is so complex that some important aspects of language cannot be learned, but are innate within the brain.

In terms of teaching, the biological or innate view is that language is a natural human phemonenon. The child's language will develop and flourish if the child is given a stimulating language environment. Language

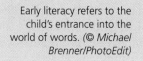
Early literacy refers to the child's entrance into the world of words. (© *Michael Brenner/PhotoEdit*)

learning is compared to learning to walk; rather than being completely acquired, some aspects of spoken language "unfold" or "flower" under appropriate developmental and environmental circumstances. Most children internalize the language system before they reach school age; they understand and respond to the language of others in a meaningful way (Fey, Windsor, & Warren, 1995; Owens, 1995). However, up to 8% of children exhibit deviations and delays in language development and require additional time and teaching to internalize the language system (Tallal, 2000; Tallal, Miller, Jenkins, & Merzenich, 1997).

Cognitive Factors

The cognitive factors of language learning highlight the links between language and thinking (Fey & Proctor-Williams, 2000; Lahey, 1988). The child's existing knowledge base, or *schema,* is an important element in language learning. The child's thoughts and language interact as the thinking process builds language meaning, and the child's language, in turn, builds the thinking process (Piaget, 1970).

For example, the infant has some existing thoughts and knowledge about the word *milk.* When the word *milk* is used by the parent, the child takes in this new word and modifies his or her knowledge base by integrating the existing concept of milk with the word *milk.* As children mature, their language becomes more sophisticated because they understand more complex language and modify it with more complex thoughts. Through language experiences, children strengthen, add to, or change their existing knowledge schema, or cognitive structure.

When a child accommodates new information with existing knowledge schema, the process is often obvious. For example, 4-year-old Aaron had gone fishing several times with his grandfather. He had the experience of catching the fish, cooking it, and eating it. When Aaron came to his grandparent's house for Thanksgiving and looked at the turkey on the table, he tried to accommodate the new information with his existing fishing schema. His thoughts led to his question, "Did you catch it with your fishing pole, Grandpa?"

In terms of language teaching, the cognitive factors suggest that language should be taught as a thinking process, promoting active experiences to build thinking and language. Parents and teachers must ascertain what the child already knows and provide active experiences to build meaning and thinking. As children use their experiences to expand their existing knowledge and language base, their language and meaning gradually develop.

Social Factors

Vygotsky (1978) explains that one important way in which language develops is through social interactions with more knowledgeable language users. Interpersonal relationships contribute to language learning, and the reciprocal interactions between the child and the parent and other persons is essential for language learning. The acquisition of language is promoted in a natural environment where human relationships help the child become an active processor of language (Lerner et al., 2003; Vygotsky, 1962/1934).

In terms of teaching, the social factors are emphasized. The child and adult have a reciprocal relationship because they influence each other in the communication process. The adult plays a mediating role, shaping learning opportunities to bring them to the attention of the young child. For example, 18-month-old Sarah knew the word *plane* and the phrase *all gone.*

While Sarah was sitting at the kitchen table with her mother, an airplane flew over the house. Her mother, initiating a conversation, pointed up questioningly as the plane flew overhead, and Sarah said, "Plane." When the noise disappeared, her mother continued the conversation, asking, "What happened?" Sarah replied, "Plane all gone," along with a gesture of extended hands to show "all gone." With her mother's guidance, Sarah produced her first sentence.

COMPONENTS OF THE LANGUAGE SYSTEM

Basic linguistic concepts and terms comprise the **components of language.** They include: (1) phonology, (2) morphology, (3) syntax, (4) semantics, and (5) pragmatics. In this section, we discusses each of these language components and how they affect language learning and language deviations.

Phonology

The component of language known as **phonology** refers to the speech sounds in a language. The smallest unit of sound in a language system is a **phoneme.** Different languages and dialects use different phonemes. The word *cat* contains three phonemes: *k-a-t*. Phoneme recognition is important in learning to read, as well as in oral language. **Phonics** is the recognition, analysis, and synthesis of phoneme elements in written words. Learning phonics is difficult for some children because they lack phonological awareness.

Morphology

The morphological component of language is known as **morphology,** and it refers to the meaning units in language. The smallest unit of meaning is a **morpheme.** Different languages indicate meaning changes through different morphological forms. For example, in **Standard English,** which is the linguistic system of English recognized by the literate culture and used in school, the word *boy* is one morpheme or meaning unit; and the word *boys* contains two morphemes or meaning units (*boy* plus plurality). A child who has not internalized the morphemic structure of Standard English might say, "There are three boy."

Children who are unaware of exceptions to morphemic rules may overgeneralize. For example, they might formulate the past tense of *fight* and *go* as *fighted* and *goed*. Typical preschool and first-grade children have well-established rules of morphology. Children can apply their morphological rules to nonsense words. For example, Berko (1958) showed each child a drawing of a birdlike creature and said, "This is a *wug.*" Next, she pointed to a drawing with two of these creatures and asked each child to complete the sentence, "There are two ____." By applying the morphological rule for plurals, children gave the answer of *wugs* by adding the phoneme /z/.

Syntax

The language component of **syntax** is the grammar system of a language—the way the words are strung together to form sentences. Different languages have different syntactic or grammatical systems. In the English language, unlike some other languages, word order is extremely important to convey meaning. Thus, "John pushes a car" differs in meaning from "A car pushes John." A child with a syntactic language disorder may not have learned how to order words in a sentence. Further, in English, we can transform the order of the words—still keeping the same subject—to generate a new meaning. The sentence "Mother is working" can be transformed to generate "Is Mother working?" A child with a syntactic language disorder may be unable to generate such sentence transformations. For example, when children with language disorders are asked to repeat the question form of "Is the boy running?" many simply repeat the simple declarative form "The boy is running."

The active form of a sentence—"Mother bakes cookies"—is easier to comprehend than the passive form, "The cookies are baked by Mother." Children with language disabilities may not understand a passive sentence. To illustrate, when first graders are shown two pictures, one of a cat chasing a dog and the other of a dog chasing a cat, and asked to point to the picture called "The cat is chased by the dog," many children choose the incorrect picture because they do not understand the passive form of the sentence.

Semantics

The language component of **semantics** refers to the vocabulary system or word meaning in a language. Pupils who have meager vocabulary understanding or usage and those who have difficulty relating a string of words to a meaningful association may have a semantic language disorder. The development of vocabulary (the semantic component) continues throughout life. In contrast, the morphology, phonology, and syntax components normally become firmly established during the preschool years.

A student with a semantic disorder may understand a concept but may not possess the appropriate word to express it. For example, referring to twins, one boy with language disabilities talked about the "two girls with the same face." He did not know the word *twin* to communicate his idea.

Pragmatics

The language component of **pragmatics** refers to the social side of language, how the speaker uses language in his or her environment. Pragmatics takes into account the relationship between speaker and listener; the speaker's assessment of the listener's degree of knowledge; behaviors, such as taking turns in conversation, staying on topic, and asking pertinent questions; and other factors, such as general appearance, involvement in the conversation, and eye contact. Some students with learning disabilities have poor skills in interpreting, inferring, comparing, and responding to the language of others, which are problems that may cause many social difficulties. These individuals have more difficulty in the social use of language, are less effective in their communication attempts, and do poorly in the listening role of a conversation. They interrupt the speaker more frequently in order to insert their own ideas in the conversation (Bryan, Wong, & Donahue, 2003).

Another element of the language system is *intonation,* or the sound patterns of spoken language, including *pitch* (melody), *stress* (accent), and *juncture* (pauses). The intonation system of each language is different. An example of intonational differences is the contrast between the sound of *White House cat* (a certain cat that lives in the residence of the president of the United States) and *white house cat* (a domesticated cat with white fur). Students who have been unable to capture the intonation system of English may speak in a monotone voice and without expression.

When listening to the intonation pattern of infants, one cannot distinguish the babbling of a 3-month-old Chinese baby from that of a Dutch or an American baby of the same age. By the age of 6 months, however, the intonation of the babbling is similar to the intonation of the language in the infant's immediate environment; the babbling is in Chinese, Dutch, or English. The "native language" of a 6-month-old baby can be identified through tape recordings of the baby's babbling. The baby's babble consists of the intonation patterns and the phonemes of the native language.

TYPES OF LANGUAGE PROBLEMS

Many children with learning disabilities and related disorders have speech and/or language difficulties. They do not do well in situations that require extensive language interactions and conversations, and they are also less skillful in maintaining a conversation. Over 55% of all preschool children (ages 3 though 5) who receive special education services are identified as speech or language impaired (U.S. Department of Education, 2002). In addition, speech and/or language disorders are a common co-occurring condition for older students with disabilities. Furthermore, adolescents and adults with learning disabilities often continue to have poor oral language and communication skills (Vogel & Reder, 1998).

In this section, we discuss: (1) language disorders versus speech disorders, (2) delayed speech, (3) phonological awareness, (4) temporal acoustical processing, (5) rapid automatized naming and word finding, and (6) language disorders. Websites that describe spoken language problems are **http://www.kidsource.com/LDAspoken-language.html** and **http://www.kidsource.com/NICHCY/speech.html.**

Language Disorders Versus Speech Disorders

Language disorders differ from speech disorders. **Speech disorders** are abnormalities of producing sounds, such as: (1) articulation difficulties (e.g., the child who cannot produce the *r* sound and says "wabbit"), (2) voice disorders (e.g., a very hoarse voice), or (3) fluency difficulty (e.g., stuttering). **Language disorders** are much broader and encompass the entire spectrum of communication, including disorders such as: (1) delayed speech, (2) receptive language disorders, and (3) expressive language disorders.

Delayed Speech

Children with a **language delay** may not speak at all, or they may use very little language at an age when language normally develops. For example, the 4-year-old child who has not yet learned to talk has a language delay. At least 8% of children fail to develop speech and language at or near the expected age (Tallal, 2000; Tallal et al., 1997). "LD Stories: Language Delay" describes Noah, a child with a language delay.

The relatively common childhood condition known as *otitis media* can seriously impair language learning in children. **Otitis media** involves an infection of the middle ear that can cause temporary hearing loss. Even if the hearing loss is temporary and mild, it can lead to language delay if it occurs at stages that are critical to language learning in young children.

Phonological Awareness

Phonological awareness (and phonemic awareness) refers to the child's ability to focus on and manipulate phonemes (or the sounds of language) in spoken words. As noted previously, phonemes are abstract units of language, the smallest units constituting spoken language. Learning to reflect about the phoneme sounds of language is more difficult than learning to understand and use language. Many children who have difficulty in learning to read are not sensitive to the phoneme sounds of language and words (Blachman, Tangel, & Ball, 2004; Mann & Foy, 2003; Lyon, Shaywitz, & Shaywitz, 2003; Torgesen, 1998). Table 10.2 illustrates the number of phonemes in several common words.

Successful beginning readers must be aware of phoneme sounds within words to appreciate that the words *cat* and *hat* differ in a single phoneme sound. Children with poor phonological abilities are unable to tap out the number of sounds within a word, such as *mop*.

If a child is unable to reflect about the sound elements of language and to perceive the sounds within words, the alphabetic system will remain a mystery. As children become aware of the phonological system, they can

LD STORIES

LANGUAGE DELAY

Noah G., age 5 years 6 months, was in kindergarten when his parents were contacted about problems he was having in school. The kindergarten teacher said that Noah did not seem to get along with the other children in class. He had no friends, would often strike out and hit his classmates, and was especially disruptive during the conversation time and story periods. He refused to participate in class activities, such as the puppet show that was being prepared for presentation to the parents. The kindergarten teacher said that when she did not know what Noah wanted, this situation often provoked a tantrum.

Mrs. G. said that Noah does not want to go to school and that it is sometimes difficult to get him to go to his class. In describing his developmental history, Mrs. G. said that Noah was born 6 weeks prematurely, weighing 4 lb 5 oz, and that he had been placed in an incubator for a short period. He was a colicky baby and had difficulty nursing. His motor development was average; he crawled at 8 months and walked alone at 12 months. Language development was slow. He spoke his first word at 24 months and did not begin speaking in sentences until age 4. Because he could not communicate with others, he often resorted to pointing and grunting to make his desires known and frequently had temper tantrums when others did not understand what he wanted. Noah does not get along well with his two older sisters. Both sisters are very verbal and do not give Noah much chance to talk. When Noah is asked a question, his sisters answer before he can respond. Mrs. G. said that the doctor suspected a hearing loss when Noah was younger. He had many colds as a toddler and had a condition the doctor called *otitis media,* with fluid behind the eardrums. The doctor put tubes in Noah's ears when he was 4, and his hearing tested normal after this procedure.

The speech teacher observed Noah during class and reported that he played alone most of the time. During the storytelling period and show-and-tell time, he wandered about the room. Often, when another child was playing with a toy, Noah would grab it. If the other child did not give the toy up readily, Noah would hit his classmate until he got it. He listened very little and did not talk to other children in the class. He seemed to tire of one activity very quickly, moving on to another.

During the multidisciplinary evaluation, the speech teacher checked Noah's hearing with an audiometer, and his auditory acuity was normal. The school psychologist tested Noah with an IQ test, the Wechsler Preschool and Primary Scale of Intelligence—Revised. His full-scale IQ score was in the normal range (FSIQ 101), with his performance IQ score (PIQ 119) substantially higher than his verbal IQ score (VIQ 84).

The case conference team recommended that Noah be placed in a developmental kindergarten and receive language therapy from the speech-language pathologist in the school, who would also work with Noah's parents and kindergarten teacher to develop language activities for the home and the inclusion kindergarten.

gain entry into the alphabetic system. Written English is an alphabetic system with written letters of the alphabet representing speech sounds. (Some written languages, such as Chinese, are pictorial—the printed symbols reflect ideas.) Research shows that there is a link between the lack of phono-

TABLE 10.2

Number of Phonemes in
Several Common Words

Word	Number of phonemes
oh	one
go	two
check	three
stop	four
checkers	five

logical awareness and poor reading in many alphabetic languages, such as English, Swedish, Spanish, French, Italian, Portuguese and others (Lundberg, 2002).

The National Reading Panel is a research group that was established by the National Institute of Child Health and Human Development to assess the status of research-based knowledge on the effectiveness of teaching children to read. After an exhaustive search of over 100,000 research-based studies, the National Reading Panel (2000) reached the following conclusions about phonological awareness:

- Can be taught and helps in reading
- Is effective in kindergarten and first grade
- Helps older students, all socioeconomic status (SES) groups, and bilingual students
- Can be successfully taught by many different methods
- Was usually used for an average instructional session of 25 min
- Can be taught by classroom teachers
- Can be used along with printed letters

Table 10.3 provides examples of several phonological awareness tasks that teachers can use in instruction (Adams et al., 1998; Blachman et al., 2004; Coyne, Kame'enui, & Simmons, 2001). The phonological tasks are listed from easiest to hardest (Coyne et al., 2001).

An informal test of phonological awareness is provided in Table 10.4. For formal tests of phonological awareness, see Table 10.5 (in the section "Assessing Oral Language.") The "Teaching Strategies" section of this chapter offers strategies for building phonological awareness.

Temporal Acoustical Processing

One explanation for why children do not develop speech and language at or near the expected ages is that some children find it difficult to process

TABLE 10.3	Task[a]	Activity
Phonological Awareness Tasks	1. Phoneme segmentation	How many phonemes are in the word *ship*?
	2. Phoneme isolation	Tell me the first sound in *paste*.
	3. Phoneme blending	What word is *s/k/u/l*?
	4. Phoneme identity	Tell me the sound that is the same in *bike, boy, bell*.
	5. Phoneme categorization	Which word does not belong: *bus, bun, run*.
	6. Rhyming	Did you ever see a fly kissing a *tie*?
	7. Phoneme deletion	Say *smile* without the *s*.

[a]Listed from the easiest to the most difficult.

sounds quickly enough to distinguish rapid acoustical change in speech, which is known as **temporal acoustical processing.** During the course of normal language, the speech sounds come in too fast for these children to recognize and decipher. A series of studies conducted by Paula Tallal and her colleagues over many years suggests that children who have delays in speech and language development may have difficulty with rapid temporal integration of acoustically varying signals and serial memory. These deficits impact central auditory processing in the millisecond time range (Tallal, 2000; Tallal, Miller, et al., 1997).

The research on temporal acoustical processing difficulties in children with language delays led to the development of a computer program called *FastForWord*. This program alters the acoustics of speech, drawing out sounds and then speeding them up, by stretching out certain speech sounds and emphasizing rapidly changing speech components by making them slower and louder. The purpose of FastForWord is to help children understand and recognize the acoustically altered speech. Children engage in specifically designed computer games in which they follow spoken commands produced by the computer. The instructions for these computer games require children to distinguish various sound cues. As each child's performance improves, these sound cues gradually become shorter in duration and spaced more closely. The researchers report that the children improved in oral language skills. The FastForWord program is for use with children ages 5 through 12 (Merzenich, Jenkins, & Tallal, 1996; Scientific Learning, 1995; Tallal, Allard, et al., 1997; Tallal, Miller, et al., 1997; Tallal, Miller, & Merzenich, 1996). The website for Scientific Learning is **http://www.scientificlearning.com.** An evaluation conducted by Marcaruso and Hook (2001) found that children who used the FastForWord program did not gain any advantages in reading and spoken language when compared with children receiving other similar kinds of reading instruction.

TABLE 10.4

Informal Test of Phonological
Awareness

Give the child two demonstration items to help him or her understand the task. For example, first say the word *cowboy;* then ask the child to say the word. You then tell the child to say the word again, but not to say *boy.*

Do the same with the word steamboat. Tell the child, "Say it again, but don't say steam." If the child answers both demonstration items correctly, give the following test.

Item	Question	Correct response
1. Say *sunshine.*	Now say it again, but don't say *shine.*	*sun*
2. Say *picnic.*	Now say it again, but don't say *pic.*	*nic*
3. Say *cucumber.*	Now say it again, but don't say *cu.*	*cumber*
4. Say *coat.*	Now say it again, but don't say /k/.	*oat*
5. Say *meat.*	Now say it again, but don't say /m/.	*eat*
6. Say *take.*	Now say it again, but don't say /t/.	*ache*
7. Say *game.*	Now say it again, but don't say /m/.	*gay*
8. Say *wrote.*	Now say it again, but don't say /t/.	*row*
9. Say *please.*	Now say it again, but don't say /z/.	*plea*
10. Say *clap.*	Now say it again, but don't say /k/.	*lap*
11. Say *play.*	Now say it again, but don't say /p/.	*lay*
12. Say *stale.*	Now say it again, but don't say /t/.	*sale*
13. Say *smack.*	Now say it again, but don't say /m/.	*sack*

Scoring: Give one point for each correct answer.

Score	Expected level
1–3	Kindergarten
4–9	Grade 1
10–11	Grade 2
12–13	Grade 3

Source: From J. Rosner, *Helping children overcome learning difficulties.* (New York: Walker & Company, 1979) Copyright 1979 by Jerome Rosner. Reprinted with the permission of Walker & Company.

Rapid Automatized Naming and Word Finding

Some children with language delays have difficulty with **rapid automatized naming (RAN)** and **word finding.** These children cannot quickly and automatically name objects and are slow at recalling the correct words. For example, when given the task of naming pictures as they are shown, these children cannot rapidly say the names of the pictures. A slowness in word finding and naming is an accurate predictor of later reading and learning disabilities. Slowness in naming is probably caused by memory retrieval problems, which make it difficult to access verbal information (deJong & Vrielink, 2004; Catts, 1993; German, 2001; Moats, 1994b).

Problems with naming and slow word retrieval affect adolescents and adults with learning disabilities, as well as children. Word-finding problems can be lifelong sources of difficulty in reading, learning, and using expressive language.

There are various resources that address these disorders. Useful instructional methods for dealing with word-finding problems in children are described by Meyer, Wood, Hart, and Felton (1998). Word-finding strategies for adults can be found in *It's on the Tip of My Tongue* (German, 2001). The *Word Finding Intervention Program* (German, 1993) is a word-finding teaching program for children. Additional information is available at **http://www.wordfinding.com**. (See Table 10.5 and the "Tests for Assessing Students With Learning Disabilities" section for a description of word-finding tests.)

Language Disorders

As noted previously, language disorders differ from speech disorders. Speech disorders are abnormalities of speech, while language disorders are much broader and include the entire range of communication disorders. Studies showed that students who had various kinds of oral language disorders as preschoolers often had later language problems in reading and writing. A website for language disorders is **http://www.kidsource.com/ NICHCY/speech.html**.

Language disorders are sometimes referred to as *childhood aphasia* or *developmental aphasia*. Because *acquired aphasia* is a medical term used to identify adults who lose the ability to speak because of brain damage from a stroke, disease, or accident, the term **developmental aphasia** is used to describe children who have severe difficulty in acquiring oral language (Kuder, 2003). In this section, we discuss: (1) receptive language disorders and (2) expressive language disorders.

Receptive Language Disorders The process of understanding verbal symbols is called *oral receptive language*. Receptive language is a prerequisite for the development of expressive language.

Some children with **receptive language disorders** cannot understand the meaning of even a single word. Others have difficulty with more complex units of speech, such as sentences or longer speech units. A child with receptive language problems may be able to understand single words, such as *sit, chair, eat,* and *candy,* but may have difficulty understanding a sentence using those words, such as "Sit on the chair after you eat the candy." Some children understand a word in one context, but they are unable to relate it to another context. The word *run* may be understood as a method of loco-motion, but the child may not get the meaning when the word is used in reference to baseball, a faucet, a woman's stocking, or a river. *Echolalia,* which is the behavior of repeating words or sentences in parrotlike fashion without understanding the meaning, is another form of a receptive language disorder.

Some children are unable to discriminate between the pitch levels of two tones (tone discrimination), and others cannot discriminate or blend isolated, single-letter sounds. Another receptive language problem is the inability to recognize small word parts within a sentence (morphemic discrimination), such as the *z* sound difference between "the cow*s* ate grass" and "the cow ate grass."

Expressive Language Disorders   The process of producing spoken language is called *oral expressive language.* Children with **expressive language disorders** may depend on pointing and gesturing to make their wants known. These children can understand speech and language produced by others, they do not have a muscular paralysis that prevents them from talking, and they do well on nonverbal tasks. Yet these children have difficulty in producing speech or in talking (Fey et al., 1995; Owens, 1995; Wiig & Semel, 1984).

Several clinical conditions are related to expressive language. **Dysnomia** is a word-finding problem or a deficiency in remembering and expressing words. Children with dysnomia may substitute a word, such as *thing,* for every object they cannot remember, or they may attempt to use other expressions to talk around the subject. For example, when asked to list the foods she ate for lunch, one 10-year-old girl used circumlocution in describing a "round red thing that rhymed with potato," but she was unable to remember the word *tomato.* Another condition is **apraxia,** in which children remember the sound of the word, but they cannot at will move or manipulate their speech musculature to make the appropriate sounds, even though they do not have a paralysis. In yet another type of expressive language disorder, a child is able to speak single words or short phrases but has difficulty formulating complete sentences.

CULTURAL AND LINGUISTIC DIVERSITY IN ORAL LANGUAGE	## Nonstandard English

A language difference, in contrast to a language disorder, can also affect school learning. For example, the student's language may be a dialect of Standard English, such as an Appalachian dialect or Black English. The student's language is similar to that of others in the student's immediate environment, is appropriate for the surroundings, and causes no difficulty in communicating with others within this environment. These students do not have a language disorder, but their language difference can interfere with |

understanding and using Standard English and with school learning (Payne & Taylor, 2002; Walker, 1999).

There can be mismatch between the student's language system and the language system used in the general environment. Abstract concepts, scientific analysis, logical thinking, and the communication of subtle ideas require a mastery of a complex, sophisticated language system. Students who use a dialect of English and have not learned Standard English may find school work difficult when it is conducted in Standard English.

English-Language Learners

English-language learners are students who are not proficient in English, and they encounter many difficulties in classes taught entirely in English. The concept of multicultural education reflects an appreciation of society as a fundamentally pluralistic democracy, which is respectful of ethnic, religious, social, linguistic, and cultural differences (Hernandez, 2001). In today's diverse society, an increasing number of students come from homes in which a language other than English is spoken. The Hispanic population increased by 58% during the past decade, which is three to four times the growth rate of the general population. Over 18% of the students with learning disabilities are identified as Hispanic (U.S. Department of Education, 2002). Spanish speakers represent 76% of the non-English language population, but there are more than 100 distinct language groups served in U.S. schools. The number of English-language learners increased to 3.4 million in the year 2000 (Jiménez, 2002).

Children who are truly *bilingual* understand and use two languages well, their native language and their second language—English. In fact, research shows that true bilingual abilities are associated with a higher level of cognitive attainment. Bilingual acquisition involves a process that builds on an underlying base for both languages. The duality of languages does not hamper overall language proficiency or cognitive development for bilingual children (Cummins, 1989; Hakuta, 1990; Jiménez, 2002).

However, the problem for many English-language learners is that they have limited English proficiency, which is a difficulty understanding and using English. Some of these students speak only in their native language; others use both English and their native language but still have considerable difficulty with English. A child's native language provides the foundation upon which English language skills are built. Students who use their native language effectively are likely to acquire and use English appropriately, but students who have problems in their native language also experience problems in English as a second language (Lundberg, 2002; Ortiz, 1997). Additionally, research shows that a student may acquire conversational English in 6 months but may not have the language proficiency to support the com-

- Be responsive to cultural and individual diversity.
- Teach English-language reading to develop English-language competence.
- Be familiar with assessment tools, recommended practices, and acceptable accommodations for English-language learners.
- Help students transfer what is learned in one language to the other language.

- Provide opportunities to move from learning and producing limited word translation and fragmented concepts to using longer sentences and expressing more complex ideas and feelings.
- Encourage home–school collaboration.
- Encourage communication among general and special education staff members.

plex demands of academic development in English. Reaching that level may take up to 2 or more years (Cummins, 1989; Jiménez, 2002; Ortiz, 1997).

English-Language Learners and Learning Disabilities In addition to their limitations in English, some linguistically diverse children also have learning disabilities. They must cope not only with learning English, but also with their underlying language disorders and learning disabilities. If a child has a language disorder in his or her primary language, the language problem will also be reflected in the second language (Gerber & Durgunoglu, 2004; Jiménez, 2002; Ortiz, 1997).

The research on the best methods for teaching students who have learning disabilities and whose native language is not English is still inconclusive. Teachers must be particularly sensitive to the needs of these students and recognize that achieving proficiency in English requires time. These teachers need competencies in both learning disabilities and in teaching students with limited English proficiency. Some suggestions for English-language learners who have learning disabilities are given in "LD in Practice: Effective Practices for Supporting English-Language Learners" (Jiménez, 2002; Ortiz, 1997).

Learning a Second Language

Methods for teaching a second language include *ESL*, *bilingual*, *sheltered English*, and *immersion* methods.

- In the **English as a second language (ESL) method,** students learn through carefully controlled oral repetitions of selected second-language patterns. When students come from many different language backgrounds, the ESL approach is used.

- In the **bilingual method,** students use their native language for part of the school day and use the second language (English) for the other portion of the school day. The objective of the bilingual program is to strengthen school learning through the native language and gradually to add the secondary language. The underlying philosophy is that students will recognize and respect the importance of their native culture and language in American society. In the bilingual method, then, schooling is provided in two languages. Academic subjects are usually taught in the native language, and the student receives oral practice in English.

- **Sheltered English** is a method of teaching children who have some proficiency in English by having students learn English more rapidly through instruction with printed materials that are written in English, typically used for a content-area subject. The rationale for this approach is that spoken language is fleeting and inconsistent over time. In written language, the text is stable and does not pass the learner by. With written text, students can reread and reconsider what is being learned. The sheltered English approach has been used with children whose native language is Spanish. The students continue to use Spanish for part of the day, while English is used in teaching certain subjects with written materials, such as reading or social studies. The teaching of English is merged with this instruction. Wide reading of high-interest stories in English helps develop English-language competence (Gersten, Brengelman, & Jiménez, 1994).

- In the **immersion method,** students are *immersed* in, or receive extensive exposure to, the second language. In fact, where there is no formal instruction for a person learning a second language, this is essentially what occurs. Individuals simply learn through this type of repeated exposure as they live daily in the mainstream of the dominant-language society. Immersion is the instructional method for schoolchildren in Canada, where it is used to teach French to English-speaking children by enrolling them in French-speaking immersion schools (Fortin & Crago, 1999).

EARLY LITERACY AND ORAL LANGUAGE

The importance of providing young children with a rich literary environment is recognized as essential to the world of language. **Early literacy** refers to the child's early entrance into the comprehensive world of words, language, books, poetry, and stories. It includes helping children become aware of print, words, and the sounds of language. The early literacy phi-

LD IN PRACTICE
ACTIVITIES TO PROMOTE EARLY LITERACY

- *Engage children in oral language activities.* Provide children with many opportunities to talk and to use oral language.

- *Surround young children with a literacy environment.* Supply and read many books, stories, and poems, and then discuss them.

- *Introduce concepts about print.* Point out that print carries meaning and can be read from left to right and from top to bottom. Show that words are separated by spaces.

- *Use word and sound games.* Play games to help children become aware that spoken words are constructed from sounds. Teach rhyming games, nursery rhymes, and poetry.

- *Build alphabet knowledge.* Help children recognize alphabet letters, and encourage them to write these letters.

- *Make children aware of letter–sound correspondence.* Help children begin to see the relationship between sounds and letters.

- *Encourage early writing.* Have materials for writing available. Children may scribble or just write letters or draw pictures.

- *Help children build a beginning reading vocabulary.* Plan activities to alert children to their first sight words. For example, compile a collection of their favorite words or logos.

losophy encourages young children to enjoy experiences with stories and books, and it encourages early writing (National Research Council, 1998).

It is especially important that children with learning disabilities be given an abundant and rich literature environment. From an early age, they should hear stories, tell stories, and even write journals and stories. Story reading helps build oral language experiences. Predictable books that have a pattern or refrain should be used, and one should encourage children to repeat the predictable elements. It is also important to read and reread favorite stories and have the children listen to them on CDs or tapes while following along in their books.

Methods that foster early literacy are described in "LD in Practice: Activities to Promote Early Literacy" (National Research Council, 1998; Richek et al., 2002).

ASSESSING ORAL LANGUAGE

The purpose of assessing oral language is to determine what language abilities the child has acquired, what language problems (if any) the child exhibits, and how well the child uses language functionally. This information helps in planning the teaching. Assessment should consider the two sides of oral language: listening and speaking. Language assessment measures include: (1) informal measures and (2) formal tests.

Informal Measures

Often the most valuable information is obtained by observing as the child uses language functionally in a real environment, such as a class or recreational setting. When rating scales are used in assessment, an informant (usually a parent) provides information about the child's language development and usage. Informal assessment measures offer valuable information about the child's language ability, but informal assessment measures are not standardized.

An informal measure of listening can be obtained by assessing the child's ability to comprehend a story that is read aloud. This listening test is often used as part of an informal reading inventory (IRI; see the chapter on reading). The procedure requires the teacher to read aloud stories that are graded for difficulty level. Then the child is asked comprehension questions to determine how well he or she understands this material. In an informal reading inventory, the child's listening level is often compared to the child's reading level (Richek et al., 2002; Spinelli, 2002).

Formal Tests

Formal tests are standardized instruments for gathering information about oral language development; a number of examples are listed in Table 10.5. (These and other language tests are described more fully in "Tests for Assessing Students With Learning Disabilities.")

Formal tests of language, along with informal language measures, are used to assess a child's language problems. These test results are included in the child's individualized education program (IEP) and become the basis for measuring progress.

TEACHING STRATEGIES

The integrated language system consists of the language forms of listening, speaking, reading, and writing. Spelling and handwriting can be considered part of writing. This chapter presents teaching strategies for the oral language skills of listening and speaking. Strategies for teaching reading are presented in the chapter on reading, and the strategies for the written language skills of writing and spelling are presented in the chapter on written language.

Oral language has two contrasting sides: (1) understanding oral language (listening) and (2) producing oral language (speaking).

TABLE 10.5

Oral Language Tests

Test[a]	Age or grade tested
Auditory discrimination tests	
■ Wepman Test of Auditory Discrimination	Ages 5–9
■ Goldman-Fristoe-Woodstock Test of Auditory Discrimination	Ages 2–16+
■ Auditory Discrimination in Depth (Lindamood)	All ages
General oral language tests	
■ Boehm Test of Basic Concepts—Revised	Grades K–2
■ Carrow Elicited Language Inventory	Ages 3–8
■ Clinical Evaluation of Language Fundamentals—Revised (CELF-R)	K–12
■ Comprehensive Receptive and Expressive Vocabulary Test	Ages 4–17
■ Detroit Tests of Learning Aptitude—4 (DTLA-4)	Ages 6–17
■ Developmental Sentence Scoring Test	Ages 2½–6
■ Oral and Written Language Scales (OWLS)	Ages 3–21
■ Test for Auditory Comprehension of Language—Revised	Ages 3–10
■ Test of Adolescent Language—3 (TOAL-3)	Ages 12–18
■ Test of Language Development—3: Intermediate (TOLD-3: Intermediate)	Ages 8½—12.1
■ Test of Language Development—3: Primary (TOLD-3: Primary)	Ages 8–11
Listening tests	
■ Listening Comprehension Scales—Oral, Written, and Language Scales (OWLS)	Ages 5–21
■ Carrow Test for Auditory Comprehension of Language, Revised	Ages 12–80
■ Peabody Picture Vocabulary Test—III	Ages 2–18
■ Sequential Tests of Educational Progress (STEP): Listening	Grades K–12
■ Test de Vocabulario en Images. Peabody (Spanish version of the Peabody Picture Vocabulary Test—III)	Ages 2½–18
Speech articulation test	
■ Goldman-Fristoe Test of Articulation	Ages 2–16+
Phonological awareness tests	
■ Bankson-Bernthal Test of Phonology	Ages 3–21
■ Comprehensive Test of Phonological Processing	Ages 5.0–21.11
■ Lindamood Auditory Conceptualization Test	Preschool–adult
■ Phonological Awareness Test	Ages 5–9
■ Test of Phonological Awareness	Grades K–2
Word-finding tests	
■ Test of Word Finding—2	Ages 6½–13
■ Test of Adolescent and Adult Word Finding	Ages 12–80

[a]These tests are described in "Tests for Assessing Students With Learning Disabilities."

LISTENING Listening is an often neglected element of language learning. Students are typically expected to acquire the ability to listen without special instruction. However, many students do not acquire functional skills in listening by themselves. Over half the people referred to medical hearing specialists for suspected deafness have no defect in hearing acuity and no organic pathology that would cause their seeming hearing impairment. In this section, we discuss: (1) listening comprehension, (2) phonological awareness of language sounds, (3) understanding words and building a listening vocabulary, (4) understanding sentences, (5) listening comprehension, (6) critical listening, and (7) listening to stories.

Listening Means Comprehension

Listening is a basic skill that can be improved through practice. An explanation for poor listening is that students today are so bombarded with constant sound that they learn to "tune out." Students who are skillful at not listening should be taught to "tune in."

For some students, a learning problem stems from a receptive language disorder, which refers to difficulty comprehending speech. These students may avoid language activities because listening is so distressing.

Listening differs from hearing, which is a physiological process that does not involve interpretation. One can *hear* a foreign language with good auditory acuity but be unable to *listen* to what is being said. In contrast to hearing, listening demands that one select appropriate meanings and organize ideas according to their relationships. In addition, listening calls for evaluation, acceptance or rejection, internalization, and, at times, appreciation of the ideas expressed. Listening is the foundation of all language growth, and the child with a deficit in listening skills will have difficulty with all the communication skills.

There are significant differences between listening and reading. The reader can reread and study the material, but the listener hears the material only once and then it is gone. (Of course, using a recording device modifies this difference.) Readers can regulate their own speed, going slower or faster as their purpose and the difficulty of the material dictate, but the listener's speed of listening is set by the speaker. The listener has additional clues from the speaker's voice, gesture, appearance, and emphasis, but the reader cannot derive such supporting information from the printed page. The listener–speaker combination also offers more opportunity for feedback, questioning, and a two-way discussion than reading offers.

When teachers ask students to *listen*, they do not want them simply to *hear* or to recognize the words being spoken. Students who are directed to listen are expected to comprehend the communication message being sent.

Teaching strategies for each of the following listening skills are described in the next sections.

- Phonological awareness of language sounds
- Understanding words and building a listening vocabulary
- Understanding sentences
- Listening comprehension
- Critical listening
- Listening to stories

Phonological Awareness of Language Sounds

Precursors for learning to read include perceiving and recognizing phonemes, which are the sounds of our language. To be successful during the beginning stages of reading, children must hear individual phoneme sounds of the language and be aware that the words they are hearing are composed of individual sounds. Abilities in phoneme awareness prepare children for learning phonics.

The following activities are designed to build phonological awareness:

1. *Nonsense.* Have children listen to and detect the slight change in the name of a familiar story or poem, such as "Baa, Baa, Purple Sheep" or "Twinkle, Twinkle, Little Car."

2. *Clapping names.* Ask children to clap out syllables in names and words. For example, clap "Jenn-if-fer" (three claps) or "Zip-pi-ty-doo-dah" (five claps).

3. *Finding things: Initial phonemes.* Use real objects or pictures of objects. Say the name of the object and ask children which picture or object begins with the same sound. Children can group those objects in one place, put them in one container, or paste their pictures into a chart. For example, the initial consonant *m* may be presented with *milk, money, moon, man,* and *monkey.*

4. *Take away a sound.* Have children say their names or a word without the initial sound. For example, say, "——enjamin." Children in the group must identify the whole word.

5. *Add a sound.* Say a word pair, with the second word adding a sound. For example, say "girl, girls" or "mile, smile."

6. *Troll talk: Blending games.* The troll talks funny, saying the sounds of words separately. The children must guess the word by blending the sounds. For example, the troll utters the phonemes "ch-ee-z," "p-e-n," "f-u-n," or "What is your n-ā-m?" The children blend the sounds and identify the word.

7. *Nursery rhymes.* Read nursery rhymes or Dr. Seuss books to children. Look at the pictures and emphasize the rhyming elements. Children enjoy the many repetitions of nursery rhymes. Occasionally leave

off the word that is the rhyming element and have the child say the word: "Jack and Jill went up the——."

8. ***Rhyming words.*** Rhyming can be a very enjoyable game for preschoolers. Songs with rhymes and nursery rhymes are valuable sources of rhyming activities. The singer Raffi (1986) has a series of delightful audiotapes that have great appeal to young children. Children find this question, which is asked in one of the songs, very funny: "Did you ever see a fly kissing a tie?" A follow-up game can be developed to think of other rhyming words as substitutes. One group of preschoolers thought of "Did you ever see a hook kissing a book?" and "Did you ever see a grandma kissing a pajama?"

9. ***Using visual cues to segment speech sounds.*** To help children recognize the speech sounds in words, put a picture representing a short word on a card. Draw a rectangle underneath the picture and divide it into the number of phonemes in the word. Have the child say the word slowly, putting a counter in each square as each sound is articulated. Figure 10.4 illustrates a card for the word *sun*.

10. ***Elkonin cards.*** Obtain counters such as buttons or pennies. Place a picture with a short word on a card. Use words with the same number of letters as sounds (e.g., *cap, run,* and *lamp*). For sound counting, say the word slowly and have the child put down a counter for each sound. One set of cards can have both pictures and words, and another can have only the pictures (Blachman, 1997; Blachman et al., 2004; Elkonin, 1973).

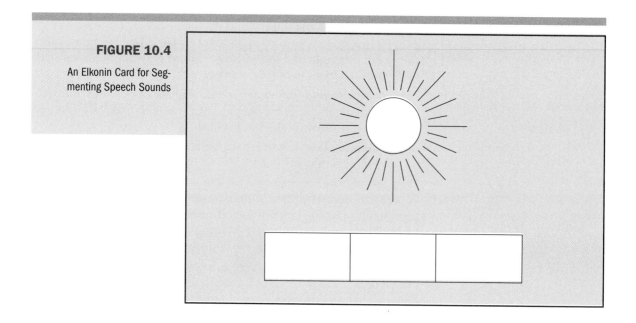

FIGURE 10.4

An Elkonin Card for Segmenting Speech Sounds

11. *Rhyming riddles and games.* The teacher selects a group of words, one to rhyme with *head* and the other to rhyme with *feet*. Then the teacher asks a riddle so that the answer rhymes with either *head* or *feet*. The children then point to the part of their body that has a name that rhymes with *head* or *feet* to answer the riddle. For example, "When you are hungry, you want to ——." The children point to their *feet* because *eat* rhymes with it. Repeat by naming other parts of the body to elicit words that rhyme with *hand* or *knee* or with *arm* or *leg* (Richek et al., 2002).

   Make up riddle rhymes and encourage students to make up others. One such example is, "I rhyme with *look*. You read me. What am I?"

   Have students listen to a series of three words, such as *ball, sit,* and *wall* or *hit, pie,* and *tie,* and tell which two words rhyme.

12. *Sound substitutions.* This activity is harder than rhyming. Raffi (1986) has a song on one of his audiotapes called "Apples and Bananas" that has great appeal for young children and uses phonemic substitution.

   > I like to eat, eat, eat
   > Apples and Bananas (Repeat)
   >
   > I like to ate, ate, ate
   > Ai-pples and Ba-nainas (Repeat)
   >
   > I like to oat, oat, oat
   > Oa-ples and Ba-noanos (Repeat)
   >
   > I like to ight, ight, ight
   > Igh-pples and Ba-nighnas (Repeat)

13. *Deleting sounds.* In this activity, children learn to take a word apart, remove one sound, and pronounce the word without that sound. For example, to remove a syllable: "Say *playground.* Now say it without *play.*" It is more difficult to remove a phoneme: "Say *ball.* Now say it without the *b.*" "Say *stack.* Now say it without the *t.*"

14. *Beginning sounds.* Giving three words like *astronaut, mountain,* and *bicycle,* have the students tell which word begins like *milk.* Ask the children to think of words that begin like *Tom,* to find pictures of words that begin like *Tom,* or to find pictures of words that begin with the sound *T.* Show them three pictures of different objects (for example, a pear, a table, and a car) and ask the students to select the picture of an object with a name that begins like *Tom.*

15. *Beating out names.* Beat the syllables in the rhythm and accent of names of the children in the group. For example, for a name like *Marilyn McPhergeson,* you might beat out the following pattern:

   Drumbeat: LOUD-soft-soft   soft-LOUD-soft-soft
             1 2 3   4 1 2 3

16. *Initial consonants: Same or different?*   Say three words, two of which have the same initial consonant—for example, *car, dog,* and *cat.* Ask the students to identify the word that begins with a different sound.

17. *Consonant-blend bingo.*   Make bingo cards with consonant blends and consonant digraphs in the squares. Read words and ask the students to cover the blend that begins each word.

18. *Hearing syllables.*   Say multisyllabic words and have students listen and determine the number of syllables in each word. Clapping or identifying the vowel sounds they hear helps students determine the number of syllables.

19. *Substitutions.*   Help the students learn to substitute one initial sound for another to make a new word. For example: "Take the end of the word *book* and put in the beginning of the word *hand,* and get something you hang coats on." (The word would be *hook.*)

20. *Same or different?*   Say pairs of words or nonsense words—such as *tag-tack, big-beg, singing-sinking, shin-chin,* and *lup-lub*—and ask the students to determine whether they are the same or different.

Understanding Words and Building a Listening Vocabulary

Listening requires that students acquire a listening vocabulary. Students must understand the names of objects, actions, qualities, and more abstract concepts. It is easier to teach words that carry primary lexical meaning (such as nouns, verbs, adjectives, and adverbs) than to teach structure or function words (such as prepositions and articles) that indicate relationships within sentences.

1. *Names of objects.*   To help students understand names, use actual objects, such as a ball, pencil, or doll. Sometimes you will have to add exaggeration and gestures to help the student with a severe receptive disorder understand the meaning of the word that symbolizes the object.

2. *Verb meanings.*   It is more difficult to teach the concept of a verb than the name of an object. You can illustrate verbs such as *hop, sit,* and *walk* by performing the activity.

3. *Pictures.*   Pictures are useful in reinforcing and reviewing the vocabulary that has been taught.

4. *Concepts of attributes.*   Words that describe the attributes of objects can be taught by providing contrasting sets of experiences that illustrate the attributes. Examples of such sets are *rough–smooth, pretty–ugly, little–big,* and *hot–cold.* Both concrete objects and pictures are useful in teaching attributes.

5. ***Development of concepts.*** If you combine experiences with particular objects, you can help students understand the concept beyond the object itself. For example, in learning about the concept of a chair, you might show the students a kitchen chair, an upholstered chair, a folding chair, a lawn chair, a doll chair, and a rocking chair. Through experiences with many chairs, the students develop the concept of chair.

6. ***Classes of objects.*** An even broader classification of objects must be made and labeled with a word. For example, the word *food* refers not to any single type of food, but to all foods. The students, therefore, could be taught objects that "are food" and could be asked to remove from a display any objects that "are not food."

Understanding Sentences

It is more difficult to understand sentences than single words. Some students with language disabilities need structured practice in understanding sentences.

1. ***Directions.*** Give simple directions in sentences to provide the students with needed experiences in understanding sentences. For example, you can say, "Give me the blue truck" or "Put the book on the table."

2. ***Finding the picture.*** Line up several pictures. State a sentence describing one of them and ask the students to point to the correct picture. You can make this exercise harder by adding more sentences to your description of the picture.

A number of activities can be used to practice oral language and speaking.
(© Charles Gupton/CORBIS)

3. *Function words.* Function or structure words establish structural relationships between parts of a sentence and grammatical meaning. They include noun determiners, auxiliary verbal forms, subordinators, prepositions, connectors, and question words. These words cannot be taught in isolation; they must be taught within a sentence or phrase. You might, for example, teach words such as *on, over, under, behind, in front of, beneath, inside,* and *in* by placing objects *in* a box or *under* a chair while saying the entire phrase to convey the meaning.

4. *Riddles.* Have students listen to a sentence and fill in the word that fits. For example, for the word *sled,* you might say, "I am thinking of a word that tells what you use to go down a snowy hill."

Listening Comprehension

Listening comprehension is similar to reading comprehension, but the information is received by hearing rather than by reading language. Thinking is a key component of listening comprehension.

1. *Following directions.* Students listen to a set of directions for making something. Have the materials ready and ask students to follow the directions step by step.

2. *Understanding a sequence of events.* Students listen to a story and are then asked to picture the different events in the order in which they happened. Pictorial series, such as comic strips, can help illustrate the events of the story, and you can mix the pictures and ask the students to place the series in the proper chronological order.

3. *Listening for details.* The teacher can read a story aloud and ask detailed questions about it. Phrase questions to ask *who, what, when, where,* and *how.* The teacher can also read aloud an instructional manual on a subject, such as how to care for a new pet, and then ask students to list all the things that should be done.

4. *Getting the main idea.* The teacher reads aloud a short but unfamiliar story and asks the students to make up a good title for the story. The teacher also reads aloud a story and asks the students to choose the main idea from three choices.

5. *Making inferences and drawing conclusions.* The teacher reads part of a story that the students do not know and stops at an exciting point to ask the students to guess what happens next.

Critical Listening

Good listening means not only understanding what is said, but also being able to listen critically and to judge and evaluate what is being said.

1. *Recognizing absurdities.* Tell a short story with a word or phrase that does not fit the story. Ask the students to discover what is funny or foolish about the story. For example, you could say, "It rained all night in the middle of the day," or "The sun was shining brightly in the middle of the night."

2. *Listening to advertisements.* Have the students listen to advertisements and determine *how* the advertiser is trying to get the listener to buy the products. Adolescents enjoy detecting propaganda techniques.

Listening to Stories

Story reading is a useful strategy for building oral language experiences. Frequently reading stories to small groups of children with language problems helps them to acquire language, figure out grammar, and learn the structure of stories (Richek et al., 2002).

1. Read stories frequently (at least once each day) to small groups of five to seven children.

2. Involve all the children in the story by asking questions appropriate to their individual levels of language acquisition.

3. Select predictable books (ones that have a pattern, refrain, or sequence) to read aloud, encouraging the children to repeat the predictable element.

4. Select well-illustrated books (ones with many illustrations closely tied to the text) to read aloud.

5. Throughout the story, ask the children thought-provoking questions.

6. Read and reread favorite stories and let the children listen to them on CDs or tapes while following along in their books.

SPEAKING Oral language is the child's first language and includes listening and speaking. The activities in this section focus on speaking and include: (1) stages of oral language development, (2) activities for natural language stimulation, (3) activities for teaching oral language, and (4) activities for improving oral language of adolescents.

Stages of Oral Language Development

A general overview of a child's oral language development provides a perspective for viewing language deviations. A child's first attempt to use vocal mechanisms is the birth cry. In the short span of time from the birth cry to the full acquisition of speech, the child goes through several stages. Table 10.6 lists speech and language milestones.

	TABLE 10.6	Age	Milestones	Activities

Age	Milestones	Activities
TABLE 10.6 Speech and Language Milestones		
1	■ Recognizes name ■ Says two words besides "mama" and "dada" ■ Imitates familiar words ■ Understands simple instructions ■ Recognizes words as symbols for objects (e.g., car, points to garage; cat, meows)	■ Respond to your child's coos, gurgles, and babbling ■ Talk to your child throughout the day ■ Read colorful books every day ■ Tell nursery rhymes, sing songs ■ Teach names of everyday objects ■ Take child to new places ■ Play games, such as peek-a-boo and pat-a-cake
1–2	■ Understands "no" ■ Uses 10 to 20 words, including names ■ Combines two words (e.g., "daddy, bye-bye") ■ Waves good-bye and plays pat-a-cake ■ Makes sounds of familiar animals ■ Gives a toy when asked ■ Uses words, such as "more" ■ Points to toes, eyes, nose ■ Gets objects when asked	■ Encourage early efforts to say new words ■ Talk to child when with child ■ Talk about new situations ■ Look at your child when child talks to you ■ Describe what your child is doing ■ Have child listen to records, tapes, CDs ■ Praise child's efforts to communicate
2–3	■ Identifies body parts ■ Carries on conversation with self and dolls ■ Asks "What's that?" and "Where's my?" ■ Uses two-word negative phrases, such as "no want" ■ Forms some plurals by adding "s" (e.g., book, books) ■ Has 450-word vocabulary ■ Gives first name, holds up fingers to tell age ■ Combines nouns and verbs (e.g., "mommy go") ■ Understands simple time concepts (e.g., "last night," "tomorrow") ■ Refers to self as "me," rather than by name ■ Tries to get adult attention, "Watch me" ■ Likes to hear same story repeated ■ May say "no" when means "yes" ■ Talks to other children, as well as adults	■ Repeat new words over and over ■ Help your child listen and follow instructions by playing games, such as pick up the ball and touch Daddy's nose ■ Take your child on trips and talk about what you see before, during, and after the trip ■ Let your child tell you answers to simple question ■ Read books every day, perhaps as part of the bedtime routine ■ Listen attentively as your child talks to you ■ Describe what you are doing, planning, thinking ■ Have the child deliver simple messages for you ■ Carry on conversations with the child, preferably when the two of you have some quiet time together ■ Ask questions to get your child to think and talk

TABLE 10.6 (cont.)

Speech and Language Milestones

Age	Milestones	Activities
2–3	■ Solves problems by talking instead of hitting or crying ■ Answers "where" questions ■ Names common pictures and things ■ Uses short sentences like "Me want more" or "Me want cookie" ■ Matches three to four colors, knows "big" and "little"	■ Show the child you understand what he or she says by answering, smiling, and nodding your head ■ Expand what the child says (e.g., if he or she says, "more juice," you say, "Adam wants more juice")
3–4	■ Can tell a story ■ Has a sentence length of four to five words ■ Has a vocabulary of nearly 1,000 words ■ Names at least one color ■ Understands "yesterday," "summer," "lunchtime," "tonight," "little–big" ■ Begins to obey requests, such as " put the block under the chair" ■ Knows his or her last name, names of street on which he/she lives and several nursery rhymes	■ Talk about how objects are the same or different ■ Help your child to tell stories using books and pictures ■ Let your child play with other children ■ Read longer stories to your child ■ Pay attention to your child when the child is talking ■ Talk about places you have been to or will be going to
4–5	■ Has sentence length of four to five words ■ Uses past tense correctly ■ Has a vocabulary of nearly 1,500 words ■ Points to colors: red, blue, yellow, and green ■ Identifies triangles, circles, and squares ■ Understands "in the morning," "next," "noontime" ■ Can speak of imagery conditions, such as "I hope" ■ Asks many questions, asks "Who?" and "Why?"	■ Help your child sort objects and things (e.g., things you eat, animals) ■ Teach your child how to use the telephone ■ Let your child help you plan activities such as what you will make for Thanksgiving dinner ■ Continue talking with your child about your child's interests ■ Read longer stories to your child ■ Let your child tell and make up stories for you ■ Show your pleasure when your child comes to talk with you
5–6	■ Has sentence length of five to six words ■ Has a vocabulary of approximately 2,000 words ■ Defines objects by their use (e.g., you eat with a fork) and can tell what objects are made of ■ Knows spatial relations, such as "on top," "behind," "far," and "near" ■ Knows own address	■ Praise your child when your child talks about feelings, thoughts, hopes, and fears ■ Comment on what you did or how you think your child feels ■ Sings songs and rhyme with your child ■ Continue to read longer stories ■ Talk with your child as you would an adult

TABLE 10.6 (cont.)

Speech and Language
Milestones

Age	Milestones	Activities
5–6	■ Identifies a penny, nickel, and dime ■ Knows common opposites such as "big–little" ■ Understands "same" and "different" ■ Counts 10 objects ■ Asks questions for information ■ Distinguishes left and right hand ■ Uses all types of sentences (e.g., "Let's go to the store after we eat")	■ Look at family photos and talk to your child about your family history ■ Listen to your child when your child talks to you

Source: From Learning Disabilities Association of America, Pittsburgh. Reprinted with the permission of the Learning Disabilities Association of America.

Babbling   Vocalization during the first 9 months of life is called *babbling.* During this stage, children produce many sounds, those in their native language as well as those found in other languages. Infants derive pleasure from hearing the sounds they make, and making such sounds gives them the opportunity to use the tongue, larynx, and other vocal apparatuses and to respond orally to others. Children who are deaf begin the babbling stage but soon stop because they receive no satisfaction from hearing the sounds they produce. Parents of children with language disorders often report that their child does not engage in the activities of babbling, gurgling, or blowing bubbles. These children should be encouraged to engage in such oral play to help them have the normal experiences of language acquisition.

Jargon   By about 9 months, the babbling softens and becomes *jargon.* Children retain the phoneme sounds that are used in the language they hear. Their vocalizations reflect the rhythm and melody of the oral speaking patterns of others around them. Although their intonational patterns may be similar to those of adults, children do not yet use words at this stage; it is as though they are pretending to talk. The parents of children who are diagnosed as having language disabilities often report that their children missed this stage of development.

Chinese children have been observed to have a mastery of basic Chinese intonation patterns by 20 months of age, a feat that is very difficult for an English-speaking adult to accomplish. Yi was a baby from China who was adopted at 10 months of age. Her adoptive parents became concerned about a possible language disorder because she displayed no signs of language play and did not engage in jargon. The problem was happily solved when the family had lunch at a Chinese restaurant. As soon as Yi heard people talking in Chinese, she spontaneously began "talking" in jargon, using Chinese sounds and intonational patterns.

Single Words Single words, such as *mama* and *dada*, normally develop between 12 and 18 months of age. The ability to *imitate* is evident at this stage, and children may well imitate sounds or words that they hear others say or that they themselves produce. Parents often report that their child with language disabilities did not engage in verbal imitation and repetition activities.

Two- and Three-Word Sentences Two- and three-word sentences, such as *Baby eat, Daddy home,* and *Coat off,* mark the next stage and follow the use of single words. Once children begin to use language, their skill in producing speech increases at a remarkably rapid pace.

Between 18 months, when a toddler first produces a two-word utterance, and age 3, many children learn the essentials of English grammar and can produce all linguistic types of sentences. The child's oral language development at age 3 appears to be almost abrupt; the child has an extensive vocabulary and uses fairly complex sentence structures. During this stage, reports become rather hazy—partly because things develop so rapidly and partly because as observers, we do not understand the underlying mechanism of language acquisition. By the time children enter school at age 6, they are fairly sophisticated users of the grammar of their native language.

Problems in Language Acquisition Most children seem to acquire language in a relatively natural and easy manner, without a need for direct teaching. Many children with language disabilities, however, do not go through the typical developmental stages of language acquisition and exhibit difficulty in acquiring one or several properties of language. Some have difficulty with the phonology of language—differentiating and producing the appropriate sounds. Others have difficulty remembering words or structuring morphological rules. Some have difficulty with grammar or syntax and in putting words together to formulate sentences. Still others have a semantic difficulty in vocabulary development.

Experiences in listening (i.e., the input, or receptive, side of language) precede speaking (i.e., the output, or expressive, side of language). Listening alone does not produce the ability to speak, but a looping or feedback process must be created in which the child both listens and speaks. The interrelationship of listening and speaking provides immediate reinforcement that shapes speaking behavior.

Activities for Natural Language Stimulation

Teachers and parents can take advantage of many opportunities in the daily life of a child in school or at home to provide natural language stimulation (Lerner et al., 2003):

1. *Expansion.* This is a technique to enlarge and enhance the child's language. In the conversation that follows, the adult expands a child's limited utterance.

    Child: "Cookie."

    Teacher or parent: " 'Cookie? I want cookie.' Well, here it is!"

2. *Parallel talk.* In this technique, the adult tries to help language development by supplying language stimulation, even when no speech is heard. As the child plays, the teacher or parent guesses what the child is thinking and supplies short phrases describing the actions, thereby placing words and sentences in the child's mind for future reference. For example, if the child is banging a block on the floor, the teacher might say: "There's a block. If I hit the block on the floor, it makes a noise. A big noise. Bang, bang, bang. Block. My block. Bang the block."

3. *Self-talk.* In this technique, teachers model language by engaging in activities that do not directly involve the child. As teachers complete their own tasks and work in close proximity to the child, they can capitalize on opportunities to use meaningful language stimulation that the child can hear. For example, while cutting some paper, the teacher might say, "I have to cut the paper. Cut the paper. I need scissors. My scissors. Open, shut the scissors. Open, shut. I can cut, cut, cut."

Activities for Teaching Oral Language

The oral language skills for talking are accomplished by: (1) building a speaking vocabulary, (2) learning language patterns, (3) formulating sentences, and (4) practicing oral language skills. The following sections provide activities to improve each of these oral language skills.

Building a Speaking Vocabulary Some children with language disorders have an extremely limited vocabulary and a very specific, narrow, and concrete sense of the meaning of words. Throughout their lives, people have a much larger listening vocabulary than speaking vocabulary. Young children are able to understand words long before they are able to produce and use them. Children with a language disorder may be able to recognize words when they hear them, but they may be unable to use those words. Adults with known brain injuries may lose their ability to remember words easily as a result of damage to the language area of the brain. This condition, as noted earlier, is *dysnomia,* meaning the inability to remember the names of objects. Children may substitute another referent like *thing, whatsit,* or *that,* or a gesture or pantomime for the word they cannot bring to mind. The following exercises can help children use words and build an accessible speaking vocabulary.

1. *Naming.* Have the children name common objects in or outside the room (chair, door, table, tree, or stone). Have a collection of objects in a box or bag. As each is removed, have the children name it. Have the children name colors, animals, shapes, and so forth. A collection or a file of good pictures of objects provides excellent teaching material. You can make pictures more durable and washable by backing them with cardboard and covering them with a self-adhesive transparent covering.

2. *Department store.* The game of department store (or hardware store, supermarket, restaurant, shoe store, etc.) gives the children an opportunity to use naming words. One child plays the role of the customer and gives orders to another, who is the clerk. The clerk collects pictures of the ordered items and names the items while giving them to the customer.

3. *Rapid naming.* Give the students a specified length of time, such as one minute, to name all the objects in the room. Keep a record of the number of words named to note improvement. You can also ask the students to rapidly name objects in pictures. Another variation could be related to sports, the outdoors, pets, and so forth.

4. *Missing words.* Have the students say the word that finishes a riddle. For example: "Who delivers the mail? *(mail carrier).* I bounce a——— *(ball)."* Read a story to the children, pausing at certain places to leave out words. Have the children supply the missing word. The use of pictures helps in recalling and naming the object.

5. *Word combinations.* Some words can best be learned as part of a group. When one member of the group is named, the children may be helped to remember the second; for example, *paper–pencil, boy–girl, hat–coat,* and *cats–dogs.* Series such as days of the week and months of the year may also be learned in this fashion.

6. *Troublesome words.* Be alert for troublesome words. When you note such a word, you may be able to give an immediate lesson on it and then plan for future exercises using that word.

Learning Language Patterns: Making Morphological Generalizations
Some children have difficulty learning to internalize and use the morphological structure of the language. We all must make generalizations concerning the systems of forming plurals, showing past tense, and forming possessives. We must also learn the exceptions where generalizations do not hold true. For example, the phoneme /s/ or /z/ is usually added to a word in English to show plurality: *three cats* or *two dogs.* In some cases, the sound of /ez/ is added, as in *two dresses,* or the root word is changed, as in *two men.* In a few cases, the word is not changed, as in *four fish.*

1. *Use pictures to build morphological generalizations.* Ask children to point to the picture that describes the sentence you say aloud. For

example, present two pictures, one that shows an activity in process and another that shows that same activity completed. Then say, "The boy is *painting* a picture," and ask students to choose one of the pictures. Follow that by saying, "The picture is now *painted*," and have them choose the appropriate picture. Similarly, you might pair "The dog is running" and "The dogs are running" to show plural forms.

2. *Use games to form plurals.* Show an object, such as a ball, and have the children say the word *ball*. Then show two of the objects and have the children say "Two balls."

Formulating Sentences Some children are able to use single words or short phrases but are unable to generate longer syntactic units or sentences. In acquiring language, children must learn to internalize sentence patterns so that they can generate new sentences. Some linguists have said that the child becomes a sentence-producing machine. To achieve this state, the child needs many skills, including the ability to understand language, to remember word sequences, and to formulate complex rules of grammar.

1. *Provide experiences with many kinds of sentences.* Start with the basic simple sentence and help the child generate transformations. For example, two basic sentences can be combined in various ways:

    Basic sentence: "The children play games."

    Basic sentence: "The children are tired."

    Combined sentences: "The children who are tired play games."
    "The children who play games are tired."

    Sentence pattern variations can also be practiced:

Statements	*Questions*
Children play games.	Do children play games?
Games are played by children.	Are games played by children?

2. *Demonstrate structure words.* As mentioned earlier, words such as *on, in, under,* and *who,* which show the relationship among parts of the sentence, are best taught within the sentence. Close observation reveals that many children have hazy concepts of the meanings of such words. You can help students understand these concepts if you ask them to put blocks *in, on,* or *under* a table or chair, and then ask them to explain what they did. Words such as *yet, but, never,* and *which* often need clarification. Give a sentence with only the key or class words and then ask the students to add the structure words, as in this example:

    "Jack—went—school—late."
    "Jack went to school, but he was late."

3. *Substitute words to form sentences.* Have students form new sentences by substituting a single word in an existing kernel sentence. For example:

"I took my *coat* off. I took my *boots* off."

"The child is *reading*. The child is *running*. The child is *jumping*."

4. *Play a detective game.* To help students learn to formulate questions, hide an object and have students ask questions concerning its location until it is found.

Practicing Oral Language Skills Students with a deficiency in oral expressive language need practice and multiple opportunities to use words and to formulate sentences. The following activities enable students to practice their speaking skills.

1. *Use oral language activities.* A number of activities can be used to practice the use of oral language and speaking, such as conversations; discussions; radio or television broadcasts; show-and-tell sessions; puppetry; dramatic play; telephoning; choral speaking; reporting; interviewing; telling stories, riddles, or jokes; giving book reports; and role playing.

2. *Discuss objects.* Help the students tell about the attributes of an object—its color, size, shape, composition, and major parts—and to compare it with other objects.

3. *Use categories.* Place items in a box that can be grouped to teach categories, such as toys, clothes, animals, vehicles, furniture, and fruit. Ask the students to find the ones that go together and tell what they are. You can vary this activity by naming the category and asking the students to find and name the items or by putting items together and asking which do not belong.

4. *Test comprehension.* Ask questions that require students to think and formulate responses. For example:

   "What would you be if you dressed funny and were in a circus?"

   "Why is it easier to make a dress shorter than it is to make it longer?"

   "Why should you put a goldfish in a bowl of water?"

5. *Ask how.* Say, "Tell me how——you brush your teeth, go to school," and so forth. Also say, "Tell me why——Tell me where we do——" Such requests can provide an opportunity for valuable practice.

6. *Finish stories.* Begin a story and let the students finish it. For example:

   "Betty went to visit her aunt in a strange city. When the plane landed, Betty could not see her aunt at the airport——."

7. *Use Peabody language kits.* These kits are boxes that contain puppets, pictures, and language lessons, all designed to develop oral language abilities. They are published by American Guidance Services.

Activities for Improving the Oral Language of Adolescents

Direct instruction in language also helps improve the oral language and communication skills of adolescents with learning disabilities. Sometimes students at the middle school or high school levels appear, at first, to have adequate oral language skills, so their true needs are often overlooked. In addition, the secondary school curriculum emphasizes performance in written language more than in oral language, so their deficiencies may go undetected. On closer observation, however, we find that the oral language of many secondary students with learning disabilities is meager. Many of the methods described earlier work for adolescents, and the following methods are also useful.

1. *Learning strategies.* Instruction in learning strategies is particularly useful for adolescents. Adolescents should be involved in setting the goals they are trying to reach and in selecting learning strategies to reach these goals. Self-monitoring, verbal rehearsal, and error analysis are the kinds of strategies that have been helpful in reading, and they can also be used for improving oral language (see the chapter on theories of learning).

2. *Vocabulary building through classification.* Adolescents can expand their oral vocabularies if they receive help in classifying and organizing words. For example, they can build lists or hierarchies of words on a topic. For the topic of space exploration, they might use words that classify space vehicles, space inventions, first events that occurred in space, and so on. There are several approaches to this activity. The teacher can supply the words for classifying, the students can supply the words, or the teacher can provide a partial classification system and the students can complete it.

3. *Listening in stages.* Read the beginning of a selection to your students. After they listen to several paragraphs, stop and ask a question: "By now you should be able to answer. . .". This activity, in turn, provides a setting for the next portion of listening.

4. *Reciprocal questioning.* This is a variation of reciprocal teaching. Instead of the teacher asking the questions, the students ask the questions. The technique encourages the development of questioning skills.

5. *Sentence combining.* Say two short sentences aloud and ask students to think of all the ways in which the sentences can be combined into one sentence.

6. *Reviewing a group discussion.* Have students hold a short discussion on an assigned topic. After the discussion, ask them to analyze the effectiveness of the discussion. Did they stay on the topic? Did they allow others to talk? Did they direct the conversation to the right people? Did they follow through when a point was made?

7. *Explaining how to play a game.* Many students with learning disabilities have difficulty giving explanations and need practice in this activity. Such practice could consist of having students explain to another person how to play a game, how to make something, or how to do something. The recipient of the explanation can be a peer or a younger child. The students could first engage in verbal rehearsal to practice the explanation and then try to be sensitive to whether the listener understands and is able to respond to questions. Examples of subjects for explanation include the rules of a video game, how to cook and peel a hard-boiled egg, or how to play checkers or bingo.

COMPUTER TECHNOLOGY FOR ORAL LANGUAGE

Computer technology can be helpful in teaching oral language skills. A few select computer software programs are described in this section. Before using these in the classroom, you may wish to review the *National Educational Technology Standards for Students* to determine how they can best be incorporated into your teaching. The website is **http://www.iste. org/standards/index.html/**.

- *Earobics.* This is an educational software program to teach auditory and phonological awareness skills. It uses a CD-ROM and six interactive games that teach oral language skills. Cognitive Concepts, Inc., may be reached at **http://www.cogcom.com**.

- *FastForWord.* This software program alters the acoustics of speech, slowing down the sounds, then speeding them up to help children recognize words. Scientific Learning Corporation may be contacted at **http://www.scientificlearning.com**.

- *Laureate learning systems.* This is a series of software programs for teaching oral language skills to young children with language disorders and to other individuals with disabilities. It trains students in cause-and-effect, turn-taking, early vocabulary, syntax, cognitive concepts, auditory processing, and reading. Laureate Learning Systems may be reached at **http://www.laureatelearning.com**.

- *Lexia software.* This is phonics-based interactive reading software that uses multisensory approaches. The website is **http://www.lexia learning.com**.

TEACHING LANGUAGE IN THE GENERAL EDUCATION CLASSROOM

Many children in general education classrooms have speech and language problems, in addition to learning disabilities and other types of disabilities and disorders. The general education classroom teacher can assist these students. Many of the teaching strategies in this chapter can be used to enhance language learning. Some ideas for the general education teacher are provided in "LD in Practice: Teaching Language in the General Education Classroom."

LD IN PRACTICE

TEACHING LANGUAGE IN THE GENERAL EDUCATION CLASSROOM

- Provide students with many opportunities for speaking, explaining, and giving their own points of view.
- Promote discussion groups on topics of interest.
- Have students explain how to do something or demonstrate how to make something.
- Have students talk about themselves and their interests.

- Teach vocabulary that is related to an area of study.
- Provide good language models.
- Use role playing and acting out of stories.
- Encourage students to talk about their interests, such as movies, television shows, books, sports, or hobbies.

CHAPTER SUMMARY

1. Language is perhaps the most important accomplishment of the human being. Language is intimately related to all kinds of learning, and an untreated language disorder may diminish an individual's capacity to learn.

2. Language plays a vital role in learning. It enhances thinking and permits us to speak of things unseen, of the past, and of the future.

3. Language encompasses the elements of listening, speaking, reading, and writing, all of which have an underlying language core. Oral language is the primary language system and consists of listening and speaking. Written language is the secondary language system and consists of reading and writing.

4. Language is a communication process. Listening and reading are receptive language modes. Talking and writing are expressive language modes. A breakdown can occur anywhere in the communication process.

5. Factors involved in language acquisition include behavioral factors, biological or innate factors, cognitive factors, and social factors.

6. Components of the language system include phonology, morphology, syntax, semantics, and pragmatics.

7. Types of language problems include delayed speech, lack of phonological awareness, problems with temporal or acoustical processing, receptive language disorders, and expressive language disorders.

8. Consider the linguistic and cultural diversity of oral language. English-language learners are students whose first language is not

English and who exhibit a limited language proficiency. Some children are English-language learners and also have a learning disability.

9. *Early literacy* refers to the child's early entrance into the world of words, language, stories, and books.

10. The "Teaching Strategies" section suggests activities for teaching listening and speaking skills.

1. Describe the communication process. Discuss the kinds of problems that a student may encounter in communicating.

2. What are the components of language? Give an example of each. What kinds of problems can a student with learning disabilities encounter with each component of language?

3. Describe a few of the problems faced by students who are English-language learners. Describe a few practices that have been shown to be helpful for English-language learners.

4. What is meant by the term *early literacy*? Describe a few methods that foster early literacy.

5. What is phonological awareness? Why is it important for young children to develop skills in phonological awareness?

KEY TERMS

apraxia *(p. 343)*

bilingual method *(p. 346)*

components of language *(p. 334)*

developmental aphasia *(p. 342)*

dysnomia *(p. 343)*

early literacy *(p. 346)*

English as a second language (ESL) method *(p. 346)*

expressive language disorders *(p. 343)*

immersion method *(p. 346)*

language delay *(p. 337)*

language disorders *(p. 337)*

morpheme *(p. 334)*

morphology *(p. 334)*

otitis media *(p. 337)*

phoneme *(p. 334)*

phonics *(p. 334)*

phonology *(p. 334)*

pragmatics *(p. 335)*

primary language system *(p. 327)*

rapid automatized naming (RAN) *(p. 341)*

receptive language disorders *(p. 342)*

secondary language system *(p. 327)*

semantics *(p. 335)*

sheltered English *(p. 346)*

speech disorders *(p. 337)*

Standard English *(p. 334)*

syntax *(p. 335)*

temporal acoustical processing *(p. 340)*

word finding *(p. 341)*

Reading

This chapter on reading is the second of three chapters on the integrated language system. Reading is an integral part of the language system and is closely linked to oral language and writing.

In the first part of this chapter, the "Theories" section, we discuss: (1) the consequences of reading disabilities and (2) dyslexia; we also discuss (3) the elements of reading, (4) phonemic awareness, (5) phonics and word-recognition clues, (6) fluency, (7) vocabulary, (8) comprehension, (9) the reading–writing connection, and (10) assessing reading.

In the "Teaching Strategies" section, we present: (1) reading strategies for the general education classroom, (2) strategies to improve word recognition, (3) strategies to improve fluency, (4) strategies to improve reading comprehension, (5) special remedial methods for reading, (6) methods to deal with specific reading problems, and (7) computers and reading.

THEORIES

THE CONSEQUENCES OF READING DISABILITIES

If our children do not learn to read, they cannot succeed in life. Without the ability to read, the opportunities for academic and occupational success are limited. Unfortunately, at least 80% of students with learning disabilities encounter difficulties in reading (Lerner, 1989). The reading of books is on a decline, with only 57% of adults reported to have read a book in 2002 (National Endowment for the Arts, 2004).

It is critical that we identify children with reading problems early and provide them with appropriate early instruction. More than 17.5% of the nation's school children—about 1 million children—encounter reading problems during the crucial first 3 years of schooling (National Reading Panel, 2000). Moreover, 74% of children who were unsuccessful at reading in third grade are still unsuccessful in ninth grade (National Institute for Child Health and Human Development, 1999). The reading problems of adolescents and adults reflect reading difficulties that were not resolved during their early years (National Research Council, 1998). The *wait-and-fail method* refers to the policy of not promptly addressing the reading difficulties of young children but, instead, waiting to do so when they are older. Lyons (2003) reported on the findings about reading disorders from research supported by the National Institute of Child Health and Human Development.

- Reading is so critical to success in our society that reading failure not only constitutes an educational problem, but it also rises to the level of a major public health problem.

- Children who are most at risk for reading failure lack phonemic awareness, lack sensitivity to the sounds of language, are not familiar with the letters of the alphabet, and may not understand the purpose of print. In addition, these children lack sufficient oral language and verbal skills and have meager vocabularies.

- Children may also be at risk for reading failure because of their linguistic and cultural backgrounds and their limited exposure to the English language.

- Early identification of young children who are at risk for reading failure and timely intervention to assist them are essential for maximizing treatment success.

Because reading is the basic skill for all academic subjects, failure in school can be traced to inadequate reading skills. Students today face more mandatory tests than ever before, and they need to earn diplomas and degrees to obtain jobs. The need to overcome these hurdles, as well as the

Children should be surrounded by the world of books and have many experiences listening to stories, reading books, and writing. (© LWA-JDC/CORBIS)

necessity of filling out application forms and taking licensing examinations, makes life for the poor reader difficult and seemingly full of impassible barriers. In today's world, high technology and automation have created a demand for highly trained people. Telecommunications, e-mail, and the Internet all require users to read written electronic information on a monitor screen.

The development of reading skills serves as the major academic foundation for all school-based learning. Efficient reading is a key skill for maintaining employment or retraining for another job. Workers in every occupation now have to retrain themselves to prepare for new jobs many times during their work careers. Poor reading skills cause many problems for individuals in the world of work. Because fewer jobs are available for unskilled and semiskilled workers, these individuals are likely to end up being chronically unemployed. Opportunities for gainful employment decrease for youth who drop out of school. They have twice the unemployment rate that high school graduates do, have fewer opportunities for continued training, and lack the qualifications to attend postsecondary school or college (Gerber, 1997; Hennesy, Rosenberg, & Tramaglini, 2003).

We should also recognize that reading is not a natural process. In contrast to other developmental achievements, such as learning to talk, learning to read requires careful instruction. Learning to read is also a relatively lengthy process. It takes several years, and the learner must persevere over a long period of time. Moreover, the process of recognizing words is complex; readers must use a variety of strategies to accomplish this purpose. Children must learn to read so that later they can *read to learn*.

In our linguistically and culturally diverse society, more students come from homes in which a language other than English is spoken. Therefore, the more knowledge and empathy that a teacher has for a student's personal background and cultural heritage, the more effective the teacher's reading instruction will be. Current information and research about reading can be found at **http://www.readingrockets.org.**

DYSLEXIA   The condition known as *dyslexia* is an unusual type of severe reading disorder that has puzzled the educational and medical communities for many years. Actually, dyslexia is one type of severe learning disability that affects some children, adolescents, and adults. "LD Stories: People With Dyslexia" provides statements from well-known individuals with dyslexia about how this problem has affected their lives.

People with this baffling disorder find it extremely difficult to recognize letters and words and to interpret information that is presented in print form. People with dyslexia are intelligent and may have very strong mathematics or spatial skills. For example, Charles Schwab, the founder of the successful and innovative stock brokerage firm, has struggled with severe reading problems throughout his life. Schwab has coped by developing

PEOPLE WITH DYSLEXIA

Adults who have suffered from dyslexia can long recall the anguish of trying to cope with this mysterious condition in a world that requires people to read.

> I remember vividly the pain and mortification I felt as a boy of 8 when I was assigned to read a short passage of scripture with a community vesper service during the summer vacation in Maine—and did a thoroughly miserable job of it.

Nelson Rockefeller
TV Guide, October 16, 1976

> I'm not lazy, I'm not stupid, I'm dyslexic. My parents grounded me for weeks at a time because I was in the bottom 3% in the country in math. On the SAT's I got 159 out of 800 in math. My parents had no idea that I had dyslexia. They never knew such a thing existed (S. Smith, 1991).

Henry Winkler
"The Fonz" in Happy Days
Actor, director, producer

> I got all C's and D's in school and I am mildly dyslexic. But I am very persistent and ambitious. When I applied to college, the admissions officer said I wasn't what they wanted. So I sat outside his office 12 hours a day until the admissions officer said he would let me in if I attended summer school. The tuition was $12,000, so I took out my wallet and gave him $12,000 in cash. I was already making good money in nightclubs. I think that having dyslexia is a competitive advantage. Dyslexic people are good at setting everything aside to pursue one goal. Ambition beats genius 99% of the time (from Jay Leno interview in

Home Business Magazine, 2001, as found at **http://www.schwablearning.org, 2001**).

Jay Leno
Comedian and late-night talk show host

> When I was young, they used to say on my report cards, "She has the ability but doesn't apply herself." Everything I learned in school was through spoken information because I had such a hard time reading and writing. I can't spell, and if I have to dial the telephone long distance, it's a hassle. You have to find the place that you can shine if you don't fit in with what everybody else is doing. I became the class clown because I could not read or write. I dropped out of school at age 16 (S. Smith, 1991).

Cher
Actress, singer, dancer

> I hardly got through school. Probably the biggest fear of my life barring none, was *not* competing in the Olympic games against the best athletes in the world, but when I was a young boy, my biggest fear was having to stand up in front of the class and read. It wasn't until later in life that I found my niche, and that was athletics. For the first time in my life, I could hold my head up high. I could get out on the football field and compete against a boy I know was a real good reader. All of a sudden, we were equal and, in most cases, I could beat him. That was very important to me (S. Smith, 1991).

Bruce Jenner
Olympic gold medalist

other skills, such as the abilities to envision, to anticipate where things are going, and to conceive a solution to a business problem. He feels that his reading disorder forced him to develop these skills at a higher level than that attained by people for whom reading comes easily (Kantrowitz &

Underwood, 1999; Morris, 2002; West, 1997). Schwab supports a website to help parents and individuals with reading disabilities: **http://www.schwablearning.org.**

Although there are a number of different definitions of dyslexia (see the chapter on medical aspects of learning disabilities), there is general agreement on several points (Hynd, 1992; Shaywitz, 2003):

1. Dyslexia has a biological basis and is caused by a disruption in the neural circuits in the brain.
2. Dyslexic problems persist into adolescence and adulthood.
3. Dyslexia has perceptual, cognitive, and language dimensions.
4. Dyslexia leads to difficulties in many areas of life as the individual matures.
5. Some individuals with dyslexia excel in other facets of life.

The life stories of corporate CEOs with dyslexia show their remarkable skills in the business world (Morris, 2002). People with dyslexia tend to find ingenious ways to hide their disability. For example, a widowed gentleman caught in the social dating whirl routinely handled the problem of dining in restaurants by putting down his menu and saying to his companion, "Why don't you order for both of us, dear? Your selections are always so delicious." This man hired professionals to handle his reading and writing matters. His friends attributed his actions to wealth, never suspecting his inability to read.

For many years, scholars strongly suspected that dyslexia has a neurobiological basis; however, until recently, they lacked the scientific evidence to support this belief. Research now offers evidence that dyslexia is caused by an abnormality in brain structure, a difference in brain function, and genetic factors (Gilger, 2003; Kibby & Hynd, 2001; Shaywitz, 2003; Shaywitz & Shaywitz, 1998, 1999; Zeffrino & Eden, 2000). The fascinating brain research studies on dyslexia and the new technologies for assessing the link between brain function and learning were discussed in the chapter on the medical aspects of learning disabilities. While neuroscientists continue their search for the causes of dyslexia, teachers must provide the instruction to teach these individuals how to read.

ELEMENTS OF READING

The National Reading Panel (2000) is a commission of reading scholars assigned by the U.S. Congress to conduct an evidence-based assessment of the research literature on reading and its implications for reading instruction. Finding that over 100,000 research studies on reading had been published since 1966, the National Reading Panel had to establish stringent criteria for the inclusion of research studies in their evidence-based assessment. (More information about their findings is available at the website

http://www.nationalreadingpanel.org.)

The research criteria for the studies selected by the assessment had to: (1) focus on reading, preschool to Grade 12, (2) be published in English in a referred journal, (3) clearly describe the participants, (4) describe the intervention in enough detail to allow for replication, (5) allow judgments about how instructional fidelity was ensured, and (6) include a careful description of outcome measures.

The National Reading Panel (2000) selected several elements of reading for its intensive study, which it concluded were important essentials for learning to read. Effective readers need to be competent in the following components of reading, each of which is discussed in this textbook.

1. Phonemic awareness (which is discussed in the chapter on oral language)
2. Phonics (which is discussed in this chapter)
3. Fluency (which is discussed in this chapter)
4. Vocabulary (which is discussed in this chapter)
5. Text comprehension (which is discussed in this chapter)

PHONEMIC AWARENESS

Phonemic awareness is the ability to notice, think about, and work with the individual sounds in spoken words. Before children learn to read print, they need to become aware of how the sounds work in words. They must understand that words are made of speech sounds, or phonemes. The term *phonological awareness* is broad and includes the ability to identify and manipulate larger parts of spoken language, such as words, syllables, and rhymes, as well as phonemes. Phonemic awareness is a part of phonological awareness; it focuses on the process of identifying and manipulating the individual sounds in words (Center for the Improvement of Early Reading Achievement, 2001). You can find more information on the National Institute for Literacy's website, **http://www.nifl.gov.**

Phonemic awareness focuses on children's hearing and using the sounds of language, which is discussed in greater detail in the chapter on oral language.

PHONICS AND WORD-RECOGNITION SKILLS

Reading requires the ability to recognize words. Once readers develop facility in word recognition, they can concentrate on the meaning of the text. Without these lower level reading skills, the higher cognitive skills cannot function (Williams, 1998). The reader who must exert much effort to recognize words will have little processing capacity remaining for comprehension.

Early attention to word-recognition skills is important because this early ability accurately predicts later skill in reading comprehension. Children who get off to a slow start rarely become strong readers (National Reading Panel, 2000). Learning word-recognition skills early leads to wider reading abilities in school and out of school. Reading a wide variety of material provides opportunities to increase one's vocabulary, develop an interest in books, and foster general reading growth (Cunningham & Stanovich, 1998; Lyon, 2003).

Readers use several **word-recognition skills** to identify words, such as: (1) phonics, (2) sight words, (3) context clues, and (4) structural analysis. The "Teaching Strategies" section of this chapter suggests methods for teaching each of these word-recognition skills.

Phonics

Phonics is an essential word-recognition skill that involves learning the correspondence of letters and sounds and applying that knowledge to recognizing words and reading. *Phonics* refers to the relationship between printed letters (**graphemes**) and the sounds (phonemes) in language. Children must learn to **decode** printed language and translate print into sounds through the alphabetic principle of the symbol–sound relationship. This process is known as *breaking the code*.

Children with reading disabilities require systematic phonics instruction. A systematic phonics program is a planned, sequential set of phonics elements, which is taught explicitly and systematically. Research shows that children who learn the sound–symbol system of English read better than children who have not mastered this skill (Chall, 1967, 1983; Lyon, 2003; Moats, 1998; National Reading Panel, 2000). As noted previously, a precursor to learning phonics is phonemic awareness, which is the child's recognition that speech can be segmented into sounds (see the chapter on oral language).

Understanding phonics helps children break the code so that they can recognize words quickly and easily. In a written alphabet language, such as English, the code involves a system of mapping, or seeing the correspondences between letters and sounds. Once a child learns these mappings, she or he has broken the code and can then apply this knowledge to figure out plausible pronunciations of printed words (Adams, 1990; Moats, 1998).

Children with reading disabilities need direct instruction in phonics and decoding that makes the relationship between printed letters and sounds explicit. Such **explicit code-emphasis instruction** assists the learning process by providing these children with a basis for remembering the order identified for useful letter strings and for deriving the meanings of printed words. (See "Teaching Strategies" later in this chapter for phonics instruction.)

Findings of the National Reading Panel on the Effectiveness of Phonics Instruction   The National Reading Panel (2000) reached the following conclusions about the effectiveness of phonics instruction:

1. Systematic phonics instruction makes a bigger contribution to children's growth in reading than other programs that provide unsystematic or no phonics instruction.

2. All systematic phonics programs are effective in promoting reading achievement, and they do not appear to differ significantly from one another.

3. Systematic phonics instruction is effective when delivered through tutoring, through small groups, or through teaching classes of students.

4. Systematic phonics instruction is effective when taught in kindergarten. It must be appropriately designed for young learners and must begin with foundational knowledge involving letters and phonemic awareness.

5. Phonics instruction is effective in helping to prevent reading difficulties among at-risk students and in helping to remediate reading difficulties in students with reading disabilities.

6. Systematic phonics instruction is beneficial to students regardless of their socioeconomic status (SES).

Teacher Knowledge About Phonics   Studies that compare methods for teaching beginning reading show that children who are taught phonics directly and systematically in the early grades receive higher scores on reading achievement tests during their primary years than children who do not receive this training (Chall, 1991; Lyon & Moats, 1997; Moats, 1998; National Reading Panel, 2000). However, many teachers lack a firm grounding in phonics and phonics generalizations (Horne, 1978; Lerner & List, 1970; Moats, 1998). Some teachers do not remember learning phonics themselves, and many did not receive adequate phonics instruction during their teacher training. (The reader may wish to take the *Foniks Kwiz* in "Phonics Quiz and Review" in the website for this book **http://college. hmco.com/education.** A brief review of phonics generalizations follows the quiz.)

Types of Phonics Approaches   There are several different types of phonics instructional approaches (National Reading Panel, 2000). Table 11.1 shows the types of phonics approaches, with an explanation of each approach and examples.

Sight Words

Unlike some other languages, written English has an inconsistent phoneme–grapheme relationship, or spelling pattern. The relationship between the letter and its sound equivalent is not always predictable. The letter *a,* for example, is given a different sound in each of the following typical first-grade words: *at, Jane, ball, father, was, saw,* and *are.* Another example of this complexity is the phoneme of the long *i,* which has a different spelling pattern in each of the following words: *aisle, aye, I, eye, ice, tie,*

TABLE 11.1

Different Types of Phonics Approaches

Phonics approach	Explanation	Example
Synthetic phonics	Teaching students explicitly to convert letters into sounds (or phonemes) and then blend the sounds to form recognizable words	Take the word *stop*. Break it into sounds: *s/t/o/p*. Then blend the sounds into the word.
Analytic phonics	Teaching students to analyze letter–sound relations in pre-viously learned words to avoid pronouncing sounds in isolation	Analyze the sounds in the whole word *making*.
Analogy phonics	Recognizing that a rhyme segment of an unfamiliar word is identical to that of a familiar word	Known word *kick* New word *brick* Known word *sing* New word *ring*
Embedded phonics	Teaching students phonics skills by embedding phonics instruc-tion in text reading; this is a more implicit approach that relies to some extent on incidental learning	Instruction in phonics skills is incidental and is taught during the read-ing of a text.
Phonics through spelling	Teaching students to segment words into phonemes and to select letters for those phonemes	Students are instructed to spell words phonemically.

Source: From *Teaching children to read: An evidence-based assessment of the scientific research literature on reading and its implications for reading instruction,* p. 8, Report of the National Reading Panel, 2000, Washington, DC: National Institute of Child Health and Human Development.

high, choir, buy, sky, rye, pine, and *type.* To further complicate the problem of learning to read English, many of the most frequently used **sight words**—which are words that are recognized instantly, without hesitation or further analysis—in first-grade books have irregular spelling patterns. A few of these words are shown in the first column of Table 11.2; the second column shows the way they would be spelled with a dependable phoneme–grapheme relationship so that readers could "sound them out." These words must thus be learned as sight words (Richek et al., 2002).

The problems caused by the undependable written form of English can be approached in two ways:

1. *Introduce only a small number of words at a time, selecting words on the basis of frequency of use.* Some beginning reading words have regular spellings, whereas others have irregular spellings. Words are learned visually through extensive review and through context, mean-

TABLE 11.2

Typical First-Grade
Sight Words

English spelling	Phonic spelling
of	uv
laugh	laf
was	wuz
is	iz
come	kum
said	sed
what	wut
from	frum
one	wun
night	nite
know	noe
they	thai

ing, and language. Basal readers, for example, rely on a controlled introduction of a small number of new words.

2. ***Simplify the initial learning phase by selecting only words that have a consistent sound–symbol spelling relationship.*** With this approach, students learn phonics and are exposed to carefully selected words with dependable spellings. Linguistic and phonetic methods use this approach and rely on selected words with a dependable spelling pattern.

Eventually, of course, the child must learn about the undependable spelling of many common English words. Through careful selection of the words for reading, students are kept from learning the awful truth about spelling until second grade or later. Inevitably, however, the reader must confront the undependable written form of English.

Context Clues

Context clues help a student recognize a word through the meaning, or context, of a sentence or paragraph in which the word appears. Redundancies in language occur when information from one source repeats or supports information from another source. These language redundancies provide hints about unknown words from the meaning of the surrounding text, which helps readers make conjectures and guesses about unfamiliar words.

Instruction in recognizing words through context is best done by actual reading. When students with reading disabilities have consistent practice in reading stories and books, they naturally learn to use context clues. The meaning of the sentence plus the initial sounds in the word may provide enough clues for the reader to recognize the word.

Structural Analysis

Structural analysis refers to the recognition of words through the analysis of meaningful word units such as prefixes, suffixes, root words, compound words, and syllables. Structural elements include compound words (*cowboy*), contractions (*can't*), word endings or inflectional suffixes (*-s, -ed, -er, -est, -ing*), word beginnings or prefixes (*in-, pre-, un-, re-, ex-*), roots (*play* in *replaying*), and syllables (i.e., breaking multisyllabic words into smaller units).

A reader may recognize structural elements of a word (e.g., the prefix *re-* and the suffix *-tion* in *repetition*). These clues, combined with the context of the sentence, may be sufficient for recognizing the word.

Combining Word-Recognition Clues

Readers should be encouraged to use all of the word-recognition clues (phonics, sight words, context clues, and structural analysis). However, they will need these strategies only when an unknown word stops the reading process. Readers usually use several clues together until they recognize the unknown word. Students with learning disabilities need practice in each of these word-recognition clues to achieve independence and flexibility and to gain fluency.

FLUENCY **Reading fluency** is the ability to read connected text rapidly, effortlessly, and automatically (Hook & Jones, 2004; Meyer, 2002; National Reading Panel, 2000). Readers must develop fluency to make the bridge from word recognition to reading comprehension (Jenkins, Fuchs, Vandern Broek, Espin & Deno, 2003). In this section, we describe: (1) sight words, (2) automaticity, (3) repeated reading, and (4) other methods to improve reading fluency. The "Teaching Strategies" section offers additional strategies to improve fluency.

Sight Words

Many poor readers have difficulty reading fluently because they do not possess an adequate sight vocabulary and must labor to decode many of the words in the reading passages. With their energies focused on recognizing words, their oral reading is filled with long pauses and many repetitions, and it is characterized by monotonous expression. Fluent reading requires that most of the words in a selection be sight words. When a selection contains too many difficult (nonsight) words, the reading material will be too arduous and frustrating for the reader (Burns, Roe, & Smith, 2002; Jenkins et al., 2003).

Table 11.3 illustrates 220 basic sight words that students should know by the end of third grade. These words are divided into groups according to their difficulty. One of the best and certainly most natural ways to learn sight words is by actually reading stories. Sight words appear many times in context. A natural way to expose children to sight words is through language experience stories, which contain many sight words. Students with reading disabilities need other direct approaches to strengthen their sight vocabulary. Some methods for teaching sight vocabulary are presented in the "Teaching Strategies" section of this chapter.

Automaticity

Automaticity is the fast, accurate, and effortless word identification at the single word level. The speed and accuracy with which single words are identified is a key predictor of reading comprehension. The range of children's skill in recognizing words is large. One research study reported that in a first-grade class, the number of words that children recognized ranged from 15 words to 1,933 words. The average skilled reader read three times as many words as the average less skilled reader (Compton & Appleton, 2004).

Recognizing Syllables A powerful tool to develop automatic word recognition is to teach students the visual patterns in the six syllable types, which are shown in Figure 11.1.

Repeated Reading

Guided oral reading procedures, such as repeated reading, clearly improve reading fluency and overall reading achievement (National Reading Panel, 2000). The "Teaching Strategies" section in this chapter describes additional strategies to improve reading fluency.

The repeated reading method is simple and straightforward, emphasizing practice and repetition to improve fluency and accuracy. Meyer (2002) notes three steps for teaching repeated reading:

1. The student reads aloud a passage at the student's instructional level several times until the desired rate of reading, measured in words per minute, is achieved

TABLE 11.3

The 220 Basic Sight Words

Preprimer	Primer	First	Second	Third
1. the	45. when	89. many	133. know	177. don't
2. of	46. who	90. before	134. while	178. does
3. and	47. will	91. must	135. last	179. got
4. to	48. more	92. through	136. might	180. united
5. a	49. no	93. back	137. us	181. left
6. in	50. if	94. years	138. great	182. number
7. that	51. out	95. where	139. old	183. course
8. is	52. so	96. much	140. year	184. war
9. was	53. said	97. your	141. off	185. until
10. he	54. what	98. may	142. come	186. always
11. for	55. up	99. well	143. since	187. away
12. it	56. its	100. down	144. against	188. something
13. with	57. about	101. should	145. go	189. fact
14. as	58. into	102. because	146. came	190. through
15. his	59. than	103. each	147. right	191. water
16. on	60. them	104. just	148. used	192. less
17. be	61. can	105. those	149. take	193. public
18. at	62. only	106. people	150. three	194. put
19. by	63. other	107. Mr.	151. states	195. thing
20. I	64. new	108. how	152. himself	196. almost
21. this	65. some	109. too	153. few	197. hand
22. had	66. could	110. little	154. house	198. enough
23. not	67. time	111. state	155. use	199. far
24. are	68. these	112. good	156. during	200. took
25. but	69. two	113. very	157. without	201. head
26. from	70. may	114. make	158. again	202. yet
27. or	71. then	115. would	159. place	203. government
28. have	72. do	116. still	160. American	204. system
29. an	73. first	117. own	161. around	205. better
30. they	74. any	118. see	162. however	206. set
31. which	75. my	119. men	163. home	207. told
32. one	76. now	120. work	164. small	208. nothing
33. you	77. such	121. long	165. found	209. night
34. were	78. like	122. get	166. Mrs.	210. end
35. her	79. our	123. here	167. thought	211. why
36. all	80. over	124. between	168. went	212. called
37. she	81. man	125. both	169. say	213. didn't
38. there	82. me	126. life	170. part	214. eyes

TABLE 11.3 (cont.)

The 220 Basic Sight Words

Preprimer	Primer	First	Second	Third
39. would	83. even	127. being	171. once	215. find
40. their	84. most	128. under	172. general	216. going
41. we	85. made	129. never	173. high	217. look
42. him	86. after	130. day	174. upon	218. asked
43. been	87. also	131. same	175. school	219. later
44. has	88. did	132. another	176. every	220. knew

Source: From "The Dolch List Reexamined," by D. D. Johnson, 1971, *The Reading Teacher, 24(5),* pp. 455–456. Reprinted with permission of Dale D. Johnson and the International Reading Association. All rights reserved.

FIGURE 11.1

Six Syllable Types

Syllable type	Example
Closed (closed with a consonant, vowel makes its **short** sound)	*pot*
Open (ends in a vowel, vowel makes its **long** sound)	*go*
Silent *e* (ends in vowel consonant e, vowel makes its **long** sound)	*cake*
Vowel combination (the two vowels together make a sound)	*coat*
Controlled *r* (contains a vowel plus r, vowel sound is changed)	*card*
Consonant + *le* (at the end of a word)	*ta/ble*

Source: Adapted from "The Importance of Automaticity and Fluency for Efficient Reading Comprehension," by P. Hook and S. Jones, *Perspectives, 28*(Winter 2002), 9–14. Reprinted with the permission of the International Dyslexia Association.

2. After reaching the criterion rate, the student reads aloud another passage at the same level of reading difficulty until that rate is attained again

3. Results are graphed to document fluency gains and provide much needed motivation

Other Methods to Improve Reading Fluency

The following list offers additional methods to improve reading fluency, such as

- *Read-along method.* The teacher and one student read a passage together orally
- *Paired reading.* Two students read in pairs, alternating pages; paired reading provides extensive reading practice for both students
- *Echo reading.* First, the teacher models an oral reading passage; the student is then asked to imitate the teacher's reading

Fluency occurs when students begin to read easily instead of laboring through reading material. Students need many opportunities to read if they are to gain fluency. Knowledge of sound–symbol associations and abundant practice contribute to fluency. However, the books read have to be at the appropriate difficulty level—not too hard, but not too easy. Students enjoy reading series books, such as the *Boxcar Children* series. They also enjoy books about horses, animals, sports figures, and books that hook them into reading independently. The *Harry Potter* series is a remarkable example of books that students like to read.

Unfortunately, because of stringent curriculum demands, less skilled readers often find themselves reading materials that are too difficult for them to enjoy or to be helpful in building their fluency. As a consequence, poor readers do not have the opportunities to read books and stories at their reading level and to practice newly acquired skills. It is essential that all children be provided with as many reading experiences as possible, regardless of their achievement levels. In fact, frequent reading not only improves reading fluency and reading skills, but it also improves verbal abilities and thinking abilities (Cunningham & Stanovich, 1998).

VOCABULARY Vocabulary occupies a central position in learning to read. The student's vocabulary has a significant effect on reading achievement and is strongly related to reading comprehension (National Reading Panel, 2000).

Vocabulary knowledge requires the reader to not only know the word, but also to apply it appropriately in context. For example, when two boys tried to make cookies, they were puzzled when their cookies stuck to the pan. They had followed the directions in the recipe and greased the bottom of the pan. Their vocabulary problem was they thought the meaning of the word *bottom* referred to the underside of the pan. The part on which they had been told to place the cookies seemed to them to be the top of the pan.

Some important facets of teaching vocabulary are:

- *Differences between oral vocabulary and reading vocabulary:* (1) *Oral vocabulary* is the words the child uses in speaking and in listening, and (2) *reading vocabulary* is the words the reader recognizes in print.

    Children enter school with a large oral vocabulary, estimated to be about 6,000 words. The average high school senior knows about 45,000 words (Stahl, 2004). Many of these words are in the student's reading vocabulary.

FIGURE 11.2

Stages of Word Learning

Stage	Level of knowledge
Unknown	Word is unfamiliar and meaning unknown
Acquainted	Word is somewhat familiar, reader understands the basic meaning
Established	Word is very familiar, reader immediately knows the meaning and uses the word correctly

- *Indirect instruction and direct instruction.* Students build their vocabulary knowledge both indirectly and directly. Methods for **indirect instruction** include the expansive use of oral language and students reading extensively on their own. In **direct instruction,** words are explicitly taught using word-learning strategies.

- *Stages of learning words.* It is important to recognize that students learn words gradually. Most words require 20 exposures in context before an adequate grasp of their meanings is acquired (McKenna, 2004). Figure 11.2 illustrates three stages of word learning.

The National Reading Panel (2000) summarized its findings about vocabulary instruction, noting that

- Instruction in vocabulary leads to gains in comprehension and the method must be appropriate for the age and ability of the reader

- Computer programs are helpful in teaching vocabulary

- Vocabulary can be learned incidentally in the context of storybook reading or by listening to others

- The instructional procedure of teaching vocabulary before reading a text is helpful

The "Teaching Strategies" section of this chapter offers some specific strategies to improve students' vocabulary.

COMPREHENSION

The purpose of reading is **comprehension;** that is, gathering meaning from the printed page. All reading instruction should provide for the development of reading comprehension. For many students with reading disabilities, reading comprehension is a major problem. Comprehension skills do not automatically evolve after word-recognition skills have been learned. Although most students with reading disabilities eventually learn the basics of word-recognition skills, many continue to have great difficulty with tasks that require comprehension of complex passages. These students need to learn strategies that will help them become active readers who understand the text. In this section, we describe: (1) the views of reading

Source: PEANUTS reprinted by permission of UFS, Inc.

comprehension, (2) strategies to promote reading comprehension, (3) comprehension of narrative materials, and (4) comprehension of expository materials.

Views of Reading Comprehension

Reading comprehension is an active process that requires an intentional and thoughtful interaction between the reader and the text. As readers try to comprehend the material they read, they must bridge the gap between the information presented in the written text and the knowledge they possess. Reading comprehension thus involves thinking. The reader's background knowledge, interest, and the reading situation affect comprehension of the material. Each person's integration of the new information in the text with what is already known will yield unique information (National Reading Panel, 2000).

Reading Comprehension Depends on What the Reader Brings to the Written Material   Reading comprehension depends on the reader's experience, knowledge of language, and recognition of syntactic structure, as well as on the redundancy of the printed passage (Richek et al., 2002). To appreciate the importance of the reader's knowledge in reading comprehension, read the following excellent illustration:

> A newspaper is better than a magazine, and on a seashore is a better place than a street. At first it is better to run than to walk. Also you may have to try several times. It takes some skill but it's easy to learn. Even young children can enjoy it. Once successful, complications are minimal. Birds seldom get too close. One needs lots of room. Rain soaks in very fast. Too many people doing the same thing can also cause problems. If there are no complications, it can be very peaceful. A rock will serve as an anchor. If things break loose from it, however, you will not get a second chance. (Bransford & Johnson, 1972, cited in Aulls, 1982, p. 52)

As a mature reader, you were able to understand every word of this paragraph, yet you probably did not understand the passage and cannot explain what it is about. The reason you had difficulty is that you did not have the appropriate background knowledge to bring to the printed text. Now, we shall expand your background knowledge by telling you that the passage is about *kites*. If you reread the paragraph now, you will find a marked improvement in your reading comprehension. The implication for teaching is that when the reader has limited knowledge to relate to the text content, no amount of rereading will increase comprehension. What students with learning disabilities need in many cases is more background knowledge to improve their comprehension.

Reading Comprehension Is a Thinking Process   The relationship between reading and thinking has been noted for a long time. In 1917, Thorndike likened the thinking process used in mathematics to that of reading:

> Understanding a paragraph is like solving a problem in mathematics. It consists of selecting the right elements of the situation and putting them together in the right relations, and also with the right amount of weight or influence or force for each . . . all under the influence of the right mental set or purpose or demands. (p. 329)

Reading can be viewed as thinking or as something akin to problem solving. As in problem solving, the reader must employ concepts, develop and test hypotheses, and modify those concepts. In this way, reading comprehension is a mode of inquiry, and methods that employ discovery techniques should be used in the teaching of reading. The key to teaching from this perspective is to guide students to set up their own questions and purposes for reading. Students then read to solve problems that they have devised for themselves. Students can be encouraged first to guess what will happen next in a story, for example, and then to read to determine the accuracy of those predictions (Stauffer, 1975). This approach, which is called a *directed reading–thinking activity,* is described in the "Teaching Strategies" section of this chapter.

Reading Comprehension Requires Active Interaction With the Text   Readers must be active participants, interacting with the text material. They must actively combine their existing knowledge with the new information of the printed text.

There is evidence that good readers generally do not read every word of a passage; instead, they "sample" certain words to determine the meaning and skip many others. They go back and read every word only when they encounter something unexpected. An excellent example of a reader interacting with the text is provided by Adler (1956):

> When people in love are reading a love letter, they read for all they are worth. They read every word three ways; they read the whole in terms of the parts, and each part in terms of the whole; they grow sensitive to context and ambiguity, to insinuation and implication; they perceive the color of words, the order of phrases, and the weight of sentences. They may even take punctuation into account. Then, if never before or after, they read. (p. 4)

Strategies to Promote Reading Comprehension

In its review of comprehension instruction strategies, the National Reading Panel (2000) recognized several strategies that had a solid scientific basis of instruction for improving reading comprehension.

1. *Comprehension monitoring.*   Students learn how to be aware of their understanding of the material.
2. *Cooperative learning.*   Students learn reading strategies together.
3. *Use of graphic and semantic organizers, including story maps.*   Students make graphic representations of the material to assist their comprehension.
4. *Question answering.*   Students answer questions posed by the teacher and receive immediate feedback.
5. *Question generation.*   Students ask themselves questions about various aspects of the story.
6. *Story structure.*   Students are taught how to use the structure of the story as a means of helping them recall story content in order to answer questions about what they have read.
7. *Summarization.*   Students are taught to integrate ideas and to generalize from the text information.

Williams (1998) suggests that students with learning disabilities require a different type of comprehension instruction than typical learners need. Just as students with learning disabilities need explicit structured instruction to learn word-recognition skills, they need explicit, highly structured instruction to learn reading comprehension skills. Incidental, literature-based instruction that is typically used to teach reading comprehension is not sufficient. Williams (1998) taught comprehension to students with learning disabilities through a "Themes Instruction Program," which consists of a series of twelve 40-min lessons. Each lesson is organized around a single story and is composed of five parts:

1. Prereading discussion on the purpose of the lesson and the topic of the story that will be read

2. Reading the story

3. Discussion of important story information using organized (schema) questions as a guide

4. Identification of a theme for the story, stating it in general terms so that it is relevant to a variety of stories and situations

5. Practice in applying the generalized theme to real-life experiences

Comprehension Activities Before, During, and After Reading Reading comprehension can be taught before reading, during reading, and after reading, as indicated in Table 11.4.

TABLE 11.4

Strategies to Promote Reading Comprehension

Before reading	During reading	After reading
Establish a purpose for reading	Direct attention to difficult or subtle dimensions of the text	Ask students to retell or summarize the story
Review vocabulary	Point out difficult words and ideas	Create graphic organizers (e.g., webs, cause-and-effect charts, outlines)
Build background knowledge	Ask students to identify problems and solutions	Put pictures of story events in order
Relate background knowledge and information to the story	Encourage silent reading	Link background information
Encourage children to predict what the story will be about	Encourage students to monitor their own comprehension while reading	Generate questions for other children
Discuss the author if such knowledge helps to set up the story	Insert author information in the story	Have students write their own reactions to stories and factual material

Before reading a story, teachers should motivate and interest students in the reading selection, review the vocabulary, build background information, and have the students predict what the story will be about. *During reading,* the teacher should direct the students' attention to the difficult or subtle dimensions of the story, anticipate difficult words and ideas, talk about problems and solutions, encourage silent reading, as well as encourage students to monitor their own comprehension. *After reading,* comprehension strategies can include having the readers summarize or retell the story, talk about what they liked and what they wished had been different in the story, create graphic organizers, put pictures of story events in order, link background information, and talk about the characters in the story (Richek et al., 2002).

Comprehension of Narrative Text

Two types of reading comprehension materials are narrative materials and expository materials. **Narrative materials** are stories, which are usually fiction, as opposed to *informational materials,* which are subject matter materials. Narratives have characters, a plot, and a sequence of events that occur during the story. To read narrative materials effectively, students must be able to identify the following (Richek et al., 2002):

- Important characters
- The setting, time, and place
- The major events in sequence
- The problems that the characters had to solve and how those problems were resolved

Sometimes narratives are inspirational. Readers can leave the limits of their everyday lives and travel to other parts of the world, to space, and to other time periods. Poor readers often respond negatively to narrative materials and have to be strongly encouraged to read stories. It is important to ask for their reactions and to find narrative materials that meet their interests. Different varieties of narrative reading materials are called *genres.* To become good readers, students need to have experiences with a variety of narrative materials, such as those outlined in "LD in Practice: Narrative Genres."

Comprehension of Informational Text

Informational materials include subject matter materials, such as textbooks used in social studies or science content areas. As students move through the grades, the reading tasks they confront change dramatically. Reading assignments in content-area textbooks take the place of narrative stories.

Students are often assigned to read textbooks independently, without supervision or help. They may be required to read a chapter, complete a written assignment on the chapter, prepare for a class activity based on the chapter, and take a test on the content of the chapter. It is not surprising that many students with learning disabilities cannot complete such assignments. A student whose reading has been limited to narrative stories will lack experience with, and the ability to do, the kind of reading that informational, content-area textbooks require.

Instruction at the secondary level places heavy demands on reading proficiency and provides little teacher direction. Major problems in content-area reading for students with learning disabilities include the following:

1. *There is a heavy emphasis on reading to obtain information.* Content-area instruction is based on presumed proficiency in reading. Students are expected to read, comprehend, and retain large amounts of information—up to 50 pages a week for each general education content classes. Furthermore, students may be required to take four content-area classes (e.g., English, science, mathematics, and history). For students with learning disabilities, the reading demand can become overwhelming.

2. *Content textbooks are generally written above the grade level in which they are used.* The textbook could be extremely difficult for the student with learning disabilities to read and understand. If a 10th-grade student is reading at a 5th-grade level, for example, and the social studies textbook is written at an 11th-grade level, there will be a 6-year discrepancy between the student's reading level and the reading level of the textbook.

3. *Content-area teachers often assume that students have adequate reading ability, and they do not teach reading skills.* At this level, there is little time spent on teaching reading skills, such as organizing or studying

an outline. Teachers can help students read content books by making the reading meaningful, connecting it to other material that the students have covered, and encouraging students to review the material to get an orientation to the text as a whole. Teachers can also introduce difficult or technical words before reading the text and alert students to monitor for comprehension as they are reading.

The "Teaching Strategies" section of this chapter provides some suggestions to help students read informational materials by using content-area textbooks.

THE READING–WRITING CONNECTION

Strong ties exist between reading and writing. As students write, their reading skills improve. Readers and writers are constructing meaning. Readers construct meaning from the author's text; writers compose or construct meaning as they write. In this section, we discuss: (1) early literacy and writing and (2) literature-based reading instruction.

FIGURE 11.3

Example of Early Alphabetic Reading–Child's Response to "What Did You Eat for Thanksgiving?"

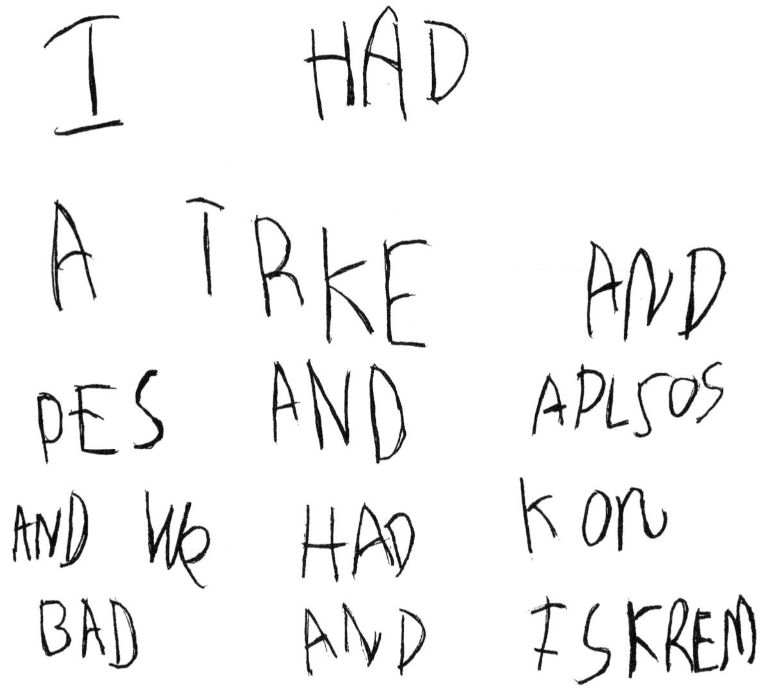

"I had a turkey and pies and applesauce, and we had corn bread and ice cream."

Writing Before Reading

The following example describes an incident involving a kindergartner who confidently used writing before learning to read. A business call was made to a client's home and the client's 5-year-old child answered the phone. The caller's side of the telephone conversation was overheard and went as follows:

"Hello, I want to speak to Mr. John Walsh . . . Oh, he's in the shower? Well, would you please write a message for him? . . . Good. Please write that . . . What? You haven't any paper? . . . Okay, I'll wait until you get a piece of paper . . . You got the paper? Good. Please write that . . . What? You haven't got a pencil? . . . Okay, I'll wait . . .Good. You found a pencil. Please write that Eugene Lerner called. I'll spell that—*E-U-G-E-N-E L-E-R-N-E-R*. My phone number is 708-555-1437. Did you write that down? . . . Good. Now would you read the message back to me? . . . What's that? You can write, but you haven't learned to read?"

Early Literacy and Writing

Young children begin to grasp the insight that alphabet letters represent abstract speech segments. At a very early stage of literacy development, young children begin to write letters for words. For example, a child might write *KR* for *car, TRKE* for *turkey,* or *PTZU* for *pizza.* Children should be encouraged to write. Acceptance of "invented spelling" encourages children's writing. Figure 11.3 shows the writing of a young child who uses the alphabetic principle. Sometimes children learn to write before they learn to read. "LD Stories: Writing Before Reading" tells the story of a kindergartner who learned to write before learning to read.

Literature-Based Reading Instruction

The literature-based approach to reading, which is also known as whole language instruction, emphasizes the importance of writing. This approach is based on the belief that children should be surrounded by a world of books and should have many experiences with listening to stories, reading books, and writing. The language-based approach to teach reading involves a number of principles:

1. ***There are strong interrelationships among the various language systems: oral language, reading, and writing.*** The links between reading and oral language and writing should be strengthened. Active experiences with writing and oral language will improve a child's reading. Developing an awareness of the interrelation of oral and written

language is a focus of *early literacy*. Children are encouraged to write as early as kindergarten and even before learning to read (see the chapters on oral language and written language). Figure 11.4 illustrates the writing of a 5 year old in kindergarten. However, children who have underlying language problems or motor difficulties are likely to encounter problems with early writing and will need more help in the early grades than many of their classmates.

2. ***Young children should be immersed in language and books from infancy.*** Children need much exposure to language, books, and stories. The value of using stories has been part of our culture from Mother Goose to Dr. Seuss. It is essential that books, stories, and poems become an integral part of a child's life. Children also benefit greatly from sharing books and hearing stories (Richek et al., 2002; see the chapter on oral language).

FIGURE 11.4

Journal of a Kindergarten Student

"Today I cut my finger with a scissors."

3. *Children should be given many experiences with writing.* Children need opportunities to engage in abundant writing and to express their thoughts and ideas in writing and in journals.

4. *Children need time for independent reading.* Children need opportunities to engage in reading for enjoyment when they are not under the supervision of a teacher.

ASSESSING READING

There are more measures and tests for assessing reading than for other areas of the curriculum. Reading can be assessed through: (1) *informal measures,* such as the informal reading inventory and portfolio assessment or through (2) *formal tests,* such as survey tests, diagnostic tests, and comprehensive batteries.

Informal Measures

One of the simplest methods of assessing reading is to observe informally as the student reads aloud. The teacher can readily detect the student's general reading level, word-recognition abilities, types of errors, and understanding of the material. This method is very practical and can be as informative as elaborate test batteries.

Informal Reading Inventory   The **informal reading inventory (IRI),** which can be administered quickly and easily, provides a wealth of information concerning the student's reading skills, reading levels, types of errors, techniques of attacking unknown words, and related behavioral characteristics (Johnson, Kress, & Pikulski, 1987).

The informal reading inventory procedure requires the examiner to choose selections of approximately 100 words in length from a series of graded reading levels. The student reads aloud from several graded levels while the teacher systematically records the errors. If the student makes more than five errors per 100 words, the student is given progressively easier selections until a level is found at which there are no more than two errors per 100 words. To check comprehension, the teacher asks the student 4 to 10 questions about each selection. By means of the following criteria, an informal reading inventory can determine three reading levels:

1. *Independent reading level.* The student is able to recognize about 95% of the words and to answer about 90% of the comprehension questions correctly. (This is the level at which the student is able to read library books or do reading work independently.)

2. *Instructional reading level.* The student is able to recognize about 90% of the words in the selection, with a comprehension score of about 70%. (This is the level at which the student will profit from teacher-directed reading instruction.)

3. *Frustration reading level.* The student is able to recognize fewer than 90% of the words, with a comprehension score of less than 70%. (If the student does not understand the material, this level is too difficult and should not be used for instruction.)

In addition to informal reading inventories developed by teachers, several standard commercial inventories are available, and they offer a convenient way to administer the reading inventory. They include the Standard Reading Inventory, and the Analytic Reading Inventory, Second Edition. They are described in "Tests for Assessing Students With Learning Disabilities." (Also see Appendix C in Richek et al., [2002], which contains a complete *informal* reading inventory that teachers are free to use.)

The IOTA Informal Word-Reading Test   The IOTA test is a public domain informal test for word-reading skills. It was originally published by M. Monroe (1932). See Figure 11.5 and Table 11.5 for information about how to administer this test.

Portfolio Assessment of Reading   Portfolio assessment is an alternative to traditional, standardized reading assessment tests. The problem with standardized reading tests is that they do not measure what students are actually doing in the reading classroom and do not closely link the assessment to the reading curriculum. Proponents of portfolio assessment propose that learning is too complex and assessment too imperfect to rely on any single index of achievement.

Specifically, *portfolio assessment* consists of keeping samples of the students' reading and writing work. It is relatively easy to collect samples of students' writing during the school year. For reading, the teacher keeps a reflective log, recording the students' reactions to books they read, along with the teacher's own reactions. The log shows the growth of each student in reading comprehension. Samples of language experience stories can be kept in the portfolio. Other assessment methods of this type are observations of students ("kid watching"), checklists, interviews with students, and collections of student work. By reviewing the students' work over a period of time, teachers, parents, and students themselves are able to evaluate progress (Richek et al., 2002).

Formal Tests

Formal reading tests can be classified as survey tests, diagnostic tests, or comprehensive batteries. *Survey tests* are group tests that give an overall reading achievement level. These tests generally give at least two scores: word recognition and reading comprehension. *Diagnostic tests* are individual tests that provide more in-depth information about the student's strengths and weaknesses in reading. *Comprehensive batteries* are tests with components that measure several academic areas, including reading.

FIGURE 11.5

The IOTA Informal Word-
Reading Test

Directions: Prepare three separate pieces of paper: one with the words on Card 1, one with the words on Card 2, and one with the words on Card 3. Use a word processor to write the words, about 16, with a large font in three columns. Duplicate the words for marking by the teacher. Show Card 1 to the student and have the student read the words, going down each column slowly and carefully and keeping place with a finger. Encourage the student to try each word, but do not offer any help. Use the same procedure for Card 2 and Card 3. Record all subvocal and vocal efforts at pronouncing these words.

Scoring: Count the number of words correctly read and convert it to a grade-level score by using the IOTA Conversion Chart. Words that the student self-corrects are counted as correct.

Card 1

dig	on	Jack
dog	saw	tack
dug	of	sack
card	for	wend
cart	who	tend
Carl	how	send

Card 2

blind	done	mare
blond	bone	fare
choke	tar	care
chuck	nip	pardon
spurt	ton	parlor
squirt	tap	target
repast	gray	tarnish
request	chew	

Card 3

as	form	pig
it	ball	bed
to	pod	sung
left	balk	plea

Source: From Marion Monroe, *Children Who Cannot Read: The Analysis of Reading Disabilities and the Use of Diagnostic Tests in Instruction of Retarded Readings.* Copyright 1932 by The University of Chicago Press. Reprinted with permission.

Table 11.6 lists some of the widely used formal reading tests in each of these categories. "Tests for Assessing Students With Learning Disabilities" provides more information on these tests.

TABLE 11.5

IOTA Conversion Chart (pupil's grade medians)

Pupil's score	Grade	Pupil's score	Grade	Pupil's score	Grade
12	1.0	26	2.0	40	3.1
13	1.0	27	2.0	41	3.2
14	1.1	28	2.1	42	3.4
15	1.2	29	2.2	43	3.5
16	1.2	30	2.3	44	3.7
17	1.3	31	2.3	45	3.8
18	1.4	32	2.4	46	4.0
19	1.5	33	2.5	47	4.2
20	1.5	34	2.5	48	4.5
21	1.6	35	2.6	49	4.7
22	1.7	36	2.7	50	5.0
23	1.7	37	2.8	51	5.3
24	1.8	38	2.9	52	5.5
25	1.9	39	3.0	53	T

Source: From Marion Monroe, *Children Who Cannot Read: The Analysis of Reading Disabilities and the Use of Diagnostic Tests in Instruction of Retarded Readings.* Copyright 1932 by The University of Chicago Press. Reprinted with permission.

TABLE 11.6

Commonly Used Formal Reading Tests

Test	Grade or age assessed
Survey tests	
■ Gates-MacGinitie Reading Tests (Fourth Edition)	Grades 1–12
■ Metropolitan Achievement Tests	Grades K–12
■ SRA Achievement Series: Reading	Grades 1–12
■ Wide-Range Achievement Test—3 (WRAT-3)	Ages 5–adult
Diagnostic tests	
■ Diagnostic Assessment of Reading With Trial Teaching Strategies (DARTTS)	Grades 1–12, adult
■ Durrell Analysis of Reading Difficulty	Grades 1–6
■ Gates-McKillop-Horowitz Reading Diagnostic Tests	Grades 1–6
■ Stanford Diagnostic Reading Test (Fourth Edition)	Grades 1–12
■ Woodcock Reading Diagnostic Battery	Ages 4–90
■ Woodcock Reading Mastery Test—Revised	Ages 5–adult
Comprehensive batteries	
■ Brigance Comprehension Inventory of Basic Skills—Revised	Grades K–9
■ Kaufman Test of Educational Achievement (K-TEA)	Grades 1–12
■ Peabody Individual Achievement Test—Revised (PIAT-R)	Grades K–12
■ Woodcock-Johnson Tests of Achievement III	Preschool–adult

TEACHING STRATEGIES

This "Teaching Strategies" section presents approaches, methods, and materials to teach reading to students with learning disabilities. It is organized by the following strategies: (1) reading strategies for the general education classroom, (2) strategies to improve word recognition, (3) strategies to improve fluency, (4) strategies to improve reading comprehension, (5) special remedial methods for reading, (6) methods to deal with specific reading problems, and (7) using computers to teach reading.

READING STRATEGIES FOR THE GENERAL EDUCATION CLASSROOM

Many children with reading disabilities are in inclusive settings in general education classrooms. In "LD in Practice: Reading Strategies for the General Education Classroom," we present some teaching tips for general education teachers to use with students who have reading and learning disabilities.

STRATEGIES TO IMPROVE WORD RECOGNITION

Building Phoneme Awareness

A child who is learning to read must first become aware of the sounds in words and language. Strategies for teaching children to become aware of the phonemes, or sounds, in language include: (1) learning to count the sounds in words, (2) learning to segment the sounds and syllables in words, and (3) learning to recognize rhyming words. These strategies are presented in the chapter on oral language.

Dynamic Indicators of Basic Early Literacy Skills (DIBELS)

Some schools are using a measurement system called **DIBELS** to assess the early reading skills of young children in Grades K–2. DIBELS stands for *Dynamic Indicators of Basic Early Literacy Skills*. DIBELS measures are designed to assess the young child's skills in phonological awareness (initial sound fluency and phonemic segmentation fluency), alphabetic principles (nonsense word fluency), and oral reading fluency. The intent of DIBELS is to monitor the early reading skills of young children frequently to identify young children who are likely to have difficulty in learning to read and to provide the appropriate intervention. More information about DIBELS can be found at **http://dibels.uoregon.edu.**

LD IN PRACTICE

READING STRATEGIES FOR THE GENERAL EDUCATION CLASSROOM

General modifications

- Increase the amount of repetition and review
- Allot more time for completing work
- Provide more examples and activities
- Introduce the work more slowly

Phonics

- Play word and rhyming games
- Analyze the phoneme elements that make up a word
- Build word families

Fluency

- Help students recognize sight words
- Find opportunities for students to reread passages aloud
- Use predictable books
- Use read-along methods
- Use the language experience method to let the children read their own language

Vocabulary

- Teach content vocabulary before reading a chapter in a science or social studies text
- Find words in the students areas of interest (sports, movies, television shows, current events) and use these words for study
- Use word webs to study vocabulary words

Reading comprehension

- Provide students with background knowledge about a story or content-area reading
- Use the K-W-L strategy to improve comprehension
- Have students predict what will happen next in a story
- Use graphic organizers to visualize the reading passage
- Show movies or videos about a book to enhance interest
- Have students act out passages in a story

Phonics Methods

Phonics systems and phonics books have been on the market for over 60 years. Many phonics programs today are repackaged as preprinted masters for duplication or as CDs, recordings, audiotapes, videotapes, computer software programs, and multimedia packages. Two phonics approaches are: (1) synthetic and (2) analytic. *Synthetic phonics* methods first teach students isolated letters and their sound equivalents. Then they teach students to synthesize or blend these individual phoneme elements into whole words. *Analytic phonics* methods teach students whole words that have a consistent sound-spelling pattern, and they then teach students to analyze the phoneme elements that make up the word.

A typical exercise in phonic materials appears in Figure 11.6. Some of the widely used phonics programs are listed next:

- *The Benchmark Program* (Benchmark School, Media, PA 19063)
- *Building Reading Skills* (McCormick-Mathers)
- *Keys to Reading* (Economy Company)
- *New Phonics Skilltexts* (Charles E. Merrill)
- *Open Count Reading Program* (SRA/McGraw-Hill)
- *Phonics We Use* (Riverside)
- *Speech-to-Print Phonics* (Harcourt Brace)
- *Sunform Alphabet* (Sundberg Learning Systems)
- *Wordland Series* (Continental Press)

Phonic Remedial Reading Lessons   Phonic remedial reading lessons consist of words with a consistent phonic pattern that the student reads (Kirk, Kirk, & Minskoff, 1985). The child simply reads words that have been

FIGURE 11.6

Example of Phonics Exercises

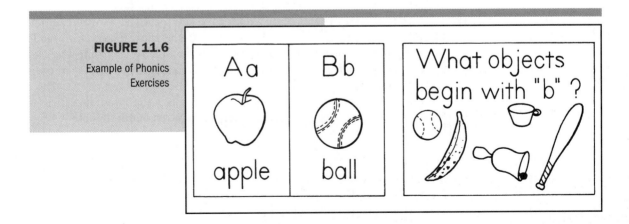

arranged across the page. Part 1 of these drills introduces the most frequent sounds, including short vowels and consonants; Part 2 consists of certain combinations of the previously learned sounds. Part 3 presents less frequently used sounds in whole words, and Part 4 provides supplementary exercises. The drills are based on the principles of minimal change, one response to one symbol, repetition, and social reinforcement. This method is to be used for only a few minutes of an instructional session for students who need practice in decoding skills. Figure 11.7 presents an example of a phonic remedial reading lesson.

The Dollar Store   Many useful reading games and materials can be found by browsing through a dollar store. These bargain items include phonics games, alphabet letters, sight word cards, and other reading-related materials. Teachers can develop a collection of these items that can be placed in an activity center or used to reinforce a reading lesson. Dollar store items can also be purchased through the Internet at **http://www.DollarBins.com.**

STRATEGIES TO IMPROVE FLUENCY   In addition to recognizing words accurately, readers must read the words quickly and fluently. Otherwise, reading is labored and not enjoyable, and the reader loses meaning. Some strategies to improve fluency include: (1) repeated reading, (2) predictable books, and (3) the neurological impress method.

Repeated Reading

Repeated reading is a strategy used to give the student repeated practice to improve his or her oral reading fluency. It is especially useful with slow, halting readers who accurately identify most words in a passage but have not developed fluency. The method involves the selection of passages that are 50 to 200 words long and at a difficulty level that enables the student to recognize most of the words. The student then reads the selection orally three or four times before proceeding to a new passage. Word-accuracy rates and reading speed are usually reported to the student after each reading, and daily practice is recommended (Richek et al., 2002). Some students particularly enjoy repeated reading when the passages are displayed on a computer screen.

   Read Naturally is a commercial fluency and training program that focuses on fluency development. Its website is **http://www.readnaturally.com.**

Predictable Books

Predictable books contain patterns or refrains that are repeated over and over. Many are based on folktales and fairy tales. For example, in *The*

FIGURE 11.7

Sample Page From Phonic Remedial Reading Lessons

Lesson 1-A

a

at	sat	mat	hat	fat
am	ham	Sam	Pam	tam
sad	mad	had	lad	dad
wag	sag	tag	lag	hag

sat	sap	Sam	sad
map	mam	mad	mat
hag	ham	hat	had
cat	cap	cad	cam

sat	am	sad	pat	mad
had	mat	tag	fat	ham
lag	ham	wag	hat	sap
sad	tap	cap	dad	at

map	hag	cat	sat	ham	tap
sap	map	hat	sad	tag	am
Pam	mat	had	tap	hat	dad
fat	mad	at	wag	cap	sag

To the teacher: This lesson introduces many of the consonant sounds. */b/, /r/, /n/, /j/, /x/,* and */v/* are introduced in Lesson 1–B. The sounds of */y/, /z/, /k/,* and */q/* are not introduced until still later.

Source: From *Phonic remedial reading lessons*, by S. A. Kirk, W. Kirk, and E. Minskoff, 1985, Novato, CA: Academic Therapy Publications. Copyright 1985 Academic Therapy Publications. Reprinted by permission.

Three Billy Goats Gruff, the question "Who is that trip-trapping over my bridge?" is asked by the troll as each billy goat goes over the bridge. A favorite predictable book is *Brown Bear, Brown Bear.* After the book has been read to young children several times, they are able to predict the wording and begin saying the refrain along with the storyteller. Using predictable books is an excellent way to actively involve children in a story even before they can read. They begin to develop language knowledge and anticipate what will be said. This experience helps develop support for word recognition when they do read the story (Richek et al., 2002).

Neurological Impress Method

Another approach to improving fluency for students with severe reading disabilities is the *neurological impress method* (Heckelman, 1969; Langford, Slade, & Barnett, 1974). It is a system of rapid-unison reading by the student and teacher. The student sits slightly in front of the teacher, and both read together out of one book. The voice of the teacher is directed into the ear of the student at a fairly close range. The student or the teacher places a finger on the word as it is read. At times, the teacher's voice may be louder and faster than the student's, and at other times the teacher may read more slowly than the student, who may lag slightly behind. No preliminary preparations are made with the reading material before the student sees it. The goal is simply to cover as many pages as possible within the time available without tiring the student. The theory underlying this method is that the auditory process of feedback from the reader's own voice and from the voice of someone else reading the same material strengthens the reading process.

In the *read-along method,* a similar process occurs. In this method, children listen to a CD or a tape recording of a story as they read along with the text. In the classroom, headphones may be used so that the tape recording does not disturb other children. There are many commercial stories and tapes available for this purpose.

STRATEGIES TO IMPROVE READING COMPREHENSION

This section describes strategies to improve reading comprehension. Comprehension is the essence of the reading act. Along with learning to recognize words, children must understand and interact with the text. The section discusses: (1) basal readers, (2) activating background knowledge, (3) language experience method, (4) the K-W-L technique, (5) building meaning with vocabulary and concepts, (6) the reading–writing connection, (7) thinking strategies, and (8) learning strategies for reading.

Using Basal Readers

Basal readers are a sequential and interrelated set of books and supportive materials intended to provide the basic material for the development of fundamental reading skills. A **basal reading series** consists of graded readers that gradually increase in difficulty, typically beginning with very simple readiness and first-grade books and going through the sixth- or eighth-grade level. The books increase in difficulty in vocabulary, story content, and skill development. Auxiliary material, such as teacher's manuals and activity books, often accompany the books. Most basal reading series incorporate an eclectic approach to the teaching of reading, using many procedures to teach readiness, vocabulary, word recognition, comprehension, and the enjoyment of literature.

As the major tool of reading instruction for the past 40 years, the basal reader has been the target of continual criticism from diverse groups, including some educators, scholars from other academic disciplines, the popular press, parent groups, political observers, moralists, and, recently, ethnic and women's groups. Critics have scoffed at and satirized the language, phonics presentation, story content, class appeal, pictures, qualities, and environment of the characters of the basal reader. In spite of this highly vocal and severe criticism, basal readers continue to be the major tool for reading instruction in elementary classrooms throughout the country.

Because most basal readers are not committed to any one teaching procedure, publishers are continually modifying them in response to the demands of the times and the consumer market. For example, more phonics and decoding activities are currently being added to basal readers. Other recent basal reader modifications have more literature-based materials and language activities in the early grades. The modifications have also made stories longer and more sophisticated and added stories that present diverse cultural and ethnic characters.

There are also series of readers produced especially for slow readers. Table 11.7 lists books that were designed for high interest but easier reading level; the symbol (S) indicates that a book is available in Spanish.

Activating Background Knowledge

The following strategies alert the student to the *background knowledge* needed for reading comprehension and build on student experiences.

Language Experience Method

The **language experience method** is well accepted as a method that builds on the student's knowledge and language base, linking the different forms of language—listening, speaking, reading, and writing. This method uses the student's own experiences and language as the raw material. Students begin by dictating stories to the teacher (or writing stories by themselves). These stories then become the basis of their reading instruction. Through the language experience approach, students conceptualize written material as follows:

What I can think about, I can talk about.

What I can say, I can write (or someone can write for me).

What I can write, I can read.

I can read what others write for me to read.

There is no predetermined, rigid control over vocabulary, syntax, or content. The teacher uses the text or stories that the student composes to develop reading skills. The language experience approach to reading has a vitality and immediacy, as well as an element of creativity. The method is

Series	Reading level
TABLE 11.7	
Reading Series for Low Reading Ability and High Interest Level	
■ Challenger (New Readers Press)	1–6
■ Edmark Reading Program (SRA; McGraw-Hill)	1–4
■ Fastbacks (Fearon)	4–5
■ Focus: Reading for Success (Spanish version: Leer para triunfar; Scott, Foresman; S)	K–8
■ High Action Reading Series (Modern Curriculum Press)	2–6
■ High Noon Books (High Noon Publishers)	1–6
■ Key-Text (Economy Company)	P–8
■ New Directions in Reading (Houghton Mifflin)	2–7
■ The New Open Highways Program (Scott, Foresman)	1–8
■ Programa de lectura en español (Spanish; Houghton Mifflin; S)	K–8
■ Quest Adventure, Survival (Raintree Publishers)	3–10
■ Rally (Harcourt Brace Jovanovich)	2–7
■ The Reading Connection (Open Court)	2–11
■ Reading for Today (Steck-Vaughn)	1–5
■ Scott, Foresman Spanish Reading Program (Scott, Foresman, S)	1–5
■ Spanish Reading Series (Economy Company; S)	1–5
■ Sprint Library (Scholastic)	3–7
■ Sprint Reading Skills Program (Scholastic)	1–5
■ Sport Close-ups (Crestwood House)	3–12

effective both in the beginning-to-read stage with young children and in corrective instruction with older pupils. The interest of the student is high because the emphasis is on reading material that grows out of the student's personal experiences and natural language in expressing these experiences. An example of a language experience story is shown in Figure 11.8. (Language experience is also discussed as a writing strategy in the chapter on written language.)

The K-W-L Technique

K-W-L is a technique for reading and studying content-area textbooks (Ogle, 1986). The letters represent three questions in three steps of a lesson:

1. *K: What I know.* Students think of and state all the knowledge they have on a subject. A group of students can pool their knowledge.

2. *W: What I want to find out.* Each student thinks of and writes on a sheet of paper what he or she wants to (or expects to) learn from the reading. Students can then compare their answers to this question.

FIGURE 11.8

Language Experience Chart

We went to the Museum of Science and Industry.

We saw baby chicks come out of eggs.

We went down a coal mine.

We played with computers.

3. *L: What I learned.* Students read the lesson silently and write what they have learned from the reading. Answers to this question can be shared by the group.

Figure 11.9 shows a K-W-L strategy sheet. Groups of students can complete what they already know (K) about a subject, what they want to find out (W), and, after completing the reading, what they have learned (L).

Building Meaning With Vocabulary and Concepts

To read effectively, readers need to have knowledge of word meanings and of the concepts underlying the words. The more students read, the more

FIGURE 11.9

K-W-L Strategy Sheet

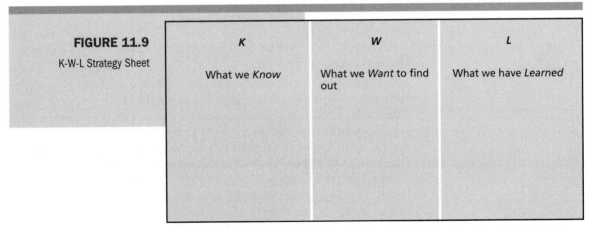

K	W	L
What we *Know*	What we *Want* to find out	What we have *Learned*

Source: From "K-W-L: Teaching Model That Develops Active Reading of Expository Text," by D. M. Ogle, 1986, *The Reading Teacher, 39,* p. 565. Copyright 1986 by the International Reading Association. Reprinted with permission.

word meanings and language they will acquire. It is important to use strategies that will build the student's vocabulary and understanding of words.

Knowledge of vocabulary and the ability to understand the concepts of words are closely related to reading achievement. Limited vocabulary knowledge can seriously hamper reading comprehension. Further, as words become more abstract, the concepts become more difficult to grasp.

Concepts are commonly explained as ideas, abstractions, or the essence of things. For example, the concept of *chair* refers to an idea, an abstraction, or a symbol of concrete experiences. A person's experiences may have included exposure to a specific rocking chair, an upholstered chair, and a baby's highchair, but the concept *chair* symbolizes a set of attributes about "chairness." The word *chair* allows a person to make an inference about new experiences with chairs, such as a lawn chair observed for the first time. The word or concept of *chair* by itself does not have an empirical reference point.

At a still more abstract level, words become further removed from concrete referents. The concept *chair* is part of a broader concept of *furniture*. Concepts even more removed from the sensory world are ideas, such as *democracy, loyalty, fairness,* and *freedom*.

A further confusion in school learning is related to the fact that textbooks present important concepts as technical terms, such as *plateau, continental divide, density of population, pollution, the law of gravity,* or *space exploration*. Problems in reading in the content areas are frequently due not to the difficulty of the words, but to the concentration and compactness of the presentation of the concepts.

Because language plays a key role in concept development, language problems are likely to be reflected in faulty conceptual abilities and limited vocabulary development. Students who have meager, imprecise, or inaccurate concepts will have difficulties understanding a reading passage. Illustrations of the consequences of imprecise concept development are given in "LD Stories: Misunderstanding of Concepts."

Expanding Vocabulary   The following activities are designed to expand and build vocabulary:

1. *Highlighting multiple word meanings.*   Multiple meanings of words often cause confusion in reading. For example, there are many meanings of the word *note*. In music, *note* means the elliptical character in a certain position on the music staff. In arithmetic or business, a *note* might mean a written promise to pay. In English or study hall, a *note* might refer to an informal written communication. In social studies, a *note* might refer to a formal communiqué between the heads of two nations. In science, one might be able to *note* the results of an experiment, meaning to observe them. In English class, the selection of literature might discuss an individual who was a person of great *note,* or importance, in the community. In any lesson, the student could be asked to make *note* of an examination date, meaning to remember it.

MISUNDERSTANDING OF CONCEPTS

- Some students confuse one attribute of an object with the concept of the object. For example, Paula could not understand the circular concept of the roundness of a plate. When told that the plate was "round" and asked to draw a circle around its edges, Paula said, "That's not round; that's a dish." Students may also confuse the concept of an object with its name. When Paula was asked if the moon could be called by another name, such as cow, she responded, "No, because the moon doesn't give milk."

- Misunderstanding a symbol that conveys multiple concepts may have unexpected consequences. Nine-year-old Susie was in tears when she brought home a medical form from the school nurse advising Susie's parents to take their daughter for an eye examination. Susie sobbed that the cause of her anguish was not that she needed eyeglasses, but that the nurse had filled in an *F* in the blank next to the word sex on the examination form. That symbol *F* conveyed the concept of a grade, and Susie feared she had failed sex.

- Students often deal with their inability to understand a concept by ignoring it. By failing to read a word they do not know, they may change the entire meaning of a passage. One high school student thought the school was using pornographic material because the people described in the following passage were nude: "The pilgrims did not wear gaudy clothes." Because the boy did not know the meaning of the word gaudy, he simply eliminated it from the sentence.

- To make pizza, Lisa and Jaime were told to put it in the microwave oven, heat it, and then bring it to the lunchroom. Thinking they were following the directions, after heating the pizza, they unplugged the microwave oven and carried it (with the pizza inside) to the lunchroom.

The teacher could make a *note,* meaning a remark, in the margin of the paper. In material on England, paper money may be called a *bank note.* The student who cannot hold the various concepts of this word in mind will have trouble understanding many areas of the curriculum. By highlighting multiple meanings—through dictionary games, sentence-completion exercises, and class discussion—teachers can offer important help to students who must develop an awareness of one word's different meanings.

2. ***Providing concrete experiences.*** To build vocabulary and develop concepts for reading, students need concrete experiences with words. A first step is to provide students with primary experiences with the word or concept. The next step is to encourage and assist students to draw conclusions from their experiences. As students progress to more advanced stages, teachers can foster skills of classifying, summarizing, and generalizing.

3. *Exploring sources of vocabulary.* Because vocabulary is woven into every phase of our lives, new words can be drawn from any aspect of a student's experience: television, sports, newspapers, advertising, science, and so on. Many students enjoy keeping lists of new words and developing word books.

4. *Expanding vocabulary through classification.* Another way to learn new words is to attach them to known words. Much vocabulary growth takes place in this manner. Vertical vocabulary expansion involves taking a known word and breaking it down into categories. For example, students take the concept *dog* and break it into many species *(collie, terrier, cocker spaniel).* Horizontal vocabulary growth refers to enrichment and differentiation. Children may first call all animals *dogs.* Then they learn to distinguish cats, horses, and other creatures.

Word Webs   A **word web** is a type of graphic organizer, which is a strategy for helping build vocabulary and making information easier to understand and learn. Word webs enrich associations with a word and deepen a student's understanding of important concepts. Figure 11.10 shows an example of a word web for *ice cream.* A group of students developed the word web by answering three questions: "What is it?" "What is it like?" and "What are some examples?"

FIGURE 11.10

Word Web

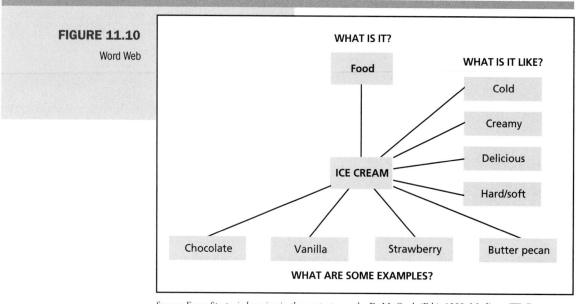

Source: From *Strategic learning in the content area,* by D. M. Cook (Ed.), 1989, Madison, WI: Department of Public Instruction (p. 132). Reprinted with the permission of the Wisconsin Department of Public Instruction, 125 South Webster Street, Madison, WI 53702, 800/243/8782.

Research shows that graphic organizers help students with learning disabilities understand reading material and improve their comprehension (Fisher et al., 1995; Sabbatino, 2004). A computer program that produces many types of graphic organizers is *Inspiration* (Inspiration Software, **http://www.inspiration.com**).

Cloze Procedure   The **cloze procedure** is a useful technique for building comprehension and language skills. It is based on the Gestalt idea of closure—the impulse to complete a structure and make it whole by supplying a missing element. When the cloze procedure is applied to the reading process, the following steps are used:

1.   Select a passage of reading material.

2.   Rewrite the material and delete every *n*th word (e.g., every 5th word or every 10th word). Replace the deleted word with a blank line; all lines should be the same length.

3.   Ask students to fill in each blank by writing the word they think was deleted.

One advantage of the cloze test over the conventional reading test or other fill-in-the-blank tests is that because words are deleted at random, both *lexical* words and *structural* words are omitted. Lexical words carry primary meaning and are roughly similar to verbs, nouns, adjectives, and adverbs. Relationships are indicated by structural words, such as articles, prepositions, conjunctions, and auxiliary verbs. What the reader supplies provides clues to his or her underlying language processes.

The cloze procedure may be modified and used for a variety of purposes. To teach vocabulary, for example, only the words of the vocabulary lesson can be deleted. In content areas, such as social studies, technical words can be deleted. Or the teacher can delete other selected categories, such as adjectives, adverbs, or prepositions. For students who have difficulty in writing, the cloze words can be printed on cards backed with felt or Velcro, which students place on the appropriate blank space in the written passage.

In the sample cloze exercise that follows, the reading material was retyped with every 10th word deleted and replaced by a standard-size line. Students supply the missing words.

Fill in the deleted words in the following passage entitled "Farming in Switzerland":

Switzerland is a country of very high, steep mountains _____ narrow valleys. In the valleys are the farms where _____ farmers raise much of the food they need for _____ and their animals. Because the valleys are tiny, the _____ are small. There is no room on them for _____ grassland that is needed for pasturing cows or goats _____ sheep during the summer.

Answers: *and, the, themselves, farms, the, or*

Source: From Paul McKee, M. Lucile Harrison, Annie McCowen, and Elizabeth Lehr, *High Roads*. Copyright 1962, renewed 1990 by Beverly McKee Eaton, Paul E. Harrison, and Gloria Royer. Reprinted with the permission of Houghton Mifflin Company. All rights reserved.

The Reading–Writing Connection

Dialogue Journals   Dialogue journals are a personal way to integrate reading and writing. To initiate this activity, the teacher gives each student a notebook, and teachers and students write personal messages to one another through the notebook. A variety of topics can be addressed; teachers may ask students how they liked a story or ask them about their pets, birthdays, holidays, or something that happened to them. Some teachers paste a picture, a cartoon, or a Polaroid photograph of the student in the journal and ask for student comments. After the student writes something, the teacher responds in the journal. The response may provide some personal information and then ask for more information or may start another topic. Typically, as students get used to the journal, they begin to write more and look forward to a regular interchange through the journal. Figure 11.11 shows a written journal from a bilingual class.

Materials Without Words   To foster reading comprehension, the teacher can use materials that do not have words, such as comic books without captions, silent films, and books of photographs. The students first figure out the story content from the pictures; then they make the transition to printed words. Once the students understand the material, words become meaningful. The students can even write their own dialogue.

Written Conversations   Instead of saying what they wish to communicate to the teacher or to friends, students can write the message and give it to their teacher or to other students. The teacher's (or classmates') responses should also be written (Richek et al., 2002). Students in junior high school often surreptitiously send small folded notes to their friends. This activity legitimizes the note exchange ventures.

FIGURE 11.11

Written Journal From a Child in a Bilingual Class

La gente digo que todo parecia
un milagro y eran muy felices.

Thinking Strategies

The Directed Reading–Thinking Activity   The **directed reading–thinking activity (DRTA)** method promotes the processes of thinking, predicting, and confirming while reading. In this activity, a sentence or a short passage is first read by a group of students. The teacher then encourages the students to predict, by making guesses and establishing hypotheses about what will happen next. Finally, the students read the next short selection to confirm or reject their predictions and also to develop a new prediction for the next part of the story. DRTA promotes group work and social learning. To enhance the group work, teachers can display the stories using big books, overhead transparencies, computer screens, or multimedia computer programs.

With this method, teaching reading becomes a way of teaching thinking, as teachers ask such questions as "What do you think?" "Why do you think so?" and "Can you prove it?" The emphasis is on teaching thinking, and pupils learn to examine, hypothesize, find proof, suspend judgment, and make decisions (Richek et al., 2002).

Self-Monitoring   In this strategy, students learn to monitor their own mistakes. Specific training is needed for students to learn how to check their own responses and become conscious of errors or answers that do not make sense. Self-monitoring requires active involvement in the learning process rather than passive learning, in which students are not conscious of incongruities. Students are taught how to scan the material before answering a question and how to stop, listen, look, and think—that is, to consider systematically the alternative approaches and answers before responding to a problem. The aim of self-monitoring is to reduce impulsive, thoughtless answers and to delay responses until a systematic search for the right response has been made.

Questioning Strategies   The types of questions teachers ask stimulate the various types of thinking in which students engage during reading. Many of the questions teachers use demand recall of details. To stimulate comprehension, teachers must also plan questions that provoke conjecture, explanation, evaluation, and judgment. The following examples illustrate the four types of comprehension questions.

1. *Literal comprehension.*   "What did little brother want to eat?"
2. *Interpretation.*   "Why was the cookie jar kept on the basement steps?"
3. *Critical reading.*   "Did Mother do the right thing in leaving the children alone?"
4. *Creative reading.*   "How would you have solved this problem?"

With *self-questioning* learning strategies, students develop their own comprehension questions. Students with learning disabilities are taught to use self-questioning strategies while reading. They ask themselves such questions as "What am I reading this passage for? What is the main idea? What is a good question about the main idea?" When students learn to monitor their reading, their comprehension improves significantly (Taylor, Alber, & Walker, 2002).

Learning Strategies for Reading

Learning strategies are discussed in greater detail in the chapters on theories of learning and adolescents and adults with learning disabilities. A major reading comprehension problem for students with learning disabilities is that they tend to be passive and to wait for teacher direction. They do not know how to interact effectively with the text or to merge the information with what they already know. They often read reluctantly, hesitating to ask questions and focusing solely on what they think the teacher wants them to remember. These students may not monitor their reading comprehension. When they are not sure of the meaning of a passage they are reading, they do not take action by going back and trying to understand. Instead, they continue to read and lose even more of the meaning. Often, they are unaware that something is wrong.

Students with disabilities in reading comprehension need instruction that helps them become actively involved in the reading and in trying to reconstruct the author's message. They need to develop metacognitive abilities by learning to recognize their loss of comprehension when it occurs and employing "fix-up" strategies. Learning strategies for improving reading comprehension help students become active, involved learners who are able to direct their own learning (Lenz & Deshler, 2003; Deshler et al., 1996).

SPECIAL REMEDIAL METHODS FOR READING   The special methods discussed in this section are designed for students with severe reading problems and are not typically used in the general education classroom. We discuss the following special methods: (1) multisensory methods, (2) the Fernald Method, (3) Reading Recovery, and (4) direct instruction programs.

Multisensory Methods

A collection of programs that are based on the Orton-Gillingham Method comprise the **multisensory methods** for students with severe reading and learning disabilities. They include the Orton-Gillingham Method, Project

READ, the Wilson Reading System, Alphabetic Phonics, the Herman Method, and the Spalding Method (Birsh, 1999; Henry, 1998). These multisensory groups have formed an umbrella organization called the International Multisensory Structured Language Council (McIntyre & Pickering, 1995). The multisensory methods have the following similar characteristics (Oakland et al., 1998):

- Help anchor verbal information by providing links with the visual, auditory, tactile, and kinesthetic pathways for learning
- Use highly structured phonics instruction with an emphasis on the alphabetic system
- Include abundant drill, practice, and repetition
- Have carefully planned sequential lessons
- Emphasize explicit instruction in the language rule systems to guide reading and spelling

The multisensory methods use several senses to reinforce learning, as indicated in the acronym **VAKT,** which is formed from the first letter of the words *visual, auditory, kinesthetic,* and *tactile.* To stimulate all of these senses, students hear the teacher say the word, say the word to themselves, hear themselves say the word, feel the muscle movement as they trace the word, feel the tactile surface under their fingertips, see their hands move as they trace the word, and hear themselves say the word as they trace it. Several of the multisensory methods are described in this section.

The Orton-Gillingham Method   The *Orton-Gillingham Method* is an outgrowth of the Orton theory of reading disability (Orton, 1937, 1976). This method focuses on a multisensory, systematic, structured language procedure for reading-decoding and spelling instruction. Initial activities focus on learning individual letter sounds and blending. The student uses a tracing technique to learn single letters and their sound equivalents. These single sounds are later combined into larger groupings and then into short words (Gillingham & Stillman, 1970; Orton, 1976).

Simultaneous spelling tasks are also part of the Orton-Gillingham Method. While writing the letters, the students say both the sounds of the letters in sequence and the letter names. The method emphasizes phonics and depends on a formal sequence of learning. Independent reading is delayed until the major part of the phonics program has been covered.

There are a number of extensions and applications of the Orton-Gillingham Method. Project READ, an adaption of the Orton-Gillingham Method in the public schools of Minnesota, reported significant gains in reading achievement (Enfield, 1988). A variation of the Orton-Gillingham Method was developed by Slingerland (1976), who offered an extensive set of materials. Another adaptation is the *Recipe for Reading* (Traub & Bloom, 1978), which is accompanied by 21 supplementary readers.

The Wilson Reading System The *Wilson Reading System* (Wilson, 1988) is a multisensory, structured language program based on the Orton-Gillingham philosophy. It provides a step-by-step method for teachers working with students who require direct, multisensory, structured language teaching. The Wilson Reading System targets students who have difficulty decoding independently, reading with fluency, or spelling words, even with the help of a spell-checker or dictionary. The program teaches students the structure of words and language through a carefully sequenced 12-step program that helps them master decoding and improve encoding in English. It directly teaches phonological awareness, phonology, and total word structure, and it takes 1 to 3 years to complete. The Wilson program is also used for adults with dyslexia.

The Fernald Method Grace Fernald (1943/1988) developed an approach to reading that uses visual, auditory, kinesthetic, and tactile senses, but it differs from the other multisensory programs in that it teaches a whole word (rather than single sounds). The student traces the entire word, thereby strengthening the memory and visualization of the entire word. As described in "LD in Practice: The Fernald Method," her method consists of four stages, but its uniqueness is most evident in Stage 1. The Fernald Method is also effective for teaching spelling (see the chapter on written language).

Reading Recovery

Reading Recovery is a reading program designed for first-graders who are having difficulty with learning to read. Reading Recovery provides special instruction for students who are in the lowest 20% of their first-grade class. All first-graders are tested during the first few weeks of first grade, and those in the lowest 20% are selected for the Reading Recovery program. Each child in the program then receives one-on-one reading instruction for 30 min each day for a period of 12 to 16 weeks (Richek et al., 2002).

Reading Recovery teachers receive an intensive training program in instructional techniques and theories in which they learn how to foster the integration of clue systems in word recognition.

Direct Instruction Programs

Direct instruction has proven to be highly effective with children who are considered to be at risk because of poverty (Carnine et al., 1990). The *Direct Instruction Reading Program* consists of six levels that roughly correspond to Grades 1 through 6. A sample page from this program is shown in Figure 11.12. Reading Mastery Level I teaches basic decoding and comprehension skills. Intensive explicit phonics instruction helps the beginning

LD IN PRACTICE
THE FERNALD METHOD

Stage 1.

It is essential that the student select the word to be learned. The teacher writes the student's word on paper with a crayon. The student then traces the word with his or her fingers, making contact with the paper, thus using both tactile and kinesthetic senses. As the student traces it, the teacher says the word so that the student hears it (using the auditory sense). This process is repeated until the student can write the word correctly without looking at the sample. Once the student learns the word, the sample is placed in a file box. The words accumulate in the box until there are enough words for the student to write a story by using them. The story is then typed so that the student can read his or her own story.

Stage 2.

The student is no longer required to trace each word, but rather learns each new word by looking at the teacher's written copy of the word and saying it to himself or herself while writing it.

Stage 3.

The student learns new words by looking at a printed word and repeating it to himself or herself before writing it. At this point, the student may begin reading from books.

Stage 4.

The student is able to recognize new words from their similarity to printed words or to parts of words previously learned. The student now can generalize the knowledge he or she has acquired through the reading skills.

reader master letter sounds, begin to sound out words, and use these words in stories.

This highly structured reading program consists of lessons based on carefully sequenced skill hierarchies. Based on principles of behavioral psychology, the program contains drills and instructional reading, as well as materials for repetition and practice. Students progress in small, planned steps, and teacher praise is used as reinforcement. Teachers are guided in

FIGURE 11.12

Sample Page From Direct
Instruction Reading Program

lots of cars

a man on a farm

has lots of cars.

hē has ōld cars.

hē has little cars.

are his cars

fōr gōats?   nō.

are his cars

fōr shēēp?   nō.

are his cars

fōr cows?   nō.

his cars are

fōr cops.

hē has lots of

cop cars.

Task 21   Teacher introduces the title
a. Pass out Storybook 1.
b. Open your book to page 56.
c. Hold up your reader. Point to the title. These words are called the title of the story. These words tell what the story is about. I'll read the title the fast way.
d. Point to the words as you read: Lots of cars.
e. Everybody, what is this story about? (Signal.) *Lots of cars.* Yes. Lots of cars. This story is going to tell something about lots of cars.

Task 22   First reading—children read the story the fast way
Have the children reread any sentences containing words that give them trouble. Keep a list of these words.
a. Everybody, touch the title of the story and get ready to read the words in the title the fast way.
b. First word. Check children's responses. (Pause three seconds.) Get ready. Clap. *Lots.*
c. Next word. Check children's responses. (Pause three seconds.) Get ready. Clap. *Of.*
d. Repeat *c* for the word cars.
e. After the children have read the title, ask: What's this story about? (Signal.) *Lots of cars.* Yes, lots of cars.
f. Everybody, touch the first word of the story. Check children's responses.
g. Get ready to read this story the fast way.
h. First word. (Pause three seconds.) Get ready. Clap. *A.*
i. Next word. Check children's responses. (Pause three seconds.) Get ready. Clap. *Man.*
j. Repeat *i* for the remaining words in the first sentence. Pause at least three seconds between claps. The children are to identify each word without sounding it out.
k. Repeat *h* through *j* for the next two sentences. Have the children reread the first three sentences until firm.
l. The children are to read the remainder of the story the fast way, stopping at the end of each sentence.
m. After the first reading of the story, print on the board the words that the children missed more than one time. Have the children sound out each word one time and tell what word.
n. After the group's responses are firm, call on individual children to read the words.

Source: From *Reading Mastery Series Guide Rainbow Edition,* 1995, Science Research Associates, Inc. Reprinted with permission of McGraw-Hill.

specific procedures and oral instruction through each step of the program. The program uses a synthetic phonics approach, and the students are first taught the prerequisite skill of auditory blending to help them combine isolated sounds into words. In addition, the shapes of some alphabet letters are modified to provide clues to the letter sounds. This special alphabet is gradually phased out as the children's reading skills improve.

The *Corrective Reading Program* (Englemann, Becker, Hanner, & Johnson, 1988) is designed for the older student (Grades 4–12). It consists of two strands: decoding, which follows the regular direction instruction format, and comprehension, which uses text materials of interest to the older student. The web address for direct instruction programs is **http://www. sra-4kids.com.**

METHODS TO DEAL WITH SPECIFIC READING PROBLEMS

Students who have great difficulty in acquiring reading skills often encounter special types of problems, such as: (1) reversals, (2) finger pointing and lip moving, (3) halting oral reading, and (4) poor silent reading. The following strategies can help students with these specific reading problems.

Reversals

Reversals are the tendency to reverse letters or words that are different only in direction, such as *b* for *d*, *no* for *on*, or *saw* for *was*. Inversions are another common type of error, such as *u* for *n*. Poor readers with this problem may even write backward, producing "mirror writing."

It is very common for beginning readers to make reversals. At the beginning stages of reading, such errors merely indicate a lack of experience with letters and words. Reversals typically disappear as the student gains experience and proficiency in reading. Therefore, teachers must decide whether the reversals are merely developmental (in which case they should be ignored) or whether they indicate a disability interfering with reading progress and requiring specific remediation. The following methods are suggested:

1. Concentrate on one letter at a time. For example, start with the letter *b*, make a large chart, and use a memory word such as *bicycle*.
2. Trace the confusing word or letter on a large card or on the blackboard, or use felt letters so that the student has kinesthetic reinforcement.
3. Underline the first letter of a confusing word or write the first letter in a color.
4. Use phonics instruction to reinforce the pronunciation of the confusing word.
5. Write the confusing word, and say it while writing.
6. Use memory devices. For example, show that the lowercase *b* goes in the same direction as the capital *B* and that one can be superimposed on the other.

Finger Pointing and Lip Moving

Both finger pointing and lip moving are characteristic normal behaviors in the early stages of reading. Moreover, when material becomes difficult, even mature and efficient readers fall back on these habits because they do help us understand difficult and frustrating material. Some students may need these aids to understand what they are reading.

However, finger pointing and lip moving inhibit fluent reading and should be discouraged when they are no longer needed. Both habits encourage word-by-word reading, vocalization, or subvocalization. Both also inhibit speed and reduce comprehension. The following remedial approaches should be considered:

1. Do not select material that is so difficult that it forces the student to use these behaviors.

2. Extensive finger pointing may be a symptom of visual difficulties. In some cases, the student may need an eye examination.

3. Students should be made aware of their habits and made to understand how they inhibit reading progress.

4. A first stage in eliminating finger pointing can be the use of markers to replace fingers and then the elimination of the marker itself. If the marker is placed *above* the line of print, readers will be able to read as quickly as they can, and the marker will not be a barrier to speed and looking ahead.

5. Students may need to be reminded that they are moving their lips. Increasing the speed of reading also acts to eliminate lip moving.

Disfluent Oral Reading

The repeated reading technique described earlier in this chapter has been found to effectively improve fluency. Poor readers often read in a very hesitant, nonfluent, halting manner. Research shows that teachers tend to interrupt poor readers much more often than they interrupt good readers, thereby discouraging oral reading fluency. To improve their oral reading, students need more practice in the skill. Make sure the material is not too difficult, have the students first read the material silently, and tell them you will not interrupt while they are reading.

Inability to Read Silently

Most purposeful reading by adults is silent. Therefore, instruction should include opportunities for students to read silently. To stress the importance of silent reading, it should be done before oral reading. Students need direct motivation to read silently. For example, you might stress the information that the student should find in the text, and follow the silent reading with questions and discussion so that the students will see it as a meaningful activity. Gradually increase the quantity of silent reading that students are expected to do.

Recorded Textbooks and Digital CD-ROMs

There are several sources for obtaining recorded books on tape or on digital CD-ROMs that are available to students with disabilities. Students who are identified as having learning disabilities are eligible to obtain, at no cost, books recorded for the blind. In addition, new titles can be recorded if needed. For students with severe reading problems, recorded textbooks can be a real boon; using recorded books allows them to keep up with content while continuing to improve their reading skills. For further information, contact Recording for the Blind and Dyslexic, 20 Roszel Road, Princeton, NJ 08540. The organization can also be reached by telephone at (866) 732-3585 or at the website **http://www.rfbd.org.**

COMPUTERS AND READING

Computers offer many instructional advantages for students with learning disabilities to learn and practice reading skills. Computer programs are motivating, they provide time for learning on a one-to-one basis, they help develop automaticity, and they offer time to think about reading passages. Computer reading programs are available for the prereading, elementary, secondary, and adult levels.

The dizzying pace of change in computer technology has created a dramatic increase in both the number and the quality of computer programs for reading instruction. Computer programs teach literacy, sight words, phonics skills, vocabulary, reading comprehension, and they improve reading rate. New advances in computer technology can help students overcome their reading difficulties (Belson, 2003; Lewis, 1998; Raskind & Higgins, 1998(b)).

Several computer programs that are useful for students with reading problems include are suggested by Belson (2003).

- Reading Blaster (Knowledge Adventure), which is a skill-and-drill software application that allows students to practice spelling and letter–sound relationships.
- The Living Books Series (The Learning Company) includes CD-based books that read stories to children in a normal (human) voice.
- READ 180 (The Scholastic Company). The student begins each lesson by viewing a video that provides background knowledge. The student then reads the text, with *clickable* vocabulary words.
- Earobics (Cognitive Concepts) is a software application designed to teach phonemic awareness through a series of activities and games.
- Inspiration and Kidspiration (Inspiration Software) provides a graphic organizer to help students organize their ideas about stories and words. The website is **http:www.inspiration.com.**

Text-to-Speech Programs

There are several computer programs that are designed to read text aloud. These programs are designed for very poor readers and for individuals with visual disabilities. Several of these programs are described in the following list.

- Recordings for the Blind and Dyslexic (RFBD) provides information on this program at **http://www.rfbd.org.** This organization is dedicated to providing books, including textbooks for individuals who are dyslexic or blind. Material is available in two formats: (1) *RFBD Classic Cassettes* are audio recordings that are played on cassette players, and (2) *RFBD AudioPlus* are digital recordings that are played on CD players.

- *Kurzweil Educational Systems* provides software programs that read text aloud. Information about Kurzweil 1000, Kurzweil 3000, and Kurzweil for Macintosh can be viewed at **http://www.kurzweiledu.com.**

With these programs, text can be scanned, and there are several electronic voices that can be chosen.

- Read Please (free) and Read Please Plus (shareware) read any electronic text. Their website is **http://www.readplease.com**. The program is available in several languages, which users can download to their computers.

- *E-Text Reader* currently allows its material to be downloaded without charge. The website is **http://www.readingmadeeasy.com**. E-Text Reader will read any electronic or scanned text. There are three excellent voice choices. It comes from Premier Assistive Technology, which also sells a more robust text-to-speech program.

CHAPTER SUMMARY

1. Reading is part of the language system and is closely linked to the other forms of language—oral language and writing.

2. Reading is a major academic difficulty for students with learning disabilities. The detrimental effects of reading disabilities have serious consequences in terms of academic achievement, employment, and success in life.

3. Dyslexia is a learning disability in which the individual has extreme difficulty in learning to read. Dyslexia is associated with neurological dysfunction.

4. Major elements of reading are phonemic awareness, phonics and word-recognition skills, fluency, vocabulary, and comprehension.

5. Readers need skills in word recognition to develop fluency in reading. Word recognition takes place through phonics, sight words, context clues, and structural analysis.

6. Reading fluency refers to the reader's ability to recognize words quickly and read text with speed, accuracy, and proper expression.

7. The purpose of reading is comprehension, which is the active understanding and involvement with the written material.

8. Narrative text is the reading of stories. Informational text is the reading of subject matter material, such as textbooks.

9. There are many ways to assess reading ability. Informal measures include informal reading inventories, miscue analysis, and portfolio assessment. Formal tests include survey tests, diagnostic tests, and comprehensive batteries.

10. The "Teaching Strategies" section of this chapter presents strategies for teaching reading to students with learning disabilities. Presented are methods for improving word recognition, improving fluency, and improving reading comprehension. This section also presents special remedial methods for readers with severe disabilities and specific reading problems and discusses the use of computers for teaching reading.

DISCUSSION AND REFLECTION

1. Describe the elements of reading. What does each element contribute to learning to read?

2. Readers use a variety of methods to recognize words. Describe the different methods of word recognition. What method(s) do you think good readers rely upon?

3. Describe reading fluency. Why is it important to teach fluency?

4. What is reading comprehension? Identify a few strategies used to promote reading comprehension. Describe how students might respond to these strategies.

5. Describe two special remedial methods for teaching reading to students with severe reading disabilities. How might students respond to these approaches?

6. What are the differences between informal and formal methods for assessing reading achievement? Describe a test or an assessment technique for each.

KEY TERMS

automaticity *(p. 383)*

basal reading series *(p. 406)*

cloze procedure *(p. 409)*

comprehension *(p. 387)*

context clues *(p. 381)*

decode *(p. 378)*

DIBELS *(p. 401)*

direct instruction *(p. 387)*

directed reading–thinking activity (DRTA) *(p. 415)*

explicit code-emphasis instruction *(p. 378)*

informational materials *(p. 392)*

grapheme *(p. 378)*

indirect instruction *(p. 387)*

informal reading inventory (IRI) *(p. 397)*

language experience method *(p. 407)*

multisensory methods *(p. 416)*

narrative text *(p. 392)*

phonemic awareness *(p. 377)*

reading comprehension *(p. 388)*

reading fluency *(p. 382)*

Reading Recovery *(p. 418)*

sight words *(p. 380)*

structural analysis *(p. 382)*

VAKT *(p. 417)*

vocabulary *(p. 386)*

word-recognition skills *(p. 378)*

word web *(p. 412)*

12

Written Language: Written Expression, Spelling, and Handwriting

CHAPTER OUTLINE

> Chewing on the pencil, feeling intimidated by the blank page, erasing holes in the paper, tearing up the page—these are common behaviors of students with writing difficulties as they labor to write. The secret to becoming a writer is to write and to keep on writing.
>
> —*Anonymous*

Written language is the third form of the integrated language system. The Theories section of this chapter considers three areas of written language: (1) written expression, (2) spelling, and (3) handwriting. Word processing as a computer skill is also discussed because it is an important dimension of written language and strengthens the connections among the forms of language. The Teaching Strategies section of this chapter presents specific instructional techniques in: (1) written expression, (2) word processing, (3) spelling, and (4) handwriting to help students with writing difficulties develop their written language skills.

THEORIES

Many people dislike writing. Their disdainful attitude is depicted in the story of the New York City taxicab driver who skillfully guided his cab past a pedestrian. The cabby then explained to his passenger why he was so careful: "I always try to avoid hittin' 'em because every time ya hit one, ya gotta write out a long report about it."

Words are the primary means of communication for human beings. Using words is the way we tell one another what we want, what we do not want, what we think, and how we feel. When words are spoken, they are a wonderful asset—quick, direct, and easy. But when words must be written, they become burdensome, part of a slow and laborious task. Many students with learning disabilities have significant problems in the acquisition and use of written language, and written language problems often continue to adversely affect their lives as adults (Harris, Graham, & Mason, 2003; Lenz & Deshler, 2003; Troia, Graham, & Harris, 1998).

Writing is the most sophisticated and complex achievement of the language system. In the sequence of language development, writing is typically the last to be learned, although the early literacy approach encourages children to write even before they learn to read. Through writing, we integrate previous learning and experiences in listening, speaking, and reading. Proficiency in written language requires an adequate basis of oral language skills, as well as many other competencies. The writer must be able to keep one idea in mind while formulating the idea into words and sentences, and the writer must be skilled in planning the correct graphic form for each letter and word while manipulating the writing instrument. The writer must also possess sufficient visual and motor memory to integrate complex eye–hand relationships. The instructional concept of "writing across the curriculum" has become a persuasive force in the teaching of writing. This means that writing is encouraged in all subjects of the curriculum, not only those in which written language is the center of instruction.

Three components of writing are addressed in this chapter: (1) written expression, (2) spelling, and (3) handwriting.

WRITTEN EXPRESSION

Ernest Hemingway, when asked about what was the most frightening thing he ever encountered, answered, "a blank sheet of paper." Success as a writer is intimately tied to the quality of writing instruction the student receives.

Writing requires many related abilities, including facility in spoken language, the ability to read, skills in spelling, legible handwriting or skill with computer keyboarding, knowledge of the rules of written usage, and cognitive strategies to organize and plan the writing.

Individuals with writing difficulties often lack many of these critical writing-related abilities and may have severe problems communicating through writing. Their writing is replete with errors in spelling, punctuation, capitalization, handwriting, and grammar. Their written products tend to be short, poorly organized, and impoverished in terms of their development of ideas. Poor skills in written communication and in sharing thoughts through writing can persist over time and into the adult years (Harris et al., 2003; Lenz & Deshler, 2003). "LD Stories: Written Language Problems," illustrates two accounts of individuals with writing difficulties.

The Writing Connection in the Integrated Language System

The links among the elements of language connect the language forms with one another and also strengthen the underlying language system. Extensive oral language experiences promote reading. Instruction in reading improves performance in writing. Experiences with writing and composing improve one's knowledge of language and skill in speaking and reading. All strengthen the underlying language system (Richek et al., 2002).

WRITTEN LANGUAGE PROBLEMS

Using a Things to Do List

Writing a list of things to do is recommended as a good organizational strategy. A recent news story from Kansas City reported a bank robbery. The police apprehended a suspect, obtained a search warrant, and went to the suspect's home, where they found a "things to do" list. Among the items on the list was "rob a bank." This was not a good organizational strategy for this bank robber.

A Written Language Disability

The following news story from Miami illustrates the importance of writing skills for successful communication. In an attempted burglary, a would-be robber handed this handwritten note to the bank teller:

A GOT A BUM. I ALSO HAVE A CONTOUR. I'M GOING TO BLOW YOU SKY HEIGHT. I'M NO KILLEN. THIS IS A HELD UP.

Unable to decipher the note, the teller asked the robber for help in reading the message. By the time the robber deciphered the words for the teller, the police had arrived and arrested the robber. To make matters worse for the robber, the police were able to trace him to other bank holdups in which the same spelling and writing errors were made in the burglary note (Miami Herald, 1980). Written language skills are required in most occupations today—even to be a successful bank robber.

(*Possible translation:* I got a bomb. I also have a control. I'm going to blow you sky high. I'm no killer. This is a holdup.)

The processes used in spoken language, reading, and writing have many similarities. In both reading and writing, people set and revise goals, refining and reconstructing meaning as they go through the material. They develop expectations about what they will read or write next, form attitudes about the text, and monitor the information they wish to remember or convey. Both reading and writing use a constructive process. Readers construct meaning as they recode the author's message into their own language; writers construct original ideas in the process of writing the message (Harris et al., 2003).

By its very nature, writing is an active process. The physical aspect of writing literally forces active involvement upon the writers. Writers perform the actions of picking up a pen or pencil (or using a computer keyboard) and recording their thoughts. While people write, they must actively work at producing something that did not exist before by using their own background knowledge and integrating their language skills. The process of revising requires rethinking and reconstruction. Much reading also occurs during the process of writing. When adults write, over half of the writing time is actually devoted to reading. As soon as good writers complete a section of writing, they reread it. They also reread to see how to connect a previously written section to one they are about to write. When these writers complete an entire text, they reread it again immediately and then reread it a short time later. The kind of reading that takes place during writing is intensive and involves much critical analysis (Harris & Graham, 1997).

Early Literacy and Writing

The term *early literacy* refers to the child's early entrance into the world of words, language, and stories. The concept of early literacy emphasizes the interrelatedness of the various forms of language in the child's development. Children develop literacy through simultaneous experiences with oral language, reading, and writing.

The early literacy philosophy suggests that writing may be easier than reading and may actually develop earlier than reading (Snow et al., 1998). Writing is a more self-involving task than reading because the meaning of a writer's message originates from within the writer and is known to the writer in advance. In contrast, reading requires that the reader be able to interpret someone else's ideas and use of language, which is a more difficult task for the beginner.

The early literacy view is that writing is beneficial, even for primary-age children, and should be encouraged (CIERA, 1998; Snow et al., 1998a). When young children write, they directly explore both the functions and the forms of written language. Writing helps children understand that, in English, print progresses from left to right. Many young children who have not yet learned this rule of written English reverse this process, writing from right to left, as shown in Figure 12.1.

FIGURE 12.1

Children Must Learn That Writing in English Goes From Left to Right

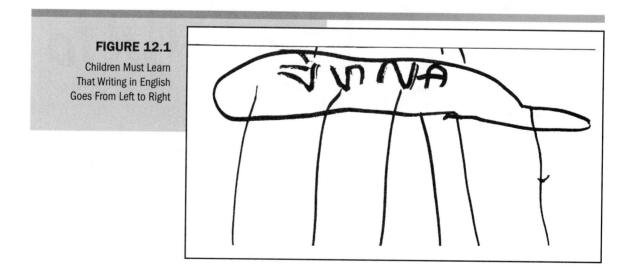

In their early writing experiences, young children should not be required to adhere to criteria of proper form or correct spelling; they should simply be encouraged to explore and to play with writing. Young children are encouraged to use "invented spelling," which means they follow their own spelling rules. Early writing also increases children's awareness of the phonological properties of language. When children attempt to put their ideas into print, they explore and learn about the alphabetic nature of written English. As they begin to realize that words can be segmented into sounds, they acquire important skills for the early stages of reading. Figure 12.2 shows an example of a child's writing in a kindergarten class using an early literacy curriculum.

The Writing Process

Current theories on the teaching of writing call for a major shift in instructional emphasis to the *process* instead of the *product* of writing (Graves,

FIGURE 12.2

Example of a Child's Writing in a Kindergarten Early Literacy Class

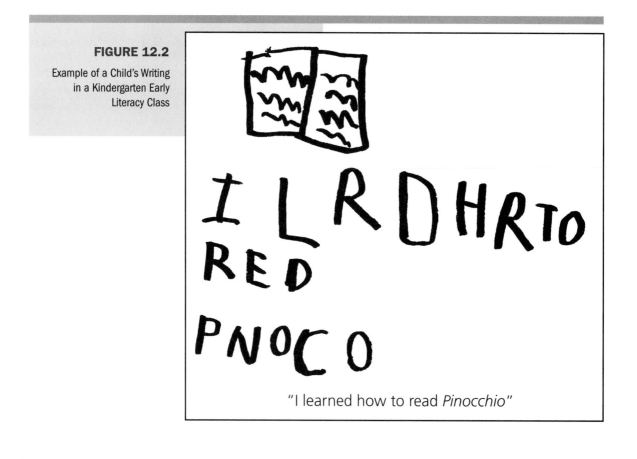

"I learned how to read *Pinocchio*"

1994; Harris et al., 2003). The traditional product approach to writing emphasized the written assignment (or product) created by the writer. In contrast, the process approach to writing focuses on the entire process that writers use in developing a written document. In the traditional product approach, teachers' checking and grading of the written product are based on certain expectations of perfection. Students are expected to spell correctly, use adjectives, and compose topic sentences. Their papers are graded on word choice, grammar, organization, and ideas. The papers are then returned to the students with corrections (often in red ink), and students are expected to learn and improve their writing skills from these grades and corrections. The more conscientious the teacher, the more conscientiously the corrections fill the students' papers. Too often, the result of applying the product approach to writing instruction is that people learn to dislike writing.

The process approach to writing is different and emphasizes the thinking processes that are involved in writing. Teachers are encouraged to understand the complexity of the writing process as they help students think about, select, and organize tasks. Students are encouraged to ask themselves questions such as "Who is the intended audience? What is the purpose of the writing? How can I get ideas? How can I develop and organize the ideas? How can I translate and revise the ideas so that the reader will understand them?"

Writing is a learned skill that can be taught in a school setting as a thinking–learning activity, with emphasis on the writing process. As a cognitive process, writing requires both backward and forward thinking. Good writers do not simply sit down and produce a text. Rather, they go through several stages of the **writing process**—prewriting, drafting, revising, and sharing with an audience, as shown in Figure 12.3 (Graves, 1994).

Stage 1: Prewriting   During this first stage, the writer gathers ideas and refines them before beginning formal writing. **Prewriting** involves a type of

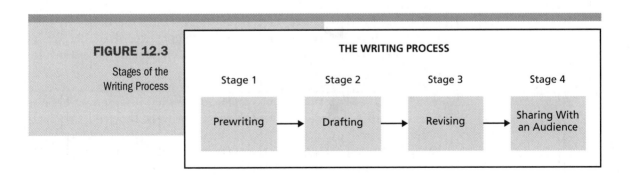

FIGURE 12.3

Stages of the Writing Process

THE WRITING PROCESS

Stage 1 — Prewriting → Stage 2 — Drafting → Stage 3 — Revising → Stage 4 — Sharing With an Audience

brainstorming, such as talking through some thoughts and ideas, jotting a few notes in a margin, or developing a graphic organizer or list of the main points. During this time, the writer also identifies an intended audience. Students are more willing to write if they choose the topic. They may write about someone they know, a special event, or themselves. Teachers can help by asking students to make a list of people who are special to them or to list activities they did during a holiday break.

Stage 2: Drafting   In the second stage of the writing process, the writer records the ideas on paper. Although many people think of this stage as "writing," it actually is only one step in the process. The term **drafting** is used instead of *writing* to emphasize that this is one version of what eventually will be written and that it will be changed. The first draft of a piece of writing is not for the reader, but for the writer. As the writer jots down words, sentences, and paragraphs, these give rise to new ideas or ways to revise ideas already written. At this stage, there may be an over-flow of ideas, with little organization or consideration of prose, grammar, and spelling.

Stage 3: Revising   Having completed the prewriting and drafting stages, the writer then refines the draft version of the text by **revising** and editing. Mature writers take the ideas of the first draft and reorganize and polish them. There may be several revisions, with different kinds of changes made in each, such as in content, the way of expressing the ideas, the vocabulary, the sentence structure, and the sequence of ideas. The last revision is editing, which includes checking for grammatical, punctuation, and spelling errors. This stage requires a very critical view of one's own work.

Students with writing difficulties are often reluctant to revise. Just writing the draft requires extensive effort, and making revisions can seem over-whelming. Rewriting of earlier drafts is greatly facilitated by using computers and word processing software programs.

To help writers learn to revise, teachers can model revisions in dictated stories or in their own work. They can have students make suggestions for revising some of the teacher's writing, make the revisions, and share the re-vised version.

Students can also make suggestions for revising the drafts of their classmates. It is important to make this a positive experience. Be sure to note some good features of a student's work before making suggestions for revision.

Stage 4: Sharing With an Audience   This fourth stage is important because it gives value and worth to the entire writing process. It provides students with the opportunity to receive feedback and to perceive themselves as au-thors who are responding to an audience. In this final stage, the writer con-siders the audience for whom the material is intended and whether the ideas will be well communicated to the reader. The amount of rewriting will depend on the intended audience. The audience could be the teacher, other students in the class, or a larger audience that is reached through publication (Graves, 1994).

Sharing with an audience or publishing can occur as a book is bound and shared with a class or placed in a classroom library. Other forms of sharing could be a presentation, a bulletin board display, a newsletter, or a puppet show.

Principles for Teaching the Writing Process

The following principles apply to planning instruction for the writing process (Harris et al., 2003).

1. *During the prewriting stage, the writing process requires much time, input, and attention.* Writers need something to write about. They need sufficient prior experiences to create and stimulate ideas for a good written production. Giving a written assignment (such as "write a 100 word theme on spring") without first supplying a prewriting buildup will not produce a rich written product. Teachers can provide input experiences through activities, such as trips, stories, discussions, and oral language activities. Sources of inspiration for writing include reading, art, content-area activities, films, television, newspapers, trips and field experiences, brainstorming, and Internet searches. Devote as much time to the prewriting stage as to the writing stage.

2. *The drafting stage frees students from undue concentration on the mechanics of writing.* Students should realize that all writers make errors in spelling and grammar in the first draft. Although such mistakes should *eventually* be corrected, they need not be fixed immediately. Instead, the student should focus on the content during the drafting stage and later clean up the work through editing.

3. *The revising stage helps students edit their work.* Students often think that their writing is finished when they have completed their first draft. When they realize that they must go through the revising stage before their work will be complete, they begin to think of writing as a process instead of a product. A teacher can demonstrate the imperfections of a first draft by exhibiting first drafts of his or her own writing to show the students that all writing needs to be edited. Students can form small groups to review and edit one another's work.

4. *Avoid excessive corrections of students' written work.* Students are discouraged from trying if their attempts to express ideas are met by having their papers returned full of grammatical, spelling, punctuation, and handwriting corrections in red ink, with heavy penalties for mistakes. As one pupil remarked, "An *F* looks so much worse in red ink."

By receiving negative reinforcements, students soon learn to beat the game—they will limit their writing vocabulary to words they know how to spell, keep their sentences simple, avoid complex and creative ideas, and keep their compositions short.

A Learning Strategy Teaching Approach to Writing

A learning strategy approach called *self-regulated strategy development (SRSD)* is an explicit, structured approach to teaching writing (Graham, Harris, & Larsen, 2001; Harris et al., 2003). Students with writing difficulties need structure and direction to acquire writing strategies. The goals of SRSD are: (1) to help students develop a knowledge of writing and the strategies involved in the writing process, (2) to support students in the ongoing development of the abilities needed to monitor and manage their writing, and (3) to promote students' development of positive attitudes about writing and about themselves as writers.

The six stages of the SRSD model of writing are (Harris et al., 2003)

1. *Develop background knowledge.* Working within a group, students think about what is known about the topic and find additional information from a variety of sources.

2. *Discuss it.* The students talk about and discuss what they have learned with one another and with their teacher. They then discuss a specific writing strategy that they plan to use. For example, they may decide to use the strategy of semantic mapping.

3. *Model it.* The students model how to use a writing strategy, thinking aloud as they work.

4. *Memorize it.* Students review and say aloud the parts of the writing strategy.

5. *Support it.* Students begin to write a story by using the writing strategy.

6. *Independent performance.* Students now use the writing strategy independently.

Strategies for Writing

Students with writing difficulties find writing tasks challenging, so teachers must provide adequate structure to help them carry out a writing assignment. A variety of writing strategies, such as: (1) written conversations, (2) personal journals, (3) patterned writing, (4) graphic organizers, and (5) picture drawing can help students find ideas for writing, share their ideas on paper, use interesting and descriptive vocabulary, and make the

writing purposeful (Graham et al., 2001; Harris et al., 2003; Richek et al., 2002).

Written Conversations   In this strategy, two students, or a student and a teacher, sit beside each other and communicate. The partners cannot speak; instead, writing is the only communication allowed. If one person's message is unclear, the partner must ask for clarification in writing. Used on a regular basis, this strategy helps students learn to record their thoughts in writing. For example, to catch up on the news, the teacher can ask the student in writing how things are going. The teacher can also write a greeting and message, and the student can answer (Richek et al., 2002). Or the student can write something, and the teacher can respond in writing. For this exchange, each writer can use a different-colored pen or pencil. Figure 12.4 shows an example of a written conversation.

Personal Journals   In a personal journal, students record personal events or experiences in writing. They practice writing by recording day-to-day accounts of events in their lives and their feelings about these experiences, which they can read later. An example of a journal entry is shown in Figure 12.5. Each student needs a journal, usually a notebook of lined paper. Students often create titles for their journals and decorate the cover or title

FIGURE 12.4

An Example of Written
Conversation

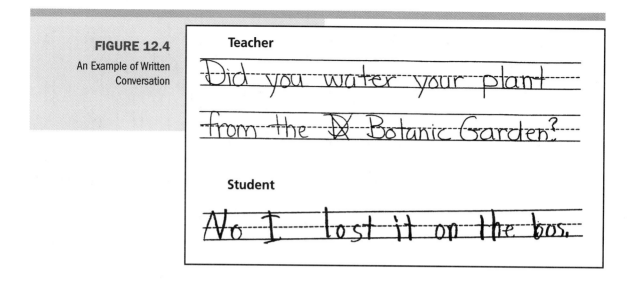

Teacher

Did you water your plant from the ⊠ Botanic Garden?

Student

No I lost it on the bos.

FIGURE 12.5

An Example of a
Journal Entry

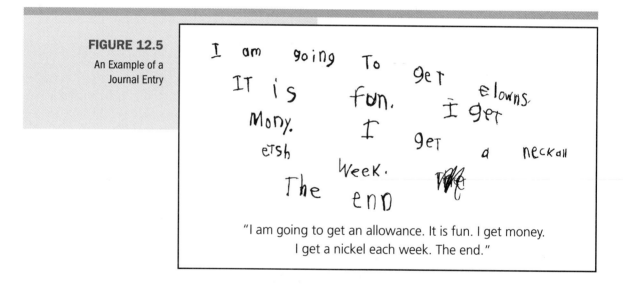

"I am going to get an allowance. It is fun. I get money.
I get a nickel each week. The end."

page. Time is set aside (usually at least a few periods a week) to record personal thoughts in journals. It is easier for students to read and write if they use only one side of a page.

Students may choose to share some of their journal entries, but they should have the choice of not doing so. If a student does not want the teacher to read a journal entry, the student can fold a page in half lengthwise, and the teacher will then not read the folded pages. Teachers should also be careful not to correct grammatical errors or spelling errors because this practice undermines the student's confidence and may decrease the amount of writing.

Some students with writing difficulties lack the confidence to maintain a journal. Teachers can help students overcome this problem by modeling journal writing and help students who cannot think of journal topics with suggestions, such as favorite places, special people, favorite stories, things I like to do, things I don't like to do, things that make me angry, and things I do well. A list of "Ideas for Writing" could be put on a chart in the room or placed in the student's journal on an "Ideas" page.

Patterned Writing   In this strategy, the students use a favorite predictable book with a patterned writing, and then they write their own version. This method gives students the security of a "frame" to use to write a personalized response. One favorite frame is *Brown Bear, Brown Bear, What Do You See?* (Martin, 1992). Each page of this book contains a refrain, such as "Brown bear, brown bear, what do you see? I see a blue bird looking at me." Students make up their own refrain and illustrate it. The finished writing of several students can be put together into a book and placed on the library table for others to read.

Graphic Organizers   **Graphic organizers** are visual displays that organize and structure ideas and concepts. In the context of reading, graphic organizers help students understand the reading material. Research shows that reading comprehension improves when students use graphic organizers. In the context of writing, graphic organizers can help students generate and organize ideas as they prepare for a writing assignment (Lenz et al., 2003; Sabbatino, 2004).

The Venn diagram is one graphic organizer in which there are two intersecting circles. This graphic is useful for preparing for a "compare and contrast" writing assignment. For example, in comparing two people in history, one puts the descriptors of one person in one circle, the characteristics of the other person in the second circle, and the common characteristics in the intersecting section. Figure 12.6 shows a Venn diagram comparing oranges and apples.

Inspiration is a software program that makes it easy for students to develop graphic organizers to plan, develop, organize, or summarize a writing project. The website for this company is **http://www.inspiration.com**. Users can download or request trial versions of this software. Students find it easier to tackle a writing assignment if they begin to organize their ideas in the prewriting stage using this graphic organizer program. A version of this software for younger children is *Kidspiration*. Figure 12.7 displays a graphic organizer of the writing process that was accomplished with Inspiration software.

Drawing Pictures   An important communication method for children with writing difficulties is the drawing of pictures. These children are often very

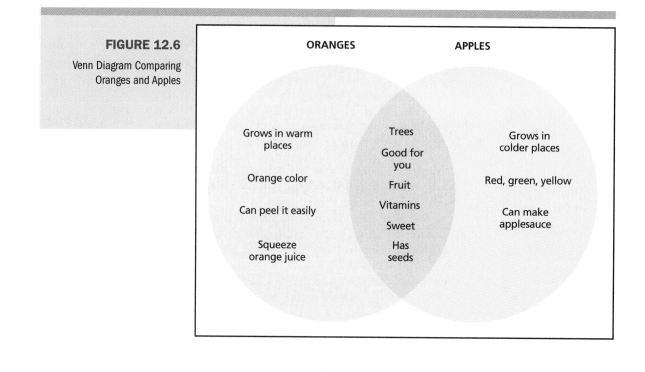

FIGURE 12.6

Venn Diagram Comparing Oranges and Apples

ORANGES   APPLES

Grows in warm places

Trees
Good for you

Grows in colder places

Orange color

Fruit

Red, green, yellow

Can peel it easily

Vitamins

Can make applesauce

Sweet

Squeeze orange juice

Has seeds

good at expressing their ideas in pictures. The visual areas of learning are often an area of strength and should be encouraged (Smith, 2001, 2005; West, 1997). Figure 12.8 is a spoof of a child's drawing of his mother.

Computers and Word Processing

Word processing is one of the most widely used computer applications. It offers an excellent means of teaching writing and integrates the language systems. With this effective tool, writing becomes a less arduous task for many individuals with writing difficulties. With a computer, students can write without worrying about handwriting and can revise without making a mess of the written document. In Figure 12.9, a fourth-grade student uses a word-processing program to describe his invention for a science project.

Electronic Keyboards   Alphasmart, Dana, and Nero are electronic keyboards that are used for word processing. These devices are lightweight, relatively low-cost devices (about $200–$400) that can be used instead of a computer. Files are stored on a disk, which can be transferred to a PC or a Macintosh computer. Pages can be printed by connecting the Alphasmart, Dana, or Nero keyboards to any printer. Many classes provide all students in the class with an Alphasmart or Dana keyboard. The web address for Alphasmart is **http:www.alphasmart.com.**

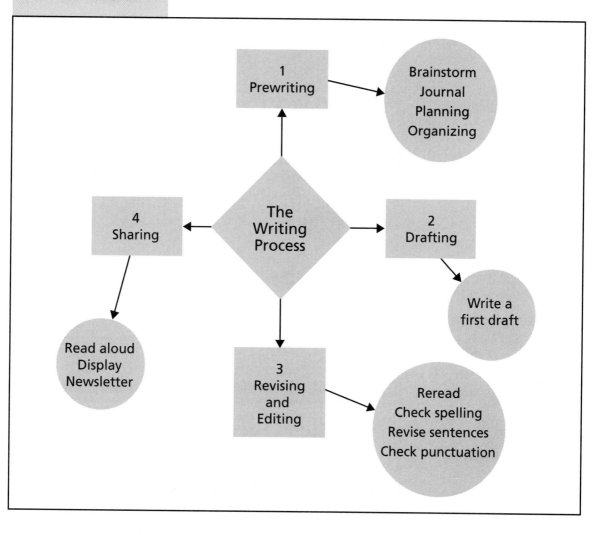

Advantages of Word Processing   As the writing tool of the contemporary classroom, word processing supports writing in the following ways (MacArthur, 1996; Richek et al., 2002):

- *Motivation.*   Students are motivated to write because word processing increases their ability to produce neat, error-free copies. It also encourages them to share their writing and to publish it in a variety of formats.

FIGURE 12.8

Expressing Ideas in Pictures

"Mrs. Hammond! I'd know you anywhere from little Billy's portrait of you."

FIGURE 12.9

"The Sanitary Sleeve," a Word-Processing Document

The Sanitary Sleeve

I invented the sanitary sleeve so people could wipe their nose on their sleeve and not ruin their shirt. You make a sanitary sleeve by gluing Velcro on the sleeve of your shirt (glue the Velcro on the left sleeve if you are a lefty and on the right sleeve if you are a righty). You'll also need special Kleenex with Velcro on it. This is an invention that your Mom will like because your shirt will stay clean even when you have a cold.

- *Collaboration.*   Students learn to collaborate in the writing process with teachers and peers because of the visibility of the screen and the anonymity of the printed text.

- *Ease of revision.*   The editing power of the computer eases the physical burden of revising, making it easier to correct, revise, and rewrite a text. The writer can readily add, correct, delete, and revise and can freely experiment until the display screen shows exactly what the writer wants to say. The writer can also work with the printed copy to make further changes, if desired, and then enter those changes into the computer.

- *Help with fine-motor problems.*   Typing is inherently easier and neater than handwriting, especially for students with fine-motor problems. At any point, by clicking "print," the writer can obtain a printed copy. Word processing eliminates the difficult task of recopying or retyping and encourages the student to expend energy on the important part of the writing process—thinking about content, editing, and revising.

- *Special features.*   Many word-processing software programs have special features, such as spell checkers, a thesaurus, grammar checkers, and speech synthesis programs that make the process of writing easier.

Keyboarding   To use a word processor for writing, students must learn typing or keyboarding skills. Keyboarding is discussed in this chapter, in the section on handwriting instruction.

Talking Word-Processing Programs   Talking word-processing programs are text-to-speech programs that allow users to hear electronic text. These programs are helpful for people who have difficulty reading print. Several text-to-speech programs are listed in Table 12.1.

Word-Prediction Programs   Word-prediction programs can be very helpful for poor writers. Word-prediction programs work together with a word processor to *predict* the word the user wants to enter into the computer. When the user types the first one or two letters of a word, the word-prediction software offers a list of words beginning with that letter. The user simply selects the desired word. The word-prediction software can also predict the next word in a sentence, even before the letters of the next word are entered. The prediction is based on syntax, spelling rules, word frequency, redundancy, and repetitive factors. The word-prediction software is helpful for students with learning disabilities who have difficulty in writing, keyboarding, spelling, and grammar (Belson, 2003; Lewis, 1998; Raskind & Higgins, 1998a). A popular word-prediction program is Co-writer (see Table 12.1).

Voice-Recognition Systems   Voice-recognition systems allow a person to operate a computer by speaking to it. Using it in combination with a word processor, the user dictates to the system through a microphone, and the spoken words are converted to text on the computer screen. The computer

TABLE 12.1

Computers and Writing

Type of computer program	Name	Company and web address
Talking word-processing programs	Write: OutLoud	Don Johnston, **http://www.donjohnston.com**
	Kurzweil 3000	Kurzweil Education Systems, **http://www.kurzweiledu.com**
	WYNN 3.0	Freedom Scientific, **http://www. freedomscientific.com/WYNN**
	ReadPlease and ReadPleasePlus	ReadPlease Corporation, **http://www.readplease.com**
	E-Text Reader	**http://www.readingmadeeasy.com**
Word-prediction programs	Co-writer	Don Johnston, **http://www.donjohnston.com**
Voice-recognition programs	Dragon NaturallySpeaking	Scansoft, **http://www.scansoft.com**
	ViaVoice	IBM Special Needs Systems **http://www.ibm.com**
Word-processing software	AppleWorks	Claris, **http://www.apple.com/ appleworks**
	Microsoft Works	Microsoft, **http://www.microsoft.com**
	Microsoft Word	Microsoft, **http://www.microsoft.com**
	WordPerfect	Corel, **http://www.wordperfect.com**

learns to recognize the speech of the individual using it. The more the system is used, the more accurate it becomes in recognizing the user's spoken language. Voice-recognition systems may be particularly helpful to those individuals who have oral language abilities that are superior to their written language abilities. Voice-recognition programs are especially useful for individuals with dyslexia (Belson, 2003; Raskind & Higgins, 1998). Some voice-recognition systems are listed in Table 12.1.

Word-Processing Software   Many excellent word-processing programs are available for students at all levels. Table 12.1 describes some of the programs used in schools.

Writing E-mail Messages   A widely used and exciting method for encouraging writing and sharing written messages with an audience is through e-mail. Many classes are linking up with other classes through the Internet, providing children with the opportunity to write to one another. In addition, there are commercial services specifically designed for telecommunication for children.

E-mail is a quick and inexpensive way to transmit information. A child can write and send a message, and the message is then stored in a mailbox within a host computer system until the receiver logs on and read his or her mail. A class in California can communicate via e-mail with a class in Alaska or Mexico. Children can develop friendships across districts, states, and even nations.

Using Presentation Software Software that allows users to develop presentation slides (such as Microsoft PowerPoint, Hyperstudio, Appleworks, and Kid Pix) provides an excellent way for students to engage in writing. Students with writing difficulties often struggle with writing, a skill that taps into many of their most severe disability areas. Secondary students with severe writing disabilities often master presentation software very quickly.

Students might, for example, develop a PowerPoint slide presentation about what they did during their winter break, recalling an experience that was recent and vivid. Presentations can be augmented with color, a variety of fonts, background colors, animations, graphics, and photos. Students can then present their PowerPoint shows to the class.

Many students with writing difficulties are enthusiastic about using PowerPoint and about making PowerPoint presentations in lieu of writing compositions. They explain that it is easier to write in short phrases rather than in long sentences; it is fun; and, most important, it is easy to share their work with an audience. Creating a presentation slide project seems to call upon the students' visual skills, an area of strength for many students with learning disabilities (Zilla & Lerner, 2001). A useful tutorial for PowerPoint is at **http://www.actden.com/pp**.

Assessment of Written Expression

The assessment of writing usually focuses on the written product. As with other areas of instruction, both informal and formal measures can be used to assess writing. Some of these measures are listed in Table 12.2; these tests are more fully described in "Tests for Assessing Students with Learning Disabilities." Written language tests usually require students to first write a passage, which is then evaluated.

SPELLING Spelling has been called "the invention of the devil." Continuing this spiritual analogy, someone has quipped that the ability to spell well is "a gift from God." Spelling is one curriculum area in which neither creativity nor divergent thinking is encouraged. Only one pattern or arrangement of letters can be accepted as correct; no compromise is possible. What makes

TABLE 12.2	Test	Age or grade assessed
Tests of Written Expression	■ Oral and Written Language Scales (OWLS)—Written Expression Scale	Ages 3–21
	■ Test of Adolescent and Adult Language—3 (TOAL-3)	Ages 12–19
	■ Test of Early Written Language	Ages 2–4
	■ Test of Written Expression (TOWE)	Ages 5–17
	■ Test of Written Language—3 (TOWL-3)	Ages 7–18
	■ Woodcock-Johnson Psychoeducational Battery—III, Tests of Achievement	Grades K–17

spelling so difficult is that the written form of the English language has an inconsistent pattern; there is not a dependable one-to-one correspondence between the spoken sounds of English and the written form of the language. Therefore, spelling is not an easy task, even for people who do not have spelling difficulties.

Spelling a word is much more difficult than reading a word. In reading, several clues—context, phonics, structural analysis, and configuration—help the reader to recognize a word in print. Spelling offers no such opportunities to draw on peripheral clues. Many individuals who have trouble spelling words are skilled in recognizing them in reading. However, individuals who are poor in decoding words in reading are almost always poor in spelling as well.

Developmental Stages of Learning to Spell

Children go through several distinct stages of spelling development, following a general progression of spelling knowledge. The rate of progression differs among children with different spelling abilities, but all children pass through the stages in order. Moreover, the spelling errors that children make reflect their current developmental stage. There are overlaps in the ages at which children pass through each developmental stage of spelling. The stages and their accompanying ages and characteristics follow:

Stage 1: Developing Prephonetic Writing, Ages 1–7 Children scribble, identify pictures, draw, imitate writing, and learn to make letters, as shown in Figure 12.10.

Stage 2: Using Letter Names and Beginning Phonetic Strategies, Ages 5–9 Children attempt to use phoneme representations but exhibit limited knowledge. They use invented spelling by letter name (e.g., *HIKT* for

FIGURE 12.10

Developing Prephonetic
Writing: Making Letters

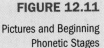

FIGURE 12.11

Pictures and Beginning
Phonetic Stages

"I'm going apple picking on Sunday"

hiked, LRN for *learn,* or TRKE for *turkey*). Children may be able to spell some sight words correctly, as shown in Figure 12.11.

Stage 3: Using Written Word Patterns, Ages 6–12 Spelling attempts are readable, pronounceable, and recognizable, and they approximate conventional spelling, even though they are not precise (e.g., *offis* for *office* or *alavater* for *elevator*). The child's invented spellings follow rules of short vowel and long vowel markers. Most sight words are spelled correctly, as shown in Figure 12.12.

FIGURE 12.12

Written Word Patterns

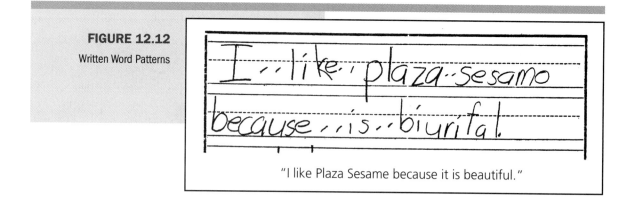

"I like Plaza Sesame because it is beautiful."

Stage 4: Using Syllable Junctures and Multisyllabic Words, Ages 8–18
Students display errors in multisyllabic words. Invented spelling errors occur at syllable juncture and *schwa* positions and follow deviational rules (e.g., *useage* for *usage*; the term *schwa* refers to unaccented syllables and reflects common spelling errors, such as *cottin* for *cotton*). Multisyllabic sight words may or may not be transferred to spelling performance.

Stage 5: Developing a Mature Spelling Perspective, Ages 10–Adult At this stage, previously acceptable invented spellings are now viewed as errors. Many individuals continue to have great difficulty with spelling, even if they follow the rules. Because of the many exceptions in English, individuals should learn to rely on backup sources, such as dictionaries, computer spelling checks, and electronic spellers. (*Franklin Spelling Tutor,* from Franklin Learning Resources, is one example of an electronic speller. For additional information, go to **http://www.franklin.com.**)

Problems Related to Spelling

Spelling requires many different abilities. For example, a child who lacks phonological awareness will not recognize that there are phonemes or sounds within spoken words and will have difficulty with the spelling-to-sound linkages that are necessary in spelling (Torgesen, 1998). Some children are initially unable to read a spelling word. Other children do not know how to apply phonics and structural analysis to spell a word. Still others are poor at visualizing the appearance of the word. Some children have poor motor facility and physical difficulty writing words.

To spell a word correctly, an individual must not only have stored the word in memory, but must also be able to completely retrieve it from memory without the help from visual clues. Poor spellers who cannot remember or visualize the letters and the order of the letters in words benefit from activities to help strengthen and reinforce the visual memory of the spelling words. Fernald (1943/1988), for example, developed a tracing technique to teach spelling by reinforcing the visual image of the word, drawing on the tactile and kinesthetic senses. (The Fernald Method is described in the Teaching Strategies section of this chapter.)

Some poor spellers have difficulty with auditory memory and cannot hold the sounds or syllables in their minds. These students need instruction that will help them recognize the sounds of words and build phonological skills.

Motor memory is also a factor in spelling because the speller must remember how the word "felt" or recall the motor movement when the word was previously written. Students with motor memory problems need additional practice with writing the spelling words.

Invented Spelling

Invented spelling is the beginning writer's attempt to write words by attending to their sound units and associating letters with them in a systematic, although unconventional, way (Richek et al., 2002). Examples of invented spellings used by young children are *evry budy* for *everybody, nabor* for *neighbor, ez* for *easy, neck all* for *nickel,* and *1000ilnd* for *thousand island.* Examples of writing with invented spelling are shown in Figure 12.13 and Figure 12.14.

Children who are encouraged to use invented spelling and to compose anything they want in whatever way they can are much more willing to write. They learn to take risks in a failure-free environment, and they come to understand that writing is a pleasurable form of communication in which thoughts are translated into symbols that mean something to other people. Figure 12.14 illustrates the writing of a first-grade student who was able to express deep emotional feeling about a ladybug. Research shows that children who were allowed to invent their own spelling at an early age tend to spell as well as, or better than, children who were not given this instruction (Ehri & Wilce, 1985). It is important that teachers who use invented spelling as an instructional technique make sure that parents understand the philosophy and purpose of the method. "LD Stories: Learning the Awful Truth About Spelling" tells of a child who was encouraged to use invented spelling and was later shocked when told that spelling has rules.

A critical factor in using invented spelling is the child's phonological awareness of the sounds of language. Young children who have phonemic awareness of the sounds of language have proficiency in invented spelling and tend to write more.

FIGURE 12.13

Example of
Invented Spelling

SUUMENN POo
I AMMGO ENN

"Swimming pool. I am going in."

Cognitive Learning Strategies for Spelling

Cognitive learning strategies for spelling include activities such as self-questioning and self-monitoring. Students are taught to ask themselves the following questions, which are listed on a prompt card:

FIGURE 12.14

Example of
Invented Spelling

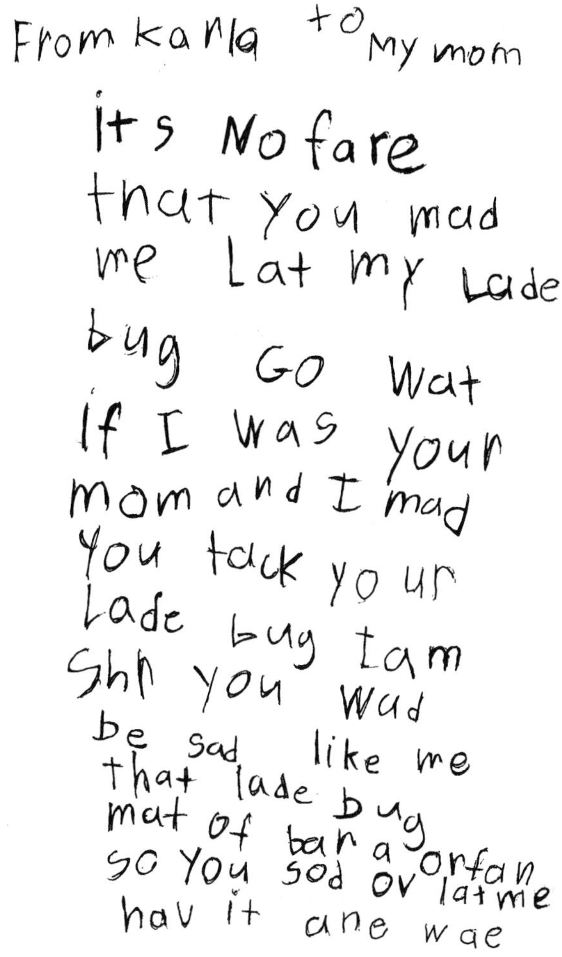

From Karla to My mom

It's No fare
that you mad
me Lat my Lade
bug Go Wat
If I was your
mom and I mad
You tack yo ur
Lade bug I am
Shr you wad
be sad like me
that lade bug
mat of bar a orfan
so you sod ov lat me
hav it ane wae

"From Karla to my mom. It's no fair that you made me let my ladybug go. What if I was your mom and I made you take your ladybug. I am sure you would be sad like me. That ladybug might have been an orphan. So you should have let me have it anyway."

1. Do I know this word?
2. How many syllables do I hear in this word? (Write down the number.)
3. I will spell out the word.
4. Do I have the right number of syllables?

LEARNING THE AWFUL TRUTH ABOUT SPELLING

Some children who use invented spelling are jolted when they realize that there are strict rules about correct spelling. Brian had been in third grade for 2 weeks in the fall semester when he asked his mother to transfer him to a different third-grade class. Brian explained that the reason for his request was that his current third-grade teacher was not a very good teacher. When his mother probed further, Brian confided that his third-grade teacher thought there was only one way to spell a word.

---

5. a. If the word has the right number of syllables, am I unsure of the spelling of any part of the word? If I am, I will underline that part and try spelling the word again. Now, does it look right to me? If it does, I will leave it alone. If it still does not look right, I will underline the part I am not sure of and try again.

    b. If the word I spelled does not have the right number of syllables, let me hear the word in my head again and find the missing syllable. Then I will go back to Step 2.

6. When I finish spelling, I tell myself I am a good worker. I have tried hard at spelling.

Multisensory Approaches to Spelling

Using several senses helps to reinforce the learning of spelling words. Multisensory learning involves the senses of visual, auditory, kinesthetic, and tactile learning. Two multisensory spelling approaches are the *multisensory method* and the *Fernald Method*, which are described in detail in the strategies for teaching spelling, later in this chapter. These methods require students to use visual, auditory, tactile, and kinesthetic learning.

Two Theories of Word Selection for Teaching Spelling

In selecting words for teaching spelling, there are two alternative approaches: (1) the *word-pattern approach* and (2) the *word-frequency approach.*

Word-Pattern Approach to Spelling The **word-pattern approach to spelling** is based on the contention that the spelling of American English is sufficiently rule-covered to warrant an instructional method that stresses phonological, morphological, and syntactic rules or word patterns. This might also be called a phonics approach to spelling because it selects words to teach phonic generalizations. This approach to teaching spelling capitalizes on the underlying regularity between the phonological and morphological elements in oral language and their graphic representations in written language.

In spite of the seemingly numerous exceptions to the rules of spelling, research demonstrates that American English spelling has predictable patterns and an underlying system of phonological and morphological regularity.

Teachers can help students discover underlying linguistic patterns by selecting words for spelling instruction based on linguistic patterns. For instance, when teaching the spelling pattern of the phoneme *oy*, the teacher should include words such as *boy, joy, Roy,* and *toy* to help students form a phonological generalization. The teaching of spelling can be merged with phonics instruction so that phonics and word-analysis skills are practiced during the spelling lesson.

Word-Frequency Approach to Spelling In the **word-frequency approach to spelling,** words for spelling instruction are chosen on the basis of frequency of use, rather than on phonological patterns. The criteria for word selection are frequency of use, permanency, and utility. A core of spelling words that are most frequently used in writing was determined through extensive investigations of the writing of children and adults (Fitzgerald, 1951).

A few words in our language are used over and over. In fact, only 2,650 words and their derivative repetitions make up about 95% of the writing of elementary-school children. A basic list of 3,500 words covers the needs of children in elementary school (Fitzgerald, 1955), and 60% of our writing consists of the 100 words shown in Table 12.3.

The word-frequency approach to spelling is based on the belief that there are so many exceptions to spelling rules that occur in the most frequently used words that it is difficult to convey patterns and rules to beginning spellers. Examples of the irregular relationship between phonemes (the spoken sounds) and graphemes (the written symbols) are easy to cite. George Bernard Shaw, an advocate of spelling reform, is credited with the suggestion that the word *fish* be spelled *ghoti: gh* as in cough, *o* as in *women, ti* as in *nation*. Following phonic generalizations, the word *natural* could be spelled *pnatchurile*. The many inconsistencies that exist in English spelling are illustrated in the following limericks:

TABLE 12.3

The 100 Most Common
Words in Written Language

a	eat	in	our	there
all	for	is	out	they
am	girl	it	over	this
and	go	just	play	time
are	going	know	pretty	to
at	good	like	put	too
baby	got	little	red	tree
ball	had	look	run	two
be	has	made	said	up
big	have	make	saw	want
boy	he	man	school	was
but	her	me	see	we
can	here	mother	she	went
Christmas	him	my	so	what
come	his	name	some	when
did	home	not	take	will
do	house	now	that	with
dog	how	of	the	would
doll	I	on	them	you
down	I'm	one	then	your

A king, on assuming his reign,
Exclaimed with a feeling of peign:
"Tho I'm legally heir
No one here seems to ceir
That I haven't been born with a breign."

A merchant addressing a debtor,
Remarked in the course of his lebtor
That he chose to suppose
A man knose what he ose
And the sooner he pays it, the bedtor!

A young lady crossing the ocean
Grew ill from the ship's dizzy mocean,
She called with a sigh
And a tear in her eigh,
For the doctor to give her a pocean.

And now our brief lesson is through—
I trust you'll agree it was trough;
For it's chiefly designed
To impress on your migned
What wonders our spelling can dough!

Source: Reprinted by special permission of Dr. Emmett Albert Betts, Phonetics Spelling Council.

One teacher found that students' spelling of the word *awful* was varied and included *offul, awfull, offel,* and *offle*. Each is an accurate phonetic transcription of the oral sounds of the word.

Assessment of Spelling

Informal Tests   Informal and teacher-constructed spelling tests are particularly useful. Curriculum-based assessment also offers a way to obtain information on spelling that is directly linked to instruction (Spinelli, 2002).

A short informal spelling test, as shown in Table 12.4, was developed by selecting 10 words from a frequency-of-use word list (Durrell, 1956). The student is asked to spell on paper words from each grade list until three words in a grade list are missed. The student's spelling level can be estimated as that at which only two words are missed.

Formal Tests   Some formal tests of spelling are individual spelling tests, and others are part of a comprehensive academic achievement battery.

TABLE 12.4

Informal Spelling Test

Grade 1	Grade 2	Grade 3	Grade 4	Grade 5	Grade 6	Grade 7
all	be	after	because	bread	build	although
at	come	before	dinner	don't	hair	amount
for	give	brown	few	floor	music	business
his	house	dog	light	beautiful	eight	excuse
it	long	never	place	money	brought	receive
not	must	in	sent	minute	except	measure
see	ran	gray	table	ready	suit	telephone
up	some	hope	town	snow	whose	station
me	want	live	only	through	yesterday	possible
go	your	mother	farm	bright	instead	straight

TABLE 12.5

Tests of Spelling

Test	Type	Age or grade assessed
■ Brigance Comprehensive Inventory of Basic Skills—Revised	Battery	Grades K–9
■ Peabody Individual Achievement Test— Revised (PIAT-R)	Battery	Grades K–12
■ Spellmaster Assessment and Teaching System	Spelling	Grades 2–adult
■ Test of Written Spelling—3 (TOWS-3)	Spelling	Grades 1–12
■ Wide-Range Achievement Test—3 (WRAT-3)	Battery	Ages 5–adult

Table 12.5 shows some commonly used spelling tests. (For further discussion, see "Tests for Assessing Students With Learning Disabilities.")

HANDWRITING

Three different ways to produce writing are currently taught in schools: (1) manuscript writing (a version of printing), (2) cursive writing (sometimes called *script*), and (3) keyboarding (or typing).

Even though the use of computer word processing is becoming more common in our schools, handwriting remains a necessary competency. Handwriting is still the major means by which students convey to teachers what they have learned. In many life situations, adults find handwriting an unavoidable necessity.

Handwriting is the most concrete of the communication skills. It can be directly observed, evaluated, and preserved, providing a permanent record of the output. The process of handwriting is intricate and depends on many different skills and abilities. Writing requires accurate perception of the graphic symbol patterns. The act of writing entails keen visual and motor skills that depend on the visual function of the eye, the coordination of eye movements, smooth motor coordination of eye and hand, and control of arm, hand, and finger muscles. Writing also requires accurate visual and kinesthetic memory of the written letters and words.

Extremely poor handwriting is sometimes called **dysgraphia,** and this condition may reflect other underlying neurological conditions. Poor handwriting may be a manifestation of fine-motor difficulties because the student is unable to execute efficiently the motor movements required to write or to copy written letters or forms. Students may be unable to transfer the input of visual information to the output of fine-motor movement, or they may have difficulty in activities that require motor and spatial judgments. Some students exhibit dystrophic problems when they cannot go from a far-point visual task of seeing a letter or word on a chalkboard to then copying that form on a piece of paper, a near-point visual task. Other underlying shortcomings that interfere with handwriting performance are poor motor skills, faulty visual perception of letters and words, and difficulty in remembering visual impressions.

Figure 12.15 illustrates the attempts of two 10-year-old boys with handwriting disabilities to copy some writing materials.

Manuscript Writing

Handwriting instruction usually begins with **manuscript writing** in kindergarten, where children begin to write letters of the alphabet. Manuscript writing usually continues in first, second, and third grade.

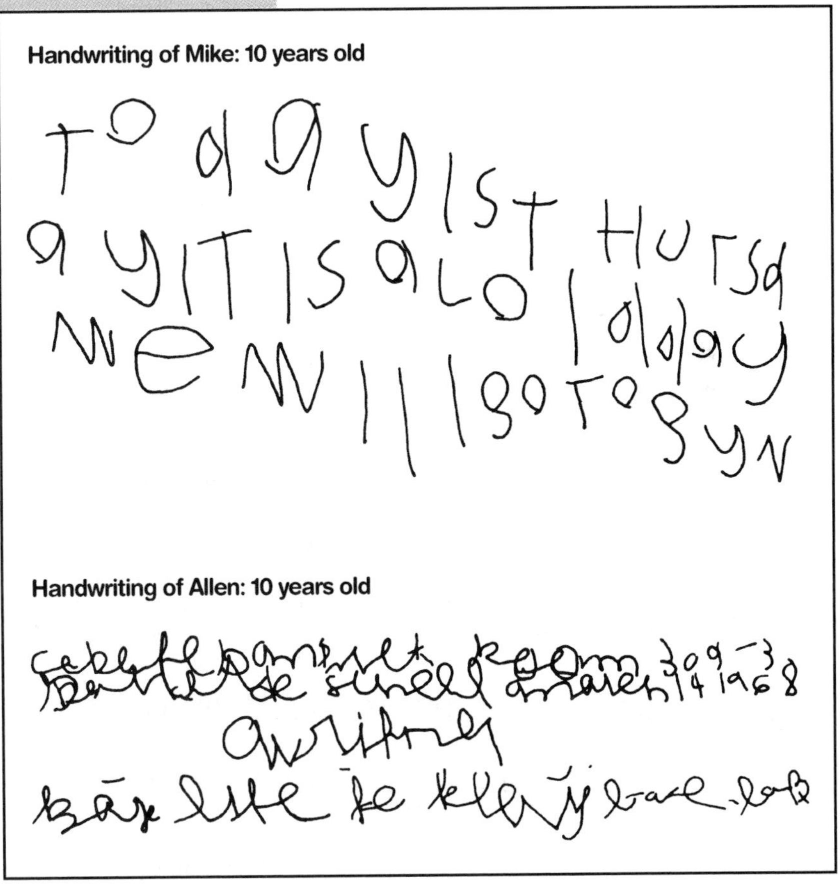

FIGURE 12.15

Illustrations of the Handwriting of Two 10-Year-Old Boys With Handwriting Disabilities (in both cases, the boys were asked to copy from a sample)

Handwriting of Mike: 10 years old

Handwriting of Allen: 10 years old

Manuscript writing has certain advantages: It is easy to learn because it consists of only circles and straight lines, and the letter forms are closer to the printed form used in reading. Some educators believe it is not essential to transfer to cursive writing at all because the manuscript form is legal, legible, and probably just as rapid. Many children with writing difficulties find manuscript writing easier than cursive writing. The manuscript letters are shown in Figure 12.16.

FIGURE 12.16

Sample Manuscript and Cursive Alphabets

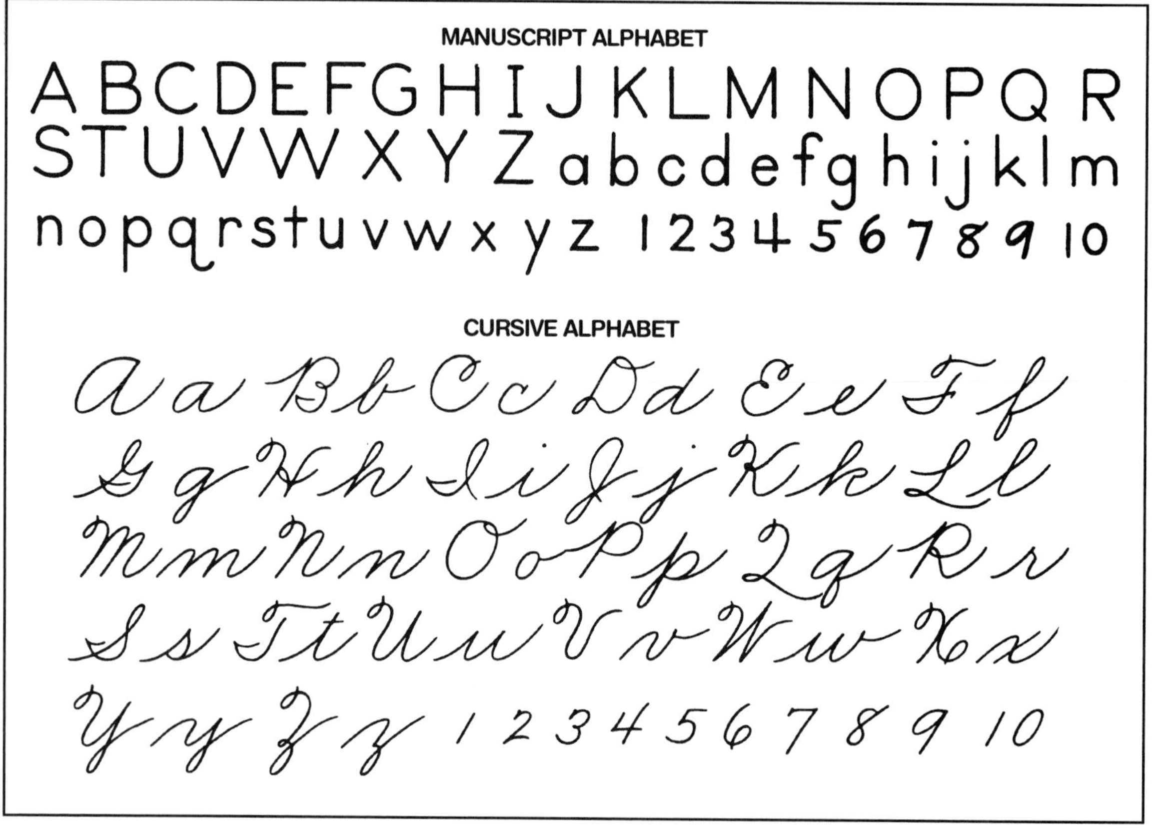
MANUSCRIPT ALPHABET
A B C D E F G H I J K L M N O P Q R
S T U V W X Y Z a b c d e f g h i j k l m
n o p q r s t u v w x y z 1 2 3 4 5 6 7 8 9 10
CURSIVE ALPHABET
Aa Bb Cc Dd Ee Ff
Gg Hh Ii Jj Kk Ll
Mm Nn Oo Pp Qq Rr
Ss Tt Uu Vv Ww Xx
Yy Zz 1 2 3 4 5 6 7 8 9 10

Source: From *Sample Manuscript Alphabet, Grade 3* and *Sample Cursive Alphabet, Grade 3*, 1958, Columbus, OH: Zaner-Bloser. Used by permission.

Cursive Writing

In **cursive writing** (sometimes called *script*), the letters are connected. The transfer to cursive writing is typically made somewhere in the third grade, although schools teach cursive writing as late as fifth grade. In an earlier era, writing instruction emphasized the flourishes of cursive writing, but today the goal is to teach functional handwriting. Cursive writing has certain advantages: (1) it minimizes spatial judgment problems for the student and (2) it has a rhythmic continuity and wholeness that are missing from manuscript writing. In addition, errors of reversals are virtually eliminated with cursive writing. However, many students with writing disabilities find it difficult to make the transfer to cursive writing after they have learned manuscript writing. Samples of cursive letters are shown in Figure 12.16.

Another handwriting form is the *D'Nealian* writing system (Hagin, 1983). This system helps students make the transition to cursive writing more easily. The D'Nealian system is a simplified cursive writing style in which manuscript letters have the basic forms of the corresponding cursive letters. Most of the manuscript letters are made with a continuous stroke that produces a kind of connected manuscript writing, and the student does not have to lift the pencil. Students with handwriting difficulties can more easily transfer from manuscript writing to this modified form of cursive writing.

The Left-Handed Student

Left-handed people encounter a special handwriting problem because their natural tendency is to write from right to left on the page. In writing from left to right, left-handers have difficulty seeing what they have written. Their hand covers up the writing and tends to smudge the writing as it moves over the paper. To avoid the smudging, some left-handed students begin "hooking" their hand when they start using pens.

Left-handedness today is accepted as natural. The student who has not yet stabilized handedness should be encouraged to write with the right hand. However, a student with a strong preference for the left hand should be permitted to write as a lefty, although this creates some special problems in writing and requires special instruction. Research shows that left-handers can learn to write just as quickly as right-handers. For manuscript writing, the paper should be placed directly in front of the left-handed student, without a slant. For cursive writing, the top of the paper should be slanted north–northeast, opposite to the slant used by the right-handed student. The pencil should be long, gripped about 1 in. from the tip, with the eraser pointing to the left shoulder. The position of the hand should be curved, with the weight resting on the outside of the little finger, and hooking should be avoided.

Many word-processing programs include adjustments to change the mouse to a left-handed clicking position.

Keyboarding or Typing Skills

The skills needed to use a computer keyboard are referred to as either **keyboarding** or *typing* skills. For students who have severe problems in handwriting, learning to use a word-processing program offers a very welcome and feasible solution to their handwriting problems. The motor skills required for keyboarding are easier than the motor skills required for cursive writing, and the output is certainly more legible for the reader. However, simply putting a student in front of a computer is not enough; it is essential to provide explicit and consistent instruction in keyboarding. Teaching students the correct finger positions is much better than allowing them to develop the bad habits of a hunt-and-peck method.

Learning to type is hard work and requires direct and regular instruction over an extended period of time, with ample opportunities for drill and practice. Sufficient time must be provided in the schedule for keyboarding instruction and for the student to practice the skills.

Good keyboarding software programs for students, such as Type to Learn (Sunburst at **http://www.sunburst.com**) and Mavis Beacon Teaches Typing (The Learning Company at **http://www.learningco.com**), are based on sound instructional principles. They begin by demonstrating how each new key should be pressed, showing a keyboard on the screen and demonstrating key strokes by highlighting specific keys. As students practice using the new keys, they receive feedback on their accuracy. There are frequent opportunities for practice, and the programs contain drills emphasizing both accuracy and speed. Good programs keep a running record of the students' proficiency level so that students can keep track of how fast they type (in words per min) and how many errors they make. Students also enjoy computer typing games.

TEACHING STRATEGIES

The balance of this chapter presents specific instructional strategies for teaching written language in the areas of: (1) writing strategies for the general education classroom, (2) written expression, (3) word processing, (4) spelling, and (5) handwriting.

WRITING STRATEGIES FOR THE GENERAL EDUCATION CLASSROOM

Many students with writing difficulties receive their writing instruction in the general education classroom. "LD in Practice: Writing Strategies for the General Education Classroom" offers some writing strategies for the general education classroom teacher.

STRATEGIES FOR TEACHING WRITTEN EXPRESSION

Many students with learning difficulties reach upper elementary or secondary levels with little exposure to, and little experience with, written expression. Intense instruction to improve poor reading skills often overshadows instruction in writing. Learning to write requires abundant time and opportunities for various kinds of writing.

Principles for Instruction in the Writing Process

The following principles guide the teaching of writing:

1. *Provide opportunities for extensive writing.* Student writers need sufficient time to think, reflect, write, and rewrite. The fact is that many students with writing difficulties spend less than 10 min per day composing. It is recommended that composing time be extended to 50 min each day, 4 days each week. Break the writing time into several smaller segments for some students.

2. *Establish a writing environment.* The atmosphere of the writing classroom should foster writing activities and encourage cooperative writing work. Teachers can also use individual writing folders containing the students' current writing projects, a list of finished pieces, ideas for future topics, and writing assistance materials, such as individual spelling dictionaries. Keep materials and books in one place, so students can begin their writing without having to request teacher assistance.

3. *Allow students to select their own topics.* Writing projects are most successful when students have a personal interest in the subject. If they need more information, reading and other source materials should be readily available.

4. *Model the writing process and thinking aloud.* The act of writing is encouraged when teachers and peers model the cognitive processes involved in writing. For example, the teacher could model the writing stages by thinking aloud: "I want to plan a mysterious setting for my story. What about a haunted house? Next, I must decide on the characters in this story . . ." (Graham & Harris, 1997).

5. *Develop a sense of audience.* In the traditional writing curriculum, students write for the teacher and think they must match the teacher's

LD IN PRACTICE

WRITING STRATEGIES FOR THE GENERAL EDUCATION CLASSROOM

Written Expression

- Allocate sufficient time for writing. Students learn to write by writing; therefore, have students write four times per week.
- Encourage students in the primary grades to use invented spelling.
- Use brainstorming to create ideas about writing topics.
- Give students a range of writing tasks. Creative writing is personal writing, while functional writing conveys information about a subject.
- Teach students the stages of the writing process: prewriting, drafting, revising, sharing.
- Use a graphic organizer, such as Inspiration, to plan a story.
- Use a presentation program, such as PowerPoint, to develop a story.
- Use the Internet to conduct research on a topic.

Spelling

- Limit the number of spelling words to be learned at one time.
- Analyze the phonemes of new words.
- Point out the syllables in multisyllabic words.
- Teach word families (e.g., *at, sat, rat, mat*).
- Provide periodic retesting and review.
- Use multisensory strategies (e.g., see the word, say the word, write the word in the air, see the word in your mind's eye, write the word on paper, and compare the word to the model).

Handwriting

- Begin with manuscript writing and explain that it consists of lines and circles.
- The teacher says the name of the letter to be written.
- Have the students trace the letter with their finger.
- Use dotted lines for a letter and have the students trace the dots with a pencil.
- The teacher gives stroke directions to the students (e.g., first we go down, then we go up).
- Have the students copy a letter (or word) on paper while looking at a model.
- The students write the letter from memory while saying the name of the letter.

standards of correctness. Expand the students' sense of audience by having them engage in peer collaboration, consulting, group sharing, and publication. Provide opportunities to discuss the writing progress with peers who are not writing experts. When the writing projects are finished, students can read their material to an audience of peers and discuss their work.

6. *Transfer ownership and control of the writing to the students.* A goal of the writing process is to transfer ownership and control to the writer. As the students learn to internalize the strategies that are being taught, they should gradually take more responsibility for their writing and be able to work without teacher direction.

7. *Capitalize on students' interests.* Teachers should be aware of students' interests and be alert for relevant events that can become the subject for writing. Interests in sports, school, local and national news, trips, family vacations, or holidays offer subjects for writing. One teacher found that trolls (the little dolls with the homely, elf-like features and colorful hair) were reemerging as a popular toy. So many students were bringing them to school that the teacher had to limit students to one troll guest a day. Capitalizing on their interest, the teacher had students design their own trolls in drawings and write stories telling why the manufacturer should adopt their troll designs.

8. *Avoid punitive grading.* Do not allow grading practices to discourage students. Consider grading only ideas, not the technical form, for some assignments, or give two grades—one for ideas and one for technical skills. If a student makes errors in many areas, you might correct only one skill, such as capitalization. When the student masters that skill, you can concentrate on another area.

9. *Differentiate between creative and functional writing.* *Creative* and *functional* writing lessons have different goals, and students should understand that different skills are required for each. In creative writing, the goal is to develop ideas and express them in written form, and there is less need for technical perfection. In contrast, a goal of functional writing is to learn the form of the output. The final product, such as a business letter, requires the writer to adhere to certain standards and structure. By separating these two goals, one can develop different kinds of writing skills for each.

10. *Provide abundant input.* Students need something to write about. Before asking students to write, make sure that they have had enough firsthand experiences, such as trips, creative activities, or watching television shows, movies, or sports events, that can be drawn upon for writing material. Talking about the experiences is also helpful.

11. *Schedule frequent writing.* Students need frequent writing experiences to develop skills in writing. An assignment to write a certain

number of pages per week in a personal journal that will not be corrected (or even read) by the teacher is an excellent technique for providing necessary practice and improving the quality of writing.

12. *Use the cloze procedure.*   The *cloze procedure* (discussed in the chapter on reading) can also be used to teach written expression. Write a sentence with a word deleted and have the students try to insert as many different words as possible. For example, "John _____ the ball." Sentences can be taken from reading material.

13. *Combine sentences.*   This approach to teaching written expression is especially useful for adolescents and adults. The teacher writes several separate kernel sentences. The students must combine those sentences into a more complex sentence by adding clauses and connectors.

STRATEGIES FOR USING WORD PROCESSING

The following list provides some suggested activities for using computer word processing to teach writing:

1. *Expanding vocabulary.*   Using a word-processing program, write a sentence or short paragraph on the computer. Use the computer thesaurus to find synonyms for several words.

2. *Learning story sequence.*   Place several sentences about a series of events in incorrect order. Have the students use the "cut" and "paste" functions to put them in the proper sequence.

3. *Beginning a story.*   Put the beginning of a story on a disk and have each student continue the narrative. Each student's story can be compared with others. In another variation, begin a story on a disk and then have one student write the next segment, another student write the following segment, and so on.

4. *Keeping an electronic diary or journal.*   Keeping a journal of daily events has proved to be an effective technique for improving reading and writing skills. Instead of writing on paper, the student can use a computer with word-processing software.

5. *Sending e-mail.*   Students can use e-mail to send personal, semipersonal, and class messages. The messages can be sent between students in the class, between the teacher and the students, or between the students and students in other classes throughout the world.

6. *Writing book reports.*   To make writing a book report on the computer easier, develop a template with key topics, such as title of the book, author, type of book, summary, and the student's name. To write the book report, the student loads the template and fills out the information next to each topic.

7. *Writing a class newsletter.*   A newsletter can be written with any word-processing program. Several commercial programs allow users to

write, illustrate, paste up, and print pages that resemble a newspaper or newsletter. Microsoft Word allows users to move two columns. Another program is the Children's Writing and Publishing Center by the Learning Company, at **http://www.broderbund.com.**

8. *Using graphics.*   Graphics can easily be added to many of the previously mentioned activities. Graphics can be found on Internet sites or photos can be taken with a digital camera. Art clips often come with word-processing software programs, or they can be purchased separately on disks. Graphics can be scanned in with a scanner or students can create their own art graphics.

9. *Expanding the writing process to the web.*   Students who have access to the Internet can find a wealth of information (such as text, pictures, photographs, and charts) about a topic of their interest. Topics such as dinosaurs, baseball, sports figures, or the history of Canada can be investigated through a search engine. With material gathered from their searches, the students can develop stories and reports or develop web pages to show their reports to others.

STRATEGIES FOR TEACHING SPELLING

The following list provides strategies for teaching spelling:

1. *Auditory perception and memory of letter sounds.*   Provide practice in auditory perception of letter sounds, strengthen knowledge of phonics and structural analysis, and develop skills in applying phonic generalizations. (See the chapter on oral language for specific techniques.)

2. *Visual memory of words.*   Help the students strengthen visual memory so that the visual image of a word can be retained. Materials should be clear and concise, and the students should be helped to focus attention on the activity. Flash cards and computer spelling software can also be used to develop speed and strengthen memory. (See the chapter on young children with learning disabilities for specific methods to develop visual perception and memory.)

3. *Multisensory methods in spelling.*   Students who are told to study spelling lessons are frequently at a loss as to what to do. The following is a multisensory approach that engages the visual, auditory, kinesthetic, and tactile senses:

    a. *Meaning and pronunciation.*   Have the students look at the word, pronounce it correctly, and use it in a sentence.

    b. *Imagery.*   Ask students to "see" the word and say it. Have them say each syllable of the word, say the word syllable by syllable, spell the word orally, and then use one finger to trace the word, either in the air or by touching the word itself.

c. *Recall.* Ask students to look at the word and then close their eyes and see it in their mind's eye. Have them spell the word orally. Then ask them to open their eyes and look at the word to see if they were correct. (If they make an error, they should repeat the process.)

d. *Writing the word.* Ask the students to write the word correctly from memory, check the spelling against the original, and then check the writing to make sure every letter is legible.

e. *Mastery.* Have the students cover the word and write it. If they are correct, they should cover and write it two more times.

4. *The Fernald Method.* This method (Fernald, 1943/1988) is a multi-sensory approach, and it is used to teach reading and writing as well as spelling. Very briefly, it consists of the following steps:

a. Students are told that they are going to learn words in a new way that has proved to be very successful. They are encouraged to select a word that they wish to learn.

b. The teacher writes that word on a piece of 4 in. by 10 in. paper, as the students watch and as the teacher says the word.

c. The students trace the word, saying it several times, and then write it on a separate piece of paper while saying the word.

d. The students write the word from memory without looking at the original copy. If the word is incorrect, students repeat Step C. If the word is correct, it is put in a file box. The words in the file box are used later in writing stories.

e. At later stages, this painstaking tracing method for learning words is not needed. Students learn a word by *looking* as the teacher writes it, *saying* it, and *writing* it. At a still later stage, the students can learn by only looking at a word in print and writing it. Finally, they learn by merely looking at the word.

5. *The "test-study-test" versus the "study-test" methods.* There are two common approaches to teaching spelling in the classroom: the "test-study-test" and the "study-test" plans. The test-study-test method uses a pretest, which is usually given at the beginning of the week. The students then study only those words that were missed on the pretest. This method is better for older students who have fairly good spelling abilities because they do not need to study words they already know. The study-test method is better for young students and for those with poor spelling abilities who would miss too many words on a pretest. The study-test method permits them to study a few well-selected words before the test is given.

6. *Listening centers, audiotapes, and CDs.* Spelling lessons can easily be put on audiotapes or CDs. After students have advanced to a level

that enables them to work by themselves, they can complete their spelling lessons in a listening laboratory. Earphones allow for individualized instruction and help many students to block out distracting auditory stimuli.

7. *Electronic spellers and computer spell-checkers.* Students should learn how to use these spelling devices as an aid in spelling.

The following list of activities are representative of useful methods for teaching handwriting:

1. *Chalkboard activities.* These activities provide practice before writing instruction is begun. Circles, lines, geometric shapes, letters, and numbers can be made with large, free movements using the muscles of the shoulders, arms, hands, and fingers. (For additional suggestions, see the chapter on young children with learning disabilities.)

2. *Other materials for writing-movement practice.* Finger painting or writing in a clay pan or a sand tray gives the students practice in writing movements. Put a layer of sand, cornmeal, salt, or nondrying clay on a cookie sheet. Use commercial or homemade finger paints for the painting practice. Students use one finger or a pointed stick to practice writing shapes, forms, letters, and numbers. A small, wet sponge can be used to draw shapes on a chalkboard.

3. *Position.* Have the students prepare for writing by sitting in comfortable chairs at a table that is at the proper height. Be sure the students' feet are flat on the floor and both forearms are on the writing surface. Each student's nonwriting hand should hold the paper at the top. Have students stand and work at a chalkboard for the initial writing activities.

4. *Paper.* For manuscript writing, the paper should be placed without a slant, parallel with the lower edge of the desk. For cursive writing, the paper is tilted at an angle—approximately 60 degrees from vertical—to the left for right-handed students and to the right for left-handed students. To help the student remember the correct slant, place a strip of tape parallel to the top of the paper at the top of the desk. It may be necessary to attach the paper to the desk with masking tape to keep it from sliding.

5. *Holding the pencil.* Many students with writing disorders do not know how or are unable to hold a pencil properly between their thumb and middle finger, with the index finger riding the pencil. They should grasp the pencil above the sharpened point. A piece of tape or a rubber band placed around the pencil can help the student hold it at the right place.

If a student has difficulty grasping the pencil, the pencil can be put through a practice golf ball (the kind with many holes). Have the student place the middle finger and thumb around the ball to practice the right grip. Large, primary-size pencils, large crayons, and felt-tip pens are useful for the beginning stages of writing. Clay might also be placed around the pencil to help the student grasp it. Short pencils should be avoided because it is impossible to grip them correctly.

6. *Stencils and templates.* Make cardboard or plastic stencils of geometric forms, letters, and numbers. Have the students trace the form with one finger, a pencil, or a crayon. (Clip the stencil to the paper to prevent it from moving.) Then remove the stencil and reveal the figure that has been made. The stencil can be cut so that the hole creates the shape or, in reverse, so that the outer edges of the stencil create the shape.

7. *Tracing.* Make heavy black figures on white paper and clip a sheet of onionskin or transparent paper over the letters. Have the students trace the forms and letters. Start with diagonal lines and circles, then horizontal and vertical lines, geometric shapes, and finally, letters and numbers. The students may also trace a black letter on paper with a crayon or felt-tip pen or they may use a transparent sheet. Another idea is to put letters on transparencies and project the images onto a chalkboard or a large sheet of paper. Students can then trace over the images.

8. *Drawing between the lines.* Have the students practice making "roads" between double lines in a variety of widths and shapes. Then ask the students to write letters by going between the double lines of outlined letters. Use arrows and numbers to show the direction and sequence of the lines.

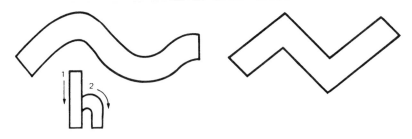

9. *Dot-to-dot.* Draw a complete figure and then draw an outline of the same figure by using dots. Ask the students to make the figure by connecting the dots.

10. **Tracing with reducing cues.** Write a complete letter or word and have the students trace it. Then write the first part of the letter or word and have the students trace your part and then complete the letter or word. Finally, reduce the cue to only the upstroke and have the students write the entire letter or word.

11. **Lined paper.** Begin by having students use unlined paper. Later, have them use paper with wide lines to help them determine the placement of letters. It may be helpful to use specially lined paper that is color cued to aid in letter placement. Regular lined paper can also be color cued to help students make letters.

12. **Template lines.** For students who need additional help in stopping at lines, tape can be placed at bottom and top lines. Windows can be cut out of cardboard to give further guidance for spacing letters. The following figure shows a template made from a piece of cardboard with three windows for one-line, two-line, and three-line letters. One-line letters are those that fit in a single-line space: *a, c, e, i, m, n*. Two-line letters are those with ascenders only: *b, d, h, k, l, t*. Three-line letters are those with descenders: *f, g, j, p, q, z, y*.

13. **Letter difficulty.** In terms of ease, cursive letters are introduced in the following order: beginning letters—*m, n, t, i, u, w, r, s, l*, and *e*; more difficult letters—*x, z, y, j, p, h, b, k, f, g*, and *q*; and combinations of letters—*me, be, go, it, no*, and so forth.

14. *Verbal cues.* Students are helped in the motor act of writing by hearing the directions for forming letters—for example, "down-up-and-around." When using this technique, teachers must take care not to distract the students with these verbal instructions.

15. *Words and sentences.* After the students learn to write single letters, instruction should proceed to writing words and sentences. Spacing, size, and slant are additional factors to consider at this stage.

CHAPTER SUMMARY

1. This chapter examined theories and teaching strategies for three areas of written language: written expression, spelling, and handwriting.

2. Written expression is considered the most complex and difficult language skill to achieve and the most common communication disability.

3. The writing process consists of the stages of prewriting, drafting, revising, and sharing with an audience. Emphasis in instruction should be on the process rather than on the product.

4. Strategies for writing include using written conversations, personal journals, patterned writing, and graphic organizers.

5. Word processors offer an excellent means of teaching writing because they integrate all the language systems.

6. Spelling is particularly difficult in English because of the irregularity between the spoken and written forms of the language. Children go through several distinct stages of spelling development. Their rates of progression differ, but they all pass through the stages in order.

7. Invented spelling is the beginning writer's attempt to write words and should be encouraged. These spellings are developmental approximations of the correct spellings.

8. Handwriting is a fine-motor skill that causes difficulty for many individuals with learning disabilities. Special consideration must be given to teaching manuscript writing and cursive writing and to instructing the left-handed student. Many students with handwriting difficulties are helped by using computers and word processors. It is important to teach students typing or keyboarding skills.

9. Specific teaching strategies are described for writing, word processing, spelling, and handwriting.

1. What are the differences between instruction that focuses on the written *product* and instruction that focuses on the writing *process*?

2. Describe the stages of the writing process.

3. How can graphic organizers help students with learning disabilities write?

4. Discuss the advantages of computer word processing for writing.

5. What is invented spelling? Do you think it should be encouraged? Why or why not?

6. Discuss how the characteristics of learning disabilities affect the writing of students with learning disabilities in written expression, spelling, and handwriting.

KEY TERMS

cursive writing *(p. 461)*

drafting *(p. 436)*

dysgraphia *(p. 458)*

graphic organizers *(p. 441)*

invented spelling *(p. 451)*

keyboarding *(p. 462)*

manuscript writing *(p. 459)*

prewriting *(p. 435)*

revising *(p. 436)*

sharing with an audience *(p. 437)*

word-frequency approach to spelling *(p. 455)*

word-pattern approach to spelling *(p. 455)*

word processing *(p. 442)*

writing process *(p. 435)*

13 Mathematics

CHAPTER OUTLINE

> **If you can't explain it simply, you don't understand it well enough.**
>
> —*Albert Einstein*

Some individuals with learning disabilities do well in language and reading, but their nemesis is mathematics and quantitative learning. Two mathematics problem areas for students with learning disabilities are identified in IDEA–2004 (PL 108–446): (1) mathematics calculation and (2) mathematics reasoning. Difficulties in either of these areas can interfere with achievement in school and with success in later life.

In the Theories section of this chapter, we examine: (1) mathematics disabilities, (2) early number concepts and number sense, (3) characteristics of mathematics disabilities, (4) mathematics disabilities at the secondary level, (5) mathematics standards, (6) learning theories for mathematics instruction, and (7) assessing mathematics ability. In the Teaching Strategies section, we discuss: (1) mathematics strategies for the general education classroom, (2) the mathematics curriculum, (3) principles of instruction for students with mathematics disabilities, (4) activities for teaching mathematics, and (5) using technology for mathematics instruction.

THEORIES

We live in a mathematical world. When students think about the scores of their favorite baseball team, compare player standings, plan to purchase a CD, or pay for a movie ticket, they rely on mathematical concepts. When adults plan their budget, balance a checkbook, or use a spreadsheet, they are using mathematics. The level of mathematical thinking and problem solving needed in the workplace and in day-to-day living has increased dramatically (National Council of Teachers of Mathematics, 2000).

Mathematics is a symbolic language that enables human beings to think about, record, and communicate ideas concerning the elements and relationships of quantity. It is also a universal language; it has meaning for all cultures and civilizations. In every culture, social class, and ethnic group, children live in a natural environment that is rich in quantitative information and events. Human beings in all cultures, language groups, social classes, and ethnic groups think about, record, and communicate ideas through quantity. Children in some cultures count blocks; children in other cultures count stones.

MATHEMATICS DISABILITIES

Many students have difficulty in acquiring and using mathematics skills. About 6% to 7% of the students in general education classes show evidence of a serious mathematics difficulty. Approximately 26% of students with learning disabilities exhibit problems in the area of mathematics. Over 50% of students with disabilities have mathematics goals written into their individualized education programs (IEPs) (Cass, Cates, Smith, & Jackson, 2003).

Mathematics difficulties that emerge in elementary school often continue through the secondary school years. Not only is a mathematics disability a debilitating problem for individuals during school years, but, as noted previously, it also continues to impair them in their daily lives as adults (Cass et al., 2003; Miller & Mercer, 1997; Shalev et al., 1998).

The term *dyscalculia* is a medically oriented term that describes a severe disability in mathematics. An analogous term in reading is *dyslexia,* which is a severe reading disability with medical connotations. **Dyscalculia** is described as a specific disturbance in learning mathematical concepts and computation associated with a neurological, central nervous system dysfunction. Without direct intervention, dyscalculia persists. Almost one half of the children who were identified with dyscalculia in the fourth grade were still classified as having dyscalculia 3 years later (Shalev et al., 1998).

It should be stressed that not all students with learning disabilities encounter difficulty with number concepts. In fact, some individuals with severe reading disabilities do well in mathematics and exhibit a strong aptitude in quantitative thinking.

The identification and treatment of mathematics disabilities has received much less attention than problems associated with reading disabilities (Cass et al., 2003). The mathematics curriculum in most general education classrooms does not pay sufficient attention to learning differences in mathematics among students. The general education mathematics curriculum does not allot enough time for instruction, for guided practice, or for practical applications. In addition, mathematical concepts are introduced at too rapid a rate. If students do not have sufficient time to fully grasp a mathematical concept and to practice it before another mathematical concept is introduced, they feel overwhelmed and become confused (Cawley & Foley, 2001; Butler, Miller, Crehan, Babbitt, & Pierce, 2003).

EARLY NUMBER CONCEPTS AND NUMBER SENSE

For some children, difficulties with number sense begin at an early age. The ability to count, match, sort, compare, and understand one-to-one correspondence hinges on the child's experience in manipulating objects. A child with unstable perceptual skills, attention problems, or difficulties in motor development may have insufficient experiences with the activities of manipulation that pave the way for understanding quantity, space, order, time, or distance.

When expected to perform mathematics assignments, some children have not yet acquired the needed early skills for mathematics learning. If these children are introduced to a number concept before they have the necessary prerequisite experiences, they will not understand, and they will be confused. Learning mathematics is a sequential process, and children must acquire skills at an earlier stage before going on to the next stage. **Early number learning** includes: (1) spatial relationships, (2) visual–motor and visual–perception skills, and (3) concepts of time and direction.

Spatial Relationships

Typically, young children learn by playing with objects, such as pots and pans, boxes that fit into each other, and objects that can be put into containers. These play activities help develop a sense of space, sequence, and order. Parents of children with mathematics disabilities often report that their child did not enjoy or play with blocks, puzzles, models, or construction-type toys as preschoolers. These children may have missed these early number-learning experiences.

Many concepts of **spatial relationships** are normally acquired at the preschool age. Children destined to have mathematics disabilities are baffled by such concepts as *up–down, over–under, top–bottom, high–low, near–far, front–back, beginning–end,* and *across.* The child may be unable to perceive distances between numbers on number lines or rulers and may not know whether the number 3 is closer to 4 or to 6.

Visual–Motor and Visual–Perception Abilities

Children with mathematics disabilities may have difficulty with activities requiring visual–motor and visual–perception abilities. Some may be unable to count objects in a series by pointing to each of them and saying, "One, two, three, four, five." These children must first learn to count by physically grasping and manipulating objects.

Some children are unable to see objects in groups (or sets)—an ability needed to identify the number of objects quickly. Even when adding a group of three with a group of four, some children with mathematics disabilities persist in counting the objects starting with the number 1 to determine the total number in the groups instead of using the *counting on* strategy. With the *counting on* strategy, children learn to add on to the number of the larger group (Bley & Thornton, 2001; Van de Walle, 2004).

The inability to visually perceive a geometric shape as a complete and integrated entity is a visual–perception problem. A square may not appear as a square shape, but rather as four unrelated lines.

Other children have difficulty in learning to perceive number symbols visually. They might confuse the vertical strokes of the number 1 and the number 4, or they may confuse the upper half of the number 2 with portions of the number 3.

Some children with poor mathematics abilities do poorly in visual–motor tasks. Because of their difficulty in perceiving shapes, recognizing spatial relationships, and making spatial judgments, they are unable to copy geometric forms, shapes, numbers, or letters. These children are likely to perform poorly in handwriting, as well as in arithmetic. When children cannot write numbers easily, they cannot properly align the numbers that they write, which leads to computation errors (Bley & Thornton, 2001).

Concepts of Time and Direction

Basic concepts of time are typically acquired during the preschool years. For example, a 4 year old counted the time until his grandmother would come to visit in terms of "sleeps" (e.g., Grandma will be here after three sleeps). Expressions such as "10 minutes ago," "in a half hour," and "later" are usually part of the preschooler's understanding and speaking vocabulary. By the end of first grade, students are expected to tell time to the half hour, and by the middle grades to the nearest minute. Many students with mathematics disabilities have a poor sense of time and direction. They become lost easily and cannot find their way to a friend's house or to their own home from school. They sometimes forget whether it is morning or afternoon and may even go home during the recess period, thinking the school day has ended. Because they have difficulty estimating the time span of an hour, a minute, several hours, or a week, they cannot estimate how long a task will take. They may not be able to judge and allocate the time needed to complete an assignment.

CHARACTERISTICS OF MATHEMATICS DISABILITIES Each student who encounters difficulties in mathematics is unique; not all exhibit the same traits. Nevertheless, a number of characteristics of learning disabilities affect quantitative learning. In this section we discuss some characteristics of mathematics disabilities, such as: (1) information-processing difficulties, (2) language and reading abilities, and (3) math anxiety.

Information-Processing Difficulties

Many of the elements of information processing are linked to mathematics disabilities, such as paying attention, visual–spatial processing, auditory processing, memory and retrieval, and motor skills (Wilson & Swanson, 2001). Table 13.1 shows how problems with elements of information processing affect mathematics performance.

TABLE 13.1

Information-Processing
Factors and Problems in
Mathematics Performance

Information-processing factors	How problems in information processing affect mathematics performance
Attention	■ Difficulty maintaining attention to do steps in algorithms or problem solving ■ Difficulty in sustaining attention during instruction
Visual–spatial processing	■ Loses place on the worksheet ■ Difficulty seeing differences between numbers, coins, or operation symbols ■ Problems in writing across the paper in a straight line ■ Problems with direction: up–down, left–right, aligning numbers ■ Difficulty using a number line
Auditory processing	■ Difficulty doing oral drills ■ Problems in "counting on" from within a sequence
Memory and retrieval	■ Cannot remember math facts ■ Forgets steps when doing a problem ■ Difficulty telling time ■ Forgets multiple-step word problems
Motor problems	■ Writes numbers illegibly, slowly, and inaccurately ■ Difficulty in writing numbers in small spaces

Source: The ideas for this table were suggested by S. Miller and C. Mercer, "Educational Aspects of Mathematics Disabilities," 1997, *Journal of Learning Disabilities, 30*(1), p. 50. Copyright 1997 by PRO-ED, Inc. Reprinted with permission.

Language and Reading Abilities

Early concepts of quantity are evidenced by the child's use of language, such as *all gone, that's all, more, big,* and *little.* Although some children with mathematics disabilities have superior verbal language skills and may even be excellent readers, for many children the mathematics disability is compounded by oral language and reading deficiencies. Their language problems may cause them to confuse mathematics terms, such as *plus, take away, minus, carrying, borrowing,* and *place value.* Mathematics word problems are particularly difficult for students with reading disabilities. If they are unable to read or do not understand the underlying language structure of the mathematics problem, they cannot plan and perform the tasks required to solve the problem (Bley & Thornton, 2001).

LD IN PRACTICE
GUIDELINES FOR DEALING WITH MATH ANXIETY

1. *Use competition carefully.* Have students compete with themselves rather than with others in the class or school. In a competitive situation, make sure that students have a good chance of succeeding.

2. *Use clear instructions.* Make sure that students understand what they are to do in math assignments. Ask students to work sample problems and be sure that they understand the assignment. When doing a new math procedure, give students plenty of practice and examples or models to show how the work is done.

3. *Avoid unnecessary time pressures.* Give students ample time to complete math assignments in the class period. Give occasional take-home tests. If necessary, reduce the number of problems to be completed.

4. *Try to remove pressure from test-taking situations.* Teach students test-taking strategies. Give practice tests. Make sure that the test format is clear and that students are familiar with the format. For example, a student may be familiar with the problem in the following format:

$$\begin{array}{r} 7 \\ +8 \\ \hline \end{array}$$

The same child may be unfamiliar with a test format that presents the same problem in a different form:

$$7 + 8 =$$

Math Anxiety

Math anxiety, an emotion-based reaction to mathematics, causes individuals to freeze up when they confront math problems or when they take math tests. The anxiety may stem from the fear of school failure and the loss of self-esteem. Anxiety has many repercussions. It can block the school performance of students with mathematics disabilities by making it difficult for them to initially learn the mathematics, it impedes their ability to use or transfer the mathematics knowledge they do have, and it becomes an obstacle when they try to demonstrate their knowledge on tests (Barkley, 1998; Slavin, 2000).

Many students and adults with learning disabilities report that anxiety is a constant companion. One individual said that she sprinkled anxiety wherever she went, making calm people nervous and nervous people fall apart. She described her feelings: "I couldn't get out the right words. I trembled, and my insides writhed" (Smith, 1991). Some guidelines for dealing with math anxiety are given in the "LD in Practice: Guidelines for Dealing With Math Anxiety."

MATHEMATICS DISABILITIES AT THE SECONDARY LEVEL

For students in junior and senior high school, the mathematics disabilities differ from those at the elementary level. The secondary mathematics curriculum becomes increasingly more sophisticated and abstract because it is based on the presumption that the basic skills have been learned. The increased mathematics requirements at the high school level and the pressure of more testing are likely to adversely affect students with mathematics disabilities (Deshler et al., 2001).

The states are increasing their high school mathematics requirements for graduation. High school graduation is contingent upon passing mathematics courses, such as algebra, that previously were required only of students in a college preparatory curriculum. Many states now include algebra as a graduation requirement for all students (National Council of Teachers of Mathematics, 2000; Witzel, Mercer, & Miller, 2003).

Many secondary students with mathematics disabilities do succeed in advanced mathematics courses, but others shy away from algebra, geometry, statistics, and calculus. In the past, students with learning disabilities who faced mathematics disabilities were advised to continue remedial or basic mathematics courses. However, because algebra is required for a high school diploma, we must consider how best to prepare students with mathematics disabilities to learn algebra.

Common mathematics difficulties at the secondary level include basic operations (including fractions), decimals and percentages, fraction terminology, multiplication of whole numbers, place value, measurement skills, and division (Cass, et al., 2003). Adolescents with learning disabilities continue to have memory deficits that interfere with the automatic learning of computation facts. Adolescents who have such difficulty appreciate techniques that will help them learn and remember calculation facts. Students with severe problems in mathematics need direct instruction, with emphasis on learning basic skills to help them acquire functional abilities for successful living.

Many students with learning disabilities can succeed in advanced mathematics courses. They need these courses because a large number will be going on to postsecondary education and college, and many will enter professions, such as engineering or computer science, that require competencies in advanced mathematics.

Effective instructional strategies in mathematics for secondary students include the following (Cass et al., 2003; Witzel et al., 2003):

- *Provide many examples.* Students need to have many examples that illustrate the concept being taught. Teachers often provide too few examples.

- *Provide practice in discriminating various problem types.* Secondary students with mathematics disabilities have problems with discrimination. They ignore the operation sign and add instead of subtract. Once a skill is learned, the mathematics problem should be placed with different problems so that the student will learn to discriminate and generalize.

- *Provide explicit instruction.* Students with mathematics disabilities need direct instruction that is organized with step-by-step presentations.

High Standards and Annual Testing

Federal and state governments now require the establishment of high mathematics standards and annual testing that uses those standards as a measure. Under the No Child Left Behind Act of 2002, schools are accountable for results and are punished or rewarded on the basis of students' test results. The scores that students receive on these mathematics tests affect high-stakes decisions, such as whether they will be promoted to the next grade or will receive a high school diploma. Garrison Keillor, the satirist, describes Lake Wobegon, where "all the women are strong, all the men are good looking, and all the children are above average." Schools in high socioeconomic areas tend to have students who do well under this mathematics approach, while schools in poor areas struggle to have their students perform at the designated levels.

Students with mathematics disabilities, in general, do not fare well under this approach to mathematics education without special considerations and accommodations (Witzel et al., 2003; Ysseldyke, Thurlow, Bielinski, House, & Moody, 2001).

Mathematics Principles and Standards From the National Council of Teachers of Mathematics

The National Council of Teachers of Mathematics (NCTM, 2000) updated its principles and standards for teaching mathematics in its 2000 report. The complete NCTM report can be viewed at **http://www.nctm.org.** We provide a brief overview of: (1) mathematics *principles* and (2) mathematics *standards* identified in this report because they have significance for students with mathematics disabilities.

NCTM Principles NCTM established six principles for school mathematics, as shown in Table 13.2.

NCTM Standards The NCTM established standards for school mathematics in Grades prekindergarten to 12. The standards include numbers and operations, algebra, geometry, measurement, data analysis and probability, problem solving, and reasoning and proof. Each standard consists of

TABLE 13.2	NCTM Principles	Description
NCTM Principles for School Mathematics	1. Equity	The school system should require high mathematics expectations and strong support for all students.
	2. Curriculum	The overall curriculum must be coherent, focused on important mathematics elements, and well articulated across the grades.
	3. Teaching	Teachers should understand what students know and need to learn. Teachers should challenge and support students to learn well.
	4. Learning	Students must learn mathematics with understanding, actively building new knowledge from experience and prior knowledge.
	5. Assessment	Tests should support learning and furnish useful information to both teachers and students.
	6. Technology	Computer technology is essential in teaching mathematics, in influencing the mathematics that is taught, and in enhancing student learning.

Source: Adapted from *Principles and Standards for School Mathematics.* Copyright 2000 by the National Council for Teachers of Mathematics. All rights reserved. Standards listed with the permission of the National Council of Teachers of Mathematics (NCTM). NCTM does not endorse the content or validity of these alignments.

several specific goals that apply across all the grades. An overview of these standards is shown in Table 13.3.

Special educators note that the NCTM principles and standards are for all students. It is important to learn how to implement these goals for students with learning disabilities, especially in general education classroom settings (Jones & Southern, 2003; Miller & Mercer, 1997).

LEARNING THEORIES FOR MATHEMATICS INSTRUCTION

Learning mathematics should be an active process that involves doing. Use of hands-on learning materials allows students to explore ideas for themselves. Manipulative materials enable students to see, to touch, and to move objects. As students become actively involved in mathematics, they should be encouraged to use mathematics for solving real-life problems. Active involvement is illustrated in "LD Stories: Active Involvement in Mathematics." This active view of mathematics learning is epitomized in the following Chinese proverb:

"I hear and I forget. I see and I remember. I do and I understand."

Progression From Concrete Learning to Abstract Learning

The learning of mathematics is a gradual process. It is not a matter of either knowing it or not knowing it. Instead, the learning of mathematics follows

TABLE 13.3

NCTM Standards for
School Mathematics

NCTM standards	NCTM goals
Numbers and operations	■ Understand numbers, ways of presenting numbers, relationships among numbers, and number systems ■ Understand meaning of operations and how they relate to one another ■ Compute fluently and make reasonable estimates
Algebra	■ Understand patterns, relations, and functions ■ Represent and analyze mathematical situations and structures using algebraic symbols ■ Use mathematical models to represent and understand quantitative relationships ■ Analyze change in various contexts
Geometry	■ Analyze characteristics and properties of two- and three-dimensional geometric relationships ■ Specify locations and describe spatial relationships using coordinate geometry and other representational systems ■ Apply transformations and use symmetry to analyze mathematical situations ■ Use visualization, spatial reasoning, and geometric modeling to solve problems
Measurement	■ Understand measurable attributes of objects and the units, systems, and processes of measurement ■ Apply appropriate techniques, tools, and formulas to determine measurements
Data analysis and probability	■ Formulate questions that can be addressed with data and collect, organize, and display relevant data to answer them ■ Select and use appropriate statistical methods to analyze data ■ Develop and evaluate inferences and predictions that are based on data ■ Understand and apply basic concepts of probability
Problem solving	■ Build new mathematical knowledge through problem solving ■ Solve problems that arise in mathematics and in other contexts ■ Apply and adapt a variety of appropriate strategies to solve problems ■ Monitor and reflect on the process of mathematical problem solving
Reasoning and proof	■ Recognize reasoning and proof as fundamental aspects of mathematics ■ Make and investigate mathematical conjectures ■ Develop and evaluate mathematical arguments and proofs ■ Select and use various types of reasoning and methods of proof

ACTIVE INVOLVEMENT IN MATHEMATICS

The following example illustrates how a young child uses estimation skills.

■ Four-year-old Lee had just had his first experience sleeping overnight in a tent. Lee, his brother, and his grandparents erected a tent, in which they placed four sleeping bags for their overnight campout. When Lee excitedly described the experience to his parents the next day, they asked if they could come along next time. Lee did not answer immediately but spent some time considering the question. After estimating the space, he responded to his parents, "No, you cannot come with us because the tent is not big enough to hold two more sleeping bags."

■ The following problems show how young children construct solutions to subtraction problems (Lindquist, 1987).

Problem A: Jane had 8 trucks. She gave 3 to Ben. How many trucks does she have left?

Problem B: Jane has 8 trucks. Ben has 6 trucks. How many more trucks does Jane have than Ben?

In Problem A, a young child counts out eight trucks and gives three away. Then the child counts the trucks that are left. In Problem B, the child counts out eight trucks for Jane and a set of six trucks for Ben. The child then matches Jane's trucks to Ben's. Finally, the child counts to see how many more trucks Jane has than Ben. The child has constructed meaning and does not ask, "Should I add or subtract?"

a continuum that gradually increases in strength. As mathematics learning progresses, knowledge slowly builds from concrete to abstract learning, from incomplete to complete knowledge, and from unsystematic to systematic thinking.

To help students progress from concrete to abstract learning, three sequential levels of mathematics instruction are suggested (Cass et al., 2003; Miller & Mercer, 1997; Witzel et al., 2003):

1. *The concrete level.* At this level, students manipulate actual materials such as blocks, cubes, marbles, plastic pieces, poker chips, or place-value sticks. Students can physically touch, move, and manipulate these objects as they work out solutions to number problems.

2. *The semiconcrete level.* Once the students master the skill on the concrete level, instruction progresses to the semiconcrete or representational level. Students use pictures or tallies (i.e., marks on the paper) to represent the concrete objects as they work on mathematics problems.

3. *The abstract level.* At this level, students use only the numbers to solve mathematics problems without the help of semiconcrete pictures or tallies.

Direct Instruction of Mathematics

Direct instruction is a method of mathematics teaching that helps students achieve mastery of mathematics skills through instruction that is explicit, carefully structured, and planned. It is a comprehensive system that integrates curriculum design with teaching techniques to produce instructional programs in mathematics (Carnine, 1997; Swanson, 1999b). The sequential nature of mathematics makes the direct instruction approach particularly adaptable to the content of mathematics.

Mathematics programs based on direct instruction are highly organized and carefully sequenced. Instruction follows an ordered plan. Teachers determine the objectives of the teaching, plan the teaching through task analysis, provide explicit instruction, and plan for continuous testing (Fuchs & Fuchs, 2001a; Swanson, 1999b).

Direct instruction has been shown to be very effective for students with learning disabilities (Jones & Southern, 2003; Marchand-Marcella, Slocum, and Martella, 2004). Teachers who use direct instruction:

1. Break tasks into small steps
2. Administer probes to determine whether the students are learning
3. Supply immediate feedback
4. Provide diagrams and pictures to enhance student understanding
5. Give ample independent practice

Learning Strategies Instruction

Learning strategies instruction helps students with mathematics disabilities to acquire specific procedures for meeting the challenges of mathematics and to take control of their own mathematics learning (Deshler, 2003). Intervention practices that use learning strategy instruction are effective in increasing achievement (Swanson, 1991). Teachers who implement a learning strategies instruction model do the following (Deshler, 2003; Mainzer et al., 2003):

1. Provide elaborate explanations
2. Model learning processes
3. Provide prompts to use strategies
4. Engage in teacher–student dialogues
5. Ask processing questions

See the chapter on adolescents and adults with learning disabilities for more information about learning strategies instruction.

Problem Solving

Problem solving is identified as the top priority for the mathematics curriculum by the National Council of Teachers of Mathematics (NCTM, 2000). Moreover, problem solving is rapidly assuming a larger part of the curriculum in both general education and special education (Cawley & Foley, 2001; NCTM, 2000; Van de Walle, 2004). Mathematics problem solving involves the kind of thinking needed to work out mathematics word problems. In addition, a current view of mathematics expands the perspective of **problem solving** to the processes by which a student resolves unfamiliar situations. Implicit in the teaching of problem solving from this perspective are these underlying beliefs about mathematics: (1) there is no single way to do mathematics, (2) there is no single way to organize mathematics for instructional purposes, and (3) important mathematical concepts are actually learned through problem solving (Van de Walle, 2004).

An example of a problem-solving task is to ask students to think about the number 8 and to draw a picture of how the number 8 can be broken in two different amounts. Then ask the students to tell a story to go with their pictures (Van de Walle, 2004).

Problem solving is the most difficult area of mathematics for many students with mathematics disabilities. These students need extensive guidance and practice to learn to combine thinking and language with the calculation skills and concepts required to solve mathematics problems.

To solve mathematics problems, students must analyze and interpret information so that they can make selections and decisions. Problem solving requires that students know how to apply mathematics concepts and use computation skills in new or different settings (Cawley & Miller, 1989).

How do students go about solving problems in mathematics? Research shows that first and second graders readily invent their own ways to solve simple word problems. However, by the middle grades, they stop their personal problem-solving attempts and begin to rely on rote procedures they have learned in school. Middle-grade students tend to automatically compute with whatever numbers are in the problems.

Middle-grade students should be encouraged to continue to create and use their own ways to solve mathematics problems, as illustrated in "LD Stories: Encouraging a Problem-Solving Attitude." To encourage a problem-solving attitude, teachers should help structure the students' responses to problems by talking with them about those responses. Encouraging such a discussion raises the level of the students' answers. Teachers can help by listening to the students' thinking aloud about the word problems. It is also

ENCOURAGING A PROBLEM-SOLVING ATTITUDE

The following example of a word problem illustrates how teachers can encourage an inventive, problem-solving attitude (Lindquist, 1987).

Problem: Rebecca wants to sell 30 boxes of Girl Scout cookies. She has sold 25. How many more must she sell? The teacher asks if anyone can draw a picture to show this problem.

One student drew the following figure to solve this problem:

important to encourage the use of different strategies to solve mathematics problems and to ask students, "How did you get your answer?"

Many of the mathematics textbooks that are used in general education classrooms today use a problem-solving approach. Because problem solving is often difficult for students with learning disabilities, they need extensive guidance and practice to learn to combine thinking and language with the calculation skills and concepts required in mathematics problem solving. To solve mathematics problems, students must analyze and interpret information so that they can make selections and decisions.

Van de Walle (2004) recommends a three-step structure to teach mathematics problem-solving lessons, which appear in the following list and are illustrated in Figure 13.1:

1. *Getting ready.* First, students attend to the problem and translate the problem into their own experiences and language. The teacher makes sure they understand what is expected.

FIGURE 13.1

Structure for a
Problem-Solving Lesson

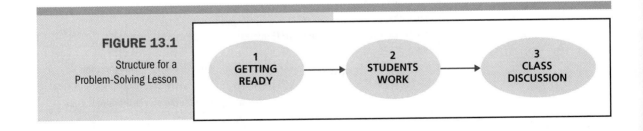

2. *Students work.* It is at this stage that students have a chance to work without constant guidance. The teacher lets go, listens carefully, and provides hints.

3. *Class discussion.* In the final step, there is a discussion of the solutions. The teacher accepts student solutions without evaluation. Students justify and evaluate their results and methods.

Some Problem-Solving Examples

1. Ask the students to view a pair of items: $5 - 2 = 3$ and $8 - 5 = 3$.

   Next, ask the students to explain how two different number combinations result in the same answer. For example, you arrived at the same answer because the answer represents the difference between the numbers in each combination (Cawley & Foley, 2001).

2. Ask students to compare the fractions $\frac{6}{8}$ and $\frac{4}{5}$. Then ask which fraction is larger? (Assume that the students have not been taught about common denominators.) One student answered, "I know that $\frac{4}{5}$ is the same as $\frac{8}{10}$ and that is $\frac{2}{10}$ away from a whole. Because tenths are smaller than eighths, $\frac{8}{10}$ must be closer to a whole, so $\frac{4}{5}$ is larger" (Van de Walle, 2004).

3. Ask students how the number 7 can be broken into different amounts. Then ask the students to draw pictures showing ways in which the number 7 can be broken into different amounts (Van de Walle, 2004).

Commercial Programs Several commercial mathematics programs are designed to address the types of mathematics problems that are encountered by students with mathematics disabilities. Table 13.4. lists some of these programs.

TABLE 13.4

Commercial Mathematics Programs for Students With Learning Disabilities

Program	Publisher	Web address
■ Computational Arithmetic Program	Pro-Ed	http://www.proedinc.com
■ Cuisenaire Rods	ETA/Cuisenaire	http://www.etacuisenaire.com
■ Key Math Early Steps Program	American Guidance Services	http://www.agsnet.com
■ Key Math Teach and Practice	American Guidance Services	http://www.agsnet.com
■ Mastering Math	Steck-Vaughn	http://www.steck-vaughn.com
■ Matter of Facts	Creative Publications	http://www.creativepublications.com
■ Semple Math	Stevenson Learning Skills	http://www.stevensonsemple.com

LD IN PRACTICE

MATHEMATICS STRATEGIES FOR THE GENERAL EDUCATION CLASSROOM

- Determine the students' basic computational skills in addition, subtraction, multiplication, and division.
- Have students use manipulatives to help them understand a concept.
- Teach the students mathematics vocabulary.
- Use visuals and graphics to illustrate concepts to the students.
- Have students make up their own word story problems.
- Teach students how to use a calculator.
- Teach money concepts by using either real money or play money.
- Teach time by using manipulative clocks.
- Provide many opportunities for practice and review.

covered in the mathematics curriculum from kindergarten through Grade 8 include numbers and numeration; whole numbers—addition and subtraction; whole numbers—multiplication and division; decimals; fractions; measurement; geometry; and computer education, a subject that is beginning to show up in many mathematics programs.

Although the sequence may vary somewhat in different programs, the general timetables of instruction are as follows:

Kindergarten. Basic number meanings, counting, classification, seriation or order, recognition of numerals, and the writing of numbers

Grade 1. Addition through 20, subtraction through 20, place value of 1s and 10s, time to the half hour, money, and simple measurement

Grade 2. Addition through 100, subtraction through 100, counting from 0 to 100, skip-counting by 2s, place value of 100, and regrouping for adding and subtracting

Grade 3. Multiplication through 9s, odd or even skip-counting, place value of 1,000s, two- and three-place numbers for addition and subtraction, and telling time

Grade 4. Division facts, extended use of multiplication facts and related division facts through 9s, and two-place multipliers

Grade 5. Fractions, addition and subtraction of fractions, mixed numbers, long division, two-place division, and decimals

Grade 6. Percentages, three-place multipliers, two-place division, addition and subtraction of decimals and mixed decimals, multiplication and division of decimals, and mixed decimals by whole numbers

Grade 7. Geometry, rounding, ratios, and simple probability

Grade 8. Scientific notation, using graphs, complex fractions, complex applications, and word problems

The Secondary Mathematics Curriculum

The content areas for Grades 9 through 12 that were identified by the Commission on Standards for School Mathematics of the NCTM (2000; see the NCTM website at **http://www.nctm.org**) are as follows:

- Geometry
- Statistics
- Probability
- Discrete mathematics

PRINCIPLES OF INSTRUCTION FOR STUDENTS WITH MATHEMATICS DISABILITIES

Several principles of mathematics learning offer a guide for effective mathematics instruction. The principles discussed here include: (1) early number learning, (2) progressing from the concrete to the abstract, (3) providing opportunity for practice and review, (4) generalizing the concepts and skills that have been learned, and (5) teaching mathematics vocabulary.

Early Number Learning

It is important to check into the previously acquired *early number learning* to ensure that the student is ready for what needs to be learned. Time and effort invested in building a firm foundation can prevent many later difficulties as the student tries to move on to more advanced and more abstract mathematics processes. The basic early number learning abilities that are essential are described in Table 13.6. If they are lacking, they must be taught.

Progressing From the Concrete to the Abstract

Pupils can best understand a mathematics concept when teaching progresses from the concrete to the abstract. A teacher should plan three instructional stages: *concrete, semiconcrete,* and *abstract* (Cass et al., 2003; Witzel et al., 2003).

TABLE 13.6

Early Number Learning

Ability	Description
■ Matching	Grouping similar objects together
■ Recognizing groups of objects	Recognizing a group of three objects without counting
■ Counting	Matching numerals to objects
■ Naming a number that comes after a given number	Stating what number comes after 7
■ Writing numerals from 0 to 10	Knowing the right sequence
■ Measuring and pairing	One-to-one correspondence, estimating, fitting objects
■ Sequential values	Arranging like objects in order by quantitative differences (e.g., by size)
■ Operations	Manipulation of the number facts to 10 without reference to concrete objects

1. In the **concrete instruction** stage, the student manipulates real objects in learning the skill. For example, the student could see, hold, and move two blocks and three blocks to learn that they equal five blocks.

2. In the **semiconcrete instruction** stage, a graphic representation is substituted for actual objects. In the following example, circles represent objects in an illustration from a worksheet:

$$OO + OOO = 5$$

3. At the **abstract instruction** stage, numerals finally replace the graphic symbols:

$$2 + 3 = 5$$

Provide Opportunity for Practice and Review

Students need many opportunities for review, drill, and practice to overlearn the math concepts because they must be able to use computation facts almost automatically. There are many ways to provide this practice, and teachers should vary the method as often as possible. Such techniques can include worksheets, flash cards, games, behavior management techniques (such as rewards for work completed), and computer practice (special software programs that give immediate feedback).

Teach Students to Generalize to New Situations

Students must learn to generalize a skill to many situations. For example, students can practice computation facts with many story problems that the teacher or students create and then exchange with each other. The goal is to gain skill in recognizing computational operations and applying them to various new situations.

Teach Mathematics Vocabulary

The vocabulary and concepts of mathematics are new to students and must be learned. The student may know the operation, but may not know the precise term applied to the operation. Table 13.7 shows the vocabulary for basic mathematics operations.

ACTIVITIES FOR TEACHING MATHEMATICS The instruction activities in this section are grouped into three categories: (1) teaching early number skills, (2) teaching computation skills, and (3) teaching word story problems.

Teaching Early Number Skills

Classification and Grouping

1. ***Sorting games.*** Give students objects that differ in only one attribute, such as color or texture, and ask them to sort the objects into two dif-

---

TABLE 13.7

Mathematics Vocabulary for Basic Operations

Operation	Terms		
Addition	3	→	addend
	+5	→	addend
	8	→	sum
Subtraction	9	→	minuend
	−3	→	subtrahend
	6	→	difference
Multiplication	7	→	multiplicand
	×5	→	multiplier
	35	→	product
Division	7	→	quotient
	6)‾42‾		
			divisor

---

ferent boxes. For example, if the objects differ by color, have students put red items in one box and blue items in another box. At a more advanced level, increase the complexity of the classification of the attributes, asking students to sort, for example, movable objects from stationary objects. Another variation is to use objects that have several overlapping attributes, such as shape, color, and size. You might present the students with cutouts of triangles, circles, and squares in three colors (e.g., blue, yellow, and red) and two sizes (e.g., small and large). Ask the students to sort them according to shape and then according to color. Then ask the students to discover a third way of sorting.

2. *Matching and sorting.* A first step in the development of number concepts is the ability to focus on and to recognize a single object or shape. Have the student search through a collection of assorted objects to find a particular type of object. For example, the student might look in a box of colored beads or blocks for a red one, search through a collection of various kinds of nuts for all the almonds, choose the forks from a box of silverware, look in a box of buttons for the oval ones, sort a bagful of cardboard shapes to pick out the circles, or look in a container of nuts and bolts for the square pieces.

3. *Recognition of groups of objects.* Domino games, playing cards, concrete objects, felt boards, magnetic boards, and cards with colored disks all provide excellent materials for developing concepts of groups.

Ordering

1. *Serial order and relationships.* When teaching the concept of ordering, ask the student to tell the number that comes after 6 or before 5 or between 2 and 4. Also, ask the student to indicate the first, last, or third of a series of objects. Other measured quantities can be arranged by other dimensions, such as size, weight, intensity, color, or volume.

2. *Number lines.* A **number line** is a sequence of numbers forming a straight line that allows the student to manipulate computation directly. Number lines and number blocks for the students to walk on are helpful in understanding the symbols and their relationships to one another.

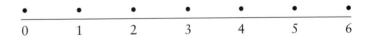

3. *Arranging by size and length.* Have the student compare and contrast objects of different size, formulating concepts of smaller, bigger, taller, and shorter. Make cardboard objects, such as circles, trees, houses, and so forth; or collect objects, such as washers, paper clips, and screws. Have the student arrange the objects by size and then estimate the size of the objects by guessing whether certain objects would fit into certain spaces.

One-to-One Correspondence: Pairing

One-to-one correspondence is a relationship in which one element of a set is paired with one, and only one, element of a second set. Pairing provides a foundation for counting. Activities designed to match or align one object with another are useful. Have the student arrange a row of pegs in a Peg-Board to match a prearranged row, or set a table and place one cookie on each dish, or plan the allocation of materials to the group so that each person receives one object.

Counting

1. *Motor activities for counting.*   Some students learn to count verbally, but they do not attain the concept that each number corresponds to one object. Such students are helped by making strong motor and tactile responses along with the counting. Looking at visual stimuli or pointing to the objects may not be enough because such students will count erratically, skipping objects or saying two numbers for one object. Motor activities to help students establish the counting principle include placing a peg in a hole, clipping clothespins on a line, stringing beads onto a pipe cleaner, clapping three times, jumping four times, and tapping on the table two times. Use the auditory modality to reinforce visual counting by having students listen to the counts of a drumbeat with their eyes closed. The students may make a mark for each sound and then count the marks.

2. *Counting cups.*   Take a set of containers, such as cups, and designate each with a numeral. Have the students fill each container with the correct number of items, using objects such as bottle caps, chips, buttons, screws, or washers.

Recognition of Numbers

1. *Visual recognition of numbers.*   Students must learn to recognize both the printed numbers (7, 8, 3) and the words expressing these numbers (seven, eight, three). They must also learn to integrate the written forms with the spoken symbols. If students confuse one written number with another, color cues may help them to recognize the symbol. You might, for example, make the top of the number 3 green and the bottom of the number 3 red. Another activity is to have the students match the correct number with the correct set of objects; felt, cardboard, or sandpaper symbols or groups of objects can be used.

2. *Parking lot poster.*   Draw a "parking lot" on a poster, numbering parking spaces with dots instead of numerals. Paint numerals on small cars and have the students park the cars in the correct spaces.

FIGURE 13.4

Part-Whole Relationship

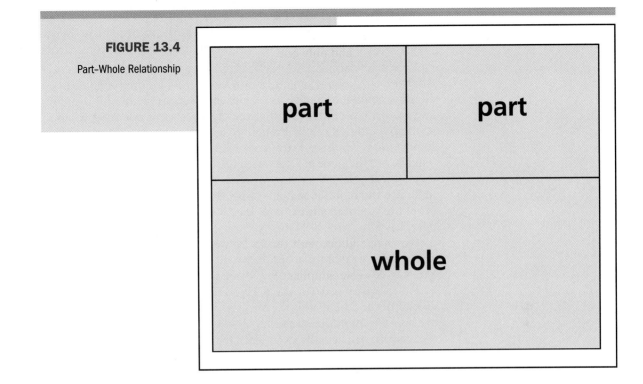

Teaching Computation Skills

1. *Part–whole concepts.* The "big concept" idea is that addition and subtraction have a **part–whole relationship;** you add to find the whole or total of two or more parts, and you subtract from the whole to find the missing part. Use Figure 13.4 to help students see the part–whole relationship. Use counters or put the figure on an overhead projector to demonstrate the part–whole relationship to the entire group. Students can use counters to demonstrate the part-whole relationship.

2. *Basic computation skills.* Many problems in mathematics are due to students' deficiencies in basic computation skills. To help students to overcome these deficiencies, teach the basic **mathematics computation** skills that the students lack: addition, subtraction, multiplication, division, fractions, decimals, and percentages.

3. *The dollar store.* An inexpensive way to teach many mathematics computation skills is to obtain mathematics games and materials from a dollar store. Online dollar stores also can be a good source. Many mathematics games can be obtained without charge (except for

shipping costs) from perusing the website **http://www.DollarBins.com.**
Mathematics games on CDs can be found at the website **http://www.
planetcdrom.com.** A collection of these games and activities can be
placed on a mathematics activities table.

4. *Addition.* Knowledge of addition facts provides the foundation for
all other computational skills. Addition is a short method of counting,
and students should know that they can resort to counting when all
else fails. Addition can be thought of as "part plus part equals whole."
Important symbols to learn are: + (plus, or "put together") and =
(equals, or "the same as"). As with the other areas, begin by using concrete objects, then use cards with sets that represent numbers, and finally use the number sentence with the numbers alone: $3 + 2 = \square$.
From this, the students can also learn that $2 + 3 = \square$; $\square + 2 = 5$; and
$3 + \square = 5$.

Teaching addition using sums between 10 and 20 is more difficult.
There are several approaches. It is easier to start with doubles, such as
$8 + 8 = 16$. Then ask what $9 + 8$ equals: One more than 16.

Another way is to "make a 10." For example, in $7 + 5$, the pupil
takes 3 of the 5, and adds the 3 to the 7 to make 10. Now the students
can see that $10 +$ the remaining $2 = 12$. Use movable objects so that
the students can actually experience the process:

$$7 + 5 = 12$$
$$10 + 2 = 12$$

The number line provides another way to teach addition. With a
number line, the students can visually perceive the addition process.

5. *Subtraction.* After the students have a firm basis in addition, introduce subtraction. An important new symbol is − (minus, or "take
away"). A student places a set of objects on the desk and then takes
away certain objects. How many are left? $6 - 2 = \square$. Then use cards
with sets on them. Find 6 by using a card with a set of 2 and a card
with a set of 4. Tell the students you have a set of 6 when the cards are
joined. Take away the set of 2 and ask the students what is left.

The number line is also useful in subtraction.

Regrouping is an important concept that is introduced in subtraction, along with the ideas of "1s," "10s," and "100s."

6. *Multiplication.* Many students with a mathematics disability do not
know multiplication facts (refer to Figure 13.3). Those students will be
unable to learn division until they master multiplication facts.

Multiplication is a short method of adding. Instead of adding $2 +
2 + 2 + 2$, the students can learn $2 \times 4 = 8$. Subtraction is not a pre-
requisite of multiplication, and a student having difficulty with subtraction may do better with multiplication. The symbol to learn is $\times$
(times).

There are several ways of explaining multiplication. One way is the *multiplication sentence.* How much are 3 sets of 2? Using sets of objects, the students can find the total either by counting objects or by adding equal addends.

The concept of reversals (turn-around) can also be introduced. The sentence $3 \times 5 = \square$ does not change in the form $5 \times 3 = \square$.

In the *equal addend approach,* ask the students to show that

$$3 \times 5 = 5 + 5 + 5, \text{ or } 15$$

In the *number line approach,* students who can use number lines for addition will probably also do well in using them for multiplication. The student adds a unit of 5 three times on the line, to end up at the 15 on the line.

The *rectangular array approach* contains an equal number of objects in each row. For example, 3×5 is shown as

$$\begin{matrix} O & O & O & O & O \\ O & O & O & O & O \\ O & O & O & O & O \end{matrix}$$

7. **Division.** This computational skill is considered the most difficult to learn and to teach. As mentioned earlier, basic division facts come from knowledge of multiplication facts. Long division requires many operations, and students must be able to do all the steps before they can put them together. The new symbol is $\div$ (divide).

There are a number of ways to approach division. Sets can be used: $6 \div 3 = \square$. Draw a set of 6 and enclose three equal sets. The missing factor is seen as 2:

How many subsets are there? How many objects are there in each set?

The number line can also be used. By jumping back a unit of 3, how many jumps are needed?

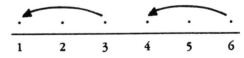

The *missing factors* approach uses known multiplication facts and reverses the process: $3 \times \square = 12$. Then change to a division sentence: $12 \div 3 = \square$.

8. **Fractions.** Geometric shapes are commonly used to introduce fractional numbers. The new symbol is shown next:

$$\frac{1}{2} \begin{matrix} \rightarrow \text{ number of special parts} \\ \rightarrow \text{ total number of equal parts} \end{matrix}$$

FIGURE 13.5

Some Common
Fractions

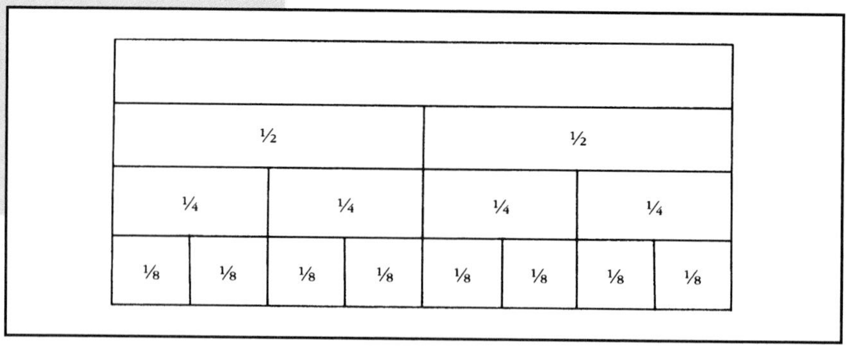

½				½			
¼		¼		¼		¼	
⅛	⅛	⅛	⅛	⅛	⅛	⅛	⅛

Start with halves, followed by quarters and then eighths. Cut shapes out of flannel or paper plates. Figure 13.5 illustrates common fractions.

9. *Learning the computational facts.*   Once the concepts behind the facts are known, the students must memorize the facts themselves. Many different learning opportunities are needed. Students can write the facts, say them, play games with facts, take speed tests, and so forth. Also helpful are flash cards, rolling dice, playing cards, or learning a fact a day. A wide variety of methods should be used.

To learn computational skills, students with mathematics disabilities require much experience with concrete and manipulative materials before moving to the abstract and symbolic level of numbers. Objects and materials that can be physically taken apart and put back together help the students to observe visually the relationship of the fractional parts of the whole.

There are 56 basic number facts to be mastered in each mode of arithmetic computation (addition, subtraction, multiplication, and division), if the facts involving the 1s $(3 + 1 = 4)$ and doubles $(3 \times 3 = 9)$ are not included. Examples of number facts are $3 + 4 = 7$; $9 - 5 = 4$; $3 \times 7 = 21$; $18 \div 6 = 3$. In the computational skill of addition, for example, there are 81 separate facts involved in the span from $1 + 1 = 2$ to $9 + 9 = 18$. Few students have trouble with the 1s $(5 + 1 = 6)$ or with the doubles $(2 + 2 = 4)$. Therefore, if these facts are omitted, there are 56 basic addition facts to be mastered. Similarly, without the 1s and doubles, there are 56 facts to be mastered in each of the other computation areas—subtraction, multiplication, and division.

FIGURE 13.6

Calendar for
Learning Facts

Sun	Mon	Tue	Wed	Thur	Fri	Sat
1	2	3	4	5	6	7
8	9	10	11	12	13	14
15	16	17	18	19	20	21
22	23	24	25	26	27	28

10. *The 2-weeks facts: 7 + 7.* Students circle 2 full calendar weeks and count the number of days in each week, as shown in Figure 13.6, to learn that $7 + 7 = 14$.

11. *Subtraction of 9s from teen numbers.* One useful technique to help students learn subtraction of 9s from the teen numbers is to have students consider the following problem: $16 - 9 = \square$. Adding the 1 and 6 gives the correct answer of 7. This technique works with subtracting 9s from all teen numbers.

12. *Arrangements.* Give students the numbers 1, 2, 3. Ask them in how many ways they can be arranged: 1-2-3; 1-3-2; 2-1-3; 2-3-1; 3-1-2; 3-2-1 (or $3 \times 2 \times 1 = 6$). Another arrangement puzzle is: If four children sit around a square table, in how many ways can they arrange themselves? ($4 \times 3 \times 2 \times 1 = 24$).

13. *Puzzle cards of combinations.* Make cardboard cards on which problems of addition, subtraction, multiplication, and division are worked. Cut each card in two so that the problem is on one part and the answer is on the other. Each card must be cut uniquely so that when the students try to assemble the puzzle, only the correct answer will fit.

14. *Rate of perception of number facts.* The use of computer programs or flash cards is a way to increase the rate of recognition of sets of objects, number symbols, and answers to number facts. A quick exposure device can be made by putting information on transparencies, then cutting the transparencies into strips and inserting them in a filmstrip projector. By covering the lens with a sheet of cardboard and exposing the material for a short period of time, students practice rapid recognition of number facts.

15. *Playing cards.* An ordinary deck of cards becomes a versatile tool for teaching number concepts. Some activities are arranging suits in sequential order by number, matching sets of numbers, adding and subtracting with individual cards, and quickly recognizing the number in a set.

Teaching Word Story Problems

The goal of mathematics instruction is to apply the concepts and skills in problem solving. The National Council of Teachers of Mathematics (2000) calls for more emphasis on problem solving at all levels. Some suggestions for teaching word story problems are provided in the following list.

1. *Word story problems.* Use word story problems that are of interest to the students and within their experience.

2. *Posing problems orally.* This method is especially important for students with reading problems.

3. *Visual reinforcements.* Use concrete objects, drawings, graphs, or other visual reinforcements to clarify the problem, demonstrate solutions, and verify the answers. Have students act out the problem.

4. *Simplifying.* Have students substitute smaller and easier numbers for problems with larger or more complex numbers so that they can understand the problems and verify the solutions more readily.

5. *Restating.* Have students restate the problems in their own words. This verbalization helps the students to structure the problems for themselves and also shows whether they understand the problems.

6. *Supplementary problems.* Supplement textbook problems with your own, which could deal with classroom experiences. Including students' names makes the problem more realistic.

7. *Time for thinking.* Allow students enough time to think. Ask for alternative methods for solving the problems. Try to understand how the students thought about the problem and went about solving the problem.

8. *Steps in solving word problems.* Many students with learning disabilities have difficulty with word problems. Although problems in reading may be a factor, the difficulty is often in thinking through the math problems. Students tend to begin doing computations as soon as they see the numbers in the problems. The following steps are helpful in teaching word problem applications:

    a. *Seeing the situations.* Have the students first read the word problem and then relate the setting of the problem. The students do not need paper and pencil for this task. They should simply describe the setting or situation.

    b. *Determining the question.* Have the students decide what is to be discovered—What is the problem to be solved?

    c. *Gathering data.* The word problem often gives much data—some relevant, some not relevant to the solution. Ask the students to read the problem aloud, or silently, and then list the relevant and irrelevant data.

    d. *Analyzing relationships.* Help the students analyze the relationships among the data. For example, if the problem states that the down payment on an automobile costing $2,000 is 25%, the students must see the relationship between these two facts. Seeing relationships is a reasoning skill that students with learning disabilities often find difficult.

    e. *Deciding on a process.* Students must decide which computational process should be used to solve the problem. Students should be alert to key words, such as *total* or *in all,* which suggest addition, and *is left* or *remains,* which suggest subtraction. They should next put the problem into mathematical sentences.

    f. *Estimating answers.* Have the students practice estimating what a reasonable answer might be. If the students understand the reasoning behind the problem, they should be able to estimate answers.

    g. *Practice and generalization.* After students have thought through and worked out one type of problem, the teacher can give similar problems with different numbers.

9. *Time.* **Time concepts** involve a difficult dimension for many students with learning disabilities to grasp, so they may require specific

instructions to learn how to tell time. Real clocks or teacher-made clocks are needed to teach this skill. A teacher-made clock can be created by using a paper fastener to attach cardboard hands to a paper plate. A sequence for teaching time might be the hour (1:00), the half hour (4:30), the quarter hour (7:15), 5-minute intervals (2:25), before and after the hour, minute intervals, and seconds. Use television schedules of programs or classroom activities and relate them to clock time.

10. *Money.* The use of real money and lifelike situations is an effective way to teach number facts to some students. Have them play store, make change, or order a meal from a restaurant menu and then add up the cost and pay for it. All of these situations provide concrete and meaningful practice for learning arithmetic.

USING TECHNOLOGY FOR MATHEMATICS INSTRUCTION

Calculators

Students must be required to learn the computation facts, but there are times for using the calculator as well. Students in school should be taught how to make efficient use of the calculator. In doing a mathematics reasoning problem, students often become so bogged down in computation that they never get to the reasoning aspects of the lesson. By using calculators, students can put their energies into understanding the mathematical concept rather than on performing the underlying calculation process.

A low-cost pocket calculator is easily accessible and handy. It can be used to compute basic facts, as well as more complicated math processes, and it is also useful for self-checking. Because it is more socially acceptable than other counting systems, it is particularly helpful for adults who have not memorized basic computation facts. Students do need instruction in the proper way to use a calculator, so lessons must be designed to teach calculation skills.

Students with mathematics disabilities may find talking calculators useful. The talking calculator is a calculator with a speech synthesizer. When a number, symbol, or operation is pressed, it is vocalized by the speech synthesizer. The user gets auditory feedback and can double-check the answers.

Secondary students and adults are likely to need programmable calculators to perform more complex math functions.

Computers

The rapid pace of change in computer applications has made computer technology especially useful for teaching mathematics.

Many mathematics software programs, although not specifically designed for students with learning disabilities, may be useful. Computers motivate students, and the mathematics software programs can individualize, provide feedback, and offer repetition (Lewis, 1998; Raskind & Higgins, 1998a). These programs should have as little clutter as possible and should offer concise, clear directions, moving from simple and concrete directions to longer and more complex ones. The programs should question the student frequently (asking, for example, "Are you sure? Do you want to change your answer?"). They should also provide immediate feedback to the student. Mathematics programs range from drill-and-practice programs to problem-solving programs.

A good source for mathematics software programs for students with learning disabilities is Closing the Gap's *Resource Directory* (2004). The website is **http://www.closingthegap.com**. Table 13.8 lists some mathematics software for students with learning disabilities.

TABLE 13.8

Selected Mathematics Software for Students With Mathematics Disabilities

Title	Publisher	Grade level	Description
The Cruncher	Davidson/Knowledge Adventure	3–8	A spreadsheet and a tutorial for spreadsheet use and development; animated onscreen helpers to guide activities
Geometer's Sketchpad	Key Curriculum Press	5–12	Enables students to create Euclidean geometric construction; users can analyze geometry and measure a sketch; drawings can be animated easily
Logical Journey of the Zoombinis	Broderbund	4–7	Animated program to explore and apply fundamental principles of logic, problem solving, and data analysis
Wide World of Mathematics	Scott Forsman	6–8	Multimedia program uses news and sports footage to show students how mathematics is used at work and in real-word events; addresses decimals, area, probability equations, bar and line graphs, rates, and proportions

Source: From "Ten tips for software selection for math instruction," by B. Babbit, *Scope: Learning Disabilities Association of Illinois* 36(4): 8, accessed at **http://www.ldonline.org/ld_indepth/technology/ babbitt_math_tips/html**.

Spreadsheets

Computer spreadsheets are an essential part of the mathematics curriculum, and their use is recommended by the National Council of Teachers of Mathematics (2000). Moreover, students with learning disabilities often do very well with spreadsheet applications, possibly because spreadsheets are a visual task, rather than a linguistic task. A **spreadsheet** displays numeric information through a grid of columns and rows. The intersection of a column and a row is called a *cell*. When numbers are placed in the cells, they can be used in mathematics computations or in mathematics formulas, such as averages. Charts and graphs, such as **pie charts, bar graphs,** or line graphs are electronically made, based on the numbers in the spreadsheets (see Figure 13.7). A *pie chart* is a circular chart cut into segments illustrat-

FIGURE 13.7

Spreadsheet, Pie Chart, and Bar Graph

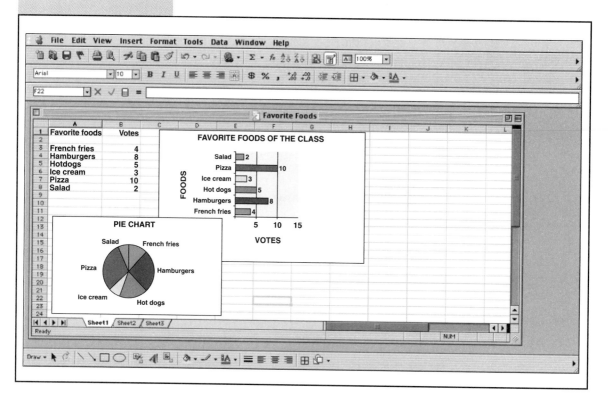

ing magnitudes or frequencies. A *bar graph* is a type of chart in which different values are represented by rectangular bars. A wide variety of student activities can be accomplished with spreadsheets, such as planning a budget, keeping records of grades, compiling an inventory of items used in a hobby, or tracking election results.

In one activity, students noted their favorite foods. These foods were then listed on a chalkboard and each student voted for his or her favorite food. The class votes were tallied (e.g., pizza, 10 votes; hot dogs, 5 votes, etc.). The favorite foods and votes were then put into Columns A and B on a spreadsheet, and the students made pie charts and bar graphs from their spreadsheets. Figure 13.7 shows the spreadsheet, pie chart, and bar graph that resulted from this activity.

CHAPTER SUMMARY

1. Some students with learning disabilities have severe difficulty in learning mathematics. For others, mathematics seems to be an area of strength. Dyscalculia is a severe disability in learning and using mathematics that is associated with a neurological dysfunction.

2. Early number learning in young children include abilities in spatial relations, visual–motor and visual–perception processing, and concepts of time and direction.

3. Characteristics of mathematics disabilities are related to information-processing difficulties, language and reading abilities, and math anxiety.

4. Views about teaching mathematics have changed over the years in response to national concerns. Today's approach is to require high standards and annual testing.

5. There are several learning theories of mathematics instruction for students with learning disabilities, which include the progression from concrete learning to abstract learning, direct instruction, learning strategies instruction, and problem-solving approaches.

6. Students' mathematics abilities can be assessed through formal tests and informal measures. Each provides a different kind of information about mathematics performance.

7. The content of the mathematics curriculum is sequential and cumulative. Different elements of mathematics are taught at different grade levels.

8. Principles of instruction in mathematics stress that the students should have early number learning. Instruction should progress from the concrete to the abstract, with ample opportunity for practice and review. The students must learn to generalize concepts that have been learned, and they should also know the vocabulary for basic mathematics operations.

9. Students should learn basic computational facts, but they should be allowed to use calculators for some purposes in the classroom. Calculator use should be part of the mathematics curriculum.

10. Computers have many useful applications in teaching mathematics to students with learning disabilities.

DISCUSSION AND REFLECTION

1. The Individuals With Disabilities Education Improvement Act (IDEA–2004) recognizes two areas in which students can have mathematics disabilities. Identify these two areas and discuss the implications for services.

2. Characteristics of learning disabilities can affect the learning of mathematics. Select four characteristics of students with mathematics disabilities and describe how these characteristics can affect mathematics learning.

3. Do you think calculators should be used in mathematics instruction? Why or why not? Discuss how they could be used.

4. How can computers be used in the teaching of mathematics?

5. Describe how students can be instructed to go from concrete learning to abstract learning.

14 Social and Emotional Behavior

CHAPTER OUTLINE

An analogy between self-esteem and poker chips exists in the game of "life." To play this "game," a person must enter adulthood with many piles of "poker chips" (self-esteem). Adults with a lot of chips have a great self-concept. Those with a meager pile of chips have a poor self-concept. How do adults acquire these chips? During childhood and adolescence, when good things happen to people (such as success, victory, and being praised), they receive poker chips. Then, when bad things happen (such as failure, frustration, and being criticized), they lose chips.

—Rick Lavoie (2000)

Learning disabilities encompass more than academic difficulties. There is a renewed recognition of related disorders that impact the individual's life, and social, emotional, and behavioral difficulties must be considered. Among the co-occurring conditions are attention deficit disorder (ADD) and Asperger's syndrome (which were discussed in the chapter on attention deficit disorders and related neurodevelopmental conditions).

In the Theories section of this chapter, we discuss: (1) nonverbal learning disorders, (2) social disorders, (3) emotional problems, (4) behavioral challenges, and (5) assessing social and emotional behaviors. Students with these disorders often suffer from depression, suicidal tendencies, anxiety, school phobia, and loneliness. Frequently, these students are taking medication that may affect school learning (Kline & Silver, 2004).

In the Theories section, we examine the characteristics of related disorders and the concepts underlying the social, emotional, and behavioral challenges of individuals with learning disabilities. The causes and effects of these problematic areas are complex and interrelated (Kline & Silver, 2004).

The Teaching Strategies section of this chapter offers various interventions that teachers can use to meet these social, emotional, and behavioral challenges, such as: (1) developing social competencies, (2) strategies for students with emotional problems, and (3) behavior management strategies.

THEORIES

Characteristics of Nonverbal Learning Disorders

The condition of *nonverbal learning disorders (NVLD)* has captured a growing interest among researchers and practitioners. NVLD are considered a subtype of learning disabilities that differs markedly from academic, linguistic, and cognitive disabilities. The condition of NVLD is identified in the field of neuropsychology as a neurological disorder that involves a dysfunction in the right hemisphere of the brain. Students with NVLD have serious difficulties with social interactions and interpersonal skills. For example, students with NVLD have difficulty understanding those subtle cues that are inherent in nonverbal communication and that play such an important role in social interaction. Children with NVLD often have high verbal intelligence, tend to be early talkers, and do well on reading and decoding in the primary years; consequently, their nonverbal learning problems are often missed. These children often have poor visuospatial abilities, poor nonverbal problem-solving abilities, and low arithmetic skills. Problems with NVLD become more evident in the later elementary school years, during adolescence, and in the adult years (Dimitrovsky et al., 1998; Rourke, 1995; Thompson, 1997; Tsatsanis, Fuerst, & Rourke, 1997).

People with NVLD often have difficulty adapting to new or novel situations. Despite their high verbal intelligence and high scores on receptive and expressive language measures, they inaccurately read nonverbal signals and cues, and they lack the social ability to comprehend nonverbal communication cues. If they do not perceive subtle cues in the environment, they do not know when something has gone far enough; they do not recognize the idea of personal space; and they cannot interpret the facial expressions of others. Normally, these social cues are intuitively grasped through observation; however, individuals with NVLD need to be taught these social skills through direct and explicit instruction (Dimitrovsky et al., 1998; Thompson, 1997; Tsatsanis et al., 1997).

Adults with NVLD often have serious difficulty in the workplace. Their problems include poor self-concept, mental health problems, difficulty in social relationships, and terse or curt response styles. Transitions are difficult because these individuals like routine and find it difficult to take on new responsibilities and assignments. Unable to reflect on the nature and seriousness of their own problems, they tend to attribute their failures, as well as their successes, to others, instead of to themselves. Their coping mechanisms are often misinterpreted as *emotional* or *motivational* problems (Price, 1997; Rourke, 1995; Thompson, 1997; Tsatsanis et al., 1997).

One mother described her daughter's NVLD as a serious difficulty in visual–spatial imagery. The mother noted that her daughter could not find her way to a friend's house nor was she able to visualize where her classroom was at school. She had to remember words and verbal labels to keep from getting lost (Martin, 2004). "LD Stories: A Nonverbal Learning Disorder" presents an example of a child with NVLD. A website about NVLD is located at **http://www.nldline.com.**

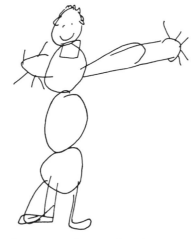

LD STORIES

A NONVERBAL LEARNING DISORDER

Nine and a half year old Jimmy is an example of a student with a nonverbal learning disorder. On the Wechsler Intelligence Scale for Children, Fourth Edition (WISC-IV), Jimmy received an IQ score of 127, putting him in a high intelligence classification. He did particularly well on the sections that required verbal and language responses. However, on the Goodenough-Harris Drawing Test, his drawing of a man ranked at the 6th percentile for his age.

Jimmy had many problems in the area of social perception. Although he performed satisfactorily in many academic subjects, his teachers consistently reported that his social behavior in school was both strange and disturbing. The speech teacher dismissed him from class because of his abnormal delight and hilarity when others in the class made mistakes. Another teacher reported that he seemed unconscious of wrongdoing, that he made odd statements totally out of context, and that he was not well accepted by other children. Another report commented that Jimmy had not developed skills in social situations. Although he wanted to be accepted by others and to have friends, Jimmy did not seem to know the appropriate manner of gaining friends and instead tended to antagonize other students. As seems to be true of some other students with NVLD, Jimmy did poorly in perceptual–motor tasks and seemed to have a poor understanding of spatial relationships. The psychologist reported poor performance in perceptual–motor and coordination activities on the Bender-Gestalt Test.

Characteristics of Social Disorders

Deficits in **social skills,** which are the skills necessary to meet the basic social demands of everyday life, are probably the most crippling type of problem that a student can have. In terms of total life functioning, a social disorder may be far more disabling than an academic dysfunction, as described in "LD Stories: Social Skills Disorders." A social disorder affects almost every aspect of life—at school, at home, and at play.

Many students with learning disabilities have poor social skills. They lack sensitivity to others, have a poor perception of social situations, and suffer social rejection (Bryan, 1997; Sridhar & Vaughn, 2001; Wong & Donahue, 2002). It is important to recognize, however, that not all students with learning disabilities encounter difficulties with social skills. In fact, for many students, the social sphere is an area of strength. They are socially competent at making and maintaining friends, and they work at pleasing teachers and parents (Haager & Vaughn, 1997). It is estimated that one third of students with learning disabilities have problems with social skills (Bryan, 1997; Voeller, 1994). Some individuals with learning disabilities have a social disorder, but they do well in academic domains; others have both social and academic disabilities.

In school, students need well-developed social and interactive skills in dealing with peers and adults; those who have social perception problems are often at a great disadvantage. (© Jeffrey W. Myers/ FPG International)

SOCIAL SKILLS DISORDERS

The following case examples illustrate social disorders. These disorders may not be recognized because they do not prevent students from using verbal language with fluency or from learning to read.

Wanda: Impulsive Behavior

The school predicted that a 12-year-old girl with a social disability would not be able to get along in a secondary school because of her poor skills in social perception. Wanda read well, performed well in math, and wrote well; she just could not get along with others. She was too impulsive. What she thought, she said. Wanda scratched where it itched. She went where she happened to look. When Wanda finally was academically ready to enter high school, she could not be sent. She would not have lasted there a day (Nall, 1971).

Samuel: Disruptive Social Behavior

Six-year-old Samuel was judged by a psychologist to have an IQ score in the high superior range. He was able to read simple stories by the time he entered first grade. However, Samuel's mother was frequently called in for parent–teacher conferences because of her son's highly disruptive social behavior. The kindergarten teacher reported that Samuel was bossy, turned other children away from him, and had been a "social problem" all year. The first-grade teacher said that Samuel found it difficult to accept *no* for an answer, he stamped his feet, cried frequently, pushed others so that he could be first in line, and alienated the other children by kissing and hugging them to gain affection.

Samuel's mother also described her son's social behavior at home as intolerable. Sitting still for even a few minutes seemed to be impossible, and he ate so rapidly that he stuffed half his sandwich into his mouth all at once. Samuel would invite a classmate to his house to play and then be so excited that he could not do much but run around. The classmate would soon tearfully beg Samuel's mother to let him go home, and Samuel would also be in tears because of the frustration of trying so hard and not knowing what went wrong. His mother also reported several other incidents typical of children with social perception deficits. Once, for example, when a neighbor girl arrived to play with Samuel, he exclaimed to her, "You sure are a fat one!" The would-be friend left in tears, but Samuel could not understand what he had done wrong. On another occasion, when Samuel was invited to a birthday party, his behavior was so antisocial that the mother of the birthday child phoned Samuel's parents to take him home.

Becky: Inept Social Behavior

Becky, a 13 year old with high average intelligence, constantly said the wrong thing at the wrong time. She seemed unaware of the consequences of her inappropriate remarks. Her parents found they could not have any personal conversations at dinner because she would tell someone about the conversation. Becky had told her Uncle Al, for example, that her parents said he was lazy and irresponsible.

Becky desperately wanted to have friends and to have people like her, but her remarks often offended others and turned them away. For instance, Becky wanted very much to go to a summer camp, but she was rejected by the camp program because she failed the intake interview. She told the interviewer that her parents wanted to get rid of her, so they could go on a vacation.

Becky's problems with social perception continued in high school. Her classmates and teachers found her behavior and remarks annoying and disruptive. She did not know how to accept constructive criticism without making an unsuitable rejoinder, and she did not know how to use socially acceptable techniques to disagree with others. During class, she constantly raised her hand to demand recognition, made challenging remarks, and commented critically in an undertone while the teacher was talking to the class.

The social disorder may be a primary and discrete disability, separate from academic problems and learning problems. It can also reflect a secondary problem if it is the failure to learn that creates emotional and social problems. In school, students need well-developed social and interactive skills to deal with peers and adults; those who have social perception problems are often at a great disadvantage. Some definitions of learning disabilities (e.g., by the Interagency Committee on Learning Disabilities, 1988) recognize the component of social disabilities. Most definitions, however, such as the federal definition in the Individuals With Disabilities Education Improvement Act (IDEA–2004; PL 108–446), do not mention social disorders or disabilities.

Asperger's Syndrome Severe social problems and difficulty in social interactions are evident in children with Asperger's syndrome (Baker & Welkowitz, 2005, Roman, 1998; Thompson, 1997). *Asperger's syndrome* is a developmental disorder affecting two-way social interaction and verbal and nonverbal communication. Asperger's syndrome is characterized by a reluctance to accept change; an inflexibility of thought; and an all-absorbing, narrow area of interest. Children with Asperger's syndrome are usually extremely good at rote memory skills (e.g., repeating facts, figures, dates, times), and many excel in mathematics and science. There is a range of severity of symptoms within the syndrome; the very mildly affected child often goes undiagnosed, and many others may just appear odd or eccentric (Baker & Welkowitz, 2005).

Asperger's disorder is recognized by the *Diagnostic and Statistical Manual of Mental Disorders, Fourth Edition (DSM-IV)* (American Psychiatric Association, 1994). It is described as a qualitative impairment in social interaction; restricted repetitive and stereotyped patterns of behavior, interest, and activities; significant impairment in social, occupational, or other important areas of functioning; and no general delay in language or cognitive development. (More information about Asperger's syndrome is in the chapter on attention deficit disorder and related neurodevelopmental conditions.) A website for Asperger's syndrome is **http://www.aspergers syndrome.org.**

Poor Social Perception   The ability to understand social situations, as well as a sensitivity to the feelings of others, is called **social perception.** Children with problems in social perception perform poorly in the kinds of social activities expected of children of the same chronological age. They are inept at judging the moods and attitudes of the people in their environment, and they are insensitive to the atmosphere of a social situation. They tend to display inappropriate behaviors, to make inappropriate remarks, and to not know how to disagree with others in acceptable ways. (See "LD Stories: A Nonverbal Learning Disorder.") Children with learning disorders typically exhibit a higher rate of psychosocial adjustment problems than their peers, such as anxiety, depression, and behavioral problems (Pearl & Bay, 1999; Wong & Donahue, 2002).

Lack of Judgment   Developing social perception is similar in some ways to developing academic skills, such as reading or mathematics. In both instances, children must learn to anticipate processes, and they must compare the actual result with the expected result. Based on this feedback, children must adjust their behavior. Children with social perception problems are likely to have difficulty in each of these steps. Because they do not anticipate the social processes of others, they are unable to confirm whether the social behavior of the person matches the anticipated behavior. In addition, they cannot adjust their own behavior in light of such comparisons. One consequence is that they appear to lack tact and sensitivity. They may, for example, inappropriately share very personal information with casual acquaintances. At the same time, they may not know how to make appropriate investments in establishing a close relationship with those with whom they wish to be friends (Osman, 1987).

Difficulties in Perceiving How Others Feel   Children with social disorders appear to be less attuned than their peers to the feelings of others. They may use inappropriate behavior or language because they do not know whether the person to whom they are reacting is sad or happy, approving or disapproving, or accepting or rejecting. In addition, they are insensitive to the general atmosphere of a social situation. Research shows that children with social disorders are poor at detecting or perceiving the subtle social cues given by others; which is an insensitivity that is a source of difficulty in interacting with peers and parents (Rourke, 1995; Silver, 1998; Thompson, 1997). For example, most children can sense a parent's emotional state by the parent's body language and then decide whether to approach or avoid a parent when the parent comes home from work. Children with social perception deficits, however, do not pick up on the subtle messages usually conveyed by facial expression, body language, or tone of voice; they miss, for example, the "not now" signal that these cues send (Silver, 1998).

Problems in Socializing and Making Friends Parents of children with social disorders report that their children have considerable difficulty making friends. During times when there are no planned activities, such as after-school hours, weekends, or holidays, their loneliness becomes especially acute (Tur-Kaspa, Weisel, & Segrev, 1998).

Research shows that the social life of children with social disorders differs from that of other children. When they attempt to initiate social interactions, they are often ignored. Even strangers can detect these youngsters after viewing them on a videotape for only a few minutes (Bryan, 1997). In conversing with others, children with social disabilities tend to make more nasty and competitive statements. When working with a partner, they tend to resist the initiatives of the partner. These children are often viewed as hostile, and they are at risk for social neglect and rejection (Vaughn et al., 2001).

Social Problems in Different Settings

A child's social problems appear in many different settings.

Family Relationships The family is the core of a child's life. Children desperately need the satisfaction and assurance of members in the primary family. Even with the intimate family, however, the numerous problems in social skills, behavior, language, and temperament make it hard for a child with social disabilities to establish a healthy family relationship. The child may not receive satisfaction from the family sphere and may even be rejected by parents, as well as by peers and teachers (Silver, 1998). Some research suggests that interventions by parents can have a positive impact on the child's self-concept (Elbaum & Vaughn 2001).

The School Setting Successful adjustment in school, especially in inclusive settings, requires competencies in social skills. Essential social competencies in school include such skills as refraining from interrupting when others are talking, communicating needs in a socially acceptable manner, sharing with others, waiting one's turn, and being able to follow directions. One of the significant reasons often given for the inclusion of students with disabilities in general education classrooms is to improve the student's self-concept, social integration, and peer relationships. However, research suggests that simple proximity is not enough to insure such social competence, acceptance, and improved self-concept (Elbaum & Vaughn, 2001; Nowicki, 2003; Vaughn et al., 2001). Placement and decisions about the services to be provided should be based on academic, as well as social, information.

Adolescents and Adults With Social Disorders   Many adolescents with learning disabilities have no social problems, and they do well in social situations (Hazel & Schumaker, 1988). However, for those who do have social disorders, along with their learning disabilities, adolescence is a particularly trying stage of life. These students engage in fewer activities related to extracurricular events, and they go out with friends less frequently than their classmates (Price, 1997). Their social problems affect friendships, employment, and family relationships; and they keep them from full and successful participation in school, work, social circles, and family (Scanlon, 1996).

During the stage of adolescence, being different is not tolerated. Instead, being exactly like everyone else in the peer group is a criterion that must be met before a sense of pride in individual differences can emerge. The emerging sense of identity as an individual is an important step in growing up. However, adolescents with learning disabilities are already different. Social acceptance may elude them because they are inept at sports, dancing, engaging in other activities with peers, making small talk, or listening to others. Some adolescents withdraw into the house, and they become content with watching television, listening to music, or reading. Other adolescents become so desperate for social acceptance that they are overly vulnerable to peer pressure, and their inappropriate acts lead to trouble (Silver, 1998).

For adults with learning disabilities, social disorders often continue to impact many aspects of their life. Feelings of inadequacy and poor self-concept continue. Studies show that difficulties in getting and keeping a job are among the major complaints of adults with learning disabilities. Social disorders also interfere with employment (Gerber & Brown, 1997; Johnson & Blalock, 1987; Price, 1997; Scanlon, 1996). Problems that continue into adulthood include the failure to make friends, to establish relationships, and to find a satisfying social life.

EMOTIONAL PROBLEMS   The student's emotional problems not only interfere with academic learning, but they can impact the student's entire life. In this section, we consider the individual's emotional problems, looking at: (1) the characteristics of emotional problems, (2) low self-concept, (3) anxiety, (4) depression, and (5) the quality of resiliency.

Characteristics of Emotional Problems

Let us compare the emotional and personality development of achieving students with the emotional development of students with learning problems. Successful achievers have a multitude of gratifying experiences to develop important basic feelings of self-worth, and they have hundreds of opportunities for self-satisfaction, as well as the enjoyment of pleasing others. When students are achieving, the parent–child relationship is mutually satisfying because normal accomplishments stimulate parental responses of approval and encouragement. As a result of their own feelings of accomplishment and their awareness of the approval of those around them, achieving students develop a sense of self-worth and a prideful identity. Successful achievers establish healthy identifications with their mothers, fathers, and other key figures in their lives. They build feelings of self-worth, a tolerance for frustration, and a consideration for others (Rock, Fessler, & Church, 1997; Silver, 1998).

In contrast, the emotional and personality development of students who encounter learning failure follow a very different pattern. If the central nervous system is not intact and is not maturing in a normal manner, disturbances in motor and perceptual development lead to dissatisfaction with one's self. Failed attempts at mastering tasks induce feelings of frustration, rather than feelings of accomplishment. Instead of building self-esteem, the thwarted attempts produce an attitude of self-derision and, at the same time, these thwarted attempts fail to stimulate the parents' normal responses of pride. Parents, therefore, may become anxious and disheartened, reactions that can result in either rejection or overprotection.

With such a developmental scenario, it is not surprising that many students with learning problems develop emotional problems. These students may react by *internalizing* their emotional problems or by *externalizing* their emotional problems. An internalizing reaction may take the form of a conscious refusal to learn, a resistance to pressure, clinging to dependency, quick discouragement, a fear of success, sadness, and withdrawal into a private world. An externalizing reaction can take the form of overt hostility, acting-out behaviors, excessive anger, fighting with other children, and defiance toward teachers. If the problems are so severe that they interfere with further learning and life activities, the student may be referred for psychological or psychiatric counseling (Silver, 1998).

Low Self-Concept

The emotional scars caused by repeated failure and the inability to achieve and develop a sense of competence and self-worth are often indelible. Research shows that students with emotional problems often have a negative view of themselves. The feelings within themselves and the response from the outside world mold a concept of a threatening environment in which they feel insecure and view themselves as inept. They do not receive the normal satisfactions of recognition, achievement, or affection. Their unsuccessful academic and/or social experiences lead to disappointment, frustration, feelings of incompetence, a lack of self-worth, and a poor self-concept (Silver, 1998). In considering these emotional issues, the critical question is—how does the student *feel*?

School is often a place that makes few allowances for the shortcomings of these students, a place where teachers often are unable to comprehend their difficulties. Ironically, the characteristic inconsistency and unpredictability of learning disabilities may account for an occasional academic breakthrough during which these students perform well. However, such random moments of achievement may serve to make matters worse. The teacher may be convinced that the student could do it "if she just tried harder." Failure now may be viewed purely in terms of bad behavior, poor

Mastery of tasks brings
respect from peers.
(© *James Carroll*)

attitude, or lack of motivation. Increased impatience and blame from the teacher intensify the student's anxiety, frustration, and confusion.

Anxiety

Students with learning disabilities display more symptoms of anxiety than their peers. The demands and pressures of school and high-stakes testing provoke increased anxiety and even panic. These students feel that events beyond their control are happening *to them*. When they encounter these situations, they feel hopeless and become frozen and panicked during these periods of intense pressure. These students may miss class, they tune out, and become disorganized. The feelings that these students experience are real and must be understood by teachers and parents (Gorman, 1999). Some test-taking tips are included in the chapter on adolescents and adults with learning disabilities in "LD in Practice: Test-Taking Tips."

Depression

Many students with learning disabilities suffer from depression and a general pervasive mood of unhappiness. Their clinical depression may be a reaction to the stress and frustration of school demands, the lack of friendship and social interactions, or they may stem from a biochemical predisposition. Signs of depression include: (1) loss of energy, (2) loss of interest in friends, (3) difficulty in concentration, and (4) feelings of helplessness, which occasionally are expressed through suicidal talk (Gorman, 1999; Learning Disabilities Association of America, 1999). For more information on depression, see the website **http://www.ldonline.com/LDInDepth.**

The Quality of Resiliency

Although a person's feeling of self-worth is threatened by continual failure, not all individuals with learning disabilities develop low self-esteem. Some have remarkable resiliency and are able to preserve self-confidence and self-worth (Brooks & Goldstein, 2002; Freiberg, 1993; Keogh, 2000). Such resilience seems to result from a mix of internal and external contextual factors (Sorensen, et al., 2003). What are the factors that enable individuals to keep on trying, and how can the school help? Self-worth is gained through mastery of a skill or task, through perceived respect from peers, and through one's feelings of competence. Students who believe that they have competencies in areas other than academic work are less likely to be devastated by school failure. To maintain their sense of self-worth, students need a support system from sources such as teachers, parents, and peers who will acknowledge that these students possess other competencies. The support system preserves their self-worth by keeping failure to a minimum; increasing the visibility of their nonacademic talents, skills, and competencies; and emphasizing *learning* goals over *performance* goals. For example, the student can be given credit for performing a task in the correct manner (a learning goal) even though the final answer may not be accurate (the performance goal).

It is fascinating to observe individuals who have achieved greatness and maintained a sense of belief in their self-worth and in what they were doing despite having faced years of rejection and ridicule. Some examples are Gertrude Stein, the famous poet, who submitted poems to editors for about 20 years before one was finally accepted for publication. Vincent van Gogh sold only one painting during his lifetime. Frank Lloyd Wright was rejected as an architect during much of his life. So, too, many individuals with learning disabilities have overcome failure and rejection because they strongly believed in themselves. The stories of adults with learning disabilities who have succeeded against the odds are inspiring, and their resilience is evident in their success (Gerber & Brown, 1997; Gerber & Reiff, 1991; S. L. Smith, 1991).

Techniques to build self-esteem and to enhance a healthy mental attitude are presented in the Teaching Strategies section of this chapter and in the chapter on clinical teaching.

BEHAVIORAL CHALLENGES

Students with learning disabilities sometimes exhibit co-occurring behavioral problems. These behavioral problems must be considered in the planning of instruction (Buck, Polloway, Kirpatick et al., 2000; Scott, 2003).

Functional Behavioral Assessment and Positive Behavioral Supports

IDEA–2004 (PL 108–446) requires that if the child's behavior interferes with his or her learning, or with the learning of others, the IEP team will consider a functional behavioral assessment and develop positive behavioral supports. **Functional behavioral assessment** involves determining the cause, or antecedent event, that triggers the child's behavior. For example, when the teacher asks Charlie to read (antecedent event), he begins to disturb others in the classroom by hitting them or Jerry swears and uses inap-

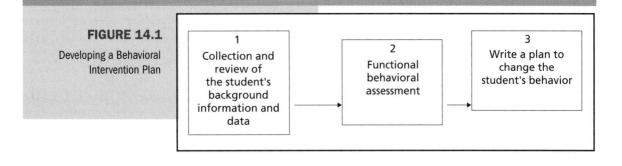

FIGURE 14.1

Developing a Behavioral Intervention Plan

1
Collection and review of the student's background information and data

2
Functional behavioral assessment

3
Write a plan to change the student's behavior

propriate language when asked to do a task. The **positive behavioral supports** are strategies to change a student's troublesome behavior. Positive behavioral supports are designed to increase positive behavior or to replace an undesirable behavior. For example, Charlie is only asked to read aloud after he has practiced and prepared to do this task. Charlie's response can be modified by rewarding him when he responds in a more suitable fashion. Jerry signs a contract to respond using appropriate language. This approach is based on the concepts of behavior management (see the chapter on assessment).

The questions that should be addressed to develop positive behavioral supports include: (1) What happened? (2) What happened before? (3) What happened after? (4) How can the response be changed? Figure 14.1 shows the steps involved in behavioral intervention planning. The steps include (1) collecting and reviewing the student's background information and data, (2) functional behavioral assessment, and (3) writing a plan to change the student's behavior (Buck et al., 2000). Websites for functional behavioral assessment can be found at **http://cie.asu.edu/volumel/number5** and **http://www.pbis.org.**

Reinforcement Theory

Reinforcement is used to increase or to change a target behavior. By identifying reinforcements that a student wants, teachers can construct a reward system that will promote the desired behavior. Positive and immediate reinforcements are the most effective in fostering the desired behavior. Stars, stickers, raisins, tokens, points, praise, flashing lights, or simply the satisfaction of knowing that the answer is correct are common reinforcers. The following list notes some examples of consequent events that have been provided by the teacher as part of a reward system:

- After Annette reads five pages, she receives *two tokens that are exchangeable for toys.*
- In teaching reading to Serena, the desired behavior is having her say the sound equivalent of the letter *a* every time a stimulus card with the letter *a* is shown. For each correct response, Serena immediately receives a positive reinforcement, such as *a piece of low-sugar cereal, stars, points, money, praise,* or *attention.*

Reinforcement theory offers a major tool for **behavior management.** The use of reinforcements provides an important strategy for teaching students appropriate behavior and for managing behavior. In applying reinforcement theory, the teacher must do the following:

1. Identify potential reinforcers that will motivate the student and accelerate performance on a specific task. Reinforcers are consequent events that increase preceding events.
2. Identify the student's responses or behaviors that should trigger the reinforcer. Responses and behaviors must be observable and clearly defined.
3. Arrange the environment so that the student receives reinforcement for the desired behavior. A reward system should be devised so that reinforcements are offered on a predetermined schedule for the desired behaviors.
4. Eventually, have the student make independent instructional decisions, such as making corrections and establishing reinforcement values. Including the student in the modification of the reward system is helpful as the student is moved to a system of naturally occurring reinforcers.

A critical view of reinforcement theory and behavior modification is expressed by Kohn (1995), in his book with the provocative title *Punished by Rewards: The Trouble With Gold Stars, Incentive Plans, A's, Praise, and Other Bribes.* Kohn argues that this method of saying, "Do this and you will get that" and dangling goodies (ranging from candy bars to sales commissions) in front of people; the same way that we train the family pet. It is a short-run solution that is ineffective in the long run. To the extent that educators do not modify reward systems to move students toward naturally occurring reinforcers, Kohn's argument is probably justified. It is critical to help students maintain desired behaviors from reinforcers that occur naturally in the environment. The following principles will assist in achieving that end:

1. Start with the reinforcer that will increase the desired behavior and that is most natural.

2. Once the behavior is securely established, begin to withdraw the reinforcer on a careful schedule of use and nonuse. (See Alberto & Troutman, 2003, for a more complete explanation of reinforcement schedules.)

3. Include the student in the revision of the reinforcement schedule, making sure they understand the benefits of the desired behavior.

Reinforcement is used to increase or change the target behavior. It allows one to construct a reward system that will promote the desired behavior. As noted previously, positive and immediate reinforcements are most effective in fostering the desired behavior. Reinforcement is always defined by its impact on a particular student. Common reinforcers are stars, stickers, raisins, tokens, points, praise, flashing lights, or simply the satisfaction of knowing that the answer is correct.

Motivation

Motivation is the force that energizes and directs one's drive to accomplish goals. Students need a strong desire to learn in school because much of academic learning requires persistent, hard work over a long period of time. Theories of motivation focus on such questions as: (1) How do students become interested enough to initiate learning? (2) What causes students to move toward a particular goal? (3) What causes students to sustain that interest over an extended period of time to reach that goal?

Students with learning disabilities may appear to be unmotivated, but their lack of motivation may actually result from chronic academic failure. The process of losing motivation begins when students first doubt their intellectual abilities. They then start to view their achievement efforts as futile, eventually asking themselves, "Why try if you know you are going to fail?" After encountering repeated failure in the classroom, these students develop negative and defeatist attitudes about school learning. As a consequence, they have fewer opportunities to experience personal control over learning outcomes and eventually begin to doubt that they are in control of their academic destinies (Groteluschen, Borkowski, & Hale, 1990; McGrady, Lerner, & Boscardin, 2001; Schmid & Evans, 1998).

Attribution Theory

Attribution theory provides one way to look at motivation. The term **attribution** refers to the way people explain to themselves the causes of their successes and failures. Research shows that poor achievers differ from their peers in terms of attribution style. They tend to attribute their successes to factors outside of their control, such as random luck or the teacher; and they blame their failures on their lack of ability, the difficulty of the task, the teacher, or other random factors (Chapman, 1988; Kistner, Osborn, & LaVerrier, 1988; Stipek, 1993).

In contrast, students who are successful achievers have a different attribution style. They attribute failure to their own lack of effort, and they attribute success to their own effort. Feeling in control of the situation, good learners persevere on difficult tasks, delay gratification, and are actively involved in the learning situation (Stipek, 1993).

Students with learning disabilities should be guided to change their attribution styles to become more persistent and independent learners. Statements that recognize the important part the students' efforts played in their success help to stabilize a budding internal attribution.

Cognitive Behavior Modification

Cognitive behavior modification is a self-instructional approach to learning. Developed by Meichenbaum (1977), cognitive behavior modification requires individuals: (1) to talk to themselves aloud, (2) to give themselves instruction on what they should be doing, and (3) to reward themselves verbally for accomplishments. Individuals learn to motivate themselves through self-talk, self-reinforcement, and self-monitoring.

The self-instructional cognitive behavior modification program involves the following steps:

1. First, the teacher models or performs a task while talking to himself or herself aloud as the students observe.
2. The students then perform the same task while talking to themselves, under the teacher's guidance.
3. The students quietly whisper the instructions to themselves while going through the task.
4. The students use inner (or private) speech while performing the task.
5. Finally, the students self-monitor their performance by telling themselves how they did. For example, "I did well" or "Next time I should slow down."

Cognitive behavior modification has often been used with adults in such settings as weight-loss programs. Students with learning problems can use the procedure for all kinds of learning, schoolwork, and homework. The goal of cognitive behavior modification is not only to change the person's behavior, but the goal is also to increase the person's awareness of their behavior and the thinking associated with the behavior. Many of the ideas inherent in cognitive behavior modification are incorporated into *learning strategies instruction.*

Helping Students With Behavioral Challenges

The Teaching Strategies section of this chapter offers strategies for helping students with behavioral challenges.

ASSESSING SOCIAL AND EMOTIONAL BEHAVIORS

Assessing a student's social skills and emotional status is difficult. Observational techniques are the most direct way to judge a student's social and emotional behaviors. In fact, teachers who have daily contact with students in the classroom are excellent judges of the students' social and emotional reactions. Other assessment methods include inventories, checklists, and rating scales. Several of these assessment instruments are listed in Table 14.1, and they are described more fully in "Tests for Assessing Students With Learning Disabilities."

Interview instruments are questionnaires that help a teacher interview the parent, the student, another teacher, or someone else who has contact with the student. *Student inventories* are given to the student to complete.

Sociometric techniques provide information about the student's popularity and acceptance by classmates. They are designed to identify the students who are the most and least liked in their classes. One sociometric technique is to ask the students to nominate the three classmates (or another number of classmates) that they like most.

TEACHING STRATEGIES

This section of the chapter presents teaching strategies: (1) for developing social competencies, (2) for students with emotional challenges, and (3) for behavior management.

DEVELOPING SOCIAL COMPETENCIES

Students who are socially competent learn social skills effortlessly through daily living and observation. Students with social deficits need conscious effort and specific teaching to learn about the social world, its nuances, and its silent language. Just as we teach students to perform schoolwork—to read, write, spell, do arithmetic, and pass tests—we can teach students with social disorders how to live with and relate to other people. Just as we must use different methods to teach different academic skills, so must we use a variety of methods to teach students how to get along with others.

The activities in this section are designed to develop social skills. They are divided into the following categories: (1) self-perception, (2) sensitivity to other people, (3) social maturity, (4) learning strategies for social skills, and (5) social skills programs.

TABLE 14.1

Instruments to Assess Social
and Emotional Behaviors

Instrument	Purpose	Age or grade assessed
Interview instruments		
■ AAMR Adaptive Behavior Scale—School, (Second Edition)	Used to assess adaptive behavior	Ages 3–21
■ Scales of Independent Behavior—Revised	Designed to measure functional independence and adaptive functioning in school, home, employment, and community settings	Ages 2–adult
■ Vineland Social–Emotional Early Childhood Scales	Designed to assess the social and emotional functioning of young children	Ages birth–11
Rating scales		
■ Burk's Behavior Rating Scales	Used to identify particular behavioral problems and patterns of problems shown by children	Grades 1–9
■ Child Behavior Checklist	Designed to assess the competencies and problems of children and adolescents through the use of ratings and reports by different informants	Ages 2–18
■ Devereux Behavior Rating Scale—School Form	Designed to evaluate behaviors typical of children and adolescents with moderate to severe emotional disturbance	Ages 5–18
■ Devereux Scales of Mental Disorders	Constructed to evaluate behaviors associated with psychopathology	Ages 5–18
■ Pupil Rating Scale (Revised): Screening for Learning Disabilities	Used to identify students with deficits in learning, subtests and scores include verbal (auditory comprehension, spoken language, and total) and nonverbal (orientation, motor coordination, personal–social behavior, and total)	Ages 5–14
Student inventories		
■ Coopersmith Self-Esteem Inventories	Designed to measure evaluative social, academic, family, and personal areas of experience	Ages 8–80
■ Piers-Harris Children's Self-Concept Scale	Designed to aid in the assessment of self-concept in children and adolescents	Grades 4–12

Self-Perception

1. *Awareness of body parts.* Have the students locate the parts of the body on a doll, on a classmate, or on themselves. Make a cardboard person with movable limbs. Put the cardboard person in various positions (e.g., with the left leg and right arm out) and have the students duplicate the positions.

2. *Completing pictures.* Have the students complete a partially drawn figure or tell what is missing in an incomplete picture.

3. *Scrapbooks.* Help the students put together scrapbooks about themselves. The students should include pictures of themselves at different stages of growth, pictures of their families and pets, a list of their likes and dislikes, anecdotes about their past, accounts of trips, awards they have won, and so on. One group of secondary students with learning disabilities enjoyed making a PowerPoint presentation entitled, "About Me."

4. *Emotional awareness.* Encourage the students to identify and name emotions that are appropriate for a particular situation.

Sensitivity to Other People

Spoken language is only one means of communication; there is also a "silent language" with which people communicate without the use of words, relying instead on gestures, stance, facial expressions, and tone of voice. Students with social deficits need help in learning how to decode the communication messages conveyed by this silent language.

1. *Pictures of faces.* Collect pictures of faces and have the students ascertain whether the faces convey the emotion of happiness or sadness. Other emotions to be shown include anger, surprise, pain, and love (Dimitrovsky et al., 1998).

2. *Gestures.* Discuss the meanings of various gestures with the students, such as waving good-bye, shaking a finger, shrugging a shoulder, turning away, tapping a finger or foot, and stretching out arms.

3. *Videos CDs and story situations.* Find pictures, short videos, or story situations in which the social implications of gesture, space, and time are presented, and help the students to identify the emotional content of communication.

4. *What the voice tells.* Help the students learn to recognize implications in the human voice, beyond the words themselves, by having the students listen to a voice on a tape recorder to determine the mood of the speaker and to decipher the communication beyond the words. Role playing with different emotions is also effective.

Social Maturity

Social development involves growing from immaturity to maturity and from dependence to independence. Among all species of animal life, the human infant is perhaps the most dependent on others for survival at birth. The road from complete dependence to relative independence is the long and gradual growth toward social maturity. **Social maturity** involves recognizing the rights and responsibilities of self and others, making friends, cooperating with a group, following procedures agreed on by others, making moral and ethical judgments, and gaining independence in the outside world. The following list provides strategies to help students develop socially.

1. *Anticipating consequences of social acts.* Role playing, creative play, stories, and discussions can help the students to see what happens if the rules of a game or the rules of manners are broken. Help the students predict the endings or the next events in stories and literature. Discuss why or why not the predictions might be accurate.

2. *Establishing independence.* Encourage the students to go places alone. Make simple maps, include the directions to follow, and talk about the various steps to take in getting to the desired location; use a walking map, if necessary. Plan activities so that the students can make simple purchases alone. In addition, plan activities that provide opportunities for the students to talk to other people, to ask directions, interview others, and so on.

3. *Making ethical judgments.* Help the students learn cultural mores and learn to make value judgments. For example, the students can discuss and analyze age-appropriate dilemmas and situations that involve acts such as telling lies, stealing, and protecting a friend. Help the students learn to differentiate how ethical mores are expressed in the various cultures and settings in which they live and work.

4. *Planning and implementing.* Have the students make plans for a trip, activity, party, picnic, or meeting. Then, help the students successfully implement the plans to gain a sense of independence and maturity.

5. *Solving the "weekend problem."* A consequence of a social disorder is that students often have difficulty making friends. Parents frequently complain of a "weekend problem," when their child appears to have nothing to do. Without companions and friends, summers and vacations can be difficult periods for such children. This situation requires the initiative and cooperation of parent groups and community organizations to develop appropriate solutions to the weekend problem. Teachers can help by fostering appropriate reciprocal friendships at school. Including students in group activities for at least part of the day and placing students with potential friends can assist in this process.

Learning Strategies for Social Skills

Learning strategies are useful for helping students acquire academic skills, and they are also effective in teaching social skills (Deshler et al., 1996; Lenz & Deshler, 2003). Social strategies instruction changes students' typical patterns of responses to social situations. Students learn to develop new cognitive responses to social problems and to think about their social actions.

Social skills learning strategies include: (1) teaching students to stop and think before responding, (2) to verbalize and rehearse social responses, (3) to visualize and imagine the effect of their behavior, and (4) to preplan social actions.

The response of many students with learning disabilities in social situations is impulsive; they act without considering what is required and without thinking through the possible solutions or the consequences of various courses of action. Through instruction in the strategies of self-verbalization and self-monitoring, students can be taught self-control to keep from giving immediate, nonreflective responses. The students are trained to verbalize and ask themselves questions such as "What am I supposed to be doing?" In other words, they are taught to stop and think before responding. Teachers can model social learning strategies by talking out such thoughts as "Does this problem have similarities to other problems I have encountered?" or "What are three possible solutions?" The students then practice these skills of self-verbalization, or thinking aloud. The self-monitoring method has been found to reduce inappropriate social responses (Deshler et al., 1996). Social skills strategies include: (1) direct instruction, (2) prompting, (3) modeling, (4) rehearsal, and (5) reinforcement (Carter & Sugai, 1988). Several social skills strategies are presented in "LD in Practice: Strategies for Teaching Social Skills in the General Education Classroom."

Social Skills Programs

A number of commercial programs are designed to help students develop social skills. Several of these programs are listed in Table 14.2.

STRATEGIES FOR STUDENTS WITH EMOTIONAL PROBLEMS

Strengthening Self-Esteem

Successful experiences build *self-esteem*, which is comprised of the feelings of self-worth, self-confidence, and self-respect. It is often of little value to try to determine whether the learning failure or the emotional problem is the primary precipitating factor in students with a low self-esteem. A more constructive approach is to help the students accomplish an educational task so that their feelings of self-worth are oriented in a positive direction.

LD IN PRACTICE

STRATEGIES FOR TEACHING SOCIAL SKILLS IN THE GENERAL EDUCATION CLASSROOM

- *Judging behavior in stories.* Read or tell an incomplete story that involves social judgment. Have the students anticipate the ending or complete the story. A short video of a social situation provides an opportunity to discuss critically the activities of the people in the video. For example, discuss the consequences of a student's rudeness when an acquaintance tries to begin a conversation, or the consequences of a student making a face when asked by her mother's friend if she likes her new dress, or the consequences of a student hitting someone at a party.

- *Grasping social situations through pictures.* A series of pictures can be arranged to tell a story that involves a social situation. Have the students arrange the pictures and explain the story. Comics, readiness books, beginning readers, and magazine advertisements all provide good source materials for such activities. The series can also include pictures that are on transparencies.

- *Learning to generalize newly acquired social behaviors.* After students learn socially appropriate behaviors, they must learn to generalize these behaviors to many settings, such as an inclusive classroom, the home environment, playgrounds, and other social situations. Students need many opportunities to practice and maintain newly acquired skills. Collaboration between special education teachers and general education teachers is needed to make plans for generalizing in inclusive classrooms.

- *Learning conversation skills.* Students must learn how to converse with others. They must learn how to extend greetings, introduce themselves, find a topic to talk about, listen actively, ask and answer questions, and say good-bye.

- *Friendship skills.* Students must learn how to make friends, give a compliment, join group activities, and accept thanks.

- *Game-playing skills.* Social skills can be taught to students through the activity of playing games with others. The instruction involves social modeling, behavioral rehearsal, and behavior transfer while playing games.

Student accomplishments can increase the ability to learn and strengthen emotional outlook. The beginning of this mutual reinforcement cycle is also the beginning of effective treatment (Silver, 1998).

Parents and teachers can help build self-esteem by providing a strong support system to promote students' feelings of control and power over their destiny. Students should be helped to develop their skills in decision making by providing opportunities to make decisions. They should learn to

TABLE 14.2 Social Skills Programs	■ ASSET: A Social Skills Program for Adolescents With Learning Disabilities (Research Press). A social skills program based on instruction in learning strategies. The website is **http://www.researchpress.com**. ■ Life-Centered Career Education (LCEE) (Council for Exceptional Children). This program provides functional activities that are work related. The website is **http://www.cec.sped.org**. ■ The SCORE Skills: Social Skills of Cooperative Groups (Edge Enterprises). Learning strategies for working in a cooperative learning curriculum. The telephone number is (877) 767-1487. ■ Skillstreaming the Adolescent: New Strategies and Perspectives for Teaching Prosocial Skills (Research Press). This program provides activities for developing social skills in adolescents. The website is **http://www.researchpress.com**. ■ Skillstreaming the Elementary School Child: New Strategies and Perspectives for Teaching Prosocial Skills (Research Press). This program provides activities for developing social skills in elementary school children. The website is **http://www.researchpress.com**. ■ Social Skills Intervention (American Guidance Services). A social skills program for students with learning disabilities. The website is **http://www.agsnet.com**. ■ The Walker Social Skills Curriculum: The Accepts Program (Pro-Ed). This program provides activities for developing social skills within the school curriculum. The website is **http://www.proedinc.com**.

recognize the causes of their success and failure so that they stop blaming themselves and begin, instead, to feel that their efforts will influence the outcome. Students need coping mechanisms and strategies that will allow them to respond constructively to failure (also see the chapter on clinical teaching).

Self-Esteem Strategies   If failure to learn is accompanied by emotional problems, the student may be the victim of a continuous cycle of failure. In this cycle, the failure to learn leads to adverse emotional responses—feelings of self-derision and anxiety—which augment the failure-to-learn syndrome. Teachers must find a way to reverse this cycle—to build feelings of self-worth, to increase self-confidence and self-concept, and to provide an experience of success. Research shows that different self-esteem strategies are effective with different age groups. *Self-concept strategies* are effective with middle-school students. *Academic interventions* are effective with elementary-aged children. *Counseling types of interventions* are effective with middle-school students and high school students (Elbaum & Vaughn, 2001).

The following "LD in Practice: Strategies for Improving Self-Esteem in the General Education Classroom" provides some self-esteem activities and approaches.

LD IN PRACTICE

STRATEGIES FOR IMPROVING SELF-ESTEEM IN THE GENERAL EDUCATION CLASSROOM

- *Therapeutic relationships.* For most students with learning problems, the teacher can provide a type of therapy through skilled and sensitive clinical teaching. (Specific techniques for building such a relationship are discussed in the chapter on clinical teaching.)

- *Bibliotherapy.* Bibliotherapy is an approach to help students understand themselves and their problems through books where the characters in the book learn to cope with problems similar to those faced by the students. By identifying with a character and working out the problem with the character, students are helped with their own problems. Books designed to explain the learning problem to the students are also useful.

- *Magic circle.* Participants are seated in a circle. They are encouraged to share their feelings, to learn to listen, and to observe others. The program seeks to promote active listening, to focus on feelings, to give recognition to each individual, and to promote greater understanding. Sample circle topics include

  It made me feel good when I . . .

  I made someone feel bad when I . . .

  Something I do very well is . . .

  What can I do for you . . . ?

- *Creative media.* Teachers can use art, dance, and music as therapy techniques for promoting the emotional involvement of students with learning disabilities.

- *Counseling.* Students' reactions to failure and to success depend in part on their attitudes, emotional status, beliefs, and expectations. Healthier emotional attitudes can be developed through counseling, both individually and in groups.

- *Psychiatric and psychological services.* The most severely affected students may need psychiatric or psychological treatment before or during educational treatment.

BEHAVIOR MANAGEMENT STRATEGIES

Behavior management strategies can be useful for students with learning disabilities. Many teachers intuitively use many of these procedures, but precise application of behavior management requires that the procedures are systematic and that the behaviors to be changed are observable and measurable. In this section, we discuss: (1) reinforcement, (2) contingency contracting, (3) time-out, and (4) home–school coordination.

Reinforcement

As noted earlier in this chapter, a *reinforcement* is a consequent event that occurs after a person makes a behavioral response. By definition, a reinforcer increases the likelihood that the preceding behavior will be repeated. A *positive reinforcement* is a consequence that is added or given to the student. A *negative reinforcement* is a consequence that is removed from an individual. The preceding behavior increases or decreases as a result of the reinforcement.

Sometimes teachers or parents inadvertently reinforce inappropriate behavior. For example, if Willie clowns around, and the teacher pays attention to him, the teacher's attention to Willie's actions, even if the teacher perceives it as negative attention, may reinforce the undesirable behavior of clowning around. "LD in Practice: Finding Reinforcers" describes some items that might be useful as positive reinforcers.

Contingency Contracting

The *contingency contract* is a written agreement between the student and the teacher. An example of a contingency contract is shown in Figure 14.2. The idea that something desirable can be used to reinforce something the student does not wish to do is the essence of **contingency contracting.** This is also called "Grandma's Rule" because grandmothers are alleged to promise, "If you finish your vegetables, you can have your dessert." For example, Dave, who likes to play ball, is allowed to play after he finishes his spelling work.

Time-Out

Time-out is a procedure in which a disruptive student is removed from the instructional activities and placed in a designated isolated area for a short period of time. Isolation does not have to be complete to be effective, but it does need to remove the student from the group. Time-out can be a powerful technique to manage disruptive behaviors in children, but it should be used cautiously. If implemented properly, time-out offers an effective means of managing behavior. Several conditions will increase the likelihood of success with this method (Alberto & Troutman, 2003):

LD IN PRACTICE
FINDING REINFORCERS

The success of behavior management depends upon finding the appropriate reinforcer to increase the target behavior. What is viewed as desirable by one student may hold little interest for another. Ways to find a successful reinforcer include observing the students to see what they choose to do in their free time and requesting information from the students and their parents. Reinforcers can be *extrinsic,* which is something external, such as food or toys; or reinforcers can be *intrinsic,* which is something internal, such as the satisfaction of mastering a task. The reinforcement can be social, such as praise or approval from a teacher or parent. It can be a token to be exchanged for a later reinforcement or it can take the form of a privilege. A good reinforcement for any individual is simply the one that works for that individual. Several suggested reinforcements are

- *Foods:* Nuts, edible seeds, low-sugar cereal, peanuts, popcorn, raisins, and fruit

- *Play materials:* Baseball cards, toy animals, toy cars, marbles, jump ropes, gliders, crayons, coloring books, clay, dolls, kits, balls, puzzles, comic books, balloons, games, and yo-yos

- *Tokens:* Marks on the blackboard or on the student's paper, gold or silver stars, marbles in a jar, plastic chips on a ring, poker chips, tickets, and washers on a string

- *Activities or privileges:* Having computer time, presenting at show and tell, going first, running errands, having free time, helping with cleanup, taking the class pet home for the weekend, leading the songs, seeing a video, listening to music, and doing artwork

- Time-out should be brief, from 1 min to 10 min, with young children requiring the least amount of time. A common rule of thumb is no more than 1 min for every year of the child's age.

- Warn the child only once by stating clearly the broken rule.

- During a time-out, the teacher and the other children should ignore the student.

- Actively assist the student's return from time-out by directly engaging the child in ongoing activities.

Home–School Coordination

Programs of **home–school coordination** are intended to improve the behavior of students by combining school and home efforts. Behavioral goals are

FIGURE 14.2

Contingency Contract

CONTRACT

This contract is an agreement between _____
(student)

and _____ .
(teacher)

_____ will _____
(student)
_____

by _____ .
(date of completion)

If the work described above is completed on time,

_____ will _____
(teacher)

_____

_____

_____

by _____ .
(date of reward)

_____   _____
Signature of student   date

_____   _____
Signature of teacher   date

established for the student, and each day the teacher indicates the goals the student has met. These behavior-management sheets are sent home, signed by the parents to acknowledge the teacher's comments, and then returned to the school. The student is reinforced at home for the positive behaviors displayed at school. A sample home–school behavior-management sheet is shown in Figure 14.3. Strategies for students with behavioral disorders are listed in "LD in Practice: Strategies for Students With Behavioral Challenges in the General Education Classroom."

LD IN PRACTICE

STRATEGIES FOR STUDENTS WITH BEHAVIORAL CHALLENGES IN THE GENERAL EDUCATION CLASSROOM

- *Seating placement.* Seat the student with minimal extraneous distraction and where you can readily ascertain if the student is attentive. Place the student away from windows and doors.

- *Plan varied activities.* Modify the classroom routine to enable the student to get up and move around the classroom periodically. Have the student pass out papers or put books away.

- *Provide structure and routine.* Establish a routine and follow it each day. If something unusual occurs, prepare the students by explaining what event will happen and when the event will occur.

- *Require a daily assignment notebook.* The assignment notebook helps the students to organize time, know what is to be done, and to designate when it has been accomplished.

- *Make sure you have the student's attention before you begin.* Use an attention signal, such as a hand sign, a light touch, or eye contact to gain the student's attention.

- *Make directions clear and concise.* Directions should be consistent with daily instructions. Simplify complex directions and avoid multiple commands.

- *Break assignments into workable chunks.* If workbook or assignment sheets are cluttered and confusing, adapt them by breaking them into smaller parts. Less material will be on the page, and the material will be better organized.

- *Give extra time as needed.* Some students may work at a slower pace and may require extra time to complete the task.

- *Provide feedback on completed work as soon as possible.*

- *Encourage parents to set up appropriate study space at home.*

- *Make use of learning aids.* Many students enjoy using computers, calculators, and other learning aids.

- *Find something that the child does well and encourage that interest.*

FIGURE 14.3

Home–School Behavior-
Management Sheet

Student: _____ Teacher: _____

Week beginning: _____

Use (S) for satisfactory performance.
Use (U) for unsatisfactory performance.
Use (N) for items that do not apply.

	Mon	Tues	Wed	Thurs	Fri
1. Homework turned in					
2. Began work within 3 min of assignment					
3. Followed directions					
4. Followed class and school rules					
5. Paid attention to teacher					
6. Raised hand to speak					
7. Other					

If 80% of applicable boxes are checked, the student will receive 20 min of computer time.

Teacher's initials: _____

COMMENTS AND SIGNATURE

	Teacher	Parent
Monday	_____	_____
Tuesday	_____	_____
Wednesday	_____	_____
Thursday	_____	_____
Friday	_____	_____

- Parent signs chart daily
- Child takes chart home daily
- Child returns chart to school daily
- Child receives daily reward

CHAPTER SUMMARY

1. A comprehensive understanding of the problems of students with learning disabilities and related disorders requires considering the effects of social, emotional, and behavioral facets of the student.

2. Nonverbal learning disorders involve problems in social learning. Students with NVLD may initially do well in academic learning, but as these students advance through the grades, and social skills become more important for ensuring their success, they tend to fall behind.

3. The characteristics of social problems include Asperger's syndrome, poor social perception, a lack of judgment, difficulty in perceiving the feelings of others, problems in socializing and making friends, and problems in family relationships and in school.

4. Students with learning disabilities often have emotional problems. These may be the consequence of experiencing continual failure. The emotional problems may include having little self-confidence, a poor self-concept, and few opportunities to develop feelings of self-worth.

5. Some students with learning disabilities display behavioral challenges. Functional behavioral assessment and positive behavioral supports are needed for these students. Other considerations are reinforcement, motivation, attribution, and cognitive behavior modification.

6. Assessment instruments for social–emotional factors include interviews, inventories, checklists, rating scales, and sociometric techniques.

7. Teaching strategies include developing social skills, helping students with emotional problems, building self-esteem, and behavior management strategies.

DISCUSSION AND REFLECTION

1. What are nonverbal learning disorders (NVLD)? What are some specific problems associated with NVLD?

2. Why do you think deficits in social skills are called "the most crippling type of problem that a student can have?" What are common indicators of social problems?

3. Describe functional behavioral assessment and positive behavioral supports.

4. What is reinforcement? How can effective reinforcers be identified?

5. Discuss "resiliency." Why is the quality of resiliency important to individuals with learning disabilities?

6. What strategies could a teacher use to help a student with challenging behaviors?

**KEY
TERMS**

attribution *(p. 533)*

behavior management *(p. 532)*

cognitive behavior modification
(p. 534)

contingency contracting *(p. 543)*

functional behavioral assessment
(p. 530)

home–school coordination
(p. 544)

positive behavioral supports
(p. 531)

reinforcement *(p. 531)*

social maturity *(p. 538)*

social perception *(p. 524)*

social skills *(p. 521)*

time-out *(p. 543)*

REFERENCE GUIDE

Case Study: The Process of Referral, Assessment, and Teaching of Adam Z.

INTRODUCTION

Case studies are useful because they provide an opportunity to apply knowledge to the assessment–teaching process in an actual situation. The case of Adam Z., a freshman high school student, follows the format outlined in Chapter 2. A case study is influenced by the theoretical orientation of the case investigators, and professionals often differ in their views of such matters as the selection of assessment instruments, the analysis of the assessment information, and the recommended intervention procedures. The case of Adam Z. is followed through six stages of the assessment–teaching process:

Stage 1: Prereferral activities

Stage 2: Referral and initial planning

Stage 3: Multidisciplinary evaluation

Stage 4: The case conference meeting—Writing the individualized education program

Stage 5: Implementing the teaching plan

Stage 6: Monitoring the student's progress

Identifying Information: Adam Z.

Name of student: Adam Z.

Age: 14 years 6 months

Current placement: High school freshman, Grade 9.4

**STAGE 1:
PREREFERRAL
ACTIVITIES**

Shortly after the semester started in September, Adam Z.'s high school departmental English teacher, Ms. Sloan, requested a prereferral staffing to discuss Adam, who was doing poorly in his general English class. The informal prereferral staffing included Adam's departmental teachers: his English teacher (Ms. Sloan), his general science teacher, his American history teacher, and his Spanish teacher. Ms. Sloan reported that Adam's problem in the English class was that he could not read his literature assignments and therefore had little knowledge of the content of this material. After discussing Adam's problem, the members of the prereferral team recommended that a classmate in the English class tape-record the assigned literature readings for Adam so that he could listen to the material. Specifically, they recommended that Adam's classmate Peter be given this assignment because Peter was particularly interested in speech and drama and read well orally.

Ms. Sloan discussed this proposal with Adam and Peter, and they both agreed to give the plan a trial. Peter recorded two of the literature assignments to help Adam study his English homework. However, about 1 week into this plan, Peter won the lead role in the school play, and frequent rehearsals kept him from making further recordings for Adam. As Peter's interest in the plan waned, so did Adam's, and he began to fall even further behind in English. At the next report period at the end of October, Adam received a failing grade in English. At this point, Ms. Sloan decided to refer Adam for a special education evaluation.

STAGE 2: REFERRAL AND INITIAL PLANNING

Ms. Sloan met with Adam's mother, Mrs. Z., to discuss Adam's failing work in English class. Mrs. Z. related that Adam had always had difficulty in school, beginning in the primary grades. During the elementary years—Grades 1 through 8—Adam had attended several schools; however, he had not received any special education services. As Mrs. Z. signed the consent form to have the evaluation, she remarked that she hoped Adam would finally receive some help now that he was in high school.

Ms. Sloan subsequently submitted the referral to the special education coordinator in the high school. The initial planning for Adam's multidisciplinary evaluation included the following assessment information: (1) classroom observation, (2) a review of health information and tests of auditory and visual acuity, (3) a conference with Adam, (4) developmental and educational history, (5) a psychological report and measures of learning aptitude, and (6) measures of present levels of academic achievement.

STAGE 3: MULTIDISCIPLINARY EVALUATION

The multidisciplinary evaluation team consisted of the school psychologist, the learning disabilities teacher, the high school guidance counselor, and the school nurse. Each member of the team was responsible for obtaining certain kinds of evaluation information. A summary of this information follows.

Classroom Observation

The special education teacher observed Adam during an American history class. The students in the class were assigned to read a passage about the U.S. Constitution and then answer 10 multiple-choice questions on the text. Adam exhibited behavior suggesting that he was completing the assignment: He appeared to be reading the selection; then he appeared to be answering the questions, exhibiting such behaviors as scratching his head and looking up at the ceiling, as if thinking, before marking each answer. Upon examination of his test paper and in discussion with him, however, it became evident that the assignment was completely beyond his current achievement level. He had learned to act appropriately and to fake the behavior of looking as though he were doing the same work that the other students were doing.

Review of Health Information and Tests of Auditory and Visual Acuity

The school nurse reviewed the health records, which showed that Adam had been absent often during the primary and elementary years because of frequent colds. Also, his mother had reported that during his early school years he had suffered from otitis media, which is an inflammatory condition of the middle ear that results in fluctuating and temporary hearing loss. The school nurse tested Adam's hearing with an audiometer and found that his auditory acuity fell within normal limits. The school nurse also gave Adam a visual screening test, and no problems were noted. The other health history indicated no unusual health problems.

Conference With Adam

The guidance counselor met with Adam to discuss the evaluation. Adam clearly recognized that he had a learning problem. He told the counselor that he did not understand why he was so different from the other kids and why he always had so much difficulty learning to read. He thought he had gotten along at his previous school because the teachers had left him alone and had never called on him. Adam also mentioned that he was worried that his parents did not like him because he caused them so much more trouble than did his sister. He confided that he had once convinced a friend to rush into his house shouting, "Help, help! Adam's been run over!" so that he could watch his mother's reaction through the window. He quite expected her to say, "Thank goodness for that." When she stood up in a panic, Adam rushed in, telling her it was only a joke. His mother was very angry about his joke, but Adam thought it was worth playing the trick to find out that she really cared.

Developmental and Educational History

The guidance counselor interviewed Mr. and Mrs. Z. and also reviewed Adam's educational history through his cumulative records.

Adam is the younger of two children. His sister is 2 years older and is an excellent student. Adam, born 2 months prematurely, weighed 4 lbs 8 oz at birth. He was a colicky baby and was put on a supplemental formula because his weight gain had been slow. He was allergic to the formula and several changes had to be made. Motor developmental milestones were accomplished within the normal range: He crawled at 8 months and walked at 12 months. His language development, however, was slow. Unlike his sister, he did not engage in such activities as cooing, verbalizing, or babbling during his infancy. By age 2, he had not learned to say any words to express himself; he only pointed and gestured. His pediatrician referred him to the University Language Disorders Clinic, where he received language therapy for 1 hour each week until he was 3 years old. At that time, the family moved to a country in Asia, where Mr. Z. was assigned for 3 years as part of his military service. During this period, Adam did not attend school or receive any language help. The family had a child-care helper who did not speak English. Mrs. Z. said that it was not until Adam was 4 years old that she was able to decipher and understand his verbalizations.

Mrs. Z. said that Adam was an extremely active child, getting into everything, and that when he was young, the family could not take him to restaurants or to the homes of friends because of his extremely hyperactive behavior. He seemed to be driven, in constant motion and touching everything. His poor communication skills and hyperactivity interfered with his ability to make friends as a young child. Adam is no longer hyperactive; however, he still is not very talkative. He does well in sports activities and is on the football team.

Adam was placed in first grade when the family returned to the United States from their overseas assignment. At the end of the school year, the school suggested that Adam repeat first grade. However, his father would not hear of it, and Adam was enrolled in the second grade of a private school. The family moved three times during Adam's elementary years because of his father's military assignments. He never did repeat a grade during elementary school.

Although Adam does not enjoy school, he does not complain, and he tries hard to succeed. Just before the conference ended, Adam's father commented that as a child he also had difficulty learning to read in school but has nevertheless done well as an officer in the military service. Mr. and Mrs. Z. said they hoped Adam could be helped through the special services of the school.

Psychological Report and Measures of Learning Aptitude

The school psychologist administered the Wechsler Intelligence Scale for Children—Third Edition (WISC-3) to assess Adam's intellectual potential and the Wide-Range Achievement Test—3 (WRAT-3) to screen his academic achievement. The psychologist found that Adam was in the above-average range of intelligence but that his abilities in performance areas were substantially higher than his abilities in language areas. Adam especially did poorly in tasks that required auditory memory abilities. The WRAT-3 indicated severe problems in reading and spelling, with less severe problems in mathematics. Adam was cooperative during the testing, was aware of his problem, and appeared to be eager to succeed in school. He was well adjusted, considering the many years of failure he had encountered. His scores on these tests follow: WISC-3 Full-Scale IQ, 104; Performance IQ, 120; Verbal IQ, 91.

Verbal subtests	Scaled score	Performance subtests	Scaled score
Information	7	Picture arrangement	13
Comprehension	6	Picture completion	14
Arithmetic	9	Block design	15
Vocabulary	7	Object assembly	14
Similarities	8	Coding	8
Digit span	6		

Wide-Range Achievement Test—3 (WRAT-3)

Reading (word recognition)	3.3
Arithmetic	6.0
Spelling	3.0

Measures of Present Levels of Academic Achievement

The special education teacher administered the following academic tests in their entirety or as partial tests: the Brigance Diagnostic Inventory of Essential Skills; the Woodcock-Johnson Psychoeducational Battery, III—Tests of Achievement; Key Math—Revised; the Clinical Evaluation of Language Fundamentals—Revised (CELF-R); the Gray Oral Reading Tests, Fourth Edition; Test of Adolescent and Adult Language—3 (TOAL-3); and the Test of Written Language—3 (TOWL-3). A brief summary of Adam's test results in several academic areas follows.

Oral Language Abilities: Receptive   Adam scored at or above average on tests of comprehension of oral language sentences and words. When visual input was included, he seemed to do better in receiving and remembering the language.

Oral Language Abilities: Expressive   Problems were evident in Adam's use of oral language, in word finding (retrieval of a precise word), and in syntax. He had difficulty repeating sentences with complex syntactical structures and words with difficult articulation patterns, and his word fluency was poor in terms of quantity, quality, and speed.

Reading   According to the oral reading inventory, Adam's instructional reading level was at the middle third grade. Although he knew basic word-recognition skills, vowels, consonants, and simple word prefixes and suffixes, his efforts to apply this information were slow and laborious. His sight vocabulary was at the third-grade level, but his recognition was somewhat slow. Adam's comprehension of the oral reading passages was surprisingly strong. Considering his difficulty with word-recognition skills, he seemed to make good use of context clues to help him understand the story.

Silent reading scores ranged from Grade 3.5 to 5.0, generally below the fifth percentile for his age and grade. Observation of Adam during silent reading showed that he spent more time studying the questions than reading the text. He seemed to be looking for words he knew.

Mathematics   Mathematics was an area of significant strength for Adam. He did particularly well in computation and in mental mathematics. However, when he had to read a mathematics word-story problem, the task became more difficult.

Written Language   Written language was an area of great difficulty for Adam. He did poorly in usage, mechanics, and spelling. Both quantity and quality of output were very meager. His handwriting, however, was legible.

STAGE 4: THE CASE CONFERENCE MEETING—WRITING THE INDIVIDUALIZED EDUCATION PROGRAM (IEP)

The case conference team met and included the following participants: the general education English teacher, the special education teacher, the school psychologist, the special education coordinator, Mr. and Mrs. Z., and Adam.

The case conference team agreed that Adam has learning disabilities and requires special education services. He exhibits a severe discrepancy between his potential and his achievement in reading, oral language, and written language.

Adam possesses a number of strengths, such as intellectual aptitude in the above-average range, with strong abilities in performance areas, mathematics concepts, and computational skills; receptive oral language; and physical and motor performance. He does not exhibit behavior problems in school and appears to have a high desire to learn.

Areas of weakness that should be considered include poor reading skills (although he has a knowledge of basic word-attack skills), inadequate skills in oral expressive language, poor written language and spelling skills, and inefficient strategies for coping with the demands of the high school curriculum.

The case conference team felt that Adam's academic problem was severe. Because he had not received any help in the past, he now needs an intensive special education intervention. The team recommended that Adam receive instruction from a special education teacher and that this teacher collaborate with the content-area teachers. The case conference team recommended that Adam be placed in a general education subject class for mathematics and physical education, and a career education class to begin planning for career and work. Adam's special education teacher will collaborate with the teachers of these classes. The individualized education program (IEP) team indicated that Adam will need accommodations of extended time in taking the statewide tests. Mr. and Mrs. Z. agreed to the plan, and an IEP was written and signed by all members of the case conference team.

STAGE 5: IMPLEMENTING THE TEACHING PLAN

The special education teacher developed more specific plans to meet the objectives written into Adam's IEP. The plans included soldifying and practicing word-recognition skills, building reading comprehension skills through reading of content-area books, enrolling Adam in a career education class, teaching learning strategies to improve his ability to help himself learn, and providing direct instruction in oral expression and in writing. The special education teacher will collaborate by planning and working with the general education, content-area teachers.

STAGE 6: MONITORING THE STUDENT'S PROGRESS

Adam's progress will be reviewed informally on a weekly basis by the special education teacher. Progress will be monitored in all classes and conferences will be held with each of the content-area teachers. The special education teacher will collaborate with the content-area teachers and provide more intensive instruction as needed. A review of Adam's progress and a reevaluation of his program will be held in 6 months.

Tests for Assessing Students With Learning Disabilities

This appendix provides an alphabetical listing of a number of tests that are useful in assessing students with learning disabilities. The list includes tests that were mentioned in this text, as well as some tests that were not discussed. The descriptive material about each test is brief and is not designed to be evaluative. Because tests are frequently revised and new forms of manuals are issued, it is desirable to obtain a current catalog from the publisher before placing an order.

When selecting tests, the user should consider the technical qualities of the test, such as: (1) its purpose, (2) reliability, (3) validity, (4) standardization procedures, (5) types of scores that are provided, (6) ease of administration and scoring, and (7) time and training needed to administer the test. The Standards for Educational and Psychological Tests (American Educational Research Association, 1999) is a comprehensive guide for test users and developers; it sets the standard for the kinds of information that should be in test manuals, for the kinds of information that should be provided on the technical adequacy of tests, and for test use. The website is **http://www. apa.org/standards.htm.**

AAMR Adaptive Behavior Scale—Second Edition. American Association of Mental Retardation. There are two editions of the AAMR Adaptive Behavior Scale: (1) the School Edition (ages 3–21) and (2) the Residential and Community Edition (ages 18–79). Assesses the total life-functioning abilities of individuals through an interview with an informant. 20 minutes.

Ammons Full-Range Picture Vocabulary Test (Forms A and B). Psychological Test Specialists. An individually administered test of receptive language vocabulary. Preschool to adult.

Analytic Reading Inventory—Second Edition. Charles E. Merrill. Criterion-referenced informal reading inventory that yields independent, instructional, and frustration reading levels and listening, miscues, and comprehension analysis. Grades 1–6.

Attention Deficit Disorder Evaluation Scale. Hawthorne Educational Services. There are two versions of the Attention Deficit Disorder Evaluation Scale: (1) the Home Version and (2) the School Version. Rating Scales: School Version, ages 4–5 to 21 years with three subscales: inattentive, impulsive, and hyperactive. Home Version, ages 4–20.

Auditory Discrimination in Depth (Lindamood). Riverside. Auditory perception skills of sounds, letters, and words. All ages.

Auditory Discrimination Test (Wepman). Western Psychological Services. An individual test of a child's ability to distinguish if two spoken words are the same or different. Ages 5–8.

Bankson–Bernthal Test of Phonology. Pro-Ed. Test of knowledge of phonology. Ages 3–12.

BASC—Behavior Assessment for Children AGS. A coordinated system of instructions that evaluates the behavior, thoughts, and emotions of children and adolescents. Ages 4–18. 20 minutes.

Basic Achieving Skills Individual Screener (BASIC). Psychological Corporation. Individual test of reading, mathematics, spelling, and writing. Grades 1–12.

Bender-Gestalt Test. Western Psychological Services. An individually administered test of a person's performance in copying designs. The Koppitz Scoring (E. Koppitz, **The Bender-Gestalt Test for Young Children,** New York: Grune & Stratton, 1963) provides a developmental scoring system for young children. Ages 5–10.

Boehm Test of Basic Concepts—Revised. Psychological Corporation. Diagnostic group test of understanding of concepts. Grades K–2.

Brigance Assessment of Basic Skills. Curriculum Associates. Tests of reading, language arts, and arithmetic. Grades K–6.

Brigance Assessment of Basic Skills—Spanish Edition. Curriculum Associates. For students with limited English proficiency. Grades K–8.

Brigance Comprehensive Inventory of Basic Skills—Revised. Curriculum Associates. Criterion-referenced tests of readiness, reading, language arts, and mathematics. Grades K–6. 15–90 minutes.

Brigance Inventory of Early Development—Revised. Curriculum Associates. Assesses functional skills of preschool children. Ages 1–7.

Brigance Diagnostic Inventory of Essential Skills. Curriculum Associates. Measures minimal academic and vocational competencies. Designed for secondary students. Grades 6–adult.

Bruinicks-Oseretsky Test of Motor Proficiency. AGS. Individually administered test of gross- and fine-motor development. Ages 4–16.

Burk's Behavior Rating Scales. Western Psychological Services. Measures 18 categories of behavior, including self-blame, anxiety, withdrawal, dependency, attention, impulse control, sense of identity, and social conformity. Ages 3–18.

California Achievement Tests: Reading and Mathematics. California Testing Bureau. A battery of group tests to assess several areas of academic achievement. Grades K–12.

Carrow Elicited Language Inventory. Riverside. Assessment of language proficiency in spoken language. Ages 3–8.

Child Behavior Checklist (T. Achenbach & C. Edelbrock, Burlington, VT: University of Vermont, Department of Psychiatry). Checklists for teachers and parents. Measures behavior and hyperactivity. Parent checklists for ages 2–3 and for ages 4–18. Teacher's Report Form, ages 5–18. 20 minutes.

Clinical Evaluation of Language Fundamentals—Revised (CELF-R). Psychological Corporation. Individual screening test and diagnostic battery to measure oral language abilities. Grades K–12.

Comprehensive Receptive and Expressive Vocabulary Test. Riverside. Individual vocabulary test with two subtests: (1) expressive vocabulary and (2) receptive vocabulary. Ages 4–17. 45 minutes.

Comprehension Test of Phonological Processing. Pro-Ed. A test used to measure phonological processing. Ages 4–9.

Conners Rating Scales. Multi-Health Systems. Conners Teacher Rating Scale, ages 3–17. Conners Parent Rating Scale, ages 3–17. Rating scales for hyperactivity. Parents and teachers provide information to determine the child's level of hyperactivity. 10–15 minutes.

Coopersmith Self-Esteem Inventories. Publishers Test Services. Self-report questionnaires that consist of short statements, such as "I can usually take care of myself." The subject answers with either "like me" or "unlike me." Measures attitude toward the self in social, academic, and personal contexts. Ages 8–80.

Denver Developmental Screening Test—Revised. Denver Developmental Materials. Identifies delays in young children in the areas of fine-motor, adaptive, gross-motor, personal–social, and language development. Ages 1 month–6 years. 20 minutes.

Detroit Tests of Learning Aptitude—4 (DTLA-4). Pro-Ed. An individual test of mental functions that has subtests measuring various areas of mental processing. In addition to an overall score, the tests yield nine composite scores. Ages 6–17. 30–60 minutes.

Developmental Sentence Scoring Test. Northwestern University Press. A speech sample from 50 complete utterances (sentences) is obtained from the child and then scored and analyzed. Ages 2½–6.

Developmental Test of Visual–Motor Integration. Western Psychological Services. A visual–motor test of the subject's abilities in copying designs. Ages 5–15.

Devereux Adolescent Behavior Rating Scale. Devereux Foundation. A scale for teacher rating of behavior of adolescents. Ages 13–18.

Devereux Child Behavior Rating Scale. Devereux Foundation. A rating scale for use by parent or teacher. Ages 8–12.

Devereux Elementary School Behavior Rating Scale. Devereux Foundation. A rating scale that identifies 11 school-related behaviors, such as disturbance, impatience, attention, withdrawal, inability to change, slowness, and quitting before completing a task. Grades K–6.

Diagnostic Assessment of Reading with Trial Teaching Strategies (DARTTS). Riverside. Identifies strengths and weaknesses in reading through six areas: word recognition, word analysis, oral reading, silent reading comprehension, spelling, and word meaning. Identifies student reading levels. 20–30 minutes. The Trial Teaching Strategies provide a series of teaching sessions to identify the most effective methods and materials for individual students. Provides three reading levels: potential, instructional, and independent. 30 minutes.

Diagnostic Mathematics Inventory: Mathematics System. CTB/McGraw-Hill. Individual inventory of student achievement in mathematics. Grades 1–12.

Diagnostic Reading Inventory. Kendall/Hunt. Individual informal reading inventory with graded word lists and graded oral and silent reading passages. Grades 1–8.

Diagnostic Tests and Self-Helps in Arithmetic. California Testing Bureau. Test designed to diagnose arithmetic difficulties. Grades 3–8.

DIAL-R. AGS Edition. Developmental Indicators for the Assessment of Learning—Revised (DIAL-R). AGS. A prekindergarten screening test to identify children with learning problems. Preschool age.

Durrell Analysis of Reading Difficulty. Psychological Corporation. A battery of diagnostic tests designed to help in the analysis and evaluation of specific reading difficulties. Grades 1–6. 30–60 minutes.

Ekwall Reading Inventory. Allyn & Bacon. Informal reading inventory of oral and silent reading. Grades Preprimary–9. 20–30 minutes.

Gates-MacGinitie Reading Tests (4th ed.). Teachers College Press. A general test of silent reading designed for group administration. Five forms. Grades 1–12.

Gates-McKillop-Horowitz Reading Diagnostic Tests. Teachers College Press. Battery of tests for individual administration, designed to give diagnostic information about a student's reading skills. Grades 1–6. 60–90 minutes.

Gilmore Oral Reading Test. Psychological Corporation. An individually administered oral reading test that gives information about word accuracy, rate, and comprehension. Grades 1–8. 15–20 minutes.

Goldman-Fristoe Test of Articulation. American Guidance Services. Tests the articulation of words and sentences. Ages 2–16+. 30 minutes.

Goldman-Fristoe-Woodcock Test of Auditory Discrimination. American Guidance Services. Tests auditory discrimination of phonemes against a quiet background and against a noisy background. Ages 2–16+.

Goodenough-Harris Drawing Test. Psychological Corporation. Provides a score of nonverbal intelligence obtained through an objective scoring of a student's drawings of a human figure. Ages 3–15. 13–15 minutes.

Gray Oral Reading Tests (4th ed.). Pro-Ed. Two forms. An individually administered oral reading test. Thirteen passages for oral reading and comprehension questions. Grades preprimary–12.

Halstead-Reitan Neuropsychological Test Battery for Children. Reitan Neuropsychology Laboratory. Designed to test brain behavior functions in children. Ages 9–14.

Illinois Test of Psycholinguistic Abilities (3rd ed.) (ITPA–3). Pro-Ed. Individually administered test containing 12 subtests of dimensions of mental processes. Scores obtained on subtests can be used for diagnostic purposes. Ages 2–10. 60 minutes.

Informal Reading Inventory (Appendix D in M. Richek, J. Caldwell, J. Jennings, & J. Lerner, *Reading Problems: Assessment and Reading Strategies,* Allyn & Bacon, 2002). An informal reading inventory of oral and silent reading, including word-recognition and reading-comprehension passages and questions. Grades preprimary–8.

Iowa Tests of Basic Skills. Riverside. Group test of several academic areas: reading, arithmetic, language, and work-study skills. Grades K–12.

Kaufman Assessment Battery for Children (K-ABC). AGS. Individual test of intelligence and achievement. Yields four major scores: sequential processing, simultaneous processing, mental processing composite, and achievement. Ages 2–12. 1 hour.

Kaufman Brief Intelligence Tests. (K-BIT). AGS. Verbal and nonverbal subtests. Provides IQ score. Ages 4–90. 15–30 minutes.

Kaufman Test of Educational Achievement (K-TEA). AGS. Individually administered tests of reading, mathematics, and spelling. Grades 1–12. Brief form: 20–30 minutes; comprehensive form: 50–75 minutes.

Key Math—Revised. American Guidance Services. Measures 14 arithmetic subskills. Individually administered. Four levels of evaluation. Grades K–6.

Keystone Visual Survey Service for Schools. Keystone View. Individually administered visual screening device to determine the need for further referral for a visual examination. Ages 2–18.

Learning Disabilities Diagnostic Inventory (LDDI). An individual rating scale to help identify intrinsic processing disorders and learning disabilities. Ages 8.0–17.11. 1–20 minutes.

Learning Styles Inventory. Price Systems. Uses responses to 100 true–false items to identify students' preferred learning conditions. Grades 3–12.

Leiter International Performance Scale. Stoelting. Nonverbal test of mental abilities. Ages 2–18. 1.5 hours.

Lincoln-Oseretsky Motor Development Scale. Stoelting. Individual tests of a variety of motor skills. Ages 6–14.

Lindamood Auditory Conceptualization Test. Riverside. Measures speech sound discrimination and perception of number, order, sameness, or difference of speech sounds. Preschool to adult. 10 minutes.

Listening Comprehension Scales. (OWLS). AGS. Measures listening comprehension and oral expression. Ages 5–21.

McCarthy Scales of Children's Abilities. Psychological Corporation. General intellectual levels and strengths and weaknesses in several ability areas. Ages 2.5–8.5. 45–60 minutes.

Metropolitan Achievement Tests. Psychological Corporation. Group-administered battery of tests that measures several areas of academic achievement: reading, spelling, and arithmetic. Grades K–12.

Monroe Diagnostic Reading Tests. Nevins. Individually administered diagnostic reading test of oral reading and word recognition. Grades 1–4. Untimed.

Monroe Reading Aptitude Tests. Riverside. Group-administered test to measure readiness for reading.

Nonreading test that assesses several areas of mental functioning. Ages 6–9.

Motor-Free Test of Visual Perception. Academic Therapy Publications. Test of visual perception that does not require a motor component. Ages 4–8. 10 minutes.

Nebraska Test of Learning Aptitude. Hiskey Publications. An individual test of intellectual potential used widely with the deaf or hard-of-hearing. Ages 7–17. 40–60 minutes.

Nelson-Denny Reading Test. Riverside. Group or individual general reading assessment. Grades 9–adult.

Nelson Reading Skills Test. Riverside. Diagnostic reading battery. Grades 3–9.

Oral and Written Language Scales (OWLS). AGS. Listening comprehension and oral expression; individual test assesses listening and oral expression skills. Ages 3–21. 1–25 minutes. Written Expression Scale; test assesses written language. Ages 5–21. 15–25 minutes.

Ortho-Rater. Bausch & Lomb. Individual visual screening test. Grades 1–12.

Otis-Lennon School Ability Test. Psychological Corporation. Group test of general mental ability and scholastic aptitude. Grades K–12. 45–80 minutes.

Peabody Developmental Motor Scales. Riverside. Early childhood development program provides in-depth assessment and an instructional program in gross-motor and fine-motor skills, eye–hand coordination, finger dexterity, reflexes, balance, and locomotion. Ages birth–83 months. 10–20 minutes.

Peabody Individual Achievement Test—Revised (PIAT-R). AGS. Individually administered test of five subjects: mathematics, reading recognition, reading comprehension, spelling, and general information. Grades 6–12.

Peabody Picture Vocabulary Test—III. AGS. An individually administered test of receptive language vocabulary. Ages 2–18.

Phonological Awareness Test. LinguiSystems. Individually administered test to diagnose deficits in phonological awareness. Ages 5–9.

Piers-Harris Children's Self-Concept Scale. Western Psychological Services. Students respond "yes" or "no" to statements such as "I am a happy person." State-

lated and rejected. This program addresses the social problems these children face and offers some practical solutions. Richard Lavoie. 1 hour. (PBS) Price: $49.95.

Print Resources

Accardo, P., Blondis, T., Whitman, B., & Stein, M. (2000). *Attention deficits and hyperactivity in children and adults* (2nd ed.). New York: Marcel Dekker.

Birsh, J. (1999). *Multisensory teaching of basic language skills.* Baltimore: Paul H. Brookes.

Deshler, D., Schumaker, J., Lenz, B., Bulgren, J., Hoch, M., Knight, J., et al. (2001). Ensuring content-area learning by secondary students with learning disabilities. *Learning Disabilities Research & Practice, 16*(2), 96–108.

Ford, A. (2003). *Laughing Alegra.* New York: Newmarket Press.

Friend, M., & Cook, L. (2003). *Interactions: Collaborative skills for school professionals* (4th ed.). Boston: Allyn & Bacon.

Fletcher, J., Couter, W., Reschley, D. & Vaughn, S. (2004). Alternative approaches to the definition and identification of learning disabilities: Some questions and answers. *Annals of Dyslexia, 54*(2), 304–331.

Graham, S., Harris, K., & Larsen, L. (2001). Prevention and intervention of writing difficulties. *Learning Disabilities Research & Practice, 16*(2), 62–73.

Lerner, J., Lowenthal, B., & Egan, R. (2003). *Preschool children with special needs: Children at-risk and children with disabilities.* Boston: Allyn & Bacon.

National Council of Teachers of Mathematics. (2000). *Principles and standards for school mathematics.* Reston, VA: Author.

National Reading Panel. (2000). *Teaching children to read: An evidence-based assessment of the scientific literature on reading and its implications for reading instruction.* Washington, DC: National Institute of Child Health and Human Development.

Office of Special Education and Rehabilitative Services. (2000). *A guide to the individualized education program.* Washington, DC: U.S. Department of Education.

Richek, M., Jennings, J., Caldwell, J., & Lerner, J. (2002). *Reading problems: Assessment and reading strategies.* Boston: Allyn & Bacon.

Salvia, J., & Ysseldyke, J. (2004). *Assessment in special and inclusive education.* Boston: Houghton Mifflin.

Shaywitz, S. (2003). *Overcoming Dyslexia.* New York: Alfred A. Knopf.

Silver, L. (1998). *The misunderstood child: Understanding and coping with your child's learning disabilities.* New York: Times Books.

Smith, S. L. (2005). *Live it learn it: The academic club methodology for students with learning disabilities and ADHD.* Baltimore, MD: Paul H. Brookes.

Spinelli, C. (2002). *Classroom assessment for students with special needs in inclusive classrooms.* Upper Saddle River, NJ: Merrill/Prentice Hall.

Swanson, L., Harris, K., & Grahm, S. (2003). *Handbook of learning disabilities.* New York: Guilford Press.

Thurlow, M. (2000). Standards-based reform and students with disabilities: Reflections on a decade of change. *Focus on Exceptional Children, 33*(3), 1–16.

Wong, Y., & Donahue, M. (Eds.). (2002). *The social dimensions of learning disabilities.* Mahwah, NJ: Erlbaum.

Organizations for Learning Disabilities and Related Disorders

Asperger's Syndrome Coalition of the United States (ASC-U.S.)
P.O. Box 2577 Jacksonville, FL 32203-2577
Phone: (904) 745-6741
E-mail: aspen@cybermax.net
> National organization that provides information and support to individuals, families, and professionals dealing with neurological communication disorders on the autism spectrum, including nonverbal learning disabilities, Asperger's syndrome, high-functioning autism, semantic-pragmatic disorder, hyperlexia, and PDD-NOS.

Association of Educational Therapists (AET)
1804 W. Burbank Blvd. Burbank, CA 91506
Phone: (818) 843-1183   Fax (818) 843-7423
> AET is a national membership organization that provides referrals to local educational therapists.

Association on Higher Education and Disability (AHEAD)
P.O. Box 21192 Columbus, OH 43221-0192
Phone: (614) 488-4972   Fax: (614) 488-1174

AHEAD is an international organization that provides training programs, workshops, conferences, and publications.

Children and Adults With Attention Deficit Disorders (CHADD)
8181 Professional Place, Suite 201 Landover, MD 20785
Toll free: (800) 233-4050   Phone: (301) 306-7070
Fax: (301) 306-7090
http://www.chadd.org

Through family support and advocacy, public and professional education, and the encouragement of scientific research, CHADD works to ensure that individuals with ADD reach their inherent potential. Local chapters hold regular meetings to provide support and information.

Council for Exceptional Children (CEC)
1920 Association Dr., Reston, VA 22091-1589
Phone: (703) 620-3660
http://www.cec.sped.org

A nonprofit membership organization with 17 specialized divisions, DLD is the division of the CEC that is dedicated to learning disabilities. The organization provides free information and holds conferences.

Council for Learning Disabilities (CLD)
P.O. Box 40303 Overland Park, KS 66204
Phone: (913) 492-8755   Fax: (913) 492-2546

CLD provides services to professionals who work with individuals with learning disabilities.

Division for Learning Disabilities (DLD)
1920 Association Dr., Reston, VA 22091-1589
Phone: (703) 620-3660
http://www.teachingld.org

A division of the Council for Exceptional Children for professionals working in the field of learning disabilities.

Educational Resources Information Center (ERIC)
1920 Association Dr., Reston, VA 22091-1589
Toll free: (800) 328-0272   Phone: (703) 264-9474

Information clearinghouse funded by the U.S. Department of Education and hosted by the Council for Exceptional Children.

International Dyslexia Association (IDA) (formerly the Orton Dyslexia Society)
Chester Building, Suite 382
8600 LaSalle Road Baltimore, MD 21286-2044
Toll free: (800) 222-3123   Phone: (410) 296-0232
http://www.interdys.org

The society has 42 branches across the country that offer informational meetings and support groups. Referrals are made for persons seeking resources; in addition, the society publishes journals and publications about dyslexia.

Learning Disabilities Association of America (LDA)
4156 Library Road Pittsburgh, PA 15234
Phone: (412) 341-1515   Fax: (412) 344-0224
http://www.ldaamerica.org

The LDA national office has a resource center with over 500 publications for sale; it also operates a film rental service. Call the national headquarters to receive a free information packet.

Association for the Education of African American Children With Learning Disabilities
P.O. Box 09521 Columbus, OH 43209
Phone: (614) 237-6021   Fax: (614) 238-0929
E-mail: info@aacld.org

National Center for Learning Disabilities (NCLD)
381 Park Avenue South, Suite 1420 New York, NY 10016
Toll free information and referral service:
(888) 575-7373   Phone: (212) 545-7510
Fax (212) 545-9665
http://www.ld.org

NCLD seeks to raise public awareness and understanding, furnish national information and referrals, and arrange educational programs and legislative advocacy. NCLD provides educational tools to heighten understanding of learning disabilities, including annual publications, quarterly newsletters, informative articles, specific state-by-state resource listings, and informative videos about learning disabilities.

National Information Center for Children and Youth With Disabilities (NICHCY)
P.O. Box 1492 Washington, DC 20013
Toll Free: (800) 695-0285   Phone: (202) 884-8200

NICHCY is an information clearinghouse that provides free information on disabilities and related issues, focusing on children and youth (birth to age 25). Free services include personal responses, referrals, technical assistance, and information searches.

National Institute for Child Health and Human Development (NICHD)
National Institutes of Health
6100 Executive Boulevard Rockville, MD 20852
Phone: (301) 496-5733

NICHD provides reviews of literature and information related to NICHD research.

National Association for Adults With Special Learning Needs (NAASLN)
1444 I St. NW, Suite 700 Washington, DC 20005
Phone: (202) 216-9623
E-mail: NAASLN@BostromDC.com

A nonprofit organization comprised of professionals, advocates, and consumers whose purpose is to educate adults with special learning needs. NAASLN publishes a newsletter and holds annual conferences.

National Association for the Education of Young Children (NAEYC)
1509 16th Street, NW Washington, DC 20036-1426
Toll free: (800) 424-2460
E-mail: aauj82@prodigy.com

NAEYC is a national membership organization that focuses on children from birth to age 8. The organization sponsors an annual conference; publishes a bimonthly journal; and has a catalog of books, brochures, videos, and posters.

Recording for the Blind and Dyslexic
www.rfbd.org
20 Roszel Road Princeton, NJ 08540
Toll free: (800) 221-4792   Phone: (609) 452-0606
Fax: (609) 520-7990

Operators provide information on over 80,000 recorded textbooks and other classroom materials, from fourth grade through postgraduate levels, that are available for loan.

Schwab Learning
1650 South Amphlett Boulevard, Suite 300 San Mateo, CA 94402
Toll free: (800) 230-0988   Phone: (650) 655-2410
Fax: (650) 655-2411
http://www.schwablearning.org

Schwab Learning, a program area of the Charles and Helen Schwab Foundation, is dedicated to helping children with learning differences be successful in learning and life. It provides reliable, research-based information and guidance. Developed especially for parents of children who are newly identified as having a learning difference, it is designed to be a parent's "guide" through the new and unfamiliar landscape of LD.

Figures and Tables

Chapter 2
Figure 2.4, p. 67: W. Otto, R. McMenemy, and R. Smith, *Corrective and Remedial Teaching*, Third Edition. Copyright 1980 by Houghton Mifflin Company. Used by permission. **Figure 2.6, p. 71:** From Inclusive Assessment and Accountability Systems by Erickson, Ysseldyke, Thurlow, & Eliot, *Teaching Exceptional Children*, 31(2), 1998, p. 8. Copyright 1998 by The Council for Exceptional Children. Reprinted with permission.

Chapter 6
Table 6.1, p. 200: *Diagnostic and Statistical Manual of Mental Disorders, Fourth Edition, Text Revision*. Washington, DC, American Psychiatric Association, 2000.

Chapter 8
Table 8.3, p. 281: From Wagner et al. (1993); The Secondary School Programs of Students with Disabilities: A Report from the National Longitudinal Transition Study of Special Education Students. Used by permission. **Table 8.7, p. 296:** "College Guides and Resources for Learning Disabilities" from *Their World*, NCLD, 1999. Reprinted with the permission of the National Center for Learning Disabilities, 381 Park Avenue South, New York, NY 10016. http://www.ncld.org.

Chapter 10
Table 10.4, p. 341: From J. Rosner, *Helping Children Overcome Learning Difficulties*. Copyright 1979 by Jerome Rosner. Reprinted by permission from Walker & Company.

Chapter 11
Table 11.3, pp. 384–385: From Johnson, D. D. (1971, February), The Dolch List reexamined. *The Reading Teacher*, 242(5), 455–456. Reprinted with permission of Dale D. Johnson and the International Reading Association. All rights reserved. **Figure 11.5, p. 399:** From Phonic Remedial Reading Lessons by S. A. Kirk, W. Kirk, and E. Minskoff. Copyright 1985 Academic Therapy Publications. Reprinted by permission. **Table 11.5, p. 400:** From The IOTA Informal Word Reading Test and IOTA Conversion Chart, Grade Medians in M. Monroe, *Children Who Cannot Read: The Analysis of Reading Disabilities and the Use of Diagnostic Tests in Instruction of Retarded Readings*, University of Chicago Press, © 1932. Reprinted by permission of The University of Chicago Press. **Table 11.6, p. 400:** From The IOTA Informal Word Reading Test and IOTA Conversion Chart, Grade Medians in M. Monroe, *Children Who Cannot Read: The Analysis of Reading Disabilities and the Use of Diagnostic Tests in Instruction of Retarded Readings*, University of Chicago Press, © 1932. Reprinted by permission of The University of Chicago Press. **Figure 11.7, p. 405:** *Source:* From "K-W-L: Teaching Model That Develops Active Reading of Expository Text," by D. M. Ogle, 1986, *The Reading Teacher*, 39, p. 565. **Table 11.7, p. 408:** From *Reading Mastery 8 Fast Cycle, Storybook 1/e* by S. Engelmann and E. Bruner, Copyright 1995 McGraw-Hill. Reproduced with permission of The McGraw-Hill Companies.

Chapter 13

Table 13.1, p. 480: The ideas for this table were suggested by S. Miller & C. Mercer, (1997). Educational Aspects of Mathematics Disabilities. *Journal of Mathematics Disabilities, 30*(1), p. 50.   Table 13.3, p. 485: *Source:* Adapted from the National Council for Teachers of Mathematics (2000), *Principles and Standards for School Mathematics,* Reston, VA: Author.

Chapter 8

p. 274: P. Rodis, A. Garrod and M. Boscardin. (2001). *Learning Disabilities: Life Stories.* Boston, Allyn & Bacon.

Chapter 12

p. 455: Reprinted by special permission of Dr. Emmett Albert Betts, Phonetics Spelling Council.

Text

Chapter 4

p. 150: From A Mother's Thoughts on Inclusion by Carr, M. N. (1993), *Journal of Learning Disabilities, 26*(9), 590–592. Copyright © 1993 by Pro-Ed, Inc. Reprinted by permission.

abstract instruction At this level of mathematics instruction, students manipulate symbols without the help of concrete objects or representational pictures or tallies.

accommodations Refers to adjustments and modifications within a general education program to meet the needs of students with disabilities. Required under Section 504 of the Rehabilitation Act.

accommodations for assessment Modifications that are made in testing students with disabilities.

active learners Students who are involved with their learning and contribute to the learning process.

active learning Dynamic involvement in the learning process.

adapted physical education Physical education programs that have been modified to meet the needs of students with disabilities.

adaptive behavior scales A rating scale of information provided by an informant who knows the child (such as the parent). It is usually obtained during an interview with the parent and provides information about the student's self-help skills, communication skills, daily living skills, socialization, and motor skills.

affect Refers to children's perception of themselves.

Americans with Disabilities Act (ADA) A federal law passed in 1990 to protect the rights of individuals with disabilities.

annual goals General estimates of what the student will achieve in one year. These goals should represent the most essential needs of the student. Annual goals are part of the written individualized education program.

antecedent event In behavioral psychology, the situation that precedes the target behavior.

aphasia Impairment of the ability to use or understand oral language, usually associated with an injury or abnormality of the speech centers of the brain. Several classifications are used, including expressive aphasia, receptive aphasia, developmental aphasia, and acquired aphasia.

apraxia Difficulty in directing one's motor movements.

Asperger's Syndrome Qualitative impairment in social interactions, impulse control, and self-motivation. Classified as high functioning autism.

assessment stages This is the stage during which tests are given (multidisciplinary evaluation) and decisions are made (the case conference or IEP meeting).

assistive technology Any technology that enables an individual with a disability to compensate for specific deficits. It includes low-tech or high-tech equipment.

Assistive Technology Act Federal Law for providing technology devices and services to increase the function capabilities of individuals with disabilities.

attention deficit disorder (ADD) Difficulty in concentrating and staying on a task. It may or may not be ac-companied by hyperactivity. Used by the U.S. Department of Education.

attention deficit hyperactivity disorder (ADHD) Difficulty in concentrating and staying on a task, accompanied by hyperactivity. The condition of ADHD is identified and defined by the American Psychiatric Association's *Diagnostic and Statistical Manual of Mental Disorders,* fourth edition.

attribution *See* attribution theory.

attribution theory A person's ideas concerning the causes of his or her successes and failures.

audiology A discipline that spans a number of functions, including the testing and measurement of hearing, the diagnosis and rehabilitation of those who are deaf and hard-of-hearing, the scientific study of the physical process of hearing, and the broadening of knowledge and understanding of the hearing process.

auditory blending The ability to synthesize the phonemes of a word in recognizing the entire word. In an auditory blending test, the individual sounds of a word are pronounced with separations between each phoneme sound. The child must combine the individual sounds to say and recognize the word.

auditory discrimination The ability to recognize a difference between phoneme sounds; also the ability to identify words that are the same and words that are different when the difference is a single phoneme element (for example, *big-pig*).

Autism Lifelong developmental disability that is best described as a collection of behavioral systems that affect verbal communication, nonverbal communication, and social interactions.

automaticity In cognitive learning theory, the condition in which learning has become almost subconscious and therefore requires little processing effort.

background knowledge Information and experiences that are gained about the topic of instruction or about a reading selection.

bar graphs A type of chart in which different values are represented by rectangular bars.

basal reading series A sequential and interrelated set of books and supportive material intended to provide the basic material for the development of fundamental reading skills.

basal reader *See* basal reading series.

basic academic skills instruction Instruction focusing on direct teaching, especially in reading and mathematics. Students receive instruction at a level that approximates their achievement or instructional level.

behavioral analysis The process of determining the subskills or steps needed to accomplish a task.

behavior management   Using behavioral strategies to direct an individual's activity in an appropriate manner.

behavioral approach   An approach to teaching that concentrates on the sequence of learning skills and on changing a child's behavior through contingencies (such as reward, punishment, and so on).

behavioral unit   In behavioral psychology, the core unit that constitutes an action and its environment. It consists of the antecedent event, the target behavior, and the consequent event.

bibliotherapy   A technique of using characters in books to help children work through personal problems.

bilingual method   A teaching approach in which students use their native language for one part of the instructional day and English for the other part of the instructional day.

brain electrical activity mapping (BEAM)   A procedure using a machine to monitor brain wave activity.

brain-injured child   A child who before, during, or after birth has received an injury to or suffered an infection of the brain. As a result of such organic impairment, there are disturbances that prevent or impede the normal learning process.

case history   A compilation of the student's background, development, and other information. Case-history information is usually obtained from parents and from the student's school and medical histories. Often this information is obtained by interview.

center-based program   A program offered at a central facility for comprehensive services for young children and delivered by staff members with expertise in disciplines related to intervention and therapy for young children.

central nervous system   The organic system comprising the brain and the spinal cord.

central nervous system dysfunction   A disorder in learning caused by an impairment in brain function.

cerebral hemisphere   One of the two halves (the right hemisphere and the left hemisphere) that constitute the human brain.

child-find   Ways of locating young children with disabilities in the community.

children at risk   Children who are at risk for poor development and learning failure. Three categories of at risk are established risk, biological risk, and environmental risk.

Children with Specific Learning Disabilities Act (PL 91–230)   A law passed in 1969 that first recognized children with learning disabilities.

clinical teaching   A method of teaching that tailors learning experiences to the unique needs of a particular child.

cloze procedure   A technique that is useful in testing, in teaching reading comprehension, and in determining readability (or difficulty level of the material). The cloze procedure involves deleting words from the text and inserting underlined blank spaces. Measurement is made by counting the number of blanks that students can correctly fill.

cognitive abilities   Clusters of human abilities that enable one to know, be aware, think, conceptualize, reason, criticize, and use abstractions.

cognitive behavior modification   A self-instructional approach to learning. It requires individuals to talk to themselves out loud, give themselves instruction on what they should be doing, and reward themselves verbally for accomplishments.

cognitive strategy   The mental processes involved in thinking and learning, such as perception, memory, language, attention, concept formation, and problem solving.

collaboration   Teachers working together to plan and teach a child, usually a general education teacher and a special education teacher.

collaborative teaming   Teachers working together. Partnerships between the general education teachers and special education teachers.

components of language   The language system includes phonology, morphology, syntax, semantics, and pragmatics.

comprehension   The purpose of reading, gathering meaning from the printed page.

computed tomography (CT)   A computerized series of X-rays that build a three-dimensional image of the brain.

conceptual disorder   Difficulty in thinking and organizing thoughts.

concrete instruction   A method of teaching in which the child manipulates real objects for learning.

concrete operations stage   In Piaget's theory, the stage at which children can systematize and organize thoughts on the basis of past sensual experience.

consequent event   In behavioral psychology, the reinforcement that follows the behavior.

constructive learning   A theory of learning that is based on the idea that children can build their own mental structures. In mathematics, they create their own number ideas.

content-area teachers   High school teachers whose primary orientation and expertise is the subject matter of their specialty. In contrast, elementary teachers tend to have an orientation and more expertise in child development.

context clues   Clues that help readers recognize words through the meaning or context of the sentence or paragraph in which the words appear.

contingency contracting   A behavioral management strategy that entails a written agreement between the student and the teacher stating that the student will be able to do something he or she wants if he or she first completes a specified task.

continuum of alternative placements   An array of different placements that should be available in a school system to meet the varied needs of students with disabilities.

co-occurring conditions   A term used to describe conditions that exist along with an attention deficit disorder. Also called *comorbidity*.

coteaching   The process of two professionals working together to seek a joint solution. Often refers to the joint efforts of the special education teacher and the general education classroom teacher.

criterion-referenced tests   Tests that measure the student's abilities in specific skills (rather than tests that compare a student to others in a norm group).

cultural and linguistic diversity   Representation by many different cultures and language groups.

current achievement level   A student's present stage of performance in an academic area.

curriculum-based measurement (CBM)   Assessment designed to measure student performance on the student's curriculum activities and materials. The student's performance on an academic task is repeatedly measured and charted to assess changes in learning performance.

cursive writing   The style of writing sometimes called script. The individual letters are joined in writing a word. Children typically learn cursive writing in third grade.

decode   The process of unlocking words into component sounds.

developmental aphasia   The term used to describe a child who has severe difficulty in acquiring oral language. This term implies that the disorder is related to a central nervous system dysfunction.

developmental delay   A term designating that a child is slow in a specific aspect of development, such as in cognitive, physical, communication, social/emotional, or adaptive development. It is considered a noncategorical label for identifying a young child for services.

developmental indicators   Early precursors or signs of learning disabilities.

developmental pediatrics   A medical specialty that combines expertise in child development with medical knowledge. The medical areas of pediatrics, genetics, neurology, and psychiatry are particularly important.

developmental variations   Differences in rate of development in different areas of learning within an individual.

developmentally appropriate practice (DAP)   Guidelines for a curriculum for young children based on a constructivist philosophy emphasizing child-initiated learning, exploratory play, and the child's interests.

diagnostic teaching   Teaching designed for the purpose of gathering further information about a student.

diagnostic tests   Tests that provide specific evaluative information about a child's functioning.

diet-related theories   Concepts of controlling hyperactivity and behavior through diet control.

differentiated instruction   Teaching that seeks to find that special method which will be successful for an individual student to help that student learn.

direct instruction   A method associated with behavioral theories of instruction. The focus is directly on the curriculum or task to be taught and the steps needed to learn that task.

direct services   The learning disabilities teacher works directly with a child to provide instructional services.

directed reading-thinking activity   A guided method of teaching reading comprehension in which readers first read a section of text, then predict what will happen next, and then read to verify the accuracy of the predictions.

discrepancy between achievement and intellectual ability   The student's achievement is compared to the student's intellectual ability. A significant difference between these two scores indicates a learning disability.

discrepancy score   A mathematical calculation for quantifying the discrepancy between the student's current achievement and his or her potential.

distractibility   The tendency to attend to irrelevant external stimuli, a practice which detracts from attending to the task at hand.

drafting   A stage in the writing process in which a preliminary version of the written product is developed.

dynamic assessment   Evaluation of a student by noting how the student performs during instruction in an interactive teaching environment.

Dynamic Indicators of Basic Early Literacy Skills (DIBELS)   A measurement system to assess early reading skills.

dyscalculia   A medical term indicating lack of ability to perform mathematical functions. The condition is associated with neurological dysfunction.

dysgraphia   Extremely poor handwriting or the inability to perform the motor movements required for handwriting. The condition is associated with neurological dysfunction.

dyslexia   A severe reading disorder in which the individual cannot learn to read or does not acquire fluent and efficient reading skills. Research suggests that there is a connection between dyslexia and neurological dysfunction.

dysnomia   A deficiency in remembering and expressing words. Children with dysnomia may substitute a word-like thing for many objects when they cannot remember the name of the object. They may attempt to use other expressions to talk around the subject.

early literacy   The child's early entrance into the world of words, language, and stories. Literacy emerges in children through simultaneous experiences with oral language, reading, and writing.

early number learning   The young child's early learning of quantitative concepts.

ecological system   The several environments within which an individual lives and grows, including home and school, as well as social and cultural environments.

Education for All Handicapped Children Act of 1975   See PL 94–142.

educational setting   The student's placement for instruction.

eligibility criteria   Standards for determining whether a student can be classified as having learning disabilities and will be eligible for learning disabilities services.

email   Electronic mail allows a user to send messages to another user's private "mailbox" within the host computer of the electronic network.

emotional intelligence   The notion that the ability to deal with one's emotions is an aspect of intelligence.

English as a second language (ESL) method   A method of teaching English to students whose native language is not English.

English–language learners (ELL)   Students who speak a language other than English and have a limited proficiency with English.

executive control   A component in the information-processing model that refers to the ability to control and direct one's own learning. It is also referred to as *metacognition*.

explicit code-emphasis instruction   Systematic and direct teaching of decoding and phonics skills.

explicit instruction   Teachers are clear about what should be taught and how it should be done. Students are not left to make inferences from experiences on their own.

explicit teaching   *See* explicit instruction.

expressive language disorders   Difficulties in using language (or speaking).

Feingold diet   A diet that eliminates artificial flavors, artificial preservatives, and artificial colors in an attempt to control hyperactivity in children. (*See* food additives.)

food additives   Artificial flavors, artificial preservatives, and artificial colors that are put into food. (*See* Feingold diet.)

formal operations stage   In Piaget's theory, the stage at which children can work with abstractions.

formal standardized tests   Commercially prepared tests that have been used with and standardized on large groups of students. Manuals that accompany the tests provide derived scores on student performance, such as grade scores, age scores, percentiles, and standard scores.

functional behavioral assessment   Evaluating a child's behavior problems by analyzing the behavioral unit.

functional behavioral supports   The provision of assistance and help to change a child's behavior.

functional magnetic resonance imaging (fMRI)   A new MRI method for studying the live human brain at work.

functional skills or survival skills   Teaching survival skills to enable students to get along in the outside world.

genetics of learning disabilities   The study of the inheritability of learning disabilities.

general education classroom   The regular class, in which most students in school receive instruction.

general education placement   The placement of a child with a disability into the regular classroom for instruction.

general tests   Tests that provide overall scores but not diagnostic information.

giftedness   Refers to children and youth who display evidence of high performance capability in areas such as intellectual, creative, artistic, or leadership spheres or in specific academic fields, and who require services or activities not ordinarily provided by the school in order to develop such capabilities.

grapheme   The written representation of a phoneme sound.

graphic organizers   Visual representations of concepts, knowledge, or information that incorporates both text and pictures to make the material easier to understand.

Head Start   A preschool program intended to provide compensatory educational experiences for children from low-income families who might otherwise come to school unprepared and unmotivated to learn. Head Start is sponsored by the Office of Child Development.

high-stakes testing   State-wide tests given to all students that result in critical decisions for the child.

home-based program   A system of delivering intervention services to very young children in their homes. Parent(s) become the child's primary teacher. A professional child-care provider goes to the child's home, typically one to three times per week, to train the parent(s) to work with the child.

home-school coordination   A behavior management strategy for helping a child learn. Progress at school is reinforced at home.

hyperactivity   A condition characterized by uncontrollable, haphazard, and poorly organized motor behavior. In young children, excessive gross-motor activity makes them appear to be on the go, and they have difficulty sitting still. Older children may be extremely restless or fidgety, may talk too much in class, or may constantly fight with friends, siblings, and classmates.

IEP meeting   A meeting attended by parents, school staff, and sometimes the student to make decisions about the individualized education plan (IEP).

immersion method   An approach in which students receive extensive exposure to a second language.

impulsivity   A characteristic of attention deficit disorder, in which the child reacts quickly without careful thought.

inattention   Not concentrating on a task.

inclusion   The policy of placing children with disabilities in regular or general education classes for instruction.

inclusive environment   Placing children with disabilities in an inclusive or regular classroom with typical children.

indirect instruction   The teaching reading of skills through incidental teaching.

indirect services   The learning disabilities teacher works with the classroom teacher as a consultant to provide services for a child with a learning disability.

individualized education program (IEP)   The written plan for the education of an individual student with learning disabilities. The plan must meet requirements specified in the rules and regulations of IDEA.

individualized family service plan (IFSP)   A plan for young children that includes the family as well as the child.

informal assessment measures   Ways of evaluating performance that are not formal standardized tests. These can include teacher-made tests, diagnostic teaching, commercial nonstandardized tests, curriculum-based assessment, and so on.

informal reading inventory An informal method of assessing the reading level of a student by having the student orally read successively more difficult passages.

information-processing model A systems approach to cognitive processing. The information processing model emphasizes the flow of information, the memory system, and the interrelationships among the elements of cognitive processes.

informational materials Reading text material that is about subject matter. Usually non-fiction.

instruction stages This stage is part of the IEP process and includes implementing a teaching plan, and reviewing and re-evaluating the student's progress.

interactive dialogues Discussions between the teacher and children in the class.

Interagency Committee on Learning Disabilities (ICLD) A committee commissioned by the U.S. Congress and made up of representatives from twelve agencies of the Department of Health and Human Services and the Department of Education to develop a federal definition of learning disabilities.

interpersonal intelligence One of the multiple intelligences that reflects the person's ability to deal effectively with other people.

invented spelling The beginning writer's attempt to write words. The young writer attends to the sound units and associates letters with them in a systematic, although unconventional, way.

keyboarding The process of typing on a computer keyboard.

kinesthetic perception Perception obtained through body movements and muscle feeling, such as the awareness of positions taken by different parts of the body and bodily feelings of muscular contraction, tension, and relaxation.

language delay Slowness in the acquisition of language. The child with a language delay may not be talking at all or may be using very little language at an age when language normally develops.

language disorders The term that refers to children with a language delay or language disabilities.

language experience method A method of teaching reading based on the experiences and language of the reader. The method involves the generation of experience-based materials that are dictated by the student, written by the teacher, and then used as the material for teaching reading.

lateral preference A tendency to use either the right or left side of the body or to favor using the hand, foot, eye, or ear of one side of the body.

learned helplessness A trait of students with learning disabilities in which they exhibit passiveness and do not take on the responsibility for their own learning.

learning differences The concept that all individuals have variations in learning abilities in various areas.

learning disabilities A disorder in one or more of the basic processes involved in understanding spoken or written language. It may show up as a problem in listening, thinking, speaking, reading, writing, or spelling

or in a person's ability to do math, despite at least average intelligence. The term does not include children who have learning problems which are primarily the result of visual, hearing, or physical handicaps, mental retardation, or emotional disturbance, or of environmental, cultural, or economic disadvantage. Individuals with learning disabilities encounter difficulty in one or more of seven areas: (1) receptive language, (2) expressive language, (3) basic reading skill, (4) reading comprehension, (5) written expression, (6) mathematics calculations, or (7) mathematics reasoning.

learning strategies approach *See* learning strategies instruction.

learning strategies instruction A series of methods to help students direct their own learning, focusing on how students learn rather than on what they learn.

least restrictive environment (LRE) A term in special education law that indicates that children with disabilities should be placed in an environment that has typical or nondisabled children.

limited English proficiency (LEP) The term used to describe students whose native language is not English and who also have difficulty understanding and using English.

linguistics The scientific study of the patterns, nature, development, function, and use of human language.

long-term memory Permanent memory storage that retains information for an extended period of time.

magnetic resonance imaging (MRI) An advanced neurology device that converts signals into a shape on a video screen, thereby permitting the study of the living brain.

manuscript writing The form of handwriting sometimes called *printing*. This form of writing, closer to the printed form, is easier to learn than cursive writing because it consists of only circles and straight lines.

mastery learning The steps of a subject are are put in sequential order. Mastery learning determines if the child has learned (or mastered) each step.

math anxiety Refers to a debilitating emotional reaction to mathematics situations.

mathematics computation The basic mathematical operations, consisting of addition, subtraction, multiplication, division, fractions, decimals, and percentages.

mathematics learning strategy Applying an instructional method to the learning of a mathematics concept.

mediation A process of resolving disputes between the parent and the school in a nonadversarial fashion.

mental retardation Significantly subaverage general intellectual functioning existing concurrently with deficits in adaptive behavior and manifest during the developmental period.

metacognition The ability to facilitate learning by taking control and directing one's own thinking process.

mild/moderate disabilities A grouping of students with different disabilities: learning disabilities for instruction, mild mental retardation, and emotional disturbances.

mind mapping A technique that employs a pictorial method to transfer ideas from a student's mind onto a piece of paper.

minimal brain dysfunction (MBD) A term that refers to mild or minimal neurological abnormality that causes learning difficulties.

miscue analysis An evaluation of the errors the student makes in oral reading.

morpheme The smallest meaning unit of a language system.

morphology The linguistic system of meaning units in any particular language; for example, the word *played* contains two meaning units (or morphemes): play + ed (past tense).

multidisciplinary evaluation The assessment process in which specialists from several disciplines evaluate a child and coordinate their findings.

multimodal treatment plan Combines several approaches to treating children with ADD/ADHD.

multiple intelligences Many different talents or intelligences, such as verbal or linguistic intelligence and visual or spatial intelligence.

multisensory methods A collection of programs based on the Orton-Gillingham method that use several sensory avenues to teaching reading.

multistore memory system The central idea in the information-processing model of learning. Information is seen as flowing among three types of memory: the sensory register, short-term memory, and long-term memory.

narrative text Reading text material that tells a story. Usually fiction.

National Joint Committee on Learning Disabilities (NJCLD) An organization of representatives from several professional organizations and disciplines involved with learning disabilities.

neurological impress method An approach for teaching reading to students with severe reading disabilities that consists of a system of rapid-unison reading by the student and the instructor.

neurology The medical specialty that deals with the functioning and development of the central nervous system.

neurons Nerves within the brain.

neuropsychology A discipline that combines neurology and psychology and studies the relationship between brain function and behavior.

neurosciences Disciplines that are involved with the study of the brain and its functions.

neurotransmitter The chemicals that transmit messages from one cell to another across the synapse (a microscopic space between nerve cells).

1999 Regulations for IDEA–1997 A clarification of the procedures for the law, IDEA–1997, developed by the U.S. Department of Education.

No Child Left Behind Act (NCLB) The latest revision of the Elementary and Secondary Education Act of 2001. Public Law 107-110.

nonverbal learning disorders (NVLD) Poor skills in nonacademic areas of learning, such as poor social skills.

norm-referenced tests Standardized tests that compare a child's performance to that of other children of the same age.

number line A sequence of numbers forming a straight line that allows the student to manipulate computation directly. Number lines help students develop an understanding of number symbols and their relationship to each other.

observation Careful watching of a student's behavior, usually in the classroom setting.

occupational therapist (OT) A therapist who is trained in brain physiology and function and who prescribes exercises to improve motor and sensory integration.

one-to-one correspondence A relationship in which one element of a set is paired with one and only one element of a second set.

one-to-one instruction Teaching with one teacher and one student.

ophthalmologist A medical specialist concerned with the physiology of the eye, its organic aspects, diseases, and structure.

oral expressive language The skills required to produce spoken language for communication with other individuals. Difficulty in producing spoken language is called *expressive language disorder*.

oral receptive language Understanding of the language spoken by others. Listening is a receptive oral language skill.

otitis media Middle-ear infection that may cause temporary hearing loss and may impede language development.

otologist The medical specialist responsible for the diagnosis and treatment of auditory disorders.

otology The medical specialty that deals with auditory disorders.

parent support groups Small groups of parents who meet to obtain information about their children with disabilities and to discuss common problems.

parents' rights Used in the 2004 IDEA for procedural safeguards to protect the rights of parents.

Part B of IDEA–2004 The part of the law (IDEA) that refers to regulations for children with disabilities. In reference to early childhood, Part B covers preschoolers with disabilities ages 3 through 5.

Part C of IDEA–2004 The part of the law (IDEA) that covers infants and toddlers from birth through age 2.

part–whole relationship Addition and subtraction have a part-whole relationship. Add to the whole or total of two parts; and you subtract from the whole to find the missing part.

passive learners Adolescents with learning disabilities who tend to wait for teacher direction instead of being actively involved in the learning situation.

peer tutoring A method of instruction in which the student is taught by a peer or classmate.

perception The process of recognizing and interpreting information received through the senses.

perceptual disorder A disturbance in the ability to perceive objects, relations, or qualities; difficulty in the interpretation of sensory stimulation.

perceptual modality concept The notion that children have preferred channels for learning (for example, auditory or visual). Information on the child's perceptual strengths and weaknesses is used in planning instruction.

perceptual motor learning The integration of motor learning and visual percetual learning.

performance standards Academic levels set by national, state, and local bodies that students should achieve on achievement tests.

perseveration The behavior of being locked into continually performing an action.

phoneme The smallest sound unit of a language system.

phonemic awareness An awareness of the sounds in words and language.

phonics An application of phonetics to the teaching of reading in which the sound (or phoneme) of a language is related to the equivalent written symbol (or grapheme).

phonological awareness A child's recognition of the sounds of language. The child must understand that speech can be segmented into syllables and phonemic units.

phonology The linguistic system of speech sounds in a particular language. The word *cat,* for example, has three sounds (or phonemes).

pie chart A circular chart showing segments that illustrate magnitude or frequencies.

place value The aspect of the number system that assigns specific significance to the position a digit holds in a numeral.

placement The selection of the appropriate setting for teaching a child.

portfolio assessment A method of evaluating student progress by analyzing samples of the student's classroom work.

positive behavioral support Methods that assist as the child learns new ways of behaving.

positron emission tomography (PET) A procedure that permits one to measure metabolism within the brain.

postmortem anatomical studies Autopsy studies of the brain of persons with a history of dyslexia.

potential for learning A term that refers to intellectual ability, whether measured by an intelligence test, a test of cognitive abilities, clinical judgment, or other means.

pragmatics The social side of language; the social context and social customs surrounding language.

precursors Early signs of learning problems in young children.

preoperational stage One of Piaget's developmental stages of learning. During this stage children make intuitive judgments about relationships and also begin to think with symbols.

prereferral activities Preventive procedures taken prior to referral for special education evaluation and intended to help regular teachers work more successfully with the child in the regular classroom.

present levels of achievement The levels at which the student is currently achieving in various developmental and academic areas. The written individualized education program must include a statement of the child's present levels of educational performance. A requirement in the student's IEP.

prewriting The first step of the writing process, in which writers evoke and gather ideas for writing.

primary language system The child's first language, usually oral language. In relation to bilingual students it can refer to the student's native language.

problem solving The kind of thinking needed to work out mathematics word problems.

procedural safeguards Regulations in federal law that are designed to protect the rights of students with learning disabilities and their parents.

progress monitoring Assessment procedures to measure the student's academic performance and evaluate the effectiveness of instruction.

psychiatrist The medical specialist who deals with emotional problems and mental health issues.

psychological processing A phrase used in the definition of learning disabilities in the Individuals with Disabilities Education Improvement Act of 2004, that refers to abilities in visual or auditory perception, memory, or language.

psychological processing disorders A phrase in the federal definition of learning disabilities that refers to disabilities in visual or auditory perception, memory, or language.

psychostimulant medications Medications, including Ritalin, that are initially prescribed for a child with attention deficit disorder.

psychotherapeutic teaching An approach to teaching that concentrates on the student's feelings and relationship with the teacher.

Public Law 94–142 Public Law 94–142 is the Education for All Handicapped Children Act. It was passed by Congress in 1975. The law guarantees a free and appropriate public education to children with disabilities. This law was reauthorized in 1990 and 1997 as the Individuals with Disabilities Education Act (IDEA). The most recent version is the 2004 Individuals with Disabilities Education Improvement Act (IDEA–2004).

Public Law 101–476 This is the Individuals with Disabilities Education Act (IDEA) passed by Congress in 1990. It updated PL 94–142, the Education for All Handicapped Children Act.

Public Law 105–17 The 1997 Individuals with Disabilities Education Act that was passed by Congress in 1997.

Public Law 108-446 The most recent federal special education law. The Individuals with Disabilities Education Improvement Act of 2004 (IDEA–2004).

rapid automatized naming (RAN) The ability to quickly and automatically name objects and pictures of objects.

rapport A close relationship between teacher and child that is based on total acceptance of the child as a human being worthy of respect.

rating scales A ranking of student behavior as judged by a parent, teacher, or other informant.

readiness The state of maturational development that is necessary before a skill can be learned.

reading comprehension Understanding of the meaning of printed text.

reading fluency   The ability to recognize words and passages readily and smoothly.

Reading Recovery   A reading program first used in New Zealand in which first graders who rank very low in reading are selected for a period of intensive reading instruction.

reasonable accommodations   The phrase used in Section 504 of the Rehabilitation Act to describe what can fairly easily be done in a setting to make adjustments for an individual with a disability.

receiving neurons   Neurons that receive information.

receptive language disorders   Difficulty understanding oral language or listening.

reciprocal teaching   A method of teaching through a social interactive dialogue between teacher and student that emphasizes the development of thinking processes.

referral   The initial request to consider a student for a special education evaluation.

referral stages   The initial stages of the IEP process. They include the prereferral activities and the referral activities.

reinforcement   An event following a response that increases the likelihood that the person will make a similar response in similar situations in the future.

residential facilities   An educational institutions in which students live away from home and receive their education. A residential facility may be sponsored by a government agency or may be privately managed.

resource room   A special instructional setting, usually a room within a school. In this room, small groups of children meet with a special education teacher for special instruction for a portion of the day. Children spend the remainder of the day in the general education classrooms.

response-to-intervention   A method of assessing children with learning disabilities. The Individuals with Disabilities Education Improvement Act of 2004 advocates teaching high risk students with scientifically-based instructional materials, in order to judge the students response to this intervention.

retrieval   Recalling information from long-term memory.

revising   A stage of the writing process in which the writer reworks a draft of a written product.

scaffolded instruction   Teacher supports for the student, particularly at the initial stage of learning a task.

scotopic sensitivity syndrome   A difficulty in processing full-spectrum light efficiently, which causes a reading disorder.

screening   A type of assessment using ways to survey many children quickly to identify those who may need special services.

secondary language system   The student's second language, usually written language. In the case of bilingual students, it may refer to their second language (English).

Section 504 of the Rehabilitation Act   Federal law that covers all agencies and institutions receiving financial assistance and that requires that no otherwise qualified handicapped individual shall be excluded from participation.

self-esteem   Feelings of self-worth, self-confidence, and self-concept that provide an experience of success.

semantics   A linguistic term referring to the vocabulary system of language.

semiconcrete instruction   The level of mathematics instruction in which the students use representational objects to refer to math concepts, such as tallies, pictures, or marks, instead of the actual objects.

sending neurons   Neurons that send information to the brain.

sensorimotor stage   One of Piaget's developmental stages of learning. During this stage children learn through senses and movements and by interacting with the physical environment.

sensory integration   A theory stemming from the field of occupational therapy that physical exercises can modify the brain.

sensory register   The first memory system in the information-processing model that interprets and maintains memory information long enough for it to be perceived and analyzed.

separate class   A special class for children with disabilities taught by a teacher with special training. Children in a separate class usually spend most of the day in this setting.

separate schools   Schools for students with learning disabilities that students attend during the day. They return home after school.

severe discrepancy   A significant difference between a child's current achievement and intellectual potetial.

sharing with an audience   A stage of the writing process in which the final written product is read by others.

sheltered English   A method of teaching children who have some proficiency in English to learn English more rapidly by having them use materials written in English.

short-term memory   A second memory storage within the information-processing model. It is a temporary storage facility serving as working memory as a problem receives one's conscious attention.

sight words   Words that a student recognizes instantly, without hesitation or further analysis.

skills sequence   The sequence of steps involved in learning a skill.

social maturity   The development of social aspects of life.

social perception   The ability to understand social situations, as well as sensitivity to the feelings of others.

social skills   Skills necessary for meeting the basic social demands of everyday life.

soft neurological signs   Minimal or subtle neurological deviations that some neurologists use as indicators of mild neurological dysfunction.

sound counting   Activities to help students count the number of sounds in a word. Counters (such as Popsicle sticks or tongue depressors) are often used.

spatial relationships   Concepts such as up-down, over-under, top-bottom, high-low, near-far, beginning-end, and across. A disturbance in spatial relationship can interfere with the visualization of the entire number system.

speech disorders disorders of articulation, fluency, or voice.

spreadsheets The display of numeric information through rows and columns, usually used in a computer program.

stages of acceptance The different emotions parents go through when they learn they have a child with disabilities.

stages of child development approach An approach to teaching that is based on a model of child development.

stages of learning The stages a person goes through in mastering material, such as acquisition, proficiency, maintenance, and generalization.

Standard English The linguistic system of English recognized by the literate culture and used in school.

standards–based education The setting of certain standards for curriculum content. Tests are based on these standards to ascertain if students reach the standard.

strategies intervention model (SIM) An instructional method for teaching learning strategies to adolescents with learning disabilities.

Strauss Syndrome A set of characteristics of brain-injured children. The term was suggested instead of using the term "brain-injured" children. It also honors Alfred Strauss.

structural analysis The recognition of words through the analysis of meaningful word units, such as prefixes, suffixes, root words, compound words, and syllables.

synapse The space between two neurons.

syntax The grammar system of a language; the linguistic rules of word order; the function of words in a sentence.

tactile perception Perception obtained through the sense of touch via the fingers and skin surfaces.

target behavior In the behavioral unit, A–B–C, the target behavior is "B," the actual behavior of the student.

task analysis A teaching approach that analyzes an activity by breaking it down into a sequence of steps.

temporal acoustical processing The ability to process sounds of language rapidly enough to distinguish speech sounds and words.

theories The purpose of theory is to bring form and coherence, and meaning to what is observed in the real world. Underlying concepts explaining what is observed.

time concepts The sense of time, which is not easily comprehended by some students with learning disabilities, who may be poor at estimating the span of an hour, a minute, several hours, or a weekend and may have difficulty estimating how long a task will take. Trouble with time concepts characterizes students with mathematics disabilities.

time out A behavior management method in which a child is removed from a group for a short period of time.

transition The process of moving from one type of program to another. In early childhood programs it can be from the birth-through-2 program to the ages

3-through-5 program, or from the ages 3-through-5 program to another educational placement. For adolescents transition refers to the passage from school to the adult world.

transition planning Planning for making the change from being a student to being an adult. Students with learning disabilities need help with this process.

tutorial instruction Teaching designed to help students meet requirements in their specific academic-content subjects and to achieve success in the regular curriculum. This teaching is usually accomplished through one-to-one instruction or in small groups.

Universal Design for Learning (UDL) A policy of designing solutions for people with disabilities that are useful for others in the general population.

VAKT The abbreviation for *visual, auditory, kinesthetic,* and *tactile* learning, a multisensory approach to teaching reading that stimulates all avenues of sensory input simultaneously.

visual discrimination The ability to note visual differences or similarities between objects, including letters and words.

visual perception The identification, organization, and interpretation of sensory data received by the individual through the eye.

vocabulary Recognition and knowledge of words. Consists of oral vocabulary and reading vocabulary.

word finding Recalling the correct words.

word finding difficulties A slowness or inability to think of words.

word-frequency approach to spelling A method of word selection and instruction for spelling. Words are selected for spelling instruction on the basis of how frequently they are used in writing.

word–pattern approach to spelling A theory of word selection and instruction in spelling. It is based on the belief that the spelling of English is sufficiently rule-covered to warrant a method of selection and instruction that stresses phonological, morphological, and syntactic rules or word patterns.

word processing Writing with a computer (as contrasted with writing by hand or on a conventional typewriter).

word-recognition skills Strategies for recognizing words, including phonics, sight words, context clues, structural analysis, and combinations of these strategies.

word web A type of graphic organizer. It helps students learn words, build vocabulary, and makes information about the word easier to understand and learn.

working memory See short-term memory.

work-study program A high school program in which students work on a job for a portion of the day and go to school for a portion of the day.

World Wide Web (WWW) Interconnected pages or sites with textual and graphic information on the Internet.

writing process The process whereby writers go through a series of stages during writing. The four stages of the writing process are (1) prewriting, (2) drafting, (3) revising, and (4) sharing with an audience.

zone of proximal development (ZPD) A term, used by Vygotsky, envisioning a range of levels of difficulty for a student. The lower end is very easy, the upper end beyond the student's capacity. The ZPD is the midpoint and is an appropriate level for learning.

REFERENCES

Accardo, P., & Blondis, T. (2000). Pediatric management of ADHD medication. In P. Accardo, T. Blondis, B. Whitman, & M. Stein (Eds.), *Attention deficits and hyperactivity in children and adults* (pp. 513–534, 2nd ed.). New York: Marcel Dekker.

Accardo, P., Blondis, T., Whitman, B., & Stein, M. (2000). *Attention deficits and hyperactivity in children and adults* (2nd ed.). New York: Marcel Dekker.

Adams, A., Foorman, B., Lundberg, I., & Beeler, T. (1998). The elusive phoneme. *American Educator, 22*(1 & 2), 18–31.

Adams, M. J. (1990). *Beginning to read.* Cambridge, MA: MIT Press.

Adams, M. (2001). Alphabetic anxiety and explicit systematic phonics instruction. In S. Neuman & D. K. Dickinson (Eds.), *Handbook of early literacy* (pp. 66–80). New York: Guilford Publications.

Adams, M. J., & Bruck, M. (1995). Resolving the "Great Debate." *American Educator, 19*(2), 7, 1–20.

Adelman, P., & Vogel, S. (1991). The learning disabled adult. In B. Wong (Ed.), *Learning about learning disabilities* (pp. 564–594). San Diego: Academic Press.

Adler, M. (1956). *How to read a book.* New York: Simon & Schuster.

Administration for Children and Families. (2001 January 25). *Fact sheet.* Washington, DC: U.S. Department of Health and Human Services.

Alberto, P., & Troutman, A. (1995, 1998, 2003). *Applied behavior analysis for teachers.* Columbus, OH: Merrill.

Alexander, D. (1999). *Keys to successful learning: A national summit of research on learning disabilities.* New York: National Center for Learning Disabilities.

Algozzine, B. (1991). Curriculum-based assessment. In B. Wong (Ed.), *Learning about learning disabilities* (pp. 40–59). San Diego: Academic Press.

Alverez, L. (1998). A short course in sensitivity training: Working with Hispanic families of children with disabilities. *Focus on Exceptional Children, 31*(1), 73–78.

American Academy of Opthalmology. (1987). Policy statement: Learning disabilities, dyslexia, and vision. *Journal of Learning Disabilities, 29*(7), 412–413.

American Academy of Pediatrics. (1991, June). The American Academy of Pediatrics definition of attention deficit hyperactivity disorder. *AAP News,* 12–13.

American Academy of Pediatrics. (1998). Learning disabilities, dyslexia, and vision. *Pediatrics, 102*(5), 1217–1219.

American Academy of Pediatrics. (2001). Clinical practice guideline: Treatment of the school-age child with attention deficit hyperactivity disorder. *Pediatrics, 108*(4), 1033–1044.

American Optometric Association. (1985). Position statement on vision therapy. *Journal of the American Optometric Association, 56*(10), 782–783.

American Psychiatric Association. (1994). *Diagnostic and Statistical Manual of Mental Disorders, Fourth Edition (DSM-IV).* Washington, DC: Author.

American Psychiatric Association. (2004). *Diagnostic and Statistical Manual of Mental Disorders, Fourth Edition, Revised.* Washington, DC: American Psychiatric Association.

Asperger, H. (1944). Die 'autistischen psychopathen' im kindesalter. *Archiv fur Psychiatrie und Nervenkrankheiten, 117,* 76–136.

Association for Persons with Severe Handicaps (TASH). (1995). Resolution on inclusive education. In J. Kauffman & D. Hallahan (Eds.), *The illusion of full inclusion* (pp. 314–316). Austin, TX: Pro-Ed.

Atkinson, R., & Shiffrin, R. (1968). Human memory: A proposed system and its control processes. In K. Spence & J. Spence (Eds.), *The psychology of learning and motivation: Advances in theory and research* (Vol. 2). New York: Academic Press.

Aulls, M. (1982). *Developing readers in today's elementary schools.* Boston: Allyn & Bacon.

Austen, F. (2001, July 19). Learning to speak their minds. *New York Times,* D-1, pp. 6–7.

Aylward, E. H., Richards, T. L., Berninger, V. W., Nagy, W. E., Field, K. M., Grimme, A. C., et al. (2003). Instructional treatment associated with changes in brain activation in children with dyslexia. *Neurology, 61,* 212–219.

Ayres, J. (1994). *Sensory integration and learning disorders.* Los Angeles: Western Psychological Services.

Babbitt, B. Ten tips for software selection for math instruction. Retrieved from http://www.ldonline.org/ld_indepth/technology/babbitt_math_tips.html.

Bagnoto, S. J., Neisworth, J., & Munson, S. (1997). *Linking assessment and early intervention.* Baltimore: Paul H. Brookes.

Baker, J., & Zigmond, N. (1990). Are regular education classes equipped to accommodate students with learning disabilities? *Exceptional Children, 56,* 515–526.

Baker, L., & Welkowitz, L. (2005). *Asperger's syndrome: intervening in schools, clinics, and communities.* Mahwah, NJ: Lawrence Erlbaum Associates.

Ball, E. W., & Blachman, B. A. (1991). Does phoneme awareness training in kindergarten make a difference in early word recognition and spelling? *Reading Research Quarterly, 26*(1), 49–66.

Barkley, R. (1995). *Taking charge of ADHD: The complete authoritative guide for parents.* New York: Guilford Press.

Barkley, R. (1998). *Attention deficit hyperactivity disorder.* New York: Guilford Press.

Baroody, A., & Ginsburg, H. (1991). A cognitive approach to assessing the mathematical difficulties of children labeled "learning disabled." In H. L. Swanson (Ed.), *Handbook on the assessment of learning disabilities* (pp. 117–228). Austin, TX: Pro-Ed.

Bateman, B. (1992). Learning disabilities: The changing landscape. *Journal of Learning Disabilities, 25,* 29–36.

Bateman, B. (1995). Who, how, and where: Special education's issues in perpetuity. In J. Kauffman & D. Hallahan (Eds.), *The illusion of full inclusion* (pp. 75–90). Austin, TX: Pro-Ed.

Bateman, B., & Linden, M. (1998). *Better IEPs. How to develop legally correct and educationally useful programs* (3rd ed.). Longmont, CO: Sopris West.

Bauer, A., Keefe, C., & Shea, T. (2001). *Students with learning disabilities or emotional/behavioral disorders.* Columbus, OH: Merrill/Prentice Hall.

Beck, I. L., & Juel, C. (1995). The role of decoding in learning to read. *American Educator, 19*(2), 8, 21–25, 39–42.

Beckman, P. (2001). *Access to the general education curriculum for students with disabilities.* (Report No. EC308681). Arlington, VA: ERIC Clearinghouse on Disabilities and Gifted Education. (ERIC Document Reproduction Service No. ED458735).

Belson, S. (2003). *Technology for exceptional learners.* Boston: Houghton Mifflin Company.

Bender, L. (1957). Specific reading disability as maturational lag. *Bulletin of the Orton Society, 7,* 9–18.

Bender, W. (2002). *Differentiated instruction for students with learning disabilities.* Thousand Oaks, CA: Corwin Press.

Berko, J. (1958). The child's learning of English morphology. *Word, 14,* 15–17.

Biegler, E. (1987). Acquired cerebral trauma, neuropsychiatric and psychoneurological assessment and cognitive retraining issues. *Journal of Learning Disabilities, 20,* 579–580.

Birsh, J. (1999). *Multisensory teaching of basic language skills.* Baltimore: Paul H. Brookes.

Blachman, B. (Ed.). (1997). *Foundations of reading acquisition and dyslexia: Implications for early instruction.* Mahwah, NJ: Erlbaum.

Blachman, B., Tangel, D., & Ball, E. (2004). Combining phonological awareness and word recognition instruction. *Perspectives: The International Dyslexia Association, 24*(9), 12–14.

Blackorby, J., & Wagner, M. (1997). The employment outcomes of youth with learning disabilities: A review of findings from the NLTS. In P. Gerber & D. Brown (Eds.), *Learning disabilities and employment* (pp. 57–76). Austin, TX: Pro-Ed.

Blalock, G., & Patton, J. R. (1996). Transition and students with learning disabilities: Creating sound futures. *Journal of Learning Disabilities, 29*(1), 7–16.

Bley, N., & Thornton, C. (2001). *Teaching mathematics to students with learning disabilities.* Austin, TX: Pro-Ed.

Bloomfield, L., & Barnhart, C. (1963). *Let's read* (Pt. 1). Bronxville, NY: C. I. Barnhart.

Bond, G., Tinker, M., Wasson, B., & Wasson, J. (1984). *Reading difficulties: Their diagnosis and correction.* Englewood Cliffs, NJ: Prentice-Hall.

Bradley, C. (1937). The behavior of children receiving benzedrine. *American Journal of Psychiatry, 94,* 577–585.

Bradley, L. (1988). Rhyme recognition and reading and spelling in young children. In W. Ellis (Ed.), *Intimacy with language: A forgotten basic in teacher education.* Baltimore: Orton Dyslexia Society.

Brainerd, C. J. (2003). Jean Piaget, learning research, and American education. In B. J. Zimmerman & D. H. Schunk, (Eds.), *Educational psychology: A century of contributions* (pp. 251–287). Mahwah, NJ: Erlbaum.

Bransford, J., & Johnson, M. (1972). Contextual prerequisites for understanding: Some investigations of comprehension and recall. *Journal of Verbal Learning and Verbal Behavior, 11,* 726–727.

Bravo-Valdivieso, L., & Müller, N. (2001). Learning disabilities studies in South America. In D. Hallahan & B. Keogh (Eds.), *Research and global perspectives in learning disabilities: Essays in honor of William M. Cruickshank* (pp. 309–326). Mahwah, NJ: Erlbaum.

Bredenkamp, S. (Ed.). (1987). *Developmentally appropriate practice in early childhood programs serving children from birth through age 8.* Washington, DC: National Association for the Education of Young Children.

Bredenkamp, S. (1993). The relationship between early childhood education and early childhood special education. *Topics in Early Childhood Special Education, 13,* 258–273.

Bredenkamp, S., & Copple, C. (Eds.). (1997). *Developmentally appropriate practice in early childhood programs*. Washington, DC: National Association for the Education of Young Children.

Bricker, D. (1998). An activity-based approach to early intervention. Baltimore: Paul H. Brookes.

Broadbent, D. (1958). *Perception and communication*. London: Pergamon Press.

Broca, P. (1879). Anatomie comparée des circonvolutions cérébrales. *Revue Anthropologique, 1*, 387–498.

Brooks, R. (2000). Self-esteem and resilience: A precious gift for our children. *The child information and resource guide* (pp. 34–37). Landover, MD: CHADD.

Brooks, R. & Goldstein, S. (2002). *Raising resilient children*. Baltimore: Paul H. Brookes.

Brophy, J. E., & Good, T. L. (1986). Teacher behavior and student achievement. In M. C. Wittrock (Ed.), *Handbook of research on teaching* (3rd ed., pp. 328–375). New York: Macmillan.

Brown, D. (2000). *Educate yourself for the world of work*. New York: Woodbine House.

Bryan, T. (1991). Social problems and learning disabilities. In B. Wong (Ed.), *Learning about learning disabilities* (pp. 190–231). San Diego: Academic Press.

Bryan, T. (1997). Assessing the personal and social status of students with learning disabilities. *Learning Disabilities Research and Practice, 12*(1), 63–76.

Bryan, T. (2003). Social factors in learning disabilities: What is this anyway? *Thalmus, 21*(1), 18–30.

Bryan, T., Sullivan-Burnstein, K., & Mathur, S. (1998). The influence of affect on social information processing. *Journal of Learning Disabilities, 31*, 418–426.

Bryan, T., Wong B., & Donahue, M. (2003). *Social dimensions of learning disabilities: Essays in honor of Tanis Bryan*. Mahwah, NJ: Erlbaum.

Bryant, B., & Rivera, D. (1997). Educational assessment of mathematics skills and abilities. *Journal of Learning Disabilities, 30*, 57–68.

Buck, J., Palloway, E., Kirkpatrick, M., Patton J., & McConnell, K. (2000). Developing behavioral intervention plans: A sequential approach. *Intervention in School and Clinic, 36*(1), 3–9.

Burns, P., Roe, B., & Smith, S. (2002). *Teaching reading in today's elementary schools*. Boston: Houghton Mifflin.

Bursuck, W. D., Rose, E., Cowen, S., & Yahaya, M. (1989). Nationwide survey of postsecondary education services for students with learning disabilities. *Exceptional Children, 56*, 236–254.

Butler, F., Miller, S., Crehan, K., Babbitt, B., & Pierce, T. (2003). Fraction instruction for students with mathematics disabilities: Comparing two teaching sequences. *Learning Disabilities Research & Practice, 18*(2), 91–111.

Carbo, M., & Hodges, H. (1988). Learning styles strategies can help students at risk. *Teaching Exceptional Children, 20*, 55–58.

Carmichael Olson, H., & Burgess, D. M. (1997). Early intervention for children prenatally exposed to alcohol and other drugs. In M. J. Guralnick (Ed.), *The effectiveness of early intervention* (pp. 109–145). Baltimore: Paul H. Brookes.

Carnegie Corporation. (1994). *Starting points: Meeting the needs of our youngest children*. New York: Author.

Carnine, D. (1997). Instructional design in mathematics for students with learning disabilities. *Journal of Learning Disabilities, 30*(2), 134–141.

Carnine, D., Jones, E., & Dixon, R. (1995). Mathematics: Educational tools for diverse learners. *School Psychology Review, 23*(3), 406–427.

Carnine, D., Silbert, J., & Kame'enui, E. J. (1990). *Direct instruction in reading*. Columbus, OH: Merrill.

Carreker, S. (1992). *Reading readiness*. Houston, TX: Neuhaus Education Center.

Carta, J. J. (1995). Developmentally appropriate practice: A critical analysis as applied to young children with disabilities. *Focus on Exceptional Children, 27*(5), 1–15.

Carter, J., & Sugai, G. (1988). Teaching social skills. *Teaching Exceptional Children, 20*(3), 68–71.

Cass, M., Cates, D., Smith, M., & Jackson, C. (2003). Effects of manipulative instruction: Solving area and perimeter problems by students with learning disabilities. *Learning Disabilities Research & Practice, 18*(2), 112–120.

Catts, H. W. (1993). The relationship between speech-language impairments and reading disabilities. *Journal of Speech and Hearing Research, 36*(5), 948–958.

Cawley, J., Hayden, S., Cade, E., & Baker-Kroczynski, S. (2002). Including students with disabilities in the general education science classroom. *Exceptional Children, 68*, 423–435.

Cawley, J., & Foley, T. (2001). Enhancing the quality of mathematics for students with learning disabilities: Illustrations from subtraction. *Learning Disabilities: A Multidisciplinary Journal, 11*(2), 47–60.

Cawley, J., & Miller, J. H. (1989). Cross-sectional comparisons of the mathematics performances of children with learning disabilities: Are we on the right track toward comprehensive programming? *Journal of Learning Disabilities, 22*, 250–254, 259.

Cawley, J. F., & Reines, R. (1996). Mathematics as communication. *Teaching Exceptional Children, 28*(2), 29–34.

Cazden, C. (1992). *Whole language plus: Essays on literacy in the United States and New Zealand.* New York: Teachers College Press.

Center for Effective Collaboration and Practice. (1998). *An IEP team's introduction to functional behavior assessment and behavior intervention plans.* Washington, DC: Author.

Center for the Improvement of Early Reading Achievement (CIERA). (1998). *Improving the reading achievement of America's children: Ten research-based principles.* Washington, DC: Department of Education.

Center for the Improvement of Early Reading Achievement (CIERA). (2001). *Early reading first, put reading first: The research building blocks for teaching children to read.* Washington, DC: Author.

Center, Y., Wheldall, K., Freeman, L., Outhred, L., & McNaught, M. (1995). An evaluation of reading recovery. *Reading Research Quarterly, 30*(2), 240–263.

Chalfant, J., & Pysh, M. (1993). Teacher assistance teams: Implications for the gifted. In C. J. Maker (Ed.), *Critical issues in gifted education: Vol. 888. Gifted students in the regular classroom* (pp. 32–48). Austin, TX: Pro-Ed.

Chalfant, J. C. (1989). Diagnostic criteria for entry and exit from services: A national problem. In L. Silver (Ed.), *The assessment of learning disabilities* (pp. 1–26). Boston: College Hill Press.

Chall, J. (1967, 1983). *Learning to read: The great debate.* New York: McGraw-Hill.

Chall, J. (1979). The great debate: Ten years later with a modest proposal for reading stages. In L. B. Resnick & P. A. Weaver (Eds.), *Theory and practice of early reading* (Vol. 1, pp. 29–55). Hillsdale, NJ: Erlbaum.

Chall, J. (1983b). *Stages of reading development.* New York: McGraw-Hill.

Chall, J. (1987). Reading development in adults. *Annals of Dyslexia, 37,* 240–251.

Chall, J. S. (1991). American reading instruction: Science, art and ideology. In W. Ellis (Ed.), *All language and the creation of literacy* (pp. 20–26). Baltimore: Orton Dyslexia Society.

Chapman, J. (1988). Cognitive-motivational characteristics and academic achievement of learning-disabled children: A longitudinal study. *Journal of Educational Psychology, 80,* 357–365.

Chapman, J. (1992). Learning disabilities in New Zealand: Where kiwis and kids with LD can't fly. *Journal of Learning Disabilities, 26*(6), 363–370.

Chomsky, N. (1965). *Aspects of the theory of syntax.* Cambridge, MA: MIT Press.

Clark, F. (2000). The strategies intervention model: A research-validated intervention for students with learning disabilities. *Learning Disabilities: An Interdisciplinary Journal, 10*(4), 209–217.

Clark, F., Mailloux, Z., & Parham, D. (1989). Sensory integration and children with learning disabilities. In P. N. Pratt & A. S. Allen (Eds.), *Occupational therapy for children* (pp. 457–507). St. Louis: C. V. Mosby.

Clark, S. (2000). The IEP process as a tool for collaboration. *Teaching Exceptional Children, 33*(2), 56–67.

Clay, M. (1985). *The early detection of reading difficulties* (3rd ed.). Portsmouth, NH: Heinemann.

Clay, M. (1993b). *Reading recovery: A guidebook for teachers in training.* Portsmouth, NH: Heinemann.

Clements, S. (1966). *Minimal brain dysfunction in children: Terminology and identification* (NINDS Monograph No. 3, Public Health Services Publication No. 1415). Washington, DC: U.S. Department of Health, Education, and Welfare.

Closing the Gap. (2003). *The 2003 resource directory.* Henderson, MN: Author.

Cole, C., & McLeskey, J. (1997). Secondary inclusion programs for students with mild disabilities. *Focus on Exceptional Children, 29*(6), 1–15.

Compton, D., & Appleton, A. (2004). Exploring the relationship between text-leveling systems and reading accuracy and fluency in second-grade students who are average and poor decoders. *Learning Disabilities Research and Practice, 19*(3), 176–184.

Cook, R. E., Tessier, A., & Klein, M. D. (2000). *Adaptive early childhood curricula for children in inclusive settings.* Columbus, OH: Merrill/Prentice Hall.

Coordinated Campaign for Learning Disabilities. (1998). *Learning disabilities: Information, strategies, resources.* Washington, DC: Communication Consortium Media Center.

Cotman, C., & Lynch, G. (1988). The neurobiology of learning and memory. In J. Kavanagh & T. Truss, Jr. (Eds.), *Learning disabilities: Proceedings of the national conference* (pp. 1–69). Parkton, MD: York Press.

Council for Exceptional Children (2001). *Professional standards.* Arlington, VA: Council for Exceptional Children.

Council for Exceptional Children (2002). *Strategy instruction.* Arlington, VA: Council for Exceptional Children. (ERIC Document Reproduction Service No. ED 474302).

Council for Exceptional Children (2004). Student progress monitoring gains supporters. *Today, 10*(7), 1, 9, 17, 19, 25.

Coyne, M., Kame'enui, E., & Simmons, D. (2001). Prevention and intervention in beginning reading: Two complex systems. *Learning Disabilities Research and Practice, 16*(2), 62–73.

Cratty, B. J. (1988). *Adapted physical education in the mainstream.* Denver: Love Publishing.

Crockett, J., & Kauffman, J. (2001). The concept of the least restrictive environment and learning disabilities? Least restrictive of what? Reflections on Cruickshank's 1997 Guest Editorial for the *Journal of Learning Disabilities.* In D. Hallahan & B. Keogh (Eds.), *Research and global perspectives in learning disabilities: Essays in honor of William M. Cruickshank* (pp. 147–161). Mahwah, NJ: Erlbaum.

Crook, W. (1983). Let's look at what they eat. *Academic Therapy, 18,* 629–631.

Crook, W. G., & Stevens, L. (1986). *Solving the puzzle of your hard-to-raise child.* New York: Life Sciences Press.

Cruickshank, W., Bentzen, F., Ratzeburgh, F., & Tannhauser, M. (1961). *Teaching methods for brain injured and hyperactive children.* Syracuse, NY: Syracuse University Press.

Cummins, J. (1989). A theoretical framework for bilingual special education. *Exceptional Children, 56,* 111–120.

Cummins, J. (1996). *Negotiating identities: Education for empowerment in a diverse society.* Los Angeles: California Association for Bilingual Education.

Cunningham, A., & Stanovich, K. (1997). Early reading acquisition and its relation to reading experience and ability ten years later. *Developmental Psychology, 33*(6), 934–945.

Cunningham, A., & Stanovich, K. (1998). What reading does for the mind. *American Educator, 22*(1 & 2), 8–17.

da Fonseca, V. (1996). Assessment and treatment of learning disabilities in Portugal. *Journal of Learning Disabilities, 29*(2), 114–117.

Dalke, C. (1993). Making a successful transition from high school to college: A model program. In S. Vogel & P. Adelman (Eds.), *Success for students with learning disabilities* (pp. 57–80). New York: Springer-Verlag.

DeFord, D. (1991). On noble thoughts, or toward a clarification of theory and practice within a whole language framework. In W. Ellis (Ed.), *All language and creation of literacy* (pp. 27–39). Baltimore: Orton Dyslexia Society.

Defries, J. C., Filipek, P. A., Fulker, D. W., Olson, R. K., Pennington, B. F., Smith, S. D., & Wise, B. W. (1997). Colorado Learning Disabilities Research Center. *Learning Disability Quarterly, 7–8,* 19.

DeFries, J. C., Fulker, D. W., & LaBuda, M. C. (1987). Reading disability in twins: Evidence for a genetic etiology. *Nature, 329,* 537–539.

DeFries, J. C., Stevenson, J., Gillis, J., & Wadsworth, S. J. (1991). Genetic etiology of spelling deficits in the Colorado and London twin studies of reading disability. *Reading Writing, 3,* 271–283.

de Hirsch, I., Jansky, J., & Langford, W. (1966). *Predicting reading failure.* New York: Harper & Row.

DeJong, P., & Vrielink, L. (2004). Rapid automatic naming: Easy to measure hard to prove (quickly). *Annals of Dyslexia, 54*(1), 39–64.

Deno, S. (2003). Developments in curriculum-based measurement. *The Journal of Special Education, 37*(3), 184–192.

Deno, S. L. (1985). Curriculum-based measurement: The emerging alternative. *Exceptional Children, 52,* 219–232.

Deshler, D. (2003). A time for modern-day pioneers. *Learning Disabilities Association Newsbriefs, 38*(3), 3–10, 24.

Deshler, D., Ellis, E. S., & Lenz, B. K. (1996). *Teaching adolescents with learning disabilities: Strategies and methods.* Denver: Love Publishing.

Deshler, D., & Schumaker, B. (1988). An instructional model for teaching students how to learn. In J. Graden, J. Zins, & M. Curtis (Eds.), *Alternative educational delivery systems: Enhancing instructional options for all students.* Washington, DC: National Association of School Psychologists.

Deshler, D., Schumaker, J., Lenz, B., Bulgren, J., Hock, M., Knight, J., et al. (2001). Ensuring content-area learning by secondary students with learning disabilities. *Learning Disabilities Research & Practice, 16*(2), 96–108.

Deuel, R. K. (1995). Developmental dysgraphia and motor skills disorders. *Journal of Child Neurology, 10*(Suppl. 1), S6–S7.

Dewey, J. (1946). *The public and its problems.* Chicago: Gateway.

Dewey, J. (1998). *How we think.* Boston: Houghton Mifflin.

Diamond, G. (1983). The birth date effect: A maturational effect? *Journal of Learning Disabilities, 16,* 161–164.

Dimitrovsky, L., Spector, H., Levy-Shiff, R., & Vakil, E. (1998). Interpretation of facial expressions of affect in children with learning disabilities with verbal or nonverbal deficits. *Journal of Learning Disabilities, 31*(3), 286–292, 312.

Di Pasquale, G., Moule, A., & Flewelling, R. (1980). The birth date effect. *Journal of Learning Disabilities, 13,* 234–238.

Disabilities Rights Advocates. (2001). *Do no harm: High-stakes testing and students with learning disabilities.* Oakland, CA: Author.

Division for Learning Disabilities and Division for Research Council for Exceptional Children. (2001, Spring). *Current practice alerts: High-stakes assessment, 4,* 1–4.

Dohrn, E., & Bryan, T. (1998). Coaching parents to use causal attributions and task strategies when reading with their children. *Learning Disabilities: A Multidisciplinary Journal, 9*(2), 33–46.

Duffy, F. (1988). Neurophysiological studies in dyslexia. In D. Plum (Ed.), *Language, communication and the brain.* New York: Raven Press.

Duffy, F., & McAnulty, G. (1985). Brain electrical activity mapping (BEAM): The search for a physiological signature of dyslexia. In F. Duffy & N. Geschwind (Eds.), *Dyslexia: A neuroscientific approach to clinical evaluation* (pp. 105–122). Boston: Little, Brown.

Dunn, L. (1968). Special education for the mildly retarded: Is much of it justifiable? *Exceptional Children, 35,* 5–22.

Dunn, R. (1988). Teaching students through the perceptual strengths or preferences. *Journal of Reading, 31,* 304–309.

Durrell, D. (1956). *Improving reading instruction.* New York: Harcourt, Brace & World.

Eastman, M., & Safran, J. (1986). Activities to develop your students' motor skills. *Teaching Exceptional Children, 19,* 24–27.

Education for all Handicapped Children Act of 1975, Public Law 142, 9th Congress.

Ehlers, S., & Gillberg, C. (1993). The epidemiology of Asperger Syndrome: A total population study. *The Journal of Child Psychology and Psychiatry and Allied Disciplines, 34*(8), 1327–1350.

Ehri, L., & Wilce, L. (1985). Movement into reading: Is the first stage of printed word reading visual or phonetic? *Reading Research Quarterly, 20,* 163–179.

Elbaum, B. (2002). The self-concept of students with learning disabilities. A metanalysis of comparisons across different placements. *Learning Disabilities Research and Practice, 17,* 216–226.

Elbaum, B., & Vaughn, S. (2001). School-based interventions to enhance the self-concept of students with learning disabilities: A meta-analysis. *Elementary School Journal, 101*(3), 303–329.

Elkins, J. (2001). Learning disabilities in Australia. In D. Hallahan & B. Keogh (Eds.), *Research and global perspectives in learning disabilities: Essays in honor of William M. Cruickshank* (pp. 181–196). Mahwah, NJ: Erlbaum.

Elkonin, D. B. (1973). U.S.S.R. In J. Downing (Ed.), *Comparative reading* (pp. 551–580). New York: MacMillan.

Ellis, E., Deshler, D., Lenz, K., Schumaker, J., & Clark, F. (1991). An instructional model for teaching learning strategies. *Focus on Exceptional Children, 23*(6), 1–23.

Enfield, M. (1988). The quest for literacy. *Annals of Dyslexia, 38,* 8–21.

Engelmann, S., Becker, W. C., Hanner, S., & Johnson, G. (1988). *Corrective reading program: Series guide.* Chicago: Science Research Associates.

Erickson, R., Ysseldyke, J., & Thurlow, M. (1998). Inclusive assessments and accountability systems: Tools of the trade in educational reform. *Teaching Exceptional Children, 31*(2), 4–9.

Erikson, E. H. (1968). *Identity: Youth and crisis.* New York: Norton.

Fabbro, F., & Masutto, C. (1994). An Italian perspective on learning disabilities. *Journal of Learning Disabilities, 27*(3), 139–141.

Farmer, T., & Farmer, M. (1996). Social relationships of students with exceptionalities in mainstream classrooms: Social networks and homophily. *Exceptional Children, 62*(5), 431–450.

Farr, R., & Carey, F. (1986). *Reading: What can be measured?* Newark, DE: International Reading Association.

Feingold, B. (1975). *Why your child is hyperactive.* New York: Random House.

Fennel, E. B. (1995). The role of neuropsychological assessment in learning disabilities. *Journal of Child Neurology, 10*(Suppl. 1), S36–S41.

Fernald, G. (1988). *Remedial techniques in basic school subjects.* Austin, TX: Pro-Ed. (Original work published 1943)

Feuerstein, R. (1979). *The dynamic assessment of retarded performers: The learning potential assessment device, theory, instruments, and techniques.* Baltimore: University Park Press.

Feuerstein, R. (1980). *Instrumental enrichment: An intervention program for cognitive modifiability.* Baltimore: University Park Press.

Feuerstein, R., Rand, Y., Jensen, M., Kaniel, S., & Tzuriel, D. (1987). Prerequisites for assessment of learning potential: The LPAD model. In C. Schneider-Lidz (Ed.), *Dynamic assessment: An interactional approach to evaluating learning potential* (pp. 35–51). New York: Guilford Press.

Fey, M., Windsor, J., & Warren, S. (Eds.). (1995). *Language intervention: Preschool through the elementary years*. Baltimore: Paul H. Brookes.

Fey, M. E., & Proctor-Williams, K. (2002). Recasting, elicited imitation, and modeling in grammar intervention for children with specific language impairments. In D. V. M. Bishop & L. B. Leonard (Eds.), *Speech and language impairments in children* (pp. 177–194). Philadelphia: Taylor & Francis Group.

Filipek, P. (1995). Neurobiologic correlates of developmental dyslexia: How do dyslexics' brains differ from those of normal readers? *Journal of Child Neurology, 10*(Suppl. 1), S62–S85.

Fisher, A., Murray, E., & Bundy, A. (1991). *Sensory integration: Theory and practice*. Philadelphia: F. A. Davis.

Fisher, J., Schumaker, J., & Deshler, D. (1995). Searching for validated inclusion practices: A review of the literature. *Focus on Exceptional Children, 28*(4), 1–20.

Fitzgerald, J. (1951). *A basic life spelling vocabulary*. Milwaukee: Bruce.

Fitzgerald, J. (1955). Children's experiences in spelling. In V. Herrick & L. Jacobs (Eds.), *Children and the language arts* (Chapter 11). Englewood Cliffs, NJ: Prentice-Hall.

Fletcher, J., Aram, D., Shaywitz, S., & Shaywitz, B. (2000). Learning, language, and attention deficit disorders in children: Comorbidity, assessment and intervention. In P. Accardo, T. Blondis, B. Whitman, & M. Stein (Eds.), *Attention deficits and hyperactivity in children and adults* (pp. 241–257, 2nd ed.). New York: Marcel Dekker.

Fletcher, J., Coulter, W., Reschly, D., & Vaughn, S. (2004). Alternative approaches to the definition and identification of learning disabilities: Some questions and answers. *Annals of Dyslexia, 54*, (2) 304–331.

Fletcher, J. M., & Foorman, B. R. (1994). Issues in definition and measurement of learning disabilities: The need for early intervention. In G. R. Lyon (Ed.), *Frames of reference for the assessment of learning disabilities* (pp. 185–200). Baltimore: Paul H. Brookes.

Fletcher, J. M., Shaywitz, S. E., Shankweiler, D. P., et al. (1994). Cognitive profiles of reading disability: Comparisons of discrepancy and low achievement definitions. *Journal of Educational Psychology, 86*, 6–23.

Fletcher, T. V., & DeLopez, C. (1995). A Mexican perspective on learning disabilities. *Journal of Learning Disabilities, 28*(9), 530–534, 544.

Foorman, B., & Torgesen, J. (2001). Critical elements of classroom and small-group instruction promote reading success in all children. *Learning Disabilities Research & Practice, 16*(4), 203–212.

Forgan, J. (1996). *Developmentally Appropriate Software for Young Children*. Presentation at the Council for Exceptional Children Annual Conference, Orlando, FL.

Fortin, J., & Crago, M. (1999). French language acquisition in North America. In O. L. Taylor & L. Leonard (Eds.), *Language acquisition across North America: Cross cultural and cross linguistic perspectives* (pp. 209–244). San Diego: Singular Publishing Co.

Fox, A. (1998). Clumsiness in children: Developmental coordination disorders. *Learning Disabilities: A Multidisciplinary Journal 9*(2), 57–63.

Frace-Blunt, M. (2000). High-stakes testing: A mixed blessing for special education students. *CEC Today, 7*, 1, 5, 7–15.

Francks, C., Fisher, S., Marlow, A., MacPhie, L., Taylor, K., Richardson, A., Stein, J., & Monaco, A. (2003). Familial and genetic effects on motor coordination, laterality, and reading-related cognition. *American Journal of Psychiatry, 160*, 1970–1977.

Frankenberger, W., & Fronzaglio, K. (1991). A review of states' criteria and procedures for identifying children with learning disabilities. *Journal of Learning Disabilities, 24*, 495–500.

Freiberg, H. J. (1993). A school that fosters resiliency in inner-city youth. *Journal of Negro Education, 62*, 364–376.

Friend, M., & Bursuck, W. (1996, 2002). *Including students with special needs: A practical guide for classroom teachers* (3rd ed.). Boston: Allyn & Bacon.

Friend, M., & Cook, L. (2003). *Interactions: Collaborative skills for school professionals* (4th ed.). New York: Longman.

Fuchs, D., & Fuchs, L. (1998). Researchers and teachers working together to adapt instruction for diverse learners. *Learning Disabilities Research & Practice, 13*(3), 126–137.

Fuchs, D., Mock, D., Morgan, P., & Young, C. (2003). Responsiveness-to-interventions: Definitions, evidence, and implications for the learning disabilities construct. *Learning Disabilities Research and Practice, 18* (3), 167–171.

Fuchs, L., & Fuchs, D. (2001a). Principles for the prevention and intervention of mathematics difficulties. *Learning Disabilities Research & Practice, 6*(2) 85–95.

Fuchs, L., & Fuchs, D. (2001b). Using assessment to account for and promote strong outcomes for students with learning disabilities. In D. Hallahan & B. Keogh (Eds.), *Research on global perspectives in learning disabilities: Essays in honor of William M. Cruickshank* (pp. 93–110). Mahwah, NJ: Erlbaum.

Fuchs, L. S., & Deno, S. L. (1994). Must instructionally useful performance assessment be based in the curriculum? *Exceptional Children, 61*(1), 15–24.

Galaburda, A. (1990). The testosterone hypothesis: Assessment since Geschwind and Behan, 1982. *Annals of Dyslexia, 40,* 18–38.

Ganschow, L., Philips, L., & Schneider, E. (2000). Experiences with the University Foreign Language Requirement: Voice of students with learning disabilities. *Learning Disabilities: A Multidisciplinary Journal, 10*(3), 111–128.

Ganschow, L., Sparks, R., & Javorksy, J. (1998). Foreign language and learning difficulties: An historical perspective. *Journal of Learning Disabilities, 31*(2), 248–258.

Garcia, S. B., & Malkin, D. H. (1993). Toward defining programs and services for culturally and linguistically diverse students in special education. *Teaching Exceptional Children, 26*(1), 52–58.

Gardner, H. (1983). *Frames of mind.* New York: Basic Books.

Gardner, H. (1993). *Multiple intelligences: The theory in practice.* New York: Wiley.

Gardner, H. (1999). *Intelligence reformed: Multiple intelligences for the twenty-first century.* New York: Basic Books.

Gardner, H., & Hatch, T. (1989). Multiple intelligences go to school. *Educational Researcher, 18,* 4–10.

Gately, S., & Gately, F. (2001). Understanding coteaching components. *Teaching Exceptional Children, 33*(4), 40–47.

Gerber, M., & Durgunoglu, A. (2004). Reading risks and intervention for young English learners: Evidence from longitudinal intervention research. *Learning Disabilities Research and Practice, 19*(4), 199–201.

Gerber, P. (1997). Life after school: Challenges in the workplace. In P. Gerber & D. Brown (Eds.), *Learning disabilities and employment* (pp. 3–18). Austin, TX: Pro-Ed.

Gerber, P., & Brown, D. (Eds.). (1997). *Learning disabilities and employment.* Austin, TX: Pro-Ed.

Gerber, P., & Reiff, H. (Eds.). (1994). *Learning disabilities in adulthood: Persisting problems and evolving issues.* Boston: Andover Medical Publishers.

Gerber, P. J., & Reiff, H. B. (1991). *Speaking for themselves: Ethnographic interviews with adults with learning disabilities.* Ann Arbor: University of Michigan Press.

German, D. (1993). *Word finding interactive programs.* Itasca, IL: Riverside Publishing.

German, D. (2001). *It's on the tip of my tongue.* Chicago: Word Finding Materials.

Gersten, R. (1998). Recent advances in instructional research for students with learning disabilities: An overview. *Learning Disabilities Research & Practice, 13*(3), 162–170.

Gersten, R., Brengelman, S., & Jiménez, R. (1994). Effective instruction for culturally and linguistically diverse students: A reconceptualization. *Focus on Exceptional Children, 27*(1), 1–16.

Gilger, J. (2003). Genes and dyslexia. *International Dyslexia Association, 29*(2), 6–8.

Gillingham, A., & Stillman, B. (1970). *Remedial training for children with specific difficulty in reading, spelling, and penmanship.* Cambridge, MA: Educators Publishing Service.

Goldey, E. (1998). New angles on motor and sensory coordination in learning disabilities: A report on the 1998 LDA medical symposium. *Learning Disabilities: A Multidisciplinary Journal, 9*(2), 65–72.

Goldstein, C. (1998). Learning at cybercamp. *Teaching Exceptional Children, 30*(5), 16–21.

Goldstein, K. (1939). *The organism.* New York: American Books.

Goleman, D. (1995). *Emotional intelligence: Why it can matter more than IQ.* New York: Bantam Books.

Gopnick, A., Meltzoff, A., & Kuhl, P. (1999). *The scientist in the crib: Minds, brains, and how children learn.* New York: William Morrow.

Gorman, C. (2003). The new science of dyslexia. *Time, 162,*(4) 52–59.

Gorman, J. (1999). Understanding children's hearts and minds: Emotional functioning and learning disabilities. *Teaching Exceptional Children, 31*(3), 72–77.

Graham, S., & Harris, K. (1997). Whole language and process writing: Does one size fit all? In J. Lloyd, E. Kame'enui, & D. Chard (Eds.), *Issues in educating students with disabilities* (pp. 239–261). Mahwah, NJ: Erlbaum.

Graham, S., Harris, K., & Larsen, L. (2001). Prevention and intervention of writing difficulties for students with learning disabilities. *Learning Disabilities Research & Practice, 16*(2), 62–73.

Graves, D. H. (1994). *A fresh look at writing.* Portsmouth, NH: Heinemann.

Greeno, J., Collins, A., & Resnick, L. (1996). Cognition and learning. In B. Berliner & R. Calfee (Eds.), *Handbook of educational psychology* (pp. 15–46). New York: Macmillan.

Greenwood, C. R. (1996). Research on the practices and behavior of effective teachers at the Juniper Gardens Child's Project: Implication for the education of diverse learners. In D. L. Speece & B. Keogh (Eds.), *Research on classroom ecologies: Implications for inclusion of children with learning disabilities* (pp. 39–67). Mahwah, NJ: Erlbaum.

Greenwood, C. R., Maheedy, L. F., & Delquardi, J. C. (2002). Class-wide peer tutoring. In G. Stoner, M. R. Shinn, & H. Walker (Eds.), *Intervention for achievement and behavior problems* (pp. 611–649). Washington, DC: National Association for School Psychologists.

Groteluschen, A., Borkowski, J., & Hale, C. (1990). Strategy instruction is often insufficient: Addressing the interdependency of executive and attributional processes. In T. Scruggs & B. Wong (Eds.), *Intervention research in learning disabilities* (pp. 81–101). New York: Springer-Verlag.

Guralnick, M. J. (Ed.). (1997). *The effectiveness of early intervention.* Baltimore: Paul H. Brookes.

Haager, D., & Vaughn, S. (1995). Parent, teacher, peer and self-reports of the social competence of students with learning disabilities. *Journal of Learning Disabilities, 28*(4), 205–215, 231.

Haager, D., & Vaughn, S. (1997). Assessment of social competence in students with learning disabilities. In J. Lloyd, E. Kame'enui, & D. Chard (Eds.), *Issues in educating students with disabilities* (pp. 129–152). Mahwah, NJ: Erlbaum.

Haber, J. (2000). *The great misdiagnosis: ADHD.* Dallas: Taylor Trade Publishing.

Hagin, R. (1983). Write right—or left: A practical approach to handwriting. *Journal of Learning Disabilities, 16,* 266–271.

Hagin, R., & Simon, J. (Eds.). (2000). Adults with learning disabilities enter the professions: Issues of diagnosis, education, accommodations, and licensing. *Learning Disabilities: A Multidisciplinary Journal, 10*(2), 35–106.

Hakuta, K. (1990). Language and cognition in bilingual children. In A. M. Padilla, H. H. Fairchild, & C. Valadez (Eds.), *Bilingual education: Issues and strategies* (pp. 47–59). Newbury Park, CA: Sage.

Hallgren, B. (1950). Specific dyslexia (congenital word-blindness): A clinical and genetic study. *Acta Psychiatrica Scandinavica Supplementum, 65,* 1–287.

Hammill, D. (1990). On defining learning disabilities: An emerging consensus. *Journal of Learning Disabilities, 23,* 74–84.

Handwerk, M., & Marshall, R. (1998). Behavioral and emotional problems of students with learning disabilities, serious emotional disturbances, or both conditions. *Journal of Learning Disabilities, 31*(4), 327–338.

Harris, K., Graham, S., & Mason, L. (2003). Self-regulated strategy development in the classroom: Part of a balanced approach to writing instruction for students with disabilities. *Focus on Exceptional Children, 35*(7), 1–16.

Harris, K. R., & Graham, S. (1997). *Making the writing process work: Strategies for composition and self-regulation.* Cambridge, MA: Brookline Books.

Harth, R., & Burns, C. (2001, July). *PACE: A non-degree college program.* Paper presented at the International Association of Special Education Conference, Warsaw, Poland.

Harth, R., & Burns, C. (2004). Vocational outcomes for young adults with multiple learning disabilities. *Learning Disabilities: A Multidisciplinary Journal, 13*(2), 49–54.

Hasbrouck, J. (1996, April 12). *Oral reading fluency: A review of literature with implications for use with elementary students who are difficult to teach.* Paper given at the Council for Exceptional Children meeting, Orlando, FL.

Hasselbring, T., & Glaser, C. (2000). Use of computer technology to help students with special needs. *The Future of Children: Children and Computer Technology, 10*(2), 102–122.

Hasselbring, T., & Goin, I. (1993). Integrated technology and media. In E. Polloway & J. Patton (Eds.), *Strategies for teaching learners with special needs* (pp. 145–162). New York: Merrill/Macmillan.

Hauser, P., Zametkin, A. J., Martinez, P., Vitiello, B., Matochik, J. A., Mixson, J. A., & Weintraub B. D. (1993). Attention deficit-hyperactivity disorder in people with generalized resistance to thyroid hormone. *New England Journal of Medicine, 328,* 14, 997–1001.

Hazel, J., & Schumaker, J. (1988). Social skills and learning disabilities: Current issues and recommendations for future research. In J. Kavanagh & T. Truss, Jr. (Eds.), *Learning disabilities: Proceedings of the national conference* (pp. 293–344). Parkton, MD: York Press.

Head, H. (1926). *Aphasia and kindred disorders of speech.* London: Cambridge University Press.

Head Start Bureau. (1993). *Head Start performance standards on services for children with disabilities.* Office of Human Development: Administration on Children, Youth, and Families. Washington, DC: U.S. Government Printing Office.

Heckelman, R. (1969). A neurological impress method of reading instruction. *Academic Therapy, 4,* 277–282.

Hennesy, N., Rosenberg, D., & Tramaglini, S. (2003). A high school model for students with dyslexia: Remediation to accommodation. *International Dyslexia Association, 29*(2), 38–40.

Henry, M. (1998). Structured, sequential, multisensory teaching: The Orton legacy. *Annals of Dyslexia, 48,* 3–26.

Hernandez, H. (2001). *Multicultural education.* Upper Saddle River, NJ: Prentice-Hall.

Hinshelwood, J. (1917). *Congenital word blindness.* London: H. K. Lewis.

Hiscock, M., & Kinsbourne, M. (1987). Specialization of the cerebral hemispheres: Implications for learning. *Journal of Learning Disabilities, 20*(3), 130–143.

Holloway, J. (2001). Inclusion and students with learning disabilities. *Educational Leadership, 57*(6), 86–118.

Hook, P., & Jones, S. (2004). The importance of automaticity and fluency for efficient reading comprehension. *Perspectives: International Dyslexia Association, 24*(2), 16–21.

Horne, M. (1978). Do learning disabilities specialists know their phonics? *Journal of Learning Disabilities, 11,* 580–582.

Hsu, C. (1988). Correlates of reading success and failure in a logographic writing system. *Thalmus, 6*(1), 33–59.

Huttenlocher, P. (1991, September 26). *Neural plasticity.* Paper presented at the Brain Research Foundation Women's Council, University of Chicago, Chicago.

Hutton, J. (1984). Incidence of learning problems among children with middle ear pathology. *Journal of Learning Disabilities, 17,* 41–42.

Hynd, G. (1992). Neurological aspects of dyslexia: Comments on the balance model. *Journal of Learning Disabilities, 25,* 110–113.

Hynd, G., Hern, L., Voeller, K., & Marshall, R. (1991). Neurobiological basis of attention deficit hyperactivity disorder (ADHD). *School Psychology, 20*(2), 174–186.

Hynd, G., & Semrud-Clickman, M. (1989). Dyslexia and brain morphology. *Psychological Bulletin, 106,* 447–882.

Individuals with Disabilities Education Act of 1990, Public Law 101-476, 101st Congress.

Individuals with Disabilities Education Act of 1997, Public Law 105-17, 105th Cong., lst Sess. (January 7, 1997).

Individuals With Disabilties Education Improvement Act of 2004, Public Law 108-446, 108th Cong. 2nd sess. (December 3, 2004).

Interagency Committee on Learning Disabilities (Ed.). (1988). *Learning disabilities: A report to the U.S. Congress.* Washington, DC: U.S. Government Printing Office.

Irlen, H. (1991). *Reading by the colors: Overcoming dyslexia and other reading disabilities through the Irlen method.* Garden City Park, NY: Avery Publishing.

Itard, J. (1962). *The wild boy of Aveyron* (G. Humphrey & M. Humphrey, Trans.). New York: Appleton-Century-Crofts. (Original work published 1801)

Iverson, S., & Tunner, W. (1993). Phonological processing skills and the reading recovery program. *Journal of Educational Psychology, 85,* 112–120.

Jackson, J. H. (1874). On the nature of duality of the brain. In J. Taylor (Ed.), *Selected writing of John Hughlings Jackson.* New York: Basic Books.

Jenkins, J., Fuchs, L., Van den Broek, P; Epsin, C. & Deno, S. (2003). Accuracy and Fluency in List and Context Reading of Skilled and RD groups: Absolute & Relative Performance Levels. *Learning Disabilities Research & Practice, 18*(4), 237–245.

Jennings, J., Caldwell, J., & Lerner, J. (2006). Reading problems: Assessment and reading strategies. Boston: Prentice-Hall.

Jiménez, R. (2002). Fostering the literacy development of Latino students. *Focus on Exceptional Children, 34*(6), 1–10.

Johns, B. (2003). NCLB and IDEA: Never the twain should meet. *Learning Disabilities: A Multidiscplinary Journal, 12*(3), 89–92.

Johnson, D. J., & Blalock, J. (1987). *Adults with learning disabilities: Clinical studies.* Orlando, FL: Grune & Stratton.

Johnson, E., Kimball, K., & Brown, S. (2001). A statewide review of the use of accommodations in large-scale, high stakes assessments. *Exceptional Children, 67,* 2, 261–264.

Johnson, M., Kress, K., & Pikulski, J. (1987). *Informal reading inventories.* Newark, DE: International Reading Association.

Jones, E., & Southern, W. (2003). Balancing perspectives on mathematics instruction. *Focus on Exceptional Children, 35*(9), 1–16.

Jones, E., Wilson, R., & Bhojwani, S. (1997). Mathematics instruction for secondary students with learning disabilities. *Journal of Learning Disabilities, 30,* 151–163.

Juel, C. (1995). The role of decoding in learning to read. *American Educator, 19,* 8–42.

Kagan, J. (1966). Reflection–impulsivity: The generality and dynamics of conceptual tempo. *Journal of Abnormal Psychology, 71,* 17–24.

Kame'enui, E. (1991). Toward a scientific pedagogy of learning disabilities: A sameness in the message. *Journal of Learning Disabilities, 24,* 364–372.

Kantrowitz, B., & Underwood, A. (1999, November 2). Dyslexia and the new science of reading. *Newsweek, 134,* 72–80.

Katz, M. (1997). *On playing a poor hand well.* New York: W. W. Norton.

Kauffman, J., Gerber, M., & Semmel, M. (1998). Arguable assumptions underlying the regular education initiative. *Journal of Learning Disabilities, 21*(1), 6–11.

Kauffman, J., & Hallahan, D. (1997). A diversity of restrictive environments: Placement as a problem of social ecology. In J. Lloyd, E. Kame'enui, & D. Chard (Eds.), *Issues in educating students with disabilities* (pp. 325–342). Mahwah, NJ: Erlbaum.

Kauffman, J., & Wiley, A. (2004). How the president's commission on excellence in special education devalues special education. *Learning Disabilities: A Multidisciplinary Journal, 13*(1), 3–6.

Kavale, K. (1990). Variances and verities in learning disability interventions. In T. Scruggs & B. Wong (Eds.), *Intervention in learning disabilities* (pp. 3–33). New York: Springer-Verlag.

Keller, H. (1961). *The story of my life.* New York: Dell.

Keogh, B., & Bess, C. (1991). Assessing temperament. In H. L. Swanson (Ed.), *Handbook on the assessment of learning disabilities* (pp. 313–330). Austin, TX: Pro-Ed.

Keogh, B. (2000). Risk, families, and schools. *Focus on Exceptional Children, 33*(4), 1–11.

Kephart, N. (1963). *The brain-injured child in the classroom.* Chicago: National Society for Crippled Children and Adults.

Kephart, N. (1967). Perceptual-motor aspects of learning disabilities. In E. Frierson & W. Barbe (Eds.), *Educating children with learning disabilities* (pp. 405–413). New York: Appleton-Century-Crofts.

Kephart, N. (1971). *The slow learner in the classroom.* Columbus, OH: Charles E. Merrill.

Kibby, M., & Hynd, G. (2001). Neurological basis of learning disabilities. In D. Hallahan & B. Keogh (Eds.), *Research and global perspectives in learning disabilities: Essays in honor of William A. Cruickshank* (pp. 25–42). Mahwah, NJ: Erlbaum.

Kirk, S. A. (1963). Behavioral diagnosis and remediation of learning disabilities. In *Proceedings of the Conference on the Exploration into the Problems of the Perceptually Handicapped Child.* Evanston, IL: Fund for the Perceptually Handicapped Child.

Kirk, S. A. (1987). The learning-disabled preschool child. *Teaching Exceptional Children, 19*(2), 78–80.

Kirk, S. A., & Elkins, J. (1975). Characteristics of children enrolled in Child Service Demonstration Centers. *Journal of Learning Disabilities, 8,* 630–637.

Kirk, S. A., Kirk, W., & Minskoff, E. (1985). *Phonic remedial reading drills.* Novato, CA: Academic Therapy Publications.

Kistner, J., Osborn, M., & LaVerrier, L. (1988). Causal attributions of learning-disabled children: Developmental patterns and relation to academic progress. *Journal of Educational Psychology, 80,* 82–89.

Klin, A., Lang, J., Cicchetti, D., & Volkmar, F. (2000). Brief report—Interrater reliability of clinical diagnosis and *DSM-IV* criteria for austistic disorder: Results of the *DSM-IV* autism field trial. *Journal of Autism and Developmental Disorders, 30,* 163–167.

Klin, A., Volkman, F., & Sparrow, S. (2000). *Asperger Syndrome.* New York: Guilford Press.

Kline, F., & Silver, L. (2004). The educator's guide to mental health in the classroom. Baltimore: Paul H. Brookes.

Kluwe, R. (1987). Executive decisions and regulation of problem solving behavior. In F. Weinert & R. Kluwe (Eds.), *Metacognition, motivation and understanding* (pp. 31–64). Hillsdale, NJ: Erlbaum.

Knackendoffel, E. A. (1996). Collaborative teaming in the secondary school. In D. Deshler, E. Ellis, & B. Lenz (Eds.), *Teaching adolescents with learning disabilities* (pp. 517–616). Denver: Love.

Kohn, A. (1995). *Punished by rewards: The trouble with gold stars, incentive plans, As, praise, and other bribes.* Boston: Houghton Mifflin.

Koppitz, E. (1973). Special class pupils with learning disabilities: A five-year follow-up study. *Academic Therapy, 8,* 133–140.

Korinek, L., & Bulls, J. A. (1996). SCORE-A: A student research paper writing strategy. *Teaching Exceptional Children, 28*(4), 60–63.

Korkunov, V., Nigayev, A., Reynolds, L., & Lerner, J. (1998). Special education in Russia: History, reality, and prospects. *Journal of Learning Disabilities, 31*(2), 186–192.

Kotulak, R. (2004, May 2). Scientists offer hope for poor readers. *Chicago Tribune,* Section 1, pp. 1, 10.

Krashen, S. D. (1992). *Fundamentals of language education.* Torrance, CA: Laredo.

Kratochvil, C., Heiligenstein, J., Dittmann, R., Spencer, T., Biederman, J., Wernicke, J., et al. (2002). Atomoxetine and methyiphenidate treatment in children with ADHD: A prospective, randomized, open-label trial. *Journal of the American Academy of Child and Adolescent Psychiatry, 41,* 1–9.

Kravetz, M., & Wax, I. (2001). *K & W guide for the learning disabled.* New York: The Princeton Review.

Kübler-Ross, E. (1969). *On death and dying.* New York: Macmillan.

Kuder, S. (2003). *Teaching students with language and communication disorders.* Boston: Allyn & Bacon.

Lahey, M. (1988). *Language disorders and language development*. Columbus, OH: Macmillan.

Lane, H. B., & Brownell, M. T. (1995). Literacy instruction: Meeting the needs of adolescents with learning disabilities. In *Secondary education and beyond: Providing opportunities for students with learning disabilities* (pp. 131–148). Pittsburgh: Learning Disabilities Association of America.

Langford, K., Slade, K., & Barnett, A. (1974). An explanation of impress techniques in remedial reading. *Academic Therapy, 9,* 309–319.

Langone, J. (1998). Managing inclusive instruction settings: Technology, cooperative planning, and team-based organization. *Focus on Exceptional Children, 30*(8), 1–15.

Latham, P., & Latham, P. (1997). Legal rights of adults with learning disabilities in employment. In P. Gerber & D. Brown (Eds.), *Learning disabilities and employment* (pp. 39–58). Austin, TX: Pro-Ed.

Lavoie, R. (2001). Poker chips and self-esteem. *Texas Key, 1044,* 9–16.

Lavoie, R. D. (1995). Life on the waterbed: Mainstreaming on the homefront. *Attention!, 2*(1), 25–29.

Lazar, I., & Darlington, R. (Eds.). (1982). Lasting effects of early education: A report from the Consortium for Longitudinal Studies. *Monographs of the Society for Research in Child Development, 27*(2–3, Serial No. 195) (Summary Report, DHEW Publication No. OHDS 80–30/79).

Learning Disabilities Association of America. (1995). *Secondary education and beyond: Providing opportunities for students with learning disabilities.* Pittsburgh: Author.

Learning Disabilities Association of America (1999). *Childhood depression fact sheet.* Pittsburgh: Author.

Lee, C., & Jackson, R. (1992). *Faking it: A look into the mind of a creative learner.* Portsmouth, NH: Heinemann.

Lenneberg, E. (1967). *Biological foundations of language.* New York: Wiley.

Lenz, B. K., Deshler, D. D. (with Kissam, B.). (2003). *Teaching content to all: Evidence-based inclusive practice in middle and secondary schools.* Boston: Pearson.

Lenz, B. K., Ellis, E. S., & Scanlon, D. (1996). *Teaching learning strategies to adolescents and adults with learning disabilities.* Austin, TX: Pro-Ed.

Lerner, J. (1989). Educational intervention in learning disabilities. *Journal of American Academy of Child and Adolescent Psychiatry, 28,* 325–352.

Lerner, J. (1990). Phonological awareness: A critical element in learning to read. *Learning Disabilities: A Multidisciplinary Journal, 1,* 50–54.

Lerner, J., Lowenthal, B., & Egan, R. (2003). *Preschool children with special needs: Children at-risk and children with disabilities.* Boston: Allyn & Bacon.

Lerner, J., Lowenthal, B., & Lerner, S. (1995). *Attention deficit disorders: Assessment and teaching.* Pacific Grove, CA: Brooks/Cole.

Lerner, J. W., & Chen, A. (1992). The cross-cultural nature of learning disabilities: A profile in perseverance. *Learning Disabilities Research and Practice, 8,* 147–149.

Lerner, J. W., & List, L. (1970). The phonics knowledge of prospective teachers, experienced teachers and elementary pupils. *Illinois School Research, 7,* 39–42.

Levine, M. (1987). *Developmental variation and learning disabilities.* Cambridge, MA: Educators' Publishing Service.

Levine, M. (1988). Learning disability: What is it? *ACLD Newsbriefs, 173,* 1–2.

Levine, M. (1993). *All kinds of minds.* Cambridge, MA: Educators Publishing Service.

Levine, M. (1994). *Educational care: A system for understanding and helping children with learning problems at home and in school.* Cambridge, MA: Educators Publishing Services.

Levine, M. (2002). *A mind at a time.* New York: Simon & Schuster.

Levine, M. (2003). *The myth of laziness.* New York: Simon & Schuster.

Levine, M., Hooper, S., Montgomery, J., Reed, M., Sandler, A., & Swartz, C. (1993). Learning disabilities: An interactive developmental paradigm. In G. R. Lyon, D. Gray, J. Kavanagh, & N. Krasnegor (Eds.), *Better understanding of learning disabilities* (pp. 199–228). Baltimore: Paul H. Brookes.

Levine, M. D., & Swartz, C. W. (1995). The unsuccessful adolescent. In Learning Disabilities Association of America (Ed.), *Secondary education and beyond: Providing opportunities for students with learning disabilities* (pp. 3–12). Pittsburgh: Learning Disabilities Association of America.

Lewis, R. (1998). Assistive technology and learning disabilities: Today's realities and tomorrow's promises. *Journal of Learning Disabilities, 31*(1), 16–26.

Lewis, T., & Sugai, G. (1999). Effective behavior support: A systems approach to proactive schoolwide management. *Focus on Exceptional Children, 31*(6), 1–24.

Liberman, A. M. (1997). How theories of speech affect research in reading and writing. In B. Blachman (Ed.), *Foundations of reading acquisition and dyslexia: Implications for early instruction* (pp. 3–20). Mahwah, NJ: Erlbaum.

Liberman, I., & Liberman, A. (1990). Whole language vs. code emphasis: Underlying assumptions and their implications for reading instruction. *Annals of Dyslexia, 40*, 51–78.

Licht, B., & Kistner, J. (1986). Motivational problems of learning-disabled children: Individual differences and their implications for treatment. In J. Torgesen & B. Wong (Eds.), *Psychological and education perspectives on learning disabilities* (pp. 225–255). New York: Academic Press.

Lindamood, P. C. (1994). Issues in researching the link between phonological awareness, learning disabilities, and spelling. In G. R. Lyon (Ed.), *Frames of reference for the assessment of learning disabilities* (pp. 351–375). Baltimore: Paul H. Brookes.

Linder, T. W. (1993). *Transdisciplinary play-based assessment: A functional approach to working with young children.* Baltimore: Paul H. Brookes.

Lindquist, M. (1987). Strategic teaching in mathematics. In B. F. Jones et al. (Eds.), *Strategic teaching and learning: Cognitive instruction in the content areas* (pp. 11–134). Washington, DC: Association for Supervision and Curriculum Development.

Lokerson, J. (2001). Learning disabilities and statewide testing: The Oregon case. *LDA Newsbriefs, 36*(2), 12.

Lovitt, T. (1991). Behavioral assessment of learning disabilities. In H. L. Swanson (Ed.), *Handbook on the assessment of learning disabilities* (pp. 95–119). Austin, TX: Pro-Ed.

Lowenthal, B. (2003). Cultural competencies for American early interventionists. *Learning disabilities: A multidisciplinary journal, 12*(3), 125–130.

Lowenthal, B., & Lowenthal, M. (1995). The effects of asthma on school performance. *Learning Disabilities: A Multidisciplinary Journal, 6*(20), 41–46.

Lundberg, I. (2002). Second language learning and reading with the additional load of dyslexia. *Annals of Dyslexia, 52*, 165–188.

Lundberg, I., & Höien, T. (2001). Learning disabilities in Scandinavia. In D. Hallahan & B. Keogh (Eds.), *Research and global perspectives in learning disabilities: Essays in honor of William M. Cruickshank* (pp. 291–308). Mahwah, NJ: Erlbaum.

Luther, S. S. (1993). Methodological and conceptual issues in research in childhood resilience. *Journal of Child Psychology and Psychiatry and Allied Disciplines, 34*, 441–453.

Lyon, G. R. (1995b). Research initiatives in learning disabilities: Contributions from scientists supported by the National Institute of Child Health and Human Development. *Journal of Child Neurology, 10*(Suppl. 1), S120–S126.

Lyon, G. R. (1996). Learning disabilities. *The Future of Children, 6*(1), 54–76.

Lyon, G. R. (1997). Progress and promise in research in learning disabilities. *Learning Disabilities: A Multidisciplinary Journal, 8*(1), 1–6.

Lyon, G. R. (1998). Why reading is not a natural process. *Educational Leadership, 55*(6) 14–18.

Lyon, G. R. (2001). Rethinking learning disabilities. In *Rethinking special education for a new century.* Available: www.ppionline.org

Lyon, G. R. (2003). Reading disabilities: Why do some children have difficulty learning to read? What can be done about it? *Perspectives: International Dyslexia Association, 29*(2), 17–19.

Lyon, G. R., Fletcher, J. M., Shaywitz, S. E., Shaywitz, B. A., Torgesen, J. K., Wood, F. B., Schulte, A., & Olson, R. (2001). Rethinking learning disabilities. In C. E. Finn, Jr., A. J. Rotherham, & C. R. Hokanson, Jr. (Eds.), *Rethinking special education for a new century* (pp. 259–288). Washington, DC: Thomas B. Fordham Foundation. Available: www.edexcellence.net/library/special_ed/index.html

Lyon, G.R., Shaywitz, S., & Shaywitz, B. (2003). Defining dyslexia, comorbidity, teachers' knowledge of language and reading. *Annals of Dyslexia, 53*, 1–14.

Lyon, G. R., & Krasnegor, N. (Eds.). (1996). *Attention, memory, and executive function.* Baltimore: Paul H. Brookes.

Lyon, G. R., & Moats, L. C. (1997). Critical conceptual and methodological considerations in reading intervention research. *Journal of Learning Disabilities, 30*(6), 578–588.

MacArthur, C. (1996). Using technology to enhance the writing process of students with learning disabilities. *Journal of Learning Disabilities, 29*, 344–354.

Mainzer, R., Deshler, D., Coleman, M., Kozleski, M., & Rodriguez-Walling, E. (2003). To ensure the learning of every child with a disability. *Focus on Exceptional Children, 35*(5), 1–12.

Mann, V. (1991). Language problems: A key to early reading problems. In B. Wong (Ed.), *Learning about learning disabilities* (pp. 130–163). San Diego: Academic Press.

Mann, V., & Foy, J. (2003). Phonological awareness, speech development, and letter knowledge in preschool children. *Annals of Dyslexia, 53*, 149–173.

Marcaruso, P., & Hook, P. (2001). Auditory processing—Evaluation of Fast For-Word for children with dyslexia. *Perspectives: The International Dyslexia Association, 27*(3), 5–9.

Marchand-Marella, N. E., Slocum, T. A., and Marcella, R. C. (Eds) *Introduction to Direct Instruction.* Boston: Pearson.

Martin, B. (1992). *Brown bear, brown bear, what do you see?* New York: Holt, Rinehart, & Winston.

Martin, R. (1995). Transition services from a legal perspective. In *Secondary education and beyond: Providing opportunities for students with learning disabilities* (pp. 82–89). Pittsburgh: Learning Disabilities Association of America.

Mastropieri, M. (1987). Statistical and psychometric issues surrounding severe discrepancy: A discussion. *Learning Disabilities Research, 3*(1), 29–31.

Mastropieri, M., & Scruggs, T. (1998). Constructing more meaningful relationships in the classroom: Mnemonic research into practice. *Learning Disabilities Research & Practice, 13*(3), 138–145.

Mather, M., & Goldstein, S. (2001). *Learning disabilities and challenging behaviors: A guide to intervention and classroom management.* Baltimore: Paul H. Brookes.

Mather, N., & Healey, W. C. (1990). Disposing aptitude-achievement discrepancy in the emperial criterion for learning disabilities. *Learning Disabilities: A Multidisciplinary Journal, 1,* 40–48.

Mayer, R. E. (1996). Learners as information processors: Legacies and implications of educational psychology, second metaphor. *Educational Psychologist, 31*(3/4), 151–164.

Mayers, S., Calhoun, S., & Crowell, E. (2000). Learning disabilities and ADHD: Overlapping spectrum disorders. *Journal of Learning Disabilities, 33,* 417–424.

McCormick, L., & Schiefelbusch, R. (1990). *Early language intervention.* Columbus, OH: Merrill.

McGough, R. (2004). Dyslexia manifests differently for Chinese readers. *Wall Street Journal,* Section D4, p. 3, September 2, 2004.

McGrady, H., Lerner, J., & Boscardin, M. (2001). The educational lives of students with learning disabilities. In P. Rodis, A. Garrod, & M. L. Boscardin (Eds.), *Learning disabilities and life stories* (pp. 177–193). Boston: Allyn & Bacon.

McIntosh, R., Vaughn, S., & Bennerson, D. (1995). FAST social skills with a SLAM and a RAP. *Teaching Exceptional Children, 27,* 37–41.

McIntyre, C., & Pickering, J. (1995). *Clinical studies of multisensory structured language education for students with dyslexia and related disorders.* Salem, OR: International Multisensory Structured Language Education Council.

McKenna, M. (2004). Teaching vocabulary to struggling older readers. *Perspectives: International Dyslexia Association, 30*(1), 13–16.

McKinney, J. D., & Hocutt, A. (1988). The need of policy analysis in evaluating the regular education initiative. *Journal of Learning Disabilities, 21*(1), 12–19.

McLean, M., Bailey, D., & Wolery, M. (Eds.). (1996). *Assessing infants and preschoolers with special needs.* Englewood Cliffs, NJ: Prentice-Hall.

McLeskey, J., Hoppery, D., Williamson, P., and Rentz, T. (2004). Is inclusion an illusion? An examination of national and state trends toward the education of students with learning disabilities in the general education classrooms. *Learning Disabilities Research and Practice, 19*(2), 109–115.

McLeskey, J., & Waldron, N. (1995). Inclusive elementary programs: Must they cure students with learning disabilities to be effective? *Phi Delta Kappan, 77*(5), 542–546.

Meece, J. L. (2002). *Child and adolescent development for educators* (2nd ed.). New York: McGraw-Hill.

Meichenbaum, D. (1977). *Cognitive behavior modification.* New York: Plenum.

Meichenbaum, D., & Goodman, J. (1971). Training impulsive children to talk to themselves: A means of developing self-control. *Journal of Abnormal Psychology, 77,* 115–126.

Meisels, S., & Fenichel, F. (Eds.). (1996). *New visions for the developmental assessment of infants and young children.* Washington, DC: Zero to Three, National Center for Infants, Toddlers, and Families.

Meltzer, L., & Montague, M. (2001). Strategic learning in students with learning disabilities: What have we learned? In D. Hallahan & B. Keogh (Eds.), *Research and global perspectives in learning disabilities: Essays in honor of William M. Cruickshank* (pp. 111–130). Mahwah, NJ: Lawrence Erlbaum.

Mercer, C., Jordan, L., Allsopp, D., & Mercer, A. (1996). Learning disabilities definitions and criteria used by the state education departments. *Learning Disability Quarterly, 19*(2), 217–232.

Merzenich, M. M., Jenkins, W. M., & Tallal, P. (1996). Temporal processing deficits of language-learning impaired children ameliorated by training. *Science, 271*(5245), 77–80.

Messerer, J., Hunt, E., Meyers, G., & Lerner, J. (1984). Feuerstein's instrumental enrichment: A new approach for activating intellectual potential in learning disabled youth. *Journal of Learning Disabilities, 17,* 322–325.

Messick, S. (1984). The nature of cognitive styles: Problems and promise in educational practice. *Educational Psychology, 19,* 59–74.

Messick, S. (1994). The matter of style: Manifestations of personality in cognition, learning, and teaching. *Educational Psychologist, 29,* 121–136.

Meyer, M. (2002). Repeated reading: An old standard is revisited and renovated. *Perspectives: International Dyslexia Association, 28*(1), 15–18.

Meyer, M., Wood, F., Hart, L., & Felton, R. (1998). Longitudinal course of rapid naming in disabled and non-disabled readers. *Annals of Dyslexia, 48*, 90–114.

Miami Herald. (1980, October 11).

Miller, S., & Mercer, C. (1997). Education aspects of mathematics disabilities. *Journal of Learning Disabilities, 30*(1), 47–56.

Moats, L. C. (1994a). Assessment of spelling in learning disabilities research. In G. R. Lyon (Ed.), *Frames of reference for the assessment of learning disabilities* (pp. 333–350). Baltimore: Paul H. Brookes.

Moats, L. C. (1994b). Honing the concepts of listening and speaking: A prerequisite to the valid measurement of language behavior in children. In G. R. Lyon (Ed.), *Frames of reference for the assessment of learning disabilities* (pp. 229–242). Baltimore: Paul H. Brookes.

Moats, L. C. (1998). Teaching decoding. *American Educator, 22*(1 & 2), 42–51.

Monroe, M. (1932). *Children who cannot read: The analysis of reading disabilities and the use of diagnostic tests in instruction of retarded readers.* Chicago: University of Chicago Press.

Montessori, M. (1912). *The Montessori method* (A. E. George, Trans.). New York: Frederick Stokes.

Montessori, M. (1964). *The Montessori method.* New York: Bently.

Montgomery, W. (2001). Creative culturally responsive, inclusive classrooms. *Teaching Exceptional Children, 33*(4), 40–47.

Moore, R., Cartledge, G., & Heckaman, K. (1995). The effects of social skill instruction and self-monitoring on game-related behaviors of adolescents with emotional or behavioral disorders. *Behavioral Disorders, 20*(4), 253–266.

Morris, B. (2003). The dyslexic CEO. *Fortune* (May 20, 2002).

Morsink, C. V., Soar, R. S., & Thomas, R. (1986). Research on teaching: Opening the door to special education classrooms. *Exceptional Children, 53*, 32–40.

Murawski, W., & Dieker, L. (2004). Tips and strategies for coteaching at the secondary level. *Teaching Exceptional Children, 36*(5), 52–58.

Murawski, W., & Swanson, H. (2002). A meta-analysis of coteaching research: Where are the data? *Remedial and Special Education, 22*, 258–267.

Myklebust, H., & Boshes, B. (1969). *Minimal brain damage in children* (final report, U.S. Public Health Service Contract 108–65–142). Evanston, IL: Northwestern University Publications.

Myles, B. S., Cook, K. T., Miller, N. E., Rinner, L., & Robbins, L. A. (2000). *Asperger's syndrome and sensory issues: Practical solutions for making sense of the world.* Shawnee Mission, KS: American Academy of Professional Coders.

Myles, B. S., & Simpson, R. I. (2001a). *Asperger's syndrome: A guide for educators and parents* (2nd ed.). Austin, TX: Pro-Ed.

Myles, B. S., & Simpson, R. I. (2001b). Effective practices for students with Asperger's syndrome. *Focus on Exceptional Children, 34* (3), 1–14.

Nall, A. (1971). Prescriptive living. In J. Arena (Ed.), *The child with learning disabilities: His right to learn* (pp. 69–77). San Rafael, CA: Academic Therapy Publications.

National Council of Teachers of Mathematics. (NCTM) (2000). *Principles and standards for school mathematics.* Reston, VA: Author.

National Council on Disability Social Security Administration. (2000). *Transition and postschool outcomes for youth with disabilities: Closing the gaps to postsecondary education and employment.* Washington, DC: U.S. Government Printing Office.

National Endowment for the Arts. (2004). *Reading at risk: A survey of literacy reading in America.* Washington, DC: Author.

National Information Center for Children and Youth (NICHCY). (1999). P.O. Box 492. Washington, DC: Author.

National Institute for Child Health and Human Development. (1999). *Keys to successful learning* (pp. 1–3). Washington, DC: National Institute for Child Health and Human Development.

National Institutes of Health. (1998). *Diagnosis and treatment of attention deficit hyperactivity disorder.* NIH Consensus Statement.

National Joint Committee on Learning Disabilities. (1994). *Collective perspectives on issues affecting learning disabilities.* Austin, TX: Pro-Ed.

National Joint Committee on Learning Disabilities. (1997). Operationalizing the NJCLD definition of learning disabilities for ongoing assessment in schools. *Perspectives: The International Dyslexia Association, 23*(4), 29–33.

National Reading Panel. (2000). *Teaching children to read: An evidence-based assessment of the scientific research literature on reading and implications for reading instruction.* Washington, DC: National Institute of Child Health and Human Development. Available: www.nichd.nih.gov/publications/nrp/smallbook.htm

National Research Council. (1998). *Preventing reading difficulties in young children.* Washington, DC: National Academy of Sciences.

No Child Left Behind Act of 2001, Public Law 110, 107th Cong. 2nd sess. (January 8, 2002).

Noll, M., Kamps, D., & Seaborn, C. (1993). Prereferral intervention for students with emotional or emotional risks: Use of a behavioral consultant model. *Journal of Emotional and Behavioral Disorders, 1*, 203–214.

Nowicki, E. A. (2003). A meta-analysis of the social competence of children with learning disabilities compared to classmates of low and average to high achievement. *Learning Disability Quarterly, 26*, 171–188.

Oakland, T., Black, J., Stanford, G., Nussbaum, N., & Balise, R. (1998). An evaluation of the dyslexia training program: A multisensory method for promoting reading in students with reading disabilities. *Journal of Learning Disabilities, 31*, 14–147.

Oas, B. K., Schumaker, J. B., & Deshler, D. D. (1995). Learning strategies: Tools for learning to learn in middle and high schools. In *Secondary education and beyond: Providing opportunities for students with learning disabilities* (pp. 90–100). Pittsburgh: Learning Disabilities Association of America.

Obrzut, J., & Boliek, C. (1991). Neuropsychological assessment of childhood learning disabilities. In H. Swanson (Ed.), *Handbook on the assessment of learning disabilities* (pp. 121–145). Austin, TX: Pro-Ed.

O'Conner, P., Sofo, F., Kendall, L., & Olsen, G. (1990). Reading disabilities and the effects of colored filters. *Journal of Learning Disabilities, 23*, 597–603.

O'Connor, R., Notari-Syverson, A., & Vadasy, P. (1998). *Ladders to literacy*. Baltimore: Paul H. Brookes.

Ogle, D. (1986). K-W-L: A teaching model that develops active reading of expository text. *The Reading Teacher, 39*, 564–570.

Olson, R. K., Gillis, J. J., Rack, J. P., DeFries, J. C., & Fulker, D. W. (1991). Confirmatory factor analysis of word recognition and process measures in the Colorado reading project. *Reading Writing, 3*, 235–248.

Opp, G. (2001). Learning disabilities in Germany: A retrospective analysis, current status, and future trends. In D. Hallahan & B. Keogh (Eds.), *Research and global perspectives in learning disabilities: Essays in honor of William M. Cruickshank* (pp. 217–238). Mahwah, NJ: Erlbaum.

Orkwis, R. (2003). *Universally designed instruction*. (Report No. EC309565). Arlington, VA: ERIC Clearinghouse on Disabilities and Gifted Education. (ERIC Document Reproduction Service No. E641).

Ortiz, A. (1997). Learning disabilities occurring concomitantly with linguistic differences. *Journal of Learning Disabilities, 30*(3), 321–232.

Orton, J. (1976). *A guide to teaching phonics*. Cambridge, MA: Educators Publishing Service.

Orton, S. (1937). *Reading, writing and speech problems in children*. New York: Norton.

Osman, B. (1987). Promoting social acceptance of children with learning disabilities. *Reading, Writing, and Learning Disabilities, 3*, 111–118.

Owens, R. E. (1995). *Language disorders: A functional approach to assessment and intervention*. New York: Merrill/Macmillan.

Palinscar, A., & Brown, A. (1984). Reciprocal teaching of comprehension-fostering and comprehension-monitoring activities. *Cognition and Instruction, 1*, 117–175.

Palinscar, A., Brown, A., & Campione, J. (1991). Dynamic assessment. In H. L. Swanson (Ed.), *Handbook on the assessment of learning disabilities* (pp. 75–94). Austin, TX: Pro-Ed.

Patten, B. (1973). Visually mediated thinking: A report of the case of Albert Einstein. *Journal of Learning Disabilities, 6*, 415–420.

Payne, K., & Taylor, O. (2002). Multicultural influences on human communication. In G. H. Shames & N. B. Anderson (Eds.), *Human communication disorders: An introduction* (pp. 106–140). Boston: Allyn & Bacon.

Pearl, R., & Bay, M. (1999). Psychosocial correlates of learning disabilities. In V. L. Scwaen & D. H. Saklofske (Eds.), *Handbook of psychosocial characteristics of exceptional children* (pp. 443–470). New York: Kluwer Academic/Plenum.

Pennington, B. (1995). Genetics of learning disabilities. *Journal of Child Neurology, 10*(Suppl. 1), S69–S77.

Pennington, B., Smith, S., Kimberling, W., Green, P., & Haith, M. (1987). Left-handedness and immune disorders in familial dyslexics. *Archives of Neurology, 44*, 634–639.

Piaget, J. (1952). *The origins of intelligence in children* (M. Cook, Trans.). New York: International University Press. (Original work published in 1936)

Piaget, J. (1970). *The science of education and psychology of the child*. New York: Grossman.

Pinker, S. (1995). *The language instinct*. New York: Harper Perennial.

Pinnell, G. S., Lyons, C. A., DeFord, D. E., Bryk, A. S., & Seltzer, M. (1994). Comparing instructional models for the literacy education of high-risk first graders. *Reading Research Quarterly, 29*(1), 8–39.

Polloway, E., Patton, J., & Serna, L. (2001). *Strategies for teaching learners with special needs*. Columbus, OH: Merrill/Prentice-Hall.

Powers, C. A. (2000). The pharmacology of drugs used for the treatment of attention deficit hyperactivity disorder. In P. Accardo, T. Blondis, B. Whitman, & M. Stein (Eds.), *Attention deficits and hyperactivity in children and adults: Diagnosis, treatment, management* (pp. 477–512). New York: Marcel Dekker.

Price, L. (1997). Psychosocial issues of workplace adjustment. In P. Gerber & D. Brown (Eds.), *Learning disabilities and employment* (pp. 275–306). Austin, TX: Pro-Ed.

Public Law 106–364 (2004). The Assistive Technology Act.

Raffi. (1986). *A children's sampler of singable songs* [cassette]. Willowdale, Ontario: Shoreline Records, a division of Troubadour Records, Ltd.

Rapkin, I. (1995). Physician's testing of children with developmental disabilities. *Journal of Child Neurology, 10*(Suppl. 1), S11–S15.

Rapp, D. J. (1986). *The impossible child in school and at home.* Buffalo, NY: Life Sciences Press.

Rappley, M. (2004). Attention deficit–hyperactivity disorder. *The New England Journal of Medicine, 352,* 165–173.

Raskind, M. (1998a). Assistive technology for individuals with learning disabilities: How far have we come? *Perspectives: The International Dyslexia Association, 24*(2), 20–26.

Raskind, M., & Higgins, E. (1998a). Assistive technology for postsecondary students with learning disabilities: An overview. *Journal of Learning Disabilities, 30*(1), 27–40.

Raskind, M., & Higgins, E. (1998b). Technology and learning disabilities: What do we know and where should we go? *Perspectives: The International Dyslexia Association, 24*(2), 1.

Raskind, M., Higgins, E., Slaff, M., & Shaw, T. (1998c). Assistive technology in the homes of children with learning disabilities: An exploratory study. *Learning Disabilities: A Multidisciplinary Journal, 9*(2), 33–56.

Raskind, M. (1998b). Literacy for adults with learning disabilities through assistive technology. In S. Vogel & S. Reder (Eds.), *Learning disabilities, literacy, and adult education* (pp. 253–274). Baltimore: Paul H. Brookes.

Rea, P., McLaughlin, V., & Walter-Thomas, C. (2002). Outcomes for students with learning disabilities in inclusion and pull-out programs. *Exceptional Children, 68,* 203–222.

Reichman, J., & Healey, W. (1983). Learning disabilities in conductive hearing loss involving otitis media. In G. Senf & J. Torgesen (Eds.), *Annual review of learning disabilities: Vol. 1. A Journal of Learning Disabilities reader* (pp. 39–45). Chicago: Professional Press.

Resnick, L. (1987). Constructing knowledge in school. In L. A. Liben (Ed.), *Development and learning: Conflict or congruence?* (pp. 19–50). Hillsdale, NJ: Erlbaum.

Resnick, L., & Klopfer, L. (1989). Toward the thinking curriculum: An overview. In L. Resnick & L. Klopfer (Eds.), *Toward the thinking curriculum: Current cognitive research* (pp. 1–18). Alexandria, VA: Association for Supervision and Curriculum Development.

Richardson, S. (2003). Are we enablers or disablers? Perspectives. *International Dyslexia Association, 29*(3), 13–14.

Richek, M., Caldwell, J., Jennings, J., & Lerner, J. (1996). *Reading problems: Assessment and teaching strategies.* Needham Heights, MA: Allyn & Bacon.

Richek, M., List, L., & Lerner, J. (1989). *Reading problems: Assessment and teaching strategies.* Englewood Cliffs, NJ: Prentice-Hall.

Richmond, J. (1990). Low-birth weight infants. *JAMA (Journal of the American Medical Association), 263*(22), 3069–3070.

Rieth, H., & Polsgrove, L. (1994). Curriculum and instructional issues in teaching secondary students with learning disabilities. *Learning Disabilities Research and Practice, 9*(2), 118–126.

Roberts, R., & Mather, N. (1995). The return of students with learning disabilities to regular classrooms: A sell-out? *Learning Disabilities Research and Practice, 10*(1), 46–58.

Robinson, G., & Conway, R. (1990). The effects of Irlen colored lenses on students' specific reading skills and their perception of ability: A 12-month validity study. *Journal of Learning Disabilities, 23,* 588–596.

Rock, E., Fessler, M., & Church, R. (1997). The concomitance of learning disabilities and emotional/behavioral disorders: A conceptual model. *Journal of Learning Disabilities, 30*(3), 245–263.

Rockefeller, N. (1976, October 16). *TV Guide,* pp. 12–14.

Rodis, P., Garrod, A., & Boscardin, M. (2001). *Learning disabilities: Life Stories.* Boston: Allyn & Bacon.

Roman, M. A. (1998). The syndrome of nonverbal learning disabilities: Clinical description and applied aspects. *Current Issues in Education, 1* (1), 1–21.

Rose, E. (1993). Faculty development: Changing attitudes and enhancing knowledge about learning disabilities. In S. Vogel & P. Adelman (Eds.), *Success for students with learning disabilities* (pp. 131–150). New York: Springer-Verlag.

Rosenshine, B. (1986). Synthesis of research on explicit teaching. *Educational Leadership, 43,* 60–69.

Rosenshine, B. (1997). Advances in research on instruction. In J. Lloyd, E. Kame'enui, & D. Chard (Eds.), *Issues in educating students with disabilities* (pp. 197–220). Mahwah, NJ: Erlbaum.

Rosenshine, B., & Stevens, R. (1986). Teaching functions. In M. Wittock (Ed.), *Handbook of research on teaching* (3rd ed., pp. 376–391). New York: Macmillan.

Rosenthal, D. (2003). Atomoxetine (Strattera) in the treatment of ADHD. *The ADHD Challenge, XVII* (2), 1–3.

Rosenthal, R., & Jacobson, L. (1968). *Pygmalion in the classroom.* New York: Holt, Rinehart and Winston.

Rosner, J. (1979). *Helping children overcome learning difficulties.* New York: Walker & Company.

Roswell, R., & Natchez, G. (1977). *Reading disability: Diagnosis and treatment.* New York: Basic Books.

Rothstein, L. (1998). Americans with Disabilities Act, Section 504, and adults with learning disabilities in adult education and transition to employment. In S. Vogel & S. Reder (Eds.), *Learning disabilities, literacy, and adult education* (pp. 29–43). Baltimore: Paul H. Brookes.

Rourke, B. P. (1989). *Nonverbal learning disabilities: The syndrome and the model.* New York: Guilford Press.

Rourke, B. P. (1995). *Syndrome of nonverbal learning disabilities: Neurodevelopmental manifestations.* New York: Guilford Press.

Runion, H. (1980). Hypoglycemia: Fact or fiction? In W. Cruickshank (Ed.), *Approaches to learning: Vol. 1. The best of ACLD* (pp. 111–122). Syracuse, NY: Syracuse University Press.

Rusch, F., & Phelps, L. (1987). Secondary special education and transition from school to work: A national priority. *Exceptional Children, 53,* 487–492.

Sabbatino, E. (2004). Students with learning disabilities construct meaning through graphic organizers: Strategies for achievement in inclusive classrooms. *Learning Disabilities: A Multidisciplinary Journal, 13*(2), 69–74.

Salend, S. (1998). Using portfolios to assess student performance. *Teaching Exceptional Children, 31*(2), 36–43.

Salvia, J., & Ysseldyke, J. (1998, 2001). *Assessment.* Boston: Houghton Mifflin.

Salvia, J., & Ysseldyke, J. (2004). *Assessment in special and inclusive education.* Boston: Houghton Mifflin.

Scanlon, D. (1996). Social skills strategy instruction. In D. Deshler, E. Ellis, & B. Lenz (Eds.), *Teaching adolescents with learning disabilities: Strategies and methods.* Denver: Love Publishing.

Scanlon, D., Deshler, D., & Schumaker, J. (1996). Can a strategy be taught and learned in secondary inclusive classrooms? *Learning Disabilities Research and Practice, 11*(1), 41–57.

Schmid, R., & Evans, W. (1998). *Curriculum and instruction for students with emotional/behavioral disorders.* Reston, VA: Council for Children with Behavioral Disorders.

Schumaker, J., Deshler, D., & Ellis, E. (1986). Intervention issues related to the education of LD adolescents. In J. Torgesen & B. Wong (Eds.), *Psychological and educational perspectives on learning disabilities* (pp. 329–366). New York: Academic Press.

Schunk, D. H. (2004). *Learning theories: An educational perspective* (4th ed.). Upper Saddle River, NJ: Pearson.

Schweinhart, L. J., Barnes, H. V., & Weikart, D. B. (1993). *Significant benefits: The High/Scope Perry Preschool study through age 27.* Monographs of the High/Scope Educational Research Foundation, No. 10. Ypsilanti, MI: High Scope Press.

Scientific Learning. (1995). *FastForWord.* Berkeley, CA: Author.

Scott, T. (2003). Making behavior intervention planning decisions in a schoolwide system of positive behavior support. *Focus on Exceptional Children, 36*(1), 1–18.

Scotti, J., & Meyer, L. (1999). *Behavioral intervention: Principles, models and practices.* Baltimore: Paul H. Brookes.

Scruggs, T., & Mastropieri, M. (1991). *Teaching students ways to remember: Strategies for learning mnemonically.* Cambridge, MA: Brookline Books.

Semb, G., & Ellis, J. (1994). Knowledge taught in school: What is remembered? *Review of Educational Research, 64*(2), 253–286.

Sequin, E. (1970). *Idiocy and its treatment by the physiological method.* New York: Columbia University Press. (Original work published 1866)

Shalev, R., Manor, O., Auerbach, J., & Grodd-Tour, V. (1998). Persistence of developmental dyscalculia: What counts. *The Journal of Pediatrics, 133*(3), 358–362.

Shannon, T., & Barr, R. (1995). Reading recovery: An independent evaluation of the effects of an early instruction intervention for at-risk learners. *Reading Research Quarterly, 30*(4), 958–996.

Shaywitz, B., Fletcher, J., & Shaywitz, S. (1995). Defining and classifying learning disabilities and attention deficit hyperactivity disorder. *Journal of Child Neurology, 10*(Suppl. 1), S50–S57.

Shaywitz, B., Shaywitz, S., Blachman, B., Pugh, K., Fulbright, R., Skudlarki, P., et al. (2004). Development of left occipitotemporal systems for skilled reading in children after a phonologically-based intervention. *Journal of Biological Psychiatry, 55*(9), 926–933.

Shaywitz, B., & Shaywitz, S. (1998b). Functional disruption in the organization of the brain for reading in dyslexia. *Proceedings of the National Academy of Sciences, 95*(5).

Shaywitz, B., & Shaywitz, S. (1999, May). *Brain research and reading: Lecture at Schwab Learning.* San Mateo, CA. Available: www.schwablearning.com

Shaywitz, S., & Shaywitz, B. (1988). Attention-deficit disorder: Current perspectives. In J. Kavanagh & J. Truss (Eds.), *Learning disabilities: Proceedings of the National Conference* (pp. 369–567). Parkton, MD: York Press.

Shaywitz, S. (2003). *Overcoming dyslexia: A new and complete science-based program for reading problems at any level.* New York: Alfred A. Knopf.

Shaywitz, S., Shaywitz, B., & Fletcher, J. (1990). Prevalence of reading disability in boys and girls: Results of the Connecticut longitudinal study. *Journal of the American Medical Association, 264,* 998–1002.

Shinn, M. R., & Hubbard, D. (1992). Curriculum-based measurement and problem-solving assessment: Basic procedures and outcomes. *Focus on Exceptional Children, 24*(5), 1–20.

Shipman, S., & Shipman, V. (1985). Cognitive styles: Some conceptual, methodological, and applied issues. In E. W. Gordon (Ed.), *Review of research in education:* Vol. 12. (pp. 229–291). Washington, DC: American Educational Research Association.

Sigel, I. E., & Brodzinsky, D. M. (1977). Individual differences: A perspective for understanding intellectual development. In H. Hom & P. Robinson (Eds.), *Psychological processes in early education* (pp. 295–329). New York: Academic Press.

Silver, A., & Hagin, R. (1966). Maturation of perceptual functions in children with specific reading disabilities. *The Reading Teacher, 19,* 253–259.

Silver, A., & Hagin, R. (1990). *Disorders of learning in childhood.* New York: Wiley.

Silver, L. B. (1987). The "magic cure": A review of the current controversial approaches to treatment of learning disabilities. *Journal of Learning Disabilities, 20,* 498–504.

Silver, L. (1998). *The misunderstood child: Understanding and coping with your child's learning disabilities.* New York: Times Books.

Silver, L. (2001). It's more than semantics: Learning differences does not equal learning disabilities. *LDA Newsbriefs, 36*(1), 2, 4.

Silver, L. (2003). Interview with Dr. Larry Silver: *Toward a common goal, 17*(1). Glen Ellyn, IL: Illinois Branch of the International Dyslexia Association.

Silver, L. (2004). *Attention deficit/Hyperactivity disorder: A clinical guide to diagnosis and treatment for health and mental health professionals.* Washington, DC: American Psychiatric Association.

Simmons, D. C., & Kame'enui, E. J. (1996). A focus on curriculum design: When children fail. *Focus on Exceptional Children, 28*(7), 1–16.

Sitlington, P. H. (1996). Transition to learning: The neglected component of transition programming for individuals with learning disabilities. *Journal of Learning Disabilities, 29*(1), 31–39.

Skinner, B. F. (1957). *Verbal behavior.* New York: Appleton-Century-Crofts.

Slavin, R. (2000). *Educational psychology: Theory and practice.* Boston: Allyn & Bacon.

Slingerland, B. (1976). *A multisensory program for language arts for specific language disability children: A guide for primary teachers.* Cambridge, MA: Educators Publishing Service.

Smith, C. (1991). *Learning disabilities: The interaction of learner, task, and setting.* Boston: Little, Brown.

Smith, C. (2000). Behavioral and discipline provisions of IDEA '97: Implicit competencies yet to be confirmed. *Exceptional Children, 66,* 403–412.

Smith, S. (2005). *Live it, learn it. The Academic Club methodology for students with learning disabilities and ADHD.* Baltimore: Paul H. Brookes.

Smith, S. L. (1991). *Succeeding against the odds: Strategies and insights from the learning disabled.* Los Angeles: Jeremy P. Tarcher.

Smith, S. L. (2001). *The power of the arts: Creative strategies for teaching exceptional learners.* Baltimore: Paul H. Brookes.

Smith, S. L., & Irvine, S. E. (1999). Technology the Lab School way: A multisensory empowering experience for students with severe learning disabilities and ADHD. *Learning Disabilities: A Multidisciplinary Journal, 9*(3), 99–107.

Smith, T., Polloway, E., Patton, R., & Dowdy, C. (2002). *Teaching children with special needs in inclusive settings.* Boston: Allyn & Bacon.

Snider, V. (1992). Learning styles and learning to read: A critique. *Remedial and Special Education, 13*(1), 6–18.

Snow, C., Burns, M., & Griffin, P. (Eds.). (1998b). *Report of the committee on the prevention of reading difficulties in young children.* Washington, DC: National Research Council, National Academy of Sciences.

Snowman, J., & Biehler, R. (2000). *Psychology applied to teaching.* Boston: Houghton Mifflin.

Sonday, A. (2000). *The Orton-Gillingham approach to teaching reading, writing, and spelling: Workshop manual.* Mendota Heights, MN: Author.

Sorensen, L. G., Forbes, P. W., Bernstein, J. H., Weiler, M. D., Mitchell, W. M., & Waber, D. P. (2003). Psychosocial adjustment over a two-year period in children referred for learning problems: Risk resilience, and adaptation. *Learning Disabilities Research & Practice, 18*(1), 10–24.

Spinelli, C. (2003). *Classroom assessment for students with special needs in inclusive settings.* Upper Saddle River, NJ: Merrill/Prentice-Hall.

Sridhar, D., & Vaughn, S. (2001). Social functioning of students with learning disabilities. In D. Hallahan & B. Keogh (Eds.), *Research and global perspectives in learning disabilities: Essays in honor of William M. Cruickshank* (pp. 65–92). Mahwah, NJ: Erlbaum.

Sridhar, D. & Vaughn, S. (2002). Bibliotherapy: Practices for improving self-concept and reading comprehension. In B. Wong & M. Donahue (Eds.), *The social dimensions of learning disabilities*. Mahwah, NJ: Lawrence Erlbaum.

Stahl, S. (2004). Scaly? Audacious? Debris? Salubrious?: Vocabulary learning and the child with learning disabilities. *Perspectives: International Dyslexia Association, 30*(1), 5–12.

Stahl, S. A., & Murray, B. A. (1994). Defining phonological awareness and its relationship to early reading. *Journal of Educational Psychology, 86,* 221–234.

Stainback, W., & Stainback, S. (Eds.). (1992). *Controversial issues confronting special education: Divergent perspectives.* Needham Heights, MA: Allyn & Bacon.

Stainback, W., & Stainback, S. (Eds.). (1996). *Inclusion: A guide for educators.* Baltimore: Paul H. Brookes.

Stanovich, K. (1993). The construct validity of discrepancy definitions of reading disabilities. In G. R. Lyon, D. Gray, J. Kavanagh, & N. Krasnegor (Eds.), *Better understanding learning disabilities* (pp. 273–307). Baltimore: Paul H. Brookes.

Stanovich, K. E. (1986). Matthew effects in reading: Some consequences of individual differences in the acquisition of literacy. *Reading Research Quarterly, 21,* 360–406.

Stauffer, R. G. (1975). *Directing the reading-thinking process.* New York: Harper & Row.

Stephens, R. (1987, September 27). *Write/read/write some more.* Paper presented at the Fourth Annual Conference on Adult Reading Problems, Chicago State University.

Sternberg, R. J. (1985). *Beyond IQ: A triarchial theory of human intelligence.* New York: Cambridge University Press.

Stevens, G., & Birch, J. (1957). A proposed clarification of the terminology to describe brain-injured children. *Exceptional Children, 23,* 346–349.

Stevens, L., & Werkhoven, W. (2001). Learning disabilities in the Netherlands. In D. Hallahan & B. Keogh (Eds.), *Research and global perspectives in learning disabilities: Essays in honor of William M. Cruickshank* (pp. 273–291). Mahwah, NJ: Erlbaum.

Stewart, A., & Lillie, P. (1995). Transition plan. In *Secondary education and beyond: Providing opportunities for students with learning disabilities* (pp. 58–81). Pittsburgh: Learning Disabilities Association of America.

Stipek, D. (1993). *Motivation to learn: From theory to practice.* Boston: Allyn & Bacon.

Stone, C. A. (1998a). The metaphor of scaffolding: Its utility for the field of learning disabilities. *Journal of Learning Disabilities, 13*(4), 344–364.

Strauss, A., & Lehtinen, L. (1947). *Psychopathology and education of the brain-injured child.* New York: Grune & Stratton.

Sugai, G., & Homer, R. (1999). Discipline and behavioral support: Preferred processes and practices. *Effective School Practice, 17,* 10–22.

Swanson, H. (1996). Informational processing: An introduction. In D. Reid, W. Hresko, & H. Swanson (Eds.), *Cognitive approaches to learning disabilities* (pp. 251–286). Austin, TX: Pro-Ed.

Swanson, H. (1999b). Instructional components that predict treatment outcomes for students with learning disabilities: Support for a combined strategy and direct instruction model. *Learning Disabilities Research & Practice, 14*(3), 129–140.

Swanson, H., & Hoskyn, M. (2001). Instructing adolescents with learning disabilities: A component and composite analysis. *Learning Disabilities Research & Practice, 16*(2), 109–119.

Swanson, H. L. (1993). Learning disabilities from the perspective of cognitive psychology. In G. R. Lyon, D. Gray, J. Kavanagh, & N. Krasnegor (Eds.), *Better understanding learning disabilities* (pp. 199–228). Baltimore: Paul H. Brookes.

Swanson, H. L. (1999a). *Intervention for students with learning disabilities: A meta-analysis of treatment outcomes.* New York: Guilford Press.

Tallal, P. (2000). The science of literacy: From the laboratory to the classroom. *Proceedings of the National Academic of Sciences. USA, 1997,* 2402–2404.

Tallal, P., Allard, L., Miller, S., & Curtiss, S. (1997). Academic outcomes of language impaired children. In C. Hulme & M. Snowling (Eds.), *Dyslexia: Biology, cognition, and intervention* (pp. 167–179). London: Whurr, British Dyslexia Association.

Tallal, P., Miller, S. L., & Merzenich, M. M. (1996). Language comprehension in language-learning impaired children improved with acoustically modified speech. *Science, 271*(5245), 81–83.

Tallal, P., Miller, S., Jenkins, W., & Merzenich, M. (1997). The role of temporal processing in developmental language-based learning disorders: Research and clinical implications. In B. Blachman (Ed.), *Foundations of reading acquisition and dyslexia* (pp. 49–66). Mahwah, NJ: Erlbaum.

Taylor, L., Alber, S. & Walker, D. (2002). The Comparative Effects of a Modified Self-questioning Strategy and Story Mapping on the Comprehension of Elementary Students with Learning Disabilities. *Journal of Behavioral Education, 11*(2), 69–87.

Taylor, O. L., & Leonard, L. (Eds.). (1999). *Language acquisition across North America: Cross-cultural and cross-linguistic perspectives.* San Diego: Singular Publishing.

Technology-Related Assistance for Individuals with Disabilities Act of 1994, Public Law 218, 103rd Cong., 2nd sess. (March 9, 1994).

Teeter, P. A., & Semrud-Clikeman, M. (1997). *Child neurology: Assessment and interventions for neuropsychological and neurodevelopmental disorders of childhood*. Needham Heights, MA: Allyn & Bacon.

Thomas, A., & Chess, S. (1977). *Temperament and development*. New York: Bruner/Mazel.

Thompson, L. (1971). Language disabilities in men of eminence. *Journal of Learning Disabilities, 4,* 34–45.

Thompson, S. (1997). *The source for nonverbal learning disabilities*. East Moline, IL: LinguiSystems.

Thorndike, E. (1917). Reading as reasoning: A study in paragraph reading. *Journal of Educational Psychology, 8,* 323–332.

Thurlow, M. (2000). Standards-based reform and students with disabilities: Reflections on a decade of change. *Focus on Exceptional Children, 33*(3), 1–16.

Tiedemann, J. (1989). Measures of cognitive styles: A critical review. *Educational Psychologist, 21,* 261–275.

Time. (1996, January 29). pp. 62–64.

Tindal, G., & Nolet, V. (1995). Curriculum-based measurement in middle and high schools: Critical thinking skills in content areas. *Focus on Exceptional Children, 17*(7), 1–22.

Torgesen, J. (1997). The prevention and remediation of reading difficulties: Evaluating what we know from research. *Journal of Academic Language Therapy, 1,* 11–47.

Torgesen, J. (1998). Catch them before they fall. *American Educator, 22*(1 & 2), 32–39.

Torgesen, J. (2001). *Empirical and theoretical support for direct diagnosis of learning disabilities by assessment in intrinsic processing weaknesses* [online]. Available: www.edexcellence.net/library/special_ed/index.html

Traub, N., & Bloom, F. (1978). *Recipe for reading*. Cambridge, MA: Educators Publishing Service.

Troia, G., Graham, S., & Harris, H. (1998). Teaching students with learning disabilities to mindfully plan when writing. *Exceptional Children, 65*(2), 235–252.

Tsatsanis, K., Fuerst, D., & Rourke, B. (1997). Psychosocial dimensions of learning disabilities: External validation and relationship with age and academic functioning. *Journal of Learning Disabilities, 30*(5), 490–502.

Tsuge, M. (2001). Learning disabilities in Japan. In D. Hallahan & B. Keogh (Eds.), *Research and global perspectives in learning disabilities: Essays in honor of William M. Cruickshank* (pp. 255–272). Mahwah, NJ: Erlbaum.

Tudge, J. R. H., & Scrimsher, S. (2003). Lev. S. Vygotsky on education: A cultural–historical, interpersonal, and individual approach to development. In B. J. Zimmerman & D. H. Schunk (Eds.), *Educational psychology: A century of contributions* (pp. 207–228). Mahwah, NJ: Erlbaum.

Tur-Kaspa, H., Weisel, A., & Segrev, L. (1998). Attributes for feelings of loneliness of students with learning disabilities. *Learning Disabilities Research and Practice, 13*(2), 89–94.

Turnbull, A., Turnbull, H., Shank, M., & Smith, S. (2004). *Exceptional lives: Special education in today's schools*. Englewood Cliffs, NJ: Prentice-Hall.

U.S. Department of Education. (1990). *To assure the free appropriate public education of all handicapped children* (Twelfth annual report to Congress on the implementation of the Handicapped Act). Washington, DC: U.S. Government Printing Office.

U.S. Department of Education. (1991). *To assure the free appropriate public education of all children with disabilities* (Thirteenth annual report to Congress on the implementation of the Individuals with Disabilities Act). Washington, DC: U.S. Government Printing Office.

U.S. Department of Education. (1997). *To assure the free appropriate public education of all children with disabilities* (Nineteenth annual report to Congress on the implementation of the Individuals with Disabilities Education Act). Washington, DC: U.S. Government Printing Office.

U.S. Department of Education. (2000). *To assure the free appropriate public education of all children with disabilities* (Twenty-second annual report to Congress on the implementation of the Individuals with Disabilities Education Act). Washington, DC: U.S. Government Printing Office.

U.S. Department of Education. (2002). *To assure the free appropriate public education of all children with disabilities* (Twenty-fourth annual report to Congress on the implementation of the Individuals with Disabilities Education Act). Washington, DC: U.S. Government Printing Office.

U.S. Office of Education. (1977). *Assistance to states for education of handicapped children: Procedures for evaluating specific learning disabilities*. (Federal Register, 42:65082–65085).

U.S. Department of Education. (1999). *Final regulation for the 1997 Individuals with Disabilities Education Act*. (Federal Register, March 12, 1999)

U.S. Department of Education. (2002). Applying positive behavioral support in schools. *To assure the free appropriate public education of all children with disabilities* (pp. III-7–III-31) (Twenty-fourth annual report to Congress on the implementation of the Individuals with Disabilities Education Act). Washington, DC: U.S. Government Printing Office.

Utley, C., Mortweet, S., & Greenwood, C. (1997). Peer-mediated instruction and interventions. *Focus on Exceptional Children, 29*(5), 1–23.

Vail, P. (1992). *Learning styles*. Rosemont, NJ: Modern Learning Press.

Van de Walle, J. A. (2004). *Elementary and middle school mathematics: Teaching developmentally.* Boston: Allyn & Bacon.

Vaughn, S., Elbaum, B., & Boardsman, A. (2001). The social functions of students with learning disabilities: Implications for inclusion. *Exceptionality, 9,* 47–65.

Vaughn, S., Gersten, R., & Chard, D. (2000). The underlying message in LD intervention research: Findings from research syntheses. *Exceptional Children, 67*(1), 99–114.

Vaughn, S., & Fuchs, L. (2003). Redefining learning disabilities as inadequate response to instruction: The promise and potential problems. *Learning Disabilities Research and Practice,* 18 (3), 137–146.

Vaughn, S., & Haager, D. (1994). The measurement of assessment of social skills. In G. R. Lyon (Ed.), *Frames of reference for the assessment of learning disabilities: New views of measurement issues* (pp. 555–570). Baltimore: Paul H. Brookes.

Vaughn, S., & Schumm, J. (1995). Responsible inclusion for students with learning disabilities. *Journal of Learning Disabilities, 28,* 264–270, 290.

Vaughn, S., & Wilson, C. (1994). Mathematics assessment for students with learning disabilities. In G. R. Lyon (Ed.), *Frames of reference for the assessment of learning disabilities* (pp. 459–472). Baltimore: Paul H. Brookes.

Vellutino, F. R., Scanlon, D. M., & Lyon, G. R. (2000). Differentiating between difficult-to-remediate and readily remediated poor readers: More evidence against the IQ–achievement discrepancy definition of reading disability. *Journal of Learning Disabilities, 33*(3), 223–238.

Villa, R., Thousand, J., Meyers, H., & Nevin, A. (1996). Teacher and administrator perceptions of heterogenous education. *Focus on Exceptional Children, 63,* 29–45.

Voeller, K. K. (1994). Techniques for measuring social competence in children. In G. R. Lyon (Ed.), *Frames of reference for the assessment of learning disabilities: New views of measurement issues* (pp. 525–554). Baltimore: Paul H. Brookes.

Vogel, S. A. (1998). Adults with learning disabilities. In S. Vogel & S. Reder (Eds.), *Learning disabilities, literacy, and adult education* (pp. 5–8). Baltimore: Paul H. Brookes.

Vogel, S. A. (1990). Gender differences in intelligence, language, visual-motor abilities, and academic achievement in students with learning disabilities: A review of the literature. *Journal of Learning Disabilities, 23,* 44–52.

Vogel, S. (2001, February). *Fairness in high stakes assessment: Lessons learned from the Oregon Case.* Presentation at the Learning Disabilities Association Annual Conference, New York.

Vogel, S., & Adelman, P. (2000). Adults with learning disabilities, 8–15 years after college. *Learning Disabilities: A Multidisciplinary Journal, 10*(3), 153–164.

Vogel, S., & Reder, S. (1998). Educational attainments of adults with learning disabilities. In S. Vogel & S. Reder (Eds.), *Learning disabilities, literacy, and adult education* (pp. 43–68). Baltimore: Paul H. Brookes.

Vogel, S. A. (1997). *College students with learning disabilities: A handbook.* Pittsburgh, PA: Learning Disabilities Association of America.

Vogel, S. A., & Adelman, P. B. (1993). *Success for college students with learning disabilities.* New York: Springer-Verlag.

Vygotsky, L. (1962, 1934). *Thought and language.* Cambridge, MA: MIT Press.

Vygotsky, L. S. (1978). *Mind in society: The development of higher psychological processes.* Cambridge, MA: Harvard University Press.

Wagner, M., & Blackorby, J. (1996). Transition from high school to work or college: How special education students fare. *The Future of Children, 6*(1), 103–120.

Wagner, M., Blackorby, J., Cameto, R., Hebbeler, K., & Newman, L. (1993). *The secondary school programs of students with disabilities: A report from the National Longitudinal Transition Study of Special Education Students.* Menlo Park, CA: SRI International.

Wagner, M., Cameto, R., & Newman, L. (2003). *Youth with disabilities: A changing population. A report of findings from the National Longitudinal Transition Study (NTLS) and the National Longitudinal Transition Study-2 (NLTS2).* Menlo Park, CA: SRI International.

Waldron, N., & McLeskey, J. (1998). The effects of inclusion school programs on students with mild and severe learning disabilities. *Exceptional Children, 64,* 395–407.

Walker, M. (1999). The acquisition of African American English: Social-cognitive and cultural factors. In O. L. Taylor & L. Leonard (Eds.), *Language acquisition across North America: Cross cultural and cross linguistic perspectives* (pp. 41–60). San Diego: Singular Publishing Co.

Walther-Thomas, C., Korinek, L., & McLaughlin, V. (2000). *Collaboration for inclusive education: Developing successful programs.* Boston: Allyn & Bacon.

Wanderman, R. (2003). Tools and dyslexia. *Perspectives, International Dyslexia Association* 29 (4), 5–9.

Wanzek, J., Dickson, S., Bursuck, W., & White, J. (2000). Teaching phonological awareness to students at risk for reading failure: An analysis of four instructional programs. *Learning Disabilities Research & Practice, 15*(4), 226–239.

Warner-Rogers, J., Taylor, A., Taylor, E., & Sandberg, S. (2000). Inattentive behavior in childhood: Epidemiology and implications for development. *Journal of Learning Disabilities, 18*(4), 520–536.

Wasik, B. (1998). Using volunteers as reading tutors: Guidelines for successful practices. *Reading Teacher, 51*(7), 262–270.

Weaver, S. M. (2000). The efficacy of extended time for post-secondary students with learning disabilities. *Learning Disabilities: A Multidisciplinary Journal, 10*(2), 47–56.

Wedell, K. (2001). British orientations to specific learning difficulties). In D. Hallahan & B. Keogh (Eds.), *Research and global perspectives in learning disabilities: Essays in honor of William M. Cruickshank* (pp. 239–254). Mahwah, NJ: Erlbaum.

Wehmeyer, M. (2002). *Self-determination and the education of students with disabilities, ERIC Digest.* EC309272. Reston, VA: ERIC Clearinghouse on Disabilities and Gifted Education.

Wehmeyer, M., & Palmer, S. (2002). *The self-determined learning model of instruction for early elementary-age students: Final report* (ED474659). Lawrence, KS: Beach Center on Families and Disabilities.

Werner, H., & Strauss, A. (1940). Causal factors in low performance. *American Journal of Mental Deficiency, 45,* 213–218.

Wernicke, C. (1908). The symptom complex of aphasia. In A. Church (Ed.), *Diseases of the nervous system* (pp. 265–324). New York: Appleton.

West, T. (1997). Slow words, quick images—Dyslexia as an advantage in tomorrow's workplace. In P. Gerber & D. Brown (Eds.), *Learning disabilities and employment* (pp. 334–370). Austin, TX: Pro-Ed.

West, T. (2003). Secret of the super successful . . . they're dyslexic. *Thalmus, 21* (1), 48–52.

West, T. G. (1997). *In the mind's eye: Visual thinkers, dyslexia and other learning difficulties, computer imaging, and the ironies of creativity.* New York: Prometheus Books.

Wiig, E., & Semel, E. M. (1984). *Language assessment and intervention for the learning disabled.* Columbus, OH: Charles E. Merrill.

Williams, J. (1991). The meaning of a phonics base for reading instruction. In E. Ellis (Ed.), *All language and the creation of literacy* (pp. 9–19). Baltimore: Orton Dyslexia Society.

Williams, J. P. (1998). Improving comprehension of disabled readers. *Annals of Dyslexia, 48,* 213–238.

Williamson, G., & Anzalone, M. (1997, April/May). Sensory integration: A key component of the evaluation and treatment of young children with severe difficulty with relating and communication. *Zero to Three, 17,* 29–36.

Wilson, B. A. (1988). *Wilson reading system.* Millbury, MA: Wilson Language Training.

Wilson, K., & Swanson, H. L. (2001). Are mathematics disabilities due to a domain-general or a domain-specific working memory deficit? *Journal of Learning Disabilities, 34*(3), 237–248.

Wingert, P., & Kantrovitz, B. (1997, October 27). Why Andy couldn't read. *Newsweek,* 56–64.

Witkin, H. A., Moore, C. A., Goodenough, D. R., & Cox, P. W. (1977). Field-dependent and field-independent cognitive styles and their educational implications. *Review of Educational Research, 47,* 1–64.

Wittrock, M. (1988). A constructive review of research on learning strategies. In C. Weinstein, E. Goetz, & P. Alexander (Eds.), *Learning and study strategies: Issues in assessment, instruction and evaluation* (pp. 287–298). San Diego: Academic Press.

Witzel, B., Mercer, C., & Miller, M. (2003). Teaching algebra to students with learning difficulties: An investigation of an explicit instructional model. *Learning Disabilities Research & Practice, 18*(2), 121–131.

Wolery, M., Werts, M. G., & Holcombe, A. (1994). Current practices with young children who have disabilities: Placement, assessment, and instructional issues. *Focus on Exceptional Children, 26*(6), 1–12.

Wolery, M., & Bailey, D., Jr. (2003). Early childhood special education research. *Journal of Early Intervention, 25*(2), 88–99.

Wong, B. (1999). Metacognition in writing. In R. Gallimore, L. Bernheimer, D. McMillan, D. Speece, & S. Vaughn (Eds.), *Developmental perspectives on children with high-incidence disabilities* (pp. 183–198). Mahwah, NJ: Erlbaum.

Wong, B. & Donahue, M. (2002). *The social dimensions of learning disabilities: Essays in honor of Tanis Bryon.* Mahwah, NJ: Lawrence Erlbaum.

Wong, B., & Hutchinson, N. (2001). Learning disabilities in Canada. In D. Hallahan & B. Keogh (Eds.), *Research and global perspectives in learning disabilities: Essays in honor of William M. Cruickshank* (pp. 197–216). Mahwah, NJ: Erlbaum.

Wong, B., & Jones, W. (1982). Increasing metacomprehension in learning-disabled and normally achieving students through self-questioning training. *Learning Disability Quarterly, 5*(3), 228–240.

Wright, P., Wright, P., & Heath, S. (2004). *No child left behind.* Hartfield, VA: Harbor House Law Press, Inc.

Yasutake, D., & Lerner, J. (1996). Teachers' perceptions of inclusion. *Learning Disabilities: A Multidisciplinary Journal, 7*(2), 1–4.

Yell, M., Rozalski, M., & Drasgrow, E. (2001). Disciplining students with disabilities. *Focus on Exceptional Children, 33*(9), 1–20.

Ysseldyke, J. (2001). Reflections on a research career: Generalizations from 25 years of research on assessment and instructional decision making. *Exceptional Children, 67*(3), 295–308.

Ysseldyke, J., Thurlow, M., Bielinski, J., House, A., & Moody, M. (2001). The relationship between institutional and assessment accommodations in an inclusive state accountability system. *Journal of Learning Disabilities, 34*(3), 212–220.

Yuan, F., & Reisman, E. (2000). Transition to adulthood: Outcomes for graduates of a non-degree, post-secondary program for young adults with severe learning disabilities. *Learning Disabilities: A Multi-disciplinary Journal, 10*(3), 153–164.

Zametkin, A., Nordahl, T. E., Gross, M., King, A. C., Semple, W. E., Rumsey, J., Hamburger, S., & Cohen, R. M. (1990, November 15). Cerebral glucose metabolism in adults with hyperactivity of childhood onset. *New England Journal of Medicine, 323,* 1361–1366.

Zeffrino, T., & Eden, G. (2000). The neural basis of developmental dyslexia. *Annals of Dyslexia, 50,* 3–30.

Zigmond, N. (1990). Rethinking secondary school programs for students with learning disabilities. *Focus on Exceptional Children, 23,* 1–22.

Zigmond, N. (1997). Educating students with disabilities: The future of special education. In J. Lloyd, E. Kame'enui, & D. Chard (Eds.), *Issues in educating students with disabilities* (pp. 275–304, 377–391). Mahwah, NJ: Erlbaum.

Zigmond, N. (2003). Where should students with disabilities receive special education services? Is one place better than another? *Journal of Special Education, 37*(3), 193–199.

Zilla, K., & Lerner, J. (2001, July). *Replacing walls with "Windows": Developing a post-secondary setting.* Paper presented at the meeting of the International Association of Special Education, Warsaw, Poland.

Zilla, K., & Lerner, J. (2004). Using Computers with Post-secondary Students with Multiple Learning Disabilities. Presentation at the Learning Disabilities Association of America. Atlanta, GA.

Delquardi, J. C., 115
Deno, S., 70, 382
Deshler, D., 104, 115, 120, 169, 181,
    187, 267, 269, 271, 272, 273, 274,
    277, 283, 285, 286, 287, 289, 416,
    430, 431, 482, 487, 539
Dewey, J., 162, 163
Diamond, G., 169
Dieker, L., 131, 148, 275
Dimitrovsky, L., 215, 519
DiPasquale, G., 169
Dohrn, E., 269
Donahue, M., 336, 521, 524
Dowdy, C., 135
Drasgrow, E., 171
Dunn, L., 134
Durgunoglu, A., 345
Durrell, D., 457

Eden, G., 309, 376
Edison, T., 4
Egan, R., 17
Ehri, L., 451
Einstein, A., 4, 476
Elbaum, B., 34, 131, 525, 526, 541
Elkins, J., 6
Elkonin, D. B., 352
Ellis, E. S., 120, 181, 287, 289
Ellis, J., 179
Enfield, M., 417
Englemann, S., 420
Epstein, F., 19
Erickson, R., 46
Erikson, E. H., 267
Espin, C., 382
Evans, W., 533

Fabbro, F., 6
Farr, R., 11
Feingold, B., 206
Felton, R., 342
Fenichel, F., 248
Fennel, E. B., 313
Fernald, G., 95–96, 97–98, 418, 451,
    468
Fessler, M., 527
Feurerstein, R., 72
Fey, M., 332, 333, 343
Filipek, P., 309
Fisher, A., 235
Fisher, J., 115, 182, 413
Fitzgerald, J., 455
Fletcher, J., 8, 11, 12, 14, 17, 54, 55,
    196

Fletcher, T. V., 6
Flewelling, R., 169
Foley, T., 477, 488, 490
Foorman, B., 135, 325
Ford, A., 150, 152
Forgan, J., 253
Fortin, J., 346
Fox, A., 232
Foy, J., 325, 337
Francks, C., 231
Frankenberger, W., 10, 11
Freiberg, H. J., 529
Friend, M., 135, 143, 146, 274, 275
Fronzaglio, K., 10, 11
Fuchs, D., 8, 12, 55, 115, 283, 487
Fuchs, L., 8, 12, 55, 115, 283, 382, 487
Fuerst, D., 519

Galaburda, A., 309
Ganschow, L., 294
Gardner, H., 14, 15, 56, 76
Garnett, K., 296
Garrand, A., 308
Garrod, A., 274
Gately, F., 146, 275
Gately, S., 146, 275
Gerber, M., 345
Gerber, P., 298, 308, 374, 526, 530
German, D., 342
Gersten, R., 105, 117, 141, 172, 181,
    182, 185, 187, 346
Gilger, J., 376
Gillingham, A., 417
Ginsburg, H., 496
Glaser, C., 36
Goldey, E., 235
Goldstein, S., 107, 152, 270, 325, 331,
    529
Goodenough, D. R., 188
Goodman, J., 188
Gopnick, A., 227
Gorman, C., 310
Gorman, J., 529
Graham, S., 430, 433, 438, 439, 463
Graves, D. H., 434, 435, 437
Greeno, J., 176, 181
Greenwood, C. R., 115, 116
Griffin, P., 142
Grodd-Tour, V., 6
Groteluschen, A., 533
Guralnick, M. J., 221, 223

Haager, D., 96, 521
Haber, J., 197

Hagin, R., 164, 296, 461
Hakuta, K., 344
Hale, C., 533
Hall, S., 152
Hallahan, D., 135
Hallgren, B., 309
Hanner, S., 420
Harris, H., 430
Harris, K., 430, 431, 432, 433, 435,
    437, 438, 439, 463
Harrison, M., 413
Hart, L., 342
Harth, R., 292
Hasselbring, T., 36
Hatch, T., 76
Hauser, P., 310
Hayden, S., 34
Hazel, J., 526
Heath, S., 30
Heckelman, R., 406
Hennesy, N., 374
Henry, M., 417
Hernandez, H., 100, 101, 344
Higgins, E., 36, 251, 423, 445, 446,
    511
Hiscock, M., 306, 307
Höien, T., 6
Holloway, J., 34, 131
Homer, R., 59
Hook, P., 340, 382, 385
Hoppey, D., 131
Horne, M., 379
Hoskyn, M., 283
House, A., 483
Hsu, C., 6
Hubbard, D., 496
Hutchinson, N., 6
Huttenlocher, P., 227
Hynd, G., 306, 307, 313, 376

Itard, J., 231

Jackson, C., 477
Jackson, R., 39
Jansky, J., 164
Javorsky, J., 294
Jenkins, J., 382, 383
Jenkins, W., 332, 340
Jenner, B., 375
Jennings, J., 189
Jiménez, R., 344, 345, 346
Johns, B., 31, 34, 135
Johnson, D. D., 385
Johnson, D. J., 526

Johnson, G., 420
Johnson, L. B., 249
Johnson, M., 389, 397
Jones, E., 484
Jones, S., 382, 385

Kagan, J., 188
Kame'enui, E. J., 104, 339
Kantrowitz, B., 4, 297, 375
Kauffman, J., 133, 135, 277
Keefe, C., 170
Keillor, G., 67, 483
Keller, H., 327
Keogh, B., 188, 227, 228, 529
Kephart, N., 234
Kibby, M., 306, 307, 313, 376
Kinsbourne, M., 306, 307
Kirk, S. A., 6, 27, 237, 403, 405
Kirk, W., 403, 405
Kistner, J., 271, 534
Klein, M. D., 233
Klin, A., 214
Kline, F., 518
Kluwe, R., 185
Kohn, A., 171, 532
Koppitz, E., 164
Korinek, L., 143
Korkunov, V., 6
Kotulak, R., 310
Kozleski, M., 104
Krasnegor, N., 176, 181
Kratochvil, C., 205
Kravetz, M., 294, 296
Kress, K., 397
Kübler-Ross, E., 153
Kuder, S., 342
Kuhl, P., 227

Lahey, M., 333
Lang, J., 214
Langford, K., 406
Langford, W., 164
Langone, J., 133, 135
La Porta, S., 296
Larsen, L., 438
Latham, P. H., 298
Latham, P. S., 298
LaVerrier, L., 534
Lavoie, R., 152, 153, 518
Lazar, I., 250
Lee, C., 39
Lehr, E., 413
Lehtinen, L., 25, 238
Lenneberg, E., 331

Leno, J., 375
Lenz, B. K., 120, 181, 187, 267, 269,
    274, 277, 283, 285, 286, 287, 289,
    416, 430, 431, 441
Leonard, L., 34, 35
Lerner, J., 5, 6, 17, 152, 189, 197, 207,
    208, 223, 226, 229, 232, 241, 245,
    247, 249, 270, 299, 308, 331, 333,
    361, 372, 379, 447, 533
Lerner, S., 152, 197
Levine, M., 12–13, 56, 102, 109, 163,
    164, 270, 313, 315
Levy-Shiff, R., 215
Lewis, R., 423, 445, 511
Lewis, T., 171
Liberman, A., 241
Liberman, I., 241
Licht, B., 271
Lillie, P., 281
Linden, M., 46
Linder, T. W., 234
Lindquist, M., 486
List, L., 379
Lowenthal, B., 17, 152, 197, 207,
    226
Lowenthal, M., 207
Lundberg, I., 6, 325, 339, 344
Lynch, G., 307
Lyon, G. R., 11, 17, 164, 176, 181,
    240, 309, 337, 373, 378, 379

MacArthur, C., 443
Maheedy, L. F., 115
Mailloux, Z., 235
Mainzer, R., 104, 120, 187, 487
Mann, V., 325, 337
Manor, O., 6
Marcaruso, P., 340
Marcella, R. C., 487
Marcharnd-Marcella, N. E., 487
Marquet, M., 20
Martin, 520
Martin, B., 441
Martin, C., 291
Mason, L., 430
Mastropieri, M., 53, 178, 179, 180
Masutto, C., 6
Mather, N., 152, 325, 331
Mathur, S., 99
Mayer, R. E., 176
Mayers, S., 196
McGough, R., 312
McGowen, A., 413
McGrady, H., 308, 533

McIntyre, C., 417
McKee, P., 413
McKenna, M., 387
McLaughlin, V., 131, 143
McLeskey, J., 34, 131, 269, 274, 275,
    283
Meichenbaum, D., 188, 534
Meisels, S., 248
Meltzer, L., 103
Meltzoff, A., 227
Mercer, C., 10, 175, 477, 480, 482,
    484, 486
Merzenich, M., 332, 340
Messick, S., 188
Meyer, L., 170
Meyer, M., 342, 382, 383
Meyers, H., 134
Miller, M., 482
Miller, N. E., 213
Miller, S., 332, 340, 477, 480, 484, 486
Minskoff, E., 403, 405
Moats, L. C., 152, 326, 342, 378, 379
Mock, D., 8, 55
Monroe, M., 398
Montague, M., 103
Montessori, M., 231
Montgomery, W., 100, 101
Moody, M., 483
Moore, C. A., 188
Morgan, P., 8, 55
Morris, B., 14, 376
Mortweet, S., 116
Moule, A., 169
Müller, N., 6
Munson, S., 247
Murawski, W., 131, 148, 275
Murray, B. A., 240, 241
Murray, E., 235
Myklebust, H., 66
Myles, B. S., 213

Nall, A., 522
Natchez, G., 107
Neisworth, J., 247
Nevin, A., 134
Newman, L., 273
Nigayev, A., 6
Nowicki, E. A., 526

Oakland, T., 417
Oas, B. K., 287
Obrzut, J., 307
Ogle, D. M., 409
Olufs, D., 296

Aptitude, transition plan and, 280
Aptitude-achievement discrepancy formulas. *See* Discrepancy, between achievement and intellectual ability method
Arithmetic skills, informal inventory of, 494
Arts, learning disabilities and, 37
Asperger's syndrome (AS), 212–213, 214, 518, 523–524
Assessment, 33. *See also* Accommodations; Individualized education program (IEP); Standardized tests; Tests; specific subjects
  accommodations for, 82–83
  alternate, 33
  areas of, 247–248
  of auditory perception, 245
  case history used for, 62–64
  in clinical teaching, 94
  criterion-referenced tests and, 75
  curriculum-based measurement for, 69–70
  diagnostic teaching and, 72–73
  dynamic, 72
  of emotional behaviors, 535
  explanation of, 44–45
  functional behavioral, 59, 171
  IEP, 49–52
  informal, 71–75
  information sources for, 62–75
  laws influencing, 45–46
  observation used for, 64–65
  of oral language, 347–348
  phases of, 245–247
  portfolio, 72
  progress monitoring for, 70–71
  purposes of, 45
  rating scales for, 65–66
  of reading, 397–400
  referral and, 45
  of social behaviors, 535
  of spelling, 457–458
  standardized norm-referenced tests for, 67–69
  of tactile and kinesthetic perception, 245
  of visual perception, 245
  of writing, 447
  of young children, 244–248
Assistive technology, 36–37, 61
Assistive Technology Act (PL 108-364, 2004), 36
Atomoxetine, 205

At risk children, 221–223, 227–228
Attention, 177
  in ADD/ADHD, 208–209
  as developmental indicator, 230–231
  increasing, 113, 211
Attention deficit disorder (ADD), 196–215, 518. *See also* Attention deficit disorder/attention deficit hyperactivity disorders (ADD/ADHD)
Attention deficit disorder/attention deficit hyperactivity disorders (ADD/ADHD)
  assessment of, 199, 200
  characteristics of, 197–199
  classroom strategies for, 211
  neuro-developmental conditions related to, 211–215
  number of children identified with, 202
  rating scales for, 200, 201
  special services for, 201
  symptoms of, 198–199
  teaching methods for, 208–211
  treatments for, 202–207
Attention deficit hyperactivity disorder (ADHD), 196. *See also* Attention deficit disorder/attention deficit hyperactivity disorders (ADD/ADHD)
  rating scales for assessing, 66
Attention deficits, among adolescents, 270
Attribution, 533–534
Attribution theory, 270–271
Audience, for writing, 436–437, 463–465
Audiologist, 319
Audiometer, 81
Audiotape
  for blind and dyslexics, 278
  for spelling, 468–469
Auditory blending, 241
Auditory discrimination, 241, 259
  tests of, 349
Auditory memory, 241, 259–260
Auditory perception, 238–239, 240–241
  activities for developing, 258–260
  assessing, 245
  spelling and, 467
  tests of, 241
Auditory processing
  activities for, 258–260

as developmental indicator, 230
Auditory-screening tests, 81
Auditory sequencing, 241
Auditory skills, observation of, 65, 122
Autism, 28, 214–215
  Asperger's syndrome and, 212–213
Automatic detector region (brain), 311, 312
Automaticity, 186, 383

Babbling, 360
Background knowledge, 286, 438
  activating, 407–413
Backward thinking, 435
Bar graphs, 512
Basal readers, 94, 406–407
Basic academic skills instruction, 283
Behavior(s). *See also* Emotional behaviors; Functional behavior assessment; Positive behavioral support; Rating scales; Social behavior
  in ABC analysis, 59, 60
  effective inclusion and classroom, 136
  functional behavioral assessment of, 58
  in language acquisition, 330–331
  neuropsychology and, 312–313
  nonverbal learning disorders and, 519–520
  positive behavioral support and, 59–60
  reinforcement and, 531–533
  social and emotional, 518–547
  of students with learning disabilities, 15–16
Behavioral analysis, 172–173
Behavioral intervention plan, 531
Behavioral pediatrics, 317
Behavioral problems, 530–535
  among adolescents, 269
  strategies in general education classroom, 546
Behavioral psychology, 170–173
  direct instruction and, 171–172
  explicit teaching and, 171
  functional behavior assessment and, 171, 173
  implications for learning disabilities, 172–173
  positive behavioral support and, 171
Behavioral temperaments, 188
Behavioral unit, 170–171

Behavior management, 532
  strategies for, 543–546
Behavior modification, 534
Bender-Gestalt Test, 316
Bias, in intelligence testing, 79
Bibliotherapy, 110
Bilingual children, 344
Bilingual education, 35, 346
Biology
  in language acquisition, 331–332
  learning disability identification and, 17
Birth-date effect, 169
Black English, 343
Blood sugar, ADD/ADHD control of, 206
Body awareness activities, 257–258
Body language, 328–329
Book reports, word processing for, 466
Books, basal reading series, 406–407
Boys, learning disabilities among, 16–17
Braille, 327
Brain. *See also* Functional magnetic resonance imaging (fMRI)
  communication process and, 330
  duality of, 306–307
  early development of, 227–228
  fMRI and, 310–312
  lateral preference and, 307
  learning in, 304
  neurochemistry of psychostimulant medications and, 207
  perceptual modality concept and, 238–240
  research on, 305, 307–312
  scientific studies of, 24–25
  traumatic brain injury and, 28
Brain-injured child, 25–26
Brainstorming, 436
Breaking the code, 378
Broca's area, 310

Calculators, in mathematics, 510
Case history
  as assessment information source, 62–64
  interview forms for, 64
Case study. *See also* Rita G. case study
  introduction to, 85
Catching activities, 256
Categorical separate classes, 140
Categorization, 188
CD-ROM technology, 38, 423
CDs, for spelling, 468–469

CEC. *See* Council for Exceptional Children (CEC)
Central nervous system, 304. *See also* Brain
  communication process and, 330
Central nervous system dysfunction, 10, 315
Cerebral dominance, 307
Cerebral hemisphere, 305–306
CHADD (Children and Adults With Attention Deficit Disorders), 196
Chalkboard, handwriting and, 469
Characteristics of learning disabilities, 14–20
Charles and Helen Schwab Foundation, 13
Charts
  mathematics and, 508
  pie chart, 512
Checking, 185
Child-find phase, 246
Childhood aphasia, 342
Child psychiatrist, 313, 319
Children. *See also* Adolescents; Elementary-age children; Young children
  brain-injured, 25–26
  clinical studies of, 24–27
  language acquisition by, 330–334
Children at risk, early intervention for, 221–223, 227–228
Chunking, for memory improvement, 179
Clarification of Policy to Address the Needs of Children With Attention Deficit Disorders Within General and/or Special Education (1991), 201, 202
Classification, 44, 45, 185
  in mathematics, 500–501
  vocabulary expansion through, 412
Class size, inclusion and, 144
Classwide peer tutoring, 116
Clinical studies, of children, 24–27
Clinical teaching, 92–93
  active learning promoted in, 117, 118
  in case study, 122–125
  characteristics of, 94–95
  cultural and linguistic environment and, 100–101
  curriculum adaptation and, 114
  differentiated instruction and, 101–105
  ecological system of, 96–101
  effective practices of, 95–96, 97–98

explicit teaching and, 116–117
  home environment and, 96
  instructional variables in, 105–107
  learning strategies for, 111–120
  peer tutoring and, 115–116
  reciprocal teaching and, 119
  scaffolding and, 117–119
  school environment and, 96
  self-esteem building and motivation in, 107–111
  social environment and, 99
  stages of teaching cycle, 93–94
  task analysis and, 120–121
  teaching strategies and, 111–114
Clonidine, 205
Cloze procedure, 413, 466
Clusters of characteristics, in student with learning disabilities evaluation, 56
Coaching, coteaching and, 147
Cognitive abilities, 173–175
  development of, 169
  object categorization and, 167
  tests of, 75–79
Cognitive behavior modification, 534
Cognitive development, 247
Cognitive factors, in language acquisition, 332
Cognitive learning theories, 103, 175, 181–182
  for spelling, 452–454
Cognitive psychology, 173–185
  cognitive learning theories, 181–182
  disorders in psychological processing, 175–176
  implications for learning disabilities, 185
  information-processing model of learning, 176–181
  metacognition, 182–185
Cognitive (thinking) skills, maturation of, 163
Cognitive styles, 188
Collaboration
  in clinical teaching, 108
  of family and school, 147
  between general and special education teachers, 142–147
  principles of, 143–144
  through word processing, 445
Collaborative teaming, 74, 276, 277–278
  prereferral, 48–49
College(s)
  attending, 281

cognitive psychology for, 186
improving self-esteem in, 542
inclusion and, 130–131
instructional strategies for students
    with learning disabilities in,
    111–120
integration of students with learning
    disabilities into, 137–138
language teaching in, 367, 368
mathematics strategies for, 497
medical information in, 319
percentage of students with learning
    disabilities in, 136, 137
as placement option, 132, 133
reading strategies for, 402
students with behavioral challenges
    in, 546
teaching social skills in, 540
teaching special-needs students in, 39
writing strategies for, 463
General education placement, 34
General education teacher
    accommodations for, 112
    collaboration with special education
        teacher, 137–138, 142–147
    supports needed for, 144–145
Generalization, 286
General tests, 69. *See also* Tests
    oral language, 349
    for reading, 79
Genetics
    in dyslexia, 310
    of learning disabilities, 309–310
Genres of literature, narrative, 393
Gestalt psychology, perception and, 238
Gesturing, 328
Gifted and talented children, with learn-
    ing disabilities, 14
Girls, learning disabilities among,
    16–17
Goals, annual (IEP), 56–57, 58
Goodenough-Harris Drawing Test, 76,
    316
Government. *See also* specific laws
    learning disabilities defined by, 6–9
Grading practices, in writing, 465
Grammar checkers, 445
Graphemes, 378
Graphic organizers, 182, 183, 390
    word web as, 412
    for writing process, 441, 443
Graphics, computers and, 467
Graphs, 508
    bar graph, 512

Gross-motor skills, 233–234
    activities for, 255–256
    assessing, 247
    as developmental indicator, 230
Gross-motor tests, 316
Grouping, in mathematics, 500–501
Group survey tests, in mathematics, 491

Halstead-Reitan Neuropsychological
    Test Battery for Children, 313
Handedness, writing and, 461–462
Handicaps, use of term, 28
Handwriting, 458–462
    strategies for, 464, 469–472
Happy failures, 105
Head Start, 249–251
Hearing, 319, 337
    vs. listening, 350
Hemispheres, cerebral, 305–306
Herman Method, 417
"Hidden curriculum," in school
    environment, 96
Hierarchical learning stages, 167–168
Hierarchical (top-down) organizers, 182
High school students. *See* Secondary
    school students
High-stakes testing, 31–33, 274
    for secondary school students,
        275–277
Hispanics, 344
HIV-infected babies, 225
Home environment, clinical teaching
    and, 96
Home/hospital setting
    description of, 141
    as placement option, 132, 133
Home-school coordination
    behavior management sheet, 547
    for social and emotional disorders,
        544–546
Hyperactivity, 197
    reducing, 210–211
    symptoms of, 200

IARLD. *See* International Academy for
    Research in Learning Disabilities
    (IARLD)
ICLD. *See* Interagency Committee on
    Learning Disabilities (ICLD)
IDEA. *See* Individuals With Disabilities
    Education Act entries
Identification
    of children with learning disabilities,
        21–22

errors in, 248
    procedures for, 21
IEP. *See* Individualized education pro-
    gram (IEP)
IEP meeting, 50, 156–157
IEP team, 50
    decisions about educational settings
        and, 134
    selection of educational setting by,
        135
Illinois Test of Psycholinguistic Abilities-
    Third Edition (ITPA-3), 76
Imagery, spelling and, 467
Immersion method, 346
Implementation
    of IEP teaching plan, 52
    of teaching plan, in clinical teaching,
        94
Impulsivity, 188, 197, 522
    managing, 209–210
    symptoms of, 200
Inattention, 197, 208–209
    symptoms of, 200
Inclusion, 34
    concerns about, 134–135
    defined, 130
    escalation of, 131
    guidelines for effective, 135, 136
    perspectives on, 130–131
    philosophical ideologies of, 134
    for secondary school students,
        274–275, 276
    supports for general education
        teachers and, 144–145
Independence stage of learning, 168
Independent performance, 438
Independent reading, level of, 397
Indirect instruction, 387
Individualized education program (IEP),
    13, 21, 135, 138, 170, 223
    accommodations for testing in, 82–83
    assessment stages of, 49–52
    assistive technology and, 61
    components of, 51
    English-language learners (ELL) and,
        60–61
    evaluation of student and, 55–57
    functional behavior assessment and,
        59
    goal setting in, 56–57, 58
    IDEA-2004 and, 54–55, 57–60
    instruction stages in, 52
    parental participation in, 152
    parents' rights in, 46, 47

positive behavioral support and, 59–60
procedural safeguards in, 46, 47
purposes of, 46
referral stages of, 47–49
Individualized family service plan (IFSP), 152, 224
Individualized transition plan (ITP), 280
Individually administered achievement tests, in mathematics, 491–492
Individuals With Disabilities Education Act (Public Law 101-476) (IDEA-1990), 6, 28, 29, 45
Individuals With Disabilities Education Act (Public Law 105-17) (IDEA-1997), 6, 28, 36, 45, 274
Individuals with Disabilities Education Improvement Act (Public Law 108-446) (IDEA-2004), 6–7, 28, 29–30. *See also* Individualized education program (IEP)
accommodations for assessment in, 82–83
ADD/ADHD and, 201
adolescents and, 275
behavioral challenges and, 530–531
behavior and, 171
continuum of alternative placements provision of, 131–133
early childhood laws and, 223–224
English-language learners (ELL) and, 60–61
free, appropriate public education and, 45–46
IEP and general education teachers in, 144
information-gathering procedures for evaluation and, 50
least restrictive environment requirement in, 130, 133–134
mathematics problem areas in, 476
parental rights in, 46, 47, 56, 150–152
physical education and, 231
psychological processing disorders and, 175
response-to-intervention method in, 54–55
role of parents in, 56
social disorders and, 523
students with learning disabilities in statewide testing and, 82
on transition from school to adult life, 279–280

Inefficient learners, 285
Inept social behavior, 522–523
Infants, early childhood intervention and, 223, 224–225
Informal arithmetic test, 74–75
Informal assessment, 244–245
definition of, 71
of mathematics, 493–496
of oral language development, 348
types of, 72–75
Informal graded word-recognition test, 73–74
Informal reading inventory (IRI), 348, 397–398
Information, for assessment. *See* Assessment
Informational text, 392–394
Information-processing difficulties, mathematics and, 479, 480
Information-processing model, 175, 176–181
Initial planning, 49
Innate factors, in language acquisition, 331–332
Inputs, 176
language, 328
Inspiration, 423
Inspiration (computer program), 413, 441
Instruction
differentiated, 101–105
direct, 103–104, 171–172
learning strategies, 120
scaffolded, 117–119
in SIM model, 287–290
Instructional planning, 45
Instructional reading, level of, 397–398
Instructional stages, IEP, 52
Instructional strategies, 93
Integrated language system, 326
teaching strategies for, 348–367
writing in, 429–433
Integration phase, of history of field of learning disabilities, 27–28
Intelligence, multiple-intelligences theory, 13, 15, 76–78
Intelligence tests
analysis of subtest scores of, 76–79
bias in, 79
types of, 75–79
Intellikeys, 252
Interactive dialogues, 189–191
Interactive learning, 287
Interagency Committee on Learning Disabilities (ICLD), 9, 523

Interests of students, transition plan and, 280
Interests of students, using materials based on, 109–111
Internalization, 105
International Academy for Research in Learning Disabilities (IARLD), 5
International Multisensory Structured Language Council, 417
Internet, 38
writing process and, 467
Interpersonal relationship. *See* Rapport
Interpersonal skills, NLVD and, 519
Interventions, 93
behavioral, 531
early, 221–223
prereferral, 48–49
Interviewer, in case history interview, 63
Interview forms, case history, 64
Interview instruments, 535, 536
Intonation, 336
Intrinsic reinforcers, 544
Intuitive judgments, 166
Invented spelling, 434, 451, 453, 454
Inventories, as mathematics tests, 493
IOTA test, 398, 399
conversion chart for, 400
IQ-achievement discrepancy, 11–12
IQ-achievement discrepancy score. *See* Discrepancy score
IRI. *See* Informal reading inventory (IRI)
It's on the Tip of My Tongue (German), 342

Jargon, 360–361
Job Corps, 290
Job Training Partnership Act (JTPA), 290
Journals
electronic, 466
personal, 439–441
reading-writing connection and, 414
Judgment, social perception and, 524
Juncture, in language system, 336
Junior high school. *See* Secondary school entries
Juvenile delinquency, 20

Kaufman Assessment Battery for Children (K-ABC), 75, 76
Kaufman Brief Intelligence Test (K-BIT), 76
K-8, mathematics curriculum for, 496–498

Keyboard, electronic, 442
Keyboarding, 445, 462
Keystone Visual Survey Service for Schools, 81
Key words, for memory improvement, 179
Kidspiration (computer software), 423, 441
Kinesthetic learning, 238
    processing activities, 261
Kinesthetic perception, 244
    assessing, 245
Kurzweil Educational Systems, 424–425
Kurzweil Reading Program, 40
K-W-L technique, 408–409

Lab School (Washington, DC), psychological processing difficulties and, 175–176
Language. *See also* Linguistic diversity
    brain and, 307
    CEC standards for, 328, 329
    as communication process, 328–330
    components of, 334–336
    as developmental indicator, 230
    forms of system, 326–328
    four forms of, 327–328
    functions of, 324–325
    immersion from infancy, 396–397
    as integrated system, 325–326
    learning styles and, 239
    mathematics difficulties and, 480
    modifying to enhance learning, 106
    observation of use, 65
    patterns of, 363–365
    silent, 537
    theories of, 324–325
Language acquisition, 324, 330–334
    behavioral factors in, 330–331
    biological (innate) factors in, 331–332
    cognitive factors in, 332
    problems in, 361
    social factors in, 332–333
Language delays, 332, 337, 338
Language development, milestones in, 358–360
Language disorders, 336–343
    expressive, 343
    phonological awareness and, 338–339
    receptive, 342–343
    vs. speech disorders, 337
Language environment, teaching and, 331–332, 333–334

Language experiences method, 407–408, 409
Language sounds, phonological awareness of, 351–354
Language tests, 80, 81
Larry P. v. Riles, bias in IQ testing and, 79
Lateral preference, 307
Laubach Literacy Action, 298
Laureate Learning Systems, 367
Law(s). *See also* specific laws
    for ADD/ADHD children, 201–202
    for adults with disabilities, 290–298
    learning disabilities and, 6–9, 28–31
    special education, 28, 45–46
    young children and, 223–228
LDAA. *See* Learning Disabilities Association of America (LDAA)
Learned helplessness, 187, 269
Learning
    active, 117, 118
    motor development and, 231–237
    potential for, 11
    of spelling, 448–450
    stages of, 168–169
    surface, 167
Learning differences, 12–13
    differentiated instruction for, 101–105
Learning difficulties, use of term, 13
Learning disabilities
    characteristics of, 14–20
    definitions of, 2, 6–12
    determining eligibility for, 52–55
    eminent people with, 3–4
    history of field, 23–28
    origins of term, 27
    percentage of children with, 22, 23
    prevalence of, 21–23
    views of, 12–14
Learning Disabilities Association of America (LDAA), 6
Learning disabilities teacher. *See* Special education teacher
Learning strategies approach, 120, 181, 185–187, 185–191, 285–286, 287–290
    in mathematics, 487–488
    for social skills, 539
    to spelling, 452–454
    to writing, 438
Learning styles, 238
Learning tasks, 10
Learning theories. *See* Theories of learning

Least restrictive environment (LRE), 34
    IDEA-2004 and, 130
    inclusion and, 133–134
Left-handed student, writing by, 461–462
Left hemisphere, 306
    reading and, 311, 312
Legislation. *See* Law(s)
Letter(s)
    recognition of, 242
    writing, 449
Letter names, spelling and, 448
Lexical words, 413
Limited English proficiency, 35, 344–345
Linguistic diversity, 34–35
    and adolescent learning disabilities, 268
Linguistic environment, clinical teaching and, 100–101
Lip moving, in reading, 421–422
Listening, 350–357
    comprehension and, 350–351
    critical, 356–357
    informal measure of, 348
Listening centers, for spelling, 468–469
Listening comprehension, 356
Listening (auditory) learning, 238
Listening skills, 212
    improving, 113–114
Listening tests, 349
Listening vocabulary, 354–355
Literacy. *See also* Early literacy
    and writing, 395, 433–434
Literacy organizations, for adult reading, 298
Literacy Volunteers of America (LVA), 298
Literature-based reading instruction, 395–396
Living Books Series, The, 423
Local education agency (LEA), 47
Long-term memory, 176, 179–181
    episodic and semantic, 179–180
Low self-concept
    in adolescents, 269
    emotional problems and, 527–529
LRE. *See* Least restrictive environment (LRE)

Mainstreaming, 134
Manifestation determination, 59
Manuscript writing, 459–460
Mapping, mind, 182, 183
Maps, concept, 182

Mastery learning, 104
Math anxiety, 481
Mathematics
    active involvement in, 486
    activities for teaching, 500–510
    analyzing errors in, 493–494
    calendar for learning facts, 507
    commercial programs for, 490
    computers in, 510–513
    curriculum for K-8, 496–498
    curriculum for secondary schools
        and, 498
    diagnostic tests of, 492–493
    direct instruction of, 487
    formal tests of, 491–493
    IEP annual goal in (sample), 58
    informal measures of, 493–496
    learning theories for, 484–490
    practice and review in, 499
    problem solving in, 488–490
    in secondary schools, 283
    spreadsheets in, 512–513
    standards in, 483–484, 485
    teaching strategies for, 496–510
    technology in, 510–513
    theories of, 476–479
    word story problems in, 508–510
Mathematics computation, 503–507
Mathematics disabilities
    characteristics of, 479–481
    at secondary level, 482–483
Maturation
    of cognitive (thinking) skills, 163,
        164–165
    developmental theory and, 167
    reading achievement by, 164
Maturational lags, 163
Maturational stage of development, of
    Piaget, 165–167
Maturity, social, 539
MBD. See Minimal brain dysfunction
    (MBD)
McCarthy Scales of Children's Abilities,
    76
Meaning
    building with vocabulary and con-
        cepts, 409–413
    spelling and, 467
Meaningful information, 180
Measurement, curriculum-based mea-
    surement (CBM), 69–70
Mediation, in IEP, 47
Medical history, 314, 315
Medical information, 304–305
    in general education classroom, 319

Medical specialists, 313. 317–320
Medical treatment, for children with
    learning disabilities, 304–305
Medication, for ADD/ADHD, 203–205,
    207–208
Medicine, advances in, 305
Memorization, 438
Memory, 176–177
    auditory, 241
    of letter sounds, 467
    long-term, 179–181
    retrieval problems, 342
    short-term, 178–179
    spelling and, 450–451
    strategies for, 287
    types of, 176
Mental retardation, classifying minority
    children as, 22
Message, sending and receiving, 329
Metacognition, 181, 182–185
    shopping behavior and, 184
Mild/moderate disabilities, use of term,
    13
Mind mapping, 182, 183
Minimal brain dysfunction (MBD),
    26–27
Minority children, classifying as men-
    tally retarded, 22
Mixed laterality, 307
Mnemonic techniques, 179
Modeling, 438
    of writing process, 463
Models of learning. See Modeling; The-
    ories of learning; specific models
Money, in mathematics, 510
Monitoring. See Progress, monitoring
Morpheme, 334
Morphological generalizations,
    363–364
Morphology, 334
Motivation, 186
    of adolescents, 270–271
    behavior and, 533
    building, 107–108
    word processing for, 443
Motor area, in brain, 305, 306
Motor coordination and development,
    observation of, 65
Motor development
    activities for, 255–258
    assessing, 247
    concepts of, 233–234
    coordination problems, 232
    learning and, 231–237
    perceptual, 234–235

through play, 234
    sensory integration and, 235–237
    skills in, 252
    tests for assessing, 237
Motor function, 313
Motor tests, 80, 81, 315–317
Movement, opportunities for, 212
Movement games, 234
MRI. See Functional magnetic reso-
    nance imaging (fMRI)
Multidisciplinary evaluation, 48, 49–50,
    122–125
Multimodal treatment plan, for
    ADD/ADHD, 202–203
Multiple-intelligences theory (Gardner),
    14, 15, 76–78
Multiple word meanings, 410–411
Multiplication, 504–505
Multiplication chart, 495
Multisensory approaches, 416–427
    perception overload and, 239–240
    in spelling, 454, 467–468
Multistore memory system, 176
Multisyllabic words, spelling of, 450
Muppet Learning Keys, 251, 252

Narrative genres, 393
Narrative text, 392
National Council for the Accreditation
    of Teacher Education (NCATE),
    31
National Council of Teachers of Mathe-
    matics (NCTM)
    Commission on Standards for
        School Mathematics of, 498
    principles and standards from,
        483–484, 485
National Institute of Child Health and
    Human Development, 373
National Institute of Child Health and
    Human Development, on devel-
    opmental variation, 164–165
National Reading Panel, 376, 377, 387,
    390
    on effectiveness of phonics instruc-
        tion, 378–379
    on phonological awareness, 339
Native language, 336
Natural language stimulation, activities
    for, 361–362
NCATE. See National Council for the
    Accreditation of Teacher Educa-
    tion (NCATE)
NCTM. See National Council of Teach-
    ers of Mathematics (NCTM)

Performance measurement, of written language, 33
Performance standards, for secondary school students, 275–277
Personal adjustment, observation of, 64–65
Personality development, 527
Personal journals, 439–441
PET. See Positron-emission tomography (PET)
Phoneme producer region (brain), 311, 312
Phonemes, 334, 378
  in common words, 339
  strategies for, 401
Phonemic awareness, 377
Phonetic strategies, 448–449
Phonic remedial reading lessons, 403–404, 405
Phonics, 239, 334, 377, 378–379
  approaches to, 379, 380
  effectiveness of, 378–379
  methods of, 403–404
  observation of abilities, 65
  remedial reading lessons for, 403–404
  spelling and, 448
  teacher knowledge about, 379
Phonological awareness, 240–241, 258–260, 337–338
  activities for, 351–354
  informal test of, 341
  of language sounds, 351–354
  tasks in, 340
  tests of, 349
Phonology, 334
Physical education, 231
Physical therapy (PT), 231
Piaget's maturational stages of development, 165–167
Pictures, as writing strategy, 441–442, 444
Pie chart, 512
Pitch, 336
Placement options, 131–133
Place value, 493–494
Planning
  inclusion and time for, 144–145
  referral and initial, 49
  of teaching task, in clinical teaching, 94
Play, motor development through, 234
Portfolio, current achievement level and, 54

Portfolio assessment, 72, 398
Positive behavioral support, 59–60, 171, 531
Positive reinforcement, in language development, 331
Positron-emission tomography (PET), 310
Postsecondary attendance, 281
Postsecondary programs, nondegree programs for adults, 291–292
Potential, vs. achievement, 11
Power Pad, 252
PowerPoint, 447
Practice, for reading fluency, 404
Pragmatics, 335–336
Predictable books, 404–406
Prediction, 185
Preoperational stage, 165, 166
Prephonetic writing, 448, 449
Prereferral activities
  in case study, 86–87
  in IEP, 47–49
Prereferral collaboration team, 48–49
Preschool children, 224
  assessing, 245–247
  computers for, 251
  with disability, 222
  early childhood intervention and, 223
  inclusion strategies for, 261, 262
  perception in, 237–244
  special education services received by, 225–226
Preschool level, characteristics of learning disabilities at, 17–19
Presentation software, 447
Present levels of achievement, determining, 54, 123–125
Prewriting, 435–436, 437
Primary language system, 327
Prior knowledge, 180
  new information and, 186
Problem solving
  examples of, 490
  lesson structure in, 489
  in mathematics, 488–490
Procedural safeguards, in IEP, 46, 47
Process approach to writing, 434–437
Processing functions, 176
Product approach to writing, 434–435
Professional development program, 13
Professional licensing, and learning disabilities, 296
Progress, monitoring, 45, 57, 70–71, 286

Project READ, 417
Pronunciation, spelling and, 467
Proprioceptive system, 237
Psychiatrist, 319
Psychological processing, as differentiated instruction, 102
Psychological processing disorders, 10, 175–176
  in federal law, 102
Psychology. See Neuropsychology
Psychostimulant medications (for ADD/ADHD), 203–204
  neurochemistry of, 207–211
Psychotherapeutic teaching, 104–105
Public Law 94-142. See Education for All Handicapped Children Act (Public Law 94-142)
Public Law 108-446. See Education for All Handicapped Children Act (IDEA-2004)
Punished by Rewards... (Kohn), 171, 532
Pupil Rating Scale (Revised): Screening for Learning Disabilities, 65

Questioning, 287
  strategies with, 415–416
Questions
  answering, 390
  generating, 390

Race/ethnicity
  children with disabilities by, 35, 227
  percentage of students with learning disabilities by, 61
Rapid automatized naming (RAN), 341–342
Rapport
  controlling, 106
  successful clinical teaching and, 108
Rating scales, 536
  of ADD/ADHD, 200, 201
  for assessment, 65–66
READ 180, 423
Read-along method, 386
Readiness, 105, 169
Reading, 372–423
  alphabetic, 394
  assessing, 397–400
  brain and, 307
  cloze procedure for, 413
  commonly-used tests of, 400
  comprehension of, 387–394
  computers and, 423–425

context clues in, 448
difficulties in adults, 20
diverse student interests in, 110–111
elements of, 376–377
fluency in, 382–386
formal tests of, 398–400
games and materials for, 404
learning as adult, 20
learning strategies for, 416
listening and, 350
mathematics difficulties and, 480
multisensory materials for, 416–420
oral language, writing, and,
325–330
portfolio assessment and, 72, 398
remedial methods in, 416–420
in secondary schools, 283
silent, 422
survey-type tests and, 79, 80
teaching strategies for, 401–425
theories of, 372–374
word-recognition skills and,
377–382
writing before, 395
Reading Blaster, 423
Reading comprehension, 388–394
reciprocal teaching and, 119
strategies for improving, 406–416
strategies for promoting, 390–392
as thinking process, 389–390
Reading failure, predicting, 164
Reading fluency, 382–386
Reading instruction, scientifically based
research for, 55
Reading problems
finger pointing as, 421–422
lip moving as, 421–422
reversals as, 421
Reading Recovery program, 418
Reading series, for low reading ability
and high interest level, 408
Reading tests
comprehensive batteries of academic
tests, 79, 80
diagnostic, 79, 80
diagnostic academic tests and test
batteries, 79–81
general survey-type, 79, 80
Reading vocabulary, vs. oral vocabulary,
386–387
Reading-writing connection, 394–397,
414
Read Please, 425
Read Please Plus, 425
Reasonable accommodations, 112

for college students, 292
Rebound effect, with psychostimulants,
205
Recall, spelling and, 468
Receptive language disorders, 342–343
Receptive language modes, 328, 329
Recipe for Reading (Traub & Bloom),
417
Reciprocal teaching, 72, 119, 190
Recognition of numbers, in
mathematics, 502
Recorded textbooks, 423
Recordings for the Blind and Dyslexic
(RFBD), 278, 424
Referral
and assessment, 45
in case study, 86–87
Referral stages, IEP, 47–49
Reflection, 188
Regrouping, 504
Regulation for the Individuals With Dis-
abilities Education Act of 1997,
The (IDEA-1997) (1999), 201
Regulations, for children with learning
disabilities, 7
Rehabilitation Act (1973) (Section 504),
30, 112, 202, 290, 291, 292
education plan under, 138
Section 504 of, 290
Rehearsal, for memory improvement,
179
Reinforcement, 531–533
as behavior management strategy,
543, 544
consequent event as, 170
negative, in writing, 437–438
Reitan-Indiana Neuropsychological
Battery for Children, 313
Related professionals, inclusion and,
145
Related services, 52, 57
Remedial reading, 416–420
phonics lessons and, 403–404
Remediation, 93
Repeated reading, 383–386
Replacement behaviors, 59–60
Report cards, 82
IEP, 52
Research, on brain, 305, 307–312
Residential facility
advantages and disadvantages of, 141
description of, 140–141
as placement option, 132, 133
Resource room
description of, 138–139

percentage of students with learning
disabilities in, 136, 137
as placement option, 132, 133
scheduling students for, 139
Response, target behavior as, 170
Response-to-intervention method, 8, 12
for determining learning disabilities
eligibility, 49, 52, 54–55
Responsibilities, of special education
teacher, 145
Restating, 508
Retrieval, long-term memory and,
179–181
Reversals, 421
visual perception and, 242–244
Review, of transition plan, 280
Review and revaluation, in IEP plan, 52
Revising, 436, 437
through word processing, 445
Reward system, 532
Right brain/left brain, 306–307
Right hemisphere, NLVD and, 519
Rita G. case study
IEP meeting, 156–157
multidisciplinary evaluation,
122–125
prereferral and referral in, 86–87
Ritalin, 204
Routine, 109

Same-age peer tutoring, 115
Scaffolded instruction, 117–119, 181.
See also Reciprocal teaching
Scheduling, of writing, 465–466
Schema, knowledge base as, 333
School(s). *See also* Educational settings
attuned, 13
environment and clinical teaching in,
96
learning disability programs in,
27–28
social disorders and, 525–526
Scientific brain studies, 24–25
Scientific research-based instruction,
response-to-intervention method
and, 54–55
Screening, 45
Screening phase, 246
Script, 461. *See also* Cursive writing
Secondary language system, 327
Secondary schools
curricula in, 283–285
learning disabilities in, 19–20
learning strategies instruction in,
285–286

mathematics curriculum for, 498
mathematics difficulties in, 482–483
teaching adolescents with learning disabilities in, 283–285
Secondary school students
in different educational environments, 271–272
diplomas and certificates for, 272
failures by students with learning disabilities, 273
inclusion in, 274
percentage with learning disabilities, 271
special issues for, 272–278
Second language, teaching methods, 345–346
Section 504 of Rehabilitation Act (1973). *See* Rehabilitation Act (1973) (Section 504)
Section 504 Plan, 138, 139
Self-concept
of adolescents, 20
emotional problems and, 527–529
enhancing, 287
low-self esteem and, 269
Self-consciousness, in adolescence, 267
Self-esteem
building, 107–108
improvement strategies for, 542
poor self-concept and, 269
strengthening, 539–541
Self-instructional cognitive behavior modification program, 534
Self-monitoring, 415
Self-perception, developing, 537
Self-questioning strategies, 416
Self-regulated strategy development (SRSD), 438
Self-talk, 362
Semantic memory, 179–180
Semantic organizers, 390
Semantics, 335
Semiconcrete instruction stage, 499
Senior high school. *See* Secondary school entries
Sensitivity, to other people, 537
Sensorimotor learning, Piaget on, 231
Sensorimotor stage, 165
Sensory integration (SI), 235–237
Sensory modality, 188
Sensory register, 176–177
Sentences
combining, 466
development of, 361
formulating, 364–365

understanding of, 355–356
Separate class
benefits of placement in, 140
description of, 139
as placement option, 132, 133
transition from, 140
Separate school
advantages and disadvantages of, 140
description of, 140
as placement option, 132, 133
Sequencing, auditory, 241
Serial order and relationships, 501
Services. *See also* Special education services
assistive technology, 61
for children with ADD/ADHD, 201
determination of, 57
for disabled college students, 295
for effective inclusion, 136
inclusion and continuum of alternative, 145
for infants and toddlers, 224
for preschool children, 224–226
related, 52, 57
Settings, for clinical teaching, 94–95
Severe discrepancy, 11
Sexuality, in adolescence, 267
Shared responsibility, in clinical teaching, 108
Sharing with an audience, 436–437
Sheltered English, 346
Shopping behavior, 184
Short-term (working) memory, 176, 178
Sight words, 379–381, 384–385, 449
in first grade, 381
fluency with, 382–383
Sign language, 329
Silent language, interpreting, 537
Silent reading, inability at, 422
SIM. *See* Strategies intervention model (SIM)
Simplifying, 508
Slosson Intelligence Test, 76
Social acceptance, effective inclusion and, 136
Social behavior
assessing, 535
assessment instruments for, 536
disruptive, 522
impulsivity and, 522
inept, 522–523
Social competencies, teaching strategies for, 535–539
Social context, of learning, 164

Social cues, children with social disorders and, 524–525
Social development, assessing, 248
Social difficulties, in adults, 20
Social disorders, 521–525. *See also* Nonverbal learning disorders (NVLD)
Asperger's syndrome as, 523–524
friendships and, 525
peer feelings and, 524–525
settings of, 525–526
Social environment, 186, 190
clinical teaching and, 96
dynamic assessment and, 72
Social factors, in language acquisition, 332–333
Social interactions, 189
Social maturity, 538
Social perception, 519–520, 524
Social problems
among adolescents, 269
Social skills
deficits in, 521
learning strategies for, 539
programs for, 539, 541
teaching in general education classroom, 540
Social skills disorders, 522
Society
early intervention and, 223
learning disabilities created by, 163–164
Sociometric techniques, 535
Soft neurological signs, 313
Software, 40. *See also* Computer technology; specific programs
mathematics, 511
presentation, 447
types of, 40
for word processing, 446
for young children, 253
Sound-symbol spelling relationship, words with, 381
Space, controlling, 105–106
Spalding Method, 417
Spanish speakers, 344
Spatial relationships, mathematics and, 478
Speaking, 357–367
in language development, 326
Speaking vocabulary, 362
Special class, percentage of students with learning disabilities in, 136, 137
Special education
collaboration with content-area teachers, 276, 277

eligibility for, 13
integrating general education with,
134–135
laws, 28, 45–46
preschool children receiving,
225–226
standards for, 31, 32
Special education programs, learning
disabilities in, 12
Special education services
for ADD/ADHD children, 201–202
determination of, 57
Special education teacher
collaboration with general education
teacher, 137–138, 142–147
competencies of, 145
responsibilities of, 145
supports needed for, 145
Special teaching technique, 104
Speech
language development and, 331
milestones in, 358–360
Speech articulation test, 349
Speech disorders, 336, 337
delayed speech and, 337
vs. language disorders, 337
Speech synthesis programs, 445
Spell checkers, 445, 469
Spelling, 434, 447–458
assessment of, 457–458
cognitive learning strategies for,
452–454
developmental learning stages for,
448–450
invented, 451, 453, 454
mature, 450
multisensory approaches to, 454
problems related to, 450–451
strategies for, 464
strategies for teaching, 467–469
tests of, 458
word-frequency approach to, 455
word patterns for, 449, 455
word selection theories for teaching,
454–457
Spreadsheets, in mathematics, 508,
512–513
SRSD. See Self-regulated strategy development (SRSD)
Stages of acceptance, for parents,
153–154
Stages of learning, 168–169
Stages of life, learning disability characteristics by, 17–20

Standard(s)
CEC language standards, 328, 329
in mathematics, 483–484, 485
from NCTM, 483–484
No Child Left Behind Act and, 82
statewide assessments and, 82
Standard English, 334, 343
Standardized tests
adequacy of, 67–69
characteristics of, 67
compared to criterion-referenced
test, 75
criticism of, 69
definition of, 67
diagnostic, 69
general, 69
survey tests in mathematics, 491
Standard Reading Inventory, 398
Standards-based education, 31–33
Stanford-Binet Intelligence Scale-Fourth
Edition, 75
Stimulus, antecedent event as, 170
Story maps, 390
Story sequence, 466
Story structure, 390
Strategies. See also specific topics
for teaching special-needs students in
general education classroom, 39
Strategies intervention model (SIM),
187, 287–290
Strattera, 205
Strauss syndrome, 26–27
Strengths, of student with learning
disabilities, 56
Strephosymbolia, 307
Stress, in language system, 336
Structural analysis, 382
spelling and, 448
Structural words, 413
Structure, 109
Student interests
transition plan and, 280
using materials based on, 109–111
Student inventories, 535, 536
Students with disabilities, composition
of, 24
Students with learning disabilities
evaluation process for, 55–57
percentage of, 22
in statewide testing, 82
"Study-test" method, vs. "test-study-
test" method, 468
Subtraction, 504
Success

in learning, 108
of learning disabled, 14
self-esteem and, 109
Summarization, 390–391
Support, 438
Supported employment, 281
Support groups
for ADD, 196–197
parent, 154–155
Supportive services, for effective
inclusion, 136
Surface learning, 167
Survey tests, 398
in reading, 79, 80
Survival skills, 283
instruction in, 284
Suspension from school, continuation of
services and, 59
Syllable junctions, spelling and, 450
Syllable types, 385
Symbols
in communication, 329
in mathematics, 476
Synapses, 207
brain development and, 227
Syntax, 335
Synthetic phonics methods, 403
Syracuse, public school curriculum
from, 27–28

Tactile defensiveness, 235
Tactile perception, 244
assessing, 245
Tactile perception tests, 317
Tactile processing, activities for, 261
Tactile system, 235
Talking word-processing programs,
445
Target behavior, 170
Task analysis, 120–121
Teachers. See also Content-area teachers; Special education teacher
culturally responsive, 101
language used by, 106
Teaching. See also Clinical teaching
coteaching, 146–147, 148
diagnostic, 72–73
explicit, 116–117
planning in clinical teaching, 94
reciprocal, 72, 119, 190
Teaching plan
development of, 57
implementation in clinical teaching,
94

Visual-motor abilities, mathematics and, 478–479
Visual-motor tests, 315–316
Visual perception, 241–244
    activities for developing, 260
    assessing, 245
    mathematics and, 478–479
    tasks in, 243
Visual processing
    activities for, 260–261
    as developmental indicator, 230
Visual-screening tests, 81, 122
Vocabulary, 386–387
    building meaning with, 409–413
    expanding, 410–413
    listening, 354–355
    mathematics, 500
    sources of, 412
    speaking, 362
    word processing for, 466
Vocalization, speech acquisition and, 360
Vocational training, 281
Voice recognition
    devices, 39
    systems, 445–446
Volunteers
    in classroom, 145
    for one-to-one instruction, 141–142
Vygotsky's social influences of learning, 189

"Wait-and-fail" method, 11–12, 229, 372–373
Walking activities, 255
Web, writing process and, 467
Wechsler Intelligence Scale for Children-Fourth Edition (WISC-IV), 75, 76
Wellbutin, 205
Wernicke's area, 310
Whole language instruction, 396
Wilson Reading System, 417, 418
WJ-III Cognitive Performance Clusters, 76, 77
WJ-III Tests of Cognitive Abilities, 76, 77
Woodcock-Johnson Psychoeducational Battery-III, Complete Battery (WJ-III), 76

Woodcock-Johnson Psychoeducational Battery III-Tests of Achievement, 81
Word(s)
    communication through, 430
    most common in written language, 456
    multiple meanings of, 410–411
    single, 361
    stages of learning, 387
    understanding of, 354
    visual memory of, 467
Word analyzer region (brain), 311, 312
Word finding, 341, 342
Word Finding Intervention Program (German), 342
Word-finding tests, 349
Word-frequency approach to spelling, 455
Word-pattern approach to spelling, 455
Word patterns, written, 449
Word-prediction programs, 445
Word processing, 38
    computers and, 442–447
    software for, 446
    strategies for, 466–467
    talking programs for, 445
Word recognition
    automaticity in, 383
    teaching strategies for, 401–404
Word-recognition clues, combining, 382
Word-recognition skills, 377–378, 379–382
    context clues, 381–382
    structural analysis and, 382
Word selection, theories for teaching spelling, 454–457
Word story problems, 508–510
Word web, 182, 412
Working memory, 176, 178
Workplace, NVLD and, 519
Work-study program, 284–285
World Wide Web. See Web
Writing, 430. See also Reading-writing connection
    assessment of, 447
    computers and, 446
    creative vs. functional, 465

cursive, 460, 461
D'Nealian, 461
early literacy and, 395, 433–434
handwriting and, 458–462
in integrated language system, 431–434
by left-handed student, 461–462
manuscript, 459–460
most common words in, 456
oral language, reading, and, 325–330
portfolio assessment and, 72
before reading, 395
reading-writing connection and, 414
spelling and, 447–458
tests of, 448
theories of, 430–431
Writing across the curriculum, 431
Writing process, 430–433, 434–437
    defined, 435
    stages of, 435–437
    teaching of, 437–438
Writing skills, 431, 435
    teaching strategies for, 462–472
Writing strategies, 430, 438–442
    computers and, 442–447
    drawing pictures, 441–442
    graphic organizers as, 441
    handwriting, 464
    patterned, 441
    personal journals as, 439–441
    spelling, 464
    written conversation as, 439
Written conversation, 439
Written English, 338–339

Young children, 220–262
    ADD/ADHD in, 198
    assessing, 244–248
    computers for, 251–254
    curriculum for, 249–253
    with disabilities by race/ethnicity, 227
    law(s) and, 223–228
    preschool inclusion strategies for, 261, 262

Zone of proximal development (ZPD), 105, 164
    scaffolded instruction and, 118

ABOUT THE AUTHORS

DR. JANET LERNER

is professor emeritus at Northeastern Illinois University. She served as professor and chairperson of the Department of Special Education at Northeastern Illinois University. She is also coeditor of *Learning Disabilities: A Multidisciplinary Journal,* a publication of the Learning Disabilities Association of America. During her extensive career in education she has authored and contributed to numerous books and articles. She has collaborated with two other authors (Lowenthal and Egan) to write *Young Children with Special Needs, Children-at-Risk,* and *Children with Disabilities* (2003), and she is a coauthor of *Reading Problems: Diagnosis and Teaching Strategies* (2002). Dr. Lerner has devoted much of her professional time to conducting workshops for in-service special education teachers. In 2004, Dr. Janet Lerner received the J.E. Wallace Wallin Special Education Lifetime Achievement Award from the Council for Exceptional Children.

DR. FRANK KLINE

is a professor at Seattle Pacific University where he serves as the associate dean for teacher education. He earned his Ph.D. in special education at the University of Kansas (the No. 1 special education graduate program in the country according to a *U.S. News & World Report* ranking). His professional interests include collaboration, instruction, and coping with mild disabilities and other forms of diversity in general education classes. Dr. Kline and Dr. Lerner have worked together on several committees, most often the program committee for the Learning Disabilities Association (LDA).